Nietzsche

VOLUMES III AND IV

The Will to Power as Knowledge
and as Metaphysics

Nihilism

HarperCollins Editions of
MARTIN HEIDEGGER

Basic Writings
Being and Time
Discourse on Thinking
Early Greek Thinking
The End of Philosophy
Hegel's Concept of Experience
Identity and Difference
Nietzsche: Volume I, The Will to Power as Art
Nietzsche: Volume II, The Eternal Recurrence of the Same
Nietzsche: Volume III, The Will to Power as Knowledge and as Metaphysics
Nietzsche: Volume IV, Nihilism
On the Way to Language
On Time and Being
Poetry, Language, Thought
The Question Concerning Technology and Other Essays
What Is Called Thinking?

MARTIN HEIDEGGER

Nietzsche

Volume III: The Will to Power as Knowledge
and as Metaphysics

Volume IV: Nihilism

Edited by
DAVID FARRELL KRELL

HarperSanFrancisco
A Division of HarperCollins*Publishers*

Acknowledgment is made for the permission of Macmillan Publishing Co., Inc., M. B. Yeats, Anne Yeats, and Macmillan Ltd., to reprint from "Nineteen Hundred and Nineteen," from *Collected Poems* by William Butler Yeats. Copyright 1928 by Macmillan Publishing Co., Inc., renewed 1956 by Georgie Yeats.

Volume Three of Martin Heidegger's text was originally published in *Nietzsche*, Erster Band, Zweiter Band, © Verlag Günther Neske, Pfullingen, 1961.

NIETZSCHE. *Volume III: The Will to Power as Knowledge and as Metaphysics.* Copyright © 1987 by Harper & Row, Publishers, Inc. Analysis copyright © 1987 by David Farrell Krell.

Volume Four was originally published in *Nietzsche*, Zweiter Band, © Verlag Günther Neske, Pfullingen, 1961.

NIETZSCHE. *Volume IV: Nihilism.* Copyright © 1982 by Harper & Row, Publishers, Inc. Analysis copyright © 1982 by David Farrell Krell.

All rights reserved. Printed in the United States of America. No part of this book may be used or reproduced in any manner whatsoever without written permission except in the case of brief quotations embodied in critical articles and reviews. For information address HarperCollins Publishers, 10 East 53rd Street, New York, NY 10022.

FIRST HARPERCOLLINS PAPERBACK EDITION PUBLISHED IN 1991.

Designed by Jim Mennick

Library of Congress Cataloging-in-Publication Data

Heidegger, Martin, 1889–1976.
   [Nietzsche. English]
   Nietzsche / Martin Heidegger. — 1st HarperCollins pbk. ed.
     p.   cm.
   Translation of: Nietzsche.
   Reprint. Originally published: San Francisco : Harper & Row, 1979—1987.
   Includes bibliographical references.
   Contents: v. 1–2. The will to power as art ; The eternal recurrence of the same / translated from the German by David Farrell Krell (1v.) — v. 3–4. The will to power as knowledge and as metaphysics ; Nihilism / edited by David Farrell Krell (1 v.)
    ISBN 0–06–063841–9 (v. 1–2). — ISBN 0–06–063794–3 (v. 3–4)
   1. Nietzche, Friedrich Wilhelm, 1844–1900. I. Krell, David Farrell. II. Title.
B3279.H48N5413   1991
193—dc20   90–49074
                                                                                   CIP

MARTIN HEIDEGGER

Nietzsche

Volume III:
The Will to Power as Knowledge
and as Metaphysics

Translated from the German by

JOAN STAMBAUGH
DAVID FARRELL KRELL
FRANK A. CAPUZZI

Edited, with Notes and an Analysis, by

DAVID FARRELL KRELL

Contents

Editor's Preface   ix

PART ONE: THE WILL TO POWER AS KNOWLEDGE   1

1. Nietzsche as the Thinker of the Consummation of Metaphysics   3
2. Nietzsche's So-called Major Work   10
3. The Will to Power as Principle of a New Valuation   15
4. Knowledge in Nietzsche's Fundamental Thought Concerning the Essence of Truth   22
5. The Essence of Truth (Correctness) as "Estimation of Value"   32
6. Nietzsche's Alleged Biologism   39
7. Western Metaphysics as "Logic"   48
8. Truth and What Is True   53
9. Tracing the Opposition of the "True and Apparent Worlds" Back to Relations of Value   57
10. World and Life as "Becoming"   64
11. Knowing as Schematizing a Chaos in Accordance with Practical Need   68
12. The Concept of "Chaos"   77
13. Practical Need as the Need for a Schema; Formation of a Horizon and Perspective   84
14. Accordance and Calculation   90
15. The Poetizing Essence of Reason   94
16. Nietzsche's "Biological" Interpretation of Knowledge   101
17. The Law of Contradiction as a Law of Being: Aristotle   111

18. The Law of Contradiction as Command: Nietzsche	115
19. Truth and the Distinction Between the "True and Apparent Worlds"	123
20. The Uttermost Transformation of Metaphysically Conceived Truth	131
21. Truth as Justice	137
22. The Essence of Will to Power; Permanentizing Becoming into Presence	150

PART TWO: THE ETERNAL RECURRENCE OF THE SAME AND THE WILL TO POWER   159

PART THREE: NIETZSCHE'S METAPHYSICS   185

1. Introduction	187
2. The Will to Power	193
3. Nihilism	201
4. The Eternal Return of the Same	209
5. The Overman	216
6. Justice	235

Analysis *by David Farrell Krell*	255
Glossary	277

Volume IV begins following page 288.

Editor's Preface

The present volume of Heidegger's *Nietzsche* consists of three parts: first, "The Will to Power as Knowledge," a lecture course presented at the University of Freiburg in the summer semester of 1939; second, "The Eternal Recurrence of the Same and the Will to Power," two lectures designed as a conclusion to all three lecture courses on Nietzsche, written in 1939 but not delivered; and third, "Nietzsche's Metaphysics," a typescript from the second half of the year 1940. These texts appear in the 1961 Neske edition of Heidegger's *Nietzsche* (referred to throughout this translation as NI, NII, with page number) at NI, 473–658; NII, 7–29; and NII, 257–333, respectively.

The holograph of "The Will to Power as Knowledge" (Archive number A 40; typescript in "Red Folder" 21) bears the title "Nietzsche: Doctrine of the Will to Power." Richardson lists the title as "Nietzsche's Doctrine of Will to Power (as Knowledge)." The plans for the *Gesamtausgabe* cite this last title without the parentheses.

"Red Folder" 21 also contains (among other unpublished materials relating to Nietzsche and to the theme of *Ereignis*) the typescript of "The Eternal Recurrence of the Same and the Will to Power." Concerning the two lectures that make up this typescript Heidegger inserted the following note at NI, 658, corresponding to the end of Part One of the present volume:

> Because of the premature end of the semester in July 1939 the presentation of the lecture course came to a close here. Volume II of this publication begins with the text of two lectures that were planned as a conclusion that would retrospectively conjoin in thought all the lecture courses that preceded them: "The Will to Power as Art," "The Eternal Recurrence of the Same," and "The Will to Power as Knowledge."

The style in which these two lectures are written suggests that they actually constitute an essay, one that would have been exceedingly difficult to communicate in lecture form. Part Two of the present volume thus serves as a bridge from Heidegger's *lectures* on Nietzsche to his *treatises* on that thinker.

As the footnote to the "Plan of the English Edition" in Volume I indicates, "Nietzsche's Metaphysics," the third and final part of the present volume, is not (as was once believed) a lecture course from the winter semester of 1941–42 but a sixty-four-page typescript dated August 1940 (see "Red Folder" 22, number 1). The typescript contains numerous corrections and additions in Heidegger's hand, from September, October, and December of 1940. A second title page of the typescript reads (in translation) as follows:

Nietzsche's Metaphysics, Interpreted on the Basis of the Stanza:

> World-play, the ruling
> Mixes "Seems" with "To Be":
> Eternally, such fooling
> Mixes *us* in—the melee!
>
> (1886?) V, 349.

At the top of the second title page a note is penciled in: "Re: Winter Semester 1938–39." This may well refer to a heretofore unlisted seminar (*Übung*, "Exercise") presented three hours per week during the winter semester of 1938–39 under the title "Toward an Interpretation of Nietzsche's Second 'Untimely Meditation': 'On the Advantage and Disadvantage of History for Life.' " Although the present text of "Nietzsche's Metaphysics" does not cite the *Welt-Spiel* stanza (see Volume IV in this series, pp. 235–37), it does close with references to Nietzsche's second *Untimely Meditation*.

The translators responsible for the first drafts of each part of the present volume are as follows: Joan Stambaugh for "The Will to Power as Knowledge," myself for "The Eternal Recurrence of the Same and the Will to Power," and Frank A. Capuzzi for "Nietzsche's Metaphysics." I have revised the translations to ensure a modicum of consistency. Heidegger's texts contain no footnotes; all such notes are my own.

Editor's Preface

I have translated afresh all passages from Nietzsche's works that are cited in Heidegger's texts. Heidegger uses the *Grossoktavausgabe* (Leipzig, 1905 ff.) throughout. In the body of the text those references appear in parentheses and are by volume and page, for example: (XII, 51). In my own footnotes I refer to that edition as GOA. Heidegger's references to *Der Wille zur Macht* (second, expanded edition, 1906) are by aphorism—not page—number, for example: (WM, 617). I have checked as many of Heidegger's references as possible against the *Kritische Gesamtausgabe* of Nietzsche's works, edited by the late Giorgio Colli and by Mazzino Montinari (Berlin: W. de Gruyter, 1967–79). The critical edition is available in a fifteen-volume paperback *Studienausgabe* (Munich: Deutscher Taschenbuch Verlag, 1980). I cite the latter throughout as CM. Fragments from Nietzsche's literary remains I cite by the full Mette-number and the fragment number [in brackets], so that readers of both the *Kritische Gesamtausgabe* and the *Studienausgabe* can locate the passage in question, for example: CM, W I 7a [65]. Occasionally I refer to the volume and page of the *Studienausgabe* where the passage can be found; for example, W II 1 [38] is located at CM, *12*, 352–53.

Part One

THE WILL TO POWER AS KNOWLEDGE

1. Nietzsche as the Thinker of the Consummation of Metaphysics

Who Nietzsche *is* and above all who he *will be* we shall know as soon as we are able to think the thought that he gave shape to in the phrase "the will to power." Nietzsche is that thinker who trod the path of thought to "the will to power." We shall never experience who Nietzsche is through a historical report about his life history, nor through a presentation of the contents of his writings. Neither do we, nor should we, want to know who Nietzsche is, if we have in mind only the personality, the historical figure, and the psychological object and its products. But was not the last thing that Nietzsche himself completed for publication the piece that is entitled *Ecce Homo: How One Becomes What One Is?* Does not *Ecce Homo* speak as his last will—that one occupy oneself with him, with this man, and let oneself be told by him those things that occupy the sections of his book?—"Why I am so wise. Why I am so clever. Why I write such good books. Why I am a destiny." Is this not the apotheosis of uninhibited self-presentation and boundless self-mirroring?

It is a gratuitous and thus often practiced procedure to take this self-publication of his own nature and will as the harbinger of erupting madness. However, in *Ecce Homo* it is a matter neither of the biography of Nietzsche nor of the person of "Herr Nietzsche." In truth, it is a matter of a "destiny," the destiny not of an individual but of the history of the era of modern times, of the end of the West. Yet it also belongs to the destiny of this one bearer of Western destiny that (at least up to now) everything that Nietzsche wanted to attain with his writings was turned into its opposite. Against his innermost will, Nietzsche, along with others, became the stimulator and perpetrator of a heightened psychological, bodily, and spiritual self-analysis and *mise-en-scène* of man. The latter has ultimately though indirectly had as its consequence the publication of all human activity in "picture and sound," through photographs and reporting, beyond all measure: a phenomenon of global dimensions that essentially shows the same traits in America and Russia, Japan and Italy, England and Germany, and is remarkably independent of the will of individuals or the type of nations, states, or cultures involved.

Nietzsche transformed himself into an ambiguous figure, and, within his world and that of the present time, he had to do this. What we must do is to grasp the forward thrust and the uniqueness, what is decisive and ultimate, behind this ambiguity. The precondition for this is that we look away from the "man" and also from the "work" insofar as it is viewed as the expression of his humanity, that is, in the light of the man. For even the work as work closes itself off to us as long as we squint somehow after the "life" of the man who created the work instead of asking about Being and the world, which first ground the work. Neither the person of Nietzsche nor even his work concern us when we make both in their connection the object of a historiological and psychological report.

What solely concerns us is the *trace* that that thought-path toward the will to power made into the history of Being—which means into the still untraveled regions of future decisions.

Nietzsche belongs among the essential thinkers. With the term *thinker* we name those exceptional human beings who are destined to think one single thought, a thought that is always "about" *beings as a whole*. Each thinker thinks only one *single* thought. It needs neither renown nor impact in order to gain dominance. In contrast, writers and researchers, as opposed to a thinker, "have" lots and lots of thoughts, that is, ideas that can be converted into much-prized "reality" and that are also evaluated solely in accord with this conversion-capability.

But the single thought of a thinker is one around which, unexpectedly, unnoticed in the stillest stillness, all beings turn. Thinkers are the founders of that which never becomes visible in images, which can never be historiologically related or technologically calculated, yet which rules without recourse to power. Thinkers are always one-sided, namely, on the sole side assigned to them in the very beginnings of the history of thinking by a simple saying. The saying comes from one of the oldest thinkers of the West, Periander of Corinth, who is accounted one of the "seven sages." The saying goes, *"Meleta to pan."* "Take into care beings as a whole."

Among thinkers, those are essential whose sole thought thinks in the direction of a single, supreme decision, whether by preparing for this decision or by decisively bringing it about. The abused and almost exhausted word *decision* is especially preferred today, now that everything has long since been decided or at least thought to be decided. Yet even the well-nigh incredible misuse of the word *decision* cannot prevent us from granting to the word that meaning by which it is related to the most intimate scission and the most extreme distinction. The latter is the distinction between beings as a whole—including gods and men, and world and earth—and Being, whose dominion first enables or denies every being whatsoever to be *the* being that it can be.

The highest decision that can be made and that becomes the ground of all history is that between the predominance of beings and the rule of Being. Whenever and however beings as a whole are thought expressly, thinking stands within the dangerous zone of this decision. The decision is never first made and executed by a human being. Rather, *its* direction and perdurance decide *about* man and, in a different way, about the god.

Nietzsche is an essential thinker because he thinks ahead in a decisive sense, not evading the decision. He prepares its arrival, without, however, measuring and mastering it in its concealed breadth.

For this is the other factor that distinguishes the thinker: only through his knowledge does he know to what extent he can *not* know essential things. However, such knowing about not-knowing, as not-knowing, must not be confused with what is acknowledged in the sciences as the limit of cognition and the bounds of factual knowledge. The latter takes into account the fact that the human conceptual faculty is finite. Ordinary factual knowledge stops where it does not know what is factually still knowable; the essential knowing of the thinker begins by knowing something unknowable. The scientific researcher inquires in order to reach useful answers; the thinker inquires in order to ground the *questionableness* of beings as a whole. The researcher always operates on the foundation of what has already been decided: the fact that there are such things as nature, history, art, and that such things can be made the subject of consideration. For the thinker there is no such thing; he stands within the decision concerning what *is* in general, what beings are.

Nietzsche stands within a decision, as do all Western thinkers before him. With them, he affirms the predominance of beings over against Being, without knowing what is involved in such an affirmation. Yet at the same time Nietzsche is that Western thinker who unconditionally and ultimately brings about this predominance of beings and thus confronts the most unrelenting acuteness of the decision. This is evident in the fact that Nietzsche anticipates the consummation of the modern age with his unique thought of the will to power.

Nietzsche is the transition from the preparatory phase of the modern age—historically, the time between 1600 and 1900—to the beginning of its consummation. We do not know the time span of this consummation. Presumably, it will either be very brief and catastrophic or else very long, in the sense of a self-perpetuating arrangement of what has been attained. There is no room for halfway measures in the present stage of the history of our planet. However, since history is essentially grounded in a decision about beings that it itself did not and can never make, this is true of every historical age in its specific, emphatic form. Different ages first derive their actual historical definition from this fact.

The previous Western position in and toward the decision between the predominance of beings and the rule of Being, which is to say, the affirmation of that predominance, unfolded and developed in a thinking that can be designated by the name *metaphysics*. In this name, *physics* means "the physical" in the original Greek sense of *ta physei onta*, "beings that as such subsist and come to presence of themselves." *Meta* means "over and away from, beyond." In the present instance, over and away from beings. Where to? To Being. Thought metaphysically, Being is that which is thought *from* beings

Nietzsche as the Thinker of the Consummation of Metaphysics

as their most universal definition and *to* beings as their ground and cause. The Christian idea of the causation of all beings through a first cause is metaphysical, especially the version of the creation story of the Old Testament as rehearsed in Greek metaphysics. The Enlightenment idea of a government of all beings under cosmic reason is metaphysical. Beings are regarded as that which lays claim to an explanation. Each time, beings take precedence here as the standard, the goal, and the actualization of Being. Even when Being is thought in the sense of an "ideal" for beings, as *what* and *how* every being is to be, the individual being is indeed subordinate to Being, but as a whole the *ideal* is in service to beings, just as every power is dependent most of all upon what it overpowers. But it also belongs to the essence of every genuine power that it overlooks and must overlook this dependency, so that it can never acknowledge it.

Metaphysics thinks beings as a whole according to their priority over Being. The whole of Western thinking from the Greeks through Nietzsche is metaphysical thinking. Each age of Western history is grounded in its respective metaphysics. Nietzsche anticipates the consummation of metaphysics. His thought-path to the will to power anticipates the metaphysics that supports the modern age as it completes itself *in* its consummation. Here "consummation" does not mean a last addition of the still missing part, nor the final repletion of a gap hitherto neglected. Consummation means the unimpeded development of all the essential powers of beings, powers that have been reserved for a long time, to what they demand as a whole. The metaphysical consummation of an age is not the mere tapering off of what is already familiar. It is the unconditioned and complete installation, for the first time and in advance, of what is unexpected and never to be expected. Compared with what has been up to now, the consummation is novel. Thus it is never seen and grasped by those who only calculate by hindsight.

Nietzsche's thought of will to power thinks beings as a whole such that the metaphysical ground of the history of the present and future age becomes visible and at the same time determinative. The determinative rule of a philosophy can be measured neither by what is familiar from hearsay nor by the number of its "followers" and "members," and least of all by the "literature" to which it gives rise. Even when Nietzsche is no longer known by name, what his thinking had to think will rule. Each thinker who thinks ahead to the decision is moved and consumed by care with respect to a need that cannot yet be felt and experienced during his lifetime, a need not yet visible in the scope of his historically ascertainable yet irrelevant influence.

In the thought of will to power, Nietzsche anticipates the metaphysical ground of the consummation of the modern age. In the thought of will to power, metaphysical thinking itself completes itself in advance. Nietzsche, the thinker of the thought of will to power, is the *last metaphysician* of the West. The age whose consummation unfolds in his thought, the modern age, is a final age. This means an age in which at some point and in some way the historical decision arises as to whether this final age is the conclusion of Western history or the counterpart to another beginning. To go the length of Nietzsche's path of thought to the will to power means to catch sight of this historical decision.

If one is oneself not forced into the thoughtful confrontation with Nietzsche, a reflective accompanying Nietzsche on his path of thought can only have as its goal consciously to draw nearer to what is "happening" in the history of the modern age. What is happening means what sustains and compels history, what triggers chance events and in advance gives leeway to resolutions, what within beings represented as objects and as states of affairs basically is *what is*. We never experience what is happening by ascertaining through historical inquiry what is "going on." As this expression tells us very well, what is "going on" passes before us in the foreground and background of the public stage of events and varying opinions. What happens can never be made historiologically cognizable. It can only be thoughtfully known by grasping what the metaphysics that predetermines the age has elevated to thought and word. What one otherwise calls Nietzsche's "philosophy" and studiously compares with previous philosophies is a matter of utter indifference. What is inevitable is what has come to word in Nietzsche's thought of will to power as the historical ground of what is happening in the context of the modern age of Western history.

Whether we incorporate Nietzsche's "philosophy" into our cultural

Nietzsche as the Thinker of the Consummation of Metaphysics

legacy or pass it by is always of no significance. It will be fatal if we, lacking the resolve for genuine questioning, simply "busy" ourselves with Nietzsche and take this "busyness" for thoughtful discussion of Nietzsche's unique thought. Unequivocal rejection of all philosophy is an attitude that always deserves respect, for it contains more of philosophy than it itself knows. Mere toying with philosophical thoughts, which keeps to the periphery right from the start because of various sorts of reservations, all mere play for purposes of intellectual entertainment or refreshment, is despicable: it does not know what is at stake on a thinker's path of thought.

2. Nietzsche's So-called Major Work

We call Nietzsche's thought of will to power his *sole* thought. At the same time we are saying that Nietzsche's other thought, that of eternal recurrence of the same, is of necessity included in the thought of will to power. Both thoughts—will to power and eternal recurrence of the same—say *the same* and think the *same* fundamental characteristic of beings as a whole. The thought of eternal recurrence of the same is the inner—but not the retrospective—completion of the thought of will to power. Precisely for this reason Nietzsche thought eternal recurrence of the same at an earlier time than he did will to power. For when he thinks it for the first time, each thinker thinks his sole thought in its completion, though not yet in its full unfolding; that is, not yet in the scope and the dangerousness that always grow beyond it and must first be borne out.

Ever since the time when Nietzsche's thought of will to power first scintillated and became decisive for him (from about 1884 until the last weeks of his thinking, at the end of 1888), Nietzsche struggled for the *thoughtful configuration* of his sole thought. As far as the writing goes, in Nietzsche's plans and sketches this configuration looked like what he himself in accordance with tradition called the "major work." But this "major work" was never finished. Not only was it never finished, it never became a "work" at all in the sense of modern philosophical works such as Descartes' *Meditationes de prima philosophia,* Kant's *Critique of Pure Reason,* Hegel's *Phenomenology of Spirit,* and Schelling's *Philosophical Investigations into the Essence of Human Freedom and the Objects Pertaining Thereto.*

Why did Nietzsche's thought-paths to the will to power fail to converge in this kind of "work"? Historiographers, psychologists, biogra-

Nietzsche's So-called Major Work

phers, and other propagators of human curiosity are not caught short of explanations in such cases. In Nietzsche's "case" especially there are ample reasons that explain the lack of the major work adequately enough for the common view.

One says that the magnitude of material, the variety and scope of individual areas in which will to power would have had to be demonstrated as the fundamental characteristic of beings, could not have been assimilated to a uniform degree by a single thinker. For ever since the middle of the last century, philosophy too cannot evade the specialization of work into one discipline—logic, ethics, aesthetics, philosophy of language, philosophy of the state and of religion—if it is to contribute more than empty, general phrases about what is already known anyhow in a more reliable fashion in the individual sciences. In Kant's time or perhaps even in Hegel's age uniform mastery in all areas of knowledge might have been just barely possible. Meanwhile, the sciences of the nineteenth century have not only broadened our knowledge of beings in a surprisingly rich and rapid way; above all, they have developed the procedures of investigating all areas of beings into such a multifariousness, fineness, and surety that a general knowledge of all the sciences can hardly graze the surface. Knowledge of the results and procedures of all the sciences is, however, necessary if anything with sufficient basis is to be decided about beings as a whole. Without this scientific foundation all metaphysics remains a castle in the air. Nietzsche himself no longer succeeded in uniformly mastering all the sciences.

One notes, furthermore, that a gift for thinking in terms of strict proofs and deductions in broad contexts—"systematic philosophizing," as it is called—was utterly lacking in Nietzsche. He himself clearly expressed his distrust of all "systematists." How could he ever succeed in producing a system of all knowledge of beings as a whole and thus a "systematic" major work?

Moreover, one ascertains that Nietzsche became the victim of an exaggerated drive for immediate recognition and impact. The success of Richard Wagner, whom Nietzsche very early—even before he really knew it himself—discovered as his true adversary, robbed him of the peace of mind necessary to go his own way, seduced him from the sovereign execution of his main task and diverted him into a kind of agitated literary production.

Finally, one emphasizes that precisely during the years when Nietzsche was wrestling to think the configuration of will to power his working powers denied him their service more frequently than before and prevented him from executing such a "work." Whereas scientific thinking, figuratively speaking, always runs along a line and can continue from the place where it stopped earlier, a thinker's thinking must in advance make a leap into the whole for each step it takes and collect itself in the center of a circle.

These and other explanations for the fact that the "work" never got written are correct. They can even be documented by Nietzsche's own remarks. However, what about the assumption with regard to which these explanations are so zealously offered? The assumption that we are talking about a "work," written in the style of already familiar philosophical "major works," is unfounded. Nor can it be founded. The assumption is untrue, because it goes against the essence and kind of thought that will to power is.

The fact that Nietzsche himself speaks of a "major work" in letters to his sister and to the few, and ever fewer, sympathetic friends and helpers does not alone prove the justifiability of that assumption. Nietzsche clearly knew that even these few "closest" friends to whom he still expressed himself could not judge what was facing him. The constantly new forms in which he tried to expound his thinking in various publications clearly show how decidedly Nietzsche knew that the configuration of his fundamental thought had to be something other than a work in the traditional sense. The lack of completion, if one may dare to assert such a thing, in no way consists in the fact that a work "about" will to power was not completed. Lack of completion could only mean that the inner form of his unique thought was denied the thinker. Yet perhaps it was not denied at all; perhaps the failure lies only with those for whom Nietzsche walked his path of thought; those who blocked this path with hasty and altogether timely interpretations, with the all-too-easy and all-too-corrupting superciliousness of all epigones.

Only on the arbitrary assumption that there is a "work" to be completed, a work that has long been guaranteed in its essence by precedents, can one take what Nietzsche left unpublished as "torso," as "fragment," as "sketch," as "preliminary study." Grant the assumption, and there is no other choice. However, if this assumption is groundless from the very beginning, and also inappropriate for the fundamental thought of this thinker, *then* these thought-paths that Nietzsche left behind take on a different aspect.

Speaking more cautiously, only then can the *question* arise as to how these paths and trains and leaps of thought are to be taken, so that we might fittingly think what was thought in them, instead of deforming it in accordance with our habits of thought.

Today there lies before the public a book with the title *The Will to Power*. This book is not a "work" of Nietzsche's. Nevertheless, it contains only what Nietzsche himself wrote down. Even the most general structural plan in which the writings of different years were ordered was drawn up by Nietzsche himself. The not completely arbitrary collection and publication in book form of Nietzsche's writings from 1882 until 1888 occurred in a first attempt after Nietzsche's death; the collection was released in 1901 as volume XV of Nietzsche's works. A substantial increase in the writings included can be found in the 1906 edition of the book *The Will to Power*, which was included in unrevised form in 1911 as volumes XV and XVI of the *Grossoktavausgabe* in place of the first edition of 1901.

Of course, the present book *The Will to Power* does not reproduce the thought-path of Nietzsche's will to power, either with regard to its completeness or, above all, with regard to its own pace and law of advance. But the book is sufficient as the basis for an attempt to follow this thought-path and to think Nietzsche's sole thought in the course of this path. Nevertheless, we have to free ourselves from the outset and throughout from the order imposed on the book.

However, we still have to follow some kind of order when we try to penetrate to the thought-path of the will to power. When we provide a differently structured selection and order of passages we are *apparently* proceeding in a no less arbitrary way than the coordinators of the present book from which we are taking our texts. But we shall initially avoid mixing up passages from very different periods—which is what the book now available does. Moreover, we shall initially keep to those passages from the years 1887–88, the time in which Nietzsche reached the point of greatest luminosity and tranquility in his thinking. From these passages we shall again choose those in which the whole of the thought of will to power comes across and is expressed in its own coherence. For this reason we cannot call these passages fragments or pieces at all. If we nevertheless retain this designation, we then note that these individual passages converge or diverge not only in content but above all according to their inner shape and scope, according to the gathering power and luminosity of thought, and according to the depth of focus and the acuity of their utterance.

Let these preliminary remarks suffice to remove the appearance of arbitrariness and fortuitousness from our procedure. We shall always distinguish sharply between the subsequently produced book bearing the title *The Will to Power* and the hidden thought-path to the will to power, whose innermost law and structure we are trying to follow. Because we do not wish to read the book *The Will to Power*, because we have to walk the *path* of thought to the will to power, we shall now open the book at a quite specific passage.

3. The Will to Power as Principle of a New Valuation

We shall focus on what Nietzsche planned to say in Part III under the title "Principle of a New Valuation," according to the arrangement discussed above. Evidently, Nietzsche wanted to express the "new," his *own* "philosophy" here. If Nietzsche's essential and sole thought is the will to power, the title of the third book immediately provides important information about what will to power is, without our yet grasping its proper essence. Will to power is the "principle of a new valuation," and vice versa: the principle of the new valuation to be grounded is will to power. What does "valuation" mean? What does the word *value* mean? The word *value* as a special term came into circulation partly through Nietzsche. One speaks of the "cultural values" of a nation, of the "vital values" of a people, of "moral," "aesthetic," "religious" "values." One does not think very much about these phrases—even though they are supposed, after all, to contain an appeal to what is supreme and ultimate.

The word *value* is essential for Nietzsche. This is immediately evident in the subtitle that he gives his thought-path to the will to power: "Attempt at a Revaluation of All Values." Value for Nietzsche means a condition of life, a condition of life's being "alive." In Nietzsche's thinking *life* is usually the term for what is and for beings as a whole insofar as they are. Occasionally, however, it also means *our* life in a special sense, which is to say, the Being of man.

Nietzsche does not see the essence of life in "self-preservation" ("struggle for existence") as do the biology and the doctrine of life of his time influenced by Darwin, but rather in a self-transcending enhancement. As a condition of life, value must therefore be thought as that which supports, furthers, and awakens the enhancement of life. Only what enhances life, and beings as a whole, has value—more precisely, *is* a value. The characterization of value as a "condition" of life in the sense of life-enhancement is initially quite undetermined. Although what conditions (value) makes what is conditioned (life) dependent upon it, it is nonetheless conversely true that the essence of what conditions (value) is determined by the essence of that which it is supposed to condition (life). Whatever essential characteristics value has as a condition of life depend on the essence of "life," on what is distinctive about this essence. When Nietzsche says that the essence of life is life-enhancement, the question arises as to what belongs to the essence of such enhancement. Enhancement, especially the kind that occurs *in* and *through* what is enhanced, is an *over-beyond-itself*. This means that in enhancement life projects higher possibilities of itself before itself and directs itself forward into something not yet attained, something first to be achieved.

Enhancement implies something like a looking ahead and through to the scope of something higher, a "perspective." Since life, that is, each being, is life-enhancement, life as such has a "perspectival character." Accordingly, this perspectival character is also appropriate to "*values*" as the conditions of life. Values condition and determine "perspectivally" in each case the "perspectival," fundamental essence of "life." This remark suggests at the same time that we must from the outset keep Nietzsche's statements about "values" as "conditions" of life out of the area of common representation, where one also often speaks of "life-conditions," for example, when one speaks of the "life-conditions" of animals at hand. "Life," "conditions of life," "values," these fundamental terms of Nietzschean thinking have their own definiteness in terms of the fundamental thought of this thinking.

"Valuation" then means determining and ascertaining those "perspectival" conditions that make life what it is, that is, assure its essential enhancement. What does a *new* valuation mean? It means that a reversal of the ancient, long-standing valuation is in preparation. Briefly stated, this old valuation is the Platonic-Christian one, the devaluation of beings at hand here and now as *mē on*, as what really ought not to be, because they represent a falling away from what truly is, from the "Ideas" and the divine order; or, if not actually a falling away, at best only a fleeting passage toward that divine order.

The old "traditional" valuation gives to life the perspective of something suprasensuous, supraterrestrial—*epekeina*, "beyond"—in which "true bliss" has its home, in contradistinction to this "vale of tears" that is called the "earth" and "world." The reversal of the valuation, the old and the new, is hinted at in a passage from Nietzsche: "What must I do to become blissful? I don't know, but I say unto you: be blissful and then do what you feel like doing" (XII, 285; from the years 1882–84).

The question posed is the Christian question of the "Gospels." The form of Nietzsche's answer is adapted to biblical language: "But I say unto you." Yet the content reverses everything, since blissfulness is not placed *after* the deed as a consequence but *before* it as a ground. However, Nietzsche does not give carte blanche for unleashing all kinds of drives that would compel and pull us in some sort of direction, but "Be blissful"—everything is contained in that.

A new valuation means to set different perspectival conditions for "life." Yet we would still understand the expression insufficiently if we thought that it was only a matter of setting new *conditions* for life. Rather, we must determine anew the essence of *life itself* and, at one and the same time, that is, as an essential consequence, the corresponding perspectival conditions for this essence. Since the essence of life is seen as life-"enhancement," all conditions that simply aim at life-preservation are downgraded to the level of those that basically hinder or even negate life and life's perspectival enhancement, to the level of those that not only preclude but undermine in advance the possibility of other perspectives. Strictly speaking, life-hindering conditions are not values but *un*values.

If life were traditionally understood merely as self-"preservation" in the service of other and later things, and if the essence of life as self-enhancement were thus misunderstood, then the traditional conditions of life, the "highest values hitherto" (XVI, 421) would not be true values; a "revaluation of all values" through a "new valuation" would be necessary. For this reason, Nietzsche plans to arrange the second book, "Critique of the (Hitherto) Highest Values," before the third book.

However, in order to decide about the necessary and sufficient conditions for life as life-enhancement, the new valuation must go back to what life itself is as self-enhancement, to what makes this essence of life possible in its ground. The ground, that with which something starts in its essence, from which it comes forth and in which it remains rooted, is called in Greek *arkhē,* in Latin *principium,* "principle."

The principle of a new valuation is what determines life, for which values are the perspectival conditions, in its essential ground. But if the principle of the new valuation is will to power, this means that life, or being as a whole, is itself will to power in its fundamental essence and essential ground—this and nothing else. Thus a note from the last year of Nietzsche's work begins with the words "If the innermost essence of Being is will to power . . ." (WM, 693; March–June, 1888).

Already in 1885 Nietzsche initiates a train of thought with the question "And do you know what 'the world' is to me?" By "world" he understands beings as a whole, often equating the term with "life," just as we like to equate "worldview" with a "view of life." He answers: "*This world is will to power—and nothing besides!* And you yourselves are this will to power—and nothing besides!" (WM, 1067).*

Nietzsche thinks the fundamental character of beings as a whole in the unique thought of will to power. The utterance of his metaphysics, that is, of the determination of beings as a whole, reads: *Life is will to power.* Something twofold and yet singular is contained in this: first, being as a whole is "life"; second, the essence of life is "will to power."

With this utterance, "Life is will to power," Western metaphysics completes itself; at its beginning stands the obscure statement "being as a whole is *physis.*" Nietzsche's utterance, "being as a whole is will to power," states concerning being as a whole that which was predetermined as a possibility in the beginning of Western thinking and

---

* See the first note on p. 164 of Volume II of this series.

became unavoidable because of an inevitable decline from this beginning. This utterance does not announce a private view of the person "Nietzsche." The thinker and sayer of this utterance is "a destiny." This means that the Being of this thinker and of every essential Western thinker consists in an almost *inhuman* fidelity to the most covert history of the West. This history is the poet's and thinker's struggle for a word for beings as a whole. All world-historical publicity essentially lacks the eyes and the ears, the measure and the heart, for the poet's and thinker's struggle for the word of Being. The struggle is in play beyond war and peace, outside success and defeat, is never touched by clamor and acclaim, and remains unconcerned about the destiny of individuals.

Being as a whole is will to power. Will to power is the principle of a new valuation. But what does "will to power" mean? We understand, after all, what "will" means inasmuch as we experience something like this in ourselves, whether in willing or even in not willing. Similarly, we attach a vague idea to the word *power*. "Will to power" is then also clear. Yet nothing would be more ruinous than to follow the usual everyday ideas about "will to power" and then to think we know something about Nietzsche's unique thought.

If the thought of will to power is the first and, in terms of rank, the highest thought of Nietzschean and thus of Western metaphysics in general, we will find our way to the decisive thinking of this first and last metaphysical thought only by traversing those paths that Nietzsche, the thinker of this thought, himself traveled. If will to power is the fundamental characteristic of all beings, it must, so to speak, be "encountered" by the thinking of this thought in every region of beings: in nature, art, history, politics, in science and in knowledge in general. Insofar as these things are beings, they must all be will to power. Science, for example, knowledge in general, is a configuration of will to power. Thoughtful reflection (in the manner of the thinker Nietzsche) about knowledge—and science in particular—must make visible what will to power is.

Therefore we ask with Nietzsche, What is knowledge? What is science? Through the answer—"It is will to power"—we learn immediately and even simultaneously what will to power means. We can ask the same question with regard to art and with regard to nature. We even *have* to ask it when we ask the question of the *essence of knowledge*. We cannot immediately comprehend why and in what way a distinctive connection exists between the essence of knowledge, the essence of art, and the essence of "nature" precisely for Nietzsche's thought.

The question of knowledge as such, and of science in particular, is now to assume priority, not only because "science" determines our most proper area of work, but above all because knowledge and knowing have attained an essential power within Western history. "Science" is not simply *one* field of "cultural" activity among others; science is a fundamental power in that confrontation by dint of which Western man as such is related to beings and asserts himself in their midst. When in the business section of today's newspaper "packing parcels" is listed as a subject "suitable" for a "science taught at the university level," this is not simply a "bad joke"; and when one works to set up a "radio science" on its own, these developments are not a degeneration of "science"; rather, they are merely bizarre stragglers in a process that has been going on for centuries, a process whose metaphysical ground lies in the fact that knowledge and knowing are conceived of as *technē* early on as a consequence of the very beginning of Western metaphysics. To ask about the *essence* of knowledge means knowingly to experience what "really" has happened in the history that we are.

According to Nietzsche, knowledge is a form of will to power. But what does he mean when he says "knowledge"? That must first be characterized and described.

However, we are not here sketching our own little "portrait" of Nietzsche's "theory of knowledge and science," in the manner of presentations in the "history of philosophy"; we are exclusively and quite strictly reflecting on his thought-paths, by way of his notes and the observations to which we have access.

Thus what this lecture course attempts is something quite simple and altogether preliminary: It is to give us directives for *thoughtfully thinking through* Nietzsche's fundamental thought. Yet the directives are not to get lost in enumerating rules and points of view as to how

The Will to Power as Principle of a New Valuation   21

this should be done. Our course is to proceed as a kind of *rigorous exercise*. When we try to think the fundamental thought, every step is a reflection on what "occurs" in Western history. This history never becomes an object in the historical contemplation of which we lose ourselves; nor is it a condition that we could psychologically prove to be the case with us. Then what is it? We will know that when we *comprehend* will to power, that is, when we are able not only to represent to ourselves what this phrase means but also to understand what the thing is: will to power—*a peculiar dominance of Being "over" beings as a whole* [in the veiled form of Being's abandonment of beings].*

---

* The bracketed phrase was apparently added in 1961. *Seinsverlassenheit des Seienden*, "the abandonment of beings by Being," is discussed in detail in Part Two of Volume IV, esp. pp. 215–21. See also section 6 of Part Two in the present volume.

4. Knowledge in Nietzsche's Fundamental Thought Concerning the Essence of Truth

Knowledge—what is it? What are we really asking about when we ask the question about the essence of knowledge? To the position of Western man in the midst of beings, to the determination, foundation, and development of this position with regard to beings, that is, to the essential determination of beings as a whole, that is, to Western metaphysics, the following unique characteristic pertains: Western man from early on had to ask the question, *Ti estin epistēmē?* "What is that—knowledge?" Only very late, in the course of the nineteenth century, did this metaphysical question become a subject for scientific inquiry, that is, a subject for psychological and biological investigations. The question about the essence of knowledge became a matter of "theory formation," on the battleground of theory of knowledge. In retrospect, stimulated by historical and philological investigation into the past, one discovered that Aristotle and Plato, and even Heraclitus and Parmenides, and then later Descartes, Kant, and Schelling "too" were in "pursuit" of such "theory of knowledge." Of course, old Parmenides' "theory of knowledge" had to be still quite "incomplete," since he did not yet have the methods and apparatus of the nineteenth and twentieth centuries at his disposal. It is correct that the greatest thinkers of antiquity, Heraclitus and Parmenides, reflected on the essence of knowledge. But it is also a "fact" that even today we hardly have any correct conception and gauge of what this reflection on the essence of knowledge meant: "thinking" as the guideline for the projection of beings as a whole upon Being, and the unrest, concealed from itself, concerning the veiled essence of *this* guideline and of the "nature of guidelines" as such.

Yet that these thinkers and, correspondingly, modern thinkers should have "pursued" the "theory of knowledge" in the manner of philosophical scholars of the nineteenth century is a childish opinion, even if one admits that Kant took better care concerning this "epistemological" business than the later "Neokantians" who "improved upon" him. We could have completely omitted mention of the twaddle of scholarly "theory of knowledge" here if Nietzsche, too, had not moved in its sultry air—in part reluctantly, in part eagerly—and become dependent on it. Since even the greatest, even the most solitary, thinkers do not live in the supraterrestrial space of a supraworldly place, they are always surrounded and touched—influenced, as one says—by contemporaries and traditions. The only really decisive question is whether one explains their true thought in terms of the influences of the milieu and the effects of their actual "life" situation, or even predominantly illumines their thought in this way, or whether one comprehends their unique thought on the basis of essentially different origins, namely, on the basis of what precisely first opens and grounds their thinking. As we follow Nietzsche's thought about the essence of knowledge, we shall not pay attention to what is in various ways "fatal," to what is contemporary or "epistemological" about him, but only to that within which the fundamental position of modern metaphysics develops and completes itself. This "metaphysical element," however, moves of itself, of its own essential weight, into a concealed historical connection with the beginning of Western thought in the Greeks. We are not thinking this connection of the fulfillment of Western metaphysics with its beginning historically as a chain of dependencies and relations among philosophical views, opinions, and "problems." We know that connection to be the very thing that now and in the future still happens and *is*.

For this reason, we must from the outset be clear about what is fundamentally being asked about when the question about the *essence* of knowledge is asked.

In Western history, knowledge is taken to be that behavior and that attitude of representing by which what is true is grasped and preserved as a possession. Knowledge that is not true is not only "untrue knowledge," but no knowledge at all; the phrase "true knowledge" is redundant. What is true and its possession—or, more succinctly, truth in the sense of a thing's being recognized as true—constitute the essence of knowledge. In the question of what knowledge is, we are basically asking about truth and its essence. And *truth*? When this or that is taken up and held to be what it actually *is*, we call this holding-for a holding-to-be-true. Here, what is *true* means what *is*. To grasp what is true means to take beings in representation and assertion and to repeat, pass on, and retain them as they *are*. What is true and truth stand in the most intimate relation to beings. The question about the essence of knowledge, as the question about what is true and truth, is a question about beings—what they themselves are as such. It questions beyond beings, but at the same time back to beings. The question concerning knowledge is a metaphysical question.

If Nietzsche's thought of will to power is the fundamental thought of his metaphysics and the last thought of Western metaphysics, then the essence of knowledge, that is, the essence of truth, must be defined in terms of will to power. Truth contains and grants that which *is*, grants beings in the midst of which man himself is a being, in such a way that he relates to beings. Thus in all relating man somehow keeps to what is true. Truth is what man strives for, it is that of which he demands that it dominate all action and letting be, all wishing and giving, experiencing and shaping, suffering and overcoming. One speaks of a "will to truth."

Because man as a being relates to beings as a whole and thus pursues and takes care of a realm of beings, and within it this or that particular being, truth is both expressly and tacitly demanded, valued, and honored. Thus one could formulate the metaphysical essence of man in the following statement: *Man is the one who honors, and consequently also the one who denies, truth.* Nietzsche's understanding of truth is thus illuminated—as though by a sudden flash of lightning—by a statement he makes about honoring truth. In a note from the year 1884, when the formation of the thought of will to power consciously begins, Nietzsche remarks "that honoring truth is already the *consequence* of an *illusion*" (WM, 602). What does this say? Nothing less than that truth itself is an "illusion," a mirage; for only if that is true can *honoring* truth be the *consequence* of an "illusion." Yet if a will to truth is vital to our "life," and if life is *enhancement* of life, the ever higher "realization" of life and thus the vitalizing of what is real, and if truth is only "illusion," "imagination," thus something unreal, truth becomes a *de-realization*, a hindrance to and even a destruction of life. Truth is then not a condition of life, not a value, but an unvalue.

But what if all barriers between truth and untruth fall and everything is of equal value, which is to say, of no value? Then nihilism becomes reality. Does Nietzsche want nihilism or does he precisely want to recognize it as such and overcome it? He wants to overcome it. If, accordingly, the will to truth belongs to life, then truth, since its essence is illusion, *cannot* be the *highest* value. There must be a value, a condition of perspectival life-enhancement, that is of greater value than truth. Indeed Nietzsche does say "that art is *worth more* than truth" (WM, 853, IV; from 1887–88).*

Art alone guarantees and secures life perspectivally in its vitality, that is, in the possibilities of its enhancement, against the power of truth. Hence Nietzsche's statement: "We have *art* in order *not to perish from the truth*" (WM, 822, 1888). Art is a higher "value," that is, a more primordial perspectival condition of "life," than truth. Here art is conceived *metaphysically* as a condition of beings, not merely aesthetically as pleasure, not merely biologically and anthropologically as an expression of life and of humanity, and not merely politically as proof of a position of power. All these interpretations of art that have appeared in the metaphysical history of the West are themselves but essential consequences of the metaphysical definition that Nietzsche utters and that is already prefigured in metaphysical thinking from the very beginning (cf. Aristotle's *Poetics*). Art stands in metaphysical opposition to truth as illusion.

But how is this? Does not art portray what is unreal, is not art in the proper sense "illusion"—to be sure, a beautiful appearance, but still a mere appearance? Is "illusionism" not taken to be the essence

---

* See Volume 1 of this series, section 12, for this and the following.

of all art in current art theories? How is art supposed to oppose and prevail against the destructive power of truth as illusion if it is of the same essence? Or are art and truth only different species of illusion? Does not everything then become "illusion," mere appearance, nothing? We dare not evade the question. We should measure right at the beginning the extent to which Nietzsche's characterization of truth as an illusion holds up. Holding one's own in the midst of the genuine exaction of thought is the first step toward thinking.

Truth, an illusion—that is a terrible proclamation, but not a mere phrase and not the manner of speaking of a presumably overwrought writer; perhaps it is already history, our most actual history, not merely since yesterday, and not only for tomorrow. Truth, always and only mere appearance? And knowledge, always the mere stabilization of sheer appearance, a taking refuge in illusion? How seldom we dare to persevere in this question, to ask it thoroughly and to seek purchase there where thoughtful thinking begins. The fact that this happens so seldom is not even due to man's customary laziness and superficiality, but rather to the busyness and the sovereignty of philosophical acumen—or what people take acumen to be. For in the face of a statement like the one just mentioned people are immediately ready to wield a devastating proof as defense. Herr Nietzsche says that truth is an illusion. And if Nietzsche wants to be "consistent"—for there is nothing like "consistency"—his statement about truth is an illusion, too, and so we need not bother with him any longer.

The idle acumen that presents itself with this kind of refutation creates an illusion that everything is settled. However, in its refutation of Nietzsche's statement about truth as illusion it forgets one thing, to wit, that if Nietzsche's statement is true, then not only must Nietzsche's own statement as true become an illusion but just as necessarily so must the true consequent statement that is brought forward as a refutation of Nietzsche be an "illusion." However, the defender of acumen will now answer; having meanwhile become *still* more clever, that our characterization of his refutation as an illusion is also for its part illusion. Certainly—and such mutual refutation can be continued endlessly, only to confirm what it already made use of with the very first step: Truth is an illusion. This statement is not only not shattered by the argumentative *tour de force* of mere acumen, it is not even touched by it.

Of course, common sense sees in this kind of refutation a very effective procedure. It is called "beating the opponent with his own weapon." Yet one overlooks the fact that with this procedure one has not yet torn away the weapon from one's opponent at all; nor *can* one tear it away, because one has renounced grasping it, that is, first *comprehending* what the statement wants to say. However, since these tricks are brought into the game again and again with regard to principles and the basic thoughts of thinkers, an interim remark about refutation was needed. We take from it four things that are important for the genuine execution of every essential reflection.

1. Such refutations have the dubious distinction of remaining ensconced in what is vacuous and without foundation. The statement "Truth is an illusion" is applied to itself solely as one "truth" among others—without reflecting on what illusion might mean here, without asking how and for what reason "illusion" as such could be connected with the essence of truth.

2. Such refutations assume the appearance of the sharpest consistency. Yet the consistency comes immediately to an end, lest it be valid for the refuter. While appealing to logic as the highest instance of thinking, one claims that this logic should be valid only for the opponent. Such refutations are the most insidious way of expelling thinking from genuine, inquiring reflection.

3. An essential statement—such as that by Nietzsche—concerning truth cannot, moreover, be refuted by statements that already as statements are subordinated to the initial statement, insofar as they are supposed to state something true; just as little can a house protest that it can dispense with every sort of foundation and yet stand firm.

4. Statements such as Nietzsche's cannot be refuted. For a refutation in the sense of a demonstration of incorrectness has no meaning here. Every essential statement refers back to a ground that cannot be shunted aside, a ground that rather demands to be grounded more fundamentally. We respect sound common sense, but there are realms that it does not penetrate, and they are the most essential ones. There are things that demand a *stricter* kind of thinking. If truth is to reign

in all thinking, then its *essence* presumably cannot be conceived by ordinary thinking and its rules of the game.

Certainly, Nietzsche's statement that honoring truth is already the consequence of an illusion, and the statement underlying this one, to the effect that truth is an illusion, even *the* illusion, sound arbitrary and alienating. These statements are not only supposed to *sound* that way, they must *be* alienating and terrible because, as thoughtful statements, they speak of what occurs in a concealed way that is always inaccessible to what is public. Hence it is necessary first of all to give the right emphasis to this first reference to Nietzsche's fundamental thought surrounding the essence of knowledge and truth. This can be done by pointing out that Nietzsche's definition of the essence of truth is not an overwrought and foundationless assertion of a man who is bent upon originality at any cost; the essential definition of truth as "illusion" is essentially connected with the metaphysical interpretation of beings and thus is as old and as primordial as metaphysics itself.

In one of the great originators of Western thinking, Heraclitus, we find a fragment (Fr. 28) whose first part (which is all that we shall consider) reads as follows: *Dokeonta gar ho dokimōtatos ginōskei, phylassei.* This saying, with its clear precision and the veiled, yet announced, play of thought in it, cannot be adequately rendered in our language, no matter how philosophical it may be. Thus we shall attempt a translation that paraphrases and clarifies right from the start: "What shows itself, what appears to one man alone, is that which the most famous one (who is held in the highest regard and fame) knows, and his knowing watches over what alone appears, holding fast to it as to what is firm and gives support." More succinctly, and more literally faithful to the Greek: "For having views / is also / the knowing of the most highly regarded one, watching over / holding fast to a view."

However, we must avoid misinterpreting this saying in a modern epistemological sense, looking for the Kantian distinction of "appearance" and "thing in itself" and ultimately even falsifying the concept of "appearance" into that of "mere illusion." The weight of the ancient Greek saying rests rather in the fact that what shows itself, what proffers an aspect, and thus the aspect itself, are taken to be what *is*. For to be "in being" means to grow, *phyein*. The rise of presencing, however, is the reign that comes to presence, *physis*. The later Greek interpretation of the beingness of beings, namely the Platonic one, can be understood only under the aegis of this primordial predetermination of beings as *physis*. For how else should the "Idea" be what is most in being of all beings if it had not already been decided that to be in being means the self-showing that arises and presences: presenting an outward appearance *(eidos)*, constituting the countenance *(idea)* that a "matter" has. *Dokeonta*, "what shows itself," is, for Heraclitus, not equivalent to mere subjective opinion in the modern sense, for two reasons: first, because *dokein* means "to show itself," "to appear," and this is said in terms of beings themselves; and second, because the early thinkers and the Greeks in general knew nothing about man as an I-subject. Precisely the most highly regarded one—and that means he who is most worthy of fame—is such a person because he has the power to look away from himself and solely to see that which alone "is." But precisely this is what shows itself, the sight and the image that proffer themselves. What is imagelike does not consist in what is fabricated, like a copied imitation. The Greek sense of "image"—if we may use this word at all—is a "coming to the fore," *phantasia*, understood as "coming to presence." With the transformations of the Greek concept of Being in the course of the history of metaphysics, the Western *concept of the image* changes accordingly. In antiquity, in the Middle Ages, in the modern period, "image" is different not only with regard to content and name but also with regard to essence. "Image" means:

1. coming to presence;
2. referential correspondence within the order of creation;
3. representational object.

For Heraclitus, knowing means to take hold of what shows itself, to guard the sight as the "view" that something proffers, the "image" in the designated sense of *phantasia*. In knowing, what is true is held fast; what shows itself, the image, is taken up and into possession; what is true is the in-formed image. Truth is imaging, the word thought now in a Greek way, not "psychologically," not epistemologically in the modern sense.

When Nietzsche says truth is "illusion," his utterance means the same as what Heraclitus in saying, and yet not the same: the same insofar as Nietzsche's saying *still* presupposes, as we shall see, the primordial interpretation of beings as a whole as *physis*; not the same insofar as the primordial Greek interpretation of beings has meanwhile essentially changed, especially in modern thinking, while nevertheless maintaining itself in this transformation. We may neither interpret Heraclitus with the aid of Nietzsche's fundamental thought nor explain Nietzsche's metaphysics simply in terms of Heraclitus and as "Heraclitean." Rather, their hidden historical affinity reveals itself only when we see or work our way through the gap that lies between both—the history of Western thought. Only then can we judge in what sense these two thinkers, one at the beginning, the other at the end of Western metaphysics, had to think "the selfsame."

Thus it is only of scant historical interest to know that Nietzsche "knew" of Heraclitus and valued him above all else all his life, and this from early on, when he was to all appearances still pursuing the business of being a professor of classical philology in Basel. One could perhaps even prove historiologically and philologically that Nietzsche's conception of truth as "illusion" "stems" from Heraclitus, or, to put it more bluntly, that he copied it from him while reading that author. We shall leave to the historians of philosophy the satisfaction of discovering such plagiaristic connections. Yet even supposing that Nietzsche took his definition of truth as "illusion" from the saying of Heraclitus, the question still remains as to why Nietzsche stumbled upon none other than this Heraclitus, whose "philosophy" was in no way appreciated in Nietzsche's day in the emphatic way that has become the fashion ever since, at least superficially. One could answer this question, too, by pointing out that already as a secondary school student Nietzsche especially venerated the poet Hölderlin, whose *Hyperion* exulted in Heraclitean thoughts. Yet the same question rises again as a retort: Why did Nietzsche have such esteem for precisely Hölderlin, at a time when this poet was known primarily

Knowledge in Nietzsche's Fundamental Thought 31

only as a name and as a romantic *manqué*? With this scholarly historical detective work, searching out dependencies, we do not advance a step; we never get to what is essential, but only get stuck in external associations and relations. What is superficial about such a procedure must be explicitly mentioned, however, because one often characterizes Nietzsche's thought as Heraclitean and thus presumes to have thought something in citing this name. And yet, neither is Nietzsche the Heraclitus of the waning nineteenth century, nor is Heraclitus a Nietzsche for the age of pre-Platonic philosophy. In contrast, what "is," what is still happening in Western history—hitherto, at present, and to come—is the power of the essence of truth. In it, beings as such show themselves and accordingly are grasped as this self-representing in representation, and one understands such representation generally as thinking. What is and what occurs consist in the strange fact that at the beginning of the consummation of modernity truth is defined as "illusion." The initial fundamental decisions concerning thought are transformed in this definition, but just as decisively their dominion is established.

5. The Essence of Truth (Correctness) as "Estimation of Value"

Our plan is still to think Nietzsche's sole thought, the will to power, initially by reflecting on the essence of knowledge. If according to Nietzsche knowledge is will to power, then the essence of will to power must also be illuminated by a sufficiently clear insight into the essence of knowledge. But knowledge is supposed to grasp what is true. Truth is what is essential about knowledge. Accordingly, the essence of truth must also strip all veils from the essence of will to power. What Nietzsche says about truth is, briefly, Truth is an "illusion." To sharpen and broaden this essential definition of truth, we cite by way of anticipation a second statement by Nietzsche. *"Truth is the kind of error* without which a certain kind of living being could not live" (WM, 493; from the year 1885).

Truth: "illusion"? Truth: "a kind of error"? Again we are about to conclude: Therefore everything is error, therefore it is not worthwhile asking about truth. Nietzsche would answer: No, precisely because truth is illusion and error, therefore there is "truth," therefore truth is a value. Strange logic! Certainly, but let us first try to comprehend before we hasten to elect as judge our all too straight and narrow understanding, condemning this doctrine of truth before it has reached our inner ear.

We must ask more clearly and more broadly what truth and knowledge, what knowing and science, are in Nietzsche. For this purpose we now set out on a route through Nietzsche's paths of thought as collected in the first section of the third book, a collection whose order, to be sure, reminds us all too clearly of the schema of theories of knowledge in the late nineteenth century—which Nietzsche could not

The Essence of Truth (Correctness) as "Estimation of Value" 33

completely escape either. The first short chapter *"a) Methods of Inquiry,"* whose title and position were invented by the editors, does contain pieces from Nietzsche's last and essential period, 1887–88, under the numbers 466–69; yet as they stand they are completely unintelligible with regard to their content and metaphysical scope. Nietzsche would certainly not have introduced his own presentation in this way.

As the point of departure for our inquiry we choose number 507 (Spring–Fall, 1887*):

> The *estimation of value* "I believe that such and such is so" as the *essence* of *"truth."* In estimations of value are expressed *conditions* of *preservation* and *growth*. All our *organs of knowledge* and *our senses* are developed only with regard to conditions of preservation and growth. *Trust* in reason and its categories, in dialectic, thus the *value-estimation* of logic, proves only their *usefulness* for life, proved by experience—*not* their "truth."
>
> That a great deal of *belief* must be present; that *judgments* may be ventured; that doubt concerning all essential values is *lacking*—that is the precondition for every living thing and its life. Therefore, what is necessary is that something *must* be held to be true—*not* that something *is* true.
>
> "The *true* and the *apparent* worlds"—I have traced this antithesis back to *value relations*. We have projected the conditions of *our* preservation as *predicates of Being* in general. Because we have to be stable in our beliefs if we are to prosper, we have made the "true" world a world not of mutability and becoming, but one of *being*.

By no means do we wish to assert that Nietzsche would have begun with this piece had he succeeded in a finished presentation. From now on we shall generally leave aside the factitious question of the supposed structure of the "work" that could not be a "work." We shall also leave aside the fact that similar passages and thoughts can be cited and adduced from other pieces written simultaneously and earlier. For all this does not tell us anything. It will not help us to advance if we persist in neglecting the attempt in *one* piece to reflect on the essential relation of truth to will to power as a whole and to fathom the significance of will to power for Nietzsche's fundamental position, that

---

* See W II 1 [38] at CM, *12*, 352–53.

is, its relation to Western metaphysics. Passage number 507 furthers the attempt, as it were, to leap into the very center of Nietzsche's interpretation of knowledge as will to power. It begins with a brief definition of the essence of truth and ends by answering the question as to why the "world" (beings as a whole) is a world of "being" and not of "becoming." This question stands at the beginning of Western thought, albeit in a different form. We shall try to think the whole piece through in its inner structure, sentence by sentence, with the intention of taking a look at the whole of Nietzsche's interpretation of truth and knowledge.

The piece begins, "The *estimation of value* 'I believe that such and such is so' as the *essence* of '*truth.*' " Every word, every underline, each aspect of the writing and the whole word-structure are important here. The introductory remark makes volumes of epistemologies superfluous, if only we can muster the quiet and the stamina and the thoroughness of reflection that such words require in order to be understood.

It is a question of the essential definition of truth. Nietzsche writes the word *truth* in quotation marks. Briefly, this means truth as it is ordinarily understood and as it has long been understood—in the history of Western thought—and as Nietzsche himself also must understand it in advance, without being conscious of this necessity, its scope, or even its ground. The essential definition of truth that since Plato and Aristotle dominates not only the whole of Western thought but the history of Western man in general down to his everyday doings and ordinary opinions and representations runs, briefly: Truth is correctness of representation, and representation means having and bringing before oneself beings, a having that perceives and opines, remembers and plans, hopes and rejects. Representing adjusts itself to beings, assimilates itself to them, and reproduces them. Truth means the assimilation of representing to *what* beings are and *how* they are.

Even though at first glance we encounter very different and even opposing conceptual definitions of the essence of truth in the thinkers of the West, they are all based on the one and only definition that truth is correctness of representing. Since, however, correctness and truth are in recent times often distinguished, we need expressly to point

The Essence of Truth (Correctness) as "Estimation of Value"

out and make clear that in the usage of this lecture course correctness [*Richtigkeit*] is understood in the literal sense of being directed toward something, the sense of suitability for beings. Sometimes in logic the word *correctness* is given the signification of "lack of contradiction," "consistency." In the first sense the sentence "This board is red" is correct but untrue; it is correct in the sense that it is no contradiction for this writing surface to be red; yet, in spite of its correctness, the sentence is untrue because it is not appropriate to the object. Correctness as consistency means that a statement is deduced from another statement in accordance with the rules of reasoning. Correctness in the sense of being free of contradiction and being consistent is also called formal "truth," not related to the content of beings, in contradistinction to the material truth of content. The concluding statement is "formally" true but materially untrue. The idea of suitability is present even in this concept of correctness (lack of contradiction, consistency), to be sure, not in the intended objective but in the rules followed in formulating propositions and drawing conclusions. Yet when we say the essence of truth is correctness, we mean the phrase in the richer sense of the suitability of the content of representation with regard to the beings encountered. Correctness is then understood as the translation of *adaequatio* and *homoiōsis*. For Nietzsche, too, it has been decided in advance and in accordance with the tradition that truth is correctness.

If this is so, then Nietzsche's first, very strange essential definition appears in a peculiar light. Nietzsche's saying that truth is an illusion, a kind of error, has as its innermost presupposition, one that is thus never uttered at all, the traditional and never challenged characterization of truth as the correctness of representing. Yet for Nietzsche this concept of truth changes peculiarly and inevitably—hence not at all arbitrarily. The first sentence of number 507 says what this necessary change looks like. Viewed grammatically, the piece begins not with a proposition but with a key word that, simply, clearly, and completely, indicates Nietzsche's position with regard to the traditional concept of truth and serves him as a directive for his own path of thought. According to this word, truth is in its essence an "estimation of value." That phrase means to appraise something as a value and posit it as such. But (according to the statement noted earlier) value signifies a perspectival condition for life-enhancement. Value-estimation is accomplished by life itself, and by man in particular. Truth as value-estimation is something that "life" or man brings about, and that thus belongs to human being. (Why and to what extent that is so still remains a question).

Nietzsche unequivocally characterizes what kind of value-estimation truth is in the words "I believe that such and such is so." This valuation has the character of a "belief." But what does "belief" mean? Belief means to *hold* such and such as *being* thus and thus. "Belief" does not mean assenting to and accepting something that one oneself has *not* seen explicitly as a being or can never grasp as in being with one's own eyes; rather, to believe here means to hold something that representation encounters as *being* in such and such a way. Believing is holding *for something,* holding it as *in being.* Thus believing here by no means signifies assent to an incomprehensible doctrine inaccessible to reason but proclaimed as true by an authority, nor does it mean trust in a covenant and prophecy. Truth as value-estimation, that is, as holding for something, as holding for something as being in this or that way, stands in an essential connection with beings as such. What is true is what is held in being, as thus and thus in being, what is taken to be in being. *What is true is being.*

If its essence is value-estimation, truth is synonymous with holding to be true. To hold something for something and posit it as such is also called *judging.* Nietzsche says, "*Judging* is our oldest belief, our most habitual holding to be true or holding to be untrue" (WM, 531; 1885–86). The judgment, an assertion of something about something, is the *essence* of knowledge; to it belongs being-true in the tradition of Western metaphysics. To hold something for what it is, to represent it as thus and thus in being, to assimilate oneself in representing to whatever emerges and is encountered, is the essence of truth as correctness. Accordingly, in the sentence we are clarifying, which says that truth is a value-estimation, Nietzsche is basically thinking nothing other than this: Truth is correctness. He seems to have completely forgotten his saying that truth is an illusion. Nietzsche even seems to be in complete agreement with Kant, who once notes explicitly in his

The Essence of Truth (Correctness) as "Estimation of Value"

Critique of Pure Reason that the explanation of truth as the "agreement of knowledge with its object" is "here granted and presupposed" (A58, B82). Briefly, for Kant the definition of truth as correctness (in the sense clarified) is incontrovertibly beyond doubt; *nota bene*, for *Kant*, who instigated the Copernican turn in his doctrine of the essence of knowledge, according to which knowledge is not supposed to conform to objects but the other way around—objects are supposed to conform to knowledge. The medieval theologians, and Aristotle and Plato too, think about "truth" in the way in which Kant explains its general essence. Nietzsche does not just *seem* to be in harmony with this Western tradition, he *is* in harmony with it; only for this reason can he, must he, distinguish himself from it. The question is why he nevertheless thinks the essence of truth differently—and in what sense differently. The key word about the essence of truth as belief does have as its *presup*position the unspoken position that truth is correctness; but it says something else, and that is what is essential for Nietzsche. For this reason, it moves immediately to the foreground by means of the sentence structure and the emphasis.

"*Estimation of value* . . . as the *essence* of 'truth' ": That means that the essence of truth as correctness (correctness as such) is really a *value-estimation*. Nietzsche's decisive metaphysical insight lies in this interpretation of the essence of correctness (of the traditional, unquestioned concept of truth). This means that the essence of correctness will by no means find its explanation and basis by saying how man, with the representations occurring in his subjective consciousness, can conform to objects that are at hand outside of his soul, how the gap between the subject and the object can be bridged so that something like a "conforming to" becomes possible.

With the characterization of truth as estimation of value, the essential definition of truth is rather turned in a *completely different direction*. We see this from the way in which Nietzsche continues his train of thought: "In estimations of value are expressed *conditions* of *preservation* and *growth.*" This sentence initially gives evidence for the characterization of the essence of "value" in general that we mentioned at the beginning: first, that it has the character of a "condition" for "life"; secondly, that in "life" not only "preservation" but also and above all "growth" is essential. "Growth" here is simply another name for "enhancement." However, "growth" sounds like merely quantitative extension and could indicate that "enhancement" is ultimately intended only in this quantitative sense of increase—although not in the manner of piecemeal accumulation, since growth points to the autonomous development and unfolding of a living being.

The "value-estimation" that is determined by the essence of truth in the sense of holding-to-be-true, any "estimation of value" whatever, is the "expression" of conditions of preservation and growth, as conditions of life. What is appraised and valued as a "value" is such a condition. Nietzsche goes still farther. Not only does "truth" revert to the scope of "conditions of life" with regard to its essence, but the faculties for grasping truth also receive here their sole determination: "All our *organs of knowledge and our senses* are developed only with regard to conditions of preservation and growth." Accordingly, truth and grasping the truth are not merely in the service of "life" according to their use and application; their essence, the manner of their organization, and thus their entire activity are driven and directed by "life."

6. Nietzsche's Alleged Biologism

We are accustomed to call a kind of thinking that interprets all appearances as an expression of life a *biological* one. Nietzsche's "world image," one says, is biologistic. Yet even if from the outset we do not in Nietzsche's case take seriously the catchword characterization of his "world image" as a biological one, because we thoroughly mistrust such labels, we still cannot deny that even the few sentences we have cited speak obtrusively enough for a "biologistic" way of thinking in Nietzsche. Moreover, we have already noted expressly and more than once his equation of the basic words *world* and *life*, both of which name beings as a whole. Life, the process of life and the course of life, are called in Greek *bios*. *Bios* in the word *biography*, "life-description," corresponds more to the Greek meaning. Biology, on the other hand, means the study of life in the sense of plants and animals. How should a thinking whose basic thought comprehends beings as a whole as "life" not be *biological*—more biological than any kind of biology we otherwise know? However, not only the basic words but also the proper intention rooted in the new estimation of value betray the "biological" character of Nietzschean thinking. Let us heed the title that stands over the fourth and concluding book of *The Will to Power*: "Discipline and Breeding." Here the idea of the conscious regulation of life, direction and "enhancement" of life in the sense of a strictly arranged life-plan, is posited as a goal and a requirement. We should not forget that Nietzsche gives the name *beast of prey* to the highest form of man and sees the highest man as the "splendid *blond beast* lustfully roving after prey and victory" (VII, 322).* There is no

---
* On the notorious "blond beast" statements in *Towards a Genealogy of Morals*, I,

longer any evading the conclusion that the "world image" of this thinker is an unconditioned biologism, not only in general and as a consequence of a harmless opinion he may have propagated but according to the innermost will of his thought.

Why should a metaphysical way of thinking not be biologistic? Where is it written that this involves an error? Is not rather a thinking that comprehends all beings as alive, as appearances of life, closest to what is really real, and thus in itself most true? "Life"—does there not resound in this word what we really understand by "Being?" Nietzsche himself once notes (WM, 582; 1885–86): " 'Being'—we have no other way of representing this than as *'living.'*—How can anything dead 'be'?"

With regard to this remark we must ask the following questions:

1. Who are the "we" who have this idea about "Being" as "life"?
2. What do these "we" mean by "life"?
3. Where does the fundamental experience come from and how is it grounded?
4. What is meant by that "Being" which is interpreted *as* "life"?
5. Where and how is the decision about this interpretation to be made at all?

From the passage cited we initially gather only that "life" is the basic measure for estimating something as being or nonbeing or notbeing. A more lively understanding of Being than that which understands it in the sense of life is not thinkable. Besides, it speaks to us in our most natural experience immediately and penetratingly. The characterization of a metaphysics as biologism thus can only confer the highest distinction and bear witness to its unbounded "nearness to life."

This ambiguous and thus specious term *biologism* obviously gets to the core of Nietzsche's thinking. How else are we to understand the thought of value in the sense of life-condition, how else posit the goal of "Discipline and Breeding," how else the archetypal determination

---

section 11 (CM, 5, 275–76), see Detlef Brennecke, "Die Blonde Bestie: Vom Missverständnis eines Schlagworts," in *Nietzsche-Studien*, V (1976), 113–45.

of man in the form of the beast of prey—than as the decided interpretation of beings as a whole as "life," the interpretation of "life" in the sense of an animality that can be bred? Now, it would actually be a very forced and even vain endeavor if one wanted to conceal Nietzsche's obvious use of biological language, or even play it down; if one wanted to bypass the fact that this use of language contains a biological way of thinking and is thus not an external covering. Yet this current and, in a way, correct characterization of Nietzschean thinking as biologism presents the *main obstacle* to our penetrating to his fundamental thought.

For this reason a preliminary discussion of the first sentence concerning the essence of truth already requires a note elucidating such current titles as "biologism," "philosophy of life," "metaphysics of life." We must not only ward off the grossest misunderstandings but above all make intelligible the fact that there are questions to be asked here. An adequate discussion of Nietzsche's fundamental thought depends on our response to them.

According to the etymology we mentioned, "biology" means "study of life"—better, "of living beings." The name now means the scientific investigation of the appearances, processes, and laws of living beings that are determined for the realms of plant, animal, and human life. Botany and zoology, the anatomy, physiology, and psychology of man form the special areas of biology before which or over which a "general biology" is sometimes placed. As a science, all biology already presupposes a more or less explicitly drawn essential delimitation of appearances that constitute its realm of objects. This realm, to repeat, is that of living beings. Underlying the delimitation of this realm there is again a preconception of what distinguishes and sets apart living beings as such, namely, life. The essential realm in which biology moves can itself never be posited and grounded by biology as a science, but can always only be presupposed, adopted, and confirmed. This is true of every science.

Every science rests upon propositions about the area of beings within which its every investigation abides and operates. These propositions about beings—about what they are—propositions that posit and delimit the area, are metaphysical propositions. Not only can they not be demonstrated by the concepts and proofs of the respective sciences, they cannot even be thought appropriately in this way at all.

Biology as such never decides *what* is living and *that* such beings are. Rather, the biologist as biologist makes use of this decision as one already made, one that is necessary for him. But if the biologist as this specific person makes a decision about what is to be addressed as living, he nonetheless does not make this decision *as a biologist,* nor with the means, the forms of thought, and the proofs of his science; here he speaks as a metaphysician, as a human being who, beyond the field in question, thinks beings as a whole.

Similarly, the art historian as historian can never decide what art is for him and why any given construction is a work of art. These decisions about the essence of art and the essential historical scope of art always lie outside the history of art, even though they are constantly made use of within the research performed by art history.

Every science is knowledge—that is, preservation of a genuine knowing that is pregnant with decision and helps to create history, above and beyond being a mere collection of information—only to the extent that it thinks metaphysically, using this word according to the traditional way of thinking. Every science that goes beyond a merely calculating mastery of its field is genuine knowledge only to the extent that it grounds itself metaphysically or understands such foundation as an indispensable necessity, as part and parcel of its essential content.

Thus the development of the sciences can always proceed along two fundamentally different guidelines. The sciences can take shape in the direction of an increasingly comprehensive and secure mastery of objects, can arrange their mode of procedure accordingly and find satisfaction in that. Yet *at the same time* the sciences can develop as genuine knowledge and on that basis set for themselves the limits of what it is scientifically valuable to know.

This digression is only to show that the field of every science—for biology, the field of the living—is staked out by knowledge and by the related propositions that have a *non*scientific character. We can call them *field propositions.* Such propositions, for example, in the field of zoology concerning the nature of the animal, when viewed from the detailed work of the research tend to give the impression of being "general," that is, indefinite and vague. For this reason most researchers, especially the "exact" ones, view such reflections with mistrust.

Actually, such metaphysical observations are indefinite and elusive only as long as they are evaluated from the perspective of science and its kind of procedure. Yet that does not mean that this characteristic of being indefinitely general pertains to the essence of such reflections. It only means that metaphysical reflection on the essence of a science's field looks amorphous and unfounded—viewed from the perspective of the science in question. But the perspective of the science in question is not only too narrow to grasp its own essence but is also in general absolutely inadequate. Thinking philosophically, the scientific researcher often believes, merely means thinking more generally and vaguely than he, the exact researcher, is accustomed to think. He forgets, or rather never knew and never learned, never wanted to know, that a different kind of thinking is required and demanded by metaphysical reflection. The transition from scientific thinking to metaphysical reflection is essentially more alien and thus more difficult than the transition from prescientific, everyday thinking to the kind of thinking we do in the sciences. The transition to metaphysics is a *leap*. The transition to science is a steady development of earlier determinations of an already existing way of representing.

The self-reflection of science has its own perspective and inquiring stance, its own form of proof and conceptual apparatus; and in all this it has its own soundness and lawfulness. To be able to carry out metaphysical reflection concerning his field, the scientific researcher must therefore transpose himself into a fundamentally different kind of thinking; he must become familiar with the insight that this reflection on his field is *something essentially different* from a mere broadening of the kind of thinking otherwise practiced in research, whether that broadening be in degree and scope, in generalization, or even in what he sees as a degeneration.

However, the demand for an essentially different thinking for reflection on a particular field does not signify regulation of the sciences by philosophy but, on the contrary, recognition of the higher knowledge concealed in every science, on which the worth of that science rests. Of course, the relationship of scientific research and metaphysical reflection on the field is not to be understood as though two different buildings stood firmly next to each other once and for all as neighbors, here "science" and there "philosophy," so that one could go in and out from one to the other in order to fetch here some information about the newest scientific discoveries and there formulations of a philosophical concept. *Science and reflection on the specific field are both historically grounded on the actual dominance of a particular interpretation of Being, and they always move in the dominant circle of a particular conception of the essence of truth.* In every fundamental self-reflection of the sciences it is always a matter of passage through metaphysical decisions that were either made long ago or are being prepared now.

The more secure the sciences become within the scope of their affairs, the more stubbornly do they evade metaphysical reflection on the specific field, and the greater becomes the danger of often unnoticeable transgressions of that field and of confusions resulting therefrom. The zenith of intellectual confusion is attained, however, when the opinion crops up that metaphysical propositions and views about reality could be grounded by "scientific insights," whereas scientific insights are, after all, only possible on the basis of a different, higher, and stricter knowledge concerning reality as such. The idea of a "scientifically founded worldview" is a characteristic offshoot of the intellectual confusion in the public mind that emerged more and more strikingly in the last third of the previous century and attained remarkable success in those half-educated circles who indulged in popular science.

However, this confused relationship between the modern sciences and metaphysics has already existed for a century and can have its ground neither in the mere divergence of science from metaphysics nor in the degeneration of philosophy. The reason for this confusion and hence the reason for the mutual separation of science and metaphysics lies more deeply concealed in the essence of modernity. If we think Nietzsche's fundamental thought decisively enough we will catch sight of the ground of this confused relationship. For now it is enough to know that the metaphysical ground of the sciences is occasionally taken notice of as such, and admitted, and then forgotten again; at other times, however, it is mostly *not* thought *at all,* or is rejected as a philosophical chimera.

When certain predominant views in biology about living beings are transferred from the realm of plant and animal life to other realms of beings, for example, that of history, one can speak of a biologism. This term designates the already mentioned extension—and perhaps exaggeration and transgression of boundaries—of biological thinking beyond its own realm. Insofar as we see an arbitrary misuse here, an unfounded violence of thinking, and ultimately a confusion in kinds of knowledge, we must ask what the reason for all this is.

What goes wrong in biologism, however, is not merely the transfer and unfounded extension of concepts and propositions from the field proper to living beings to that of other beings; what goes wrong already lies in the failure to recognize the metaphysical character of the propositions concerning the field, propositions by which all biology that is genuine and restricted to its field points beyond itself. Thus biology proves that, as a science, it can never gain power over its own essence with the means at its disposal. Biologism is not so much the mere boundless degeneration of biological thinking as it is total ignorance of the fact that biological thinking itself can only be grounded and decided in the metaphysical realm and can never justify itself scientifically. The same sort of thing occurs when, in the most exceptional cases, all customary and scientific thinking loses its truth by proceding illogically and superficially. The reason for the degeneration of scientific thinking, particularly in the form of popular science, always lies in the failure to know the level on which a science moves and can move, which is also at the same time in the failure to know the unique element that is required in all essential reflection and for its foundation.

If Nietzsche's use of language and way of thinking extensively and even consciously give rise to the illusion of biologism, we must *ask*:

On the one hand, whether Nietzsche directly adopts and extends concepts and key propositions from the biological science of his time without realizing that these biological concepts themselves already contain metaphysical decisions. If Nietzsche does *not* proceed in this way, the talk about biologism becomes untenable.

On the other hand, whether Nietzsche, although he appears to speak and think biologically and to give life a privileged position, does not want first to ground this privileged position of life in terms of a ground that has nothing more to do with the phenomena of life in plants and animals.

Finally, we must ask why the grounds of this pre-eminence of life and of living beings comes into its own precisely in the consummation of Western metaphysics.

As strange as it may sound at first, the truth of the following assertion can be founded by sufficient reflection: when Nietzsche thinks beings as a whole—and prior to that Being—as "life," and when he defines man in particular as "beast of prey," he is not thinking biologically. Rather, he grounds this apparently merely biological worldview *metaphysically.*

The metaphysical foundation of the pre-eminence of life has its ground not in an eccentric, far-fetched biological view of Nietzsche's but in the fact that be brings the essence of Western metaphysics to completion on the historical path that is alloted to it, the fact that he can bring to words what was preserved unspoken in the primordial essence of Being as *physis.* The latter was attained as an inevitable thought in the subsequent interpretation of beings that stretched along the entire course of the history of metaphysics.

By referring to the kinds of unasked and undecided questions that for Nietzsche—and not only for him—are concealed behind the catchword *biologism,* the illusion that he does, after all, think exclusively in a patently biologistic way is by no means extinguished. Now for the first time we take note of the illusion, and that is important. On the basis of what we have said it also becomes intelligible that and why the many writers who whether consciously or unconsciously expound and copy Nietzsche's treatises invariably fall prey to a variety of biologism. They are moving in the foreground of Nietzschean thinking. Because this foreground gives rise to a biological illusion, the biological element is taken to be what is unique and real; moreover, the illusion is amplified, thanks to the progress that biology has meanwhile attained. Whether one votes yes or no on Nietzsche's "biologism," one always gets stuck in the foreground of his thinking. The predilection for this state of affairs is supported by the form of Nietzsche's own publications. His words and sentences provoke, fascinate, penetrate, and stimulate. One thinks that if only one pursues one's impressions one has understood Nietzsche. We must first unlearn this abuse that is supported by current catchwords like *biologism*. We must learn to "read."

7. Western Metaphysics as "Logic"

We are asking about Nietzsche's essential definition of knowledge. Knowledge is grasping and retaining what is true. Truth as well as grasping truth are "conditions" of life. Knowledge takes place when we think and make assertions; such thinking, as representing beings, prevails in all kinds of sense perception, in nonsensuous intuition, in every type of experience and sensation. Everywhere and always, man is related in such behavior and attitudes to beings; everywhere and always, what man is related to is perceived as in being. To perceive means here to take something in advance as being in this or that way or else not, or as differently in being. What is perceived in such perception are beings; they have the character of that of which we say that it *is*. Conversely, beings as such open themselves only to such a perceiving. This is what Parmenides' saying means: *To gar auto noein estin te kai einai.* "Perceiving and Being are the same." To be the same means to belong together in essence; beings are not in being as *beings*, that is, as present, without perceiving. But neither can perceiving take hold where there are no beings, where Being does not have the possibility of coming into the open.

Every Western thinker after Parmenides had to think this saying again. Each has thought it uniquely in his own way, and no one will ever exhaust its depth. But if we want to preserve the saying's depth, we must always try to think it anew in the Greek way instead of deforming it with modern ideas. If one translates it in the seemingly literal way "Representing and Being are the same," one is tempted to read into it as the saying's content the superficial Schopenhauerian thought that the world is merely our representation—it "is" nothing in itself and for itself. But neither does the saying merely mean the opposite—in contradistinction to that subjective interpretation—to the effect that thinking is also a being and hence belongs to Being. Rather, the saying means what was already said: Beings are only where perceiving is, and perceiving is only where beings are. The saying means a third or a first thing that sustains the cohesion of both, namely, *alētheia*.

From our remembrance of this saying we now take just this one thing: grasping and defining beings have since ancient times been attributed to perceiving—to *nous*. For this we have the German word *Vernunft*, reason. Reason, apprehending beings as beings, takes hold of them in various respects: now as constituted thus and thus, that is, with respect to their constitution (quality, *poion*), now as thus and thus extended or in size (quantity, *poson*), now as thus and thus related to others (relation, *pros ti*).

When a being, for example, a rock lying at hand, is taken as hard, or as gray, it is addressed with respect to its constitution. When a man, for example, a slave, is perceived as subservient to his master, he is addressed with respect to his relation.

To address something as something is called in Greek *katēgorein*. The respects with which beings are addressed as beings—constitution, extension, situation (quality, quantity, relation) are thus called "categories," or more explicitly *ta skhēmata tēs katēgorias*, the forms into which addressing something as something (*hē katēgoria*) places what is addressed. Beings are always addressed as being thus and thus. For this reason the *skhēmata tēs katēgorias* are nothing other than *genē tou ontos*, species, kinds of provenance of beings, that from which, and thus in return to which, beings are: as thus constituted, that large, thus related, and so on. Perceiving beings as such unfolds in thinking, and thinking expresses itself in the assertion, in the *logos*.

The categories themselves can be thought through and discussed in their various possible relations. Such thinking through and discussion of the *genē tou ontos*, the "origins of beings" (as such), has since Plato been called "dialectic." The last and at the same time most powerful attempt at this thinking through of the categories, that is, of the respects in which reason thinks beings as such, is Hegel's dialectic, gathered into a work that bears the genuine and appropriate name *Science of Logic.* This title means the self-knowing of the essence of reason as the thinking of "Being." In such thinking the unity and coherence of the determinations of Being develop into the "absolute concept" and are grounded therein.

Western metaphysics, that is, the reflection on beings as such and as a whole, determines beings in advance and for its entire history as what is conceivable and definable in the respects of reason and thinking. Insofar as all customary thinking is always grounded in a form of metaphysics, everyday and metaphysical thinking alike rest on "trust" in this relation, on the confidence that beings as such show themselves in the thinking of reason and its categories, that is to say, that what is true and truth are grasped and secured in reason. Western metaphysics is based on this priority of reason. Insofar as illuminating and determining reason may and, in fact, must be called "logic," we can also say that Western "metaphysics" is "logic"; the essence of beings as such is decided in the scope of thinking.

How does Nietzsche stand with regard to this fundamental essence of Western metaphysics? The following sentence of our passage, whose first part has now already been illuminated, gives the answer: "*Trust* in reason and its categories, in dialectic, thus the *value-estimation* of logic, proves only their *usefulness* for life, proved by experience—*not* their 'truth.'"

This sentence contains two things: on the one hand, a reference to the basic process of Western history, whereby the human beings of this history are supported by trust in reason; on the other hand, an interpretation of the nature of the truth of reason and logic.

We must not conceive of the trust in reason and the powerful dominance of *ratio* one-sidedly as rationalism, for irrationalism too belongs within the scope of trust in reason. The greatest rationalists are most likely to fall prey to irrationalism, and conversely, where irrationalism determines the worldview, rationalism celebrates its triumphs. The dominion of technology and susceptibility to superstition belong together. Not merely irrationalism, but rationalism most of all—albeit more covertly and skillfully—"live" and protect themselves out of *anxiety in the face of the concept.*

Yet what does "*trust* in reason" mean in Nietzsche's statement? A basic constitution of man is meant by this trust. In accordance with this constitution, the capacity that brings man *before* beings and that represents beings as such for man is delivered over to reason.

Only what represents and secures rational thinking has a claim to the sanction of a being that is *in being*. The sole and highest court of appeal, in whose field of vision and speech is decided what is in being and what is not, is reason. We find in reason the most extreme pre-decision as to what Being means.

Hence the basic process in which all the fundamental positions and key sayings of the various stages of Western metaphysics resonate can be fixed in the formula *Being and Thinking.**

This "*trust* in reason" and in thinking thus understood remains on the hither side of any currently prevailing assessment of understanding and intellect. The rejection of intellectualism, of the degeneration of the uprooted and aimless understanding, always occurs under appeal to "sound" common *sense*, thus again to an "understanding," that is, by laying claim to "rationalism." Here too reason is the measure of what is, what can be, and what should be. If a procedure, a measure, a demand are proven or asserted to be "logical," such things are taken to be correct, that is, binding. People are impressed by that of which one can say it is "logical." Here "logical" does not mean thought in accordance with the rules of school logic but calculated on the basis of trust in reason.

How does Nietzsche interpret what he calls "*trust* in reason"? Nietzsche says "*trust* in reason" does not prove the "truth" of reason's knowledge. Again, *truth* is put in quotation marks to indicate that it is understood here in the sense of correctness. When physics, for example, thinks beings in certain categories—matter, cause, reciprocity, energy, potential, affinity—and in such thinking "trusts" these categories from the start, and through such confident research continually attains new results, such trust in reason in the form of science does not prove that "nature" reveals its essence in *anything* that is objec-

---

* See *Einführung in die Metaphysik* (Tübingen: M. Niemeyer, 1953), IV, 3. English translation by Ralph Manheim, *An Introduction to Metaphysics* (Garden City, N.Y.: Doubleday Anchor, 1961), pp. 98–164.

tively shaped and represented by the categories of physics. Rather, such scientific knowledge only demonstrates that our thinking about nature is "useful" for "life." The "truth" of knowledge consists precisely in the usefulness of knowledge for life. This says clearly enough that what generates practical use is true, and the truth of what is true is to be estimated only according to its degree of usefulness. Truth is not at all something for itself that can then be estimated; it consists in nothing other than estimability for an attainable use.

However, we may no more take the idea of use and usefulness in Nietzsche in this crude, everyday (pragmatic) sense than we may take his use of biological language in a biologistic sense. That something is useful here means simply that it pertains to the conditions of "life." And for the essential determination of these conditions, the ways of their conditioning, and the character of their conditioning in general, everything depends upon the way in which "life" itself is defined in its essence.

Nietzsche does not mean that the knowledge of physics is "true" because and only insofar as it is useful for daily life, for example, in the production of an electric device that heats living rooms in winter and cools them in summer. For practical deployments are already consequences of the fact that scientific knowledge is useful *as such*. Practical exploitation is possible only on the basis of theoretical "utility." What does "utility" mean here? That scientific knowledge and the thinking of reason posit and have posited something, namely nature, as *being* in a sense that *secures* modern technological success in advance.

8. Truth and What Is True

The question remains as to what we are to think of this positing of beings as beings. This question implies the still more essential one of what beings, in being, and Being mean here. Nietzsche's statement—the whole passage in which it stands—wants to urge the interpretation of the essence of truth in another direction. This differently oriented interpretation of the traditional concept of truth does not eradicate the latter but presupposes it and posits it more firmly, entrenches it. Trust in reason does not prove the truth of rational knowledge in the sense that the latter reproduces what is real in appropriate images; trust in reason only gives evidence that something like holding-to-be-true belongs to the essence of "life." To be themselves, living beings—especially the living being called *man*—must relate to beings and orient themselves to beings. Then Nietzsche does free himself from the traditional interpretation of truth as correctness after all! But no—we must not jump to such premature conclusions, especially since we have hardly yet thought through the essence of truth in the sense of correctness.

Correctness means the adequacy of representation to beings. Above all, this means that true representation is a representing of beings. But how this can happen, how correctness is possible and in what it consists, is still the question. Above all, it remains questionable whether correctness consists in the fact that representations arise in the soul as images of objects outside the soul. It is questionable whether the image-like correspondence of representations inside us with objects outside can ever be ascertained—and by whom. Image-like assimilation to objects can only be brought about by the objects' themselves coming to be given. Yet this only happens by our representing them, thus having representations of them in us. The question returns as to whether these representations of the objects by which the adequacy is to be measured—whether these representations of objects do indeed copy the objects or not. Briefly, and in essence, the question remains as to how the essence of correctness, which for its part expresses the essence of truth in one respect, is itself to be grasped; that is, how the *adequacy* to beings is to be understood.

Perhaps it is only a crude, unfounded preconception to think that adequacy has to have the character of an *image*. Nietzsche by no means penetrates to the essential content of the traditional and fundamental metaphysical conception of truth. The essential content of the traditional concept of truth, however, does not mean, as one readily and almost universally thinks, that truth is the *image* of things outside brought about by representations in the soul. The essential content of the metaphysical concept of truth means a great deal more. It means:

1. Truth is a characteristic of reason.
2. The basic feature of this characteristic consists in assembling and representing *beings as such*.

The essential origin of this definition of truth cannot be discussed here. Our primary question is, What do *beings* and *being* signify here? How are beings in general related to "life"? In what sense and why must beings be representable and represented to man? In what does such representing consist, and how is it determined on the basis of the essence of "life"?

Nietzsche's reflection on the essence of truth circles around these and only these questions, at times more clearly formulated, sometimes less so. The two final paragraphs of passage number 507 give us the answer in broad outline. These paragraphs provide us with the guidelines for interrogating Nietzsche's conception of truth in its innermost ground.

> That a great deal of *belief* must be present; that *judgments* may be ventured; that doubt concerning all essential values is *lacking*—that is the precondition for every living thing and its life.

Initially, these are mere assertions, and yet we must admit that they capture something essential. For what is to become of "life" if all "truth" and "belief," every agreement to something, every holding on to something, and thus every support and every possibility of taking a stance have disappeared from "life"? That there is a holding-to-be-true, that something is perceived and taken and retained as being, is not an arbitrary manifestation of life but the "precondition for every living thing and its life." Nietzsche is saying that truth is the structural ground, the basic structure into which life as life is and must be admitted. Thus truth and what is true are not first determined *subsequently* in terms of a practical use merely *accruing* to life; rather, truth must already prevail in order that what is alive can live and life as such can remain alive.

Who would want to withhold assent from this appraisal of truth? Yet our assent quickly begins to totter if we consider the statement with which Nietzsche summarizes the reference to the grounding necessity of truth and of holding on to something indubitable. "Therefore, what is necessary is that something *must* be held to be true—*not* that something *is* true." Accordingly, what is believed and held to be true can ("in itself") be a deception and untrue; it suffices for it merely to be believed and, best of all, for it to be believed unconditionally and blindly.

Does Nietzsche then want every "swindle" to be valid as truth if it only have the "luck" to secure the necessary "belief" for itself? Does Nietzsche thus want the destruction of all truth and every possibility of truth? And even if this suspicion in no way applies to him, is not his conception of truth full of contradictions and—to be blunt—quite mad? Just now Nietzsche demanded as the essential ground of every living thing *that truth exist.* And now he explains with metaphysical cynicism that it is not important for *something to be true,* that it is sufficient for something to be held to be true. How can these two statements go together?

Truth must exist, but what is true about this truth does not need to be "true." If all this is not to be called absurd, it is at least difficult to understand. Certainly. But then who says that what is most essential—to which perhaps the essence of truth belongs—must be easy to understand? "Easy to understand" means effortlessly accessible to our fortuitous everyday understanding, with its habitual ideas.

Yet if the most essential is indeed the most simple, but precisely on that account the most difficult, we must be prepared to encounter strange things when we reflect on the essence of truth. This means that we must first work our way to *that* perspective in whose scope what Nietzsche says about the essence of truth becomes comprehensible in a unified way. Only thus can we judge why and to what extent truth is indeed a *necessary* value, yet *not the highest* value. Granted that we have decided on an essential reflection, we must persist in the scope of Nietzsche's thought even if we fail to find a quick way out of these seemingly confusing and self-contradictory thoughts about the essence of truth. In the realm of truly thoughtful thinking, ways out are always signs of evasion and flight.

Or should we first gesture toward the universal historical condition of our planet to make it clear that Nietzsche is expressing something totally different from a far-fetched and exaggerated personal opinion when he says, "Therefore, what is necessary is that something *must* be held to be true—*not* that something *is* true." This sentence oppresses us in an unsettling and obscure way, even though it could be confirmed in the general historical condition of the planet by way of palpable manifestations in the very foreground of our lives—for example, the gigantic propaganda wars, or the character of sheer facade, of pomp and circumstance, in which all of life makes itself known. One cannot dismiss all this as mere externality and superficiality, wrinkling one's nose and remaining with old, familiar facts; in it speaks the depths of the abyss of the modern essence of Being. The above statement names what is happening in such a way that actual historical situations and conditions are seen as merely the *consequences* of this hidden history; as *consequences,* they have no control over their ground.

If this is so, then not only is a boundless disturbance of all trust and trustworthiness sweeping across the globe—on the very basis of "trust in reason"—but we must also think to the dimension of things that are concealed. Not merely some specific truth has been *shattered,* but the very *essence of truth.* And man must undertake to bring about a more primordial grounding of that essence.

9. Tracing the Opposition of the "True and Apparent Worlds" Back to Relations of Value

First of all, we must understand the reason for the essential import of the statement that expresses Nietzsche's conception of truth in an extreme form. In order to make this reason comprehensible, we must first bring it into view. If it already is in view, it must first be known and decided upon *as* this reason. Nietzsche's statement says that the fact that there is truth is necessary, but that what is true in this truth need not be true. What is the basis for this statement?

Nietzsche gives his reason for it in the first words of passage number 507 when he says that the essence of truth is an *"estimation of value."* The essential determination of everything essential is based on "value-estimations." What is essential is conceived *as* essential exclusively with regard to its character as *value*.

Previous to the revaluation of all traditional values that Nietzsche assumes as his metaphysical task, there is a more original turnabout: the *essence* of all beings is posited from the very beginning as *value* in general.

In the concluding paragraph of passage number 507, Nietzsche again takes up the decisive content of the crucial essential determination of truth mentioned at the beginning. He makes it into a fundamental statement, one that transposes the whole discussion about the essence of truth into the inner center of the history of metaphysics.

"The *true* and the *apparent* worlds"—I have traced this antithesis back to *value relations*. We have projected the conditions of *our* preservation as *predicates of Being* in general. Because we have to be stable in our beliefs if we are to prosper, we have made the "true" world a world not of mutability and becoming, but one of *being*.

"The *true* and the *apparent* worlds"—Nietzsche bases this opposition on value relations. He understands truth here in the sense of what is true, the "true world," and places it in an opposition. The formulation of the opposition, "the *true* and the *apparent* worlds," is again placed in quotation marks, indicating that we are dealing with traditional and generally known material. The opposition whose new determination Nietzsche is uttering here is that between what properly and truly is and what can be called a being only in a derivative and improper way. In this opposition of two worlds—the "true world" and the "apparent world"—we can discern the distinction of two realms within whatever in some way *is* in general, having as its sole limit opposition to total, vacuous nothingness. This distinction is as old as Western thinking about beings. It becomes current to the degree that the primordial Greek conception of beings congeals into something well known and taken for granted in the course of Western history to date. This division of beings as a whole into two worlds is called the "two-world doctrine" by the Schoolmen. We need not follow in detail this two-world doctrine and its historical transformations, which coincide with the main stages of Western metaphysics. But we shall observe three things.

1. This distinction between the true and the apparent worlds is the supporting structure that first makes room in advance for something like meta-physics; for a *meta (ta physika)*, a beyond, that is, a going beyond something initially given *to* something else, is possible only if the former and the latter in their *distinguishability* are used as a basis, if throughout beings as a whole there is a distinction in accordance with which the one is separated from the other in the *khōrismos* [gap].

2. Plato's philosophy gave this "doctrine of two worlds" a "classic" form, if you like, for all of Western thought.

3. Nietzsche's attitude toward this distinction is everywhere based on a particular interpretation of this doctrine of Platonism.

It is true that Nietzsche's interpretation of the opposition of the "true and apparent worlds" is rough, that it does not penetrate to the inner constitution and manner of interrogation of the fundamental metaphysical position in question with regard to either the pre-Platonic or the Platonic and post-Platonic Western doctrine of beings. Yet with this opposition Nietzsche hits upon something essential.

Plato distinguishes between the *ontōs on* and the *mē on*, the being that is in being and also *that* kind of "being" that should not be, or should not be called such. The *ontōs on*, being that is in being, being proper, that is, being that is in accordance with the essence of Being, is *to eidos*, the outward appearance in which something shows its form, its *idea*, that is, what something is, *whatness*. The *mē on* is also in being and accordingly also presents itself—thought in a Greek way—also shows an outward appearance and form, an *eidos*; but the form is warped and twisted, the outward appearance and view are overshadowed and sullied; the *mē on* is thus *to eidōlon*. So-called real things that are at hand for man—this house, that ship, that tree, this sign, and so on—are, when thought in Plato's sense, all *eidōla*, outward appearances, that only look like the outward appearance proper. They are *mē onta*, beings indeed, things present in a certain sense, having their forms, but whose outward appearances are thus-and-thus *impaired* because they must show themselves in the form of sensuous matter. Yet in this specific house that is so-and-so big and manufactured out of this or that building material, what is *houselike* still shows itself; the house-being of this house consists in the presence of the houselike. The houselike, what makes a house be a house, is what is really in being with regard to it; what is truly in being is the *eidos*, the "Idea."

In Nietzsche's language, the "true world" means "the true," truth. It is what is grasped in knowledge, it is being; the "apparent world" signifies what is untrue and not in being. But what makes beings be real beings? Of what do we say and has one said from times of old: This "*is*"? What does one take as in being even when one has fallen away from the *primordial* Platonic way of perceiving? We say something *is* of that which we always and in advance encounter as always already at hand; what is always present and has constant stability in this presence. What really is, is what already in advance can never be removed, what stands fast and resists any attack, survives any accident. The beingness of beings signifies *permanent presence*. What is *thus* in being is the true, the "truth" one can always and truly hold on to as what is stable and does not withdraw, on the basis of which one can gain a foothold. Even if Nietzsche does not penetrate explicitly to the realm of the given interpretation and does not gauge its scope in his conception of the essence of beings—as little as other metaphysicians before him—he thinks "beings," the "true," in the direction indicated, as what remains and is stable. Accordingly, the "apparent world," what is not in being, stands for what is inconstant and without stability, what constantly changes and in appearing already disappears again.

The Christian faith's distinction between the perishability of the earthly and the eternity of heaven and hell is only a developed form—shaped by a definite faith in redemption and salvation—of the distinction under discussion, between the true and the apparent worlds. Nietzsche's critique of Christianity has as its presupposition the interpretation of Christianity as a degenerate form of Platonism; his critique consists in nothing other than this interpretation.

However, Nietzsche's thought does not aim at positing another interpretation in the place of the Christian interpretation of true beings, replacing the Christian God and his heaven with another god while retaining the same God-*head*. Nietzsche's questioning rather is concerned with determining in its provenance the distinction between the true and the apparent worlds *as* this distinction. Two things remain decisive for Nietzsche's thought: first, *that* he raises at all the question of the origin of this distinction as such; and second, *how* he raises, understands, and answers the question. His answer is that the distinction between the "true" world as the constant world and the "apparent" world as the inconstant world must be derived from "value relations." This means that positing what is constant and stable as being and the corresponding opposition of what is inconstant and changing as nonbeing and merely apparent being is a specific *valuation*. Indeed, what is constant and stable is preferred as the higher value to what is changing and flowing. The valuation of the value of what is constant and inconstant is guided by the basic interpretation of what is valuable and what value is.

Nietzsche understands "value" as a condition of "life." Here condition is not the accomplishment of a *thing* occurring outside of life that first accrues to it as a factor and an occasion, or else fails to do so. To condition, being a condition, here signifies as much as constituting the essence. Insofar as life has an essence determined thus and thus, it stands of itself under certain conditions; it posits and preserves these as its own and with them it preserves itself. If, like Nietzsche, one comprehends these conditions as values and calls them so, this means that life in itself is *value-positing,* by way of procuring satisfaction for its essence. Value-positing thus does not mean a valuation that somebody imputes to life from the outside. *Valuation* is the fundamental occurrence of life itself; it is the way life brings its essence to fruition and fulfills it.

Yet life, and here especially human life, will in advance direct the positing of its proper conditions and thus the positing of the conditions of securing its vitality according to how life itself determines its essence for itself. If life as such is first of all and constantly and only concerned with maintaining itself and being perpetually secured in its constancy, if life means nothing other than securing the constancy that has come down to it and been taken over by it, then life will make whatever suffices for and serves the securing of its constancy its most proper conditions. What conditions most of all in this way is what has the highest value. If life is concerned in its life with constantly maintaining itself as such in its constancy, it must not merely have secured the corresponding individual conditions. Only what has the character of maintaining and securing constancy in general can be taken as a condition of life, that is, as a value. Only this can be addressed as "in being." But if the true is taken for what is in being, everything that is to be true must have the character of being constant and stable; the "true world" must be a constant one, one that is removed from mutability and transformation. This clarifies the initially comprehensible sense of those statements in which Nietzsche discusses the extent to which he traces the antithesis of "the true world—the apparent world" back to *value relations.* Nietzsche says, "We have projected the conditions of *our* preservation as *predicates of Being* in general." "Our" means not the life-conditions of men living right now or of men in general, but of the men of the Western, Greek, Roman-Christian, German-Romance-modern "world." Since it is somehow primarily and ultimately concerned with constancy, perpetuity, and eternity, this human race has transposed its life-concern into the "world," into the "whole." The way and manner in which the essence of beings is interpreted, namely, as permanence, arises from the way and manner in which human life understands itself in what is most of all its own: as the securing of its own permanence. These determinations alone— permanence and perpetuity and stability—thus stipulate what *is* and may be addressed as *in being*, that about which the determinations "in being" and "being" can be uttered.

The subsequent statement of Nietzsche's *seems* to be merely a general repetition of the previously mentioned one. But it says more, for it first gives Nietzsche's own interpretation of the fact *that* beings "are" and *what* they are in their essence, what he calls "conditions of preservation" of human life.

Thought Platonically, the "Ideas" are not only guiding representations for human thought, something that we "have in our heads"; they also constitute the essence of beings and in their constancy grant to all nongenuine beings their temporary and impure subsistence. They allow the *mē on* too to "be" an *on*.

However, Nietzsche's interpretation takes another direction. That beings are—the "condition of preservation" for life—need not be thought in such a way that beings are something constant, existing in and for themselves "above" and beyond life. The only condition is that life instill of itself and in itself a belief in something it can constantly hold on to in all matters.

Hence it is clear that Nietzsche traces the antithesis of the true and apparent worlds still farther back beyond value relations to the valuing life itself. *This* tracing back consists in nothing less than an essential statement about life, which runs as follows: To be able to be as life, life needs the constant fixity of a "belief," but this "belief" calls for holding something to be constant and fixed, taking something as "in being." Since life posits values, yet is at the same time concerned about its own securing of permanence, a valuation must belong to life

Tracing the Opposition of the "True and Apparent Worlds" 63

in which it takes something as constant and fixed; that is, as in being; that is, as true.

Let us now return to the beginning of passage number 507:

> The *estimation of value* "I believe that such and such is so" as the *essence of "truth."* In estimations of value are expressed *conditions* of *preservation* and *growth*.

We can now say that truth is the essence of the true; the true is that which is in being; to be in being means to be that which is taken as constant and fixed. The essence of the true lies originally in such taking-as-fixed-and-secure. Yet this taking-as . . . is not some arbitrary activity; it is rather the behavior necessary for securing the constancy of life itself. As holding-for and positing a *condition* of life, such behavior has the character of a positing of valuation and estimation-of-value. *Truth is in its essence an estimation of value.* The antithesis of true and apparent beings is a "value relation" originating from *this* estimation of value.

What we have said seems simply to say the same thing again and again and to go in circles. Not only does it seem so, it is so. However, this must not mislead us into thinking that we have already understood almost *too clearly* what Nietzsche's guiding principle says: *Truth is in its essence an estimation of value.* Until we gain insight into the metaphysical connection between the essential determination of "life" and the role of the idea of value, Nietzsche's interpretation of truth and knowledge is in danger of declining to a triviality of practical and sound common sense, whereas it is ultimately something quite different, to wit, *the most hidden and extreme consequence of the first beginning of Western thought.*

That Nietzsche himself offers "the two-world doctrine" of metaphysics as the background for an interpretation of the essence of truth contains for us a directive. We must enhance what is strange in this interpretation of truth and gather what is worthy of question to its sharpest interrogative focus.

10. World and Life as "Becoming"

The representation of something as in being in the sense of the constant and the stable is a valuation. To elevate what is true of the "world" to something permanent, eternal, and immutable in itself means at the same time to transpose truth to life itself as a necessary condition of life. Yet if the world were constantly changing and perishing, if it had its essence in the most perishable of what perishes and is inconstant, truth in the sense of what is constant and stable would be a mere fixation and coagulation of what in itself is becoming; measured against what is becoming, such fixating would be *in*appropriate and merely a distortion. The true as the correct would precisely *not* conform to Becoming. Truth would then be incorrectness, error—an "illusion," albeit a perhaps necessary one.

Thus we look for the first time in the direction from which that strange saying speaks—Truth is an illusion. At the same time we see that in this saying the essence of truth in the sense of correctness is retained; correctness means representing beings in the sense of adequation to that which "is." For only if truth in its essence is correctness can it be *in*correctness and illusion according to Nietzsche's interpretation. Truth in the sense of the true, as alleged beings in the sense of the constant, stable, and immutable is *then* illusion if the world "*is*" not in being, but in "becoming." A knowledge that—as true—takes something to be "being" in the sense of the constant and stable restricts itself to beings and yet does not get at the actual: the world as a becoming world.*

---

* The text of NI (p. 548, lines 22–24) is corrupt: an entire line of the typescript is missing between lines 22 and 23. The oversight occurred presumably because the miss-

World and Life as "Becoming" 65

Is it—in truth—a *becoming* world? Nietzsche indeed affirms this question and says that the world is—"in truth"!—a "becoming" world. There is nothing in "being." Yet he not only affirms the world as a world of "becoming," he also knows that this affirmation, as an interpretation of the world, is a valuation. Thus at the time of the note we have been discussing (WM, 507) he jots down the following:

> Against the *value* of that which remains eternally the same (*vide* Spinoza's naiveté; Descartes' also), the value of the briefest and most transient, the seductive flash of gold on the belly of the serpent *vita*. (WM, 577; Spring–Fall, 1887)*

Here Nietzsche unequivocally pits one value against another, and the "value" he posits is, as a value, that is, as a condition of life, again taken and gleaned from life, albeit within a different perspective on the essence of life: life not as the fixating and fixated, securing itself and secured in its permanence, but "life" as a serpent, as what coils and winds itself and wills back into itself as into its own essential ring; always *rolling into itself* and always rolling on in the ring as ring, as what eternally becomes—life as the serpent whose rest is merely apparent, merely the self-restraint before a darting and leaping up. The serpent is thus a companion of Zarathustra's solitude.

Nietzsche opposes what becomes to what is true, that is, what is secured, agreed upon, and fixed and in this sense is in being. As opposed to "Being," Nietzsche posits Becoming as a higher value (see WM, 708). From this we initially conclude only one thing, namely, that truth is not the highest value: "To transform the belief 'it *is* thus and thus' into the will 'it *shall become* thus and thus' " (WM, 593;

---

ing line was an emendation that Heidegger jotted on the righthand side of the holograph, designating it for insertion into the body of the text. Later printings of NI (e.g., the fourth, n.d., ca. 1980–83) have inserted the line with yet another error, placing the close-quotation after the word *sich* instead of after *seiend*. (The holograph does not place either of these words in quotation marks: Heidegger apparently added them to *seiend* at either the typescript or proof stages of the book.) I have translated the text on the basis of the following corrected version of the German: *Eine Erkenntnis, die als wahre etwas für "seiend" nimmt im Sinne des Beständigen und Festen, hält sich an Seiendes und trifft gleichwohl nicht das Wirkliche: die Welt als werdende.*

* See W II 1 [26] at CM, *12*, 348.

from the years 1885–86). Truth as holding-to-be-true, committing oneself to a once-and-for-all fixed and decided "it is thus," cannot be life's highest form, because it denies life's vitality, its will to self-transcendence and becoming. To concede to life its vitality, that it might come to be something becoming *as* becoming and not merely be as a being, that is, lie fixed as something at hand—this is what *that* valuation evidently aims for compared with which truth can only be a deposed value.

Nietzsche often expresses this thought pointedly and exaggeratedly in the quite misleading form "There is no 'truth' " (WM, 616). Yet here too he writes *truth* in quotation marks. This "truth," according to its essence, is an "illusion," but, as illusion, a necessary condition of "life." So is there "truth" after all? Certainly, and Nietzsche would be the last to want to deny that. Consequently, his saying that there is no "truth" means something more essential, namely, that truth cannot be what is initially and properly decisive.

In order to comprehend in Nietzsche's sense and evaluate in accord with his meaning why truth cannot be the highest value, it is necessary first to ask more decidedly to what extent and in what way it is still a necessary value. Only if and because truth is a necessary value does that exertion of thought which shows that it *cannot* be the highest value have its scope. Since for Nietzsche the true is synonymous with beings, we will also discover by answering the questions posed in what sense Nietzsche understands beings, that is to say, what he means when he says "in being" and "Being." Furthermore, if the true cannot be the highest value, and if the true is equivalent to beings, then beings cannot constitute the essence of the world either. The world's actuality cannot consist in some sort of Being.

Truth is holding-to-be-true, taking something as in being, securing beings for oneself by representing them, that is, by knowing them. When in the modern period *verum* becomes *certum*, when truth becomes certainty, when truth becomes holding-to-be-true, the question of the essence of truth is transformed to the essential determination of knowledge, to the question of what and how certainty is, of what being certain of oneself consists in, of what indubitability means, of what absolutely unshakable knowledge is based on. Conversely, where truth first constitutes the range of play for knowledge, the essential determination of knowledge is rooted in the concept of truth as point of departure.

Accordingly, our question about Nietzsche's concept of truth narrows down to the question, How does Nietzsche define knowledge? The fact that we have to ask it in this way shows that Nietzsche thinks in a thoroughly modern way, in spite of his high esteem for early Greek, pre-Platonic thought. For this reason, to avoid confusion, we must emphasize again and again that for modern thought the essence of truth is determined on the basis of the essence of knowledge; for incipient Greek thought the essence of knowledge is determined on the basis of the essence of truth, albeit for a brief historical moment and only at the outset.

For Nietzsche, truth as value is a necessary condition of *life*, a valuation that life brings about for its own sake. Thus with the question of knowledge and in the shape of this question we encounter at the same time the more focused question of the essence of life. Briefly, in one sentence, we can say: Our questioning is concerned with life as knowing.

11. Knowing as Schematizing a Chaos in Accordance with Practical Need

To ask what human knowledge is means to want to know cognition itself. Frequently people find such intentions nonsensical, absurd, paradoxical—comparable to Münchhausen's intention of pulling himself out of the swamp by his own hair.* In pointing out this absurdity, they think themselves especially astute and superior. Too late they realize their own amply dubious astuteness. For knowing is for man not something that he first on some occasion gets acquainted with and knows, indeed, only when he starts to erect a theory of knowledge; rather, knowing itself already implies a *self*-knowing.

Representing beings as such is not a procedure that, so to speak, merely occurs in man. It is a mode of behavior in which man stands, indeed, in such a way that the inherence in such behavior sets man out in the open region of this relation. Thus it also sustains his being human. This means that in the representing mode of behavior toward beings man always already relates himself—whether with or without his own "theory," whether with or without self-observation—to himself as well. More essentially, this means that knowing as such is always already known; to want to know cognition is not absurd, but an intention with a lofty character of decision. Everything depends on experiencing knowing in the attempt to delineate explicitly the essence of cognition precisely in the way it has already been known before any reflection about it, and the way it lies open according to its own es-

---

* The humorous and satirical sketches of the Baron K. F. H. von Münchhausen (1720–1797) have by now, after many tellings, translations, and dramatizations, become part of the standard repertory of German folk literature.

sence. If one thus explains purely formalistically, merely arguing with words and phrases, to the effect that to know cognition is absurd and impossible, this already contains an essential misunderstanding of knowing. For knowing is *reflective in itself* and never only in retrospect; it always already stands in the luminosity of its own essence through the power of this reflectiveness.

To know cognition in its essence means, rightly understood, to go back into its already open, though not yet unfolded, essential ground. It does not mean to apply an already finished and clarified mode of behavior once more—raised to a higher power—to itself.

However, the essence and history of Western man are distinguished by the fact that knowing and cognition belong to his basic relation to beings as a whole; thus lucidity in the essential sense, according to which the essence of Western man is in part decided and shaped by reflectiveness, also belongs to that relation. Because this is so, historical Western man can also be overwhelmed by a lack of reflectiveness, a disturbance of lucidity, a destiny that is thoroughly spared an African tribe. Conversely, rescuing and grounding Western historical man can only grow out of the supreme passion of reflection. To this reflection belongs above all the cognizing of cognition, the reflection on knowing and the essential ground in which it has been moving for two thousand years, thanks to the power of its essential history.

The reflection on knowing has nothing to do with erecting a boring and esoteric "theory of knowledge" in which the question of knowing asks about something that has always already been finally or temporarily predecided for the questioner in one way or the other.

Formally viewed, knowing consists in the relation of a knower to what is knowable and known. Yet this relation does not lie somewhere indifferently by itself, like the relation of a felled tree trunk in the forest to a rock lying nearby, a relation we may or may not come across. The relation that distinguishes knowing is always the one in which we ourselves are related, and this relation vibrates throughout our basic posture. This basic posture expresses itself in the way we take beings and objects in advance, in the way we have determined what is decisive in our relation to them.

If, guided by a suitable note of Nietzsche's, we now pursue the question of how he comprehends knowing and thus holding-to-be-true, hence truth, we must pay heed to the following: first, in what way he determines in advance what is encountered as the knowable, surrounding man and his life; second, in what he sees the criterion of the knowing relation to what is encountered, and to man's surroundings.

Both the preliminary determination of what is encountered and the determination of the relational character to it will be interconnected and will refer back to a common essential ground, namely, the kind of basic experience of human life as such that becomes relevant here, and the way human life belongs to the whole of the "world." The basic experience of these things is thus not a mere background for interpreting the essence of cognition, but what comes first and decides everything else in advance.

What does knowing mean for Nietzsche? How does he view in advance man's representing relation to the world? Is knowing a process in the rational living being that we call *man*? If so, what unfolds itself in this process? Is it the case that in it and through it pictures of the surrounding world are taken in, so to speak, and then taken away and transported to the soul and the spirit, so that knowing would be a kind of copying and picturing of reality? Or is knowing for Nietzsche *not* this kind of knowing? His answer to this question—asked not expressly but, so to speak, silently in advance—reads: "Not 'to know' but to schematize—to impose upon chaos as much regularity and as many forms as our practical needs require" (WM, 515; March–June 1888*).

In these words lies what is decisive about Nietzsche's conception of knowledge, just as the saying at the beginning of the note discussed earlier ("The *estimation of value* 'I believe that such and such is so' as the *essence* of '*truth*' ") says what is decisive about truth. We must grasp these words and what was cited earlier in their inner coherence and mutual rootedness. In so doing, we should in no way be concerned with the question of what has influenced Nietzsche in these interpre-

---

* This note, crucial for the following sections of Heidegger's course, appears at CM, *13*, 333–34, as W II 5 [152]. Although the GOA text diverges slightly from CM in some formal respects, I have allowed Heidegger's quotations to remain as is, noting only the most serious changes.

tations of truth and knowing historically; rather, what concerns us is the question as to what this interpretation of truth and knowing points to within Nietzsche's basic metaphysical position and what with respect to the question of truth is thus put to a more acute decision, a decision that has only now become visible. Not "where does he *get* it from?" but "what is he *saying* with it?"

"Not 'to know' but to schematize." Let us observe once again that "to know" is also put in quotation marks, as was the word *"truth"* in the other note. This means that to know is not "to know"—namely, in the supposed sense of a receptive, imitative copy—but "to schematize." We have already encountered the concept of *skhēma* in the context of a first clarification of the essence of reason and thinking in the sense of representation according to *categories* and their schemata. Nietzsche's interpretation of knowing as "schematizing" will presumably be historically connected with the essence of reason and the use of categories—*historically*, meaning that this interpretation of knowledge as "schematizing" abides with Platonic-Aristotelian thought in the same region of decision, even though Nietzsche did not "get" the concept of schema *historiologically*, by looking up past opinions, from Aristotle.

What Nietzsche understands by "schematizing" he specifies straightaway in the following words: "to impose upon chaos as much regularity and as many forms as our practical needs require." How and in what respects does this essentially define knowing understood as "schematizing"? Schematizing is discussed as imposing a certain measure of "regularity" and certain "forms." Schemata are here coinages that as such contain a regularity and a rule. But equally important, or even more essential, is what Nietzsche says in two additional points.

First, regulating forms are to a certain extent imposed on what Nietzsche calls "chaos." What gets schematized by the imposition of regulating forms is what knowing initially meets, what comes toward it in the first instance, what knowing encounters. What is encountered has the character of "chaos." We are startled, provided that we are not thoughtlessly hearing mere sentences in this discussion of Nietzsche's words but rather considering and thinking these things through on our own, on the basis of our own cognizant attitude, pondering the question of *what* encounters us in what is to be known. If we simply look around, knowingly, here in the lecture hall, on the street, in the forest, and elsewhere, do we, knowing and taking notice, encounter "chaos"? Do we not rather find an ordered, articulated region out of which objects that pertain to one another stand over against us in a surveyable, handy, available, and measurable way? We encounter all these objects in a way that is all the richer and more ordered, more adapted to and inclined toward each other, the more we let everything stand before us in a pure lingering, that is, the more we re-present the "world," as we call it, to ourselves, even if it is only a small and narrow world. But, after all, it is not "chaos"!

Second, Nietzsche says that the standard according to which regulating forms are imposed upon "chaos" is determined by our *"practical needs."* Thus practical behavior, the *praxis* of life, not "theoretical" re-presentation is the attitude from which the knowing mode of behavior arises and is determined.

The essential framework of knowledge now has its firm outlines: knowing is schematizing, what is to be known and is knowable is chaos, and what knows is the *praxis* of life. Yet these statements go against what we found a moment ago in the immediate view of our customary everyday representing of the "world."

How does Nietzsche arrive at his characterization of the essence of knowledge? Has he not and have other thinkers before him not seen the world immediately surrounding them; have they not paid heed to their own everyday experience of this world? Have they closed off the view of our essential form of knowing in favor and in honor of a preconceived opinion concerning knowledge?

Or can knowing indeed be seen from another perspective? Does knowing *have* to be seen from another perspective so that what is knowable appears in its scope as chaos, and knowing as the imposition of regularities and forms?

What is this other perspective from which the essence of knowledge here is viewed? Nietzsche himself seems to indicate the perspective from which his thinking is determined when he says that our "practical needs" are decisive for knowing. Yet precisely when we keep to our everyday activities, doings, opinions, business, and calculations, thus to "praxis" and its "world," it is most of all evident that what we are related to in a knowing way, what we attentively have to do with, what we move about in with alert senses and common sense, what we perhaps dash around in or perhaps rest in, is in any case not chaos but a structured world, a range of objects geared to each other and of things that refer to each other, things of which one "gives" the other.

The more decisively we rid ourselves of all philosophical theories about beings and knowledge, the more penetratingly the world shows itself to us in the way described. To what standpoint has thinking and reflecting about knowledge ranged, so that it can arrive at such peculiar statements as this—knowing is a schematizing of chaos carried out in accordance with practical life-needs?

Or is this characterization of the essence of knowledge not really so deranged after all? Does it not even have the tradition of metaphysical thinking on its side, so that all great thinkers agree with Nietzsche's view of knowledge? If this conception of knowledge so little agrees with our everyday mode of behavior and with what the latter knows of itself, this can no longer strike us as strange, since we know that philosophical thinking may not be measured upon the standard of sound common sense. What then are we talking about when we say that our everyday knowing and learning are related not to a chaos but to a structured, ordered realm of objects and objective connections? Are we not speaking about the world as already *known*? Is not precisely this the question of the essence of knowledge, to wit, how we first arrive at representing the objects that surround us, both the things that are the objects of our concern and thus already known and familiar and their broader scope? When we assure ourselves that in representing we are related to a structured and ordered world, do we not thus betray the fact that order and structure have and must have already occurred; do we not presuppose precisely what obviously originated from imposing regulating forms, from schematizing? If we do not get stuck on the surface but reflect in a fundamental way, knowing as representing and as bringing a world before us is basically "schematizing" chaos in accordance with practical needs. Nietzsche's interpretation of the essence of knowledge would then be nothing strange, but also nothing his own, so that we would have no right and no duty to deal with a special Nietzschean doctrine of knowing and truth.

We would merely have to ask why we encounter "chaos" first, how practical need is decisive for knowing, and why knowing is "schematizing." But, asking this way, are we able to get behind the state of our knowing mode of behavior into the sort of state from which knowing first originates: can we get behind this knowing that overcomes the unfamiliar and unknowing mode of relation to beings, the very knowing that produces and takes up a relation in general to "something," that is, to what somehow "is"?

Obviously, there lies in Nietzsche's determination of the essence of knowledge, as in the essential determinations that other thinkers—we are reminded of Kant—have posited about the essence of knowledge, a return to something that makes possible and supports that initial and for the most part familiar representing of an ordered and structured world. Thus the attempt is ventured—knowingly to get behind knowing. Knowing, understood as schematizing, is derived from practical life-needs and from chaos as the condition of the possibility and necessity of those needs. If we grasp life-praxis on the one side and chaos on the other as something that in any case is not nothing, thus a being that unfolds essentially in one way or another, such a characterization of the essence of knowledge implies a derivation of its essential structure from beings that are already in being, perhaps even from beings as a whole.

Such knowing of knowing indeed goes back "behind" knowing. But what kind of return is this? Knowing is explained in terms of its provenance and "conditions," becomes something explained and *known*. Does it thus become more knowing, does it come to master its own essence? Is this return of the kind that places knowing back in its own essential luminosity? Or does knowing become more obscure through this explanatory return? So obscure that all *light*, every trace of the essence of knowing is extinguished? Is the knowing of knowing perhaps the venture of a seriously consequential step that once in thousands of years someone takes by advancing into a matter as yet unquestioned? We may suspect that this is so, because in spite of the innumerable epistemological standpoints that the historians report on there is, at

Knowing as Schematizing a Chaos

bottom, so far only a *single interpretation* of the essence of knowledge—the one for which the first Greek thinkers laid the ground by definitively determining the Being of beings. In the midst of these beings all knowing plays, as an existing mode of behavior of a particular being that relates to beings.

This renewed, supplemental reference to the scope of the question of the essence of knowledge may suffice to make it clear that in this question great decisions are being made and have already been made in previous Western thinking. We want to see how Nietzsche carries out the most extreme consequences of these decisions, and must do so, in that he thinks *metaphysically* about knowledge—in the sense of the tradition of thought in the West and according to the need of his own age and of modern humanity.

The guiding questions for our discussion of Nietzsche's concept of knowledge have been posed: Why does chaos play an essential role in and for knowing? To what extent are practical needs of foremost importance for knowing? Why is knowledge schematizing in general? Of course, these questions are only enumerated here. Nothing has been decided about their proper order, provided there is one—which seems likely.

Is knowing schematizing because chaos is already rife and because an order must be attained? Or is the given as such understood as chaos only because it has already been decided that knowing must be schematizing? If it must be schematizing, *why*? Because order is to be attained? But why order, and in what sense? One question produces another; none of these questions is to be answered by appealing to existent and generally admitted facts. All the questions place us before decisions.

The *question* of the essence of knowledge *is*, everywhere and always, already a thinking *project* of the essence of man and his position within beings, as well as a projection of the essence of these beings themselves. If we fail to reflect on this from the outset and ever more penetratingly, then Nietzsche's presentations on knowledge are indeed similar to investigations that are made somewhere in a psychological or zoological institute concerning processes of life and knowledge, except that these institutional investigations into processes of knowledge—whether in humans or animals—can claim to be exact, whereas Nietzsche makes do with a few general biological figures of speech. If we are moving in the framework of psychological and epistemological claims to explain knowing, we are also reading Nietzsche's statements as though they were to explain to us something about cognition. We fail to see that something is being decided and has been decided in them about contemporary man and his stance vis-à-vis knowledge.

12. The Concept of "Chaos"

Knowing means imposing regulating forms on chaos. What does Nietzsche mean by the term *chaos*? He does not understand this word in the primordial Greek sense, but in the later and especially the modern sense. At the same time the word *chaos* has its own significance originating from the basic position of Nietzsche's thinking.

The Greek word *khaos* originally means "the gaping"; it points in the direction of a measureless, supportless, and groundless yawning open. (See Hesiod, *Theogony,* 116.*) A discussion as to why the fundamental experience that this word names did not and could not become dominant lies outside the present task. It will be sufficient to heed the fact that the long-since current meaning of the word *chaos,* and that always means the perspective opened up by this word, is not an original one. For us, the chaotic means the jumbled, the tangled, the pell-mell. Chaos means not only what is unordered but also entanglement in confusion, the jumble of something in shambles. In its later significance, chaos *also* always means some kind of "motion."

How does chaos come to assume precisely the role cited—of what is knowable in the essential determination of knowledge? For the reflection on knowing, whence the occasion and the impetus to characterize what knowing encounters as chaos, and indeed as absolute "chaos" itself, not simply some sort of "chaos" in some respect? Is it the counterconcept to "order"?

Again, let us keep to a familiar example: We enter this room—let us say for the first time—and ascertain that this blackboard has been covered with Greek letters. In the case of such knowledge we do not first encounter a chaos; we see the blackboard and the letters. Perhaps

---

* See the note on pp. 91–92 of Volume II in this series.

not everyone is able to ascertain that these are Greek letters, but even then we are not confronted with a chaos: rather, we confront something visible, something written, that we cannot read. Certainly, one will admit, immediate perceiving and asserting are related to the blackboard here present with such-and-such qualities, and not to a chaos. This admission indeed corresponds to the state of affairs; however, it presumes that the real question has already been decided. "*This blackboard*"—what does that mean? Does it not already mean the knowledge attained: the thing *as* blackboard? We must have already cognized this thing as a blackboard. How does it stand with *this* cognition? The statements about the blackboard are all already based on the cognition of this thing as a blackboard. To know this thing as a blackboard, we must already have ascertained what we encounter as a "thing" as such, and not, say, as a fleeting occurrence. We must have perceived in our first meeting up with it what is taken in advance as a thing in general, what we encounter, what we confront and what strikes and concerns us in *what and how it is*. We encounter black things, gray, white, brown, hard, rough things, things resonant (when struck), extended, flat, movable things—thus a manifold of what is given. Yet is what is given what gives itself? Is it not *also* already something *taken*, already taken up by the words *black, gray, hard, rough, extended, flat*? Must we not also *take back* this invasion by what we encounter through the words in which we have taken hold of what was encountered, in order to possess what is *purely* encountered, to let it *be* encountered? What *is* encountered—can anything be said about it at all? Or does the region of what can no longer be said, the region of renunciation, begin here where we can no longer or not yet decide upon what is in being, in nonbeing, or not in being? Or has one not yet given up the naming word with regard to the thing encountered, indeed not naming what is *itself* encountered but characterizing it according to what *brings* it *to* us: sight, hearing, smell, taste, touch, and every kind of feeling? What is given is called the manifold of "sensations." Kant even speaks of the "*mass* of sensations," meaning by that the chaos, the jumble, that crowds us, keeps us occupied, concerns us, washes over and tunnels through us—one says, with apparently greater precision, through "our bodies"—not only in the moment of perceiving this blackboard, but constantly and everywhere. For at the same time, and together with what we have been given in the so-called outer senses that we have cited, crowd and mill, drift and float, detain and push, pull and support "sensations" of the "inner" sense that one—again seemingly precisely and correctly—ascertains as bodily states.

If we thus venture just a few steps in the direction indicated, behind, so to speak, what appears so harmlessly and quietly and conclusively to us as an object, such as this blackboard or any other familiar thing, we do meet up with the mass of sensations—chaos. It is what is nearest. It is so near that it does not even stand "next" to us as what is over against us, but we ourselves, as bodily beings, are it. Perhaps this body as it lives and bodies forth is what is "most certain" (WM, 659) in us, more certain than "soul" and "spirit," and perhaps it is this body and not the soul about which we say that it is "inspired" [*"begeistert"*].*

Life lives in that it bodies forth. We know by now perhaps a great deal—almost more than we can encompass—about what we call the body, without having seriously thought about what *bodying* is. It is something more and different from merely "carrying a body around with one"; it is that in which everything that we ascertain in the processes and appearances in the body of a living thing first receives its own process-character. It may be that *bodying* is initially an obscure term, but it names something that is *immediately* and *constantly* experienced in the knowledge of living things, and it must be kept in mind.

As simple and as obscure as what we know as gravitation is, gravity and the falling of bodies, the bodying of a living being is just as simple and just as obscure, though quite different and correspondingly more essential. The bodying of life is nothing separate by itself, encapsulated in the "physical mass" [*Körper*] in which the body can appear to us; the body [*der Leib*] is transmission and passage at the same time. Through this body flows a stream of life of which we feel but a small and fleeting portion, in accordance with the receptivity of the momentary state of the body. Our body itself is admitted into this stream of life, floating in it, and is carried off and snatched away by this

---

* See Volume I, p. 99, including the note.

stream or else pushed to the banks. That chaos of our region of sensibility which we know as the region of the body is only *one section* of the great chaos that the "world" itself is.

We may thus gather that for Nietzsche "chaos" speaks as a name that does not signify some arbitrary jumble in the field of sensations, perhaps no jumble at all. Chaos is the name for bodying life, life as bodying writ large. Nor does Nietzsche mean by chaos what is tangled as such in its confusion, the unordered, arising from the removal of all order; rather, chaos is what urges, flows, and is animated, whose order is *concealed*, whose law we do not descry straightaway.

Chaos is the name for a peculiar preliminary projection of the world as a whole and for the governance of that world. Again, it seems, and here most of all, an uninhibited "biological" thinking is at work. It represents the world as a gigantic "body," as it were, whose bodying and living constitutes beings as a whole and thus lets Being appear as a "Becoming." Nietzsche declares often enough in his later years that the body must be made *the guideline* of observation not only of human beings but of the *world*: the projection of world from the perspective of the animal and animality. The fundamental experience of the world as "chaos" has its roots here. But since the body is for Nietzsche a structure of dominance, "chaos" cannot mean a turbulent jumble. Rather, it means the concealment of unmastered richness in the becoming and streaming of the world as a whole. The suspicion that obtrudes everywhere, the suspicion of biologism, thus seems to gain unequivocal and complete confirmation.

However, we must again emphasize that with the explicit or tacit characterization of this metaphysics as biologism, nothing is being thought, and all Darwinistic thought processes must be extruded. Above all, Nietzsche's idea of viewing man and world as such primarily from the perspective of the body and animality in no way means that man originates from the animal and more precisely from the "ape"—as if such a "doctrine of origin" could say anything about man at all!

The abyss that separates Nietzsche from all this is indicated in a note from the period of *Thus Spoke Zarathustra* (XIII, 276; 1884):

"The apes are too good-natured for man to have originated from them." The animality of man has a deeper metaphysical ground than could ever be inferred biologically and scientifically by referring man to an existent animal species that appears to be similar to him in certain external respects.

"Chaos," the world as chaos, means beings as a whole projected relative to the body and its bodying. In laying this foundation for world projection, everything decisive is included. Thus the thinking that as revaluation of all values strives for a new valuation also includes the positing of the highest value. If truth cannot be the highest value, that highest value must be yet above truth, that is, in the sense of the traditional concept of truth: it must be nearer and more in accordance with true beings, that is, with what becomes. The highest value is *art*, in contradistinction to knowledge and truth. It does not copy what is at hand, does not explain matters in terms of beings at hand. But art transfigures life, moves it into higher, as yet unlived, possibilities. These do not hover "above" life; rather, they awaken life anew out of itself and make it vigilant. For "only through magic does life remain awake" (Stefan George, *Das Neue Reich*, p. 75*).

Yet what is art? Nietzsche says it is "an excess and overflow of blossoming bodily being into the world of images and desires" (WM, 802; Spring–Fall, 1887). We must not take this "world" in an objective or a psychological sense; we must think it metaphysically. The world of art, the world as art discloses it by erecting it and placing it in the open, is the realm of what transfigures. What transfigures, transfiguration, however, is what becomes. It is a becoming that lifts beings, that is, what has become fixed, stable, and congealed over and beyond to new possibilities. The latter do not constitute a goal, to be striven after merely as though they were a supplement and an afterthought,

---

* Heidegger cites the final line of Stefan George's brief dramatic poem *Der Mensch und der Drud* ("The Human and the Wood Sprite"), taken up into the collection *Das Neue Reich* (ca. 1914–1919). The *Drud* is a Nordic wood sprite of a foreboding sort, related in the eighteenth century both to the Greek *dryad* and the Celtic *druid*. In George's poetic drama the Drud warns a self-confident humanity not to overestimate the role cleverness plays in the technological subjugation of nature. See Stefan George, *Werke*, 2 vols. (Düsseldorf: H. Küpper [earlier G. Bondi], 1968), I, 432.

for life-enjoyment and "lived-experience." They are the prior, preeminent, attuning ground of life.

Thus art is creative experience of what becomes, of life itself. And philosophy too, as thoughtful thinking, is nothing other than "art," philosophy viewed metaphysically, not aesthetically. Art, says Nietzsche, is worth more than truth. This means that it comes closer to what is actual, what becomes, to "life," than what is true, what has been fixed and immobilized. Art ventures and wins chaos, the concealed, self-overflowing, unmastered superabundance of life, chaos that seems at first a mere tangled mass, and for particular reasons must appear so.

Our initial point was that in direct statements about an everyday object like the blackboard, *the blackboard* already lies at the very basis, as knowledge. Our characterization of knowledge had to first of all ask what lies in the knowledge of what is thus given and encountered. It then became clear how what is encountered, the manifold of sensations, can be grasped as chaos. At the same time, we had to show how broadly and essentially Nietzsche takes the concept of chaos. What is to be known and what is knowable is chaos, but we encounter chaos bodily, that is, in bodily states, chaos being included in these states and related back to them. We do not first simply encounter chaos in bodily states; but, living, our body bodies forth as a wave in the stream of chaos.

Within its modern range of significance, "chaos" has a double meaning. In its proper, straightforward sense, the term means for Nietzsche "the world" as a whole, the inexhaustible, urgent, and unmastered abundance of self-creation and self-destruction (WM, 1067) in which law and anarchy are first formed and dissolve. Superficially, "chaos" means this selfsame abundance, but first in the illusion of the tangled and confused, as encountered by individual living beings. These living beings are, when thought in a Leibnizian way, "living mirrors," "metaphysical points" in which the whole of the world gathers and shows itself in the circumscribed luminosity of each perspective. In trying to clarify how chaos came to be posited as what is knowable and to be known, we happened to stumble across what knows—the living being that grasps the world and takes it over. That is not a matter of chance, for what is knowable and what knows are each determined in their essence in a unified way from the same essential ground. We may not separate either one, nor wish to encounter them separately. Knowing is not like a bridge that somehow subsequently connects two existent banks of a stream, but is itself a stream that in its flow first creates the banks and turns them *toward* each other in a more original way than a bridge ever could.

13. Practical Need as the Need for a Schema; Formation of a Horizon and Perspective

In the introductory statement of note 515 in *The Will to Power* [see p. 70, above], Nietzsche indeed calls chaos that to which knowing as schematizing responds. Yet he does not say that it is the body and bodily states that distinguish the one who knows and his bearing. Rather, he speaks of "our practical need," which the regulating form is supposed to satisfy. "Chaos" lies on the one side and "practical need" on the other. What does "practical need" mean?

Here too we must reflect more clearly, since everyone seems to know what "practical need" is. We can now fix the direction of this reflection in terms of what has been said. If what encounters knowing has the essential character of chaos, indeed in the double sense mentioned, and if chaos is encountered in relation back to something living, to its bodying and its life; and if on the other hand "practical need" is what in schematizing responds to the chaos encountered; then the essence of what Nietzsche here calls "our practical need" must stand in an essential connection, even in essential unity, with the vitality of bodying life.

Every living being, and especially man, is surrounded, oppressed, and penetrated by chaos, the unmastered, overpowering element that tears everything away in its stream. Thus it might seem that precisely the vitality of life as this pure streaming of drives and pulsions, proclivities and inclinations, needs and demands, impressions and views, wishes and commands pulls and sucks the living itself into its own stream, there to exhaust its surge and flow. Life would then be sheer dissolution and annihilation.

However, "life" is the name for *Being*, and Being means presencing, subsistence, permanence, withstanding disappearance and atrophy. If life therefore *is* this chaotic bodying and oppressive urging, if it is supposed to *be* what properly is, it must at the same time and just as originally be the concern of the living to withstand the urge and the excessive urge, lest this urge propel toward mere annihilation. This cannot happen because the urge would thus remove itself and hence could never *be* an urge. In the essence of this excessive urge lies a kind of urge that is suited to its nature, that urges life *not* to submit to the urgent onslaught but to stand fast in it, if only in order to be able to *be* urged and to urge beyond *itself*. Only what stands can fall. But withstanding the urgent onslaught urges toward permanence and stability. Permanence and the urge toward it are thus nothing alien or *contradictory* to the life-urge, but *correspond* to the essence of bodying life. In order to live, the living must for its own sake *be propelled toward the permanent*.

Nietzsche says that "our practical need" demands the schematization of chaos. How is this expression to be understood if we are to remain at the designated level of metaphysical thinking?

"Practical need" can initially mean the need for practical activity. Yet such activity pertains to life's need only if "praxis" in general belongs to the essence of life, in such a way that its execution grants the vitality of life its appropriate satisfaction. What does *praxis* mean? We usually translate the Greek term as "deed" and "activity," understanding by this the actualization of goals, carrying out of plans and aiming at outcomes and results. We measure all this according to how our "praxis" immediately, palpably, and visibly changes and "sets up" the actual that is at hand. Yet precisely in this way "praxis" and the practical are always taken merely as a consequence of praxis in the essential sense.

When thought in an original way, praxis does not mean mere activity and actualization; rather, such activity is grounded in the occurrence of life itself, "occurrence" in the sense of the vitality of life. "Practical need" now means such needing or being necessary that lies in the essence of praxis as life-occurrence. The living being needs on the basis of and for its vitality what is crucial for it as a living being, namely, that it "live," that it "be," that—as we saw—it not succumb to the torrent of its own characteristic chaos but erect itself and come to stand in that chaos. Such standing in the torrent entails a stance against the onrush, bringing it somehow to a stand; not in such a way that life comes to a standstill and ceases, but in such a way that it is secured in its stability precisely as a living being. *As life-occurrence, praxis is in itself the securing of stability.*

Because this securing is possible only through making chaos stable and fixed, praxis as the securing of stability demands that what is overwhelming us be transposed into something standing, into forms, into schemata. *Praxis is in itself, as the securing of stability, a need for schemata.* Thought metaphysically, "practical need" means being intent upon forming schemata that make the securing of stability possible—in short, the need for a schema. The need for a schema already looks for what stabilizes and thus limits. In Greek, what limits is called *to horidzon*. A *horizon* belongs to the essence of living beings in their vitality, to the securing of stability in the form of the need for a schema. Accordingly, the schema is not a limit imposed on the living being from without, not a limit with which life-activity collides so as to stunt its growth.

Forming horizons belongs to the inner essence of living beings themselves. Initially, horizon simply means setting limits to the unfolding occurrence of life with a view to stabilizing the onrushing and oppressing torrent. The vitality of a living being does not cease with this *limiting* scope, but constantly takes its start from it. The schemata take over the elaboration of the horizon.

A sufficiently lucid clarification of the essential constitution of life in Nietzsche is, of course, made particularly difficult by the fact that he often speaks only generally of living beings and thus does not expressly heed the boundary between man and animal. Nietzsche can proceed in this way without compunction, all the more so because, according to the metaphysical way of thinking, man too is posited as an animal in essence. For Nietzsche, man is the animal that is not yet firmly defined. We must first decide wherein animality consists

Practical Need as the Need for a Schema 87

and in what sense the traditional essential definition of the animal "man," the distinction of rationality, is to be understood.

The significance of the word and concept *life* oscillates in Nietzsche. Sometimes he means by it beings as a whole; sometimes he means only living beings (plant, animal, human); sometimes he means only human life. This ambiguity has essential grounds; thus it is confusing only as long as we fail to follow Nietzsche's *path* of thought. Following our guiding question as to Nietzsche's determination of truth and knowledge, we shall initially limit our discussions of life and living beings to man.

With reference to the need for a schema and forming a horizon, something else may be said that complements and anticipates later considerations. The horizon, the scope of the constant that surrounds man, is not a wall that cuts man off; rather, the horizon is *translucent*. It points as such to what has not been fixed, what becomes and can become, the possible. The horizon pertaining to the essence of living beings is not only translucent, it is somehow also always measured and "seen through," in a broad sense of "seeing and looking." As an occurrence of life, praxis moves in such seeing-through, in "perspectives." The horizon always stands within a perspective, a seeing-through to something possible that can arise out of what becomes, and only out of it, hence out of chaos. The perspective is a way of looking through, cleared in advance, in which a horizon is formed. *The character of looking through and looking ahead, together with the formation of a horizon, belongs to the essence of life.*

Nietzsche often equates horizon and perspective; thus he never reaches a clear portrayal of their distinction and their connection. This lack of clarity has its foundation not only in Nietzsche's way of thinking, but also the very matter itself. For horizon and perspective are necessarily related to each other and intertwined, so that one can often stand for the other. Above all, both are founded in a *more original essential configuration* of human being (in *Da-sein*), which Nietzsche sees and can see as little as all metaphysics before him.

Limiting ourselves to Nietzsche, and sharpening our focus, we can say that the perspective, looking through toward the possible, goes toward chaos in the sense of the urgent and becoming world, yet always within a horizon. The horizon that prevails in the schematization is for its part always only the horizon of a perspective. The horizon, which sets limits and stabilizes, not only fixes chaos in certain respects and thus secures the possible, it also first lets chaos appear *as* chaos through its transparent stability. The stable *as* such is only perceptible in the perspective of something becoming, and something becoming only reveals itself *as* such on the transparent basis of something stable.

Both what becomes and what is stable point back to a more original commencement of their essential unity—provided that they are to be thought with equal essentiality in their relatedness. Because forming a horizon and imposing a schema have their essential ground in the essence of life-occurrence, in praxis as the securing of stability, praxis and chaos essentially belong together.

The connection of the two is by no means to be represented in such a way that here we have a living being at hand in whose inside, as in a compartment, "practical needs" arise, and there, "outside" this living being, chaos. Rather, the living being as praxis, that is, as the perspectival-horizonal securing of stability, is first installed in chaos *as* chaos. Chaos as the onrushing urge of living beings for its part makes the perspectival securing of stability necessary *for* the survival of the living being. The need for schematizing *is in itself* a looking for stable things and their ascertainability, that is, their perceptibility. This "practical need" is reason.

Accordingly, reason is in its essence "practical reason," as Kant saw with increasing clarity in the course of his thinking. Reason means the projective perception of what in itself is out to make life possible. To project the law of morality in practical reason means to make possible the human being as a person who is determined by regard for the law. Reason unfolds its concepts and categories according to the actual direction of the securing of stability. Thus it is not reason itself, not its essence, that first develops out of the need to master chaos; reason is in itself already the perception of chaos, inasmuch as the turbulent throng only becomes at all perceptible in the scope of order and permanence. As what oppresses us in this or that way, it implies and demands this or that fixation, this or that schema-formation.

Practical Need as the Need for a Schema

If knowing has traditionally been taken as re-presentation, this essence of knowing is retained also in Nietzsche's concept of knowledge; but the emphasis of re-presenting shifts to re-*presenting*, to bringing-before-oneself as a *setting* in the sense of *fixing*, that is, fixating, representing in the framework of a configuration. For this reason, knowing is not "cognizing," that is, not copying. Knowing is what it is as a mustering of stable elements, as subsuming and schematizing. The boundary of the limiting horizon-formation is drawn in praxis itself by the securing of stability, which, as the occurrence of life, prefigures the direction and extent of schema-formation according to the essential state and essential elevation of the living being.

The "essential state" is the way that the living being has projected its perspective in advance. In accordance with that perspective, the scope of decisive possibilities is opened and, with it, the realm of decisions through which arises the incisive sense for what is important. The essential incisive sense is thus not a goal hovering above life, a goal one occasionally squints up at or not. The incisive sense supports life always in the sole way appropriate to it. It supports and bears life beyond itself to a possibility already seized upon, a possibility on the basis of which the actual horizon-formation first regulates itself and thus itself becomes a rule and a schema.

14. Accordance and Calculation

In what direction does the securing of stability of the living being "man" go? In a twofold direction that is already prefigured in the essence of man, in that as man he is related to his fellow men and to things. Even the individual man as an individual is always already and always only he who is related to his fellow men and surrounded by things.

Nevertheless, it is seldom possible to begin a priori with this complete essence of man. The tendency is always to start with the "individual" and then to let relations to others and things accrue to him. Nor is anything gained by assuring ourselves that man is a communal being and a herd animal, for even here the community can still be grasped as a mere collocation of individuals. And it must be said in general that even the more complete starting point of *that kind* of man who relates to others and to things and thus to himself still gets stuck in the foreground if we fail from the outset to refer to what indicates the ground on which the simple-complex relation to others, to things, and to oneself rests in general. (According to *Being and Time,* this ground is the *understanding of Being.* It is not the ultimate, but merely the first point from which the grounding of the ground takes its departure in order to think Being as the abyss.)

Like every thinker before him, Nietzsche sees the relation of man to his fellow men and to things; yet like every thinker before him, he begins with the individual and from there executes a transition to the relations mentioned. Man stands in relation to man, man stands in relation to things. The initial relation is one of mutual accordance. Yet this mutual conformity is not only related to men among themselves but always at the same time also to the things to which men relate.

To reach an accord about something means to have the same opinion concerning something; in case of a disparity of opinions, to fix the respects in which there is concordance as well as divergence. In each case accordance is concordance with regard to something as *the same*. Accordance in this essential sense is even the precondition for a divergence of opinions, for disputes; for only if the opponents mean the same thing in general can they diverge with regard to *this one thing*. The concord and discord of men are accordingly based on fixing the same and the stable. If we were entirely prey to a passing flood of mutable representations and sensations, if we were swept away by them, we would never be ourselves. Just as little could the others ever come toward one another and to us as the others they are. In the same way, that *about which* the same men were supposed to reach accord among themselves *as the same thing* would be without constancy. Since misunderstanding and lack of understanding are only deviant forms of accordance, the confluence of the same human beings in their sameness and selfhood must be based on accordance, thought in accord with its essence.

Accordance in the essential sense and agreement as a mere meeting of minds are fundamentally different. The former is the ground of historical human being, whereas the latter is always only a consequence and a means; the former is supreme necessity and decision, the latter only an auxiliary and occasion. Current opinion, however, holds that accord is already capitulation, weakness, forfeiting the debate. It knows nothing of the fact that accordance in the essential sense is the highest and most difficult struggle, more difficult than war and infinitely remote from all pacifism. Accordance is the highest struggle for the essential goals that historical humanity sets up over itself. Thus, in the present historical situation, accordance can only mean having the courage for the single question as to whether the West still dares to create a goal above itself and its history, or whether it prefers to sink to the level of the preservation and enhancement of trade interests and entertainments, to be satisfied with appealing to the status quo as if this were absolute.

Just as accordance as such fixes men in their selves as the same and initially supports the stability of kinships, groups, alliances, and associations, thus securing the survival of men among men in the foreground of their daily lives, what Nietzsche almost casually calls *"calculation"* proceeds to fixate what compels us, what changes, into things that can be calculated, things to which man can revert again and again as the same, things that he can use and make serviceable in this or that way as the same.

Basically, accordance in the usual sense is *being able to count on* man, just as association with things is being able to count *with* objects. The securing of stability has a pervasive characteristic that we may designate as *placing on account.* This involves thinking ahead to a horizon that contains directives and rules in accordance with which what throngs toward us is caught and secured. As the directives for man's relation to men and things, directives placed in advance on account and first regulating calculation, the schemata are not impressed on chaos as a stamp; rather, they are thought out in advance and then sent out to meet what is encountered, so that the latter first appears always already in the horizon of the schemata, and only there. Schematizing in no way means a schematic ordering in readymade compartments of what has no order, but the invention that places on account a range of configurations into which the rush and throng must move in order thus to provide living beings with something constant, and thus to *afford* them the possibility of their own permanence and security.

We can now read with a clearer eye the sentence with which the second paragraph begins, the paragraph that clarifies the intial statement of note 515: "In the formation of reason, logic, the categories, it was *need* that was definitive: the need, not to 'know,' but to subsume, to schematize, for the purpose of accordance and calculation. . . ." This sentence does not contain a Darwinistic explanation of the origin of the faculty of reason; it circumscribes what Nietzsche sees as the essential sphere of reason and knowing. That is praxis, as the occurrence of life, an occurrence that lets living beings perdure in a kind of permanence by bringing fixed things to presence. Yet according to tradition, fixed things are called beings. Representing beings and thinking rationally are *the* praxis of life, the primordial securing of permanence for itself. Bringing objects to a stand and grasping them in re-presentation, thus "concept formation," is no remote, specialized occupation of a theoretical intellect, nothing foreign to life, but the basic law of the occurrence of human life as such.

From here we can gauge how it stands with one widespread interpretation of Nietzsche, according to which Nietzsche is supposed to understand "spirit as the adversary of the soul," that is, of life; meaning that, basically, he denies and negates the concept.* If such formulas may be used at all, we would have to say that the spirit is not the "adversary" but the *pacemaker* of the soul, in such a way that the fixated and the constant compel the living being, not confusedly to sense its open possibilities and precipitously to announce them, but to preshape them by means of supreme reflecting and founding. To this extent the spirit is an adversary of the soul, and a very hard one at that, yet not an adversary *against* life but *for* life. The spirit is also an adversary *against* life if such life, as mere effervescence, the spume of lived experience, is claimed as its *essence*. Nietzsche cannot be hailed as the opponent of the sciences, and not at all as the enemy of knowledge, provided we think him in his proper and ownmost thoughts. Whoever has advanced through *that knowledge* in which Nietzsche persevered and perished will find the characterization of his thinking as "philosophy of life" utterly thoughtless.

No modern thinker has wrestled more vigorously than Nietzsche in order to know and to oppose all hazy and exasperated forms of ignorance—this at a time when alienation from knowledge was promoted by science itself, pre-eminently by way of that attitude we call *positivism*. Such positivism has by no means been overcome today. It has become veiled, hence more effective.

---

* Heidegger is here referring to the interpretation of Ludwig Klages. See Volume I in this series, pp. 23, 127, and 242–43.

15. The Poetizing Essence of Reason

With the publication of the second of his *Untimely Meditations,* "On the Advantage and Disadvantage of History for Life" (1873), Nietzsche's thinking gives the false impression that he is fighting against "science" in favor of so-called life, whereas in truth he is fighting for knowledge in honor of an originally conceived "life" and reflection on "life." This indicates that we sufficiently understand the necessity of knowledge for life, and of truth as a necessary value, only if we keep to the *one* path that simultaneously leads to a more original grasp of knowing in its essential unity with life. Only thus do we retain the criterion for evaluating the weight of Nietzsche's individual utterances, even against their initially apparent intent. In the course of note number 515, Nietzsche adds a remark set in parentheses: "(The development of reason is adjustment, invention, in order to make similar, identical—the same process that every sense impression goes through!)"

Bracketing this sentence could mislead us into reading past it, as if it were an incidental, basically dispensable remark.* However, in truth Nietzsche is indicating the step that leads to a still more essential conception of reason and knowing. The same thing that was meant by the expression "formation of reason" in the preceding sentence is now expressed by the phrase "development of reason." "Development" is not intended biologically in the sense of origination but metaphysically as the unfolding of essence. Reason consists in adjustment, *invention* of what is identical.

---

* Note that the parentheses were added by Nietzsche's editors. In the notebooks the jotting appears as a separate paragraph, without brackets of any kind.

The Poetizing Essence of Reason

Assuming that we frequently come across a lone tree outside on a meadow slope, a particular birch, the manifold of colors, shades, light, atmosphere has a different character according to the time of day and year, and also according to the changing perspective of our perception, our distance, and our mood; and yet it is always this "identical" tree. It *is* "identical," not subsequent to our ascertaining the matter through comparisons (as though it proved to be, after all, the "identical" tree), but the other way around; our way of approaching the tree always already looks for the "identical." Not as though the changing aspects escaped us; on the contrary, only if in advance we posit something beyond the variability of what gives itself, something that is not at hand in the self-giving given, an "identity," that is, a selfsame, can we experience the magic of the change of aspects.

Such positing of the tree as the same is in a way a positing of something that does not exist, namely, in the sense of something to be found at hand. Such positing of something "identical" is thus a creation and an invention. In order to determine and think the tree in its actually given appearance, its sameness must have been created beforehand. This irrepressible presupposing of a selfsame, that is, of a sameness, this creative character, is the essence of reason and thinking. For this reason, creation must always occur before there can be thinking in the usual sense.

In that we know what is encountered as a thing, as thus and thus constituted, as related to others in this or that way, as thus and thus elaborated, thus and thus large, we have already in advance created thinghood, constitution, relation, effect, causality, and size for what is encountered. What is created in such creativity are the categories. What properly appears to us and shows itself in its outward appearance, this same thing in its thinghood thus constituted—in Greek, this "Idea"—is of a created origin. It is thus of a higher origin, one that lies *above* everything that our most familiar doings already immediately take up, believing that they are only taking up what is handy and itself at hand. This creative essence of reason was not first discovered by Nietzsche but only emphasized by him in some particularly blunt respects, and not always adequately. Kant first explicitly perceived and thought through the creative character of reason in his doctrine of the transcendental imagination.* The conception of the essence of absolute reason in the metaphysics of German Idealism (in Fichte, Schelling, and Hegel) is thoroughly based on the Kantian insight into the essence of reason as a "formative," creative "force."

However, Kant's thought only expresses what had to be said about the essence of reason on the basis of modern metaphysics. Experienced in the modern sense, reason becomes synonymous with the subjectivity of the human subject; it means the self-certain representing of beings in their beingness, that is, *objectivity*. Representing must be self-certain because it now becomes the *re-presenting* of objects that is established purely on itself, that is, as bound up with a subject. In self-certainty, reason makes certain that with its determination of objectivity it secures what is encountered. It thus places itself in the scope of a ubiquitously calculable certainty. Thus reason becomes more explicitly than ever before the faculty that forms and images to *itself* everything that beings are. Hence it becomes the imagination, without qualification, understood in this way. If we emphasize that Kant "only" more clearly foresaw and expressed this essence of reason for the first time as a whole and in terms of the actual dimension of its capacities as a faculty, this "only" should in no way diminish the Kantian doctrine of transcendental imagination. The only thing we wish to do and can do here is to concentrate on rescuing this step of Kantian thinking by noting that it is incomparable.

The talk about the poetizing essence of reason does not, of course, mean a *poetic* essence. Just as little as all thinking is thoughtful is every poetizing and inventing automatically poetic. However, the poetizing essence of reason refers all human, that is, all rational knowing to a higher origin, whereby "higher" means essentially lying beyond our everyday habitual taking up and copying. What is apprehended in reason, namely, beings *as* beings, cannot be taken into possession by mere discovery. Thought Platonically, beings are what is present, the "Idea." When Plato tells, for example, in his dialogue *Phaedrus*,

---

* See Martin Heidegger, *Kant und das Problem der Metaphysik*, 4th expanded edition (Frankfurt am Main: V. Klostermann, 1973), pp. 125–27.

of the descent of the "Idea" from a supracelestial place, *hyperouranios topos,* into the soul of man down below, this myth, thought metaphysically, is nothing other than the Greek interpretation of the poetizing essence of reason, that is, its *higher origin.*

Nietzsche is thinking the Platonic doctrine of the Ideas all too externally and superficially, in accordance with Schopenhauer and the tradition, when he believes he must distinguish his doctrine of the "development of reason" from the Platonic doctrine of a "pre-existent Idea." Nietzsche's interpretation of reason too is Platonism, albeit transposed to modern thinking. This means that Nietzsche too must retain the *poetizing* character of reason, the "pre-existent," that is, preformed and prestabilized character of the determinations of Being, the schemata. Yet the determination of the *provenance* of this poetizing, preforming character is different in Plato and Nietzsche. For Nietzsche, this character of reason is given with the course of life—with praxis (he calls it "utility" in this passage, which is misleading); life, however, he takes as that which man himself, based on himself, has in his power. For Plato too the essence of reason and the Idea originate from "life," from *dzōē,* as the governance of beings as a whole; but human life is only a decline from true, eternal life, is merely a deformation of the latter. If we consider that human life, for Nietzsche, is only a metaphysical point of life, life in the sense of the "world," his doctrine of the schemata comes so close to the Platonic doctrine of Ideas that it is only a certain kind of reversal of the Platonic doctrine; that is to say, it is identical with it in *essence.*

Nietzsche writes: "It is not a pre-existent 'Idea' that has been at work here but utility: only if we see things in a rough and undifferentiated way are they calculable and manipulable for us." Thus he places the everyday calculability of things under an "if," that is, under the higher condition of the invention and inventability of things. In the parenthetical remark he calls this invention a "process that every sense impression goes through." How is this so? The example of the perception of the tree showed how the manifold of given color impressions is related to something identical and selfsame. But now Nietzsche thinks that every individual color impression, for example, a sensation of red, has already undergone some sort of invention. This also assumes that the individual sensations of red are each time necessarily different according to the strength of the impression, the intensity of the hue varying with its proximity to a similar color, varying with the transformation of what we have just invented as identical by lending it the word *red*, ignoring the finer gradations and tones. On the other hand, in certain kinds of painting, the artist seeks the broadest richness of differentiation within one color in order then to allow a seemingly simple, univocal red to originate in the total impression of the objective picture. Yet every *sense impression* goes through this process of being poetized into something identical—red, green, sour, bitter, hard, rough—because as an *impression* it enters nothing other than that area of reason prevailing in advance as essentially poetizing and elevating to identity and sameness. The sensuous crowds and overwhelms *us* as rational living beings, as those beings who have always already been intent on making things identical without expressly carrying out such an intention. For only what is identical offers the guarantee of the same; only the same secures constancy, while making constant effects the securing of permanence. Accordingly, even the sensations themselves that constitute the initially pressing "tumult" are a fictionalized manifold. The categories of reason are horizons of poetizing, and such poetizing first clears for what is encountered that free place from which and upon which it can appear as something constant, as an ob*ject* [*Gegen*stand].

"*Finality* in reason is an effect, not a cause." This sentence, at first obscure, is suddenly there as if it had been shot from a pistol. This is the case even when we know that "finality" (purposiveness) is one of the categories of reason and thus as *one* schema among others pertains to what is to be clarified under the heading of schematization or poetization. For we ask ourselves why Nietzsche cites precisely this category explicitly. If we have followed the previous interpretation of the essence of knowledge, we already possess the answers to the questions that must be posed here: First, how does Nietzsche come to emphasize expressly that finality is not a "cause" but rather an "effect"? Second, why does he mention finality with such emphasis at all?

With regard to the first, has anyone ever claimed that "finality" (purposiveness) is a cause? They have. This has been a fundamental doctrine of metaphysics since Plato and Aristotle. Purpose is a cause; in Greek, the *hou heneka* is *aition, aitia; finis est causa—causa finalis*. Thought in a Greek way, *aition* means "what is responsible for" something. In contrast, the common meaning of our word *cause* is one-sided: by it we mean what brings about an effect, the *causa efficiens*. The *on account of which* is what is responsible for the fact that something else happens and is done on account of it; it is that at which something aims, for example, a hut to grant shelter. Purpose is what is represented in advance, hence in the present case being sheltered and protected against the weather. What is represented in advance contains the directive that the hut in our example be covered, have a roof. The purpose, what is intended in advance, granting shelter, causes the fitting and finishing of a roof. Purpose is a cause. Purposiveness (finality) has the character of cause.

In contrast, Nietzsche says that finality is an effect, "not a cause." Here too we have before us Nietzsche's favorite procedure—abbreviation of a rich and essential consideration. Nietzsche has no intention of denying what we have just clarified, namely, that the purpose, what is represented in advance, has the characteristic, *as* something *re*-presented, of directing and thus causing. What he primarily wants to emphasize is this: the on-account-of-which and the for-this-reason that are represented in advance originate as such, that is, as what has been fixed in advance, from the poetizing character of reason, from its being intent on something constant; thus they are produced by reason and *for such reason* are an effect. As a category, finality is something *poetized* and thus effected (an effect). Yet what is thus poetized, the category "purpose," has the horizontal characteristic that it gives directives for the production of something else; hence it *causes* the effecting of something else. Precisely because finality as a kind of cause is a category, it is an "effect" in the sense of a poetized schema.

With regard to the second, why does Nietzsche mention finality in an emphatic way? Not only with the intention of expressing the opposite of the customary opinion in the abbreviated and very misleading form we have noted, thus introducing a "paradox," but because "finality," that is, being intent on something, looking ahead to something upon which everything depends, fundamentally characterizes the essence of reason. For all being intent on constancy is fundamentally a constant setting before oneself of something *aimed* at; it is the stake driven in the middle of the target, "purposes," the purpose.* If reason, as the representing apprehending of the actual, wanted to break out into the purposeless and to dissipate itself in the aimless and the inconstant, thus to relinquish the poetizing of the identical and the orderly, it would be overpowered by the torrent of chaos; life would come to swerve and slide in its essential process, in the securing of its permanence, would give up its essence and thus turn out badly: "with every other kind of reason, toward which there are again and again tentative starts, life miscarries—it becomes too difficult to survey—too unequal."

The special emphasis on the category of finality shows that Nietzsche understands it not only as *one* category among others but as the *fundamental category* of reason. This distinguishing of finality, of the *hou heneka (finis)*, itself moves in the fundamental direction of Western metaphysical thought. The fact that Nietzsche must attribute this privileged role to finality results from the way he posits the essential origin of reason, equating its essence with the process of life as securing permanence.

---

* *Der Zweck*, "purpose," derives from the Middle High German *zwec*, a wooden peg or plug placed as the "bull's eye" at the center of a target. From the fifteenth century onward it is equated with the word *das Ziel*, something "aimed at," the target, end, or aim. Kant's word for teleological causality or entelechy is, of course, *Zweckmässigkeit*. It is the central concept (the bull's eye, as it were) of the "doctrine of transcendental method" and the "canon" of the *Critique of Pure Reason* and of the entire *Critique of Judgment*.

16. Nietzsche's "Biological" Interpretation of Knowledge

With the determination of the essence of reason now clarified, everything is ready for Nietzsche to state in the next section of the note what is essential to the categories in general and their truth: "The categories are 'truths' only in the sense that they are conditions of life for us: as Euclidean space is a conditioned 'truth.' "*

The categories are thus not "true" in the sense that they copy something present at hand in itself—thinghood, quality, unity, plurality—the essence of their "truth" is rather gauged according to the essence of that for which "truth" remains the distinguishing characteristic, namely, knowledge. Knowledge is schema-forming, the schematization of chaos that originates from and pertains to the perspectival securing of permanence. Securing permanence, in the sense of making constant what is unarticulated and flowing, is a condition of life.

Roughly speaking, the categories, thinking in categories, and the rules and articulation of such thinking, that is, logic—all of these life procures for itself in order to maintain itself. Is not this doctrine concerning the provenance of thinking and the categories biologism?

We do not want to close our eyes to the fact that Nietzsche is thinking in a concretely biological way here and speaking that way without misgivings. This is especially true at the conclusion of the passage in which he attempts to raise everything to the essential level, to that which provides the ground for the essence of life and its development. "(An aside: since no one will maintain that there is any

---
* GOA has "a conditioning 'truth,' " CM "a conditioned 'truth.' " Here I have followed CM rather than Heidegger's citation of the GOA.

necessity for men to exist, reason, as well as Euclidean space, is a mere idiosyncrasy of a certain species of animal, one idiosyncrasy among many . . .)."

Nietzsche ascertains that the particular species of animal called man happens to be at hand. An unconditioned necessity for there being such living beings at all cannot be seen, much less shown to be founded. This species of animal, extant ultimately by chance, is so constituted in its own life that it reacts in a special way to the collision with chaos, namely, in this definite way of securing permanence, specifically by way of devising categories and adapting itself to three-dimensional space—both of these as forms of stabilizing chaos. "In itself" there is no three-dimensional space, there is no equality among things, there are no things at all as fixed and constant items with their own fixed qualities.

With the last paragraph of note 515, Nietzsche risks a step into the innermost essence of reason and thinking, unambiguously expressing their biological nature. "The subjective compulsion by which we are unable to contradict here is a biological compulsion. . . ." Again, this sentence is formulated in so compressed a fashion that it would almost have to be incomprehensible if we were not coming at it from a more clarified realm. "The subjective compulsion by which we are unable to contradict here": Where is "here"? and "unable to contradict" what? And why "contradict"? Nietzsche says nothing about this because he has something other in mind than would appear.

The transition between the penultimate and the last paragraph is lacking; more precisely, it is not explicitly expressed because it is clear on the basis of what preceded. Nietzsche thinks tacitly as follows: All thinking in categories, all nascent thinking in schemata, that is, in accordance with rules, is *perspectival*, conditioned by the essence of life; hence it is also thinking in accordance with the fundamental rule of all thought, that is, the law of the avoidance of contradiction. Whatever binding directive, whatever necessity of thought this axiom contains has the same character as all rules and schemas.

Following the thread of the note, that is, pursuing his reflection on the essence of the schemata, on the forward-reaching regulation of thinking as such and the origin of that regulation, Nietzsche arrives, not suddenly and not without mediation, at the fundamental rule to which all knowing is subject. He begins by referring to situations in which the role of the law of contradiction as a rule of thinking becomes especially clear.

Nietzsche wants to say that there are cases in which we are not able to contradict; that means cases in which we cannot fall prey to a contradiction, cases in which we must avoid the contradiction. In these cases, we cannot affirm and deny the same thing. We are compelled to do one or the other. We can affirm and deny the same thing, but not at the same time and in the same respect. In such not being able, a compulsion prevails. Of what sort?

The compulsion to the one or the other, says Nietzsche, is a "subjective" one, a compulsion lying in the constitution of the human subject; and this subjective compulsion to avoid contradiction in order to be able to think an object at all is "a biological one." The law of contradiction, the rule of avoidance of contradiction, is the fundamental law of reason; the essence of reason thus expresses itself in this fundamental rule. However, the law of contradiction does not say that "in truth," that is, in actuality something self-contradictory can never be actual at the same time; it merely says that man is compelled for "biological reasons" to think this way. Roughly speaking, man must avoid contradiction in order to escape confusion and chaos or in order to master it by imposing on it the form of what is unified and identical, free of contradiction. Just as certain sea animals, for example, jellyfish, develop and extend their tentacles for grasping and catching, the animal "man" uses reason and its grasping instrument, the law of contradiction, in order to find his way around in his environment, in that way securing his own permanence.

Reason and logic, knowledge and truth, are biologically conditioned appearances in the animal we call man. With this biological ascertainment, reflection on the essence of truth would be concluded and the biological nature of this reflection demonstrated. It would have been shown that reflection consists in nothing other than the explanatory reduction of all appearances to *life*, a manner of explanation that fully convinces everyone who is used to biological (that is, scientific) thinking, who takes facts for what they are, namely, for facts, and who also lets all metaphysical elucidations be what they are, which is to say, phantoms that are not brought to light in their own true provenance.

We wanted to establish Nietzsche's biological way of thinking in every respect. But we also wanted to show above all that Nietzsche seeks to grasp the essence of reason from the perspective of the highest principle of thinking, the law of contradiction, entirely in the sense of the tradition of Western metaphysics.

Hence, in order to penetrate to the essential *core* of the essence of reason, thus of the praxis of "life," and thus to the essence of securing permanence, we must now think further along these lines. Nietzsche's apparently merely biological explanation of the categories and of truth thus moves of itself all the more clearly into the area of metaphysical thinking, the area of the guiding question that sustains and animates all metaphysics. The fact that the reflections of note 515 culminate in an interpretation of the law of contradiction and thus reach the summit of metaphysical considerations, but that at the same time the interpretation of this law seems to support biologism in its crudest form, drives our own reflection to its ultimate limits. In the note that is correctly placed after the one we have been treating (see WM, 516; Spring–Fall, 1887 and 1888*), Nietzsche treats the law of contradiction more explicitly.

The fundamental law of reason was first completely and explicitly expressed and discussed as the axiom of all axioms by Aristotle. Its presentation is handed down to us in Book IV of the *Metaphysics* (chapters 3–10).

Ever since the Aristotelian elucidation of the law of contradiction the one question has haunted us as to whether this law is a logical principle, a highest rule of thinking, or whether it is a metaphysical law, that is, a law that decides something about beings as such—about Being.

It is simply a univocal sign of the significance of this law *that* its

---

* See W II 1 [67]; CM, *12*, 389–91. Here again I have altered Heidegger's quotations only in a few instances—all of them "formal," having to do with punctuation, underlining, etc., and not with the sense of the passages.

elucidation returns at the consummation of Western metaphysics. On the other hand, the consummation of Western metaphysics is characterized by the *way* in which this elucidation is carried out.

On the basis of what has been presented thus far, we can already anticipate the direction in which Nietzsche's interpretation of the law of contradiction and his position with regard to it will have to lie. For supposing that the law is a principle of logic, it must together with logic and the essence of reason have its origin in life's securing of permanence. Hence we are tempted to say that Nietzsche grasps the law of contradiction not logically but biologically. However, the question remains whether, precisely in this elucidation of the apparently biologically understood principle something does not come to light that prevents any kind of biological interpretation. Reflection on Nietzsche's elucidation of the law of contradiction should be for us a first way—with regard to this question that is so decisive for metaphysics—finally to get beyond what is apparently merely biological in his interpretation of the essence of truth, knowledge, and reason, and thus to clarify that interpretation in its ambiguity. The first short paragraph of note number 516 sounds strange, however, for it in no way corresponds to what follows. It reads: "We are unable to affirm and to deny one and the same thing: this is a subjective empirical principle, the expression not of any 'necessity' *but only of an inability.*"

On the basis of our previous elucidations, we note that it is possible to affirm and deny one and the same thing, but it is not possible to affirm and deny one and the same thing at the same time with regard to the selfsame and in the same respect. Or is even this ultimately possible? It is. For if this were never possible, no one would ever have thought in contradictions; there would never have been something like a thinking that contradicted itself. If any statement is ever valid according to the testimony of experience, it is this one: human beings contradict themselves in their thinking, asserting the opposite about one and the same thing at the same time. That there are contradictions is an experiential proposition. That this affirmation and denial of the same is all too possible for us is true; hence so is the fact that the "subjective compulsion" to avoid contradiction is often quite readily lacking. Then there is presumably no compulsion at all, but a peculiar *freedom* that is perhaps not only the reason for the *possibility* of self-contradiction but also the reason for the *necessity* of the principle of noncontradiction.

But why facts and the appeal to facts? They are all secured solely on the basis of our following the law of noncontradiction. The fact that there are contradictions, that self-contradictory thinking occurs none too seldom, is an experience that contributes nothing to reflection on the essence of this principle. However, what the law of contradiction expresses, what is posited in it, does not rest on experience— just as little, indeed even less so, than the statement 2 × 2 = 4 rests on experience, that is, on a cognition that is always valid only as far and as long as our knowledge extends at the time. If 2 × 2 were an experiential statement, then when we wanted to think the statement while doing justice to its essence we would have to think each time, "2 × 2 = 4, as far as we know till now; it is possible that one day 2 × 2 = 5 or 7." Yet why do we not think this way? Perhaps because it would be too complicated? No, because we (in thinking 2 × 2) *already* think *that* which we call 4. What we think in the law of contradiction, which is the very rule for the thinkability of that equation, we do not know from experience at all, that is, in the way and in the sense that what we think in it could one day be different and thus that what is thought is valid only as far as our state of knowledge extends at the time. What then do we think in the law of contradiction?

Aristotle discovered and expressed what is thought in this law for the first time in the following formulation (*Metaphysics* IV 3, 1005b 19 ff.): *To gar auto hama hyparkhein te kai mē hyparkhein adynaton tō autō kai kata to auto.* "That the same thing come to be present and not come to be present at the same time is impossible in the same and with respect to the same." In this statement, an *adynaton*, an *impossible*, is thought and said. What kind of impossibility this impossible has is evidently partly determined by that whose impossibility is meant here: presencing and not presencing at the same time *(hama hyparkhein te kai mē hyparkhein).* The impossible concerns being present and presence. However, according to the basic experience of Greek thinkers, not explicitly expressed at first, presence is the essential unfolding of Being. The law of contradiction deals with the Being of beings. The *adynaton* is an incapability in the Being of beings. *Being is incapable of something.**

In any case, Nietzsche sees one thing clearly—that in the law of contradiction an impossibility is what is decisive. Accordingly, an interpretation of this law must first throw light on the manner and the essence of this *adynaton*. According to the first paragraph, cited above, Nietzsche comprehends this "impossible" in the sense of an "inability." He remarks explicitly that it is not a matter of a "necessity" here. This means that the fact that something cannot be something and its opposite at the same time depends upon the fact that we are not able "to affirm and deny one and the same thing." Our inability to affirm and deny the same thing has as its consequence the fact that something cannot *be represented, fixated* as something and its opposite at the same time, that is to say, cannot *"be."* But our not being able to think otherwise in no way arises from the fact that what is thought of itself requires that we must think it in this way. The "impossible" is an inability in our thinking, thus a subjective not-being-able and in no way an objective prohibition on the part of the object. With the word "necessity" Nietzsche means this objective impossibility. The law of contradiction thus has only "subjective" validity; it depends on the constitution of our faculty of thinking. In the event of a biological mutation of our thinking faculty, the law of contradiction could lose its validity. Has it not lost it already?

Did not that thinker who together with Nietzsche brought about the fulfillment of metaphysics, that is, *Hegel*, abrogate the validity of the law of contradiction in his metaphysics? Did not Hegel teach that contradiction belongs to the innermost essence of Being? Is not this also the essential doctrine of Heraclitus? Yet for Hegel and for Heraclitus "contradiction" is the "element" of "Being," so that we already distort everything if we talk of a contra*diction* of speaking and saying instead of an oppositionality of Being. But the same Aristotle who first

---

* See Heidegger's 1931 lecture course, *Aristotle's Metaphysics, Theta, 1–3: On the Essence and Actuality of Force* (Frankfurt am Main: V. Klostermann, 1981), esp. sections 12 and 16. See also Walter Brogan, "Heidegger's Interpretation of Aristotle: The Finitude of Being," in *Research in Phenomenology*, XIV (1984), 249–58.

explicitly formulated that principle concerning the Being of beings also speaks of *antiphasis*. He also formulates the principle differently from the way we have cited it, in ways that make it appear as if it were actually only a matter of contrasting assertions—*phaseis*.

However these questions are to be answered, we conclude the following from them: the law of contradiction and what it says concern a fundamental question of metaphysics. Thus, whether Nietzsche interprets the impossibility designated by this law in the sense of a subjective inability of man—crudely put, as a given biological determination—or whether this interpretation is again only a foreground, Nietzsche is moving in the realm of metaphysical thinking, a thinking that has to decide about the essence of beings as such. Nietzsche does not move in this realm reluctantly or even unknowingly, but knowingly, so decisively knowingly that he penetrates to essential areas of decision in metaphysics in the following paragraphs of note number 516. The external indication of this is that he introduces the discussion proper by mentioning Aristotle. This implies not only a historiological connection with an earlier opinion, but a certain regaining of the historical ground on which Nietzsche's own interpretation of the essence of thinking, of holding-to-be-true and of truth, rests.

> If, according to Aristotle, the *law of contradiction* is the most certain of all fundamental principles, if it is the ultimate and most basic, upon which every demonstrative proof rests, if the principle of all other axioms lies in it; then one should consider all the more rigorously what sorts of assertions it already fundamentally *presupposes*. Either it asserts something about actuality, about being, as if one already knew this from another source; that is, as if opposite attributes *could* not be predicated of it. Or, perhaps the proposition means: opposite attributes *should* not be predicated of it? In that case, logic would be an imperative, *not* to know the true, but to posit and devise a world that *is to be called true for us*.

Nietzsche remarks explicitly that Aristotle takes the law of contradiction to be the "principle of all other axioms." Aristotle says this clearly enough at the end of *Metaphysics* IV 3, 1005b 33–34, where he concludes the positive discussion of this principle with the following words: *Physei gar arkhē kai tōn allōn axiōmatōn hautē pantōn.* "For, according to its essence, this is the point of departure for and ruling force over the other axioms, indeed thoroughly so." However, in order to judge the scope of Aristotle's estimation of the law of contradiction, that is, initially to see correctly the realm of its scope, one has to know in what context Aristotle treats this axiom of the highest rank. According to a centuries-old prejudice, the law of contradiction is supposed to be a rule of thinking and an axiom of logic. That it appears to be so is obvious. This appearance was widespread already by Aristotle's time, a fact that indicates that the appearance does not come about by chance. Aristotle discusses the law of contradiction in the treatise already mentioned [Book Gamma], which begins with the following words: *Estin epistēmē tis hē theōrei to on hē on kai ta toutō hyparkhonta kath' hauto.* "There is a kind of knowledge that looks at beings insofar as they are beings (beingness) and thus discusses what belongs to beingness itself and constitutes it."

Knowing the beingness of beings—in short, Being—Aristotle calls *prōtē philosophia*, "philosophy of the first order," that is, true philosophical knowledge and thinking. In the course of developing such knowledge about the beingness of beings, Aristotle asks whether to this knowing and asking there also belongs the discussion of what are called the *bebaiotatai arkhai*, the things that constitute the firmest point of departure and ruling force for all Being. What we call the law of contradiction belongs among these. Aristotle answers the question in the affirmative. That means that this "axiom" is the estimation of what belongs to the Being of beings in advance. The law of contradiction says "something" about Being. It contains the essential projection of the *on hē on*, of beings as such.

If we understand the law in the sense of the tradition that has become dominant—thus in a way that is not strictly and completely Aristotelian—it says something merely about the way thinking must proceed in order to be a thinking of beings. But if we understand the law of contradiction in an Aristotelian way, we have to ask what this law properly presupposes and posits in such a way that it can then *as a consequence* be a rule for thinking.

As we have shown clearly enough, Nietzsche takes the law as a fundamental of logic, as a "logical axiom," and notes that according to Aristotle it is the "most certain" of all principles. Aristotle says nothing about "certainty," of course, because he could not have done so, inasmuch as "certainty" is a modern concept—although, to be sure, the Hellenistic and Christian thought of the certainty of salvation paved the way for it.

17. The Law of Contradiction as a Law of Being: Aristotle

In accordance with the general style of his discussions of the essence of thinking, reason, and truth, Nietzsche's position with regard to the law of contradiction takes the following form: If the law of contradiction is the highest of all principles, then we must ask "what sorts of assertions it already fundamentally *presupposes*." The question that Nietzsche demands that we ask here has long since been answered—indeed by Aristotle—so decisively that what Nietzsche is asking about constitutes the sole content of this law for Aristotle. For according to Aristotle the law says something essential about beings as such: that every absence is foreign to presence because it snatches presence away into its nonessence, thus positing impermanence and hence destroying the essence of Being. But Being has its essence in presence and in permanence. For this reason, the aspects according to which beings are to be represented as beings will have to take into account this presence and permanence by means of the *hama*, the "at the same time," and the *kata to auto*, the "in the same respect."

Something present and permanent necessarily gets lost as such if its presence and its presentness are disregarded by the perspective on another point in time, if its permanence is disregarded by the perspective on something impermanent. If this happens, the result is that the same thing is affirmed and denied of a being. Man is thoroughly capable of something like this. He can contradict himself. But if man maintains himself in a contradiction, what is impossible does not of course consist in the fact that yes and no are thrown together, but that man excludes himself from representing beings as such and forgets *what* he really wants to grasp in his yes and no. Through contradictory assertions, which man can freely make about the same thing, he displaces himself from his essence into nonessence; he dissolves his relation to beings as such.

This fall into the nonessence of himself is uncanny in that it always seems harmless, in that business and pleasure go on just as before, in that it doesn't seem so important at all what and how one thinks; until one day the catastrophe is there—a day that needs perhaps centuries to rise from the night of increasing thoughtlessness.

Neither moral nor cultural nor political standards extend to the dimension of responsibility in which thinking is placed in accordance with its essence. Here—in interpreting the law of contradiction—we are only skimming the surface of this area and attempting to bring to our attention something slight yet not to be circumvented: the law of noncontradiction asserts something about beings as such, indeed nothing less than the following. *The essence of beings consists in the constant absence of contradiction.*

Nietzsche knows that the law of contradiction is a law concerning the Being of beings. Yet Nietzsche does not know that this interpretation of the law of contradiction was expressed by precisely that thinker who for the first time posited and conceived the law entirely as a law of Being. If Nietzsche's not-knowing were only a historiological oversight, we would pay no further attention to it. But it means something else. It means that Nietzsche fails to recognize the historical ground of his own interpretation of beings and does not judge the scope of his own positions. Thus he cannot make out his *own standpoint,* so that he also cannot get at the opposition he wants. For an opponent must first of all be grasped and attacked on the basis of his very own position.

Aristotle, however, thought in a *Greek* manner: Being was seen immediately in its essence as presence. It was sufficient for him simply to see the Being of beings in its essence as *ousia, energeia,* and *entelekheia* and to say and show what he had seen. This was all the more sufficient in that the Greek thinkers knew that Being, the essence of beings, could never be calculated and derived in terms of any beings at hand, that it must rather show itself of its own accord as *idea.* Even then Being was accessible only to an appropriate gaze.

Aristotle did not first have to ask for the presuppositions of the law of contradiction, because he already conceived this law as the prepositing of the essence of beings. For the commencement of Western thought was consummated precisely in *such* a positing.

We are hardly capable of saying which is greater and more essential in this stance of thinking adopted by the Greeks in their thinking of Being: the immediacy and purity of the original envisaging of the essential configurations of being or the lack of any need explicitly to ask about the truth of this envisaging; the lack of any need—thought in a modern way—to go *back behind* its own positing. The Greek thinkers "only" show the first steps *forward*.

Since then no one has taken a step beyond the space that the Greeks first measured out. It belongs to the mystery of the first commencement to throw so much brightness around itself that it needs no limping explanations. This also means that if a more original consideration of Being should become necessary because of a real historical need of Western man, such thinking can only occur in confrontation with the first beginnings of Western thought. This confrontation will not succeed, will remain inaccessible in its essence and necessity, as long as the greatness, that is, simplicity and purity of the corresponding fundamental mood of thinking and the power of the appropriate saying, are denied us.

Because Nietzsche in an immediate way comes closer to the essence of the Greeks than any metaphysical thinker before him, and because at the same time he thinks in a *modern* way, thoroughly and with the hardest stringency, it might seem that the confrontation with the beginning of Western thought occurs in his thinking. Yet as a modern confrontation it is not the one we mentioned; rather, it inevitably becomes a mere reversal of Greek thought. Through this reversal, Nietzsche only entangles himself all the more, inextricably, in the obverse. A confrontation does not take place. There is no grounding of the fundamental position that *emerges* from the incipient one in such a way that it does not reject the latter but lets it first stand in its uniqueness and solidity, in order thus to erect itself *on it*.

This interim remark was needed lest we take too lightly Nietzsche's position with regard to Aristotle in the question of the interpretation of the law of contradiction, and in order that we make the effort to reiterate Nietzsche's own step as clearly and univocally as possible. For it is a matter here of deciding about the uppermost fundamental principle of metaphysics and—though this amounts to the same thing—of the innermost essence of metaphysical thinking, of thinking and truth as such.

18. The Law of Contradiction as Command: Nietzsche

Nietzsche recognizes that a law touching beings as such is presupposed in the law of contradiction, but he fails to recognize that *this* presupposition is the true and sole positing of the law on the part of Aristotle. However, let us leave this failure aside for now. Instead, we shall ask something else. When Nietzsche urges us so decidedly to follow *that which is presupposed* in the law of contradiction, he must be asking along these lines himself. He must clarify *what* is being said about beings if it is true that the presupposition of the law of contradiction sits in judgment over beings. Yet Nietzsche does not ask what is decided about beings in this presupposition. For the truth of the law cannot in his view consist in what the proposition entails; what is true about the proposition consists in the way this law is a holding-to-be-true, in the way it posits what is posited. For this reason, Nietzsche asks the question as to whether such a positing that decides what beings are in their essence is possible at all and, if so, what nature the positing must have. Only when the positing nature of *that* positing which constitutes the presupposition of the law of contradiction has been characterized is the holding-to-be-true that expresses itself in the law of contradiction in Nietzsche's sense understood in its essence. Thus the decisive paragraph of number 516 reads:

> In short, the question remains open: are the axioms of logic adequate to reality or are they a means and measure for us to first *create* reality, the concept "reality," for ourselves?—In order to be able to affirm the former one would, as already said, have to have a previous knowledge of beings— which is simply not the case. The proposition therefore contains no *cri-*

terion of truth, but an *imperative* concerning that which **should** count as true.

With this, Nietzsche indeed affirms the possibility of a positing that determines how beings are to be grasped in essence. But this positing does not depend on representing and thinking adapting themselves to beings in order to learn from the latter their own essence. To do this we would already have to know in what the essence of beings consists; and every subsequent adaptation and ascertainment would be superfluous. The law of contradiction is not an adaptation to what is actual and somehow comprehensible, but is itself a positing of the measure. It expresses what beings are and what alone can count as in being, which is to say, what *does not contradict itself.* The law first gives the directive as such for what counts as in being. It expresses an ought, an imperative.

The interpretation of the law of contradiction as an imperative that declares what is to count as in being harmonizes with Nietzsche's conception of truth as a holding-to-be-true. Only this interpretation of the law of contradiction and our discussion of it lead us to the innermost essence of holding-to-be-true. For if truth cannot be a copying adaptation and is supposed to be a *holding-to-be-true,* what is the latter to hold on to? Robbed of every measure and every hold, does it not expose itself to the abyss of its own arbitrariness?

Thus holding-to-be-true needs a guiding measure in itself and for itself that determines what is held to be in being, that is, held to be true, what is to count as true. But insofar as holding-to-be-true is set on its own, this guiding measure can only come from a more original holding-to-be-true that pre-posits of itself what is to count as in being and true.

Whence does this original positing of a standard take its law? Is it blind chance, somehow arbitrarily achieved by someone and ever since binding on the basis of such factuality? No. For in this case the essential determination of Being by means of an insidious appeal to a being already at hand and secured as such would have again crept in, merely in a different form. The being in this case would be the "law" factually at hand and "universally" acknowledged. Yet the essence of

The Law of Contradiction as Command: Nietzsche

this law is determined by the kind of positing ruling in it. The positing of the standard contained in the law of contradiction, the standard for what is supposed to be able to count as in being, is an "imperative"—thus a *command*. The latter directs us to an altogether different area.

However, now we really have to ask of Nietzsche: Who is commanding here, and to whom? Whence and how do we at all come upon commands, something that has the nature of a command, in the realm of thinking, knowing, and truth?

We can see only this much now: If the law of contradiction is the uppermost fundamental principle of holding-to-be-true, if as such it supports and makes possible the essence of holding-to-be-true, and if the positing character of this law is a command, then the essence of knowledge has the essential nature of command deep within it. But knowing as re-presenting beings and what is constant is, as the securing of permanence, part of the necessary essential constitution of life itself. Hence life in itself—in its very vitality—contains the essential trait of commanding. Accordingly, the securing of permanence in human life takes place in a decision about what is to count as in being as such, what is called Being.

How does this decision take place? Does it occur as the setting up of a definition of "Being," or in a clarification of the meaning of the word *Being?* Far from it! That fundamental act, and thereby what is essential about the securing of permanence, consists in the fact that it transposes the living being "man" to the viewpoint of a perspective on beings and sustains him on that path. The basic act of founding a perspective occurs in representing what the law of contradiction already expresses subsequently in a proposition. No, we may now no longer take the law as a plausible axiom valid in itself; we must take its positing nature quite seriously. The law is a *command*. Even if we do not yet know how we are to understand the nature of this command in its essential provenance, from what has been said we can select four things and fashion them, so to speak, into a rung on which we can climb one step higher, in order to gain possession of the inner prospect onto the full essence of truth.

1. It now becomes clearer in what sense knowledge is necessary for life. Initially, and above all according to the immediate wording of

Nietzsche's sentences, it looks as if knowledge as the securing of permanence were forced on the living being from without, inasmuch as it brings advantage and success to the living being in the "struggle for existence." Yet advantage and usefulness can never be the reason for the essence of behavior, because every advantage and every positing of a useful purpose is already posited from the perspective of such behavior, and is thus always merely a consequence of an essential constitution.

Indeed, Nietzsche does frequently enough, in the wording of his often—and often necessarily—exaggerated statements, revert to the most ordinary of all opinions, to wit, that something is true because and to the extent that it is useful to that much-touted thing called "life." Yet Nietzsche's wording means something altogether different. The securing of permanence is necessary, but not because it yields an advantage; knowledge is necessary for life because it enables a necessity to arise in and from itself, and carries out that necessity, inasmuch as knowledge is in itself *commanding*. And it is commanding because it stems from a command.

2. How are we to make the commanding nature of knowledge comprehensible in terms of what has been said thus far? Our interpretation of the law of contradiction yielded the following: The definitive delineation of a horizon, the delimitation of what are called beings and what thus, as it were, embraces the range of all individual beings, is itself an *imperative*. How does this jibe with what earlier, in note 515, turned out to be the essence of reason, that is to say, with the poetizing nature of knowing? Commanding and poetizing, the commando and the freely playing formation—do they not exclude each other like water and fire? Perhaps, even certainly, as long as our concepts of commanding and poetizing extend only to what is generally familiar and current. In that case, we even speak of commanding where a so-called command is simply passed on, a "command" that perhaps is itself only called such and is not one at all, assuming that we grasp commanding in its essence, finding this essence only where a possibility of comportment and a stance are first elevated to a law, first created as a law. Then the word *command* does not mean merely *making* a demand *known* and requiring its fulfillment.

Commanding is in the first instance the erecting and the venturing of this demand, the discovery of its essence and the positing of the right that first creates that demand. Such commanding in the essential sense is always more difficult than obeying in the sense of following the command already *given*. True commanding is obedience to what is taken on in free responsibility, perhaps even first created. Essential commanding first posits the whither and wherefore. *Commanding* as making known a demand already directed, and *commanding* as founding this demand and taking on the decision contained in it, are fundamentally different. Original commanding and being able to command always arise only from *freedom* and are themselves fundamental forms of true being free. Freedom—in the simple and profound sense that Kant understood its essence—is in itself *poetizing:* the groundless grounding of a ground, in such a way that it grants itself the law of its essence. But commanding means nothing other than this.

The double reference to the commanding and poetizing nature of knowledge thus points to a unified, simple, and concealed essential ground for holding-to-be-true and truth.

3. Through the characterization of the positing nature of the law of contradiction as an "imperative," and through the reference to the essential harmony of commanding and poetizing, the concluding paragraph of note number 515, which we have passed over up to now, also is illuminated:

> The subjective compulsion of not being able to contradict here is a biological compulsion: the instinct for the utility of inferring as we do infer is part of our flesh, we almost *are* this instinct. But what naiveté to extract from this a proof that we are thereby in possession of a "truth in itself"!— Not being able to contradict is proof of an incapacity, not of a "truth."

Nietzsche speaks here of "not being able to contradict." This means that we are not able to persist in contradiction, hence that we must avoid contradiction—"here," namely, when beings are to be thought and represented. The case is not an arbitrary and isolated one, but an essential and constant one; it is *the* case in which what is alive in the manner of man lives. What now does this not being able to do otherwise mean, namely, to think otherwise than *free of contradiction*?

Nietzsche answers with the concluding sentence: "Not being able to contradict is proof of an incapacity, not of a 'truth.'"

"Incapacity" and "truth" are opposed to each other here. However, the word *incapacity* is a very misleading expression, since it suggests the idea of merely not being able, in the sense that some sort of behavior is hindered, whereas precisely a *must*, a necessary behaving-in-such-and-such-a-manner is intended. Why Nietzsche nonetheless speaks of an incapacity can be explained by his intention to create the most pointed opposite of the traditional concept of truth, in order to differentiate his interpretation of knowing and holding-to-be-true so strikingly that it almost becomes an affront. What Nietzsche contraposes under the words *incapacity* and *truth* is the same thing he means in number 516. There he says that the law of contradiction is not an axiom that is valid on the basis of its adapting to what is real. The axiom is not an *adequatio intellectus et rei*, not truth in the traditional sense. Rather, it posits a standard. The impact of the opposition lies in emphasizing the nature of positing, poetizing, and commanding in contrast to merely copying and imitating something at hand. The exaggerated talk of an "incapacity" precisely wants to say that freedom from contradiction and its observance come not from the idea of the absence of contradictory things but from a necessary capacity for command and the *must* posited in it.

Here and in many other similar passages one could express the almost peevish question, Why does Nietzsche choose his words so unintelligibly? The answer is clear: Because he is not here writing a primer and schoolbook on the "propaedeutics" of an already finished "philosophy," but speaking immediately in terms of what is to be truly known. In the range of his path of thought, the sentence in question is as univocal and as terse as possible. Of course, a decision is still open here as to whether a thinker should speak in *such* a way that absolutely everyone understands him without further ado, or whether what is thoughtfully thought should be said in such a way that those following in thought must first go a long way, a way on which everyman necessarily remains behind and only individuals perhaps reach the neighborhood of the goal.

Another question is implied here, one that is more essential and

The Law of Contradiction as Command: Nietzsche

historically decisive: Whether as many as possible, even all, are satisfied with the greatest possible superficiality of thinking, or whether particular individuals find themselves on the way. Every position with regard to the possibly offensive unclarity contained in the concluding sentence of number 515, indeed even in the entire note, comes under the decision of these questions. For this note offers the most concrete evidence of Nietzsche's "biologism," which although it does not constitute Nietzsche's fundamental position still belongs to it as a necessary ambiguity.

4. Being guided to the commanding and poetizing nature of knowing granted us a view of the peculiar necessity that rules in the essence of knowledge and that alone explains why and in what way truth as holding-to-be-true is a necessary *value*. Necessity—the *must* of commanding and poetizing—arises from freedom. Being-together-with-itself pertains to the essence of freedom, that a *free* being can coincide with itself, that it can give itself to itself in its possibilities. Such a being is outside the realm that we usually call "biological," the plant and animal realm. To freedom pertains that which according to a certain direction of interpretation in modern thought becomes visible as "subject." Nietzsche also speaks (in number 515, final paragraph) of the "subjective compulsion" to avoid contradiction; namely, with regard to the constant essential case of the subject man, the case in which the subject represents objects, that is, thinks beings.

"Subjective compulsion" means the compulsion appropriate to the essence of subjectivity, that is, freedom. But Nietzsche says, after all, "The subjective compulsion . . . is a biological compulsion"; he calls reasoning according to the law of contradiction an "instinct"; and he says in the preceding section that reason, the faculty of thinking, is "a mere idiosyncrasy of a certain species of animal." However, Nietzsche also says unambiguously that this law of contradiction, whose necessity and validity are in question as to their essence, is an "imperative." That means that it belongs to the realm of freedom, and that this realm does not lie ready-made somewhere, but is grounded by freedom itself. The essence of the compulsion mentioned in the law of contradiction is never determined by the biological realm.

If Nietzsche still says that this compulsion is a "biological" one, it is perhaps, after all, neither violent nor forced, provided we ask the *question* as to whether the term *biological* does not mean something other than what is alive, representing the latter as plant and animal. When we collide against the fact again and again that Nietzsche emphasizes holding-to-be-true, the nature of life's activity as poetizing and commanding, in contradistinction to the traditional concept of truth, does it not seem plausible that we are to hear something different in the word *biological*—namely, that which shows the essential traits of poetizing and commanding? Is it not plausible to determine for once the essence of life—mentioned so often—in terms of its own essential traits, instead of keeping a vague and confused concept of "life" at the ready in order to explain everything and thus nothing?

To be sure, Nietzsche relates everything to "life"—to the "biological." Yet does he still think life itself, the biological, "biologically," in such a way that he explains the essence of life in terms of plant and animal phenomena? *Nietzsche thinks the "biological," the essence of what is alive, in the direction of commanding and poetizing, of the perspectival and horizonal: in the direction of freedom.* He does *not* think the biological, that is, the essence of what is alive, biologically at all. So little is Nietzsche's thinking in danger of biologism that on the contrary he rather tends to interpret what is biological in the true and strict sense—the plant and animal—*nonbiologically*, that is, *humanly*, pre-eminently in terms of the determinations of perspective, horizon, commanding, and poetizing—in general, in terms of the representing of beings. Yet this verdict concerning Nietzsche's biologism would need a more comprehensive clarification and foundation.

We shall allow the question "biologism or not?" to answer itself, as we pursue the guideline of our sole question—the question of the essence of knowledge and of truth as a configuration of will to power.

19. Truth and the Distinction Between the "True and Apparent Worlds"

It has become clear so far that truth is holding-to-be-true; the latter is in essence the perspectival and horizonal intention and anticipation of identity and selfsameness as the ground of permanence. As the horizonal making-constant within the perspective of permanence, knowledge also constitutes the essence of human life insofar as the latter relates to beings. Because it also constitutes the essential stability of human life, knowledge is an intrinsic condition of this life. Nietzsche understands truth as holding-to-be-true; that is, he understands taking-as-in-being as a *necessary, although not the highest, value.*

Thus from Nietzsche's interpretation of the essence of truth there indeed results a demotion in its rank. This may well seem thoroughly alienating in the light of the traditional metaphysical dominance of the true, as what is in itself eternally in being and valid. Yet Nietzsche's metaphysical projection lies before us in a clear and unforced way: as a making constant, truth is proper to life. Human life itself, belonging to chaos, truly pertains to chaos as an overwhelming Becoming, in the manner of art. What truth cannot do, *art* accomplishes: the transfiguration of what is alive to higher possibilities, hence the actualization and activity of life in the midst of the truly actual—chaos.

When Nietzsche speaks *here* of *art,* that is, with a view to thinking beings as a whole metaphysically, he means *not only* art in the narrower sense of familiar genres of art. Art is the name for every form of transfiguring and viable transposition of life to higher possibilities; in this sense, philosophy too is "art." If we say that the supreme value for Nietzsche is art, this statement is meaningful and correct only if art is understood metaphysically and if at the same time it remains open which paths of transfiguration have priority.

For a time Nietzsche was inclined to think that his fundamental metaphysical position was decided and secured by an opposition of rank between truth and art.* Truth fixates chaos and maintains itself in the apparent world by dint of this stabilization of what becomes. As transfiguration, art opens up possibilities, frees what becomes into its becoming and thus moves about in the "true" world. Thus the inversion of Platonism is accomplished. Granted the presupposition of Nietzsche's interpretation of Platonism in the sense of the distinction between the "true and the apparent worlds," we can say that the true world is the world of becoming; the apparent world is the stable and constant world. The true and the apparent worlds have exchanged their places and ranks and modes; but in this exchange and inversion the precise *distinction* of a true and an apparent world is preserved. The inversion is possible only with this distinction as its foundation.†

If Nietzsche had not been a thinker, he would not have stood firm in the concealed center of beings as a lone watchman with openly questioning eyes; if as an "eternal convalescent" he had only put together and arranged a worldview and a world-structure for cultivated and uncultivated contemporaries out of a hundred books, in order to put himself at ease before or even in this task, and in order to iron out "contradictions"; he would have had to close his eyes to the abysses on whose edges his world-projection made him stand. Yet Nietzsche did not close his eyes; he went toward what he had to see. In the last two years of his thinking he trod to the utmost extreme this now inevitable path that he had cleared for himself.

We scarcely know about the final steps of his thinking and can gauge their scope still less, misguided above all by the view that has by now become dogmatic, that after *Thus Spoke Zarathustra* Nietzsche no longer "developed" but "only" tried to expand what he already had.

---

* Cf. sections 12 and 19 of Volume I, where the opposition of truth and art is taken to be more than what Nietzsche "for a time" believed.

† Cf. section 24 of Volume I, which differs significantly from the above, if not from what is now to follow.

Truth and the Distinction Between "Worlds"

Yet all talk of notions of "development" is altogether inappropriate here. If people insist on thinking this way, then we must say that Nietzsche's *last* "development," which is still unknown to us, leaves behind all the overturnings that he had survived on the path of his thinking.

The above intimates that *in the present case too* our portrayal of Nietzsche's conception of the essence of truth could not be the last word, that we must first take the decisive step on his thought-path, and that we can do so only if we know the preceding steps; for Nietzsche's most extreme step in the essential determination of truth does not come out of nowhere. However, it also does not result of "itself," as one might assert afterward—it arises from the unremitting refusal to compromise in his thinking. For thoughtful thinking has its *own* continuity. It consists in the sequence of ever more original beginnings, a kind of thinking that is so remote from scientific thought that one cannot even say that it is opposed to that thought. Now, if the thought-path to the will to power guides Nietzsche's sole thought, knowledge and truth must first show themselves unveiled as a configuration of will to power when they themselves are thought in their most extreme essence.

We have intentionally already referred several times to a peculiar ambiguity in Nietzsche's concept of truth, one that Nietzsche never wants to hide but that he does not immediately master in its abyssal nature. We saw that what is true in this truth is not the true, since what is true in this truth signifies what is re-presented as constant, what has been fixated as being. This stable element in the leading perspective on chaos proves to be a fixation of what becomes; the fixation becomes a denial of what flows and surges beyond itself; this fixation turns away from the properly actual. As fixated fixating, the true excludes itself from harmony with the properly actual through the denial of chaos. With respect to chaos, "the true" of such truth is not appropriate to that chaos; hence it is untrue, thus error. Nietzsche expresses this unequivocally in the sentence already quoted: "*Truth is the kind of error* without which a certain kind of living being could not live" (WM, 493; from the year 1885). This sentence should be sufficiently clear and evident after our previous discussion.

Yet what is ambiguous about it? The unequivocal determination of truth as a kind of error goes against ordinary, one-track everyday thinking; to put it in a Greek manner, it is a *paradoxon*. The interpretation of truth, expressed again and again as error, illusion, lie, and semblance, is only too clear. We can speak of ambiguity only where one and the same thing is thought in terms of a double and different significance. An essential ambiguity—one that does not rest on a mere negligence of thinking and saying—exists only where the double meaning of the same is inevitable.

Yet it is clear here that truth is a "kind of error." And error suggests passing by the truth, missing what is true. Certainly, and for this reason error leaves truth by the wayside.

If only truth did not constantly and ever more intrusively encroach on us in error—and even more essentially in it than in the true! Error is dependent on the true and truth; how could error be a mistake, how could it miss the truth, pass *it* by and go past *it* if *it* did not exist? All error thrives primarily—namely, in its *essence*—on truth. Thus when Nietzsche says unequivocally that truth is a kind of error, he must also think in this concept "error": missing truth, straying away from truth.

Truth, conceived as error, was defined as the fixated, the constant. Yet this kind of error necessarily thinks truth in the sense of harmony with the actual, that is, with becoming chaos. Truth as error misses the truth. *Truth* misses the *truth*. In the unequivocal essential definition of truth as error, truth is necessarily thought twice, and each time differently, hence ambiguously: once as fixation of the constant, and then as harmony with the actual. Only on the basis of this essence of truth as harmony can truth as constancy be an error. The essence of truth here underlying the concept of error is what has been determined since ancient times in metaphysical thinking as correspondence with the actual and harmony with it, *homoiōsis*. Harmony need not necessarily be interpreted in the sense of copying and imitating correspondence. When Nietzsche rejects the concept of truth in the sense of copying adequation, and rightly so, he need not thus already reject truth in the sense of harmony with the actual. In no way does he reject this traditional and, as it might seem, most natural essential

Truth and the Distinction Between "Worlds"

determination of truth. Rather, it is the guideline for positing the essence of truth as fixation, in contradistinction to art, which as transfiguration is a *harmony* with what becomes and its possibilities. Precisely *on the basis* of this harmony with what becomes, art as transfiguration is a *higher* value. Yet Nietzsche speaks here with regard to what art constructs in its constructions not about "truth" but about semblance. Nietzsche knows that the work of art too, as bound to configuration, must *fixate* and thus also becomes semblance, albeit a "semblance" in which the higher possibilities of life blaze and shine, that is, radiate. The concept of radiant semblance too becomes ambiguous.

We are now in a double crisscross ambiguity: truth as the fixation of beings (errorlike truth) and truth as harmony with what becomes. Yet the harmony with what becomes that is attained in art is semblance, semblance as seemingness (the fixated work is not what itself becomes) *and* semblance as the shining forth of new possibilities in that semblance. Just as truth as error needs truth as harmony, so does semblance as radiance need semblance in the sense of seemingness. This all seems very entangled, not to say confusing, and yet it is simple in its relations, provided that we *actually* think and thus descry the *whole structure* of the *essence* of truth and semblance and their reciprocity.

However, if in truth grasped in an errorlike way truth is at the same time presupposed in the sense of harmony, and if such truth too turns out to be semblance and seemingness, then does not everything finally become error and semblance? All truths and kinds of truths are only various kinds and stages of "errors" (cf. WM, 535). Then there are indeed no truths and no truth. Everything is but seemingness and appearance in different modes and stages.

It is necessary to go to this extreme. The extreme is not nothing—as a thinking that has no stamina might think—and the "nihilism" announcing itself here is no phantasm of confused thoughts. It is rather the assumption of an extreme position in which metaphysically conceived "truth" attains its last possible essence. How clearly Nietzsche discerns this path to an extreme fundamental position, how immediately he gauges the scope of this thoughtful deed in terms of history, in what direction he seeks the transformation of the essence of metaphysical truth—all are exhibited in a passage that is included in the book *The Will to Power* (WM, 749; Spring-Fall, 1887; revised Spring-Fall, 1888*). We will, of course, only understand it—and even then only approximately—when we have actually walked all the way on Nietzsche's thought-path toward the essence of truth; for we are not there *yet*, although it might seem that everything is already dissolving and destroying itself and thus that no further extreme of the interpretation of truth is possible at all.

Truth as holding-to-be-true is error, albeit *necessary* error. Truth as harmony with Becoming, art, is semblance, albeit a *transfiguring* one. There is no "true world" in the sense of something remaining the same in itself and eternally valid. The thought of the true world, as what is primarily and of itself definitive for everything, thinks vacuous nothingness. The thought of a true world thus conceived must be abolished; then only the *apparent* world remains, the world as partly a necessary, partly a transfiguring semblance: truth and art as the fundamental forms in which the appearing of the apparent world comes to appearance. What about this world of seemingness? Can we still say that the *apparent* world remains for us after the true world has had to be abolished? How is something to be left over if there is nothing else besides it? Does not what remains *then* constitute everything, the whole? Is not the apparent world then the *sole* world for itself? What are we to hold concerning it and how are we to maintain ourselves in it?

Our question is, How do matters stand with the "apparent world" that still remains after the abolition of the "true world"? What does apparentness mean here?

The elucidation of the essence of life in terms of the securing of permanence peculiar to it led us to refer to the fundamental *perspectival* character of life. What is alive always stands and maintains itself in a perspective on a range of possibilities that are in each case fixated in such and such a way, whether as "the true" of knowledge or as the "work" of art. In each case this delimiting, the drawing of an horizon,

---

* W II 2 [94], in CM, *12*, 510, is discussed in section 20, below.

is an installation of semblance. What is figured looks like the actual; yet *as* something *figured* and fixed it is precisely no longer chaos but *determinate* urging. Semblance originates in the space of the actual perspective in which a definite point of view, to which the horizon is "relative," prevails. Accordingly, Nietzsche says in *The Will to Power*, number 567 (1888):

> The *perspectival* therefore lends the character of the "appearance." As if a world would still remain after one deducted the perspectival! By doing that one would deduct the *relativity*!

But we might ask, What difference would it make if *relativity* were omitted? Would not the absolute thus be gained? As though by the relative's remaining absent, the greatly sought absolute would already enter on the scene. But why is it so important to Nietzsche to save *relativity*? What does he mean by relativity? Nothing other than the provenance of perspective, on the basis of life's creating a perspective and always looking forward and from a viewpoint. "Relativity" here expresses the fact that the horizon-like scope of perspectives, the *"world,"* is nothing other than a creation of the *"action"* of life itself. The world arises from the life-activity of what is alive and *is* only *what* and *how* it arises. What follows from this? The seemingness of the world can no longer be understood as semblance. Nietzsche says, a few paragraphs further: "No shadow of a *right* remains to speak here of *appearance*." Why? Because opening a perspective and drawing a horizon do not result from adapting to a world subsisting in itself or subsistent at all, that is, a "true" world. If there is no longer a measuring and estimating with regard to something true, how is the world that arises from the "action" of life still supposed to be branded and comprehended as "semblance" at all? With the insight into this impossibility, the decisive step has been taken, a step before which Nietzsche hesitated a long time, the step to a knowledge that must utter what it knows in all simplicity *thus*: With the abolition of the "true world" the "apparent world" also is abolished. But what remains when along with the true world the apparent world topples too, and thus the distinction as such? The concluding sentence of note 567, from the last year of Nietzsche's creative life, replies: "The antithesis of the apparent world and the true world reduces itself to the antithesis 'world' and 'nothing.' " Truth and semblance are in the same position; truth and lie are removed in the same way. Initially, it looks as if both truth and semblance were dissolved into nothingness, as if dissolution meant annihilation and annihilation the end and the end nothingness and nothingness the most extreme alienation from Being.

Thinking this way, we are too hasty. We forget that truth as error is a *necessary value* and that semblance in the sense of artistic transfiguration is the *higher value* when compared with truth. Since necessity here means belonging to the essential constituency and essential activity of life, if such belonging constitutes the content of the concept *"value,"* then the *higher* the rank a value has, the deeper the necessity it represents.

20. The Uttermost Transformation of Metaphysically Conceived Truth

Truth and semblance, knowledge and art, thus cannot have disappeared with the abolition of the "true and apparent worlds" as an antithesis. However, the essence of truth must have changed. But in what sense, and in which direction? Evidently in the direction that is determined by *the* guiding projection of life and thus of Being and actuality in general, the projection that already underlies the abolition of the true and the apparent world as an antithesis. This projection presumably is the first really to go to the extreme of metaphysical thinking—if the interpretation rooted in it and the apparent dissolution of truth do go this way. In the realm of the extreme there is only one question, to wit, how it is to be survived, whether it is to be understood in its concealed essence as an end and hence saved in some appropriate way, that is, rescued in another commencement. But long before that we must first learn where Nietzsche himself stops on his way to the outermost point.

What happens at this extreme where the distinction between a true and an apparent world disappears; what happens on the *grounds* of this distinction and its disappearing? What happens to the essence of truth? With this question, we arrive at the place where the above-mentioned passage must be cited, in which Nietzsche intimates the direction of the last metaphysical transformation of that truth which is metaphysically grounded as *homoiōsis*.

The passage is number 749, in the third chapter of the third book of *The Will to Power*. The editors gave this chapter the title "The

Will to Power as Society and Individual." The first section, to which the passage is assigned, was given the title "Society and State." The passage reads:

> The princes of Europe should indeed consider carefully whether they can do without our support. We immoralists—we are today the only power that needs no allies in order to achieve victory; thus we are by far the strongest of the strong. We do not even need to tell lies; what other power can dispense with that? A powerful seduction fights on our behalf, perhaps the most powerful there is—the seduction of truth.— "Truth"? Who has put this word in my mouth? But I repudiate it; but I disdain this proud word; no, we do not need even this; we would come to power and victory even without truth. The spell that fights on our behalf, the eye of Venus that charms and blinds even our opponents, is *the magic of the extreme,* the seduction that everything extreme exercises; we immoralists—we are *the ones at the outermost point.*

Nietzsche speaks here of the supreme and unique power of the most powerful. They no longer need allies, not even those that every power as such otherwise needs. Since every power is the organization of force under the semblance of law, it needs the lie, the dissimulation, the veiling of its intentions; it needs to display goals that are ostensibly sought after, in order to make those whom it subjugates happy. The most powerful ones to whom Nietzsche refers do not need this alliance; "truth" itself fights for them, truth as seduction. Here truth need no longer be called *truth,* for with the overcoming of the metaphysical distinction "truth" has been elevated to the uttermost form of *homoiōsis.* "The magic" of the extreme fights on behalf of the most powerful. Magic transports us to another world with its enchantment and there brings the enchanted ones to themselves in a different way. Enchantment is not stupefaction. Enchantment occurs here in the establishment of the uttermost. The latter forces those who have decided for the true into enchantment every bit as much as those who find satisfaction in the seeming.

The double ambiguity of truth and semblance, compels us to something that is neither one nor the other, neither truth nor semblance; while it makes both possible in their ambiguous reciprocity, in itself

The Uttermost Transformation

it can never be explained *in terms of* them. These most powerful ones who dare to establish the extreme call themselves "the outermost ones," the "immoralists." The correct understanding of the latter name helps us to get a clearer conception of the manner of these extreme ones and of what leads their extreme to victory by means of its magic.

"Immoralist"—this word designates a metaphysical concept. "Morality" here means neither a "moral code" nor a "doctrine of moral codes." "Morality" has for Nietzsche the broad and essential meaning of positing an ideal, indeed with the signification that the ideal, as the suprasensuous grounded in the Ideas, is the standard for the sensuous, whereas the sensuous counts as the lesser, the valueless, hence something to be fought and exterminated. Since all metaphysics is grounded on the distinction of the suprasensuous world as true in opposition to the sensuous one as apparent, all metaphysics is "moral." The immoralist removes himself from the "moral" distinction that grounds all metaphysics; he is the denier of the distinction between true and apparent worlds and the hierarchy of values posited in it. *"We immoralists" means we who stand outside the distinction that sustains metaphysics.* The title of the work that Nietzsche published in his last years, *Beyond Good and Evil,* is also to be taken in this sense.

Not to allow the distinction between a true and an apparent world, to be an immoralist, means to go to that extreme where goals and standards may no longer be read off superficially *from* a true world in itself and *for* an untrue and imperfect world. Nietzsche says that the "European princes" (the shapers and leaders of the history and the destinies of peoples) should consider whether they can still do without the support of the immoralists. This means that they should be clear about whether the goals they set or allow to prevail for their nations are still real goals, whether these sanctimonious appeals to morality, to cultural values, and to civilization and progress do not have as their background a metaphysics that has long since become delapidated. The "princes" should consider whether these are still groundable goals at all or whether they are not simply facades, remnants of a moribund metaphysical world no longer undergirded by thought. They should consider whether goals can be created on the basis of "this world" and for it, whether a knowledge is still alive that can know the essence of goals and their grounding.

When Nietzsche names the "European princes," he thinks in the direction of that which "grand politics" means for him: the determination of man's place in the world and of his essence. "Grand politics" here is simply another name for Nietzsche's own most intrinsic metaphysics. Yet what is the reflection of the immoralists meant to achieve?

The decision about the distinction between a "true world" and an "apparent world," which grounds metaphysics itself, falls within such a reflection. The decision comes to abolish both worlds and their distinction. This abolition demands nothing other than thinking the traditional essential determination of truth to the extreme, taking seriously the essential consequences with which thinking at the outermost point confronts us.

In note number 749, this uttermost thinking lies before us, couched, to be sure, in a mysterious mode of utterance, one that indicates that the thinker knows *still more essential things* about the extreme concept of truth. The note is accessible only to a sustained and reiterated thinking; nevertheless, even a first reflection can see that it deals with the essence of truth and the utterly extreme decision about it.

The editors of the book *The Will to Power* were thinking all too superficially or not at all when, obviously misled by the first words of the passage "The European princes," they immediately thought simply of the "state" and "society," and proceeded to place the passage in the totally false position where it now stands. The content and weight of this passage are concealed by their seemingly harmless error; the all-decisive question that it contains is unable to come out in the open, to wit, the question: *What happens when the distinction between a true world and an apparent world falls away? What becomes of the metaphysical essence of truth?*

Nietzsche replied in the work *Twilight of the Idols*, which was written and printed a few days before September 3, 1888, but appeared only in 1889 after his breakdown. In this work we find a section with the title "How the 'True World' Finally Became a Fable: The History of an Error." This history is told in six brief paragraphs.* The last paragraph reads (VIII, 82–83):

> 6. The true world we abolished: which world was left? the apparent one perhaps? . . . But no! *along with the true world we have also abolished the apparent one!* (Midday; moment of the shortest shadow; end of the longest error; highpoint of humanity; INCIPIT ZARATHUSTRA.)

Again, what is decisive is in brackets, namely, the positive reference to what *is, after* the fundamental metaphysical distinction has fallen away.

The answer to our question as to what has happened to the *essence* of truth after the abolition of the true and the apparent worlds reads: *"Incipit Zarathustra."* Yet Nietzsche's reply is initially for us only a tangle of questions. Only now—with the abolition of the distinction that sustained Western metaphysics—does Zarathustra begin. Who is "Zarathustra"? He is the thinker whose figure Nietzsche prophetically poetized—and had to poetize because he is the extreme, namely, what is uttermost in the history of metaphysics. *"Incipit Zarathustra"* says that with the thinking of this thinker that essence of truth becomes necessary and dominant which Zarathustra has already uttered. One may no longer speak "about" this essence once such thinking has begun. For a consequence of this essence of truth is that one must *act by way of thinking* with the *"Incipit."* The *"Incipit Zarathustra"* assumes another name: *"Incipit tragoedia"* (see *The Gay Science,* number 342†).

Again, obscure words, which we cannot think through as long as we fail to realize that Nietzsche is thinking in the sense of Greek tragedy here, as long as we do not comprehend and ponder the fact *that* tragedy always *begins* with the *"going under"* of the hero, and *why* it does so. With the abolition of that distinction between the true and the apparent worlds, metaphysics begins to go under. However, "going under" is not stopping and ending; it is end as uttermost fulfillment of essence. Only what has supreme essence can "go under."

---

* Again, see Volume I, section 24.
† See section 4 of Volume II, *The Eternal Recurrence of the Same.*

We ask again: What now happens to the metaphysical essence of truth in *going under?* What does the one who goes under—whom Nietzsche calls Zarathustra—say about truth? *Which thought* does Nietzsche think concerning the essence of truth in the formative years of *Thus Spoke Zarathustra* (1882–85)? Nietzsche thinks the essence of truth at the outermost point as something he calls "justice."

21. Truth as Justice

The thought of justice* already dominates Nietzsche's thinking in his early years. It can be historiologically shown that it dawned on him in his reflections on pre-Platonic metaphysics, especially that of Heraclitus. Yet the fact *that* precisely this Greek thought of justice, of *dikē*, sparked in Nietzsche and continued to glow throughout his thinking in an ever more concealed and silent way, constantly igniting his thinking, has its ground not in the "historiological" work with the pre-Platonic philosophers but in the historical determination that the last metaphysician of the West obeys. For this reason, Nietzsche *poetized* the ideal of such thinking, unattainable for himself, in the figure of Zarathustra. Hence the thought of justice is most decisively uttered during the *Zarathustra* period, albeit very rarely. These few main thoughts on "justice" were not published. They can be found as brief notes in jottings from the period of *Zarathustra*. In his last years, Nietzsche is completely silent about what he calls justice. Above all, nowhere is the slightest attempt to be found to bring the thought of

---

* In Volume IV of this series (*Nihilism*, pp. 144–45), the word *Gerechtigkeit* is translated as "justification." In order to avoid confusion with the word *Rechtfertigung*, it will here be rendered (more literally) as "justice." "Rightness" would also preserve the connection with the German root, *Recht*. Of utmost importance is the connection between "justice" (or "rightness") and "correctness": Heidegger sees in Nietzsche's use of the word *Gerechtigkeit* a transformation in the history of truth as *Richtigkeit*, indeed, the final transformation of that history. Perhaps it would not be amiss to view the word *Gerechtigkeit* as homologous with *Ge-stell* and *Ge-birg: Ge-recht-igkeit* embraces the whole range of notions that derive from the extreme (that is, Nietzschean) form of *homoiōsis*. On "justice," see the final section of Part Three, "Nietzsche's Metaphysics," pp. 235–51; and for a detailed discussion of *Gerechtigkeit* in the history of truth, a history in which Nietzsche plays a crucial role, see Heidegger's 1942–43 lecture course *Parmenides* (*Gesamtausgabe*, vol. 54, Frankfurt am Main: V. Klostermann, 1982), esp. pp. 84–86.

justice into an articulated connection with discussions on the essence of truth. Nietzsche never does this explicitly and in terms of the first foundations of his thinking. There is no reference at all to the fact *that* and the question of the extent to *which* the abolition of the metaphysical distinction between a true and an apparent world forces us back into the traditional metaphysical essential determination of truth as *homoiōsis*, and at the same time into the interpretation of truth as "justice."

Nevertheless, these connections and their necessity can be made visible by thinking through in a way that is sufficiently decisive Nietzsche's concept of truth. They *must* be made visible. For only a clarified look at them will reveal the essence of truth and knowledge as a configuration of will to power, and the latter itself as the fundamental trait of beings as a whole. However, the presupposition and guide for our procedure remains historical reflection that comprehends the beginning and the end of Western metaphysics in their historic oppositional unity by asking the grounding question of philosophy. This more original reflection thinks no longer metaphysically; it asks and transforms the guiding question of metaphysics, What are beings? on the basis of the (no longer metaphysical) grounding question of the truth of Being. Thus the following path of thought has already been articulated.*

First, we shall try to think the essence of truth to the extreme by asking what happens to truth after the abolition of the distinction between a true and an apparent world. From there we have to see that and how in this extreme the thought of "justice" becomes inevitable. Everything depends on our grasping justice in *Nietzsche's* sense and fitting his rare utterances about it into the previously characterized realm of the metaphysical question of truth. Our understanding and possible execution of these steps depend on our success with the first step. Nietzsche is of no help to us here, because he was unable to discern the historical roots of the metaphysical question of truth in general, and those of his own decisions in particular.

We shall now think truth, grasped metaphysically, by following two

---

* On the "guiding" and "grounding" questions, see Volume I, section 11.

Truth as Justice

paths to its *extreme:* the first way will begin from Nietzsche's ownmost concept of truth; the other way will revert to the metaphysical determination of the essence of truth that is everywhere guiding, tacitly and most generally, in the first.

The first way. Nietzsche understands truth as holding-to-be-true. Traced more fundamentally to the ground of its possibility, the latter is the poetizing presupposition of a horizon of beingness, the unity of the categories as schemata. Poetizing presupposition has its basic activity in what the law of contradiction says, that is, in the fixation of what beingness as such is supposed to mean. Beingness is supposed to mean permanence, in the sense of such fixation. Fixation is that primordial holding-to-be-true that gives to all knowing the directive toward beings as such. Holding-to-be-true originally has the character of a command. Whence does commanding take its criterion? What can indicate to it the direction at all? Does not holding-to-be-true as commanding become the plaything of an opaque and rootless arbitrariness?

Where does the essence of truth wind up if it is traced back to a commanding that is without ground or direction? After the abolition of the metaphysical distinction, all flight to our adapting to something true at hand "in itself" is blocked; but so likewise is the estimation of what is fixated in representing as what only "seems." Does holding-to-be-true still attain validity and binding force from somewhere and for itself? If it still can and does attain them, then it does so only *on the basis of itself.* Thus the still more original rootedness of the commanding nature of holding-to-be-true must contain and produce something like a *standard.* Or else it must make such a thing dispensable without, however, falling back into the pure fortuitousness of what is completely rootless. To the extent that such holding-to-be-true—with all its distancing from the realm of the distinction between a true and an apparent world—is supposed to hold on to the traditional essence of truth in some sense, that essence of truth also has to gain ascendancy in the fundamental act of holding-to-be-true.

The other way. The interpretation of truth as holding-to-be-true revealed *re*-presenting as the re-*presenting* of what urges, and thus as the permanentizing of chaos. What is true in this holding-to-be-true fixates Becoming and thus precisely does *not* correspond to the nature of Becoming as chaos. What is true in such truth is noncorrespondence, untruth, error, illusion. However, this characterization of the true as a kind of error is founded on the assimilation of the re-*presented* to what is to be fixated. There too, where the true of holding-to-be-true is understood as the untrue, the most general essence of truth in the sense of *homoiōsis* provides the foundation. Yet if the "true world" of beings in themselves collapses, and with it the distinguishability of a merely apparent world also, does not the most general essence of truth in the sense of *homoiōsis* get pulled into this collapse as well? By no means. Rather, this essence of truth now first attains its unrivaled exclusiveness.

For knowledge as the securing of permanence is necessary, although art as the higher value is still more necessary. Transfiguration creates possibilities for the self-surpassing of life at any given point of limitation. Knowledge in each case posits the fixated and fixating boundaries so that there can be something to surpass, whereas art is able to retain its higher necessity. Art and knowledge require each other reciprocally in their essence. *Art and knowledge in their reciprocity first bring about the full securing of permanence of the animate as such.*

But after all we have said, what is the securing of permanence now? Neither simply fixation of chaos in knowledge nor transfiguration of chaos in art, but both together. Yet both are in essence one: namely, the assimilation and the direction of human life to chaos, *homoiōsis*. Such assimilation is not imitative and reproductive adaptation to something at hand, but *transfiguration that commands and poetizes, establishes perspectival horizons, and fixates.*

If truth in its essence is assimilation to chaos, and if this assimilation is a commanding and poetizing one, the question arises with more trenchancy: Whence do holding-to-be-true and being true as assimilation take their measure and direction; on what basis is something *right* at all? Asking this, we bring to their outermost point holding-to-be-true as commanding and *homoiōsis* as assimilation to chaos. The thought that assimilation itself alone could and must give the measure and provide "justification," that is, decide in general about measure and direction in essence, becomes inevitable. As *homoiōsis*, truth must be what Nietzsche calls "justice."

What does Nietzsche mean by this word *justice*, which we immediately connect with right and adjudication, with morality and virtue? For Nietzsche, the word *justice* has neither a "legal" nor a "moral" significance; rather, it characterizes what is to take over the essence of *homoiōsis* and activate it, namely, assimilation to chaos, that is, to "beings" as a whole, and hence these beings themselves. To think beings as a whole in their truth and to think *the truth in them*—that is metaphysics. "Justice" is here the *metaphysical* name for the *essence* of truth, for the way in which the essence of truth must be understood at the end of Western metaphysics. Fixating the essence of truth as *homoiōsis*, and interpreting the latter as justice, constitute the metaphysical thinking that produces this interpretation as the consummation of metaphysics.

Nietzsche's thought of "justice," as the formulation of truth in the extreme, is the final necessity and inmost consequence of the fact that *alētheia* had to remain unthought in its essence and the truth of Being unquestioned. The thought of "justice" is the occurrence of Being's abandonment of beings within the thinking of beings themselves.

We may comprehend Nietzsche's thought of justice most readily, and least hindered and misguided by prejudices, by keeping to the following definition: The just is the unified nexus of what is right— "right," *rectus*, is the "exact," the suitable, what makes sense, what fits—the nexus of what points in the right direction and what conforms to that direction. To direct is to point out a direction and to set someone going in that direction.

By justice Nietzsche understands what makes truth in the sense of holding-to-be-true, that is, assimilation to chaos, possible and necessary. Justice is the essence of truth, "essence" metaphysically intended as the ground of possibility. When Nietzsche seeks to understand the essence of truth during the last years of his thinking, after the publication of *Thus Spoke Zarathustra*, he always and everywhere thinks it in terms of the ground of its possibility, in terms of justice.

He knows of justice most profoundly, and yet he seldom speaks of it. If we disregard occasional remarks, hardly intelligible by themselves, there are only two almost contemporary notes that delimit the essence of justice—that, however, with the utmost precision.

The first note bears the title *"The ways of freedom"* (XIII, number 98, pp. 41 f.), and comes from the year 1884.* According to the unexpressed context, "justice" is understood here as the proper way to be free, although nothing explicit is said about freedom itself. Yet we know from the first part of *Thus Spoke Zarathustra* what and *in what way* Nietzsche was thinking around this time (1882–83) about freedom, namely, from the section "On the Way of the Creator." We cite it in order to make immediately visible the connection between freedom and justice:

> You call yourself free? Your dominant thought I want to hear, and not that you have escaped from a yoke.
>
> Are you one who had the *right* to escape from a yoke? There are some who cast off their last value when they cast off their servitude.
>
> Free from what? As if that mattered to Zarathustra! But your eyes should tell me brightly: free *for* what?
>
> Can you give yourself your own evil and your own good and proclaim your own will over yourself as a law? Can you be your own judge and avenger of your law?
>
> It is terrible to be alone with the judge and avenger of one's own law. Thus is a star cast into the void and into the icy breath of isolation.
>
> Injustice and filth they throw after the lonely one: but, my brother, if you would be a star, you must not shine any the less for them on that account.

Freedom is understood here as freedom to and freedom for, as the binding ejection into a "perspective," a going out beyond oneself. According to the note *"The ways of freedom,"* proper freedom is "justice," for the following is said of it: *"Justice* as a constructive, exclusive, annihilative mode of thought, arising from estimations of value: *supreme representative of life itself."*

Justice "as a mode of thought," though indeed not merely "one"

---

* See the entire note, W I 1 [484], in CM, *11*, 140–41.

Truth as Justice

among many. Nietzsche wants to emphasize that justice as he understands it has the fundamental character of thinking. However, thinking was more closely determined for us as poetizing and commanding. It is such when we are not talking about everyday thinking, in the sense of a calculating that simply wanders back and forth *within* a fixed horizon without seeing it, yet still within its limits. Thinking is poetizing and commanding when we are talking about that thinking in which a horizon is established as such and in advance, a horizon whose permanence provides a condition of the vitality of what lives. Nietzsche is talking about that kind of thinking when he comprehends justice as a way of thinking. For he says explicitly that justice is a way of thinking "arising from estimations of value."

According to our various elucidations, value-estimation means positing conditions of life. By "values" Nietzsche does not mean arbitrary circumstances, not something that occasionally and in some respect is valued in this or that way at a particular time. "Value" is the name for the essential conditions of what lives. "Value" is here synonymous with "essence" in the sense of making possible, *possibilitas*. "Value-estimations" thus do not mean the values posited in the scope of our everyday calculation of things and in human efforts to reach accordance. Rather, they mean those decisions that occur in the ground of what lives—here, man—concerning the essence of man himself and of all nonhuman beings.

Justice is thinking that arises from such estimations of value. Nietzsche speaks unconditionally here when he invokes "justice" as a way of thinking that arises from *such* value-estimations; that sounds essentially different from saying that justice is *"one"* way of thinking in terms of estimations of value.

However, thinking "arising from estimations of value" could still be misunderstood, as if it were purely and simply the consequence "of" the valuations, whereas it is precisely nothing other than the activity of estimating itself. For this reason, such thinking has a distinctive manner, one that Nietzsche emphasizes succinctly and strikingly with three adjectives that, moreover, he designates successively in an essential sequence.

First and foremost, thinking is "constructive." Generally, that means that this thinking first *fashions* what does not yet stand and exist as something at hand, something that perhaps never was at all. It does not appeal to and depend upon something given for support; it is not an assimilation but is what announced itself to us as the poetizing nature of positing a horizon within a perspective. "Constructing" means not only producing something that is not yet at hand but also setting up and erecting, rising to the heights—more precisely, first gaining a height, securing it, and thus positing a "right direction." Thus "constructing" is a commanding that first raises the claim to command and creates a realm of command.

Insofar as construction fashions, it must at the same time and even prior to this be founded on a ground. Together with rising to the heights, it at the same time forms and opens a vista onto its surroundings. The essence of construction lies neither in piling up layers of building materials nor in ordering them according to a plan, but solely in the fact that when we set up a new space another atmosphere opens up, precisely through what is set up. Whenever that fails to happen, what has been built has to be explained afterward as a "symbol" for something else; it is established as such by the newspapers for the public. Construction in these two cases is never the same. Justice as the positing of something right, a positing that constructs—that is, founds, erects, and opens a vista—is the essential origin of the poetizing and commanding nature of all knowing and forming.

The thinking that constructs is at the same time "*exclusive.*" Thus constructing never moves in a vacuum; it moves within something that obtrudes and intrudes as something ostensibly definitive, something that would not only like to hinder construction but make it unnecessary. As erecting, construction must at the same time always make *incisive decisions* about measures and heights. Accordingly, it must separate *out* and first form for itself the leeway in which it sets up its measures and heights and opens its vistas. Construction advances through decisions.

The thinking that constructs and excludes is at the same time "*annihilative.*" It removes what once had secured the permanence of life. Such removal clears the way of fixations that could hinder the activity of erecting a height. The thinking that constructs and excludes can

Truth as Justice

and must bring about this removal because, as erecting, it fixates stability already in a higher possibility.

Justice has the essential constitution of the thinking that constructs, excludes, and annihilates. In this way, it brings about value-estimations; that is, it estimates whatever is to be posited as essential conditions for life. And "life" itself? In what does its essence consist? The answer to this question is already given with the essential characterization of justice. For Nietzsche concludes his note on justice by making a transition to the underlined words by way of a colon: *"the supreme representative of life itself."*

According to the context of the entire note, life is initially understood as human life. The latter itself—in its essence—represents itself, portrays itself, in justice and as justice.

"Representative" does not mean a "substitute," a "facade" and pretext for something that it itself is *not*. Nor does "representative" here mean an "expression." Rather, it means that in which life itself presents its essence, because it *is* nothing other than "justice" in the ground of its essence. Justice is the *"supreme"* representative; beyond it the essence of life cannot be thought.

Yet the statement that the essence of human life is justice does not mean that man is "just" in all his doings in the customary moral and legal sense, as if man acted everywhere only rightly and fairly.

The statement that the essence of human life is justice is of a metaphysical nature, and means that the vitality of life consists in nothing other than that thinking which constructs, excludes, and annihilates. Such grounding, which clears the way and decisively erects, grounds a height that opens onto a vista. It is the grounds for the fact that thinking exhibits the essential manner of poetizing and commanding, in which perspectives open and horizons form. With the insight into the essence of justice as the *essential ground* of life, *the* aspect is fixed in which *alone* it can be decided whether and how and within what limits Nietzsche's thinking is "biologistic."

Justice is that into which life, when set on its own, is grounded. Holding-to-be-true takes its law and rule from *justice*. Justice is the essential ground of truth and knowledge, but only, of course, when we think "justice" metaphysically in Nietzsche's sense and try to understand to what extent it means the constitution of the Being of what lives, that is, of beings as a whole.

The three determinations—constructing, excluding, annihilating—characterize the *way* of thinking by which justice is understood. These three determinations, however, are not only ordered in a certain hierarchical sequence, they tell at the same time and above all of the inner animation of this thinking. By constructing, it set itself up (first erecting the height) in this movement; thus, what thinks in this way surpasses itself, separates itself from itself, and brings what is fixated under and behind itself. This way of thinking is a self-surpassing, a becoming master of oneself from having climbed and opened a higher height. We call such self-surpassing heightening *overpowering*. It is the essence of power.

By power one usually understands the ordered, planning, calculating introduction of force. Power is taken as *a kind of force*. Increase of power and overpowering then mean accumulation and preparation of means of force and their possible calculative deployment. Whatever does violence—what is active and forceful in the exercise of force—breaks loose in an arbitrary, incalculable, blind way. Whatever erupt in such a way are called "energies." Force is then the storing up of energies that compel their way toward eruption; force is *not* in control of itself. But energy means the ability to do work. However, to work an effect means to change something at hand into something else. Energies are effective points, "point" suggesting the gathering toward a node that dissipates with a kind of compulsion and only *is* in the field of such dissipation. Power can be understood in this way as a kind of force, force as energy, and energy as a blind tumult of compulsions not further intelligible and yet experienced in its efficacy and its effects.

The reference to this possible and indeed current direction of interpretation in thinking the concept of power is necessary because Nietzsche often—frequently in passages where he wants to give *his own* thought of power particular trenchancy and emphasis—speaks of "energy" and "expressions of energy," instead of power and power relations. To customary ears, many passages sound as if Nietzsche were striving for a general dynamics of "explosions" of "centers of force," a dynamics expanded to the totality of the world. It is as if he were representing the world as energy very much in the "worldviews" emerging in his time, worldviews that were especially keen to "have a scientific basis," whether physics or chemistry or biology assumed the task of providing the leading representations.

If we think Nietzsche's thought of power in the scope of the general concept of energy, both very indefinite and yet somehow current, we remain thoroughly in the foreground, so much so that we falsely take precisely this foreground for the center. The center, the essence of what Nietzsche calls by the name "power" and also often "energy," is in truth determined by the essence of justice. With our gaze thus directed to the essence of power as self-surpassing unto essence, we possess the preconditions for understanding the second passage in which Nietzsche expresses himself about justice.

The second note is nearly contemporaneous with the first. It belongs among the reflections occurring in the time between the composition of the third and fourth parts of *Thus Spoke Zarathustra* (1884; XIV, 80*). The passage reads: "*Justice*, as the function of a panoramic power that looks beyond the narrow perspectives of good and evil, and thus has a broader horizon of *advantage*—the intention to preserve something that is *more* than this or that person." At the outset we notice a certain similarity of both definitions. The first one said "justice . . . *supreme representative of life itself.*" Now Nietzsche says, "justice, as the function of a panoramic power." "Function," "to function," means execution, carrying out—the way in which the power we are referring to *is* power and empowers. Here "function" does not mean something dependent on this power and a subsequent addition to it but power itself in its empowering. What power does Nietzsche mean when he speaks of "a" power? He does not mean "one" among and beside others, but that one power yet to be named that empowers beyond all others; the one that, corresponding to the designation "supreme representative," is the supreme power.

Such power is *panoramic* and is thus totally different from a blindly urging form of energy set loose somewhere. Being panoramic does not

---

* See W I 2 [149], from Summer–Fall, 1884; CM *11*, 188.

mean merely looking about, a gaze that roams back and forth among things that are at hand. Being panoramic is a *looking beyond* narrow perspectives. It is thus itself all the more perspectival, that is, a looking that opens up perspectives.

Whither this looking ahead that opens up? What vista does it offer? Nietzsche answers indirectly at first by naming *those* perspectives that are looked beyond, namely, "the narrow perspectives of good and evil." Good and evil are names for the basic distinction of "morality." Nietzsche understands morality metaphysically. The "good" is the "Ideal," the Idea and what lies still beyond it—being proper, the *ontōs on*. "Evil" is the metaphysical name for what is not supposed to be a being, the *mē on*. But herein lies the distinction between the true (being-in-itself) and the apparent world. That distinction designates perspectives that justice sees beyond. Justice looks beyond these narrow perspectives to a broad one. Looking beyond previous perspectives corresponds to the *exclusive* nature of the constructive way of thinking by which we earlier defined justice. But construction now becomes clearer through the nature of perspectival panorama, of opening up a broad perspective. Justice does not "have" a perspective; it *is* itself a perspective as an erecting, opening, and keeping open of it.

Earlier we referred to the connection between perspective and horizon. Every perspective has its horizon. Justice has "a broader horizon of *advantage*." We are startled. A justice that is looking for *advantage* sounds strange and at the same time clearly like utility, avidity, and expedience—very like a business transaction. And Nietzsche has even underlined the word *advantage*, leaving no doubt that "advantage" is essential to the justice spoken of here. The emphasis must fortify us in our efforts not to think the *concept* denoted by this word in terms of everyday representations. Moreover, according to its genuine, though now lost, significance, the word *"advantage"* [*Vor-teil*] means what has been alloted *to* someone in a distribution, before the actual dividing takes place. In justice, as the opening of perspectives, an all-embracing horizon spreads, the delineation of that which is already apportioned in advance to all representing, calculating, and forming, indeed as what is to be *maintained* everywhere and always. Maintain-

Truth as Justice 149

ing here means at the same time attaining, receiving, and preserving, depositing in permanence.

What is that which is apportioned before everything else, that which cannot be transcended and overtaken by any horizon? Nietzsche does not say directly *what* it is. He only says that the horizon-like intending of justice aims for something that is *more* than this or that purpose, more than the happiness and fate of individuals. All this is shunted aside in justice.

If individuals are not important, is it then the community that is so? Just as little. We can judge what Nietzsche means solely on the basis of what he says about the perspective of justice. Justice looks beyond the distinction between the true and the apparent worlds and thus looks into a higher essential determination of the world, thus into a broader horizon in which the essence of man—namely, of modern Western man—is "more broadly" determined at the same time.

What may we derive from these two quite essential utterances of Nietzsche's concerning justice? As the empowering of a perspectival power, as the highest and broadest constructive and foundational erection, it is the basic trait of life itself, "life" understood initially as human life.

We wanted to ask in what the commanding nature of human knowledge and the poetizing essence of human reason have their justifying and standard-setting ground. The answer was—in justice. According to the constitution we characterized, justice is the ground of the possibility and necessity of every kind of harmony of man with chaos, whether such harmony be the higher one of art or the equally necessary one of knowledge.* Commanding explanation and poetizing transfiguration are "right" and just, because life itself at bottom is what Nietzsche calls justice.

---

* See the correction of NI, 648, 1.3 by Otto Pöggeler, *Der Denkweg Martin Heideggers*, second ed. (Pfullingen: G. Neske, 1983), p. 122. Before the words *der Erkenntnis* Pöggeler inserts: *die gleichnotwendige*.

22. The Essence of Will to Power; Permanentizing Becoming into Presence

Is the commanding and poetizing element, the fact that knowledge is somehow groundlessly set on its own, overcome by justice? Does what is here called justice offer a guarantee against the blind eruption of a merely compulsive arbitrariness? But then does such justice in the end vouch for what is right? Asking this way, we seem to take the reflection more seriously than Nietzsche does. Yet with this question we have already placed ourselves back on a standpoint that justice, thought as the basic trait of life, no longer admits. We are asking about what is right about this justice, and have before our minds a standard that is already fixed and binding also for justice.

We may no longer question in this way, but neither should the whole matter degenerate into arbitrariness again. As matters now stand, everything "right" must come from justice. The two notes that we elucidated say nothing directly about *what* is constructed, opened up, and envisaged in justice. They everywhere emphasize solely the distinctive *how* of this "way of thinking." What is right about justice, presuming we may somehow distinguish that from justice itself, is determined, if at all, only in terms of justice itself, on the basis of the innermost core of its essence. But we will get at this only by venturing a new attempt to comprehend the manner of this "thinking," and thus to look at how and in what guise justice "functions." The constructive assigning of what is apportioned before all else is the function of a power. Which power? In what does the essence of a power consist? Our reply must be: *The power intended here is the will to power.*

How are we to understand this? Power can at best, after all, be *what* the will to power wills; thus, the goal distinguished from this willing and set before it.

If power were the will to power, that would mean that the will itself is to be understood as power. Then we could just as well say that power is to be understood as will. Yet Nietzsche does not say power is will, just as little as will is power. He thinks neither will "as" power nor power "as" will. Just as little does he merely set the two next to each other as "will and power." Rather, he thinks *his* thought of the "will to power."

If justice is the "function," the basic trait and the execution of will to power, we must think the thought of will to power in terms of the essence of justice; thus we must think justice back to its essential ground. Hence it is not sufficient for us to ward off the significations that occur to us whenever we hear the words *will* and *power* and instead to think the determinations that Nietzsche names. Precisely when we think the basic words *will* and *power* in Nietzsche's sense and, as it were, correctly according to his dictionary, the danger of completely flattening the thought of will to power is most acute; that is, the danger of merely equating will and power, of taking will as power and power as will. Thus what is decisive, will *to* power, the "to," does not come to the fore.

With such interpretations, one can at best ascertain for Nietzsche a new essential determination of the will, above all, one that is different from that of Schopenhauer. The *political* interpretations of Nietzsche's fundamental thought further this flattening process the most, if they do not actually cancel out the *essence* of will to power. And it does not matter whether these political counterfeits feed a hatred of Germans or "serve" a love of Germans. The panoramic power whose empowering occurs in the thinking that constructs, excludes, and annihilates is the "will" to power. What "power" means must be understood in terms of will to power, and what "will" means must similarly be understood in terms of will to power. Will to power is not the result of a fusion of "will" and "power," but the reverse: "will" and "power" are always merely conceptual fragments that are artificially sundered from the originally unified essence of "will to power." We can easily see that this is so from the way in which

Nietzsche defines the essence of will. He thoroughly rejects a determination of, so to speak, the isolable essence of will. For Nietzsche emphasizes again and again that *will* is merely a word that veils a manifold essence, due to the simplicity of its phonemic structure. Taken by itself, "will" is a piece of fiction; there is no such thing as "will."

> I laugh at your free will and at your unfree one, too: what you call will is delusion to me; there is no will. (XII, 267; from the *Zarathustra* period)

> At the beginning stands the great fatality of error—that the will is something that *is effective*, that will is a *faculty*. . . . Today we know that it is merely a word. (*Twilight of the Idols;* VIII, 80)

Yet Nietzsche must say in what respect that which is named in the word *will* is to be thought if the word is not to remain a mere sound. And Nietzsche does say this: Will is command (see, for example, XIII, numbers 638 and ff.).* In commanding, "the innermost conviction of superiority" is what is decisive. Accordingly, Nietzsche understands commanding as the fundamental mood of one's being superior; indeed, not only superior with regard to others, those who obey, but also and always beforehand superior with regard to oneself. The latter means excelling, taking one's own essence higher in such a way that one's very essence consists in such excelling.

The essence of power was determined as the panoramic gaze into the comprehensive vista, as overpowering. In thinking the essence of will, we do not think will alone, but will to power. The same holds true when we think the essence of power. Will and power are *selfsame* in the metaphysical sense that they cohere in the one original essence of will to power.

They can so belong only if they are held in tension and thus are precisely *not* the same in the sense of an empty sameness of coinci-

---

* On will as command, see Volume I in this series, sections 6–10, esp. p. 41. See also below, section 2 of Part Three, esp. pp. 194–96. Several of the fragments Heidegger refers us to here, including GOA, XIII, 638, are to be found in notebook W I 1, from Spring, 1884. See W I 1 [389], at CM, *11*, 113–14, which begins: "Will—a commanding: yet insofar as an unconscious act underlies this conscious act we also need to think the former efficaciously." The note goes on to question the "optics" of science.

The Essence of Will to Power

dence. Will to power means empowering to the excelling of itself. Such overpowering to excelling is at the same time the fundamental act of excelling itself. For this reason, Nietzsche constantly speaks of power being in itself "enhancement of power"; the powering of power is empowering to "more" power.

Taken superficially, this all sounds like a merely quantitative accumulation of force and indicates a mere ebullition, eruption, and raging of blind urges and pulsions. Will to power then looks like an ongoing occurrence that rumbles like the inside of a volcano and threatens to erupt. In this way, of course, nothing of its proper essence is intelligible. However, empowering to the excelling of oneself means that empowering brings life to a stand and an autochthony, but to a standing in something that, as excelling, is in motion.

However, in order not to think the original, unified essence of will to power in an empty and abstract way, we must think will to power in its supreme configuration as justice, think justice as the ground of truth in the sense of *homoiōsis* and *homoiōsis* as the ground of the reciprocal relationship of knowledge and art. In view of the concept of will to power that we have now attained, we must think through the whole path of the lecture course again in retrospect. We must thereby become aware that from the first step onward, in all the subsequent steps, will to power was always and only thought in its essence.

Thinking through the essence of will to power in the configuration of knowledge and truth had as its goal the insight *that* and *to what extent* Nietzsche, by thinking his sole thought of will to power, became the one who completed Western metaphysics. Metaphysics thinks beings as a whole, thinks what and how they are. So far, we have only thought knowledge as the securing of the permanence of human life back to justice, and thus to will to power. However, human life is what it is solely on the basis of its being directed to chaos; the latter, the whole of beings, has the fundamental character of will to power. What we must see is "that will to power is what also guides the inorganic world, or rather, that there is no inorganic world" (XIII, number 204; 1885).

In spite of the fact that his efforts frequently *seem* to do so, Nietzsche does not prove *that* "the innermost essence of Being is will to power" (WM, 693; 1888) by concluding on the basis of an inductive examination of all the regions of beings that beings are everywhere in their Being will to power. Rather, as a thinker, Nietzsche always and from the outset thinks on the basis of the projection of beings as whole to their Being as will to power.

But what about the truth of this projection? What about the truth of the metaphysical and of all projections of thought in general? As we can readily see, that is a—if not *the*—decisive question. Even today, philosophy lacks all the essential presuppositions for unfolding and mastering that question. The question cannot be asked adequately within metaphysics, and thus also not within Nietzsche's fundamental position. On the contrary, we must point in another direction.

If justice is "the supreme representative of life itself," if the will to power reveals itself properly in human life, does not the extrapolation of justice to the fundamental power of beings in general and the thoroughgoing interpretation of beings as a whole as will to power amount to an anthropomorphizing of all beings? Is not the world thought according to the paradigm of man? Is not such thinking pure anthropomorphism? To be sure. It is anthropomorphism in the "grand style," the style that has a sense for what is rare and long in coming. Nor may we think that this anthropomorphism should be held against Nietzsche as a reproach. Nietzsche knows about the anthropomorphism of his metaphysics. He knows about it not simply as a way of thinking that he stumbled upon accidentally and out of which he could no longer find his way. Nietzsche *wants* this anthropomorphizing of all beings, and wants only that. This we can see clearly in a brief note from the year 1884: "To 'humanize' the world, that is, to feel ourselves more and more masters within it—" (WM, 614). Such anthropomorphizing does not, of course, proceed by following the paradigm of some arbitrary, everyday, average man. It proceeds on the basis of an interpretation of that human being which, grounded in "justice," is in the grounds of its essence *will to power.*[*]

Anthropomorphism pertains to the essence of the history of the end

---

[*] The theme of anthropomorphism is fully developed in Heidegger's fourth and final lecture course on Nietzsche: see "European Nihilism," Part One of Volume IV in this series, esp. sections 11–13.

of metaphysics. It determines indirectly the decision of the transition, inasmuch as the transition brings about an "overcoming" of the *animal rationale* together with the *subiectum*. Indeed, it is the pivoting of a pivotal "point" first attained by means of these notions. The pivoting is: beings–Being; the fulcrum of the pivoting is: the truth of Being. The pivoting is not a turnabout; it is a turning into the other ground, as abyss. *The ground-lessness of the truth of Being* historically becomes the abandonment by Being, which consists in the fact that the revealing of Being as such remains in default. The latter culminates in the forgottenness of Being, if we understand forgetting purely in the sense of the default of commemorative thought. The grounds for the positing of man as mere man, the grounds for the anthropomorphizing of beings, are primordially to be sought in this realm.

This ruthless and extreme anthropomorphizing of the world tears away the last illusions of the modern fundamental metaphysical position; it takes the positing of man as *subiectum* seriously. Nietzsche would certainly and justly reject the reproach that his thought is a banal subjectivism that exhausts itself in proclaiming whoever happens to be there—whether an individual or community—the standard and purpose of everything. Nietzsche would claim with equal right to have brought a metaphysically necessary subjectivism to completion by making the "body" the guideline of his interpretation of the world.

In Nietzsche's thought-path to the will to power, not only modern metaphysics but *Western* metaphysics as a whole is accomplished. Its question, from the very beginning, was, What are beings? The Greeks defined the Being of beings as the permanence of presence. That definition of Being remains unshaken throughout the entire history of metaphysics.

However, have we not heard again and again that for Nietzsche the essence of beings as a whole is chaos, hence "Becoming," and precisely *not* "Being" in the sense of what is fixed and constant, which he thinks as the untrue and unreal? Being is crowded out, in favor of Becoming. The very nature of becoming and motion is determined as will to power. Can one then still call Nietzsche's thinking a consummation of metaphysics? Is it not its denial, or even its overcoming? Away from "Being"—and on to "Becoming"?

Nietzsche's philosophy is indeed often so interpreted. And if not exactly in this way, then one says that in the history of philosophy there was already very early, with Heraclitus, and later immediately prior to Nietzsche, with Hegel, a "metaphysics of Becoming" instead of the "metaphysics of Being." In a rough and ready way, that is correct; but at bottom it is as thoughtless as the first position.

As opposed to all that, we must consider anew what will to power means: empowering to the excelling of one's own essence. Empowering brings excelling—Becoming—to a stand and to permanence. In the thought of will to power, what is becoming and is moved in the highest and most proper sense—life itself—is to be thought in *its* permanence. Certainly, Nietzsche wants Becoming and what becomes, as the fundamental character of beings as a whole; but he wants what becomes precisely and before all else as *what remains,* as "being" proper, being in the sense of the Greek thinkers. Nietzsche thinks so decisively as a metaphysician that he also knows this fact about himself. Thus a note that found its final form only in the last year, 1888 (WM, 617*), begins as follows:

Recapitulation:
To *stamp* Becoming with the character of Being—that is the supreme *will to power.*

We ask: Why is this the *supreme* will to power? The answer is, because will to power in its *most* profound essence is nothing other than the permanentizing of Becoming into presence.

In this interpretation of Being, the primordial thinking of Being as *physis* advances through the extreme point of the fundamental position of modern metaphysics, thus coming to its completion. Rising and appearing, becoming and presencing, are in the thought of *will to power* thought back to the unity of the essence of "Being" according to its initial and primordial meaning, not as an imitation of the Greek but as a transformation of the modern thinking of being to its allotted consummation.

---

* See the full presentation of this note in Volume II, pp. 201–2. Note that the title, *"Recapitulation,"* was added by the editors of Nietzsche's *Nachlass.* Finally, I can find nothing in CM to corroborate Heidegger's assertion that the note, which CM dates between the end of 1886 and Spring, 1887, "found its final form" only in 1888.

The Essence of Will to Power

This means that the primordial interpretation of Being as the permanence of presencing is now rescued by being placed beyond question.

The question as to where the truth of this first and last metaphysical interpretation of Being is grounded, the question as to whether such a ground is ever to be experienced within metaphysics, is now *so* far away that it cannot be asked as a question at all. For now the essence of Being appears to be so broadly and essentially grasped that it is also equal to whatever becomes, to *"life,"* indeed as its concept.

In the consummation of Western metaphysics through Nietzsche, the all-sustaining question of truth, in whose essence Being itself in its various metaphysical interpretations essentially unfolds, not only remains unasked—as was previously the case—but also is totally buried in its character as worthy of question. For this reason, the consummation of metaphysics becomes an end. Yet this end *is* the need of the other commencement. It is up to us and to those coming after us whether we experience its necessity. Such an experience requires first of all that we understand the end as consummation. This means that we dare not plunder Nietzsche merely for the sake of some contemporary spiritual counterfeit; nor can we, ostensibly in possession of eternal truth, pass him by. We must think him. That is to say, we must always think his sole thought, and thereby the unitary guiding thought of Western metaphysics, to its own intrinsic limit. Then we will experience first and foremost how decisively Being is already overshadowed by beings and by the predominance of the so-called actual.

The overshadowing of Being by beings derives from Being itself—as Being's abandonment of beings, in the sense of the refusal of the truth of Being.

Yet by descrying this shadow *as* a shadow we already stand in another light, without finding the fire from which its radiance comes. Thus the shadow is itself already something else. It is not gloom.

> Many wanderers tell of it,
> And the deer stray in crevices,
> And the horde sweeps over heights;

> But in holy shadow,
> On the green slope dwells
> The shepherd and looks to the summit.
>
> Hölderlin, "To Mother Earth"
> (Hellingrath IV, 156 f.)*

---

* Hellingrath's text has the word *Herde* in line 3, rather than the Beissner–Schmidt reading, *Horde*. Heidegger thus took the third line to read, "And the herd roves over the heights." If Beissner and Schmidt are correct, however, it is not a "roving herd" but a "horde" that roams over the mountains. The shadow in which the shepherd dwells would thus be set in sharper and far more drastic relief. See the text of Friedrich Beissner and Jochen Schmidt, *Hölderlin Werke und Briefe* (Frankfurt am Main: Insel, 1969), I, 140.

Part Two

THE ETERNAL RECURRENCE OF THE SAME AND THE WILL TO POWER

At first there seems to be not a trace of truth in the claim that Nietzsche's philosophy is the *consummation* of Western metaphysics.* For by abolishing the "suprasensuous world" that has served heretofore as the "true" world his philosophy appears rather to reject all metaphysics and to take steps toward its ultimate abnegation. To be sure, Nietzsche's fundamental thought, "the will to power," still refers in some way to an interpretation of the beingness of beings as a whole, namely, as will. Willing goes together with knowing. In the context of Schelling's and Hegel's projects, knowing and willing constitute the essence of reason. In the context of the Leibnizian projection of the substantiality of substance, knowing and willing are thought as *vis primitiva activa et passiva* [the originary active and passive force]. However, the thought of will to power, especially in its biologistic configuration, appears to abandon the realm of this project; rather than consummating the tradition of metaphysics, it seems to truncate that tradition by disfiguring and trivializing it.

What the word *consummation* means; what precisely may *not* be used as a standard for taking its measure; to what extent we can fasten onto a "doctrine" in it; in what way the consummation keeps to the guiding projection (beings' coming to light in Being†) that articulates and grounds metaphysics as such; whether the consummation fulfills the guiding projection in its ultimate possibilities, thereby allowing it to stand outside all inquiry—none of these things can be discussed here.

The belief that Nietzsche's philosophy merely distorts, trivializes, and dogmatically abjures prior metaphysics is simply an illusion, albeit

---

* In a note, Heidegger reminds us that the present text pertains to the lecture course "The Will to Power as Knowledge," which came to an abrupt close in the summer of 1939. See the Editor's Preface to this volume.

† *Seiendes gelichtet im Sein.* Whether *gelichtet* should be translated with some form of the word "clearing," *Lichtung,* is an important and difficult question. Because Heidegger here stresses the traditional metaphysical "guiding projection" (*Leitentwurf*), and not his own further thinking of it, I have preserved the problematic reference to *lumen.*

a very stubborn one, one that persists as long as we represent his fundamental thought superficially. The superficiality arises from our postponement of a historical meditation on Western metaphysics, as well as from our practice of reflecting on the various projections that evolved from particular fundamental positions solely within the limits of what is asserted in those projections. In doing the latter, we forget that these utterances inevitably speak out of a background, a background from which they emerge; such utterances do not explicitly interrogate that background but return to it unwittingly in their very speech. The various fundamental positions understand the beingness of beings in a projection that was cast long before they themselves emerged, as far back as our Greek beginnings. These positions take the Being of beings as having been determined in the sense of permanence of presence. If we think these fundamental metaphysical positions within the scope of this guiding projection, we can preserve ourselves from the temptation to grasp Nietzsche's philosophy superficially and to pigeonhole it with the help of the usual historiological labels—as "Heraclitean," as a "metaphysics of the will," or as a "philosophy of life."

If we think in terms of the guiding projection of the beingness of beings, the projection that sustains the entire history of metaphysics even as it surpasses that history at its very commencement, then we will recognize what is metaphysically necessary and ultimate in the doctrine of the eternal recurrence of the same. When we define the interconnection of this doctrine with the fundamental thought of will to power, we bring Nietzsche's philosophy to the fore as the final distinctive position in the history of Western metaphysics. Given such an insight, Nietzsche's philosophy impels us toward the necessity of that confrontation in and for which Western metaphysics, as the totality of a history that has been accomplished, is consigned to what has been, that is to say, is consigned to an ultimate futurity. What has been liberates what apparently is merely past into its essence; specifically, it trans-lates the commencement, which apparently has foundered once and for all, into its character as a commencement. Because of this character, the commencement surpasses everything that follows it, and hence is futural. The past as *essentially unfolding*, that is, beingness projected in sundry ways as the veiled truth of Being, holds sway over everything that is taken to be current and actual, the latter by virtue of its actuating power.

In order to define the interconnection of eternal recurrence of the same and will to power, our reflections must execute the following six steps:

1. In terms of the history of metaphysics, the thought of eternal recurrence of the same anticipates in thought the fundamental thought of will to power; that is to say, it thinks that thought to the point of consummation.
2. In terms of metaphysics, in its modern phase and in the history of its end, both thoughts think the selfsame.
3. In the essential unity of the two thoughts, the metaphysics that is approaching consummation utters its final word.
4. The fact that their essential unity remains unspoken founds the age of consummate meaninglessness.
5. This age fulfills the essence of modernity; now, for the first time, modernity comes into its own.
6. Viewed historically, such fulfillment—cloaked in concealment and running counter to bemused popular opinion—is the need characteristic of the transition that embraces all that has been and prepares what is to come. It is transition to guardianship over the truth of Being.

— I —

Will to power is the essence of power itself. It consists in power's overpowering, that is, its self-enhancement to the highest possible degree. Will does not hover beyond power; it is rather the empowering command within the essence of power to exercise power. The metaphysical determination of Being as will to power remains unthought in its decisive import, and falls prey to misinterpretation, as long as Being is posited solely as power or merely as will, and as long as will to power is explained in the sense of will as power or power as will.

To think Being, the beingness of beings, as will to power means to conceive of Being as the unleashing of power to its essence; the unleashing transpires in such a way that unconditionally empowering power posits the exclusive preeminence of beings over Being. Whereas beings possess objective actuality, Being collapses into oblivion.

What this unleashing of power to its essence is, Nietzsche is unable to think. Nor can any metaphysics think it, inasmuch as metaphysics cannot put the matter into question. On the contrary, Nietzsche thinks his interpretation of the Being of beings as will to power in an essential unity with that determination of Being which arose in the rubric "the eternal recurrence of the same."

Reckoned chronologically, Nietzsche pursued the thought of eternal return of the same before he conceived of will to power, even though intimations of the latter may be found every bit as early. Yet the thought of return is above all earlier *in terms of the matter;* that is to say, it is more forward-reaching, although Nietzsche himself was never able explicitly to think through its essential *unity* with will to power as such, nor to elevate it into a metaphysical conception. Just as little did Nietzsche recognize the truth of the thought of return in terms of the history of metaphysics. The reason for this is not that the thought remained in any way obscure to him, but that like all metaphysicians prior to him Nietzsche was unable to find his way back to the fundamental traits of the guiding metaphysical projection. For the general traits of the metaphysical projection of beings upon beingness, and thereby the representation of beings as such in the domain of presence and permanence, can be known only when we come to experience that projection as historically cast. An experience of this kind has nothing in common with the explanatory theories that metaphysics every now and again proposes concerning itself. Nietzsche too elaborates only these kinds of explanations—which, however, we dare not level off by calling them a "psychology of metaphysics."

"Recurrence" thinks the permanentizing of what becomes, thinks it to the point where the *becoming* of what becomes is secured in the *duration of its becoming.** The "eternal" thinks the permanentizing

---

* *"Wiederkehr" denkt die Beständigung des Werdenden zur Sicherung des* Werdens

of such constancy in the direction of its circling back into itself and forward toward itself. Yet what becomes is not the unceasing otherness of an endlessly changing manifold. What becomes is the same itself, and that means the one and selfsame (the identical) that in each case is within the difference of the other. The presence of the one identical element, a presence that comes to be, is thought in the same. Nietzsche's thought thinks the constant permanentizing of the becoming of whatever becomes into the only kind of presence there is—the self-recapitulation of the identical.

This "selfsame" is separated as by an abyss from the singularity of the unrepeatable enjoining of all that coheres. Out of *that* enjoining alone does the difference commence.

The thought of return is not Heraclitean in the sense usually expounded by our historians of philosophy. But it thinks—in a way that has meanwhile become foreign to anything Greek—the formerly projected essence of beingness (permanence of presence), thinks it in its exitless and involuted consummation. Thus the beginning is brought to the fulfillment of its end. Thought concerning truth, in the sense of the essence of *alētheia*, whose essential advent sustains Being and allows it to be sheltered in its belonging to the commencement, is more remote than ever in this last projection of beingness. In Nietzsche's thinking, "truth" has petrified and become a hollow essence: it has the sense of a univocal accord with beings as a whole, in such a way that within this univocity the unstrained voice of Being can never be heard.

The history of the truth of Being ends when its primordial essence is utterly lost. That loss was prepared by the sudden collapse of ungrounded *alētheia*. Yet at the same time the historical illusion necessarily arises that the primordial unity of *physis* in its original configuration has been recovered once again. For in the very early period of metaphysics it was sundered into "Being" and "Becoming." What was sundered in this way was distributed between the two definitive realms, to wit, the true and the apparent worlds.

---

des Werdenden in seiner Werdedauer. For a similar constructon, see Volume II of this series, *The Eternal Recurrence of the Same*, pp. 200–1.

But, people say, what else can the cancellation of the distinction between the two, the crossing out of these two distinct worlds, mean than the fact that we are finding our way back to the commencement and thereby overcoming metaphysics? Nevertheless, Nietzsche's doctrine does not overcome metaphysics: it is the uttermost unseeing adoption of the very guiding projection of metaphysics. Yet precisely for that reason it is also something essentially other than a flaccid historiological reminiscence of ancient doctrines concerning the cyclical course of cosmic processes.

As long as we designate the thought of return as an unproven and unprovable eccentricity, and as long as we account it one of Nietzsche's poetic and religious caprices, we drag the thinker down to the flatlands of current opinion. If that were the end of the matter, then we might have to resign ourselves to this demotion as the result of those always inevitable misinterpretations by contemporary know-it-alls. Yet something else is at stake here. Inadequate interrogation of the meaning of Nietzsche's doctrine of return, when viewed in terms of the history of metaphysics, shunts aside the most intrinsic need that is exhibited in the course of the history of Western thought. It thus confirms, by assisting those machinations that are oblivious to Being, the utter abandonment of Being.

When that happens we forfeit the very first precondition that anyone would have to satisfy in order to grasp as Nietzsche's fundamental metaphysical thought the ostensibly more accessible thought of will to power. For if will to power constitutes the essential character of the beingness of beings, it must think whatever it is that the eternal recurrence of the same is thinking.

— II —

When in our meditations we bring the guiding projection of all metaphysics to closer inspection, we see that both thoughts think the same thing—will to power in terms of modernity, eternal recurrence of the same in terms of the history of the end. That guiding projection places beings as such in the open region of permanence and presence, representing them in their universal character with a view to their beingness. Which realm it is that yields our representations of permanence and presencing, indeed, the permanentizing of presence itself, never troubles the guiding projection of metaphysics. Metaphysics keeps strictly to the open region of its projection and interprets the permanentizing of presencing variously in accord with the fundamental experience of the already predetermined beingness of beings. Yet if a meditation stirs that gradually gets into its purview that which lightens, that which propriates all the openness of what is open, permanentizing and presencing will themselves be interrogated with a view to their essence. Both will show themselves as essentially bound up with time. Simultaneously, they will demand of us that we rid ourselves of whatever it is we usually designate in the word *time.* *

Will to power may now be conceived of as the permanentizing of surpassment, that is, of Becoming; hence as a transformed determination of the guiding metaphysical projection. The eternal recurrence of the same unfurls and displays its essence, so to speak, as the most constant permanentizing of the becoming of what is constant. Yet, to be sure, all this emerges solely within the scope of that interrogation that has put beingness into question with a view to its projective realm and the grounding of that realm. For such interrogation, the guiding projection of metaphysics and thus metaphysics itself have already been thoroughly overcome; they are no longer admitted as constituting the primary and solely definitive realm.

And yet we may initially try to be guided toward the identity of

---

* These lines reveal something of that way "from 1930 to the 'Letter on Humanism' " that Heidegger cites as the trajectory of his *Nietzsche* volumes "considered as a whole." (See Volume I of this series, *The Will to Power as Art*, p. xvi.) Note that "lightens" here translates *das Lichtende*, a nominalization of the present participle, hence a more active, forceful form of the word *Lichtung*. The phrase *das Lichtende . . . , das jede Offenheit des Offenen ereignet* encapsulates the central theme of a large manuscript on which Heidegger had been working between 1936 and 1938: *Contributions to Philosophy: "Of Ereignis."* The limitations of the translation of *ereignen* as "to propriate" are nowhere so apparent as here: far from being an act of aggrandizement, *Ereignis* is the granting or dispensing of Time and Being, never thought within the guiding projection of metaphysics as such. See now *Contributions*, MHG 65.

"eternal recurrence of the same" and "will to power" within the perspectives of metaphysics and with the help of its distinctions. The lecture courses *"The Will to Power as Art"* and *"The Eternal Recurrence of the Same"* pursue a path by which we may see the *inner unity* of these two. From the outset, the eternal recurrence of the same and will to power are grasped as fundamental determinations of beings as such and as a whole—will to power as the peculiar coinage of "what-being" at the historic end, and eternal recurrence of the same as the coinage of "that-being." The *necessity* of grounding this distinction is surely recognized in an unpublished lecture course I taught during the year 1927; nevertheless, the essential origin of the distinction remains concealed there.*

This distinction—and the prepotence of the elements thereby distinguished—rules unchallenged throughout the entire history of metaphysics and grows ever more self-evident. In what does it have its ground? What-being (*to ti estin*) and that-being (*to estin*) are coextensive in their differentiation with the distinction that everywhere sustains metaphysics, the distinction that is firmly established in the Platonic differentiation of *ontōs on* [being in its Being] and *mē on* [nonbeing]. Although first established in Platonism, established there once and for all, the distinction proves capable of transformation—to the point of unrecognizability. (See Aristotle, *Metaphysics* Z 4, 1030a 17.†) The *ontōs on,* that which has the character of being—and that

---

* The lectures Heidegger refers to here (delivered in the months following the publication of *Being and Time* in April of 1927) have now been published as *Die Grundprobleme der Phänomenologie* (Frankfurt am Main: V. Klostermann, 1975); translated into English by Albert Hofstadter as *The Basic Problems of Phenomenology* (Bloomington, Ind.: Indiana University Press, 1982). See chapter two, sections 10–12. Here Heidegger discusses the distinction between *essentia* and *existentia* in Aquinas, Scotus, and Suarez, a distinction that goes back to the Aristotelian *to ti estin* (or *to ti ēn einai*) and *to estin* (or *hoti estin*). Heidegger here provides a careful historical account of the prevailing view of *existentia* as *Vorhandensein,* being-at-hand. Note that Nietzsche's doctrines of eternal recurrence and will to power are *not* mentioned here, even though Kant and Hegel are cited (e.g., at the end of section 11) as inheritors of the Scholastic distinction.

† Here Aristotle discusses the *to ti ēn einai* of *ousia,* usually rendered as the "essence" of "substance," in terms of a thing's "definition" *(horismos).* At lines 17 ff. he asks

means "true" being, "true" in the sense of *alētheia*—is a "vision," a profile that comes to presence. In such presence there occurs essentially at one and the same time *what* a being is and *that* it—in the presentness of its profile—is. The "true world" is the world decided in advance with regard to its *that*. Yet insofar as it is true, and thus distinguished from the semblant; and insofar as the merely apparent world *manifests* what-being only in a hazy sort of way, hence "truly" "*is*" not, even if at the same time it is not merely nothing but a being; insofar as all this is the case, the "*that* it is" comes to obtrude precisely in the *mē on*. It comes to appear as a stripping away of the pure "visage" in which the "what" shows itself. The *to ti estin* and the *to estin* (the *ti* [what] and the *hoti* [that]) go their separate ways with and in the distinction of the *ontōs on* and the *mē on*. That-being becomes the distinguishing characteristic of each "this" (*tode ti*) and of the *hekaston* [each] as such; at the same time, these cause the relevant what-being (*eidos*) to appear, in this way alone determining a *that* for Being, and thus determining a being as a particular given. The *idea* now explicitly becomes an *eidos* in the sense of the *morphē* [form] of *hyle* [matter], in such a way that beingness is transposed to a *synolon* [gathered whole] that does not cancel the distinction. (With regard to the original Greek sense of *morphē*, which is quite different from the later distinction between *forma* and *materia*, see Aristotle, *Physics* B 1*). Under many guises, "form" assumes center stage in subsequent times, in particular because of the biblical notion of creation, as *existentia*, *essentia*, and the *principium individuationis*. What-being and that-being evanesce to vacuous "concepts of reflection" as the unquestioned acceptance of beingness waxes. They persevere with a power that be-

---

whether definitions, like the "what-being" of things, are not multiple in meaning, sometimes referring to "substance" or a "this," other times indicating every sort of "predication" of quantity, quality, and "whatever such there may be."

* Heidegger defines that "original Greek sense" of *morphē* in "On the Essence and Concept of *Physis*," in *Wegmarken* (Frankfurt am Main: V. Klostermann, 1967), pp. 309–71, esp. pp. 343–53. In the context of *eidos* and *logos*, *morphē* is there taken to be a mode of presencing, that is, of Being. See also *Der Ursprung des Kunstwerkes* (Stuttgart: P. Reclam, 1960), pp. 20–25; in *Poetry, Language, Thought*, translated by Albert Hofstadter (New York: Harper & Row, 1971), see pp. 26–30.

comes all the more tenacious as metaphysics is increasingly accepted as something self-evident.

Is it any wonder that the distinction between what-being and that-being once again comes to the fore most conspicuously at the consummation of Western metaphysics? Yet the *distinction as such* is forgotten, so that the two fundamental determinations of beings as a whole—will to power and eternal recurrence of the same—are uttered in such a way that although they are metaphysically homeless, as it were, they are posited unconditionally.

Will to power says *what* the being "is." The being is that which (as power) it empowers.

Eternal recurrence of the same designates the *how* in which the being that possesses such a "what" character is. It designates its "factualness" as a whole, its "that it is." Because Being as eternal recurrence of the same constitutes the permanentizing of presence, it is most permanent; it is the unconditioned *that*.

We must at the same time recall something else: the fulfillment of metaphysics tries on the very basis of that metaphysics to overcome the distinction between the "true" and the "merely apparent" worlds. At first it tries to do this simply by inverting those two worlds. Of course, the inversion is not merely a mechanical overturning, whereby the lower, the sensuous realm, assumes the place of the higher, the suprasensuous—an overturning in which these two realms and their locales would remain unchanged. The inversion transforms the lower, the sensuous realm, into "life" in the sense of will to power. In the essential articulation of will to power the suprasensuous is transformed into a securing of permanence.

In accordance with this overcoming of metaphysics, that is, this transformation of metaphysics into its final possible configuration, the very distinction between what-being and that-being is inevitably shunted aside. It thus *remains unthought*. What-being (will to power) is nothing "in itself" to which that-being, by some happy circumstance, is allotted. What-being, as essence, conditions the very animation of life (value). In such conditioning, what-being is at the same time the sole proper *that* of animate beings—and here that means beings as a whole.

On the basis of this cohesion of that-being and what-being (a cohesion that is now quite the opposite of the primordial encompassment of the *estin* by the *einai* of the *ontōs on* as *idea*), will to power and eternal recurrence of the same may no longer merely cohere as determinations of Being: they must say the *selfsame* thing. At the end of the history of metaphysics, the thought of eternal recurrence of the same expresses precisely what will to power, as the fundamental trait of the beingness of beings, says at the consummation of modernity. Will to power is self-surpassment into the possibilities of becoming that pertain to a commandeering which now begins to install itself. Such self-surpassment remains in its innermost core a permanentizing of Becoming as such. Self-surpassment stands opposed to all mere continuation into the endless, which is foreign and inimical to it.

As soon as we are in a position to think through the pure self-sameness of will to power and eternal recurrence of the same in every direction and in every one of its adopted guises, we shall find the basis for first measuring both of these fundamental thoughts in their particularity and in accord with their metaphysical scope. These thoughts provide an occasion for thinking back to the first commencement. For they constitute the fulfillment of that commencement, empowering unconditionally the nonessence that already emerges on the scene with the *idea*. From that fulfillment unfolds a meditation on the perennially undefined and ungrounded truth of Being. Thus begins the transition toward an interrogation of this truth.

— III —

The selfsame utterance in the essential unity of will to power and the eternal recurrence of the same is the final word of metaphysics. "Final," in the sense of exhaustive consummation, must also in a certain sense mean "first." The latter, *physis*, commences by rending itself straightaway into the ostensible opposition of Being and Becoming. Upsurgent presencing, unexamined, and not projected upon its character as "time," is always and everywhere apprehended with a view to one thing alone: coming to be and passing away, becoming and change, remaining and enduring. In this last-mentioned respect the Greeks view Being proper; indeed, for them every change is at first called *ouk on* [not-being], later *mē on* [nonbeing], but still defined as *on*. Being and Becoming are divided into two realms that are separated by a *khōrismos* [gap]. Thus they belong to a locale that is defined by these realms; here they take up their residence. To what extent does Aristotle overcome the *khōrismos* in the *ousia* of the *tode ti* [the "this"] and the *hekaston* [the "each"]? To the extent that Being becomes *ousia* solely as *entelekheia* and *energeia*.*

Being ultimately steps into the arena with its opponent, Becoming, inasmuch as the latter claims Being's place. The opposition of the two unfolds on the plain of the "actual," a terrain that is never expressly perceived as such. Being's own actuality makes a claim on it, since it stands opposed to the nonactual, the null; yet such actuality also demands for itself the character of Becoming, since it does not wish to be a petrified, "life"-less thing at hand. Hegel executes the first step in the surpassment of this opposition on behalf of "Becoming," although he grasps the latter in terms of the suprasensuous and the absolute Idea, as its self-presentation. Nietzsche, inverting Platonism, transposes Becoming to the "vital" sphere, as the chaos that "bodies forth." That inversion, extinguishing as it does the opposition of Being and Becoming, constitutes the fulfillment proper. For now there is no way out, either in such rending or in a more appropriate fusion. This becomes manifest in the fact that "Becoming" claims to have usurped the prerogative of Being, whereas the prepotence of Becoming puts a final seal on the ultimate confirmation of Being's unshaken power. Being is the permanentizing (securing) of presencing, inasmuch as the interpretation of beings and their beingness as Becoming permanentizes Becoming as unconditioned presence. In order to shore up its prepotence, Becoming heeds the beck and call of permanentizing pres-

---

* For a fuller account, see "The Essence and the Concept of *Physis*," *Wegmarken*, esp. pp. 351–57; this entire essay expands the horizon projected in Part IV of *Einführung in die Metaphysik* (*An Introduction to Metaphysics*, cited with publisher's information on p. 51, above).

encing. The primordial truth of Being holds sway in this particular permanentizing, albeit unrecognized and ungrounded, deviant in its utterly oblivious nonessence. Such empowering of Becoming to the status of Being deprives the former of its ultimate possibility for preeminence and restores to the latter its primordial essence (as bound up with *physis*); an essence, to be sure, that is consummate nonessence. Now beingness is all there is, and beingness sees to it all: alteration *and* permanence. It satisfies unconditionally the claims of being (as "life"). Providing such satisfaction, beingness appears to be beyond all question. It offers the most spacious quarters.

The essential sequence in this final phase of metaphysics, that is, the final phase of the projection of beingness upon permanentizing of presencing, is announced in the corresponding definition of the essence of "truth." Now the last reverberations of any intimation of *alētheia* fade. Truth becomes rightness, in the sense of a commanding absorption by the one who commands into the compulsion to self-surpassment. All correctness is merely a rehearsal of and an opportunity for such surpassing; every fixation merely a foothold for dissolving all things in Becoming, hence a purchase for willing the permanentizing of "chaos." Now the sole appeal is to the vitality of life. The primordial essence of truth is transformed in such a way that its metamorphosis amounts to a shunting aside (though not an annihilation) of essence. Verity dissolves in the presence of an empowering of power, a presence caught up at some point of its recurrence. Truth is once again the very same as Being, except that the latter has in the meantime been overtaken by the fulfillment of its nonessence. Yet when truth as correctness and as unconcealment has been leveled to "life-size"; when it is shunted aside in this way; then the *essence* of truth has surrendered its jurisdiction altogether. It no longer rises to the challenge of inquiry. It wanders without prospect in the region of "perspectives" and "horizons" that are bereft of every clearing. But what *then*? Then the bestowal of meaning gets under way as a "revaluation of all values." "Meaninglessness" is the only thing that makes "sense." Truth is "rightness," that is to say, supreme will to power. Only an unconditioned dominion over the earth by human beings will be right for such "rightness." Instituting planetary dominion, however, will itself be but the consequence of an unconditioned *anthropomorphism*.

— IV —

Precisely here the age of *consummate meaninglessness* begins. In such a designation the word *meaninglessness* is to be taken as a concept of thought that thinks the history of Being. Such thinking leaves metaphysics as a whole (with all its inversions and deviations in the direction of revaluations) behind. According to *Being and Time,* "meaning" designates the realm of projection, designates it in accord with its own proper intent (that is, in accord with its unique question concerning the "meaning of Being"), as the clearing of Being, the clearing that is opened and grounded in projection. Such projection is that in the thrown project which propriates as the essential unfolding of truth.*

Meaninglessness is lack of the truth (clearing) of Being. Every possibility of such a projection founders because metaphysics has shunted aside the essence of truth. When the very question concerning the essence of the truth of *beings* and of our comportment toward beings is decided, meditation on the truth of Being, as the more original question concerning the essence of truth, can only remain in default. Advancing through a metamorphosis from *adaequatio* to certitude, truth has established itself as the *securing* of beings in their *perfectly accessible disposability.* That transformation ordains the prepotence of beingness, thus defined, as *malleability.* Beingness as malleability re-

---

* *Dieses Entwerfen aber ist jenes, das im geworfenen Entwurf als Wesendes der Wahrheit sich ereignet.* Heidegger is here referring to pp. 151–52 of *Sein und Zeit,* 12th ed. (Tübingen: M. Niemeyer, 1972), a crucial juncture in his fundamental ontology. In these pages of section 32, "Understanding and Interpretation," the understanding of Being that characterizes Dasein is interpreted explicitly in terms of meaning, *Sinn.* The analysis looks back to that "lightedness" of Dasein (p. 147) and forward to that "*clearing* of Dasein" that *is* disclosure, unconcealment, "truth." It takes up explicitly the question of the meaning of Being—the sole purpose of existential analysis as such. See also the "Letter on Humanism" in *Wegmarken,* esp. pp. 156–60; in *Basic Writings* (New York: Harper & Row, 1977), pp. 205–8.

mains at the beck and call of that Being which has released itself into sheer accessibility through calculation, into the disposability of the beings appropriate to it by way of unconditioned planning and arranging.

The prepotence of Being in *this* essential configuration is called *machination.** It prevents any kind of grounding of the "projections" that are under its power and yet are themselves none the less powerful. For machination is the prepotence of all unquestioning self-assurance and certitude in securing. Machination alone can hold the stance it adopts toward itself under its unconditioned self-command. Machination makes itself permanent. When meaninglessness comes to power by dint of machination, the suppression of meaning and thus of all inquiry into the truth of Being must be replaced by machination's erection of "goals" (values). One quite reasonably expects new values to be propagated by "life," even though the latter has already been totally mobilized, as though total mobilization were something in itself and not the organization of unconditioned meaninglessness by and for will to power.† Such positings and empowerings of power no longer conform to "standards of measure" and "ideals" that could be grounded in themselves; they are "in service" to sheer expansion of power and are valued purely according to their estimated use-value. The age of consummate meaninglessness is therefore the era in which "worldviews" are invented and promulgated with a view to their power. Such worldviews drive all calculability of representation and production to the extreme, originating as they do essentially in mankind's self-imposed instauration of self in the midst of beings—in the midst of mankind's unconditioned hegemony over all sources of power on the face of the earth, and indeed its dominion over the globe as such.

---

* *Machenschaft,* all that has the quality of doing or making, prevails in the realm of purely accessible *(ausmachbaren)* beings, beings characterized by sheer disposability *(Machbarkeit)* and malleability *(Machsamkeit),* where everything is "do-able" *(machbar)* by way of securement and calculation. See the note on p. 196 of Volume IV, *Nihilism.*

† These words are in reply to Ernst Jünger's books, *Total Mobilization* (1930) and *The Worker: Domination and Configuration* (1932), in which the experience of total mobilization in World War I was taken as a prototype of the technology that is about to enmesh mankind entirely. See Section II of the Analysis at the end of this volume.

Whatever beings in their individual domains may be, whatever used to be defined as their *quiddity* in the sense of the "Ideas," now becomes something that the self-instauration can reckon with in advance, as with that which gauges the *value* of every productive and representative being as such (every work of art, technical contrivance, institution of government, the entire personal and collective order of human beings). Calculation on behalf of this self-instauration invents "values" (for our culture and for the nation). Value translates the essentiality of essence (that is, of beingness) into an object of calculation, something that can even be estimated in terms of quantity and spatial extension. Magnitude now attains to the very essence of grandeur—in the gigantic. The gigantic does *not* first of all *result from* the enhancement of the miniscule; it is not something that grows by accretion. It is the essential ground, the motor, and the goal of enhancement, which in turn consists in something other than quantitative relations.

The fulfillment of metaphysics, that is, the erection and entrenchment of consummate meaninglessness, thus remains nothing else than ultimate submission to the end of metaphysics—in the guise of "revaluation of all values." For Nietzsche's completion of metaphysics is *from the first* an inversion of Platonism (the sensuous becomes the true, the suprasensuous the semblant, world). But insofar as the Platonic "Idea" in its modern dress has become a "principle of reason" and hence a "value," the inversion of Platonism becomes a "revaluation of all values." Here inverted Platonism becomes blindly inflexible and superficial. *All that is left is the solitary superficies of a "life" that empowers itself to itself for its own sake.* If metaphysics begins as an explicit interpretation of beingness as *idea*, it achieves its uttermost end in the "revaluation of all values." The solitary superficies is what *remains after* the abolition of the "true" *and* the "semblant" worlds. It appears as the selfsame of eternal recurrence of the same and will to power.

As a revaluator of all values, Nietzsche testifies to the fact that he belongs ineluctably to metaphysics and thereby to its abyssal separation from *every possibility* of another commencement. Nietzsche himself does not know the distance that is measured out in this final step.

And yet—did not Nietzsche succeed in positing a new "meaning" beyond all the teetering goals and ideals of earlier times, and thus beyond their annihilation? Did he not in his thinking anticipate "overman" as the "meaning" of the "earth"?

However, "meaning" is once again for him "goal" and "ideal." "Earth" is the name for the life that *bodies forth*, the rights of the sensuous. "Overman" is for him the consummation of what was the last man, making fast what was long *not yet* firmly defined, namely, that animal which still craved and lunged after ideals somewhere at hand and "true in themselves."* Overman is extreme *rationalitas* in the empowering of *animalitas;* he is the *animal rationale* that is fulfilled in *brutalitas*. Meaninglessness now becomes the "meaning" of beings as a whole. The unquestionability of Being decides what beings are. Beingness is left to its own devices as liberated machination. Not only must humanity now "make do" without "a truth" but the *essence* of truth itself is dispatched to oblivion. For that reason, it is all a matter of "making do," and of some sort—any sort—of "values."

And yet the age of consummate meaninglessness possesses greater powers of invention, more forms of activity, more triumphs, and more avenues for getting all these things into the public eye than any age hitherto. It is therefore destined to fall prey to the presumption that it is the first age to discover "meaning," the first age to "bestow" meaning on everything that is "worth serving." Of course, the kind of wage it demands for its services has become exorbitant. The age of consummate meaninglessness insists on paving the way for its own essence, insists on it quite boisterously, and even violently. It seeks unthinking refuge in its own peculiar "superworld." It proceeds to the final confirmation of the prepotence of metaphysics in the form of

---

* In both *Beyond Good and Evil* (number 62) and *Toward a Genealogy of Morals* (III, 13; in CM, 5, 81 and 367) Nietzsche defines man as the *"not yet firmly defined animal."* Cf. p. 86, above, and p. 229, below. Heidegger refers to this repeatedly in his later work: see *Was heisst Denken?* (Tübingen: M. Niemeyer, 1954), pp. 24 ff.; in the English translation by Fred D. Wieck and J. Glenn Gray, *What Is Called Thinking?* (New York: Harper & Row, 1968), section VI of Part One; see also the Trakl article in *Unterwegs zur Sprache* (Pfullingen: G. Neske, 1959), pp. 45–46. On the theme of *animalitas* as *brutalitas*, broached in the next lines, see Volume IV, section 22.

Being's abandonment of beings. Thus the age of consummate meaninglessness does not stand on its own. It fulfills the essence of a concealed history—no matter how gratuitously and high-handedly our age seems to treat that subject on the highways and byways of its "histories."

— V —

The essence of modernity is fulfilled in the age of consummate meaninglessness. No matter how our histories may tabulate the concept and course of modernity, no matter which phenomena in the fields of politics, poetry, the natural sciences, and the social order they may appeal to in order to explain modernity, no historical meditation can afford to bypass two mutually related essential determinations within the history of modernity: first, that man installs and secures himself as *subiectum*, as the nodal point for beings as a whole; and secondly, that the beingness of beings as a whole is grasped as the representedness of whatever can be produced and explained. If it is Descartes and Leibniz who give essential shape to the first explicit metaphysical founding of modern history—Descartes by defining the *ens* as *verum* in the sense of *certum*, that is, as the *indubitatum* of *mathesis universalis;* Leibniz by interpreting the *substantialitas* of *substantia* as *vis primitiva* with the fundamental character of a "two-pronged" representing or *repraesentatio**—then the fact that in a history of Being we designate these names and give some thought to them suggests something quite different from the usual observations that have been made

---

* Heidegger refers to Leibniz's *doppel-"stelliger" Vorstellung*, that is, his "two-digit" mode of representation. That may simply refer to the ambiguity by which "representation" designates both the *faculty* and the *content* of representation. More technically, the two prongs in question could be the expansive and even *ecstatic* character of appetitive "primal force" in the monad, which is compelled outward and thus "puts itself forward" (*Vor-stellen*), and the circumspective or *encompassing* character of primal force as *perceptio*. See section 5c of *Metaphysische Anfangsgründe der Logik im Ausgang von Leibniz* (Frankfurt am Main: V. Klostermann, 1978); English translation by Michael Heim, *Metaphysical Foundations of Logic* (Bloomington, Ind.: Indiana University Press, 1984).

in the history of philosophy or in intellectual history concerning these figures.

Those fundamental metaphysical positions are not some supplementary, tangential, or even transcendent conceptual formulation of a history that has its origins elsewhere; nor are they pre-established doctrines that modern history somehow obeys or actualizes on its way to be. In either case the truth of metaphysics, a truth that grounds history, is being thought too extrinsically and too superficially in terms of its immediate impact. Whether we play down or exaggerate its value, we underestimate the matter in question by essentially misunderstanding it. For the determination of man as *subiectum* and of beings as a whole as "world picture" can only have sprung from the history of Being itself—here meaning the history of the transformation and the devastation of its ungrounded truth. (On the concept of "world picture," see the 1938 lecture "The Grounding of the Modern Picture of the World in Metaphysics," published in *Holzwege* in 1950 under the title "The Age of the World Picture."*) Whatever the degree and the direction of any given scientific insight into the transformation of fundamental metaphysical positions; whatever the manner and the extent of any active reordering of beings in the light of this transformation of human beings and of beings as a whole; none of these things ever enters into the orbit of the history of Being itself. They always serve as mere foregrounds that, when understood in terms of the task of the meditation, always merely give themselves out to be the real thing.

The meaninglessness in which the metaphysical articulation of modernity is consummated becomes something we can know as the essential fulfillment of this age only when it is apprehended together with the transformation of man to *subiectum* and the determination of beings as the represented and produced character of the objective. Then it becomes clear that meaninglessness is the prefigured consequence of the finality of modern metaphysics in its very beginnings.

---

* The parenthetical note was added in 1961. See *Holzwege* (Frankfurt am Main: V. Klostermann, 1950), pp. 69–104. An English translation appears in *The Question of Technology and Other Essays*, trans. William Lovitt (New York: Harper & Row, 1978).

Truth as certitude becomes the monotony that is injected into beings as a whole when they are served up for man's securing of permanence, man now having been left to his own devices. This monotony is neither imitation nor empathy with regard to a being that would be true "in itself." Rather, it is a (mis)calculating overpowering of beings through the liberation of beingness into machination. Machination itself means the essence of beingness that is disposed toward the malleability in which everything is made out ahead of time to be "do-able" and altogether at our disposal. Corresponding to this process, representation is the (mis)calculating, securing pacing-off of the horizons that demarcate everything we can perceive along with its explicability and its use.

Beings are released to their possibilities to become; in these possibilities they are made permanent—in accord with machination. Truth as securing univocity grants machination exclusive pre-eminence. When certitude becomes the one and only, beings alone remain essential; never again beingness itself, to say nothing of its clearing. *When Being lacks the clearing, beings as a whole lack meaning.*

The subjectivity of the *subiectum*, which has nothing to do with an individuation that is bound up with the ego, is fulfilled in the calculability and manipulability of everything that lives, in the *rationalitas* of *animalitas*, in which the "overman" finds his essence. The extremity of subjectivity is reached when a particular illusion becomes entrenched—the illusion that all the "subjects" have disappeared for the sake of some transcendent cause that they now all serve. With the completion of modernity history capitulates to historiology, which is of the same essential stamp as technology. The unity of these powers of machination founds a position of power for man. That position is essentially violent. Only within a horizon of meaninglessness can it guarantee its subsistence and, ceaselessly on the hunt, devote itself entirely to one-upmanship.

— VI —

The essential, historic culmination of the final metaphysical interpretation of beingness as will to power is captured in the eternal recurrence of the same, captured in such a way that every possibility for the essence of truth to emerge as what is most worthy of question founders. Meaninglessness now attains power, defining in unconditional terms the horizon of modernity and enacting its fulfillment. The latter does not by any means become perspicuous to itself—that is, to the consciousness that essentially impels and secures historiologically and technologically—as a petrifaction and demise of something that was once achieved. It announces itself rather as an emancipation that step-by-step leaves its former self behind and enhances every thing in every way. The measureless has now disguised itself as self-overpowering power, as that which alone has permanence. Under such a cloak, the measureless can itself become the standard. When the standard of measure is shaped in such a way (as the measurelessness of one-upmanship), measuring rods and pegs can be cut to size, so that everyone now can measure up as painlessly as possible, demonstrating to everyone else all the impressive things he can do and proving to himself that he really must be all right. Such proofs are simultaneously taken to be a verification of goals, avenues, and realms of established efficacy. Everything we can do confirms all that we have already done, and all that we have done cries out for our doing it; every action and thought has committed itself totally to making out what it is that can be done. Everywhere and always machination, cloaking itself in the semblance of a measured ordering and controlling, confronts us with beings as the sole hierarchy and causes us to forget Being. What actually happens is that Being abandons beings: Being lets beings be on their own *and thereby refuses itself.*

Insofar as this *refusal* is experienced, a clearing of Being *has already occurred.* For such refusal is not nothing, is not even negative; it is not some lack, is not something truncated. It is the primordial and initial revelation of Being as worthy of question—of Being as Being.

Everything depends on our inhering in this clearing that is propriated by Being itself—never made or conjured by ourselves. We must overcome the compulsion to lay our hands on everything. We must learn that unusual and singular things will be demanded of those who are to come.

Truth announces the dominion of *its* essence: the clearing of self-concealing. History is the history of *Being*. Those who are struck by the clearing of refusal, those who do not know which way to turn in the face of it, are those who flee meditation: duped too long by beings, they are so alienated from Being that they cannot even come up with a reason to be suspicious of it. Still trapped in utter servitude to a metaphysics they think they have long since suppressed, they seek escape routes to some arcane realm, some world beyond the sensuous. They flee into mysticism (which is the mere counterimage of metaphysics) or, frozen in the posture of calculation, they appeal to "values." "Values," utterly transformed into calculable items, are the only ideals that still function for machination: culture and cultural values as grist for the mill of propaganda, art products as serviceable objects—at exhibitions of our achievements and as decorations for parade floats.

We neither know nor risk something other, something that in times to come will be the *one and only: the truth of Being*. For, however ungrounded it may be, it haunts the first commencement of our history. We neither know nor risk inherence in that truth from which alone world and earth strive to acquire their essence for man. Man experiences in such strife the response of his essence to the god of Being. Prior gods are the gods that have been.

The consummation of metaphysics as the essential fulfillment of modernity is an end only because its historical ground is itself a transition to the other commencement. The latter does not leap outside the history of the first, does not renounce what has been, but goes back into the grounds of the first commencement. With this return it takes on another sort of permanence. Such permanence is not defined in terms of the preservation of any given present thing. It bends to the task of preserving what is to come. What has been in the first commencement is thereby compelled to rest in the abyss of its heretofore ungrounded ground. It thus for the first time becomes history.

Such transition is not progress, nor is it a dreamy voyage from the prior to the new. The transition is seamless, inasmuch as it pertains to the decision of primordial commencement. The latter cannot be grasped by historical retrogressions or by historical maintenance of what has come down to us. Commencement only *is* in commencing. Commencement is the handing-over that is tradition. Preparation of such a commencement takes up that questioning by which the questioner is handed over to that which answers. Primordial questioning itself never replies. For primordial questioning, the sole kind of thinking is one that attunes man to hear the voice of Being. It is a thinking that enables man to bend to the task of guardianship over the truth of Being.

Part Three
NIETZSCHE'S METAPHYSICS

1. Introduction

Like all Western thought since Plato, Nietzsche's thinking is metaphysics. As arbitrary as it might seem at first, let us consider the concept of the essence of metaphysics, while leaving the origin of the concept in obscurity. Metaphysics is the truth of beings as such and as a whole. Truth brings what being is (*essentia*, beingness), the fact that it is, and the way it is as a whole into the unconcealment of *idea*, *perceptio*, representation, and consciousness. But the unconcealed is itself transformed in accordance with the Being of beings. Truth is defined as this very unconcealment in its essence, in disclosure, in terms of the beings it sanctions; it shapes each configuration of its own essence on the basis of Being thus defined. In its own Being, therefore, truth is historical. Truth always demands a humankind through which it is enjoined, grounded, communicated, and thus safeguarded. The truth and its safeguarding belong essentially, indeed historically, together. In this way humankind in each case accepts the decision regarding its allotted manner of being in the midst of the truth of beings. Such truth is essentially historical, not because human being elapses in the course of time, but because mankind is transposed (sent) into metaphysics, and because metaphysics alone is able to ground an epoch insofar as it establishes and *maintains* humankind in a truth concerning beings as such and as a whole.

Beingness (what beings as such are) and the totality of beings (that and how beings as a whole are), as well as the essential mode of truth, the history of truth, and finally, mankind's being transposed into truth for the sake of truth's preservation—these constitute the fivefold way in which the unitary essence of metaphysics unfolds and reconstitutes itself again and again.

Metaphysics, as that truth of beings which belongs to Being, is never primarily the viewpoint and judgment of a single person; it is never merely the doctrinal systems and the expressions of an age. Metaphysics is all these things, but only as aftereffect or veneer. However, the way in which someone who is called upon to preserve truth in thought undertakes the rare joining, grounding, communicating, and safeguarding of truth in its antecedent existential-ecstatic projection, thus indicating and preparing a place for mankind within the history of truth, may be described as the *fundamental metaphysical position* of a thinker. If therefore metaphysics, which belongs to the history of Being itself, is identified with the name of a thinker (as with Plato's metaphysics or Kant's metaphysics), this is not to say that metaphysics is in each case the accomplishment and property or even the personal distinction of these thinkers as personalities engaged in a cultural activity. The identification means that these thinkers are what they are insofar as the truth of Being has been entrusted to them in such a way that they utter Being, that is, utter *the Being of beings* within metaphysics.

With *Daybreak*, published in 1881, a light dawns over Nietzsche's metaphysical path. That same year—"6,000 feet above sea level and much higher above all human things!"—insight into "the eternal return of the same" comes to him (XII, 425). From then on, for almost a decade, he wends his way in the most luminous brightness of this experience. Zarathustra comes to speak. As the teacher of "eternal return" Zarathustra teaches the "overman." He establishes and clarifies the fact that the basic character of beings is "will to power" and that all interpretations of the world, to the extent that they are kinds of *valuations,* derive from will to power. European history reveals its fundamental feature as "nihilism" and plunges toward the necessity of a "revaluation of all values hitherto." The new valuation, stemming from the now decisive, self-professed will to power, demands that its own justification be legislated on the basis of a new "justice."

During the years of Nietzsche's acme, the truth of beings as such and as a whole seeks to come to expression in his thought. One plan for the way to proceed supersedes another. One outline after another reveals the complex that the thinker wants to say. At first the rubric

Introduction

is "eternal return of the same"; it then becomes "will to power" or "the revaluation of all values." When one of these key phrases begins to pall, it appears as a title for the final segment of the entire work, or as a subtitle to the main title. Yet everything comes to bear on the education of those human beings who will "themselves undertake the revaluation" (XVI, 419). They are the "new truth tellers" (XIV, 322), the bearers of a new truth.

Nietzsche's plans and outlines cannot be taken as signs of something unfinished and unmastered. Their alternation does not signify the uncertainty of a first attempt. These sketches are not programs but records in which unmooted yet unmistakable paths are preserved, paths along which Nietzsche had to wander in the realm of the truth of beings as such.

"Will to power," "nihilism," "the eternal return of the same," "the overman," and "justice"* are the five fundamental expressions of Nietzsche's metaphysics.

"Will to power" is the word for the Being of beings as such, the *essentia* of beings. "Nihilism" is the name for the history of the truth of beings thus defined. "Eternal return of the same" means the way in which beings as a whole are, the *existentia* of beings. "Overman" describes the kind of humanity that is demanded by this whole. "Justice" is the essence of the truth of beings as will to power. At the same time, each of these key expressions indicates what the remaining expressions say. Only when what *they* say is also thought *along with* the expression in question will the connotative force of each key expression be exhausted.

The following attempt can be adequately thought only if it is also thought on the basis of the fundamental experience of *Being and Time*. That experience consists in ever-increasing but perhaps also—in a few places—self-clarifying bewilderment in the face of this one event: In the history of Western thought, from its inception, the Being of beings has indeed been thought, but the truth of Being as Being remains unthought; not only is such truth denied as a possible ex-

---

* On *Gerechtigkeit,* here rendered as "justice," see the notes on p. 137, above, and on p. 144 of Volume IV.

perience for thinking, but Western thought, as metaphysics, expressly though unwittingly conceals the occurrence of this refusal.

The following interpretation of Nietzsche's metaphysics must therefore first try to reflect upon Nietzsche's thought as metaphysics in terms of the fundamental experience we have identified; that is to say, in terms of the fundamental features of the history of metaphysics.

Our attempt to interpret Nietzsche's metaphysics therefore aims at both a proximate goal and the most distant goal our thinking can visualize.

Around 1881 or 1882 Nietzsche jotted in his notebook: "The time is coming when the struggle for world domination will be carried on— it will be carried on in the name of *fundamental philosophical doctrines*" (XII, 207). At about the time he wrote this note, Nietzsche began to recognize and discuss these "fundamental philosophical doctrines." The fact that they are evoked in a particular way and in a particular sequence has never been considered. The question as to whether this sequence must have had its basis in the essential unity of these fundamental doctrines has therefore never been asked. The question as to whether the way in which they are evoked casts any light on their essential unity requires a meditation of its own. The hidden unity of the "fundamental philosophical doctrines" constitutes the essential jointures of Nietzsche's metaphysics. On the basis of this metaphysics, and according to the direction it takes, the consummation of the modern age unfolds its history. Presumably, it will be a long history.

The proximate goal of the meditation attempted here is recognition of the inner unity of those fundamental philosophical doctrines. In order to reach this goal, each of these "doctrines" must first be discerned and discussed separately. But the ground that unifies them receives its determination from the essence of metaphysics in general. Only if the dawning age comes to stand on this ground without reservation and without obfuscation can it conduct the "struggle for world domination" on the basis of supreme *consciousness*. For the latter corresponds to the Being that sustains and governs our age.

The struggle for world domination and the unfolding of the meta-

Introduction

physics that sustains it bring to fulfillment an era of earth history and of historical mankind. For here are realized the extreme possibilities of world dominion and of the attempt that man undertakes to decree his own essence purely on his own terms.

With this consummation of the age of Western metaphysics, a still distant yet fundamental historical position is determined that, *following* the outcome of the struggle for power over the earth itself, can no longer hold open and sustain a realm for the struggle. The fundamental position in which the era of Western metaphysics is completed is thus in turn drawn into a contest of a wholly different kind. The contest is no longer a struggle to master beings. Such mastering goes its way and interprets everything "metaphysically," without being able to cope with the essence of metaphysics. Now the contest becomes a confrontation between the power of beings and the truth of Being. To prepare such a confrontation is the farthest goal of the meditation attempted here.

The proximate goal, meditation on the inner unity of Nietzsche's metaphysics as the completion of Western metaphysics, subserves the farthest goal. In terms of chronological order, of course, the goal remains infinitely far from the demonstrable events and circumstances of the present age. But this merely means that it belongs to the historical remoteness of another history.

The farthest remove is nonetheless nearer than what is usually nearby and even closest—granted that historical humanity belongs to Being and its truth; granted that Being never needs to surpass the nearness of beings in the first place; granted that Being is the sole, though still unstipulated, goal of essential thought; and granted that such thought is primordial, that in its other commencement thought must precede even poetic creation in the sense of poetry.

In the following text exposition and interpretation are interwoven in such a way that it is not always immediately clear what has been taken from Nietzsche's words and what has been added to them. Of course, every interpretation must not only take things from the text but must also, without forcing the matter, be able quietly to give something of its own, something of its *own* concerns. This something extra is what the layman, comparing it to what he takes to be the content of the text devoid of all interpretation necessarily deplores as interpolation and sheer caprice.

2. The Will to Power

Anyone at any time can discover for himself what "will" is: willing is striving for something. Each of us knows from his daily experience what "power" is: power is the exercise of force. Finally, what "will *to* power" means is so clear that one hesitates to furnish a special explanation for this conjunction of the words. "Will to power" is evidently striving for the possibility to exercise force, striving for possession of power. Yet the "will *to* power" expresses a "feeling of deficiency." The will "to" is not yet power itself, because it still does not explicitly hold power. To long for something that is not yet there is taken to be symptomatic of romanticism. However, as a drive to seize power, will to power is also at the same time sheer lust for violence. Such interpretations of "will to power," in which romanticism and malevolence would meet, corrupt the sense of this key expression in Nietzsche's metaphysics. For he is thinking something else when he says "will to power."

How should we understand "will to power" in Nietzsche's sense? Will is normally taken as a mental faculty that psychological theory long ago distinguished from understanding and feeling. In fact, Nietzsche too conceives of will to power psychologically. However, he does not describe the essence of will according to traditional psychology; rather, he defines the essence and the task of psychology according to the essence of will to power. Nietzsche demands that psychology be the "morphology and *doctrine of the development of will to power*" (*Beyond Good and Evil,* number 23).

What is will to power? It is "the innermost essence of Being" (WM, 693). That is to say, will to power is the basic character of beings as such. The essence of will to power can therefore be examined and thought only with regard to beings as such; that is, metaphysically. The truth of this projection of beings upon Being in the sense of will to power has a metaphysical character. It tolerates no grounding that would refer it to the nature and disposition of particular beings, because a being invoked *as such* can only be identified if in the first place beings have already been projected upon the basic character of will to power as Being.

Is the projection then simply left to the discretion of an individual thinker? So it would seem. This impression of caprice also afflicts the portrayal of what Nietzsche is thinking when he utters the phrase *will to power*. Yet Nietzsche himself in his published works scarcely spoke of will to power. This may be taken as a sign that he wanted to protect as long as possible what was most intrinsic to his recognition of the truth concerning beings, and to take it into the custody of a uniquely simple saying. Will to power is mentioned, but not yet singled out as a key expression, in the second part of *Thus Spoke Zarathustra* (1883). The title of the episode in which the first sovereign insight into the essence of will to power is achieved offers a clue for the correct understanding of it. In the section "On Self-Overcoming" Nietzsche says: "Where I found the living, there I found will to power, and even in the will of those who serve I found the will to be master." According to this, will to power is the basic character of "life." Nietzsche uses "life" as another word for Being. " 'Being'—we have no other way of representing this than as *'living.'*—How can anything dead 'be'?" (WM, 582). To will, however, is to will to be master. This will prevails even in the willing of one who serves, not insofar as he strives to free himself from his role as underling, but precisely insofar as he is underling and servant, and as such still has the object of his labor beneath him, as an object that he "commands." And insofar as the servant makes himself indispensable to the master as such and so obligates and orients the master to himself (the underling), the underling dominates the master. Being a servant is still a form of will to power. Willing would never be a willing to be master if the will were merely a wishing and striving, instead of being—from top to bottom—a command.

Yet in what does the command have its essence? To command is to be master, to have disposition over the possibilities, kinds, ways, and means of efficacious action. What is commanded in the command is the execution of such disposition. In the command, the one who commands obeys the disposing and thus obeys himself. In this way the one who commands is superior to himself, in that he hazards himself. Commanding is self-overcoming; it is sometimes more difficult than obeying. Only he who cannot obey himself must be commanded. An unsteady light falls on the essence of will to power from the command-character of the will.

However, power is not the goal *toward* which the will tends, as to something outside it. The will does not strive for power; rather, it comes to pass solely within the essential domain of power. Nonetheless, will is not simply power, and power is not simply will. Instead, we can say the following: The essence of power is *will to* power, and the essence of willing is will *to power*. Only on the basis of such knowledge of its essence can Nietzsche say "power" instead of "will," and instead of "will" say simply "power." Yet he never means to assert the equivalence of will and power. Nietzsche does not couple the two as if they were separate at first and only subsequently posited together as a construct. Rather, the combination of words *will to power* names precisely the inseparable unity of a conjoined, unique essence: the essence of power.

Power empowers solely by becoming master over every stage of the power reached. Power is power only if and as long as it is enhancement of power, taking command over the increase in power. Even a mere pause in the enhancement of power, a coming to rest at any stage of power, announces the onset of impotence. To the essence of power pertains the overpowering of itself. Such overpowering arises from power as such, insofar as power is command. As command, power empowers itself for the overpowering of the sundry stages of power. Power is thus continually under way "to" itself—not only to the next stage of power, but also to the attainment of power over its pure essence.

The counteressence of will to power is therefore not "possession" of power, as opposed to mere "striving for power," but "impotence for power" (see *The Antichrist*, VIII, 233). But then will to power signifies nothing else but power for power. Of course. Except that power does not mean the same thing in these two cases; rather, power for power suggests empowering for overpowering. Only when power for power is understood in this way does it touch on the full essence of power. The essence of will as command is bound up with the essence of power. But insofar as commanding is obedience to oneself, the will, corresponding to the nature of power, can be conceived of as the *will-to-will*. "Will" here too suggests different things: on the one hand, commanding, and on the other hand, having disposition over effective possibilities.

Yet if power is power for power and will is will for willing, are not power and will the same? They are the same in the sense of their essential coherence in the unity of *one* essence. They are not the same if that should mean a causal oneness of kind between two otherwise separate entities. There is no more a will for itself than there is power for itself. Will and power, when posited apart, congeal into conceptual fragments that have been artificially sundered from the essence of "will to power." Only will for willing is will, namely, will to power in the sense of power for power.

"Will to power" is the essence of power. Though never merely a *quantum* of power, the *essence* of power is of course the goal of willing, in the essential sense that the will can only be will within the essence of power itself. Thus the will necessarily needs this goal. Consequently, a *horror vacui* reigns in the essence of willing. Vacuity consists in the obliteration of willing, that is, in not-willing. Hence it is said of willing that it "will rather will *nothingness* than *not* to will—" (*Genealogy of Morals*, III, 1). To will "nothingness" here means to will diminution, negation, nullification, and desolation. In such volition power still secures for itself the possibility of command. In this way, negation of the world is itself merely a surreptitious will to power.

Everything that lives is will to power. "To have and to want to have more—in one word, *growth*—that is life itself" (WM, 125). Every mere preservation of life is thus already a decline in life. Power is the command to more power. However, in order that will to power as overpowering be able to advance a stage, that stage must not only be reached but also established and secured. Only from such certainty of power can achieved power be heightened. Therefore, enhancement of power is at the same time in itself the preservation of power. Power can only empower itself to an overpowering by commanding *both* enhancement *and* preservation. This implies that power itself and power alone posits the conditions of enhancement and preservation.

What is the nature of these conditions of the will to power, conditions posited by the will to power itself and thus conditioned by it? Nietzsche answers this question in a note from the final year of his lucid thinking, from 1887 to 1888: "The viewpoint of 'value' is the viewpoint of *conditions of preservation/enhancement* with a view to complex forms of relative life-duration within Becoming" (WM, 715).

The conditions that will to power posits for the empowering of its own essence are viewpoints. Such viewpoints come to be what they are only through the "punctuation" of a particular seeing. Such pointed seeing adopts its "view to complex forms of relative life-duration within Becoming." The seeing that posits such viewpoints provides itself with a prospect on "Becoming." For Nietzsche, the pallid term *Becoming* is replete with a content that proves to be the essence of will to power. Will to power is the overpowering of power. *Becoming* does not mean the indefinite flux of an amorphous alternation of fortuitously occurring states. But neither does *Becoming* mean "development toward a goal." Becoming is the powering advancement through sundry stages of power. In Nietzsche's language, *Becoming* means the animation—holding sway on its own terms—of will to power as the fundamental trait of beings.

Hence all Being is "Becoming." The broad vista onto Becoming is a preview of and perspect into the powering of will to power. It intends only that will to power "be" as such. But this vistalike perspect into the will to power pertains to will to power itself. As the empowering *for* overpowering, will to power is, as Nietzsche says, "perspectival" in a way that previews and "sees through." But the "perspective" is never the mere angle of vision from which something is seen; rather, this perspectival vista looks toward "conditions of preservation/enhancement." As conditions, the "viewpoints" posited in such "seeing" are of such kind that they must be reckoned *on* and reckoned *with*. They take the form of "numbers" and "measures," that is, values. Values "are everywhere *reducible* to this numerical and mensural scale of force" (WM, 710). Nietzsche always understands "force" in the sense of power; that is, as will to power. Number is essentially "perspectival form" (WM, 490). Thus it is bound up with the "seeing" that is proper to will to power, a seeing that in its very essence is reckoning with values. "Value" has the character of "viewpoint." Values "are" not, nor do they have validity "in themselves," in order also occasionally to become "viewpoints." Value is "essentially the viewpoint" of the powering-reckoning seeing of will to power (WM, 715).

Nietzsche speaks of the conditions of will to power when he calls them "conditions of preservation/enhancement." He purposely does not say conditions of preservation *and* enhancement, as if two different things had been brought together, for of course there is really only one. This single, unitary essence of will to power rules the nexus that is proper to it. Both what is overcome, as sundry stages of power, and what overcomes pertain to over-powering. What is to be overcome must put up some resistance; hence it must itself be something constant, which maintains and preserves itself. But what overcomes must also take a stand and be stable, otherwise it could not surpass itself; nor could it advance without wavering and be certain of the possibility for advancement. And, vice versa, all envisaging of preservation is purely for the sake enhancement. Because the Being of beings as will to power is in itself this nexus, the conditions of will to power, that is, values, are tied to "complex constructs." Nietzsche designates these configurations of will to power—for example, science (knowledge), art, politics, and religion—"constructs of domination."

Often he describes as values not simply the conditions of these constructs of domination, but the very constructs of domination themselves. For they provide the ways and means, hence the conditions, under which the world—which is essentially "chaos," and not "organism"—is ordered as will to power. In this way, the initially surprising statement that "science" (knowledge, truth) and "art" are "values" becomes intelligible.

"What is the objective measure of *value*? The quantum of *enhanced* and *organized power* alone" (WM, 674). Insofar as will to power is the fluctuating nexus of preservation and enhancement of power, every construct of domination governed by will to power is both permanent (as what enhances itself) and impermanent (as what preserves itself). Its inner permanence (duration) is therefore essentially relative. Such "relative duration" is proper to "life." Because life prevails only "within Becoming," that is, within will to power, "a fluctuating assessment of the limits of power" accompanies it (WM, 492). Because the character of beings as Becoming is determined on the basis of will to power, "every occurrence, every movement, every becoming" is "as an establishment of relationships of degree and force" (WM, 552). The "complex constructs" of will to power are constructs of "relative life-duration within Becoming."

In this way, every being, because it occurs essentially as will to power, is "perspectival." It is "perspectivism" (that is, the constitution of beings as a reckoning seeing that posits viewpoints), "by virtue of which every center of force—and not only man—construes all the rest of the world from *out of itself;* that is to say, measures, touches, and shapes according to its own force" (WM, 636). "If one wished to escape the world of perspectives one would perish" (XIV, 13).

Will to power is in its innermost essence a perspectival reckoning with the conditions of its possibility, conditions that it itself posits as such. Will to power is in itself value positing. "The question of values is *more fundamental* than that of certainty: the latter becomes serious only if we presuppose that the question of its value has already been settled" (WM, 588). And "*willing* in general is the same as willing to become *stronger,* willing to grow—and *in addition* willing the *means* to do this" (WM, 675).

But the essential "means" are those "conditions" under which the will to power, according to its essence, stands: "values." "In all willing there is estimating—" (XIII, 172). Will to power—and it alone—is the will that wills *values.* It must therefore at last explicitly become and remain what all evaluation proceeds from, and what governs all value estimating: it must become the "principle of valuation." Hence as soon as the basic character of beings is expressly recognized as such in will to power, and as soon as will to power dares to acknowledge itself in this way, then the way we think through beings as such in their truth, that is, truth as the thinking of will to power, inevitably becomes thinking according to values.

The metaphysics of will to power—and it alone—is rightly and necessarily a value thinking. In reckoning with values and in estimating according to relations of value, will to power reckons with itself. The self-consciousness of will to power consists in value thinking, whereby the name *consciousness* no longer signifies a neutral representing, but the powering and empowering reckoning with itself. Value thinking belongs essentially to the very being of will to power, in such a way that it is the *subiectum* (founded on itself, underlying everything). Will to power manifests itself as the subjectivity that is characterized by value thinking. As soon as being as such is experienced by way of such subjectivity, that is, as will to power, all metaphysics must be viewed as the truth concerning beings as such for value thinking in general, that is, for valuation. The metaphysics of will to power interprets all the fundamental metaphysical positions that precede it in the light of valuative thought. Every metaphysical dispute proves to be a decision concerning the hierarchy of values.

3. Nihilism

Plato, with whose thought metaphysics begins, understood beings as such, that is, the Being of beings, as "Idea." The ideas are the *one* in the many, which first appears in the light of the many and only in so appearing *is*. As this unifying one, the ideas are also at the same time the permanent, the true, in contrast with the fluctuating and semblant. Conceived in terms of the metaphysics of will to power, the ideas must be considered as values; and the supreme unities must be thought as the uppermost values. Plato himself clarifies the essence of the idea in terms of the *highest idea,* the idea of the good (*agathon*). For the Greeks, however, "good" meant what makes a thing good *for* something, and thus makes it possible. The ideas, as Being, make beings good for visibility; it makes them be present, that is, makes them be beings. *From that time, Being, as the unifying one in all metaphysics, has had the character of "condition of possibility."* With his determination of Being as objectiveness (objectivity), Kant rendered this character of Being an interpretation defined by the subjectivity of the "I think." On the basis of the subjectivity of will to power, Nietzsche comprehended these conditions of possibility as "values."

Yet Plato's concept of the good did not contain value thinking. Plato's "Ideas" are not values; for the Being of beings is not yet projected as will to power. Nonetheless, on the basis of *his own* fundamental metaphysical position, Nietzsche can regard the Platonic interpretation of beings, the "Ideas," and therefore the suprasensuous, as values. Under this interpretation, all philosophy since Plato becomes the metaphysics of values. Beings as such and as a whole are conceived in terms of the suprasensuous, which at the same time is recognized as true being, whether it be God, as the Christian Creator and Redeemer, or the moral law, or the authority of reason, or progress, or the happiness of the greatest number. The perceptible, that which is immediately present, is measured against desirability, that is, against an ideal. All metaphysics is Platonism. Christianity and all its modern secular forms are "Platonism for the 'people' " (VII, 5). Nietzsche thinks these desirable things as the "uppermost values." Every metaphysics is a "system of value-estimations" or, as Nietzsche says, morality "understood as the doctrine of the relations of supremacy under which the phenomenon 'life' comes to be—" (*Beyond Good and Evil*, number 19).

The interpretation of all metaphysics elaborated by valuative thought is a "moral" interpretation. Yet Nietzsche pursues this interpretation of metaphysics and its history, not as a scholarly, historiological theory of the past, but as a historical decision concerning what is to come. If valuative thought becomes the guideline for a historical meditation on metaphysics as the ground of Western history, then the first thing this implies is that will to power is the sole principle of valuation. When will to power dares to acknowledge itself as the fundamental trait of beings, everything must be assessed in terms of the question of whether it enhances will to power or diminishes and hinders it. As the fundamental trait of beings, will to power conditions all beings in their Being. This highest condition of beings as such is the definitive value.

Insofar as prior metaphysics has not expressly acknowledged it as the principle of valuation, will to power becomes the "principle of a new valuation" for the metaphysics of will to power. Because the metaphysics of will to power conceives of all metaphysics in a moral sense as valuation, such metaphysics comes to be valuation, indeed a "new" valuation. Its novelty consists in its being a "revaluation of all values hitherto."

This revaluation constitutes the complete essence of nihilism. But does not the name *nihilism* already imply that in this doctrine everything is nullity and nothingness, that every willing and every deed are in vain? According to Nietzsche's conception of it, however, nihilism is not a doctrinal tenet; it especially does not mean what a superficial understanding of the term would lead us to imagine, namely, the dissolution of everything into sheer nothingness.

Nietzsche, whose knowledge of nihilism arose from and essentially adhered *to* his metaphysics of will to power, did not exhibit that knowledge in connection with the encompassing metaphysical view of history that hovered before his mind's eye. Moreover, we do not know and are no longer able to extrapolate the pure form of that view from the preserved fragments of his writing. Yet Nietzsche nonetheless did think through what within the domain of his thought was meant by the name *nihilism* in all the aspects, stages, and modes that were essential to him. He set down these thoughts in scattered writings of varying scope and with varying degrees of intensity.

One such note (WM, 2) says: "What does nihilism mean? *That the uppermost values devaluate themselves.* The aim is lacking; the 'why?' receives no answer." Nihilism is the process of the devaluation of the highest values hitherto. The decline of these values is the collapse of all prior truth concerning beings as such and as a whole. The process of the devaluation of the highest values hitherto is therefore not one historical occurrence among many others but is rather the fundamental event of Western history, which has been sustained and guided by metaphysics. Insofar as metaphysics received a particular theological stamp through Christianity, the devaluation of the highest values hitherto must also be expressed theologically through the statement "God is dead." Here "God" means the suprasensuous realm in general, which as the "true" and eternal world "beyond" proclaims itself in opposition to this "earthly" world the only viable goal. If the faith of the Christian Church has grown weary and has forfeited its worldly dominion, the dominance of its God has not yet disappeared. Rather, its form has been disguised and its claims have hardened beyond recognition. In place of the authority of God and Church looms the authority of conscience, or the domination of reason, or the God of historical progress, or the social instinct.

That the highest values hitherto are devalued means that these ideals lose their capacity to shape history. But if the "death of God" and the decline of the uppermost values is nihilism, how can one still assert that nihilism is nothing negative? What drives annihilation more decisively into nullifying nothingness than death, especially the death of God? Although the devaluation of the highest values hitherto is surely proper to nihilism as the fundamental occurrence of Western history, *such devaluation nonetheless does not exhaust its essence.*

The devaluation of the highest values hitherto first of all makes the world seem valueless. These values are indeed devalued, but beings as a whole remain, and the need to establish a truth concerning beings simply grows more pronounced. The indispensability of new values becomes obvious. The positing of new values is announced. A transitional state then arises, through which the contemporary history of our world is passing. This transitional period betrays the fact that the return of the former world of values is still hoped for, indeed still pursued, even though the presence of a new world of values has been detected and—albeit unwillingly—already acknowledged. This intermediate state, in which the historical peoples of the earth must decide on their destruction or on a new beginning, will last as long as the illusion persists that the historic future is still to be rescued from catastrophe by means of a compromise that will mediate between old and new values.

However, the devaluation of the highest values hitherto does not signify a merely relative loss of validity; rather, "the devaluation is the utter collapse of prior values." The collapse implies the absolute necessity of the positing of new values. The devaluation of the highest values hitherto is merely the historical prelude to a historic process whose fundamental feature comes to prevail as revaluation of all prior values. The devaluation of the highest values hitherto is from the start embedded in the concealed yet anticipated revaluation of all values. Nihilism thus does not strive for mere nullity. Its proper essence lies in the affirmative nature of a liberation. Nihilism is the devaluation of previous values, a devaluation that turns to a complete reversal of all values. The basic feature of nihilism as history is concealed in this turning to, which is always deciding itself by reaching far back and at the same time stretching ahead of itself.

But then what meaning is the negative word *nihilism* supposed to have for something that is in essence affirmative? The name secures for the affirmative essence of nihilism the supreme pinnacle of the absolute, which repudiates every mediation. Nihilism then proclaims the following: *Nothing* of the prior valuations shall have validity any longer; all beings must be differently posited *as a whole;* that is, they must as a whole be posited on other conditions. As soon as the world seems to be valueless, due to the devaluation of the highest values hitherto, something extreme comes to the fore, which in turn can be superseded only by some other extreme (WM, 55). The revaluation must be absolute and must transpose all beings into an original unity. The original, anticipatory, unifying unity constitutes the essence of totality. In this unity reigns the determination of the *hen* [the one] that has characterized Being since the dawn of the Western world.

Because the mastery of chaos by the new valuation is brought under the law of the totality through the valuation itself, every human role in establishing the new order must in itself bear the mark of distinction of totality. Historically, therefore, the dominance of the "total" makes its appearance with nihilism. This reveals the emergent fundamental feature of the authentically affirmative essence of nihilism. Naturally, totality never signifies a mere increase in halfway measures; but neither does it mean the amplification of what is familiar, as if the total could be attained through quantitative expansion and an alteration of what already exists. The totality is always grounded in the anticipatory decisiveness of an essential reversal. That is why failure greets every attempt to calculate by means of prior modes of thinking and experiencing the new situation that is to arise in the absolute reversal.

Yet even with the recognition of the affirmative character of European nihilism we have not yet attained to its innermost essence. For nihilism is not merely *one* history, nor even the *fundamental feature* of Western history; it is the lawfulness of this historic occurrence, its "logic." The positing of the uppermost values, their falsification, devaluation, deposition, the appearance of the world as temporarily valueless, the need to replace prior values with new ones, the new positing as a revaluation, and the preliminary stages of this revaluation— all these things describe the proper lawfulness of those value-estimations in which an interpretation of the world is to be rooted.

Such lawfulness marks the historicity of Western history experienced in terms of the metaphysics of will to power. As the lawfulness of history, nihilism develops in itself as a sequence of sundry stages and configurations. Hence the bare name *nihilism* says too little, because it oscillates in ambiguity. Nietzsche rejects the idea that nihilism is the cause of the decline by indicating that nihilism, as the "logic" of the decline, surpasses the decline itself. Rather, the cause of nihilism is morality, in the sense of the positing of supernatural ideals of truth, goodness, and beauty that are valid "in themselves." The positing of the highest values simultaneously posits the possibility of their devaluation, which already begins when these values show themselves to be unattainable. Life thus appears to be unsuitable and utterly incompetent for the realization of these values. For that reason, pessimism is the "preliminary form" of nihilism proper (WM, 9).

Pessimism negates the existing world. Yet its negating is ambiguous. It can simply will decay and nothingness, but it can also renounce what exists and thus open a path for a new formation of the world. In the latter way pessimism proves to be "strong." It keeps an eye out for what is. It sees what is dangerous and uncertain and searches for conditions that promise mastery over our historical condition. A capacity for "analysis" characterizes the pessimism of strength, by which Nietzsche does not mean an agitated dissection and disentanglement of our "historical situation," but the cool—cool because cognizant—explanation and demonstration of the reasons why things are as they are. In contrast, the pessimism that sees only decay comes from "weakness"; it looks on the dark side of everything; it is on the lookout for new opportunities for failure, so that it can predict how they will all turn out. It understands everything, and for everything that occurs it can cite an analogous event from the past. To distinguish it from "analysis," Nietzsche characterizes it as "historicism" (WM, 10).

Now, quite extreme positions develop as a result of this ambiguity in pessimism. They circumscribe a realm from which the proper essence of nihilism emerges in several stages. The immediate outcome is once again an "intermediate state." At first, only "imperfect nihilism" emerges; then "extreme nihilism" ventures forth. Although "imperfect nihilism" denies the highest values hitherto, it nonetheless merely posits new ideals in the old places (in place of "early Christianity" it posits "communism"; in place of "dogmatic Christianity" it posits "Wagnerian music"). Such halfway measures postpone the decisive overthrow of the uppermost values. Such prolongation conceals what is decisive, namely, that with the devaluation of the highest values hitherto the place accorded them—the "suprasensuous" realm existing in itself—must above all be eliminated.

In order to become perfect, nihilism must pass through "extremes." "Extreme nihilism" recognizes that there is no "eternal truth in itself." Insofar as it rests content with this insight, and merely observes the decline of the highest values hitherto, it remains "passive." In opposition to it, "active" nihilism now takes charge and revolts by removing itself from the former way of life; straightaway it endows whatever wants to die with a "longing for the end" (WM, 1055).

And yet such nihilism is not supposed to be negative? Does not Nietzsche himself confirm the purely negative character of nihilism in that impressive description of the nihilist that says: "A nihilist is a man who judges of the world as it is that it ought *not* to be, and of the world as it ought to be that it does not exist" (WM, 585 A)? Here absolutely everything is negated in a twofold negation: first the world at hand and then just as quickly the suprasensuous world, the ideal world desired by this existing world. Yet behind this double negation there stands the simple affirmation of the one world that dispenses with what has gone before and installs the new from out of itself, no longer acknowledging an inherently subsistent superior world.

Extreme but active nihilism evicts prior values together with their "space" (the suprasensuous) and offers prime possibilities to the new valuation. With regard to this character of extreme nihilism, which makes space and steps into the open, Nietzsche also speaks of "ecstatic nihilism" (WM, 1055). While giving the impression of remaining a simple negation, such nihilism affirms neither something at hand nor an ideal, but the *"principle of value-estimation,"* to wit, the will to power. As soon as this is expressly conceived as the ground and measure of all valuation, nihilism has accommodated itself to its affirmative essence, has overcome and incorporated its imperfection, and so has completed itself. Ecstatic nihilism becomes "classical nihilism." That is how Nietzsche conceives of his own metaphysics. Where will to power is the professed principle of valuation, nihilism comes to be the "ideal of the *supreme degree of powerfulness* of spirit" (WM, 14). Inasmuch as every being that would exist in itself is denied, and will to power as the origin and measure of creating is affirmed, "nihilism could . . . *be a divine way of thinking*" (WM, 15). Here Nietzsche is thinking the divinity of the god Dionysos.

The affirmative essence of nihilism simply cannot be stated more affirmatively. According to its full metaphysical concept, then, nihilism is the history of the annihilation of the highest values hitherto on the basis of the anticipatory revaluation that knowingly acknowledges will to power as the principle of valuation. Revaluation therefore does not mean merely that new values are posited in the old familiar place of the prior values, but first and foremost *that the place itself is newly determined.*

This implies that values are first posited *as* values in the "re-valuation"; that is, they are conceived in their essential ground as conditions of will to power. The essence of will to power offers the possibility of thinking "the Dionysian" metaphysically.

Strictly considered, re-valuation re-thinks beings as such and as a whole on the basis of "values." This implies that the fundamental character of beings as such is will to power. Only when it is "classical" does nihilism attain its proper essence. Considered as "classical," "nihilism" is at the same time the title for the historical essence of metaphysics, insofar as the truth concerning beings as such and as a whole is fulfilled in the metaphysics of will to power and the history of that truth interpreted by means of such metaphysics.

Yet if being as such is will to power, how does Nietzsche define the entirety of beings as a whole? Posed in terms of the valuative, revaluative metaphysics of classical nihilism, this question asks: What value does the totality of beings have?

4. The Eternal Return of the Same

The total value of the world cannot be evaluated (WM, 708).
This principle of Nietzsche's metaphysics does not merely mean to say that it is beyond human capacities to discover the total value, which nevertheless exists in some hidden way. Surely, it is inherently impossible even to search for a total value of beings, since the concept of a total value is a nonconcept, inasmuch as value is essentially the condition posited by, and thus conditioned by, will to power for its own preservation and enhancement. To posit a total value for the totality would mean to subjugate the absolute under conditioned conditions.

Hence it follows that "Becoming" (that is, beings as a whole) *"has no value at all"* (WM, 708). Again, this does not say that beings as a whole are null or indifferent. The sentence has an essential sense. It expresses the value-lessness of the world. Nietzsche conceives all "meaning" as "purpose" and "end," and conceives of purpose and end as values (cf. WM, 12). Consequently, he can say that "absolute *val*uelessness, that is, *mean*inglessness" (WM, 617), "aimlessness in itself," is "a fundamental tenet of faith" for the nihilist (WM, 25).

However, in the meantime we have learned no longer to think nihilism "nihilistically" as complete dissolution into vacuous nothingness. Neither, then, can valuelessness or aimlessness any longer signify a lack or mere vacuity and absence. These nihilistic epithets touching beings as a whole mean something affirmative that occurs essentially; that is, they mean the *way in which* the whole of beings comes to presence. The metaphysical expression for this is the eternal return of the same.

What is strange in this thought, which Nietzsche himself in a multiple sense called the "most burdensome thought," can only be grasped by one who is first of all concerned to preserve its strangeness; indeed, to recognize that strangeness as the reason why the thought of the "eternal return of the same" pertains to the truth concerning beings as a whole. Almost more important at first than the explanation of its content, therefore, is insight into the context within which alone the eternal return of the same, as the definition of beings as a whole, is to be thought.

We observe that being, which *as such* has the fundamental character of will to power, can *as a whole* only be eternal return of the same. And, vice versa, being, which *as a whole* is eternal return of the same, must *as being* manifest the fundamental character of will to power. The beingness of beings and the entirety of beings in turn evoke from the unity of the truth of being the form of their particular essence.

The will to power posits perspectival conditions of its own preservation and enhancement, that is, values. In their character as ends, posited and therefore conditioned ends, values must plainly correspond to the essence of power. Power knows no ends "in themselves" in which it could come to rest. In coming to rest, it would repudiate its innermost essence, namely, overpowering. Of course, ends are what power is concerned with. But the concern is for overpowering. Such overpowering develops to its apex wherever there are obstacles. Thus the ends of power always betray the character of impediments. Because the ends of power can only be impediments, they always already lie within the radius of will to power. The impediment, even when it is not "taken" as such, is still essentially overcome by empowering. Thus for being as will to power there are no ends outside its own, to which it progresses and from which it sallies forth.

Overpowering itself, will to power essentially *goes back into itself* and so grants beings as a whole, that is, "Becoming," its unique character of animation. The movement of the world thus arrives at no final state that might exist somewhere for itself, assimilating Becoming, as it were, like the delta of a river. On the other hand, will to power does not merely posit its conditioned ends on occasion. As overpowering it is continually under way toward its essence. It is eternally active and must at the same time be end-less, insofar as "end" means a state

The Eternal Return of the Same

subsisting independently outside it. However, the end-less and eternally empowered character of will to power is at the same time finite in its positions and configurations (XII, 53). For if it were infinite in these respects, then it would also, in accord with its essence as enhancement, have to be "infinitely expanding." Yet from what surplus could such enhancement come, if all being is will to power alone?

Furthermore, the essence of will to power itself requires for its preservation, and thereby precisely for any possibility of its enhancement, that it be delineated and determined in a fixed form; that is, that as a whole it already be something self-limiting. Freedom of ends, and therefore endlessness in general, pertain to the essence of power. Yet the freedom of ends, precisely because it alone goes on demanding the conditioned positing of ends, cannot tolerate an unrestrained flood of power. The whole of beings, whose fundamental character is will to power, must therefore be a fixed magnitude. Instead of "will to power," Nietzsche sometimes also says "force." He always understands force (especially natural forces) as will to power. "Something *un*fixed with respect to power, something undulant, is *totally unthinkable for us*" (XII, 57).

Who is meant by "us"? "We" are those who think being as will to power. "Our" thought, however, is a fixing and a delimiting. "The world as force dare not be thought of as unbounded, for it *cannot* be so thought of; we forbid ourselves the concept of an *infinite* force *as incompatible with the concept 'force.'* Thus—the world also lacks the capacity for eternal novelty" (WM, 1062). Who is forbidden here to think will to power as unlimited? Who arrogates the power to claim that will to power and the whole of beings determined by it are finite? Who? Those who have experienced their own Being as will to power, those for whom "every other representation remains indefinite, and therefore *useless—*" (WM, 1066).

If being as such is will to power and thus eternal Becoming, and if will to power demands end-lessness and excludes endless progress toward an end in itself; if at the same time the eternal Becoming of will to power is delimited in its possible configurations and constructs of domination, because it cannot be new unto infinity; then being as a whole as will to power must permit the same to recur and must be an eternal return of the same. This "circuit" embodies the "primal law" of beings as a whole, if being as such is will to power.

Eternal return of the same is the way in which the impermanent (that which becomes) as such comes to presence; it comes to presence in the highest form of permanence (in circling), with the sole determination of securing its possiblity to be empowered. The recurrence, arrival, and departure of beings, defined as eternal return, everywhere has the character of will to power. The equivalence of the recurring same thus first of all consists in the fact that in every being the empowering of power commands and, as a result of this command, conditions an equivalence in the qualities of beings. Return of the same never means that for some observer, whose being would not be determined by will to power, something that was previously at hand comes to be present again and again.

"Will to power" says *what* a being as such is, namely, what it is in its constitution. "Eternal return of the same" says *how* being is as a whole when it is so constituted. The "how" of the Being of all beings is determined in tandem with the "what." The "how" affirms from the outset *that* every being at every moment receives the character of its "that" (its "factuality") from its "how." Because eternal return of the same distinguishes beings as a whole it is a fundamental character of Being, belonging as one with will to power, even though "eternal recurrence" designates a "Becoming." The same that recurs has only relative stability and is therefore essentially unstable. Its recurrence, however, signifies a continual bringing back into stability, that is, a permanentizing. Eternal recurrence is the most constant permanentizing of the unstable. Since the beginning of Western metaphysics, Being has been understood in the sense of permanence of presencing, whereby permanence has ambiguously meant both fixity and persistence. Nietzsche's concept of the eternal recurrence of the same expresses the same essence of Being. Nietzsche of course distinguishes Being as the stable, firm, fixed, and rigid, in contrast to Becoming. But Being nonetheless pertains to will to power, which must secure stability for itself by means of permanence, solely in order to be able to surpass itself; that is, in order *to become*.

Being and Becoming are only apparently in opposition, because the character of Becoming in will to power is in its innermost essence eternal recurrence of the same and thus the constant permanentizing of the unstable. Hence Nietzsche can say in one of his most decisive notes (WM, 617*):

> *Recapitulation.* To *stamp* Becoming with the character of Being—that is the supreme *will to power.*
>
> *Twofold falsification,* one by the senses, the other by the mind, in order to preserve a world of being, of perdurance, of equivalence, etc.
>
> That *everything recurs* is the closest *approximation of a world of Becoming to one of Being: peak of the meditation.*

At the apex of his thought, Nietzsche must follow the fundamental lines of that thought to its extreme and define the world with regard to its *Being.* Thus he projects and enjoins the truth of beings in the direction taken by metaphysics. Yet at the same time it is stated at the "peak of the meditation" that in order to preserve a world of beings, that is, of what is perdurantly present, a *"twofold falsification"* is necessary. The senses grant us something that is fixed in sense impressions. Mind fixes what is objective by means of representation. What occurs in each case is a different fixation of what is otherwise animated and in Becoming. As such a permanentizing of Becoming, the "supreme will to power" would be a falsification. Something false and illusory must have been installed at the "peak of the meditation," where the truth concerning beings as such and as a whole is decided. Accordingly, truth would be an error.

As a matter of fact, it is. The truth is indeed essentially error for Nietzsche, especially that definite "kind of error" whose character is adequately delineated only when the origin of the essence of truth is expressly acknowledged in terms of the essence of Being, and that here means in terms of will to power. The eternal recurrence of the same

---

* See the note on WM, 617 in Volume II of this series, pp. 201–2, and my comment in a long note on p. 257 of that volume. The Analysis in the present volume takes up this important matter once again. Meanwhile, note that in the following quotation and its discussion Heidegger does *not* omit the statement that begins "Twofold falsification. . . ." The first line of WM, 617 is cited on p. 156, above, and p. 245, below.

says *how* the universe of beings, which has no value and no end in itself, *is* as a whole. The value-lessness of beings as a whole, apparently a merely negative determination, is grounded in an affirmative determination by which the entirety of the eternal return of the same is allotted in advance to beings. However, this fundamental trait of the character of beings as a whole also forbids us to think the world as an "organism," for it is enjoined in no self-subsistent context and points to no final state in itself. "We must think it [the universe] as a totality at the greatest possible distance from the organic" (XII, 60). Only if being as a whole is chaos will the ongoing possibility of forming itself "organically" in delimited constructs of dominance of relative duration be guaranteed it as will to power. "Chaos," however, does not mean blindly raging confusion, but the manifoldness of beings as a whole, which is always pressing for the ordering of power, always demarcating boundaries of power, and always weighted toward a decisive outcome in the struggle to delineate power.

The thought that such chaos in its totality is the eternal return of the same first becomes the strangest and most frightful thought when we attain and take seriously the insight that the thinking of this thought must have the essential form of a metaphysical projection. The truth concerning beings as such and as a whole is defined solely by the Being of beings itself. It is not a thinker's personal experience, confined to an area where personal points of view are valid; nor is it a truth that can be proven "scientifically," that is, by researching individual regions of beings, such as nature or history.

That Nietzsche himself, in his passionate desire to lead his contemporaries to this "peak" of his metaphysical "meditation," had recourse to such proofs merely indicates how rarely and with what difficulty one is able to maintain oneself as a thinker on the path of any projection—and its grounding—demanded by metaphysics. Nietzsche had lucid knowledge concerning the ground of the truth of that projection which thinks beings as a whole as eternal return of the same: "Life itself created the thought which is most burdensome for life; it wants to *surpass* its greatest obstacle!" (XII, 369). "Life itself": that is will to power, surpassing itself toward itself by overpowering sundry stages of power to its zenith.

The will to power must learn to confront itself as will to power, indeed in such a way that the supreme condition for the pure empowering toward its extreme overpowering stands before it as its greatest obstacle. This happens when the purest form of permanentizing stands before it, not merely once, but continually, and always as the same. In order to secure this supreme condition (value), will to power must be the explicitly appearing "principle of valuation." It lends whatever weight survives to *this* life alone, not to a life beyond. "To re*teach* in this regard is now always the main concern:—perhaps *if* metaphysics touched upon *this* life with the *heaviest* accent,—according to my teaching!" (XII, 68).

This is the doctrine promulgated by the teacher of the eternal return of the same. Will to power itself, the fundamental character of beings as such, and not "Herr Nietzsche," posits the thought of eternal return of the same. The supreme permanentizing of the unstable is the greatest obstacle for Becoming. Through this obstacle, will to power affirms the innermost necessity of its essence. For in this way the eternal return of the same in turn brings its conditioning power to bear on worldplay. Under the pressure of this heavy burden, in which the relation to beings as such and as a whole essentially determines individual beings, the Being of beings must be experienced as will to power. Yet the being that is determined through that relation is man. The experience mentioned transfers mankind to a new truth concerning beings as such and as a whole. However, because the relationship to beings as such and as a whole distinguishes man, he first attains his essence when he inheres in such a relationship and commits himself to history for that history's consummation.

5. The Overman

The truth concerning beings as such and as a whole is taken up, enjoined, and safeguarded by humanity. Metaphysics is unable to think or even to ask why this is so; it is scarcely capable of thinking *that* it is so. The affinity of the human essence to the preservation of beings is in no way captured in the fact that in modern metaphysics every being is an object for a subject. The interpretation of beings in terms of subjectivity is itself metaphysical and is already a hidden consequence of the concealed relationship of Being itself with the essence of man. This relationship cannot be thought in terms of the subject-object relation. For the latter is precisely the necessary mistaking and ongoing concealment of both the relationship and the possibility of experiencing it. Therefore, the essential provenance of anthropomorphism, which is necessary for the completion of metaphysics, and its result, to wit, provenance of the dominion of anthropologism, are riddles for metaphysics that metaphysics cannot even perceive as such. Because man belongs to the essence of Being and from such belonging is destined to an understanding of Being, beings in their different regions and hierarchies are subject to the possibility of research and mastery by man.

However, the human being who in the midst of beings comports himself toward that being which as such is will to power and as a whole is eternal return of the same is called *the overman*. His actualization implies that being, in will to power's character as Becoming, appears in the light of the most luminous brightness of the thought of eternal recurrence of the same. "When I had created the overman, I arranged about him the great veil of Becoming and let the midday sun stand over him" (XII, 362). Because will to power, as the principle of revaluation, permits history to appear in the basic lineaments of classical nihilism, the mankind of this history must also confirm itself to itself within it.

The *over* in the name *overman* contains a negation; it signifies a going up and "over" man as he has been heretofore. The no of this negation is absolute, in that it comes from the yes of will to power. It directly concerns the Platonic, Christian-moral interpretation of the world in all its overt and covert transformations. Thinking metaphysically, this negative affirmation steers the history of mankind toward a new history. The universal, though not exhaustive, concept of "overman" means primarily the essence of that mankind which in the *history* of nihilism thinks itself in a modern way, that is to say, wills itself. Thus the herald of the doctrine of overman bears the name *Zarathustra*. "I had to give Zarathustra, a *Persian*, the honor: the Persians were the first to *think* history as a whole, in broad outline" (XIV, 303). In his "Prologue," which previews everything that is to be said, Zarathustra states: "Behold, I teach you the overman! The overman is the meaning of the earth. Let your will say: the overman *shall be* the meaning of the earth!" (*Thus Spoke Zarathustra*, "Prologue," section 3). The overman is the expressly willed negation of the previous essence of man. Within metaphysics man is experienced as the rational animal (*animal rationale*). The "metaphysical" origin of this essential definition of man, a definition that sustains all Western history, has to this hour not been understood, has not been made a matter of decision for thinking. This means that our thought has not yet emerged from the division between the metaphysical question of Being, which asks about the Being of beings, and the question that inquires more primordially; that is, inquires into the truth of Being and thus into the relationship of the essence of Being with the essence of man. Metaphysics itself refuses to question this essential relationship.

The overman certainly negates the former essence of man, but he negates it nihilistically. His negation concerns the distinctive feature of man hitherto, his reason. The metaphysical essence of reason consists in the fact that being as a whole is projected as a guideline for representational thought and is interpreted as such.

Metaphysically understood, thought is the perceptual representation of that in which being is in each case being. Nihilism, on the contrary, conceives of thought (understanding) as the reckoning that is proper to will to power, a reckoning on and with the securing of permanence as valuation. In the nihilistic interpretation of metaphysics and its history, thought, that is, reason, therefore appears as the ground and standard of the positing of values. The "unity" of all beings existing "in itself," the final "purpose" of all present beings "in itself," the truth for all beings valid "in itself"—these derive as such from values posited by reason. However, the nihilistic negation of reason does not exclude thought (*ratio*); rather, it relegates thought to the service of animality (*animalitas*).

Yet animality too is likewise already inverted. It no longer passes for mere sensuality and what is base in man. Animality is the body bodying forth, that is, replete with its own overwhelming urges. The name *body* identifies the distinctive unity in the constructs of domination in all drives, urges, and passions that will life itself. Because animality lives only by bodying, it is as will to power.

To the extent that will to power constitutes the fundamental trait of all beings, animality first destines man to be a true being. Reason is living reason only as bodying reason. All man's faculties are metaphysically predetermined as ways of enjoining power over what is empowered. *Thus Spoke Zarathustra,* Part One, "On the Despisers of the Body":

> But the awakened and knowing say: I am body entirely, and nothing else; soul is merely a word for something about the body. The body is a great reason, a plurality with one meaning, a war and a peace, a herd and a shepherd. An instrument of your body is also your little reason, my brother, which you call "spirit"—a little instrument and toy of your great reason.

The essential distinction of man in prior metaphysics, his rationality, is transposed into animality in the sense of bodying will to power.

Yet Western metaphysics does not define man simply and homologously in every epoch as a creature of reason. The metaphysical inception of the modern age first manifests the historic unfolding of that role in which reason attains its full metaphysical rank. Only on the basis of that rank can we estimate what it is that happens when reason reverts to an animality that has itself been reversed. The status of reason as modern metaphysics alone, reason having developed into the absolute, conceals the metaphysical origin of the essence of overman.

The metaphysical inception of the modern age is a change in the essence of truth, a change whose ground remains hidden. Truth comes to be certitude. Certitude lies solely and entirely in securing represented beings, a securing that can fulfill itself in representation. The jointure of the essence of representation wholly conforms to the change within the essence of truth. From the beginning of metaphysics until now, representation (*noein*) has been that perceiving which does not take beings in passively, but which can actively give to itself what is present as such in its outward appearance (*eidos*) by gazing up at it.

Such perceiving now becomes perception in the judgmental sense of being correct and asserting correctly. Representation inspects everything encountering it from *out* of itself and with reference *to* itself, inspects it with regard to whether and how it relates to what representation—as a bringing before oneself in order to make secure—requires for its own certainty. Representation is now no longer a mere guideline for the perception of beings as such; that is to say, it is no longer perception of the permanent that comes to presence. Representation comes to be the tribunal that decides about the beingness of beings and declares that in the future only what is placed before it in and through representation and thus is secured for it may be considered a being. Nevertheless, in such placing-before-itself representation necessarily *co*represents itself; but it does not represent itself only subsequently, and certainly not as an object; rather, it represents itself first of all as that before which everything has to be mustered and within whose radius alone any particular thing can be secured.

Of course, self-representing representation can decide about the beingness of beings in such a way only because as a tribunal it not only passes judgment according to a law, but also itself proclaims the law of Being. Representation can decree this law only because it already possesses it. And it possesses the law insofar as it has first of all made itself its own law. The transfer of the jointure of the essence of prior representation consists in the fact that the representing bringing-before-oneself of all that ever encounters us establishes itself as the Being of beings. Permanence of presencing, that is, beingness, now consists in representedness through and for such representation; it consists in such representation itself.

Formerly every being was a *subiectum*, something lying before us on its own basis. For that reason alone it underlay (*hypokeimenon, substans*) everything that arises or passes away, everything that comes into Being (into presencing, by way of lying-before) or departs from it. The beingness (*ousia*) of beings in all metaphysics is subjectivity in that original sense. The more familiar name for this, but one that does not suggest anything different, is *substantiality*. Medieval mysticism (Tauler and Seuse) translates *subiectum* and *substantia* as *understand* [what stands beneath] and in a correspondingly literal way *obiectum* as *gegenwurf* [thrown over against]. *

At the inception of the modern age the beingness of beings changed. The essence of that historical inception consists in this very change. The subjectivity of the *subiectum* (substantiality) is now defined as self-representing representation. Yet it is man, as rational creature, who is in a distinctive sense self-representing representation. Thus man becomes a distinctive being (*subiectum*), becomes the "definitive" "subject." Through the designated change in the metaphysical essence of subjectivity the name *subjectivity* preserves and maintains its unique meaning for the future: the Being of beings consists in representation. Subjectivity in the modern sense is contrasted with substantiality and is finally absorbed in it. Hence the decisive demand made by Hegel's metaphysics runs like this: "According to my own view, which can be justified only in the exposition of the system itself, everything depends on our grasping and expressing the true, not as *substance*, but every

---

* Note that *understand* is not the English word (which is obviously related to the present context!) but a Middle High German construction meaning, literally, "what *stands under* or *undergirds* a thing." Heinrich Seuse (or Suso) and Johann Tauler were Meister Eckhart's most influential disciples, Seuse in Constance (1300–1336), Tauler in Strasbourg (1300–1361).

The Overman

bit as much, as *subject.*"* The metaphysical essence of subjectivity is not fulfilled in "I-ness," much less in the egoism of man. The "I" is always only a possible, and in certain situations the proximate, occasion in which the essence of subjectivity professes itself and seeks an accommodation for its profession. Subjectivity, as the Being of any particular being, is never merely "subjective" in the pejorative sense of being the random opinion of an individual I.

Therefore, if with regard to subjectivity so understood we wish to speak of the subjectivism of modern thought, we must completely reject any notion that it is a question here of something "merely subjective," of egoistic and solipsistic opinion and affectation. For the essence of subjectivism is objectivism, insofar as everything becomes an object for the subject. The nonobjective—the nonobjectival—too is determined by the objective, by a relation of opposition to it. Because representation puts into representedness what encounters us and shows itself, the being that is mustered in this way comes to be an "object."

All objectivity is "subjective." This does not mean that being comes to be a mere point of view and opinion set down by some casual and arbitrary "I." That all objectivity is "subjective" means that what encounters us comes to be established as an object standing in itself. "Beingness is subjectivity" and "Beingness is objectivity" say the selfsame thing.

Inasmuch as representation is first of all concerned with securing everything that encounters us as something represented, it continuously expands the range of what is to be represented. In this way representation proceeds by extending itself beyond itself. Thus representation is *in itself,* not extrinsically, a striving. It strives for the fulfillment of its essence, that it might define in terms of representation,

---

* Heidegger cites Hegel's *Phenomenology of Spirit* in the following editions: "*System der Wissenschaft. Erster Teil, die Phänomenologie des Geistes*" (Berlin: Duncker und Humblot, for the *Verein von Freunden des Verewigten*), 1832, II, p. 14; in the first edition of 1807, published in Bamberg and Würzburg by Joseph Anton Goebhardt, p. xx. Today see the "Philosophische Bibliothek" edition (Hamburg: F. Meiner, 6th ed., 1962), p. 19.

as representing its beingness, everything that encounters us and is self-impelled. Leibniz defines subjectivity as a striving representing. With this insight the full inception of modern metaphysics is first reached (see the *Monadology,* paragraphs 14 and 15*). The monad, that is, the subjectivity of the subject, is *perceptio* and *appetitus* (cf. also *Principes de la Nature et de la Grace, fondés en raison,* paragraph 2). Subjectivity as the Being of beings means that outside the legislation of self-striving representation there may "be" and can "be" nothing that might still condition such representation.

Now, however, the essence of subjectivity of itself necessarily surges toward absolute subjectivity. Kant's metaphysics resists this essential thrust of Being—while at the same time laying the ground for its fulfillment. That is because Kant's metaphysics for the first time subsumes utterly the concealed essence of subjectivity, which is the essence of Being as conceived in metaphysics, under the concept of Being as beingness—in the sense of the condition of the possibility of beings.

As such a condition, however, Being cannot itself be conditioned by a being, that is, by something that is itself conditioned. Being can only condition itself. Only as absolute self-legislation is representation—that is to say, reason in the sovereign and wholly developed fullness of its essence—the Being of all beings. Self-legislation, however, characterizes the "will," insofar as its essence is determined on the horizon of pure reason. Reason, as striving representation, is at the same time will. The absolute subjectivity of reason is willful self-knowledge. This means that reason is absolute spirit. As such, reason is the absolute reality of the real, the Being of beings. Reason itself

---

* Paragraph 14 of Leibniz's *Monadology* (1714) begins: "The passing state, which involves and represents a multitude in unity or in the simple substance, is nothing else than what is called *perception,* which must be distinguished from apperception or consciousness. . . ." Paragraph 15 reads: "The action of the internal principle which causes the change or the passage from one perception to another, may be called *appetition*; it is true that desire cannot always completely attain to the whole perception to which it tends, but it always attains something of it and reaches new perceptions." These points are reiterated in the Leibnizian text cited below, *The Principles of Nature and of Grace, Founded in Reason,* also from the year 1714, in paragraph 2. See also Heidegger's discussion, including my suggestion for further reading, on pp. 178–79.

is solely in the mode of Being that is enjoined by it, in that it brings itself to appearance in all the stages of self-striving representation that are essential to it.

"Phenomenology" in Hegel's sense is Being's bringing-itself-to-concept as absolute self-appearing. Here phenomenology does not mean a particular thinker's way of thinking, but the manner in which absolute subjectivity as absolute self-appearing representation (thinking) *is* itself the Being of all beings. Hegel's *Logic* belongs within the *Phenomenology* because in it absolute subjectivity's appearing to itself becomes absolute only when the conditions of all appearance, the "categories," are in their most proper self-representation and disclosure, as "logos," brought into the visibility of the absolute idea.

The absolute and complete appearance of self in the light that it itself is constitutes the essence of the freedom of absolute reason. Although reason is will, here it is reason as representation (idea) that nonetheless decides the beingness of beings. Representation distinguishes what is represented in contrast to and for the one who is representing. Representation is essentially this differentiating and dividing. Hegel therefore says in the "Preface" to the whole "System of Science": "The act of dividing is the force and the labor of the *understanding*, of the most wonderful and grandest, or rather, of absolute power."*

Only if reason in this form develops metaphysically as absolute subjectivity, and thus as the Being of beings, can the reversal of the earlier preeminence of reason into the preeminence of animality of itself become absolute—which is to say, nihilistic. The nihilistic negation—not the utter elimination—of absolute reason's metaphysical *preeminence*, which determines Being, is affirmation of the absolute role of the body as the command post of all world interpretation. *Body* is the name for that configuration of will to power in which the latter is always immediately accessible, because it is always within the province of man identified as "subject." Nietzsche therefore says: "Essential: to start from the *body* and employ it as the guideline" (WM, 532; cf.

---

* Heidegger cites Hegel's *Werke* (1832–45), II, p. 25; cf. "Philosophische Bibliothek," p. 29.

also 489 and 659*). However, if the body becomes the guideline for interpreting the world, this does not imply that the "biological" and "vital" are transposed to beings as a whole and that beings are being thought "vitally"; rather, it means that the special domain of the "vital" is conceived metaphysically as will to power. "Will to power" is nothing "vital" and nothing "spiritual." On the contrary, "vital" ("living") and "spiritual" are determined as beings by Being in the sense of will to power. Will to power subsumes reason in the sense of representation under itself by taking it into its service as calculative thinking (the positing of values). The rational will that previously served representation is altered in essence to the will that commands itself as the Being of beings.

In the nihilistic inversion of the preeminence of representation to the preeminence of the will as will to power, the will first achieves absolute dominion in the essence of subjectivity. The will is no longer merely self-legislation for representational reason, which is active only as representing. The will is now pure self-legislation of itself: a command to achieve its essence, which is commanding as such, the pure powering of power.

Through this nihilistic inversion, not only is the inverted subjectivity of representation reversed to the subjectivity of willing, even the previous essence of absoluteness is assailed and transformed through the essential priority of willing. The absoluteness of representation is

---

* For WM, 489 (that is, N VII 3 [56]; Summer 1886 to Fall 1887), see now CM, *12*, 205–6:

> Everything that enters consciousness as a "unity" is by that time a vastly complicated thing: we always have merely an *illusion of unity*.
>
> The phenomenon of the *body* is the richer, clearer, more palpable phenomenon: methodologically to be placed first, without determining anything about its ultimate significance.

WM, 659 consists of two fragments (W I 4 [35–36]; June–July 1885), in CM, *11*, 565–66, the first bearing the title *"On the Guideline of the Body."* It concludes with the observation: "The body is a more astonishing thought than the old 'soul.'" The second fragment, too long to be reproduced here yet richly deserving of study, concludes:

> Suffice it to say that the body in the meantime commands a yet stronger belief than belief in the spirit; whoever wants to bury belief in the body thereby also buries utterly—belief in the authority of spirit!

still always conditioned by what presents itself to our representing. Yet the absoluteness of the will alone empowers what may be mustered as such. The essence of absolute subjectivity first reaches its fulfillment in such inverted empowering of the will. This does not signify perfection, inasmuch as perfection would still have to be measured against a measure that subsisted in itself. Fulfillment here means that the extreme, hitherto suppressed possibility of the essence of subjectivity becomes the essential center. Will to power is therefore both absolute and—because inverted—consummate subjectivity. Such consummation at the same time exhausts the essence of absoluteness.

The inception of modern metaphysics conceives of *ens* (the being) as *verum* (the true) and interprets the latter as *certum* (the certain). The certitude of representation and what is represented comes to be the very beingness of beings. Up to Fichte's *Foundations of Science in General* (1794), such certitude remained restricted to the representing of the human *cogito sum,* which because it is human can only be something created, hence conditioned. In Hegel's metaphysics, the subjectivity of reason is elaborated to the point of its absoluteness. As the subjectivity of absolute representation, it of course acknowledges sensuous certainty and corporeal self-consciousness, but only in order to absorb them into the absoluteness of absolute spirit and thus simply to deny them any possibility of absolute preeminence. To the extent that in the absolute subjectivity of reason the extreme counterpossibility of the absolute and essential dominance of an independent, self-commanding will is excluded, the subjectivity of absolute spirit is indeed absolute, but still essentially incomplete.

Only its inversion to the subjectivity of will to power exhausts the final essential possibility of Being as subjectivity. By the same token, representing reason is acknowledged in it through the transformation to valuative thinking, but only in order to be placed at the service of the empowering of overpowering. With the inversion of the subjectivity of absolute representation to the subjectivity of will to power the preeminence of reason as a guideline and tribunal for the projection of beings topples.

The consummate subjectivity of will to power is the metaphysical origin of the essential necessity of the "overman." In accordance with the prior projection of beings, true being is reason itself as creative and ordering spirit. The absolute subjectivity of reason can therefore know itself as the absolute of that truth which Christianity teaches concerning beings. According to that teaching, being is the creation of the creator. The supreme being (*summum ens*) is the Creator himself. Creating is conceived of metaphysically in the sense of productive representation. The collapse of the preeminence of representational reason contains the metaphysical essence of that event which Nietzsche calls the death of the Christian-moral God.

However, the same inversion of the subjectivity of absolute reason to the unconditioned subjectivity of will to power at the same time conducts subjectivity to the unrestricted plenipotence of the exclusive development of its proper essence. Now subjectivity as will to power simply wills itself as power in the empowering for overpowering. To will itself means here to bring itself before itself in the supreme consummation of its own essence and in that way *to be* this essence itself. Consummate subjectivity must therefore posit its own essence beyond itself on the basis of what is most inherent in it.

Yet complete subjectivity rejects anything outside itself. Nothing has a claim on Being that does not stand in the power radius of consummate subjectivity. Indeed, the suprasensuous domain and the realm of a transcendent God are subverted. Man, because *he alone* is in the midst of beings as such and as a whole *as a representational, valuative will*, must extend to consummate subjectivity the abode of its pure essence. As consummate subjectivity, therefore, will to power can only deposit its essence in the subject that is man, particularly that man who supersedes the humanity of the past. Lodged in its supremacy in this way, will to power as consummate subjectivity is the supreme and only subject, to wit, the overman. Not only does he draw away from and beyond the human essence as it has been heretofore, but as the reversal of that essence he surpasses himself at the same time to what is absolute for him, that is, to the entirety of beings, the eternal return of the same. If in the midst of being, which in general is end-less and as such is will to power, the new kind of man wills himself and in his own way wills an end, he must necessarily will the overman: "Not 'humanity' but *overman* is the goal!" (WM, 1001). The "overman" is no transcendent ideal; nor is he a person who announces himself at a particular time or shows up at a particular place. As the supreme subject of consummate subjectivity, he is the pure powering of will to power. The thought of "overman" therefore does not arise from the "arrogance" of "Herr Nietzsche." If one really wants to consider the origin of this thought from the viewpoint of the thinker, that origin lies in the innermost decisiveness by which Nietzsche submits himself to the essential necessity of consummate subjectivity; that is to say, the necessity of the first metaphysical truth concerning beings as such. The overman lives because the new mankind wills the Being of beings as will to power. It wills such Being because it is itself willed by that Being—the Being that is absolutely left to itself as mankind.

Thus Zarathustra, who teaches the overman, concludes the first part of his teaching with the words: "*Dead are all gods: now we will that overman live*—at some great midday let this be our ultimate will!—" (*Thus Spoke Zarathustra,* end of Part I). At the time of the most luminous brightness, when beings as a whole show themselves as eternal recurrence of the same, the will must will the overman; for only within the prospect of the overman is the thought of eternal return of the same to be borne. The will that wills here is not a yearning and striving, but will to power. The "we" who are willing in it are those who have experienced the basic character of beings as will to power, those who know that at its zenith will to power itself wills its own essence and thus is concordant with beings as a whole.

Now for the first time the demand posed in Zarathustra's Prologue becomes clear: "Let your will say: the overman *shall be* the meaning of the earth!" Being, which proclaims this "shall be," is commanded; and because the command is essentially will to power, Being is itself a kind of will to power. "Let your will say" first of all means: let your will be will to power. Yet as the principle of the new valuation, will to power is the reason that the being in question is not a suprasensuous beyond but is rather the earth here below, and in particular the object of the struggle for dominion over the earth; will to power is the reason why the meaning and aim of this being becomes the overman. Aim no longer means a purpose existing "in itself"; it is equivalent to saying "value." Value is a condition for itself, conditioned by will to power itself. The highest condition of subjectivity is that subject in which subjectivity itself invests it own absolute will. Such will proclaims and posits what beings as a whole are. Nietzsche dedicates the following words to this law of willing, words that were written in the years 1887-88 and that serve as an epigram to Book II of *The Will to Power:*

> All the beauty and sublimity we have bestowed on real and imaginary things I wish to reclaim as the property and product of man—as his fairest apology. Man as poet, as thinker, as god, as love, as power: O with what regal liberality he has lavished gifts upon things so as to *impoverish* himself and make *himself* feel wretched! His most selfless act hitherto has been to admire and worship and know how to conceal from himself that it was *he* who created what he admired.—

However, is not being as a whole thereby interpreted in man's image and thus made "subjective"? Does not the humanization of beings as such and as a whole imply a diminution of the world? But a counterquestion proclaims itself: Who is the human being here through whom and with reference to whom being is humanized? In what sort of subjectivity is the "subjectivization" of the world grounded? How would matters stand if, by means of a uniquely nihilistic reversal, man as he has been hitherto must first be transformed into the overman; and if overman, as the supreme will to power, should will to let beings be as beings? "No longer will to preservation, but to power; no longer the meek expression 'Everything is *merely* subjective,' but 'It is also *our* work!—Let us be proud of it!' " (WM, 1059). Of course everything is "subjective," but in the sense of the consummate subjectivity of will to power, which empowers beings to be beings. "To 'humanize' the world, that is, to feel ourselves more and more masters within it—" (WM, 614). However, man does not become "master" here through an arbitrary coercion of things via random impulses and desires. Becoming master first of all means submitting oneself to a command for the sake of the empowering of the essence of power. Drives first find their essence in the form of will to power as great passions, that is to say, passions that in their essence are replete with pure power. They "hazard themselves therein" and are themselves their own "judges, avengers, and victims" (*Thus Spoke Zarathustra*, Part II, "On Self-

Overcoming"). Petty pleasures are foreign to great passions. It is not merely the senses, but the character of power in which they are sustained that decides: "The strength and power of the senses—this is the most essential thing in a well-constituted and complete human being: the splendid 'animal' must be granted first—otherwise what could any 'humanization' matter!" (WM, 1045).

If man's animality is referred back to will to power as its essence, man himself finally becomes the "firmly defined animal." "To define firmly" here means to constitute and circumscribe and thus at the same time to make an essence permanent, to bring it to a stand, in the sense of the absolute independence of the subject of representation. In contrast, man as he has been hitherto, seeking his distinctiveness only in reason, is the *"not yet firmly defined animal"* (XIII, 276). "Humanization," when thought nihilistically, therefore means to make man what he is by inverting the preeminence of reason to the preeminence of the "body." At the same time this implies the interpretation of beings as such and as a whole according to such inverted humanity. Nietzsche can therefore say: " 'Humanization'—is a word full of prejudices, and in my ears has a sound almost the opposite of its sound in your ears" (XIII, 206). The inversion of humanization, namely, humanization through the overman, is "dehumanizing." It frees beings from the valuations of prior man. Such dehumanization reveals being "nakedly" as the powering and struggling of the constructs of domination in will to power, that is, in "chaos." Thus, in terms of the essence of its Being, being is purely "nature." Consequently, Nietzsche expresses the matter in a preliminary sketch of the doctrine of the eternal return of the same as "Chaos *sive* natura: *'On the dehumanizing of nature'* " (XII, 426).

The firm metaphysical definition of man as animal signifies the nihilistic affirmation of overman. Only where being as such is will to power and being as a whole is eternal return of the same *can* the nihilistic conversion of earlier man into overman be carried out; and only there *must* overman be established as the supreme subject of itself and for itself by means of the absolute subjectivity of will to power.

Overman does not portend an abrupt inflation in customary acts of fortuitous violence in the style of earlier man. Unlike every mere foray of existing man into measureless excess, the step to overman changes man as he has been hitherto into "the reverse." Nor does the latter merely specify a "new type" of man. Rather, nihilistically inverted man *is* for the first time man as *type*. "It is a matter of type: humanity is merely the experimental material, the vast surplus of botched specimens: a field of ruins" (WM, 713). The consummate absoluteness of will to power requires for its own essence as a condition that the kind of humanity proper to such subjectivity will itself, and that it can will itself only by willfully and consciously giving shape to itself as the breed of nihilistically inverted man.

What is classical in this self-shaping of man that takes man himself in hand consists in the straightforward and rigorous simplification of all things and men into a unity, a unity that absolutely empowers the essence of power for *dominion over the earth*. The conditions of such dominion, namely, all values, are posited and realized through a total "mechanization" of things and the breeding of human beings. Nietzsche recognizes the metaphysical character of machines and expresses his insight in an "aphorism" in the work *The Wanderer and His Shadow,* from the year 1880 (III, 317):

> *The machine as instructress.*—The machine itself teaches the intermeshing of human groups in activities in which each one has merely one thing to do: it provides a model for party organizations and the conduct of war. On the other hand, it does not promote the self-glorification of individuals: from many parts it makes one machine, and out of every individual it makes an instrument for *one* purpose. Its most universal effect is to teach the usefulness of centralization.

Mechanization makes possible a mastery of beings that are everywhere surveyable, a mastery that conserves—and that means stores—energy. The sciences too belong in its essential domain. The sciences do not merely retain their value; nor do they simply take on a new value. Rather, they are now for the first time themselves a value. As the industrially organized and controlled investigation of all beings, they define beings, and through their firm definitions they condition the securing of permanence of will to power. The breeding of human beings is not a taming in the sense of a suppression and hobbling of sensuality; rather, breeding is the accumulation and purification of energies in the univocity of the strictly controllable "automatism" of every activity. Only where the absolute subjectivity of will to power comes to be the truth of beings as a whole is the *principle* of a program of racial breeding possible; possible, that is, not merely on the basis of naturally evolving races, but in terms of the self-conscious *thought* of race. That is to say, the principle is metaphysically necessary. Just as Nietzsche's thought of will to power was ontological rather than biological, even more was his racial thought metaphysical rather than biological in meaning.

Correlative to the will to power, the metaphysical essence of every mechanical arrangement of things and the racial breeding of man therefore rest on the simplification of all beings on the basis of the original simplicity of the essence of power. Will to power wills itself alone from the single apex of this singular willing. It does not lose itself in the plurality of things unsurveyable. It knows very little about the decisive conditions for securing its own enhancement. Paucity here is not something inferior and deficient, but the abundance of the supreme possibility of command, which on the basis of its simplest decisions is most widely receptive to the possibilities of the whole. "An old Chinese said he had heard that when empires were doomed they had many laws" (WM, 745).

Out of the simplicity proper to the will to power come the clear lines, refinement, and firmness of all its castings and shapes. What is well cast and thus typical arises from and corresponds to will to power alone. And the way in which the nihilistic, classical revaluation of all values prethinks, describes, and realizes conditions for absolute dominion over the earth is "the grand style." It defines the "classical taste," to which

> a quantum of coldness, lucidity, hardness belongs: logic above all else, happiness in intellectuality, the "three unities," concentration, hatred of feeling, sensibility, *esprit*, hatred of the manifold, uncertain, rambling, intuitive, as well as of what is brief, pointed, cute, good-natured. One should not play with artistic formulas: one should recreate life so that afterward it *has to* formulate itself (WM, 849).

The grandeur of the grand style derives from the scope of its power to simplify, which is always to intensify. But because the grand style precasts the form of the all-encompassing dominion over the earth, and remains tied to the whole of beings, something gigantic pertains to it. The genuine essence of the gigantic, however, does not consist in a merely quantitative collocation of the superfluous many. The immensity of the grand style corresponds to the paucity that contains the proper fullness of the essence of simplicity; to master such simplicity is the distinctive trait of the will to power. The gigantic is not susceptible to a quantitatitve determination. The immensity of the grand style is that "quality" of the Being of all beings that accords with the consummate subjectivity of will to power. What is "classical" in nihilism has therefore also overcome all the romanticism that every "classicism" still conceals within itself, inasmuch as classicism merely "strives" for the "classical." "—Beethoven, the first great romantic, in the sense of the *French* conception of romanticism, as Wagner is the last great romantic—both instinctive opponents of classical taste, of the severe style—to say nothing of the 'grand style' " (WM, 842).

The grand style is the way in which will to power from the start dictates the arrangement of all things and the breeding of mankind as the mastery of essentially end-less beings as a whole, subjecting them to its own power, and on this basis overpowering and prescribing every step in its ongoing enhancement. Metaphysically considered, such dominating mastery over the earth is the absolute permanentizing of the whole of Becoming. Such permanentizing, however, resists the desire to establish a final state of unvarying uniformity that would endure indefinitely; for will to power would thereby cease to be itself, because it would deprive itself of the possibility of enhancement. The "same" that recurs has its sameness in a continuously new command. The accountable and controllable "relative duration" of the respective constructs of domination is essentially different from the harmless permanence of a lame persistence. The constructs are bound firmly to a definite time, which is nonetheless controllable. Such firmness always exhibits the possibility of controlled change within the sphere of an essentially calculative power.

In the grand style, the overman testifies to his own unique determination. If one measures this supreme subject of consummate subjectivity against the ideals and desires of the earlier valuation, then the configuration of overman disappears from view. In contrast, where every definite end and every path and every construct are merely conditions and means of an absolute empowering of will to power, the sole meaning of the one who as legislator first posits the conditions of domination over the earth consists precisely in not being defined by such conditions.

The apparent incomprehensibility of the overman illustrates the keenness with which the proper subject of will to power is permeated by an essential counterwill that is opposed to all fixity, a counterwill that characterizes the very essence of power. The greatness of the overman, who does not know the fruitless isolation of one who is a mere exception, consists in the fact that he invests the essence of will to power in the willing of a mankind which, in such willing, wills itself as master of the earth. In overman there is "a . . . jurisdiction of its own, which has no higher court above it" (WM, 962). The status and type of individual, of groups and their interrelation, the rank and law of a people and of national groups are defined according to the degree and mode of their power to command, on the basis of which they are pressed into the service of the realization of man's absolute dominion over himself. The overman is the casting of that mankind which first of all *wills* itself *as* a casting and even casts itself as such casting. But to do this overman requires a "hammer" with which the casting be struck and tempered, and with which everything previous, because it is inappropriate to the overman, be shattered. Nietzsche thus begins the concluding section of one of his plans for his "major work" in the following way: "Fourth Book: The Hammer. How must men be constituted who evaluate in reverse?—" (XVI, 417; from the year 1886). In one of the final plans (XVI, 425), the "eternal return of the same" is still the all-pervasive determination of beings as a whole. The concluding fragment here is entitled "The Inverted Ones: Their Hammer 'The Doctrine of Return.' "*

---

* The first "plan" cited here (XVI, 417) is actually a conflation of sketches for the third and fourth books of a particular plan dated "Sils-Maria, Summer 1886." See CM,

If being as a whole is eternal return of the same, then for mankind, which must conceive of itself as will to power within this whole, there remains only the decision as to whether it would sooner will a nihilistically experienced nothingness than no longer will at all, thereby in the latter case surrendering its essential possibility. If mankind wills nothingness as understood in terms of classical nihilism (the end-lessness of beings as a whole), then under the hammer of the eternal return of the same it fabricates for itself a situation making the inverted species of man necessary. Within the meaning-less whole, this human type posits will to power as the "meaning of the earth." The final period of European nihilism is a "catastrophe" in the affirmative sense of an overturning: "The advent of a doctrine that *sifts* men *out* . . . , that drives the weak to firm resolutions, and the strong as well—" (WM, 56).

If being as such is will to power, then being as a whole, eternal recurrence of the same, must overpower every relation to beings.

If being as a whole is eternal return of the same, then the fundamental trait of being as will to power has made itself manifest.

If the eternal recurrence of the same governs being as will to power in general, the absolute and consummate subjectivity of will to power must be humanly situated in the subject of the overman.

The truth of beings as such and as a whole is defined by will to power and eternal recurrence of the same. That truth is safeguarded by overman. The history of the truth of beings as such and as a whole, and consequently the history of mankind included in its domain, manifest the basic trait of nihilism. Yet whence does the truth of beings as such and as a whole, fulfilled and preserved in such a way, derive its own essence?

W I 8 [100]. The second (XVI, 425) appears in CM as Mp XVII 3b [45]. For both fragments, see CM, *12,* 109 and 309.

6. Justice*

Nietzsche reserves the rubrics "true" and "truth" for what Plato calls "true being" (*ontōs on, alēthōs on*), by which is meant the Being of beings, namely, the idea. Therefore, "the true," "beings," "Being," and "truth" mean the same thing for Nietzsche. Yet because he thinks in a modern way, truth is not merely a general determination of representational knowledge; rather, in accord with the change of representation to a securing mustering, truth consists in positing what is stable. Holding the "truth" is a representational holding-to-be-true (WM, 507). The true is what is made fast and therefore permanent in representational thought. Yet after the nihilistic revaluation the permanent no longer has the character of the suprasensuous that is present in itself. The permanent secures the duration of what is living, insofar as everything living needs a fixed horizon upon which it is preserved.

However, preservation is not the essence of what is alive, but merely one basic feature of this essence, which in its most proper sense remains enhancement. Because preservation posits something fixed as the necessary condition of preservation *and* enhancement, while the positing of such conditions necessarily derives from the essence of will to power; and because preservation, as the positing of conditions, has the character of valuation; the true, as what is permanent, has the character of value. *Truth is a necessary value for will to power.*

In each case, however, permanentizing congeals Becoming. Hence the true, because it is what is permanent, represents the actual that unfolds essentially in Becoming, but represents it in a way in which it is *not*. The true is not adequated to being in the sense of becoming, that is, of the properly actual, and so it is false—especially if the

---
* See the note on p. 137, above.

essence of truth is thought in accord with the long familiar metaphysical definition of it as the approximation of representation to the thing. And in fact Nietzsche thinks the essence of truth in this sense. How else could he express his corresponding delineation of the essence of truth in the following way: "*Truth is the kind of error* without which a certain kind of living being could not live. The value for *life* ultimately decides" (WM, 493). Truth is of course a necessary value for will to power. "Yet truth does not count as the supreme standard of value, much less as the supreme power" (WM, 853, section III).

Truth is a condition for the preservation of will to power. Preservation is of course necessary, but it is never adequate, never a way of powering in the will to power that properly supports its own essence. Preservation is essentially subservient to enhancement. Enhancement in every case exceeds what is preserved and its preservation; but not through mere accretion, never merely through more power. The "more" in power consists in the fact that enhancement reveals new possibilities of power beyond the present power, transfigures will to power into these higher possibilities, and at the same time incites it to go thence to its own proper essence—which is to be the overpowering of itself.

In the essence of enhancement of power thus conceived, the "higher concept" of art is fulfilled. The essence of art is to be seen in the "work of art, where it appears *without* an artist, for example, as body, as organization (the Prussian officer corps, the Jesuit order). To what extent the artist is only a preliminary stage" (WM, 796). The essence of the properly fundamental trait of will to power, namely enhancement, is art. It first determines the basic character of beings as such, which is to say, the metaphysical in being. That is why early on Nietzsche calls art the "*metaphysical* activity" (WM, 853, section IV). Because being as such (as will to power) is in essence art, beings as a whole must therefore in the direction indicated by the metaphysics of will to power be conceived of as "artwork": "The world as a work of art that gives birth to itself—" (WM, 796). The metaphysical projection of being as such and as a whole from the perspective on art has nothing in common with an aesthetic view of the world—unless one understands aesthetics as Nietzsche wants it to be understood, that is, "psychologically." At that point aesthetics is transformed into a dynamics that interprets all beings according to the "body" as its guideline. But dynamics here means the powering of will to power.

Art is the sufficient condition of itself when conditioned by will to power as enhancement. It is the value that is decisive to the essence of power. Insofar as enhancement is more essential in the essence of will to power than preservation, art is also more a condition than truth—although from another point of view truth, for its part, also conditions art. Thus the character of value is "more" appropriate to art than truth; that is to say, "more" appropriate in an essential sense. Nietzsche comprehends "that art is *worth more* than truth" (WM, 853, section IV; cf. WM, 822).*

As a necessary value, however, truth bears an essential relation to art within the unified essence of will to power, just as preservation does to enhancement. The full essence of truth can therefore be grasped only when its relation to art—and art itself within the full essence of truth—are also thought. The essence of art, in turn, points toward the initially defined essence of truth. Art as transfiguration opens up higher possibilities of surmounting any given stage of will to power.

What is possible here is defined by neither the noncontradiction of logic nor the feasibility of praxis, but by the illumination of what is still unhazarded and therefore not yet at hand. What is posited in transfiguring openness has the character of *radiant appearance*. Let this word retain its essential ambiguity: *Schein* in the sense of illumination and shining (as in sunshine) and *Schein* in the sense of mere seeming-so (a bush near a path at night appears to be a man but is really only a bush). The former is radiance as *refulgence*, whereas the latter is appearance as *illusion*. Yet because transfiguring appearance in the sense of refulgence always fixes and makes permanent the whole of beings in its becoming on the basis of definite possibilities, it remains at the same time an appearance that is not adequate to what becomes. Thus the essence of art as the will to refulgent appearance also professes to have a connection with the essence of truth, insofar

---

* See Volume I, *Will to Power as Art*, section 12, for a more detailed treatment.

as the latter is conceived as the error that is necessary for securing permanence; that is to say, is conceived as sheer illusion.

The full essence of what Nietzsche calls truth, and for the most part describes as necessary appearance relative to power, does not merely contain a relation to art; rather, it can achieve the unified ground of its determination only in what first of all sustains truth *and* art as united in their essential interrelation. But this is the sole essence of will to power itself, now of course conceived as the bringing-to-shining-and-appearing of whatever conditions its empowering of the overpowering of itself. At the same time, however, adequation to beings emerges as a guiding determination for the essence of truth in what Nietzsche identifies as "truth" and interprets as "error." In the same vein, the interpretation of art in the sense of transfiguring appearance unwittingly appeals to opening-up and bringing-into-the-open (revealing) as its guiding determination.

Adequation and revealing, *adaequatio* and *alētheia*, reign in Nietzsche's concept of truth as the still reverberating yet entirely unheeded resonance of the metaphysical essence of truth.

In the beginning of metaphysics something was decided concerning the essence of truth as *alētheia* (unconcealment and revealing), namely, that the essence of truth would in future times retreat before the determination of truth as approximation (*homoiōsis, adaequatio*), which alone took root in it. This essence would retreat yet never disappear. Metaphysics has never disputed the essence of truth that has reigned since then, as the adequative opening-up of beings through representation; yet it has also allowed the character of opening-up and revealing to sink unexamined into oblivion. In a way that corresponds to its essence, however, such oblivion entirely forgets itself from the historical moment representation is transformed into the self-securing mustering of everything representable, that is, transformed into certitude in consciousness. Everything else in which representation as such might still be grounded is denied.

Yet denial is the opposite of overcoming. Hence the essence of truth in the sense of unconcealment can never really be reintroduced into modern thought precisely because it *has always* held sway and *still* continues to reign in it—although transformed, inverted, displaced, and therefore unrecognized. Like everything forgotten, the forgotten essence of truth is not nothing. What is forgotten alone brings the metaphysics of absolute and consummate subjectivity from its concealed commencement to the point where it shifts to the extreme counteressence of the primordial determination of truth.

Truth as securing permanence of power is essentially related to art as enhancement of power. Truth and art are one in essence on the basis of the simple unity of will to power. The full essence of truth has the hidden ground of its determination here. What is innermost, what drives will to power to its uttermost, is the fact that it wills itself in its own overpowering: it is absolute but inverted subjectivity. Since the time being as such and as a whole began to unfold in the mode of subjectivity, man has come to be the subject. Because by virtue of his reason he relates to beings as the one representing, man *is* in the midst of beings as a whole; he is in their midst when he musters beings before himself, thereby necessarily putting himself into every representation.

The manner by which man in the sense of subjectivity *is* at the same time defines *who* he is: the being before whom all beings are brought and through whom they are justified as such. Thus man comes to be a ground founded on himself, and a measure of the truth concerning beings as such. This also implies that with the development of Being as subjectivity, the history of Western mankind begins as a liberation of humanity to a new freedom. Such liberation is the way in which the transformation of representation—from apprehending as taking in (*noein*) to apprehending as trial and adjudication (*perceptio*)—is carried out. The metamorphosis of representation, however, is itself the consequence of a transformation in the essence of truth. The ground of this event, from which the new freedom arises, is concealed from metaphysics. Yet the new freedom emerges from it.

Viewed negatively, the liberation to a new freedom is an escape from the Christian Church's assurance of redemption based on belief in revelation. Within the scope of this assurance, the truth of salvation does not restrict itself to a relation of faith, a relation to God; rather, the truth of salvation at the same time decides about beings. What is then called philosophy is the handmaid of theology. Beings in their sundry orders are the creation of a creator God, a creation rescued from the Fall and elevated to the suprasensuous realm once again through the redeemer God. However, because it exposes man to the free space of insecurity, whereby he takes the risk of choosing his own essence, the liberation from truth as assurance of salvation must inevitably go in the direction of a freedom that now really for the first time achieves a surety for man and defines his security anew.

Surety can now be perfected only by and for man himself. In the new freedom mankind wishes to be certain of the absolute self-development of all its faculties for unrestricted dominion over the entire earth. On the basis of such security man is sure of beings and of himself. Such certitude not only accomplishes the appropriation of a truth in itself but also is the essence of truth itself. Truth comes to be the securing of beings, a securing that is secured by man himself for his dominating installation of self in the midst of beings as a whole. The new freedom points toward the development of the new essence of truth, which at first installs itself as the self-certitude of representational reason.

Yet because the liberation to a new freedom, in the sense of the self-legislation of mankind, begins as the liberation *from* the Christian, otherworldly certitude of salvation, the liberation remains tied to Christianity even as it repels it. To a merely retrospective gaze, therefore, the history of modern humanity readily shows itself as the secularization of Christianity. Yet the profanation of what is Christian by the "world" requires a world that in the first place is projected on the basis of non-Christian claims. Secularization can be introduced and developed only within such a world. Mere renunciation of Christianity signifies nothing if a new essence of truth has not previously been determined for that renunciation, and if being as such and as a whole is not made to appear in terms of this new truth. But this truth of Being in the sense of subjectivity unfolds its essence unreservedly only when the Being of beings is brought to power completely and unconditionally as subjectivity.

Therefore, only in the metaphysics of will to power does the new freedom begin to elevate its full essence to the law of a new lawfulness.

With this metaphysics, the new age for the first time exalts itself in complete control of its own essence. What precedes is foreplay. Consequently, up to the time of Hegel modern metaphysics remains the interpretation of beings as such; remains ontology, the *logos* of which is experienced in a Christian theological way as creative reason, grounded in absolute spirit (onto-theo-logy). To be sure, Christianity will in the future still be a phenomenon in our history. Through transformations, assimilations, and compromises it is in every instance reconciled with the modern world; and with every step forward it repudiates ever more decisively its former history-shaping force. For the explanation of the world to which it lays claim stands beyond the ken of the new freedom.

In contrast, as soon as the Being of beings as will to power is conducted to the truth that is appropriate to it, the new freedom can carry out the justification of its essence in terms of the Being of beings as a whole thus defined. At the same time, the essence of such justification must correspond to this Being. The new justification of the nascent freedom requires a novel justice as the ground of its determination. This is the decisive course of liberation into the new freedom.

In a note from the year 1884 that bears the title "The Paths of Freedom," Nietzsche says: "*Justice* as a constructive, exclusive, annihilative mode of thought, arising from estimations of value: *The supreme representative of life itself*" (XIII, 42*). As a "mode of thought," justice is a representing, that is, an establishing in terms of estimations of value. Values, the perspectival conditions of will to power, are firmly established in this mode of thought. Nietzsche does not say that justice is *one* mode of thought among others in terms of (arbitrary) estimations of value. In his own words, justice is a thinking in terms of "sundry" explicitly performed valuations. Justice is thought *as such* in the sense of the will to power that alone posits values. Such thinking not only follows from estimations of value, it performs the estimating itself. This is attested to in the way Nietzsche distinguishes

---

* See p. 142, above.

the essence of this "mode of thought." Three striking determinations, named moreover in an essential sequence, offer an essential view of its formulation.

The mode of thought is "constructive." It fashions the sort of thing that is not yet, and perhaps never is, simply at hand. To fashion is to erect. It rises to the heights, in such a way that the heights are first attained and opened as such. The heights ascended in construction assure the clarity of the conditions under which the possibility of command stands. From the clarity of these heights alone can commands be issued in such a way that in the command everything that obeys is transfigured in willing. These heights point in the right direction.

"Constructive" thought is at the same time "exclusive." In this way it fixes and maintains what can support the edifice and fends off what endangers it. In this way it secures the foundation and selects the building materials.

Constructive-exclusive thought is simultaneously "annihilative." It destroys whatever stoppages and restraints hinder the constructive rising to the heights. Annihilation offers security against the pressure of all conditions of decline. Construction demands exclusion. Every constructing (as a creating) embraces destruction.

The three determinations of the essence of justice as a mode of thought are not only arranged in order of their rank; they also, and above all, speak from the inner animation of such thinking. As the constructive thought towers toward the heights, it establishes these heights as such; thus it overreaches itself, differentiates itself from what is inappropriate and uproots it in its very conditions. As such thinking, justice is a becoming master over itself in towering ascent to the supreme heights. Such is the essence of will to power itself. Thus the colon in the quotation cited above leads to the emphatic note on justice that summarizes what we have said: justice is *"the supreme representative of life itself."* For Nietzsche, "life" is merely another word for Being. And Being is will to power.

To what extent is justice the highest representative of will to power? What does "representative" mean here? The word does not mean a proxy for something, something that the proxy itself is not. Nor does it signify an expression that, precisely as an expression, is never that which is itself expressed. If it were what is expressed, then it could not be, dare not be, an expression. The "representative" attains its genuine essence only where "representation" is essentially necessary. Such a thing occurs universally as soon as Being is defined as re-presenting (*re-praesentare*). Such re-presentation, however, has its complete essence in bringing itself before itself, bringing itself to presence in that openness that it alone shapes and measures. The essence of Being is thus determined as subjectivity. As representation, it demands the representative who, by representing, brings the being itself in its Being, its presence, its *parousia,* to appearance—such that it *is* a being.

Will to power, the essential complex of enhancement of power and preservation of power, brings its own essence to power, that is, to appearance in beings, by empowering itself for overpowering. Will to power is representation that posits values. Yet construction is the supreme mode of enhancement. Differentiating and conserving exclusion is the supreme mode of preservation. Annihilation is the supreme mode of the counteressence of preservation and enhancement.

The essential unity of these three constitutive modes of justice is will to power itself at the pinnacle of its essence. At its pinnacle, however, it posits its own conditions. Will to power empowers itself to its own essence by positing "viewpoints" as conditions. In that way it brings what is firmly fixed and what becomes in their twofold shining to appearance in a unity. But by letting beings appear in such a way, will to power brings itself to appearance, as what most intimately *is* this empowering letting-appear, in the twofold radiance of refulgence and illusion.

The essence of truth that all metaphysics assumes and preserves—even if it is still in total oblivion—is a letting-appear. It is the revealing of what is concealed. It is unconcealment. Thus "justice," because it is the supreme mode of will to power, is the proper ground for the determination of the essence of truth. In the metaphysics of the absolute and consummate subjectivity of will to power truth occurs essentially as "justice."

Of course, in order to think the essence of justice in accord with this metaphysics, we must exclude all notions of justice that derive from Christian, humanistic, Enlightenment, bourgeois, and socialist moralities. The just is simply what accords with the "righteous." But the righteous, which points the right way and gives us a measure, does not exist in itself. The righteous gives us a right *to* something. Yet the righteous is for its part defined in terms of what is "right." Nevertheless, Nietzsche delineates the essence of the right in the following way: "Right = the will to make a given ratio of power eternal" (XIII, 205). Justice, then, is the ability to posit right, thus understood; it is the ability to will such a will. This willing can only be as will to power.

Thus in a second, nearly contemporary note on justice (from the year 1884) Nietzsche says the following: "*Justice,* as the function of a panoramic power that looks beyond the narrow perspectives of good and evil, and thus has a broader horizon of *advantage*—the intention to preserve something that is *more* than this or that person" (XIV, 80).*

The similarity of the two determinations of the essence of justice is hardly to be missed: justice—"*supreme representative of life itself,*" and justice—"function of a panoramic power."

Function here means an "operating," the process of an essential development, hence the way in which the power identified here is power proper. Function means the "panoramic power" itself.

How panoramic is its scope? In any case it sees "beyond the narrow perspectives of good and evil." "Good and evil" are names for the viewpoints of previous valuations that recognize a suprasensuous realm in itself as binding law. The vista that opens onto the highest values hitherto is "narrow" in comparison with the grandeur of the "grand style," in which the ways are prescribed by which the nihilistic-classical revaluation of all earlier values will come to be the fundamental feature of a dawning history. As perspectival, that is, positing values, panoramic power surpasses all previous perspectives. It is that from which the new valuation proceeds and what governs every new valuation: *the principle* of the new valuation. Panoramic power is self-proclaiming will to power. In a list of items that are to be considered

---

* See p. 147, above.

"Toward a History of the Modern Eclipse," there stands the succinct comment (WM, 59): "Justice as will to power (breeding)."

Justice is a passage *beyond* previous perspectives, a passage that posits viewpoints. In what horizon does this "constructive way of thought" posit its points of view? It has a "broader horizon of *advantage*." We are startled. A justice that looks out for advantage points shamelessly and crudely enough to the regions of utility, avidity, and expedience. Furthermore, Nietzsche even underlines the word *advantage* in his note, so as to leave no doubt that the justice meant here refers essentially to it.

The word *advantage* [*Vor-teil*] in its genuine significance, which has in the meantime been lost, means what has been previously *allotted* for a dividing and distributing, before these actions themselves are performed. Justice is an allotment that precedes all thinking and acting, an allotment of that alone to which it directs its gaze. Justice intends "to preserve something that is *more* than this or that person." Justice does not direct its gaze to either vulgar utility, an individual person, a community, or "humanity."

Justice looks beyond to that sort of mankind which is to be forged and bred into a type, a type that possesses essential aptitude for establishing absolute dominion over the earth. For only through such dominion will the absolute essence of pure will come to appear before itself, that is to say, come to power. Justice is the preconstructive allotment of conditions that firmly secure a preservation, that is, an attaining and maintaining.

However, the "something" that will be preserved in this justice is the permanentizing of the absolute essence of will to power as the fundamental character of beings. Will to power has the character of Becoming. "To *stamp* Becoming with the character of Being—that is the supreme *will to power*" (WM, 617).

Supreme will to power, which is the permanentizing of beings as a whole, unveils its essence as justice. Because it sustains and governs all letting-appear and every revealing, *it is the innermost essence of truth*. The character of Being is stamped on Becoming when being in its entirety comes to appearance as "eternal return of the same." Yet earlier we said that the permanentizing of Becoming was a "falsification," and that at "the peak of the meditation" everything amounted to illusion. Nietzsche himself grasped the essence of truth as a "kind of error." This was occasioned and justified in its own way by the ground of the determination of the essence of truth, that is, by justice.

However, truth is a kind of error and illusion only as long as it is thought in terms of its familiar though undeveloped concept as adequation to reality. As opposed to this, the projection that thinks beings as a whole as "eternal return of the same" is "thinking" in the sense of that distinctive constructive, exclusive, and annihilative mode of thought. Its truth is the "supreme representative of life itself." Of the thought that thinks this truth Nietzsche says: "Life itself created the thought that is most burdensome for life." It is true because it is in the right; it brings to appearance the essence of will to power in its supreme configuration. Will to power as the fundamental trait of beings justifies the eternal return of the same as that "radiance" in whose brilliance the supreme triumph of will to power scintillates. In this victory the consummate essence of will to power itself appears.

The mode of justification proper to the new justice is decided on the basis of the essence of that new justice. Such justification consists neither in adequation to what is at hand nor in the appeal to laws that would be valid in themselves. Every claim to justification of the latter kind has no basis or resonance in the domain of will to power. Rather, justification consists solely in what satisfies the essence of justice as the "highest representative of the will to power." This is representation. By virtue of the fact that a being is produced as a configuration of will to power in the realm of power, it is already in the right, that is, in the will that commands for itself its own overpowering. Only in this way can one say of it that it is a being, in the sense of the truth of beings as such and as a whole.

The five key expressions, "will to power," "nihilism," "eternal return of the same," "overman," and "justice," correspond to the fivefold division in the essence of metaphysics. The essence of this unity remains within metaphysics, though concealed from it. Nietzsche's thought heeds the hidden unity of metaphysics, whose fundamental position he must discern, occupy, and renovate by not conceding to any of the five key expressions the exclusive priority of a main title that, taken alone, could guide every articulation of his thoughts. Nietzsche's thinking abides in the inner movement of truth, in that he always exhibits the whole accompanying each key word and perceives the harmony of them all. The essential restlessness of his thought certifies that Nietzsche resisted the greatest danger that threatens a thinker: the danger that he abandon the place primordially assigned to him for the determination of his fundamental position and make himself understood on the basis of what is foreign to him and far behind him. If strangers wish to smother his work with alien formulas, let them do so to their hearts' content.

However, if what we have attempted here as an indication of the hidden unity of Nietzsche's metaphysics proceeds to call that metaphysics the absolute and consummate subjectivity of will to power, are we not forcing ourselves into the very thing that Nietzsche avoided? Are we not forced into historical classification, which comes from without and looks only backwards, or even into the historiological (mis)calculation of history, which is always captious and usually carping? And all of this on the basis of a concept of metaphysics that Nietzsche's thought indeed fulfills and confirms, yet does not itself ground and never itself projects!

These questions merely urge the following specific questions: In what does the essential unity of metaphysics in general have its ground? Where does the essence of metaphysics have its origin? The way we cope with these questions will have to decide whether such a reflection merely supplies a belated theory about metaphysics, thus remaining gratuitous, or whether this reflection is a meditation and hence a decision as well.

If Nietzsche's metaphysics is distinguished as the metaphysics of will to power, does it not show a preference for *one* key expression? Why precisely this one? Is the preeminence of the key expression grounded in the fact that here Nietzsche's metaphysics is experienced as the metaphysics of absolute and consummate subjectivity? Why should not the key word *justice*, which certainly identifies the basic feature of the truth of this metaphysics, distinguish Nietzsche's metaphysics, if metaphysics in general is the truth of beings as such and as a whole?

Nietzsche explicitly developed the essence of justice on the basis of will to power only in the two notes that we have discussed, notes he himself never published. Nowhere did he express the new justice as the ground for determining the essence of truth. Yet around the time both of those interpretations of the essence of justice were drafted, Nietzsche was convinced of one thing, namely, that *one* decisive insight had not yet come to real clarity for him. In a fragment (from the years 1885-86) for a retrospective preface to his book *Human, All-Too-Human* (first published in 1878) he wrote:

> It happened quite late in my life—I was already out of my twenties—that I discovered what is completely and entirely lacking in me: namely, *justice*. "What is justice? And is it possible? And if it were not possible, how would life be bearable?"—I asked myself questions like this incessantly. It profoundly disturbed me to find, wherever I excavated within myself, only passions, only narrow perspectives, only my unthinking acceptance of whatever is alien to the very preconditions for justice: but where was lucidity [*Besonnenheit*]?—the lucidity that arises from comprehensive insight [*aus umfänglicher Einsicht*]. (XIV, 385 f.)*

Yet light from this belated insight falls back on the early premonition reigning everywhere in Nietzsche's thought, which in the second *Untimely Meditation* ("On the Advantage and Disadvantage of History for Life," section 6) expressly puts "justice" in place of the repudiated "objectivity" of the historical sciences; does so, however, without conceiving the essence of subjectivity metaphysically, and without yet knowing about the basic character of justice, that is, about will to power. †

---

* See W I 7a [65], from August–September, 1885, which appears in CM, *11*, 663–64. The text of the critical edition, which I have followed here, differs slightly from that in the GOA. In the foreword to the second edition of *Human, All-Too-Human* (CM, *2*, 20) we read: "You should learn to grasp the necessary injustice in every pro and con, injustice as ineluctably present in life, life itself being *conditioned* by the perspectival and its injustice. . . ."

† Nietzsche's second *Untimely Meditation,* on which Heidegger conducted a seminar

Granted, however, that the essence of will to power comes to be conceived as absolute and, because inverted, as consummate subjectivity; granted, further, that the essence of the subjectivity of the subject is thought metaphysically; granted, finally, that the forgotten essence of metaphysical truth is again remembered as the revealing of what is concealed (*alētheia*), and is not merely mentioned and repeated; granted all this, then does not the import of those succinct notes on "justice"—succinct because they are truly formulated—outweigh all of Nietzsche's other discussions about the essence of truth, which merely echo contemporary "theories of knowledge"? Nevertheless, because in Nietzsche's thought it remains veiled as to whether and how "justice" is the essential trait of truth, the key word *justice* may not be raised to the rank of the main heading in Nietzsche's metaphysics.

Metaphysics is the truth of beings as such and as a whole. Without saying it, the metaphysics of absolute and consummate subjectivity thinks its own essence, that is, the essence of truth, as justice. The truth of beings as such and as a whole is therefore truth about beings; in such a way, of course, that its own essence is decided in terms of the fundamental trait of beings, by way of will to power as the supreme configuration of beings.

Is then every metaphysics necessarily the truth of beings as such and as a whole in this twofold sense? Truth about *beings*, inasmuch as truth emerges from the *Being* of beings? If so, does this provenance of the essence of truth say something about itself? Advancing in this way, is it not inherently historical? Does not this provenance of the essence of truth say something about the essence of metaphysics? It certainly does. And what it says can be expressed first of all only by way of opposition, specifically as follows.

Metaphysics is not a human artifact. Yet that is why there must be thinkers. Thinkers are in each case preeminently situated in the unconcealment that the Being of beings prepares for them. As a result

---

or "exercise" in 1938–39, is an essential source for Heidegger's own thoughts on, and practice of, historical interpretation. See, for example, Nietzsche's remarks (in section 6) at CM, *1*, 285, 289, and 293–94. Note also Heidegger's use of "The Advantage and Disadvantage of History for Life" in *Sein und Zeit*, at p. 396, lines 16 ff. See also the note to the "Plan of the English Edition" at the front of this volume.

of its historical essence, "Nietzsche's metaphysics," that is to say, the truth of beings as such and as a whole, which has now been preserved in words derived from his fundamental position, is the fundamental trait of the history of our age, which is inaugurating itself only now in its incipient consummation as the age of modernity: "A period when the old masquerade and moral *maquillage* of the affects arouses antipathy: *naked nature;* where the *quanta of power* are simply admitted as *decisive* (as *determining rank*); where the *grand style* again appears as the consequence of *grand passion*" (WM, 1024).

The question remains as to which peoples and what kinds of humanity ultimately and even initially will rally to the law of this fundamental trait and thus pertain to the early history of dominion over the earth. What Nietzsche outlined around 1881–82, when in *Daybreak* the thought of the eternal return of the same came to him, is no longer a question but has already been decided: "The time is coming when the struggle for dominion over the earth will be carried on— it will be carried on in the name of *fundamental philosophical doctrines*" (XII, 207).

That is not to say, however, that the struggle for unrestrained exploitation of the earth as a source of raw materials or the cynical utilization of "human resources" in service to the absolute empowering of will to power will explicitly appeal to philosophy for help in grounding its essence, or even will adopt philosophy as its facade. On the contrary, we must presume that philosophy will disappear as a doctrine and a construct of culture, and that it can disappear only because as long as it was genuine it identified the actuality of the actual, that is, Being, on the basis of which every individual being is designated to be what it is and how it is. "Fundamental philosophical doctrines" means what is taught in those doctrines, in the sense of something portrayed in a presentation that interprets beings as a whole with a view to Being. "Fundamental philosophical doctrines" means the essence of self-consummating metaphysics, which in its fundamental traits sustains Western history, shapes it in its modern European form, and destines it for "world domination." What is expressed in the thinking of European thinkers can also be historiologically reckoned in terms of the national character of those thinkers; but it can never be promulgated as a peculiarity of nationality. Descartes' thought, the metaphysics of Leibniz, Hume's philosophy, are all European and therefore global. In the same way, Nietzsche's metaphysics is at its core never a specifically German philosophy. It is European, global.

ANALYSIS AND GLOSSARY

Analysis

By DAVID FARRELL KRELL

> The thesis of Heidegger's *grand livre* [i.e., *Nietzsche*] is much less simple than people have generally tended to say.
>
> JACQUES DERRIDA, *Spurs*

Perhaps the most obstinate questions that confront us with regard to the theme of "will to power as knowledge and as metaphysics" are the following: If Heidegger in 1936-37 identifies the configuration of will to power as *art* as essential to Nietzsche's fundamental metaphysical position, an art that expresses itself most effulgently in Nietzsche's thinking of eternal return, why in 1939 does Heidegger revert to the configuration of will to power as *knowledge*? If the "peak" of Nietzsche's *and* Heidegger's meditations is the eternal recurrence of the same, why the deliberate descent to the themes of knowledge and metaphysics? How can these show the way to "the new interpretation of sensuousness," which at the end of his first lecture course on Nietzsche Heidegger proclaims the task of thinking in the grand style?

Ornery as such questions may be, they tend to forget the context of Heidegger's own inquiry into art, namely, the nexus of *truth as unconcealment*—a nexus that presumably has something to do with both knowledge and metaphysics. Heidegger would of course argue that Nietzsche's own conception of art as form-engendering force is itself bound up with fixation, fixation being the very essence of knowledge and the will to truth. On both accounts, it would not be so easy to pursue *art* by ignoring *knowledge*. Perhaps a brief reminder of the trajectory of each text in the present volume is therefore in order.

I. THE STRUCTURE AND MOVEMENT OF THE LECTURE COURSE, THE CONCLUDING LECTURES, AND THE ESSAY

The Lecture Course

"The Will to Power as Knowledge" consists of twenty-two unnumbered sections. (The numbers have been added throughout the translation to facilitate reference.) No other internal divisions or articulations mark the text. Heidegger's third lecture course on Nietzsche progresses steadily toward the question of the *essence* of truth by interpreting Nietzsche's view of truth as error as the extreme metaphysical transformation of correctness. Precisely how that extreme is to be understood, whether as a biologistic reduction of cognition and adequation, as a mere inversion of the Platonic hierarchy (truth over semblance, being over nonbeing), or as an incipient return to the commencement of metaphysics as such, remains Heidegger's principal concern.

The course opens with the claim that in Nietzsche we confront the consummation (*die Vollendung*: fulfillment, completion, end and accomplishment) of metaphysics, that is, of the realm of decisions concerning beings as a whole (section 1). Nietzsche's decision about beings, though never culminating in a confident magnum opus, centers on the notion of will to power (section 2). The latter is the principle of the new valuation (section 3) that is to establish the conditions and perspectives for self-preserving, self-enhancing life. The question concerning the essence of knowledge (section 4) arises insofar as knowledge and truth are values, albeit not the supreme values. For the tradition, truth is correctness of assertions about beings (section 5); for Nietzsche, truth is illusion, an illusion that is essential yet also ultimately inimical to life. Nietzsche's thought is not so much a biologism (sections 6 and 16) but a metaphysics of life, the consummation of Western thought on *physis*. Though metaphysics is preeminently "logical," not "physical" (section 7), Nietzsche reduces the categories of logic to schemata devised by and for the preservation of a particular species. His understanding of the value of truth as a holding-to-be-true (sections 8 and 9) cannot be dismissed as relativism or skepticism, for that understanding marks the end of the "two-world" theory that subtends occidental ontology. The question, of course, is: *How* does

Nietzsche close the gap, the *khōrismos*, between the true and the apparent worlds? Even if life and the world *are* Becoming rather than Being, so that the appeal to truth (whatever is true and in being) is itself illusory, "the true" as the correct is somehow retained in Nietzsche's asseverations on Becoming. Heidegger writes (section 10): "For only if truth in its essence is correctness can it be *in*correctness and illusion according to Nietzsche's interpretation."

All value-estimation, including the value-estimation of holding-to-be-true, makes a claim concerning beings as a whole as *chaos* (section 11). Although Heidegger's interpretation of knowing as a founded mode of being-in-the-world (see *Being and Time*, section 13) makes him less susceptible to Nietzsche's notions of "schemata" and "practical need" than perhaps Kant would have been, Heidegger hesitates to reject Nietzsche's claim concerning chaos. It is precisely his insistence on *das leibende Leben,* "bodying life," precisely the fact that a human being is some body who is alive, that Heidegger wants to heed (section 12). Thus the reference to life's bodying forth brings Heidegger back to the question of art and the new interpretation of sensuousness.

Yet Heidegger soon (section 13) reverts to the questions of perspective and horizon as modes of securing stability and permanence within chaos. After showing that accordance *(Verständigung)* with fellow human beings and calculation of things secures the needed stability (section 14), Heidegger examines the "inventive" or "poetizing" trait of human reason according to Nietzsche's philosophy—a trait reminiscent of the (creative) role of the transcendental imagination in Kant (section 15). Most illuminating in this regard is the difference between the Aristotelian and Nietzschean approaches to the law of noncontradiction (sections 16–18), as a law of Being and a command of valuative will to power, respectively.

At this point (section 19) Heidegger takes up the theme with which his first lecture course on Nietzsche had concluded, that of Nietzsche's overturning of the Platonistic distinction between the "true" and the "apparent" worlds. He now appears to vacillate on two crucial points of his earlier analysis of will to power as art: first, whether Nietzsche's fundamental metaphysical position can be characterized as such in terms of the raging discordance between art and truth; and second, whether Nietzsche merely inverts the two elements of the Platonic distinction and hence does not "twist free" of Platonic structures of thought. Heidegger now argues that alongside Nietzsche's notion of truth as error there is another (creative-artistic) notion of truth as harmony (*Einstimmigkeit*) with Becoming. Such harmony in fact (section 20) proves to be the extreme transformation of *homoiōsis* (truth as correctness) in the history of metaphysics.

After introducing the familiar yet crucial passages on the sixth and final stage of the "History of an Error" (*Twilight of the Idols,* as cited in section 24 of Volume I in this series) and on the inception of Zarathustran tragedy (*The Gay Science,* number 342, as cited in section 4 of Volume II in this series), Heidegger now (section 21) makes an unexpected move to the notion of truth as "justice," *Gerechtigkeit.* As suggestive as the reference to the pre-Platonic notion of *dikē* may be, Heidegger abandons it in order to pursue two paths to the extreme moment and uttermost transformation of *Richtigkeit,* or correctness. The first path inquires whether Nietzschean holding-to-be-true, the commanding perspective of knowledge, can save itself from a collapse into sheer arbitrariness. The "other" path shows that both art and knowledge are fixations of horizons, boundaries, and perspectives: both are forms of securing permanence; both are assimilations to chaos. The raging discord of art and truth thereby seems to cease. The conjunction between art and truth is now defined as *"transfiguration that commands and poetizes, establishes perspectival horizons, and fixates."* Both art and truth would aim at "justice," provided we are able to hear the word as a metaphysical rubric for "the *essence* of truth." Justice is a mode of thinking that constructs, excludes, and annihilates; it is the *"supreme representative"* of life; it is the "panoramic power" of self-surpassing, excelling will to power itself. Yet whether such justice provides a standard for the commanding and poetizing element in cognition (section 22) is to be doubted. For enhancement, not preservation, of power remains the metaphysical desideratum of will to power. If self-overpowering be derided as anthropomorphism—far beyond all biologism—Heidegger regards such unbridled anthropomorphism as the consummation of Western metaphysics as such, granted that metaphysics is the project of securing the permanence of all Becoming by means of Being, the latter being projected as permanence of presencing. Precisely in this way the consummation of metaphysics in Nietzsche's philosophy is unwittingly bound up with what Heidegger in the late 1930s (in the *Beiträge zur Philosophie*) envisages as "the other commencement."

One might summarize the movement of the 1939 lecture course, "The Will to Power as Knowledge," by noting the paragraph breaks in my own account of it here. Proceeding from the notion of will to power as the truth or beingness of beings (as correctness), Heidegger investigates the nature of the perspectivism of commanding, bodying life; yet the emphasis falls on fixation rather than transfiguration, so much so that the latter appears to be a kind of harmony (if not monotony, since *Einstimmigkeit* might mean both), with "justice" as the ostensible point of convergence of art and truth. If Nietzsche's philosophy of will to power expresses the final truth of beingness, it is nonetheless deaf to the question of the *essence* of truth. And yet it propels that very question in the direction of another beginning.

The Concluding Lectures

Heidegger projected two lectures to serve as the conclusion to all three lecture courses, "The Eternal Recurrence of the Same and the Will to Power"; the conclusion as we now have it consists of a general introduction and six sections. The overriding claim is that Nietzsche's philosophy is the consummation of Western metaphysics. Such metaphysics rests on the guiding projection of the beingness of beings as permanence of presencing *(Beständigkeit des Anwesens)*. The doctrines of will to power and eternal return converge as *the final* fundamental metaphysical position. That convergence is elaborated in six stages.

Eternal recurrence is said to "anticipate" the fundamental thought of will to power (section 1). While the latter is the unconditioned empowering of power as command, eternal recurrence remains cast within the guiding metaphysical projection of permanence in presencing as "the self-recapitulation of the identical." The thought of return does not cancel the distinction between Being and Becoming in such a way as to revert to the commencement as a positive possibility of thought. It does not envisage *alētheia*. Rather, it confirms the abandonment of and by Being.

Will to power marks the final metaphysical position of modernity; eternal recurrence implies the end of metaphysics as such (section 2). Will to power may, at least "initially," be identified as quiddity, the "what-being" of beings; recurrence as their existence or "that-being." This distinction coincides with the all-sustaining metaphysical distinction between *ontōs on* (proper being) and *mē on* (nonbeing), insofar as the "what?" becomes the guiding question of Western metaphysics. Nietzsche's celebration of Becoming thus actually transforms Becoming into Being; it remains within the purview of beingness as permanence of presencing and of truth as correctness (section 3). The truth of Being is value, that is, the value-estimation of supreme will to power. The latter is unrestrained anthropomorphism, seeking as it does absolute dominion over the earth and ushering in the age of consummate meaninglessness (section 4).

In this age the clearing of Being all but vanishes in the vapors of ultimate adequation—the malleability, manipulability, and disposability of beings, the machination *(Machenschaft)* of beingness. Having begun with the interpretation of beingness as Idea, specifically, the Idea of the Good, metaphysics ends with revaluation: "The solitary superficies is what *remains after* the abolition of the 'true' *and* the 'semblant' worlds." Overman defines the Good as *animalitas*, *animalitas* as *brutalitas*. Superman fashions his superworld. Yet all machination mimes the concealed yet already written history of the (non)essence of Being (section 5) which we call "modernity" *(die Neuzeit, das Neuzeitliche)*. The latter consists essentially in the instauration of man as *subiectum* and of beingness as representedness. Modernity proves to be an essentially violent, incessant rivalry of self against self within the horizon of meaninglessness.

Meaninglessness is the measurelessness of self-overpowering power (section 6). Being, refusing itself, abandons beings to their own devices. Nevertheless, the refusal of Being is something that we experience; it occurs as a peculiar kind of clearing. The clearing of Being is inherently self-concealing. Hence the revelation of Being *as* Being transpires as what is *fragwürdig*, both dubious and worthy of question.

And the style of questioning? "We must overcome the compulsion to lay our hands on everything." By accepting not dominion but guardianship over the clearing, we undergo seamless transition to "the other commencement," the onset of questioning by way of commemorative thought.

The Essay

The treatise "Nietzsche's Metaphysics" reiterates a number of themes from the 1939 lecture course (such as biologism, anthropomorphism, and justice) and relates them to the remaining lecture courses (will to power as art, eternal recurrence of the same, and European nihilism) and to the broadly cast concluding lectures we have just now summarized. Heidegger begins by emphasizing that Nietzsche's thought *is* metaphysics inasmuch as it thinks beings as a whole in their truth. Moreover, Nietzsche's metaphysics is unified, whether at any particular time the dominant rubric be "will to power," "eternal return," or "revaluation of all values." Heidegger introduces his thesis (section 1) in the following way:

> "Will to power," "nihilism," "the eternal return of the same," "the overman," and "justice" are the five fundamental expressions of Nietzsche's metaphysics.
>
> "Will to power" is the word for the Being of beings as such, the *essentia* of beings. "Nihilism" is the name for the history of the truth of beings thus defined. "Eternal return of the same" means the way in which beings as a whole are, the *existentia* of beings. "Overman" describes the kind of humanity that is demanded by this whole. "Justice" is the essence of the truth of beings as will to power.

In addition, Heidegger now introduces the essential context of the present essay, to wit, the "fundamental experience" (*Grunderfahrung*) explicated in his own major work, *Being and Time:*

> The following attempt can be adequately thought only if it is also thought on the basis of the fundamental experience of *Being and Time*. That experience consists in ever-increasing but perhaps also—in a few places—self-clarifying bewilderment in the face of this one event: In the history of Western thought, from its inception, the Being of beings has indeed been

thought, but the truth of Being as Being remains unthought; not only is such truth denied as a possible experience for thinking, but Western thought, as metaphysics, expressly though unwittingly conceals the occurrence of this refusal.

Rather than summarizing the structure and movement of this treatise in any detail, I will now merely list some of the crucial words that qualify the five key expressions. By moving quickly, I hope to capture the slow, painstaking movement of the treatise itself.

Will to power. The what-being of beings, as life, command, overpowering, enhancement; as viewpoints within Becoming, perspectives, constructs of domination, value thinking: subjectivity.

Nihilism. Devaluation; absolute revaluation as affirmative, extreme, active, ecstatic, classical: Dionysos.

The Eternal Return of the Same. The "value-lessness" of the world, the "how" of beings, that-being, Being as permanentizing: "peak of the meditation."

Overman. Human being and the essence of truth, anthropomorphism, *animal rationale,* the body bodying forth; representation, self-legislation, consummate yet inverted subjectivity, humanization/dehumanization, mechanization, dominion: the hammer.

Justice. "The true," "being," permanence vs. enhancement, error vs. art, fixation vs. transfiguration, *homoiōsis* vs. *alētheia*; liberation to the new freedom, justification; construction, exclusion, annihilation: supreme representative of life itself, panoramic power.

It will not do to exclude from this minimal résumé of the structure and movement of the essay what is most important for the *rhythm* not only of "Nietzsche's Metaphysics" but also of the other two parts of the present volume. It will not do to exclude Heidegger's own awareness of the *dangers* involved in his own interpretive practice. After elaborating the five key expressions of Nietzsche's metaphysics, Heidegger concedes the following:

> However, if what we have attempted here as an indication of the hidden unity of Nietzsche's metaphysics proceeds to call that metaphysics the absolute and consummate subjectivity of will to power, are we not forcing ourselves into the very thing that Nietzsche avoided? Are we not forced into historical classification, which comes from without and looks only

backwards, or even into the historiological (mis)calculation of history, which is always captious and usually carping? And all of this on the basis of a concept of metaphysics that Nietzsche's thought indeed fulfills and confirms, yet does not itself ground and never itself projects!

Are we wise to treat such statements as mere rhetorical ploys designed to allay readers' fears, as *captatio benevolentiae,* as minor interruptions on the way to a confident, self-assertive "Nietzsche interpretation"? We note that the treatise "Nietzsche's Metaphysics" closes with a series of *questions* concerning the ground and origin of metaphysics in general. If there is a conviction behind the questions it is that Nietzsche's metaphysics, far from being the eccentric views of a thinker on the fringes of the tradition, embodies the final truth of beings as such and as a whole.

II. CONTEXTS

That said, we know that during the year 1939 Heidegger jotted down a large number of notes that reflected his growing disenchantment with the thinker of will to power and revaluation. In fact, Heidegger now came to doubt whether Nietzsche's celebration of art in the grand style was anything but the modern metaphysical cult of genius combined with a technicist "stimulation" of "life." He placed these notes alongside materials designated for his *Contributions to Philosophy: "Of Ereignis,"* organized about such themes as the oblivion of Being, technological will-to-will, machination and—in opposition to these—intimations of Being, the other commencement, and the poetizing-commemorative thought of *sigetics* (the practice of silence).

Part Two of the present volume, with its grim analysis of disposability and its desperate invocation of the self-concealing clearing of Being, testifies eloquently to Heidegger's waxing distress. Early in these concluding lectures Heidegger cites the theme of "total mobilization." If Nietzsche's notion of will to power is now taken to be not self-assertive *life* but consummate *subjectivity;* if it is now defined no longer as transcendence but simply as will-to-will; and if revaluation now appears to be the culminating act in the drama of European nihilism, and not by any means a new beginning; then the context created for Nietzsche by Ernst Jünger becomes a matter of supreme importance.[1]

No doubt the richest philosophical sources for the Heidegger-Jünger relationship are Ernst Jünger's "Over the Line" (1950) and Heidegger's reply to that piece, "About 'The Line' " (1955).[2] Both texts—Jünger's only more obviously than Heidegger's—reflect the situation of postwar *Katastrophe* in Germany. Yet precisely for this reason I want to focus on writings and events that preceded the catastrophe, events to which both Heidegger and Jünger were totally blind and that only painful hindsight would reveal—unless Heidegger's waxing distress in the late 1930s may be taken as a premonition concerning what was to come.

In "About 'The Line,' " Heidegger praises Jünger's works *Total Mobilization* (1930) and *The Worker: Dominion and Configuration* (1932) for having revealed the "planetary" or "global" tendency of European nihilism. Taking as his point of departure the massive destruction of matériel during the pitched battles of World War I, Jünger attempted to describe the new technological era as such. Heidegger emphasizes that Jünger's books had a lasting effect on his thought, citing his own influential essay "The Question Concerning Technology" as an example. He also mentions in passing a small circle of university teachers with whom he read and discussed *The Worker*. The discussion group met during the winter semester of 1939–40, the

---

[1] In spite of several monographs in French and German on the Heidegger-Jünger relationship—e.g., Christian Graf von Krockow, *Die Entscheidung: Eine Untersuchung über Ernst Jünger, Carl Schmitt, Martin Heidegger* (Stuttgart: F. Enke, 1958); and Jean-Michel Palmier, *Les écrits politiques de Heidegger* (Paris: l'Herne, 1968)—this theme surely demands further research. See the perceptive account of Karsten Harries, "Heidegger as a Political Thinker," in Michael Murray, ed., *Heidegger and Modern Philosophy* (New Haven: Yale University Press, 1978), pp. 304–28, esp. p. 310 n. 16 and p. 326.

[2] Jünger's essay appears in *Anteile: Martin Heidegger zum 60. Geburtstag* (Frankfurt am Main: V. Klostermann, 1950), pp. 245–84. Heidegger's reply first appeared in a *Festschrift* for Jünger's sixtieth birthday (in 1955); under the title "Zur Seinsfrage" it appears now in Martin Heidegger, *Wegmarken* (Frankfurt am Main: V. Klostermann, 1967), pp. 213–53. For a discussion of Heidegger's reply, see the Analysis of Volume IV in this series, pp. 286–91. I will cite *Wegmarken* as W, with page number, in parentheses in the body of my text.

very season of "Nietzsche's Metaphysics." Heidegger reproduces a note that he sketched during those winter months of *Blitzkrieg* (W, 218):

> Ernst Jünger's book *The Worker* is important because it achieves what all prior Nietzsche literature was unable to achieve, and does so in a way that differs from Spengler. It manages to communicate an experience of beings and of the way beings are in the light of Nietzsche's projection of being as will to power. Of course, this in no way enables us to grasp thoughtfully Nietzsche's metaphysics. It does not even indicate the paths that will lead us there. On the contrary, instead of becoming worthy of question, that metaphysics is viewed as self-evident and hence apparently superfluous.

Heidegger's reservations do not mean to deny the "perdurant impact" of Jünger's writings—including the 1934 sequel, *On Agony*—on Heidegger's thinking. In the present context I will restrict myself to some observations on *The Worker*, especially one division of the second part, entitled "Technology as Mobilization of the World by the Configuration of the Worker."[3]

Much of the rhetoric of Jünger's book grates against our ears, and for good reason: domination, economy and destiny, totality, freedom as the right to work, attacks on the existence of the individual, a new breed of humanity, a new and superior race. Though it would be mistaken to identify all this as National Socialism (see sections 68–71, but also section 80), one can hardly help but think of Dedalus' response to Mr. Deasy: "I fear those big words which make us so unhappy."

The themes of technology and technicity are in some sense the steeled heart of the book. "In order to possess a real relation to technology, one must be something more than a technician" (149). For "technology is the way in which the figure of the worker mobilizes the world" (150). Only technology, only the elemental figure of the

---

[3] Ernst Jünger, *Der Arbeiter: Herrschaft und Gestalt* (Hamburg: Hanseatische Verlagsanstalt, 1932), pp. 149–94. See also the useful table or *"Übersicht"* on pp. 295–300. Again I stress that the Heidegger-Jünger relationship remains one of the most important areas for future research. My own remarks here will be meager, and are intended only as pointers. (Note that I will cite *Der Arbeiter* simply by page number in parentheses in the body of the text.)

technologized worker, escapes the destruction of the Great War and the attrition of the postwar years. The expansion of that figure is "global" or "planetary" (156).

> Wherever man comes under the spell of technology he sees himself confronted by an unavoidable either-or. For him it is either a matter of accepting the means that are peculiar to it, and of learning how to speak the language of those means, or of perishing. But if one accepts the challenge—and this is very important—then one makes oneself not only the subject but also simultaneously the object of technical procedures. Application of such means draws a particular style of life in its wake, one that embraces both the great and the small things of life. (158–59)

It is here that one finds the similarities with Heidegger's thinking on technology quite striking. Compare to Heidegger's necrology of the Rhine and its hydroelectric plant the following from Jünger: "The field that is plowed by machines and fertilized by nitrogen produced in factories is no longer the same field" (159). And compare both to John Steinbeck's dramatic depiction—also in 1939—of the mechanical rape of the land in *Grapes of Wrath.* Yet it is also here that the difference between Heidegger and Jünger comes into relief. Apart from the notorious reference to the "greatness" of National Socialism in the 1935 *Introduction to Metaphysics,* where do we find anything in Heidegger to match Jünger's confidence in the positive nature of technology, the expectation that "technology is itself cultic in origin," hence possessed of futuristic "symbols" and religious numinosity (161)? For Jünger, the most important of these symbols is the very "language" of technology—a "language" that Heidegger in "About 'The Line' " takes to be the decisive flaw in Jünger's analysis of nihilism. And if the language of technology dominates our world totally, if technology is the only kind of "power" that can be "willed" (161), then it is clear why Heidegger's call for an utterly new relation to language is issued against will to power as will-to-will. If Jünger demands that his contemporaries "grasp their world picture [*Weltbild*] as a finished and quite limited totality" (164), one cannot help but think that Heidegger's "The Age of the World Picture," cited in Part Two of the present volume, is a retort. If Jünger stresses the "provisional, workshoplike character" and "dynamic restiveness" of that world image and of its "landscape in transition" (165), Heidegger is surely much less sanguine than he about the swath of destruction that technology cuts through this landscape.

However much one perceives ways in which Jünger's views may have influenced Heidegger elsewhere—see, for example, Jünger's remarks on architecture (180–81) with a view to Heidegger's "Building Dwelling Thinking"—there is one overwhelming point with which this context may (at least for the moment) come to a close. In the concluding section to his division on technology Jünger writes (192–94):

> The preoccupation with technology will be worthwhile only when it is recognized as the symbol of a superior power.... There is no way out, no lateral way, no way back. What we must do is enhance the momentum and the velocity of those processes in which we are caught up. Hence it is good to sense that behind the dynamic excesses of our time an immovable center lies concealed.

When in "The Question Concerning Technology" Heidegger insists that the essence of technology is nothing technological, that it is rather a "destining of revealing" and hence a turning toward the "saving power" of disclosure as such, is there not a tendency and a hope to reach that "immovable center" of technology—its core, its heart, its saving grace, its meaning?

Whatever the answer to that question may be, it is important here to emphasize Heidegger's reluctance to assume Ernst Jünger's embattled yet heroic posture. Indeed, Jünger's Nietzscheanism is one that Heidegger can neither embrace nor even recognize. On the contrary, Jünger's ostensible Nietzscheanism goes a long way to explaining why Heidegger comes to take will to power as will-to-will and machination, eternal return as a symbol of the dynamo, and overman as the technical giant bent on world conquest. Given this sort of context, it becomes increasingly difficult to hear the music of Zarathustra's new lyre.

Thus, by way of summary, one must locate the shift in Heidegger's relationship with both Nietzsche and Jünger more precisely than Otto Pöggeler has done in his recent book, *Heidegger and Hermeneutical Philosophy*. There Pöggeler writes:

As National Socialism unleashed its struggle for world dominion, Heidegger, in company with Nietzsche and with Ernst Jünger's writings on total mobilization and the worker, became convinced that the worker and the soldier, absorbed in various coordinated modes of planning, had in the meantime in fact come to define the very figure of man. To the planned economy of total warfare (from which peace was becoming less and less distinguishable) corresponded the "leadership in literary matters" in the politics of culture and the technical control of intimate life—whether in "leadership in matters of child-bearing" or in the slaughter of life in the death camps. In spite of everything, [Heidegger's] thinking hoped for a turn. What it sought under the present circumstances was not the deeds of grand creators. Rather, it hoped to see where we had all gone astray, to pay heed to nascent and pristine beginnings.[4]

By 1939 Heidegger was surely less confident than Jünger about the figure of man outlined in the "coordinated modes of planning" for the worker and soldier. Though the 1933 *Rektoratsrede* bristles with such confidence, and though the first Nietzsche lectures of 1936–37 still betray some hope in "the deeds of grand creators," by 1939 the sole hope lies in the other commencement—of commemorative thought and questioning.[5]

A brief word now concerning developments in a second important context: In the Analyses to earlier volumes I have noted Heidegger's resistance to Alfred Baeumler's *Nietzsche: Philosopher and Politician*,

---

[4] Otto Pöggeler, *Heidegger und die hermeneutische Philosophie* (Freiburg and Munich: K. Alber, 1983), pp. 18–19. See also Pöggeler, *Der Denkweg Martin Heideggers* (Pfullingen: G. Neske, 1983), pp. 132–33.

[5] Yet this is not to say that Heidegger simply leaves Jünger behind. Pöggeler rightly reminds us of Heidegger's *Spiegel* interview in 1966. There (*Der Spiegel*, 30, 23, 31 May 1976, p. 206) Heidegger expresses his doubts concerning the adequacy of "democracy" to confront the challenges of our technological age. Pöggeler cites this remark as evidence of the *lasting* impact of Jünger's thought on Heidegger: "However else he may criticize Ernst Jünger, Heidegger's stance thoroughly squares with his: Jünger too takes advantage of the delicate balance in favor of freedom in today's world, without identifying himself with any of the efforts devoted to preserving that balance." See *Hermeneutische Philosophie*, p. 32. On the inability of a liberal parliamentary democracy to cope with the totalizing demands of technology, see Jünger, *Der Arbeiter*, p. 187.

published in 1931.[6] In 1936–37 Heidegger rejects Baeumler's exclusion of the doctrine of eternal recurrence from the canon of Nietzsche's philosophy. Yet, as we have seen, in the 1937 course on eternal return Heidegger comes perilously close to Baeumler's interpretation when he reads WM, 617 (the "Recapitulation" note) as the imposition of Being on Becoming. And even in his first lecture course on Nietzsche Heidegger praises Baeumler as one of those "few commentators who reject [Ludwig] Klages's psychological-biologistic interpretation of Nietzsche." It may therefore be necessary for future research to examine the Baeumler-Heidegger relationship more minutely.

Baeumler's work is itself in reaction to Ernst Bertram's attempt to "mythologize" Nietzsche.[7] Baeumler's monograph means to be an "unlegendary" account of Nietzsche as "the last great European thinker" (5, 8, and 78–79 n.). As the title would suggest, the book falls into two parts, "The Philosopher" (16–87) and "The Politician" (88–177); it opens with a preface and introduction and closes with an epilogue. Here I will consider only the first half—not that I have anything against politicians—and its seven chapters, as follows: (1) "Realism," (2) "Being and Becoming," (3) "Consciousness and Life," (4) "Perspectivism," (5) "Will as Power," (6) "The Heraclitean World," (7) "Dionysos: The Eternal Return." Three topics emerge as essential in the present context: first, Baeumler's interpretation of Nietzsche's literary remains and of their relation to the published works; second, the relation of will to power and eternal return as one of Becoming to Being; and third, Nietzsche's critique of subjectivity in modern philosophy and his notion of "justice."

Not only in his monograph but also in his afterword to *Der Wille*

---

[6] See Volume I in this series, pp. 21–23 and 241; Volume II, pp. 256–57; and Volume IV, pp. 269–72. The German text is: Alfred Baeumler, *Nietzsche der Philosoph und Politiker* (Leipzig: P. Reclam, 1931). I will cite the book merely by page number in parentheses within my text.

[7] See Ernst Bertram, *Nietzsche: Versuch einer Mythologie* (Berlin: Georg Bondi, 1918), especially pp. 1–10, "Einleitung: Legende." See also the Analysis to Volume I, pp. 239–40. In what follows I will cite Bertram's book by page number in parentheses.

zur Macht and introduction to Die Unschuld des Werdens Baeumler proclaims the *systematic* nature of Nietzsche's (preeminently unpublished) philosophy.[8] Nietzsche's published books are altogether protean, showing a variety of faces. Only when one adduces the unpublished notebooks does the "unity of Nietzsche's production" come to light (7). "What Nietzsche immediately provides is always foreground; he is a master of foreground" (9; cf. Heidegger in Volume I, p. 9: "What Nietzsche himself published during his creative life was always foreground"). In his afterword to *The Will to Power* (699; Heidegger, Volume I, p. 10, calls it "a sensible afterword"), Baeumler writes; "*The Will to Power* is Nietzsche's philosophical magnum opus. All the principal results of his thought are united in this book." Even though Heidegger in each of his lecture courses argues *against* this celebration of the (non)book *Der Wille zur Macht,* he nonetheless accepts Baeumler's assertion that the concept of will to power is the systematic "creative center" of Nietzsche's thought. Or, if that is saying too much, one may at least wonder whether Heidegger himself may have been drawn to Book III of *The Will to Power*—the basic text for the first and third lecture courses on will to power as art and knowledge—by Baeumler's observation (707) that Book III is "perhaps the most important book." For Heidegger's treatment of *Thus Spoke Zarathustra* as the "vestibule" to his planned major work ("vestibule" being Nietzsche's own word; see Volume I, p. 12), Baeumler's excerpts from Nietzsche's correspondence (*Unschuld,* xxxv–xxxvii) may have been the crucial source. In his monograph Baeumler writes (14):

> Even *Zarathustra* was only meant to be a preparation for the major metaphysical work! This magnum opus places the world before us in precise

---

[8] These two publications appeared as volumes 78 and 82–83 of the *Kröner Taschenausgabe* (Leipzig, 1930–31). They were reissued after World War II with a substantially revised afterword and introduction (Stuttgart, 1964 and 1978). Baeumler's afterword to *Der Wille zur Macht* was in fact totally recast, with extensive additions and striking deletions: a study of those deletions would be a particularly useful, though dismal, undertaking. I shall cite (in parentheses) the *first* editions of these volumes (the "Nachwort" to *Der Wille zur Macht,* pp. 699–709, and "Zur Einführung," *Die Unschuld des Werdens,* pp. xi–xl) since these are the editions (difficult to locate nowadays) that Heidegger himself read.

visages. The "Will to Power" is a genuine philosophical system, a rigorously coherent set of thoughts. . . .

Finally, in his introduction to *Die Unschuld des Werdens,* Baeumler asserts: "Thus we realize that the relation between the works and the literary remains is in Nietzsche's case entirely off the norm: from the philosophical point of view these posthumous materials are more important than the works!"[9]

Turning now to the second area of Baeumler's importance, the problems of Becoming and Being, will to power, and eternal return, I note the following points. Baeumler (20 ff.) takes Being and Becoming as sheer opposites. It is a matter of Plato versus Heraclitus, with Nietzsche struggling to defeat the former in order to restore to his rights the latter. Heidegger is therefore constrained to show, against Baeumler, that Nietzsche unwittingly views Becoming in a Platonic way, so that his return to the commencement (Heraclitus) is frustrated. In his fifth chapter (46 ff.) Baeumler affirms (as Heidegger repeatedly does) that power is not merely the *goal* of will, that will is essentially self-overpowering; yet, strangely, this does not induce Baeumler to see

---

[9] See p. xxxiii. Again, lest any of the above appear to imply "guilt by association," I must note that the problem of the Nietzschean *Nachlass* is inordinately complex, as is Heidegger's relation to it. Many of the arguments presented by the leading editor of the new *Kritische Gesamtausgabe,* the late Giorgio Colli, are certainly compatible with Heidegger's own position. For example, Colli views the relation of the notes from 1885–88 to Nietzsche's published works in terms of "esoteric," as opposed to "exoteric," productions (see CM, *13,* 651). Although he qualifies the remark as being a helpful oversimplification, he does refer to the published works as productions of Nietzsche the *artist* and the notebook materials as meditations of Nietzsche the *philosopher* (656). Whereas the final works (*Twilight of the Idols, The Antichrist*) are "polemical, tempestuous, and decadent," the notebooks contain "pure reflection," their tone being "unusually sober, almost contemplative" (657, 662). Recall that Heidegger (in Part One, section 2, above) refers to the period 1887–88 as the one in which Nietzsche's thinking achieves the greatest *Helle und Ruhe,* "lucidity and tranquility." There are many other such points of agreement in Colli's and Heidegger's views of the *Nachlass,* but they will require separate, more detailed treatment. Let me simply note here the essential agreement in this regard between Heidegger and Nietzsche's editors early and late. On the striking difference in style of writing and tempo of thinking between the last notebooks and the final published works, August Horneffer, Alfred Baeumler, and Giorgio Colli are in complete accord. Colli: "sober, almost contemplative." Horneffer: "a tranquil, almost indifferent tempo." Baeumler: "the accelerated tempo is missing, [as is] a certain heatedness, a certain intensity and forcefulness of intention."

any connection between will to power and recurrence of the same—the bone of contention between himself and Heidegger. Ironically, it is in chapter 7 (79 ff.: "Dionysos: The Eternal Return") that Baeumler's discussion appears to be most significant in the present context. That chapter opens as follows:

> At its pinnacle, the philosophy of will to power, the philosophy of eternal *Becoming*, undergoes a transition to the concept of *Being*. Becoming is. . . . The problem of the transition from Becoming to Being greatly preoccupied Nietzsche. Among the most famous elements of his philosophy is the doctrine of eternal return; objectively considered, it is nothing other than an attempt to cancel the image of eternal Becoming and to posit in its place an image of eternal Being.

Baeumler now cites WM, 617 in the form in which Heidegger often (but not always: see p. 213, above) cites it, omitting the second sentence ("Twofold falsification . . .") and the rest of the note. Yet because eternal recurrence threatens to "cancel the system" and to impose Platonic Being on Heraclitean flux, Baeumler derides it as a piece of contemptible "Egyptianism" (a term he borrows from Nietzsche), as a "subjective," "personal," "religious" experience that any sound politician would suppress. Eternal return is "without importance" when viewed from the standpoint of the system (80–81). Will to power, on the contrary, is a "formula for occurrences in general." It has "objective sense."

It is crucial to note that Heidegger's thesis on the essential unity of will to power and eternal return is at least in part a response to Alfred Baeumler's dismissal of the latter notion. The question that arises is whether Heidegger's own formalistic reduction of eternal return of the same to a metaphysical expression—the *existentia* of beings—distracts Heidegger from insights attained during his own 1937 lecture course, distracts him until the early 1950s when in *What Calls for Thinking?* he again takes up Nietzsche's "thought of thoughts."[10]

There is yet a third area of possible influence. In the course of his exposition of Nietzsche's "theory of knowledge" as "the most important accomplishment of Anti-Cartesianism in recent philosophy" (31),

---

[10] Cf. Volume II, p. 257 n. 2.

Baeumler develops the notion of Nietzsche's "perspectivism" by referring at some length to Leibniz (36 ff.) It may well be that Heidegger's many references to Leibniz in this *Nietzsche* volume (as well as those in Volume I, section 25) are indebted to Baeumler—even though Heidegger certainly had independent access to Leibniz long before Baeumler's monograph appeared. More significant is the fact that Baeumler's sixth chapter (see 65–78) contains a long section on *Gerechtigkeit,* "justice," as a fundamental component of Nietzsche's metaphysics. "Will to power," he writes, "is merely another expression for supreme justice" (78). He now cites the first of the two notes cited by Heidegger (on justice as *"the supreme representative of life itself"*) much in the way that Heidegger does. Yet this particular aspect of the Baeumlerian context is complicated by the fact that Ernst Bertram here assumes special importance. However much Baeumler tries to contrapose his own account to that of Bertram, it is clear that Bertram's discussion of "justice" is by far the more original and decisive one.

Bertram chooses *Gerechtigkeit* as the title of his fourth chapter (91–101). He offers a sensitive, nuanced account of that notion in Nietzsche's writings from the early 1870s until the end—the "end" here meaning the doctrine of *amor fati* and the exaltation of justice as *"supreme representative,"* with which aphorism Bertram's chapter in fact ends. The importance Bertram attaches to the notion of "justice" is indicated by the fact that not a single other rubric of Nietzsche's philosophy—neither will to power nor eternal return nor nihilism—appears in his book's table of contents. The interesting and important question as to whether Heidegger was familiar with Bertram's chapter can only be answered speculatively and ambiguously: although he must have known Bertram's book, which dominated the discussion of Nietzsche throughout the 1920s and early 1930s (see Volume I, pp. 238–40), Heidegger may well have relied on Baeumler in this regard.

The upshot is that if *Gerechtigkeit* seems incapable of fulfilling the task that Heidegger assigns it—to be the horizon upon which will to power as both art and truth can be projected—one must wonder whether it was not Baeumler, aided and abetted by Bertram, who once again distracted Heidegger from his own best insights. Or, to put it the other way around, if Heidegger's move to "justice" seems surprising in terms of the dynamics of "Will to Power as Knowledge" and "Nietzsche's Metaphysics," there is nonetheless a considerable amount of "external" precedent for that move.

III. QUESTIONS

Why in 1939 did Heidegger revert to will to power as knowledge when art had already been identified as the locus of the essential question, to wit, a "new interpretation of sensuousness"?

Even if we grant the importance of the question of truth (whether as the extreme impasse of *homoiōsis* or as the other commencement of *alētheia*), this question remains troubling. Does not Heidegger's identification of will to power with both the technological will-to-will and the brutalization of *animalitas* make it impossible for him to advance to the question of sensuousness? Furthermore, does not the discussion of will to power within the context of a (Baeumlerian) systematic metaphysics cause Heidegger so to formalize the relation of will to power and eternal return that virtually nothing is left of Nietzsche's "most burdensome thought"?

If we must answer these questions in the affirmative, however reluctantly, then we must venture the following question: Does not Heidegger's *Nietzsche,* viewed as a whole, proceed as a *decline* from the first two lecture courses to the second set, and from thence to the treatises on Nietzsche's metaphysics and nihilism? If there is anything to this suspicion, would it not be the gravest folly to abandon the lecture courses for the sake of the later "summary" statements? Finally, if the guiding question of these Analyses (see Volume I, p. 247) is Nietzsche's role in awakening the question of *Being and Time* (and, I should add, Heidegger's later thinking of the history of Being as well), would it be true to say that the lecture courses on will to power as art and the eternal recurrence of the same are the most fertile parts of Heidegger's *grand livre?* Which, nevertheless, is much less simple than people have generally tended to say?

I will not attempt to answer such sweeping questions here, questions that are directed to Heidegger's Nietzsche interpretation as a whole.[11] I will simply insert the reminder that Heidegger's lecture course on will to power as art itself raises the question of knowledge, *Erkenntnis*, at every crucial juncture, so that it would be utterly naive to believe that it is a matter of opting for art rather than truth. Nor do we confront the interpretation of Nietzsche's metaphysics as *the consummation of the Western tradition* merely by invoking the "contexts" for Heidegger's questioning. Let me try to develop another set of questions, rather more specific questions.

When in a note sketched in 1939 Heidegger cites "justice" as one of Nietzsche's "fundamental concepts" (justice along with value positing, Becoming, law, and legislation), does this merely reflect Heidegger's disaffection from Nietzsche, his disenchantment, or is Heidegger in fact here pursuing Nietzsche's own path of thought? Assuming that Nietzsche's thought has a path of its "own," one path, which we can map. Be that as it may, do not Nietzsche's own plans for a Vulcanic celebration of "midday and eternity" become the clinkers and ash of "legislation" and "revaluation"? Is there not some "justice" in the remark that Nietzsche's once delicate and fragile instrument for testing the solidity or speciousness of values and ideas eventually becomes a bludgeon—Maxwell's Silver Hammer? Indeed, sometimes it seems as though the "new interpretation of sensuousness" is postponed not only by Heidegger—who constantly invokes some body who is alive, yet never pursues the matter, never tells us any more about it—but also precisely in Nietzsche, Nietzsche "himself."[12] Moreover, is not Heidegger's complaint, to the effect that Nietzsche's

---

[11] In chapter eight of my book, *Intimations of Mortality: Time, Truth, and Finitude in Heidegger's Thinking of Being* (University Park, Penn.: The Pennsylvania State University Press, 1986), I have tried to pose these more sweeping questions and to reply to them. Questions such as the following: What role does Nietzsche play in reawakening the question of the *meaning*—and the *truth*, that is to say, the *history*—of Being? How are we to conceive of Nietzsche as *a* metaphysician, that is, as one among others, but also as *the last* metaphysician, the one who compels the question of Being and Time? And what can Heidegger possibly mean when he calls Nietzsche "the last *thinker* of the West"?

[12] See Krell, *Postponements: Woman, Sensuality, and Death in Nietzsche* (Bloomington and London: Indiana University Press, 1986), especially chapters 1 and 4.

extreme reduction of truth to semblance and error somehow relies on *semblance as radiant disclosure,* a sound one? Is it not "justified"? Would we squelch that complaint by facile references to the sheer multiplicity of Nietzsche's paths or styles? Or does not the question of the essential unfolding of truth, *das Wesen der Wahrheit,* here become crucial for the first time?

If we are still unhappy about "justice" as the proper conjunction of art and truth, if "harmony" seems too monotonously metaphysical a notion to come even close to Nietzschean creativity and rapture in the grand style, then how are we to dismantle in a precise and positive way Heidegger's formulation of the *"transfiguration that commands and poetizes, establishes perspectival horizons, and fixates"?* How can we—and *can* we—extricate artistic transfiguration from the economy of permanentizing? Can we, to put the matter negatively, envisage self-preserving, self-enhancing *life* at that mysterious threshold where fixation becomes petrifaction rather than a fulguration of form-engendering force? Conversely, how can we—and *can* we—both imagine and tap the creative energies of life-enhancing art, beyond every form of fixation?

Is there nothing in the metaphysical tradition, the tradition which projects Being as permanence of presencing, that can help us answer these questions? Surely, nothing can prevent our commencing to *ask* them—unless it be anxiety in the face of the solitary superficies of bodying life?

Glossary

abandonment by Being	die Seinsverlassenheit
abode	die Unterkunft
absence	die Abwesenheit
absolute	unbedingt, absolut
abysmal, abyssal	abgründlich
accomplishment, fulfillment	die Vollendung
accordance, agreement	die Verständigung
actual, real	wirklich
actuating power, efficacy	die Wirksamkeit
to address	ansprechen
advent	die Ankunft
advocate	der Fürsprecher
affinity, coherence, cohesion	die Zusammengehörigkeit
animate	lebendig
anthropomorphizing	die Vermenschlichung
appearance, semblance, radiance	der Schein, die Erscheinung
approximation, assimilation, adequation	die Angleichung
to arrange, install	einrichten
articulation	das Gefüge
aspect	der Gesichtspunkt
to assimilate	aneignen, angleichen
at hand	vorhanden
basic experience	die Grunderfahrung
basic occurrence	das Grundgeschehen
basic trait	der Grundzug

beatitude	die Seligkeit
Becoming	das Werden
Being	das Sein
being(s)	das Seiende
a being	(ein) Seiendes
being(s) as a whole	das Seiende im Ganzen
beingness	die Seiendheit
bodying (-forth)	das Leibende
bounded	begrenzt
to bring under control	bewältigen
burden	das Schwergewicht
burdensome	schwer
to calculate	errechnen, berechnen
capable	gewachsen
cast	geworfen
casting	der Schlag, typos
center	die Mitte
center of gravity	das Schwergewicht
claim	der Anspruch
clarification	die Verdeutlichung
the clearing	die Lichtung
cognition, knowledge	die Erkenntnis
coherence, cohesion	die Zusammengehörigkeit
coinage	die Prägung
collective	Gesamt-
commemorative thought	das Andenken
commencement	der Anfang
communication	die Mitteilung
completion, consummation	die Vollendung
computation	die Errechnung
concealing	die Verbergung
concealment	die Verborgenheit
conception	die Auffassung, der Begriff
concord	die Eintracht

Glossary 279

concordance	die Übereinkunft
configuration	die Gestalt
to confront	begegnen
confrontation	die Auseinandersetzung
constancy	die (Be-) Ständigkeit
consummation	die Vollendung, die Vollbringung
correspondence	die Entsprechung
countermovement	die Gegenbewegung
counterthought	der Gegengedanke
to create poetically	dichten
creation	die Schöpfung, das Schaffen
creative	schöpferisch
cycle	der Umlauf, der Kreislauf
deduction	die Schlussfolgerung
default	das Ausbleiben
to define, determine	bestimmen
definitive	massgebend
dehumanization	die Entmenschung
deification	die Vergöttlichung
difference	die Differenz, der Unterschied
differentiation	die Unterscheidung
difficult	schwierig
discerning	klug
discord(ance)	die Zwietracht, der Zwiespalt
dismay	der Schrecken
disposability	die Machbarkeit
disposition	die Verfügung
distinction	der Unterschied, die Auszeichnung
domain, realm	der Bereich

dominance, dominion	die Herrschaft
duration	die Dauer
eidos	*das Aussehen*
emblem	*das Sinnbild*
embodiment	*das Leiben*
to encounter in thought	*entgegendenken*
end, goal	*das Ziel*
energy	*die Kraft*
enhancement	*die Steigerung*
enjoining	*die Ver-fügung*
essence	*das Wesen*
essential definition, determination	*die Wesensbestimmung*
essential unfolding	*das Wesen* (verbal)
to esteem, estimate	*(ab-, ein-) schätzen*
estimations of value	*die Wertschätzungen*
eternal recurrence of the same	*die ewige Wiederkehr des Gleichen*
eternal return	*die ewige Wiederkunft*
(propriative) event	*das Ereignis*
evidentiary	*der Beweis-*
exaction	*die Zumutung*
to excell	*(sich) überhöhen*
exigencies	*die Notwendigkeiten*
explicit(ly)	*ausdrücklich*
to express	*ausdrücken*
expressly	*eigens*
the extreme, uttermost	*das Äusserste*
feeling	*das Gefühl*
final	*endgültig*
finite	*endlich*
fixation	*die Festmachung*
fixity	*die Festigkeit*
force	*die Kraft, die Gewalt*
fore, to come to the	*zum Vorschein kommen*

forgottenness, oblivion	die Vergessenheit
form	die Form, die Gestalt
to found	stiften, begründen
free space, region	das Freie
fright	die Furcht, die Furchtbarkeit
fulfillment, accomplishment	die Vollendung
full, replete	voll
fundamental	Grund-
fundamental metaphysical position	die metaphysische Grundstellung
futurity	die Zukünftigkeit
gathering	die Versammlung, legein
genesis, gestation	die Entstehung
genuine	echt
the gigantic	das Riesenhafte
global, planetary	planetarisch
grandeur	die Grösse
to grapple, cope with	bewältigen
to grasp	begreifen, fassen
to ground, found	begründen
ground(s)	der Grund
grounding question	die Grundfrage
guardianship	die Wächterschaft
guideline	der Leitfaden
guiding question	die Leitfrage
to harbor, conceal	bergen
harmony, monotony	die Einstimmigkeit
to heed	achten, beachten
hierarchy	der Rang, die Rangordnung
historicity	die Geschichtlichkeit
historiological	historisch

history of Being	die Seinsgeschichte
to hold fast to	sich halten an
to hold firm in	sich halten in
to hold-to-be-true	für-wahr-halten
humanization	die Vermenschung
Idea, idea	die Idee, idea
ill will, revulsion	der Widerwille
illusion	der Anschein, die Illusion
image	das Bild, das Sinnbild
impact	die Wirkung, die Tragweite
incipient	anfänglich
the incisive sense	der Bescheid
incorporation	die Einverleibung
individuation	die Vereinzelung
inherence	das Innestehen
inherently	in sich
insight	die Erkenntnis, der Einblick
insistence	die Inständigkeit
to install, arrange	(sich) einrichten
instauration (of self)	die (Selbst)einrichtung
interpretation	die Auslegung, die Deutung
to invert	umdrehen, umkehren
isolation	die Absonderung
jointure	der Fug
justice	die Gerechtigkeit
justification	die Rechtfertigung
to keep to oneself	an sich halten
to know	wissen

knowing, knowledge	*das Wissen, die Erkenntnis*
last, final, ultimate	*letzt*
lawfulness	*die Gesetzlichkeit*
to lighten, clear	*lichten*
the lighting	*das Lichtende*
the living, the animate	*das Lebende*
locale	*der Ort, die Ortschaft*
loneliness, solitude	*die Einsamkeit*
lucidity	*die Besonnenheit*
magnitude	*das Grosse*
main, major work; magnum opus	*das Hauptwerk*
malleability	*die Machsamkeit*
manipulability	*die Einrichtbarkeit*
mastery	*das Herrsein, die Herrschaft*
matter (of thought)	*die Sache (des Denkens)*
to matter	*angehen, anliegen*
measure, standard of	*das Mass*
measureless	*masslos*
to mediate	*vermitteln*
to meditate	*besinnen*
metamorphosis	*die Verwandlung*
midday	*der Mittag*
midpoint, center	*die Mitte*
(mis)calculation	*die Verrechnung*
moment	*der Augenblick*
monotony	*die Einstimmigkeit*
mood, attunement	*die Stimmung*
to muster, bring to	*zustellen*
mystery	*das Geheimnis*
need, calamity	*die Not*
to negate	*verneinen*

nexus, connection	der Zusammenhang, die Verflechtung
notes	die Aufzeichnungen
the nothing	das Nichts
vacuous nothingness	das leere Nichts
nullity	das Nichtige, die Nichtigkeit
oblivion, forgottenness	die Vergessenheit
to occur essentially	wesen
on hand, handy	zuhanden
one-upmanship	die Überbietung
open (region)	das Offene
openness	die Offenheit
origin	der Ursprung
original	ursprünglich
outward appearance	das Aussehen, eidos, idea
overcoming, overturning	die Überwindung
overman	der Übermensch
panoramic	weitumherschauend
to pass away	vergehen
permanence, constancy	die Beständigkeit
to permanentize, stabilize	beständigen
pertinent	zugehörig
pervasive	durchgängig
phenomena	die Erscheinungen
to pivot	drehen
plan, project(ion)	der Entwurf
plenipotence	die Vollmacht
to portray, present	darstellen
prepotence	die Vormacht
presence	die Anwesenheit
presencing	das Anwesen
what is present	das Anwesende

the present (temporal)	die Gegenwart, das Gegenwärtige
to present, portray	darstellen
to preserve	bewahren, verwahren
presumption	die Anmassung
to prevail	herrschen, walten
primordial	anfänglich
profile	das Aussehen, eidos
project(ion)	der Entwurf
proof	der Beweis
proper	eigentlich
to be proper to	gehören
proposition, statement	der Satz
to propriate	(sich) ereignen
propriative event	das Ereignis
provenance	die Herkunft
proximity, nearness	die Nähe
questionable, dubious	fragwürdig
quiddity, what-being	das Wassein, to ti estin
radiance	das Scheinen, das Aufleuchten
to radiate	scheinen
real, actual	wirklich
reality, actuality	die Realität, die Wirklichkeit
realm, domain	der Bereich
to recognize	erkennen
redemption	die Erlösung
reflection, meditation	die Besinnung
reflectiveness	die Besinnlichkeit
refulgence	der Aufschein
refusal, denial	die Verweigerung
to reign, rule	walten
to relate	sich verhalten

relation	*das Verhältnis, die Beziehung*
relationship	*der Bezug*
remote, far remove	*die Ferne*
replete	*voll*
to represent	*vorstellen*
representation	*das Vorstellen, die Vorstellung, repraesentatio*
resolutely open	*ent-schlossen*
resoluteness	*die Entschiedenheit, die Entschlossenheit*
resonance	*das Aufklingen, der Widerhall*
to respond	*entsprechen, entgegnen*
revealing	*das Entbergen*
the right	*das Recht*
the righteous	*der Rechte*
rise	*der Aufgang*
to rule, reign	*walten*
to secure	*sichern*
securement	*die Sicherstellung*
securing of permanence, stability	*die Bestandsicherung*
to seem, appear	*scheinen*
the selfsame	*das Selbe*
semblance, illusion	*der Schein*
sense, meaning, direction	*der Sinn*
sensuous	*sinnlich*
sketches	*die Aufzeichnungen*
solitude, loneliness	*die Einsamkeit*
stability	*der Bestand*
stance	*die Haltung*
standard (of measure)	*das Mass*
statement, proposition, law (of logic)	*der Satz*

strength, force	die Kraft
subjectivity	die Subjektivität
subsistence	der Bestand
suprasensuous	übersinnlich
surety	die Sicherung
to surpass, surmount	überhöhen, übersteigen, aufheben
surveyability	die Übersehbarkeit
to take-to-be-true	für-wahr-halten
task	die Aufgabe, das Aufgegebene
that-being	das Dassein, to estin
thinking	das Denken
thought	der Gedanke
transcendent	übersinnlich
transfiguration	die Verklärung
transformation	der Wandel
transiency	das Vergängliche
transition	der Übergang
the true, what is true	das Wahre
truth	die Wahrheit, alētheia
ultimately	im Grunde
the unconcealed	das Unverborgene
unconcealment	die Unverborgenheit
unconditioned	unbedingt, bedingungslos
the underlying	das Zugrundeliegende, hypokeimenon, substantia, understand
to unfold	entfalten, entwickeln
univocity	die Einstimmung
upsurgence	das Aufgehen, das Anheben, physis
usage	der Brauch, das Brauchen

utterance, saying	das Sagen, die Sage
uttermost, extreme, outermost	äusserst
vacuous	leer
valuation	die Wertsetzung
valuative thought	der Wertgedanke
value	der Wert
value thinking	das Wertdenken
value-estimations	die Wertschätzungen
to venture	wagen
viewpoint	der Gesichtspunkt, der Blickpunkt
visage, vision	das Gesicht, eidos
vitality	die Lebendigkeit
the void	die Leere
weighty	gewichtig
what-being, quiddity	das Wassein, to ti estin
to will, want	wollen
will to power	der Wille zur Macht
will-to-will	der Wille zum Willen
withdrawal	der Entzug
to withhold	vorenthalten
worthy of question	fragwürdig

MARTIN HEIDEGGER

Nietzsche

Volume IV: Nihilism

Translated from the German by
FRANK A. CAPUZZI

Edited, with Notes and an Analysis, by
DAVID FARRELL KRELL

Contents

Editor's Preface   v

PART ONE: EUROPEAN NIHILISM   1

1. The Five Major Rubrics of Nietzsche's Thought   3
2. Nihilism as the "Devaluation of the Uppermost Values"   13
3. Nihilism, *Nihil*, and Nothing   18
4. Nietzsche's Conception of Cosmology and Psychology   24
5. The Provenance of Nihilism and Nihilism's Three Forms   30
6. The Uppermost Values as Categories   36
7. Nihilism and the Man of Western History   43
8. The New Valuation   47
9. Nihilism as History   52
10. Valuation and Will to Power   58
11. Subjectivity in Nietzsche's Interpretation of History   69
12. Nietzsche's "Moral" Interpretation of Metaphysics   76
13. Metaphysics and Anthropomorphism   85
14. The Statement of Protagoras   91
15. The Dominance of the Subject in the Modern Age   96
16. The Cartesian *Cogito* as *Cogito Me Cogitare*   102
17. Descartes' *Cogito Sum*   111
18. The Fundamental Metaphysical Positions of Descartes and Protagoras   119
19. Nietzsche's Position vis-à-vis Descartes   123
20. The Inner Connection Between the Fundamental Positions of Descartes and Nietzsche   136

21.	The Essential Determination of Man, and the Essence of Truth	139
22.	The End of Metaphysics	147
23.	Relations with beings and the Relationship to Being. The Ontological Difference	150
24.	Being as *A Priori*	159
25.	Being as *Idea*, as *Agathon*, and as Condition	167
26.	The Interpretation of Being as *Idea*, and Valuative Thought	173
27.	The Projection of Being as Will to Power	178
28.	The Differentiation Between Being and beings, and the Nature of Man	183
29.	Being as the Void and as Abundance	188

PART TWO: NIHILISM AS DETERMINED BY
THE HISTORY OF BEING   197

Analysis by David Farrell Krell   253
Glossary   295

Editor's Preface

The final volume of Martin Heidegger's *Nietzsche* comprises two parts: first, a lecture course taught at the University of Freiburg during the first trimester[1] of 1940, entitled "Nietzsche: The Will to Power (II. European Nihilism)";[2] second, a treatise composed during the years 1944–46 but not published until 1961 under the title "Nihilism as Determined by the History of Being." Both texts originally appeared in Martin Heidegger, *Nietzsche*, 2 vols. (Pfullingen: Günther Neske Verlag, 1961), II, 31–256 and 335–98. (Throughout these English volumes, the Neske edition is cited as NI or NII, with page number.)

Dr. Capuzzi and I have translated the passages from Nietzsche's works in Heidegger's text afresh. But we are grateful to have had the late Walter Kaufmann's exemplary renderings for comparison. With the sole exception of the footnote on the first page of the lecture course, all footnotes are my own. The glossary, which should be used solely in order to check back to the German text, is also my own work.

Heidegger's references to *Der Wille zur Macht*, the text on which he based the lecture course, are designated by the abbreviation WM, followed by the aphorism number, not page number; e.g., (WM, 12). His references to all other Nietzschean texts are to the *Grossoktavausgabe* (Leipzig, 1905 ff.), cited in the text by volume and page—e.g., (XIV, 413–67)—and in the footnotes as GOA. I have checked most of the more important—but by no means all—of the references to the

---

[1] The change from the semester to the trimester system was a wartime measure of brief duration.

[2] The Roman numeral II presumably refers to the second chapter of Book One of *Der Wille zur Macht*, "Toward the History of European Nihilism," although the course is by no means restricted to that part. Current plans for the lecture in the Heidegger "Complete Edition" drop the numeral.

Grossoktavausgabe against the *Kritische Gesamtausgabe* of Nietzsche's works, edited by the late Giorgio Colli and Mazzino Montinari (Berlin: Walter de Gruyter, 1967 ff.), cited in the notes as CM, with volume and page number, except where the *Nachlass* fragments are concerned. For the latter, I adopt the full designation in CM of manuscript and fragment number; e.g., W II 5 [14]. Perhaps it is not out of place to mention the recent release of a fifteen-volume paperback edition of the *Kritische Gesamtausgabe* (Deutscher Taschenbuch Verlag, 1980). Readers would do well to check Heidegger's references to the *Nachlass* against this edition, even though the exclusion of the hardcover edition's concordances to *Der Wille zur Macht* makes that task formidable indeed.

Part One
EUROPEAN NIHILISM

1. The Five Major Rubrics of Nietzsche's Thought

The first philosophical use of the word *nihilism* presumably stems from Friedrich H. Jacobi. The word *nothing* appears quite frequently in Jacobi's letter to Fichte. There he says, "Truly, my dear Fichte, it would not annoy me if you or anyone else wished to say that what I set against Idealism—which I deplore as *Nihilism*— is *Chimerism*."*

Later the word *nihilism* came into vogue through Turgeniev as a name for the notion that only what is perceptible to our senses, that is, only beings that one experiences oneself, only these and nothing else are real and have being. Therefore, anything grounded on tradition, authority, or any other definitive value is negated. Usually, however, the name *positivism* is used to designate this point of view. Jean Paul, in his *Elementary Course in Aesthetics* (sections 1 and 2) employs the word in describing romantic poetry as poetic nihilism. We might compare this usage to Dostoievsky's *Foreword* to his Pushkin Lectures (1880). The passage in question runs thus:

> As far as my lecture itself is concerned, I simply want to make the following four points regarding Pushkin's importance for Russia:
> 1. That Pushkin, with his profound, penetrating, and highly compassionate mind, and through his truly Russian heart, was the first to see and recognize for what it is a significant, morbid manifestation among our intelligentsia, our rootless society which seems to hover high above the common people. He recognized it, and enabled us to place graphically before our

---

* Friedrich H. Jacobi, *Werke* (Leipzig, 1816), III, 44; from the section "Jacobi to Fichte," which first appeared in the fall of 1799. I am grateful to Dr. Otto Pöggeler, who provided the reference to Jacobi while working on the proofs of the present book. — M. H.

eyes the typical, negative Russian character: the character who finds no rest and cannot be satisfied with anything permanent, who does not believe in his native soil nor in the strength of his native soil, who fundamentally denies Russia and himself (or rather, his social class, the entire stratum of the intelligentsia, to which he too belongs, and which has detached itself from our folk heritage), who will have nothing to do with his own people, and who sincerely suffers from all this. Pushkin's Aleko and Onegin have evoked a great many characters like themselves in our literature.... (Dostoievsky, *Werke*, edited by Moeller v. d. Bruck, Division Two, XII, 95f.)

For Nietzsche, though, the word *nihilism* means something substantially "more." Nietzsche speaks about "European nihilism." He does not mean the positivism that arose in the mid-nineteenth century and spread throughout Europe. "European" has a historical significance here, and means as much as "Western" in the sense of Western history. Nietzsche uses *nihilism* as the name for the historical movement that he was the first to recognize and that already governed the previous century while defining the century to come, the movement whose essential interpretation he concentrates in the terse sentence: "God is dead." That is to say, the "Christian God" has lost His power over beings and over the determination of man. "Christian God" also stands for the "transcendent" in general in its various meanings—for "ideals" and "norms," "principles" and "rules," "ends" and "values," which are set *"above"* the being, in order to give being as a whole a purpose, an order, and—as it is succinctly expressed—"meaning." Nihilism is that historical process whereby the dominance of the "transcendent" becomes null and void, so that all being loses its worth and meaning. Nihilism is the history of the being itself, through which the death of the Christian God comes slowly but inexorably to light. It may be that this God will continue to be believed in, and that His world will be taken as "real," "effectual," and "determinative." This history resembles the process in which the light of a star that has been extinguished for millennia still gleams, but in its gleaming nonetheless remains a mere "appearance." For Nietzsche, therefore, nihilism is in no way some kind of viewpoint "put forward" by somebody, nor is it an arbitrary historical "given," among many others, that can be historically documented. Nihilism is, rather, that event of long duration in which the truth of being as a whole is essentially transformed and driven toward an end that such truth has determined.

The truth of being as a whole has long been called *metaphysics*. Every era, every human epoch, is sustained by some metaphysics and is placed thereby in a definite relation to being as a whole and also to itself. The end of metaphysics discloses itself as the collapse of the reign of the transcendent and the "ideal" that sprang from it. But the end of metaphysics does not mean the cessation of history. It is the *beginning* of a serious concern with that "event": "God is dead."* That beginning is already under way. Nietzsche himself understood his philosophy as an introduction to the beginning of a new age. He envisioned the coming century—that is, the current, twentieth century—as the start of an era whose upheavals could not be compared to anything previously known. Although the scenery of the world theater might remain the same for a time, the play in performance would already be a different one. The fact that earlier aims now disappear and former values are devalued is no longer experienced as sheer annihilation and deplored as wasteful and wrong, but is rather greeted as a liberation, touted as an irrevocable gain, and perceived as a *fulfillment*.

"Nihilism" is the increasingly dominant truth that all prior aims of being have become superfluous. But with this transformation of the erstwhile relation to ruling values, nihilism has also perfected itself for the free and genuine task of a *new* valuation. Such nihilism, which is in itself perfected and is decisive for the future, may be characterized as "classical nihilism." Nietzsche describes his own "metaphysics" with this name and conceives it to be *the* counterstroke to all preceding metaphysics. The name *nihilism* thus loses the purely nihilistic sense in which it means a destruction and annihilation of previous values, the mere negation of beings and the futility of human history.

"Nihilism," thought now in its classic sense, calls for freedom *from* values as freedom *for* a *revaluation* of all (such) values. Nietzsche uses the expression "revaluation of all values hitherto" alongside the key

---

* On the *Ereignis* of nihilism, see Heidegger's remarks during the first lecture course on Nietzsche (winter semester, 1936–37), in Martin Heidegger, *Nietzsche*. Vol. I: *The Will to Power as Art* (New York: Harper & Row, 1979), p. 156 n.

word *nihilism* as another *major rubric* by which he assigns his own fundamental metaphysical position its definite place within the history of Western metaphysics.

From the rubric "revaluation of values," we expect that altered values will be posited in place of earlier ones. But for Nietzsche "revaluation" means that the very "place" for previous values disappears, not merely that the values themselves fall away. This implies that the nature and direction of valuation, and the definition of the essence of value are transformed. The revaluation thinks Being for the first time as value. With it, metaphysics begins to be value thinking. In accordance with this transformation, prior values do not merely succumb to devaluation but, above all, the *need* for values in their former shape and in their previous place—that is to say, their place in the transcendent—is uprooted. The uprooting of past needs most assuredly takes place by cultivating the growing ignorance of past values and by obliterating history through a revision of its basic traits. "Revaluation of prior values" is primarily the metamorphosis of all valuation heretofore and the "breeding" of a new need for values.

If such revaluation of all prior values is not only to be carried out but is also to be grounded, then it has need of a "new principle"; that is, the establishment of a basis for defining beings as a whole in a new, authoritative way. But if the interpretation of beings as a whole cannot issue from a transcendent that is posited "over" them from the outset, then the new values and their standard of measure can only be drawn from the realm of beings themselves. Thus beings themselves require a new interpretation through which their basic character may be defined in a way that will make it fit to serve as a "principle" for the inscription of a new table of values and as a standard of measure for suitably ranking such values.

If the essence of metaphysics consists in grounding the truth of being as a whole, then the revaluation of all values, as a grounding of the principle for a new valuation, is itself metaphysics. What Nietzsche perceives and posits as the basic character of being as a whole is what he calls the "will to power." That concept does not merely delimit *what* a being in its Being *is:* Nietzsche's phrase, "will to power," which has in many ways become familiar, contains his interpretation of the *essence of power.* Every power is a power only as long as it is more power; that is to say, an increase in power. Power can maintain itself in itself, that is, in its essence, only if it overtakes and overcomes the power level it has already attained—*overpowering* is the expression we use. As soon as power stalls at a certain power level, it immediately becomes powerless. "Will to power" does not mean simply the "romantic" yearning and quest for power by those who have no power; rather, "will to power" means the accruing of power by power for its own overpowering.

"Will to power" is a single name for the basic character of beings and for the essence of power. Nietzsche often substitutes "force" for "will to power" in a way that is easily misunderstood. His conception of the basic character of beings as will to power is not the contrivance or whim of a fantast who has strayed off to chase chimeras. It is the fundamental experience of a *thinker;* that is, of one of those individuals who have no choice but to find words for what a being *is* in the history of its Being. Every being, insofar as it *is,* and is *as* it is, is "will to power." The phrase names that from which all valuation proceeds and to which it returns. However, as we have said, the new valuation is not a "revaluation of all prior values" merely in that it supplants all earlier values with power, the uppermost value, but first and foremost because power and *only power* posits values, validates them, and makes decisions about the possible justifications of a valuation. If all being is will to power, then only what is fulfilled in its essence by power "has" value or "is" a value. But power is power only as enhancement of power. To the extent that it is truly power, alone determining all beings, power does not recognize the worth or value of anything outside of itself. That is why will to power as a principle for the new valuation tolerates no end outside of being as a whole. Now, because all being as will to power—that is, as incessant self-overpowering—must be *a continual "becoming,"* and because such "becoming" cannot move "toward an end" *outside* its own "farther and farther," but is ceaselessly caught up in the cyclical increase of power to which it reverts, then being as a whole too, as this power-conforming becoming, must itself always recur again and bring back the same.

Hence, the basic character of beings as will to power is also defined as "the eternal recurrence of the same." The latter constitutes yet another major rubric in Nietzsche's metaphysics and, moreover, implies something essential: *only* through the adequately conceived essence of will to power can it become clear why the Being of beings as a whole must be eternal recurrence of the same. The reverse holds as well: only through the essence of the eternal recurrence of the same can the innermost core of will to power and its necessity be grasped. The phrase "will to power" tells *what* beings are in their "essence" (in their constitution). The phrase "eternal recurrence of the same" tells *how* beings of such an essence must as a whole be.

It remains for us to observe what is decisive here; namely, that Nietzsche had to think the eternal recurrence of the same *before* the will to power. The most essential thought is thought first.

When Nietzsche himself insists that Being, as "life," is in essence *"becoming,"* he does not intend the roughly defined concept of "becoming" to mean either an endless, continual progression to some unknown goal, nor is he thinking about the confused turmoil and tumult of unrestrained drives. The vague and hackneyed term *becoming* signifies the overpowering of power, as the essence of power, which powerfully and continually returns to itself in its own way.

At the same time, the eternal recurrence of the same offers the keenest interpretation of "classical nihilism," which absolutely obliterates any end above and beyond beings. For such nihilism, the words "God is dead" suggest the impotence not only of the Christian God but of every transcendent element under which men might want to shelter themselves. And that impotence signifies the collapse of the old order.

With the revaluation of all past values, an unrestricted challenge has been issued to men: that unconditionally from, through, and over themselves, they raise "new standards" under which the accommodation of being as a whole to a new order must be effected. Because the "transcendent," the "beyond," and "heaven" have been abolished, only the "earth" remains. The new order must therefore be the absolute dominance of pure power over the earth through man—not through any arbitrary kind of man, and certainly not through the humanity that has heretofore lived under the old values. Through what kind of man, then?

With nihilism—that is to say, with the revaluation of all prior values among beings as will to power and in light of the eternal recurrence of the same—it becomes necessary to posit a new essence for man. But, because "God is dead," only man himself can grant man his measure and center, the *"type,"* the "model" of a certain kind of man who has assigned the task of a revaluation of all values to the individual power of his will to power and who is prepared to embark on the absolute domination of the globe. Classical nihilism, which as the revaluation of all values hitherto understands beings as will to power and can admit eternal recurrence of the same as the sole "end," must take man himself—that is, man as he has been until now—out of and "over" himself and must fashion as his measure the figure of the "Overman." Hence, in *Thus Spoke Zarathustra* Nietzsche says, "Now then, you higher men! Only now is the mountain of man's future in labor. God died: now *we* will that Overman live." (See Part Four, "On the Higher Man," second paragraph; VI, 418.)

The Overman is the supreme configuration of purest will to power; that is to say, of the one and only value. The Overman, the absolute rule of pure power, is the "meaning" (the aim) of what alone has being; namely, "the earth." "Not 'mankind' but *Overman* is the *goal*" (WM, 1001, 1002). From Nietzsche's point of view, the Overman is not meant to be a mere amplification of prior man, but the most unequivocally singular form of human existence that, as absolute will to power, is brought to power in every man to some degree and that thereby grants him his membership in being as a whole—that is, in will to power—and that shows him to be a true "being," close to reality and "life." The Overman simply leaves the man of traditional values behind, *overtakes* him, and transfers the justification for all laws and the positing of all values to the empowering of power. An act or accomplishment is valid as such only to the extent that it serves to equip, nurture, and enhance will to power.

The five main rubrics we have mentioned—"nihilism," "revaluation of all values hitherto," "will to power," "eternal recurrence of the same," and "Overman"—each portrays Nietzsche's metaphysics from just *one* perspective, although in each case it is a perspective that defines the whole. Thus Nietzsche's metaphysics is grasped only when what is named in these five headings can be thought—that is, essentially experienced—in its primordial and heretofore merely intimated conjunction. We can learn what "nihilism" in Nietzsche's sense is only if we also comprehend, in their contexts, "revaluation of all values hitherto," "will to power," "eternal recurrence of the same," and "Overman." By starting from an adequate comprehension of nihilism and working in the opposite direction, we can also acquire knowledge about the essence of revaluation, the essence of will to power, the essence of the eternal recurrence of the same, and the essence of the Overman. But to have such knowledge is to stand within the moment that the history of Being has opened up for our age.

When we speak here about "concepts" and "grasping" and "thinking," it is certainly not a question of a propositional delimitation of what is represented when we name these major rubrics. To grasp here means consciously to experience what has been named in its essence and so to recognize in what moment of the hidden history of the West we "stand"; to recognize whether we do *stand* in it, or are falling, or already lie prostrate in it, or whether we neither surmise the one nor are touched by the other two, but merely indulge in the illusions of common opinion and the daily round, floundering in utter dissatisfaction with ourselves. Thoughtful knowing, as a supposedly "abstract doctrine," does not simply have some practical behavior as its consequence. Thoughtful knowing is in itself *comportment,* which is sustained in being not by some particular being but by Being. To think "nihilism" thus does not mean to produce "mere thoughts" about it in one's head, and as a mere spectator to retreat from reality. Rather, to think "nihilism" means to stand in that wherein every act and every reality of this era in Western history receives its time and space, its ground and its background, its means and ends, its order and its justification, its certainty and its insecurity—in a word, its "truth."

The necessity of having to think the essence of "nihilism" in the context of the "revaluation of all values," "will to power," "eternal recurrence of the same," and the "Overman" lets us readily surmise that the essence of nihilism is in itself manifold, multileveled, and multifarious. The word *nihilism* therefore permits many applications. It can be misused as an empty slogan or epithet that both repels and discredits and that conceals the user's own thoughtlessness from him. But we can also experience the full burden of what the name says when uttered in *Nietzsche's* sense. Here it means to think the history of Western metaphysics as the ground of our own history; that is, of future decisions. Finally, we can ponder more essentially what Nietzsche was thinking in using this word if we grasp his "classical nihilism" as *that* nihilism *whose "classicism" consists in the fact that it must unwittingly put itself on extreme guard against knowledge of its innermost essence.* Classical nihilism, then, discloses itself as the fulfillment of nihilism, whereby it considers itself exempt from the necessity of thinking about the very thing that constitutes its essence: the *nihil,* the nothing—as the veil that conceals the truth of the Being of beings.

Nietzsche did not present his knowledge of European nihilism in that exhaustive context he surely glimpsed by means of his inner vision, a context whose pure form we neither know nor can ever "open up" with the fragments of his work that have been preserved.

Nevertheless, in the realm of his thinking, Nietzsche thought through what he meant by the word *nihilism* in all its essential tendencies, levels, and configurations, and he put his thoughts down in notes of varying scope and intensity. A portion of these, but only a scattered, *arbitrarily* and *randomly* selected portion, were later collected into the book that after Nietzsche's death was pasted together from his posthumous writings and that is known by the title *The Will to Power.* The fragments chosen vary widely in character: reflections, meditations, definitions, maxims, exhortations, predictions, sketches for longer trains of thought, and brief reminders. *These selected pieces* were divided into four "books" under different titles. However, this way of dividing the book, which was first published in 1906, did not arrange the fragments in the order determined by the time of their writing or revision, but assembled them according to the editors' murky and in any case irrelevant personal plan. In this fabricated "book," thoughts from entirely different periods of time and from wholly divergent levels and aspects of a question are capriciously and mindlessly juxtaposed and intermingled. True, everything published in this "book" is Nietzsche's, but he never thought it *like that.*

The selections are numbered consecutively from 1 to 1067, and, thanks to this numeration, are easy to locate in the various editions. The first book, "European Nihilism," comprises numbers 1 through 134. We needn't raise the question here as to what extent other notes —whether they have been placed in subsequent chapters of this posthumous book or are not included in it at all—might with equal or greater right belong under the title "European Nihilism." For we wish to contemplate *Nietzsche's* thoughts about nihilism, as the knowledge of a thinker who thinks in the direction of world history. Such thoughts are never the mere viewpoint of that one person; still less are they the celebrated "expression of one's time." The thoughts of a thinker of Nietzsche's stature are reverberations of the still-unrecognized history of Being in the word which that historical man utters as his "language."

We today do not know the reason why the inmost core of Nietzsche's metaphysics could not be made public by him, but lies concealed in posthumous notes—*still* lies concealed, although his literary remains have for the most part become available to us, albeit in a very misleading form.

2. Nihilism as the "Devaluation of the Uppermost Values"

From what has been said about the character of the posthumous work *The Will to Power*, we can easily deduce that it will be impossible for us to deal with the individual notes in their exact order. By proceeding in such a way, we would merely be surrendering ourselves to the pointless confusion of the editors' textual arrangement. We would continue haphazardly to jumble together thoughts from different periods, that is, from different levels and thrusts of a question or discourse. Let us instead choose individual fragments. There are three criteria governing the choice:

1. The fragment must stem from a time of utter lucidity and keen insight. These are the two final years 1887 and 1888.
2. The fragment must so far as possible contain the essential core of nihilism, analyze it with sufficient scope, and show it to us from all relevant points of view.
3. The fragment must be suitable for bringing our confrontation with Nietzsche's thought on nihilism to its proper place.

These three conditions are not arbitrarily proposed: they arise from the *essence* of Nietzsche's fundamental metaphysical position, as determined by his meditation on the beginning, the career, and the completion of Western metaphysics as a whole.

In our own meditation on European nihilism we are not attempting an exhaustive presentation and elucidation of all the pertinent statements Nietzsche made. We would like to grasp the innermost essence of the history that is called *nihilism* so as to approach the Being of what is. If we occasionally connect parallel statements or similar notes, we must always bear in mind that for the most part they derive from distinct strata of thinking and that a statement yields its full import only when the often subtly shifting stratum is also co-defined. It does not matter whether we come to know all the "passages" on the "theme" of nihilism, but it is vital that by means of suitable fragments we establish a durable relationship with what it is they are addressing.

Note 12 satisfies the three conditions we have set. It was sketched in the period between November 1887 and March 1888 and bears the title "The Decline of Cosmological Values."* We cite in addition notes 14 and 15 (XV, 152 f.; spring–fall, 1887). We introduce this meditation with a note of Nietzsche's written about the same time and correctly placed by the editors at the beginning of the book.† It runs, "What does nihilism mean? *That the uppermost values devaluate themselves.* The aim is lacking; the 'why?' receives no answer" (WM, 2).

This brief note contains a question, an answer to the question, and an explanation of the answer. The question asks about the essence of nihilism. The answer is *"that the uppermost values devaluate themselves."* We immediately perceive that in the answer there is something decisive for any understanding of nihilism: nihilism is a *process,* the process of devaluation, whereby the uppermost values become valueless. Whether or not that exhausts the essence of nihilism is left undecided by the description. When values become valueless, they collapse on themselves, become untenable. The character exhibited by this process of "decline" of "the uppermost values," the extent to which it is a *historical* process and in fact the basic process of our Western history, the way in which it constitutes the historicity of the history of our own era—all these can be comprehended only if we first

---

* CM lists the title of this aphorism (W II 3 [99]), which Nietzsche reworked during the summer of 1888, simply as "Critique of Nihilism." Otherwise GOA (XV, 148–51) reproduces the text adequately.

† "Correctly placed by the editors" is perhaps an exaggeration: WM, 2 is part of a much larger note consisting of WM, 23, 2, 22, and 13 (cf. CM, W II 1 [35]), and even its two sentences are presented in inverse order.

know what something such as "value" really "is," whether there are "uppermost" ("highest") values, and *which ones* these are.

To be sure, the explanation of the answer offers a clue. The devaluation of values, hence nihilism too, consists in the fact that "an aim" is lacking. However, the question remains: Why an "aim"? An "aim" for what purpose? What is the inner connection between value and aim? The explanation says that the " 'Why?' receives no answer." The question "why?" asks why something is this or that way. The answer provides what we call the "grounds." The question repeats itself: Why must there be grounds? How and why is the ground a ground? In what way does this exist—a ground? What is the inner connection between ground and value?

We have already seen, thanks to our introductory remarks about the essential connection between "nihilism" and the "revaluation" of all prior and indeed uppermost values, that the concept of value plays a major role in Nietzsche's thought. As a result of the impact of his writings, valuative thought is familiar to us. One speaks of the "vital values" of a people, or the "cultural values" of a nation. It is said that the supreme values of mankind are worth protecting and preserving. We hear that things of "great value" are carried to safety, meaning that works of art, for example, are guarded from air attacks. In this case, "value" means the same as "goods." A "good" is a being that "has" a particular "value"; a good is a good on grounds of value, is that in which a value becomes an object and thus a "valuable."

What is a value? We know, for example, that the freedom of a people is a "value," but here again we basically take freedom to be a good that we possess or do not possess. Freedom would not be a good if it were not as such first a value, the sort of thing we esteem as something worthwhile, something valid, something that "matters." Value is what validates. Only what is valid is a value. But what does "validate" mean? What is valid plays the role of a standard of measure. The question is whether a value is valid because it is a standard of measure, or whether it can be a standard of measure because it is valid. If the latter, then we ask anew: What does it mean to say that a value is valid? Is something valid because it is a value, or is it a value because it is valid? What is value itself, that it should be valid? "To be valid" is of course not nothing, but the mode and manner in which value, indeed *as* value, "is." To be valid is a mode of *Being*. There can be value only in being-a-value.

The question about value and its essence is grounded in the question of Being. "Values" are *accessible* and capable of being a standard of measure only where things such as values are esteemed and where one value is ranked above or below another. Such esteeming and valuing occurs only where something "matters" for our behavior. Here alone is the kind of thing educed to which any comportment first, last, and always returns. To esteem something, to hold it worthwhile, also means to be *directed* toward it. Such direction *toward* has already assumed an "aim." Thus the essence of value has an *inner* relation to the essence of aim. Once again we encounter the vexing question: Is something an aim because it is a value, or does something only become a value insofar as it has been posited as an aim? Perhaps this either-or formulation betrays a question that is still insufficient and does not yet reach out into the truly questionable.

The same reflections might result from a consideration of the relation between value and ground. If value is what always matters in everything, then it also shows itself to be that in which everything that matters is grounded and derives its sustenance and permanence. Here the same questions present themselves: Does something become a ground because it has validity as a value, or does it succeed in validating values because it is a ground? The either-or fails here too, perhaps because the essential limits of "value" and "ground" cannot be determined on the same plane.

No matter how these questions are resolved, they at least sketch in outline form an inner bond connecting value, aim, and ground. However, the most pressing issue that still remains unclarified is why Nietzsche's valuative thought has far and away dominated all "world view" thinking since the end of the last century. In truth, the role that valuative thought plays is *by no means self-evident*. That is already demonstrated in the historical recollection that valuative thought was first advanced expressly in these terms during the second half of the nineteenth century and that it progressed to the status of a truism. We are all too willing to be diverted from that fact, because every historical investigation usurps a currently dominant mode of thought and makes it the guiding principle according to which the past is examined and rediscovered. Historians are very proud of these discoveries and fail to notice that they had already been made before the historians began to ply their belated trade. And so as soon as valuative thought emerged, there came—and still comes—the empty talk about the "cultural values" of the Middle Ages and the "spiritual values" of antiquity, even though there was nothing like "culture" in the Middle Ages nor anything like "spirit" and "culture" in ancient times. Only in the modern era have spirit and culture been deliberately experienced as fundamental modes of human comportment, and only in most recent times have "values" been posited as standards for such comportment. It does not follow, of course, that earlier periods were "uncultured" in the sense that they were submerged in barbarism; what follows is that with the schemata "culture" and "lack of culture," "spirit," and "value," we never touch in its essence the history, for example, of the Greeks.

3. Nihilism, *Nihil*, and Nothing

If we remain with Nietzsche's note, then we must first of all answer the one central question we posed earlier: What does nihilism have to do with values and their devaluation? In its literal sense, "nihilism" surely says that all being is *nihil,* "nothing," and presumably a thing can only be worth *nothing* because and inasmuch as it is already null and nothing in itself. The determination of value and the valuation of something as valued, as valuable or valueless, are first grounded on a determination of *whether* and *how* something *is,* or whether it is *"nothing."* Nihilism and *nihil* are not necessarily or essentially connected with valuative thought. Why is nihilism nonetheless (and with no particular justification) conceived of as "devaluation of the uppermost values" and as a "decline" of values?

Now, it is true that for us the word and concept *nothing* usually carries the concomitant tone of a value, namely, of disvaluation. We say *nothing* when some desired, anticipated, sought, demanded, expected thing is *not* at hand, *is* not. When a well is drilled somewhere for a "petroleum find," for example, and the drilling is fruitless, one says "Nothing was found"; that is, the anticipated finding, the find—the entity that one sought—was not found. "Nothing" implies a thing's not being at hand, its not being. "Nothing" and *nihil* therefore mean beings in their *Being* and are concepts of *Being* and not of *value*. (We should keep in mind what Jacob Wackernagel says in his *Lectures on Syntax,* Series II, (second edition, 1928), p. 272: "In the German *nicht[s]* . . . lies the word which in its Gothic form *waihts* . . . serves to translate the Greek *pragma.*")*

---

* Hermann Paul's *Deutsches Wörterbuch,* 6th ed. (Tübingen: Niemeyer, 1966), describes the word *nicht* as a contraction of the Old High German expression *ni (eo) wiht,*

Nihilism, Nihil, and Nothing

The root meaning of the Latin word *nihil*, which even the Romans pondered (*ne-hilum*), has not been clarified up to the present day. At any rate, according to the concept of the word, *nihilism* is concerned with the nothing and therefore, in a special way, with beings in their nonbeing. But the nonbeing of beings is considered to be the negation of beings. We usually think the "nothing" only in terms of what is negated. In drilling for oil, "nothing" was found; that is to say, *not* the entity sought. In that case, one answers the question "Is oil present?" with "No." True, in drilling for oil "nothing" was found, but in no way did we find *"the nothing,"* because it was not drilled for, and cannot be drilled for, especially not with the help of mechanical drilling rigs or other such contrivances.

Does the nothing ever let itself be found, or even searched for? Or is it the case that it does not need to be sought and found at all, because it "is" *that* which we least—that is to say, never—lose?

The nothing here signifies, not the particular negation of an individual being, but the complete and absolute negation of all beings, of beings as a whole. But, as the "negation" of everything "objective," nothingness "is" for its part not a possible object. To talk about the nothing and to pursue it in thought are shown to be projects *"without object,"* vacuous word games that furthermore do not seem to notice that they are always flatly contradicting themselves, because no matter what they stipulate about the nothing they always have to say that the nothing *is* such and such. Even when we say simply that the nothing "is" nothing, we are apparently predicating an "is" of it and making it into a being; we attribute what ought to be withheld from it.

No one would want to deny that such "reflections" are easily followed and are "striking," especially as long as one moves in the realm of facile explanations, putters about with mere words, and lets oneself be struck by all such thoughtlessness. In fact, we cannot treat the

---

literally, "not any thing." (Compare the English word *nothing*.) The word *wiht* is a close relative of the English "wight," a thing, creature, or being, anything that has a modicum of "weight"—another related word. In its article on the archaic substantive "wight," the *Oxford English Dictionary* in fact derives the Gothic word *waihts* from *two* of the principal Greek words for being, *eidos* and *pragma*. The words *nichts* and *nothing* thus preserve their reference to being—as does the ostensibly negative English expression, "Not a whit!"

nothing as the counteressence to all beings except by saying that the nothing "is" such and such. But for the most part this has "only" a limited and precise meaning: the nothing too, even the nothing, still remains rooted in the "is" and in Being. What, then, do "Being" and the "is" mean? By correctly reciting these statements, so plausible and seemingly incisive, bearing on the impossibility of saying something about the nothing without thereby proclaiming it a being, one suggests that the essence of "Being" and the "is," which one is supposedly misattributing to the nothing by speaking about it, is the most evident, well-clarified, and indisputable matter in the world. One gives the impression that one has a clear, demonstrative, and unshakable hold on the truth of the "is" and of "Being." This opinion has long been endemic to Western metaphysics. It co-constitutes the ground on which all metaphysics rests. Most often, therefore, one dispenses with "the nothing" in a brief paragraph. It seems to be a universally convincing fact that "nothingness" is the opposite of all being.

On closer inspection, the nothing turns out also to be *the negation of beings*. Denying, nay-saying, nullifying, negation—all that is the opposite of affirmation. Both negation and affirmation are basic forms of judgment, assertion, *logos apophantikos*.* The nothing, as a

---

* Aristotle (*On Interpretation*, 17a, 1-4) distinguishes *logos apophantikos* from *logos sēmantikos* in the following way: while the latter includes all meaningful statements, such as questions, commands, or requests, *logos apophantikos* is restricted to statements "that have truth or falsity in them," statements of predication, or, as the tradition calls them, "propositions." A recurrent problem in Heidegger's thought is the relationship between *logos apophantikos* and the "truth" (*alētheuein*) or "falsity" (*pseudesthai*) that are somehow "in" it. Heidegger suggests that truth is not located in propositions, as traditional logic insists, but that our speech in some way addresses primordial truth as disclosure, *a-lētheia*. Thus in his first logic course (winter semester, 1925-26) Heidegger defines *apo-phainesthai* literally as "letting (a being) be seen . . . on its own terms," and equates it with *a-lētheuein*, uncovering, unveiling, or removing (a being) from concealment. The word *phainesthai* thus points toward the very origins of the discipline that calls itself *phenomenology*, and it also suggests a kind of thinking that will have to devote itself to *alētheia*. The key text is Martin Heidegger, *Being and Time*, tr. John Macquarrie and Edward Robinson (New York: Harper & Row, 1962), section 7B, "The Concept of Logos"; section 33, "Assertion as a Derivative Mode of Interpretation"; and section 44b, "The Original Phenomenon of Truth and the Derivative Character of the Traditional Concept of Truth." See also the detailed analyses in Heidegger's first logic course, now published as Martin Heidegger, *Logik: Die Frage nach der Wahrheit* (Frankfurt am Main: V. Klostermann, 1976), §§ 9-12, pp. 62-161, and esp. section 11, pp. 127-35.

product of negation, has a "logical" origin. Certainly man needs "logic" in order to think correctly and methodically, although what one merely thinks does not have to be; that is, does not have to occur as something actual in reality. The nothing of negation or no-saying is a mere mental image, the most abstract of abstractions. The nothing is purely and simply "nothing," what is most null, and so unworthy of any further attention or respect. If the nothing is nothing, if it is not, then neither can beings ever founder in the nothing nor can all things dissolve in it. Hence there can be no process of becoming-nothing. Hence nihilism is an illusion.

Were that so, then we would be able to consider Western history saved and would be able to renounce all thoughts of "nihilism." But perhaps the matter is quite different with nihilism. Perhaps it is still as Nietzsche says in *The Will to Power* (WM, 1, from 1885–86): "Nihilism stands at the door: whence comes to us this uncanniest of all guests?" In note 2 of the Preface (XV, 137), Nietzsche says, "What I shall relate is the history of the next two centuries."

Certainly the prevailing opinion and the traditional convictions of philosophy are right to insist that the nothing is not a "being," no "object." But that does not satisfy the question as to whether this nonobjective matter really "is," inasmuch as it determines the essential unfolding of Being. The question remains whether what is not an object and never can be an object therefore "is" simply *nothingness,* and this in turn a "nullity." The question arises whether the innermost essence of nihilism and the power of its dominion do not consist precisely in considering the nothing merely as a nullity, considering nihilism as an apotheosis of the merely vacuous, as a negation that can be set to rights at once by an energetic affirmation.

Perhaps the essence of nihilism consists in *not* taking the question of the nothing seriously. In point of fact, if one leaves the question undeveloped, one remains obstinately fixed in the interrogative scheme of that familiar either-or. With general approbation, one says that the nothing *either* "is" something thoroughly null *or* it must be a being.

Among the references to *apophainesthai* in Heidegger's later thought, see "Logos," in Martin Heidegger, *Early Greek Thinking,* tr. D. F. Krell and F. A. Capuzzi (New York: Harper & Row, 1975), p. 64.

But because the nothing obviously can never be a being, the only other alternative is that it is the purely null. Who would wish to repudiate such compelling "logic"? All due respect to logic! But correct thinking can be called on as a court of last resort only if one has previously established that *what* is to be "correctly" thought according to the rules of "logic" also exhausts everything thinkable, everything that is to be thought and is given over to thinking.

What if in truth the nothing were indeed not a being but also were not simply null? And what if the *question* about the essence of the nothing, with the help of that either-or, had not yet been adequately formulated? Finally, what if the *default* of a developed question about the essence of the nothing were *the grounds* for the fact that Western metaphysics had to fall prey to nihilism? Then nihilism, conceived and experienced in a more original and essential way, would be that history of metaphysics which is heading toward a fundamental metaphysical position in which the essence of the nothing not only *cannot* be understood but also *will* no longer be understood. Nihilism would then be the essential nonthinking of the essence of the nothing. Here, perhaps, is the reason why Nietzsche was forced into what from his point of view was "complete" nihilism. Because Nietzsche surely recognized nihilism as a movement of modern Western history but was unable to think about the essence of the nothing, being unable to raise the question, he had to become a classical nihilist who expressed the history that is now happening. Nietzsche knew and experienced nihilism because he himself thought nihilistically. Nietzsche's concept of nihilism is itself nihilistic. Consequently, in spite of all his insights, he could not recognize the hidden essence of nihilism, because right from the outset, *solely* on the basis of valuative thought, he conceived of nihilism as a process of the devaluation of the uppermost values. Nietzsche had to conceive of nihilism that way because in remaining on the path and within the realm of Western metaphysics, he thought it to its conclusion.

In no sense did Nietzsche interpret nihilism as a process of devaluing the uppermost values merely because valuative thought played a role in the course of his education or in his "private" views and positions. Valuative thought played this part in Nietzsche's thought be-

Nihilism, Nihil, and Nothing

cause Nietzsche thought *metaphysically,* on the path of the history of metaphysics. But it is no accident that valuative thought took precedence in metaphysics, at the core of Western philosophy. In the concept of value there lies concealed a concept of Being that contains an interpretation of the whole of beings as such. In valuative thought the *essence* of Being is—unwittingly—thought in a definite and necessary aspect; that is, in its nonessence. This is to be shown in the following reflections.

4. Nietzsche's Conception of Cosmology and Psychology

Nietzsche's note 2, which we mentioned earlier, gives us a preliminary glimpse into the nihilistically thought essence of nihilism, an insight into Nietzsche's orientation in thinking about nihilism. Nihilism is the process of the devaluation of the uppermost values. Nihilism is the inner lawfulness of this process, the "logic" according to which the decline of the uppermost values is played out according to its essence. In what is such lawfulness grounded?

To understand the Nietzschean concept of nihilism at all as the devaluation of the uppermost values, we must now come to know what is meant by such values, to what extent they contain an interpretation of the being, why we necessarily arrive at that valuative interpretation, and what transformation is wrought in metaphysics by means of it. We shall reply to these questions by way of an elucidation of note 12 (November 1887–March 1888). The fragment, entitled "Decline of the Cosmological Values," is divided into two sections (A and B) of unequal scope, and is rounded off by a concluding remark.

The first section (A) runs thus:

> *Nihilism* as a *psychological state* will have to enter on the scene, *first*, when we have sought a "meaning" in all events that is not in them: so that the seeker eventually becomes discouraged. Nihilism, then, is the recognition of the long *squandering* of strength, the agony of the "in vain," the insecurity, the lack of any opportunity to recuperate and to regain tranquillity—being ashamed of oneself, as if one had *deceived* oneself all too long. . . . That meaning could have been: the "fulfillment" of some supreme ethical canon in all events, the ethical world order; or the growth of love and harmony in social intercourse; or the gradual approximation to a

state of universal happiness; or even the departure toward a state of universal nothingness—any goal constitutes at least some meaning. What all these notions have in common is that something is to be *achieved* in the process —and now one grasps the fact that becoming aims at *nothing* and achieves *nothing*. . . . Thus disappointment regarding an ostensible *purpose of becoming* as the cause of nihilism: whether with regard to a specific purpose or generalized insight into the fact that all previous hypotheses about purposes that concern the whole "evolution" are inadequate (man *no longer* the collaborator, let alone the center, of becoming).

Nihilism as a psychological state arises, *secondly,* when one has posited a *totality,* a *systematization,* indeed any *organization* in all occurrences, and beneath all occurrences, so that a soul that craves to adore and revere wallows in the general notion of some supreme form of domination and governance (if the soul be that of a logician, complete consistency and a *Realdialektik* quite suffice to reconcile it to everything). Some sort of unity, any form of "monism": and in consequence of such faith, man, rapt in the profound feeling of standing in the network of, and being dependent on, a totality that is infinitely superior to him, as a mode of the deity. . . . "The well-being of the universal demands the devotion of the individual"—but behold, there *is* no such universal! At bottom, man has lost faith in his own value when no infinitely valuable totality works through him; that is to say, he conceived such a totality *in order to be able to believe in his own value.*

Nihilism as psychological state has yet a *third* and *final* form. Given these two *insights,* that becoming aims at no goal and that underneath all becoming there is no grand unity in which the individual could submerge completely as in an element of supreme value, one *escape* remains: to condemn the whole world of becoming as a deception and to invent a world that would lie beyond it, as the *true* world. But, as soon as man finds out how that world is fabricated, solely out of psychological needs, and that he has absolutely no right to it, the final form of nihilism emerges: it embraces *disbelief in any metaphysical world* and thus forbids itself any belief in a *true* world. Having reached this standpoint, one concedes the reality of becoming as the *only* reality, forbids oneself every kind of clandestine access to afterworlds and false divinities—but one *cannot endure this world, which, however, one does not want to deny.* What has happened, at bottom? The feeling of *valuelessness* was attained with the realization that the overall character of existence may not be interpreted by means of the concept of *"purpose,"* the concept of *"unity,"* or the concept of *"truth."* Existence aims at nothing and achieves nothing; a comprehensive unity in the plurality of

occurrences is lacking; the character of existence is not "true," is *false*. ...
One simply lacks any grounds for convincing oneself that there is a *true*
world. ... In short, the categories *"purpose," "*unity," "Being," by which
we used to invest some value into the world—we *withdraw* again; and now
the world seems *valueless*.

According to the inscription, the matter in question is the decline of
"cosmological" values. It appears that a *special* class of values has been
named, the decline of which constitutes nihilism. In the more orthodox articulations of metaphysical doctrine, "cosmology" embraces a
particular region of beings, the "cosmos" in the sense of "nature," the
earth and stars, plants and animals. "Psychology," as the study of soul
and spirit, and especially of man as a rational creature, differs from
"cosmology." "Theology" parallels and surpasses psychology and cosmology, not as the canonical interpretation of biblical revelation, but
as the "rational" ("natural") interpretation of the biblical doctrine of
God as the first cause of all beings, of nature and of man, of history
and its works. But, just as the frequently quoted expression *Anima
naturaliter christiana* ["The soul is naturally Christian"] is not a purely
indubitable "natural" truth, but is a *Christian* truth, so too natural
theology has the ground of its truth only in the biblical teaching that
man was fashioned by a creator God who also endowed him with
knowledge of his Creator. Because natural theology as a philosophical
discipline cannot validly permit the Old Testament to be the source of
its truths, the contents of that theology must be diluted to the statement that the world must have a first cause. That does not prove that
the first cause is a "God," assuming that a God would ever let Himself
be debased into an object of proofs. It is important to have some insight into the essence of rational theology, because Western metaphysics is theological even where it opposes church theology.

The words *cosmology, psychology,* and *theology*—or the threesome
of *nature, man,* and *God*—circumscribe the realm in which all Western representation operates when it thinks beings as a whole in a metaphysical way. Consequently, when we read the inscription "Decline of
Cosmological Values" we immediately suppose that from the three
traditional domains of metaphysics Nietzsche has selected one in par-

ticular—cosmology. This supposition is erroneous. Here cosmos does not mean "nature" as distinct from man and God; rather, it signifies the "world," and "world" is the name for beings as a whole. "Cosmological values" are not a separate class of values ranked with or above others. They determine "where . . . [human life], 'nature,' 'world,' the whole sphere of becoming and transience, belong" (*Toward a Genealogy of Morals*, 1887, VII, 425). They designate the widest circle that encloses everything that is and becomes. Outside it and beyond it nothing exists. Nihilism, as the devaluation of the *uppermost* values, is the decline of *cosmological* values. If we understand its title correctly, the fragment concerns the essence of nihilism.

Section A is divided into four paragraphs, the fourth of which summarizes the other three with respect to their essential import; namely, the meaning of the decline of cosmological values. Section B affords us a view of the essential consequences of the decline. It shows that with the decline of cosmological values the cosmos itself does not fall away but is merely freed from the valuations of prevailing values and made available for a new valuation. Thus nihilism does not at all lead us into nothing. Decline is not simply collapse. But what must occur if nihilism is to lead to a rescue and recovery of beings as a whole is intimated by the concluding remark appended to the entire fragment.

The first three paragraphs of section A begin in a similar fashion: "*Nihilism* as a *psychological state*"—"will have to enter on the scene," "arises *secondly*," "has yet a *third* and *final* form." For Nietzsche, nihilism is the covert, basic law of Western history. In this fragment, however, he expressly defines it as a "psychological state." So the question arises as to what he means by "psychological" and "psychology." For Nietzsche, "psychology" is not the psychology being practiced already in his day, a psychology modeled on physics and coupled with physiology as scientific-experimental research into mental processes, in which sense perceptions and their bodily conditions are posited, like chemical elements, as the basic constituents of such processes. Nor does "psychology" signify for Nietzsche research into the "higher life of intelligent mind" and its processes, in the sense of one kind of research among others. Neither is it "characterology," as the doctrine of various human types. One could sooner interpret Nietzsche's concept of psychology as "anthropology," if "anthropology" means a *philosophical* inquiry into the essence of man in the perspective of his essential ties to beings as a whole. In that case, "anthropology" is the "metaphysics" of man. But, even so, we have not hit on Nietzsche's conception of "psychology" and the "psychological." Nietzsche's "psychology" in no way restricts itself to man, but neither does it extend simply to plants and animals. "Psychology" is the question of the "psychical"; that is, of what is living, in that particular sense of life that determines becoming as "will to power." Insofar as the latter constitutes the basic character of all beings, and inasmuch as the truth of the whole of beings as such is called "metaphysics," Nietzsche's "psychology" is simply coterminous with metaphysics. That metaphysics becomes a "psychology," albeit one in which the "psychology" of *man* has definite preeminence, lies grounded in the very essence of modern metaphysics.

Western history has now begun to enter into the completion of that period we call the *modern,* and which is defined by the fact that man becomes the measure and the center of beings. Man is what lies at the bottom of all beings; that is, in modern terms, at the bottom of all objectification and representability. No matter how sharply Nietzsche pits himself time and again against Descartes, whose philosophy grounds modern metaphysics, he turns against Descartes only because the latter *still* does *not* posit man as *subiectum* in a way that is complete and decisive enough. The representation of the *subiectum* as ego, the I, thus the "egoistic" interpretation of the *subiectum,* is still not subjectivistic enough for Nietzsche. Modern metaphysics first comes to the full and final determination of its essence in the doctrine of the Overman, the doctrine of man's absolute preeminence among beings. In that doctrine, Descartes celebrates his supreme triumph.

Because the will to power unfolds its pure powerfulness without restraint in man—that is to say, in the figure of the Overman—"psychology" in Nietzsche's sense as the doctrine of will to power is therefore always *simultaneously* and *from the outset* the realm of the *fundamental questions of metaphysics.* Thus Nietzsche can say, in *Beyond Good and Evil* (VII, 35 ff.),

> All psychology to date has got stuck in moral prejudices and fears: it has not dared to descend into the depths. To conceive of psychology as the morphology and *doctrine of the development of will to power,* as I do—no one has yet come close to this in his thought.

At the end of the section, Nietzsche says it is imperative "that psychology be recognized again as the queen of the sciences; the other sciences must minister to her. For psychology is once again the path to the fundamental problems." We could also say that the path to the fundamental problems of metaphysics is the Cartesian *Meditationes* on man as *subiectum.* Psychology is the name for the metaphysics that posits man (that is, mankind as such, not simply the individual "I," as *subiectum*) as measure and center, as ground and aim of all being. If nihilism is construed as a "psychological state," this means that nihilism concerns the position of man amid beings as a whole, the way in which man puts himself in contact with the being as such, the way he forms and sustains that relationship and thereby himself. But that implies nothing less than the way in which man is historical. That way is determined by the basic character of beings as will to power. Taken as a "psychological state," nihilism is inherently viewed as a configuration of *will to power,* as the occurrence in which man is historical.

If Nietzsche speaks of nihilism as a "psychological state," he will also operate with "psychological" concepts and speak the language of "psychology" when he explains the essence of nihilism. That is not accidental and is therefore not an extrinsic form of communication. Nonetheless, we must detect a more essential content in such language, because it refers to the "cosmos," beings as a whole.

5. The Provenance of Nihilism and Nihilism's Three Forms

In the first three paragraphs of note 12(A) Nietzsche identifies three conditions under which nihilism enters on the scene. In asking about such conditions, he is seeking to illuminate the *provenance* of nihilism. Here provenance does not mean the "whence" but the "how"— the form and manner in which nihilism comes to be and is. In no way does provenance mean a historically reckoned genesis. Nietzsche's question about the provenance of nihilism, as a question about the cause of nihilism, is nothing other than the question of its essence.

Nihilism is the process of the devaluation of the uppermost values hitherto. If these uppermost values, which grant all beings their value, are devalued, then all beings grounded in them become valueless. A feeling of futility, of the nullity of everything, arises. Hence nihilism, as the decline of cosmological values, is at the same time the emergence of nihilism as a *feeling* of utter valuelessness, as a "psychological state." Under what circumstances does the state arise? Nihilism "must enter on the scene," *first,* "when we have sought a 'meaning' in all events that is not in them." Thus a precondition for nihilism is that we seek a "meaning" in "all events"; that is, in beings as a whole. What does Nietzsche intend by "meaning"? An understanding of the essence of nihilism, which Nietzsche often identifies with the rule of *"meaninglessness"* (see WM, 11), depends on the answer to this question. "Meaning" signifies the same thing as value, since in place of "meaninglessness" Nietzsche also says "valuelessness." Still, we lack an adequate determination of the essence of "meaning." "Meaning," one would like to think, is understood by everyone. And, in the milieu of everyday thought and vague opinions, it is. But as soon as we become aware that man seeks a "meaning" in all events, and as soon as Nietzsche indicates that this search for "meaning" is frustrated, we cannot circumvent questions about what meaning means, about why and to what extent man seeks meaning, why he cannot accept possible disappointment in this matter with indifference, but is troubled and endangered, even shattered by it in his very substance.

By "meaning," Nietzsche understands "purpose" (see paragraphs 1 and 4). We think of purpose as the why and wherefore of every action, comportment, and event. Nietzsche enumerates what the desired "meaning" could have been; that is, what from the historical point of view *has been* and in its remarkable transformations *still is:* the "ethical world order"; "the growth of love and harmony in social intercourse"; pacifism, eternal peace; "the gradual approximation to a state of universal happiness" as the greatest good of the greatest number; "or even the departure toward a state of universal nothingness." For even *this* departure toward *this* aim still has a "meaning": "any goal constitutes at least some meaning." Why? Because it has a purpose, because it *is* itself a purpose. Is nothingness an aim? Certainly, because the will to will nothingness still allows the will its *volition*. The will to destruction is will nonetheless. And, because volition is to will oneself, even the will to nothingness still permits willing—that *the will itself* be.

Human will "*needs an aim*—and would sooner will *nothingness* than *not* will at all." For "will" is will to power: power to power, or as we might also say, *will to will,* will to stay on top and retain command. The will shrinks, not from nothingness, but from *not willing,* from the annihilation of its ownmost possibility. This trepidation before the emptiness of not-willing—this *"horror vacui"*—is "the fundamental fact of human will." It is precisely from the *"fundamental fact"* of human will—that it prefers *to will the nothing* rather than *not to will*—that Nietzsche derives the basic proof for his statement that the will is in its essence will to power. (See *Toward a Genealogy of Morals,* 1887; VII, 399.)* "Meaning," "aim," and "purpose" are what allow and enable will to be will. Where there is will, there is not only a way, but first of all an aim *for* the way, even if this is "simply" the will itself.

---

* At the beginning of the third and last division of his *Genealogy of Morals,* "What Is the Significance of Ascetic Ideals?" Nietzsche writes,

But those absolute "purposes" have never yet been attained in the history of man. Every effort and pursuit, every enterprise and activity, every stride on life's way, every proceeding, all "processes"—in short, all "becoming"—achieves *nothing,* attains nothing in the sense of the *pure* realization of those *absolute* purposes. Expectations in that regard are disappointed; every attempt seems valueless. One begins to doubt whether there is any purpose at all in positing a "purpose" for beings as a whole or in seeking a "meaning." What if not only the effort to fulfill purposes and accomplish meaning but even the search for a positing of purpose and meaning are all delusions? The uppermost value would thereby be made to totter, to lose its indubitable character, and to "devalue itself." The "purpose" toward which everything is supposed to tend, which is in itself absolutely valid *prior to* and *for* everything, the uppermost value, becomes untenable. The decrepitude of the uppermost values edges toward *consciousness.* In accord with the new consciousness, the relation of man to being as a whole and to himself is changed.

Nihilism as a psychological state, as a "feeling" of the valuelessness of beings as a whole, "arises *secondly* when one has posited a *totality,* a *systematization,* indeed any *organization* in all occurrences, and beneath all occurrences," which is never realized. What is now introduced as the highest value for beings as a whole has the character of *"unity,"* understood here as an all-pervasive unification, arrangement, and organization of all things into one. Such "unity" appears to be less

---

But the fact that the ascetic ideal has meant so much to man is an expression of the fundamental fact concerning the human will, namely, its *horror vacui: it needs an aim*—and it would sooner will *nothingness* than *not* will at all.

And, at the conclusion of that division (as of the book itself):

One simply cannot hide those things which were willed by a willing that took its orientation entirely from the ascetic ideal: such a hatred of the human, and even more of the animal, and still more of the material; such revulsion before the senses, and before reason itself; fear in the face of happiness and beauty; longing to escape from all semblance, change, becoming, death, desire, and from longing itself—it all signifies (let us dare to grasp it) a *will to nothingness,* a counterwill to life, rebellion against life's fundamental presuppositions; but it is and remains a *will!* And, to say again at the end what I said at the beginning: man would rather will *nothingness* than *not* will at all.

questionable in its essence than "meaning," the first "cosmological value" named. Nevertheless, even here we immediately ask ourselves why and to what extent man *"posits"* such a "ruling" and "dominant" "unity," how such positing is grounded, whether it can be grounded at all, and, if not, how it can be legitimately posited.

At once a further question arises as to whether and how this "positing" of a "unity" for beings as a whole is bound up with the previously mentioned "quest" for "meaning," whether these two are the same, and if they are, why this "same" is construed in different concepts. It can always be shown *that* man searches for meaning and posits a supreme, all-pervasive unity for beings. Nonetheless, the question of *what* the quest is and in what it is grounded must be kept open for now. At the end of the second paragraph, which describes the positing of "unity," for which Nietzsche also uses the similarly bland term "universality," he gives an indication of the *ground* of this positing, so that he might at the same time point out what happens when what is posited is *not* verified or fulfilled. Only if the *whole of beings* "works" through man, only if man is drawn into "unity" and is "submerged" in it "as in the element of highest value," only then does man have a "value" for himself. Thus, Nietzsche concludes, man must take into account such a totality and unity of beings *"so that he can believe in his own value."*

It is presupposed that man's capacity to believe in his own "value" is necessary. It is necessary because there is everywhere a concern for man's self-assertion. For man to remain certain of his own value, he must posit an uppermost value for beings as a whole. But if the belief in a unity that pervades reality is disappointed, this gives rise to the insight that nothing is aimed at by any given act or deed ("becoming"). What is implied in such an insight? Nothing less than the idea that all such realizing and becoming are nothing "real" and not truly in being, but are mere delusion. "Realizing" is therefore unreal. "Becoming" now appears to be not only aimless and meaningless but also of no consequence in itself, therefore *unreal*. However, to be able to rescue such unreality and secure for man his own value, one must in spite of everything posit *a true world* beyond "becoming," beyond the "mutable," the properly unreal and merely apparent, a world in which the permanent is preserved, untouched by any change, lack, or disappointment. Of course, the positing of this "true world," the transcendent beyond, proceeds at the expense of the earthly "world." The latter is condemned to a brief odyssey—brief when measured against eternity—through the transitory, a sojourn whose toil will find its recompense in eternity, insofar as it obtains its value from there.

From the positing of a "true world," as the world of permanent beings in themselves above a false world of change and appearance, there springs "yet a *third* and final form" of nihilism; namely, when man discovers that this "*true* world" (the "transcendent," the beyond) has been fabricated solely out of "psychological needs." Nietzsche does not explicitly name these "psychological needs" here. He has already identified them in explaining the dethronement of unity and totality. A value must be placed on beings as a whole in order that the self-worth of man remain secure; there must be a world beyond in order that this earthly world can be endured. But when it is recounted to man how, by counting on a "true world" beyond, he has only been accounting for himself and his "wishes" and has elevated a merely desirable thing into a being in itself, then the "true world"—the uppermost value—begins to totter.

It is no longer a mere matter of feeling the valuelessness and aimlessness of becoming or of feeling the unreality of becoming. Nihilism now becomes outright disbelief in anything like a *meta*-physical world, that is, a world set "above" what is sensuous and what becomes (the "physical"). Such disbelief prohibits any clandestine paths to an afterworld or heaven. Thus nihilism arrives at a new stage. It is no longer simply a matter of feeling the valuelessness of the world of becoming, of feeling its unreality. Rather, when the *supersensuous*, "true" world has fallen, the world of becoming shows itself to be the "*only* reality"; that is, the one authentic "true" world.

A peculiar transitional state emerges: first, *the world of becoming*—that is, life as lived here and now, along with its changing realms—can no longer be denied as *real;* but, second, this world, which *alone* is real, has at the outset no aims and values and so is not to be endured. It is not simply the feeling of the valuelessness of reality that dominates but also a feeling of *helplessness* within what alone is real. What is missing is an insight into the grounds for the predicament and the possibility of overcoming it.

It should already be clear from our elucidation of section A so far that Nietzsche has not juxtaposed just any "three forms" of nihilism. Nor does he merely want to describe three ways in which the hitherto uppermost values are posited. We can easily see that the three forms of nihilism designated sustain an inner relation to one another and together constitute a particular movement; that is to say, *history*. True, nowhere does Nietzsche identify any historically recognized and demonstrable forms of the positing of the uppermost values, nor the historically representable contexts of such positings, which we might describe as fundamental metaphysical positions. Nevertheless, he has such a thing in mind. He wants to show how nihilism not only arises on the ground of the inner relation of these positings of the uppermost values but also becomes a unique history that drifts toward an unequivocal historical state. Nietzsche sums up his portrayal of the three "forms" of nihilism thus:

> What has happened, at bottom? The feeling of *valuelessness* was attained when one grasped the fact that the overall character of existence may not be interpreted by means of the concept of *"purpose,"* the concept of *"unity,"* or the concept of *"truth."* Existence aims at nothing and achieves nothing; a comprehensive unity in the plurality of events is lacking: the character of existence is not "true," is *false*. . . . One simply lacks any grounds for convincing oneself that there is a *true* world.

It does seem, in this summary, as if the search for meaning, the positing of a unity, and the ascent to a "true" (supersensuous) world are merely three equivalent interpretations of the "overall character of existence" in which "nothing" is ever "achieved."

How little Nietzsche is thinking of merely defining various brands of nihilism and the conditions for their emergence is betrayed by the concluding sentence of this summary: "In short, the categories *'purpose,' 'unity,' 'Being,'* by which we used to invest some value into the world—we *withdraw* again; and now the world seems *valueless.*"

Before we show how the whole of section A is to be understood in accord with this concluding sentence, the wording of the sentence must be explained in two specific respects.

6. The Uppermost Values as Categories

Nietzsche abruptly calls the uppermost values *categories,* without giving the term a more precise explanation that might establish why the uppermost values are apprehended also in that way, and why "categories" can be conceived of as uppermost values. What are "categories"? The word, of Greek derivation, is familiar yet foreign to us. We say, for example, that someone belongs in the category of malcontents. We are speaking about a "particular category of people," and we understand *category* here to signify "class" or "sort," which are also foreign words, except that they are Romanic; they stem from the Latin. Depending on the matter at hand, the terms *category, class,* or *sort* are used to delineate a region, schema, or pigeonhole into which something is deposited and so classified.

This use of the word *category* corresponds neither to its original concept nor to the related meaning that it has preserved as a key philosophical word. Nonetheless, our current usage of the word derives from philosophical usage. *Katēgoria* and *katēgorein* arise from *kata* and *agoreuein. Agora* means a public gathering of people as opposed to a closed council meeting, the *openness* [*Öffentlichkeit*] of deliberations, of court proceedings, of the market, and of communication. *Agoreuein* means to speak openly, to announce something openly to the public, to make a revelation. *Kata* implies going from above to something below, a view onto something. *Katēgorein* therefore means that, in an explicit view on something, we reveal what it is and render it open. Such revelation happens through the word insofar as the word addresses a thing—any being at all—with regard to what it is, and identifies it as being in one way or another.

This kind of addressing and setting forth, of making public in words, is most emphatically present when charges are preferred against someone in open court proceedings, stating that he is guilty of something or other. Addressing and setting forth has its most striking and therefore most common form in such open charges. Thus *katēgorein* especially signifies a setting forth, an address, in the sense of a "charge," which implies the basic meaning of a claim that reveals something. The noun *katēgoria* can be used in that sense. *Katēgoria* is then the addressing of a thing to what it is, in such a way that through the address the being itself is, as it were, brought into words in what *it itself* is; that is to say, it comes into appearance and into the openness of publicity. A *katēgoria* in this sense is the word *table,* or *chest, house,* or *tree,* or any similar word; or *red, heavy, thin, bold*—in short, any word that addresses some being in its particularity and so proclaims how that being looks and is. The aspect in which a being shows itself as what it is, is called in Greek *to eidos* or *hē idea*. A category is the addressing of a being to the particularity of its aspect, and so is its *proper name* in the widest sense. The word is also used by Aristotle in this sense (*Physics,* B 1, 192b 17), although that in no way makes it an expression reserved for philosophical language (a "term").

A *katēgoria* is a word in which a thing is "indicted" as what it is. This prephilosophical meaning of *katēgoria* is far removed from that lifeless and superficial foreign word *category* that still persists in our language. The Aristotelian usage just cited corresponds much more fully to the spirit of the Greek language, which, to be sure, is implicitly philosophical and metaphysical and is therefore, along with Sanskrit and cultivated German, distinguished above every other language.

Now, philosophy as metaphysics deals with "categories" in a special sense. It speaks of a "doctrine of categories" and "table of categories"; Kant, for example, in his major work, *The Critique of Pure Reason,* teaches that the table of categories can be derived and deduced from the table of judgments. What does *category* mean here, in the language of the philosophers? How is the philosophical term *category* related to the prephilosophical word *katēgoria?*

Aristotle, who also used the word *katēgoria* in its usual meaning as the address of a thing in its aspect, for the first time and in a way that was decisive for the next two thousand years raised the prephilosophical expression *katēgoria* to the rank of a philosophical term that names what philosophy, in keeping with its essence, must ponder in its thinking. The elevation in rank of the word *katēgoria* was carried out in a genuinely philosophical sense. Presumably no merely derivative, arbitrarily conceived, and—as we love to say—"abstract" meaning was foisted onto the word. The thrust of the word itself, in the spirit both of the language and of the matter itself, points toward a potentially, perhaps necessarily, different and more essential meaning. When we address "that thing there"—that "door," for instance—as a door, there is another, prior claim in regarding it so. What claim? We already identified it when we said "that thing there" is addressed as a door. In order that we can address the named as a "door" and not as a window, what is meant must have already shown itself as *"that thing there"*—as what is present in some way or other. Before we address the thing meant as a "door," the unexpressed claim has already been made that it is a "that thing there"—a thing. We could not regard the named as a door if we did not first of all let it encounter us as a thing existing for itself. The claim (*katēgoria*) that it is a thing underlies the address "door." "Thing" is a more fundamental and original *category* than "door," a "category" or claim that states in what mode of Being a designated being shows itself: that it is a being for itself, or, as Aristotle says, a something that of itself is for itself—*tode ti.*

A second example. We ascertain that this door is brown (not white). To be able to address the thing named as brown, we must regard it in its color. But even the coloration of a thing appears to us as this color and as no other only if the thing confronts us as being constituted in a particular way. If the thing were not already addressed in its constitution, then we could never address it as "brown"; that is, as brown-colored, as constituted (qualified) in a particular way.

Underlying and sustaining (as its ground) the prephilosophical address (*kategoria*) of something as "brown" is our addressing it as "constituted in a particular way," the category "constitution," *poiotēs, poion, qualitas.* In relation to the category "quality," the prior claim is identified as a category in that it names what must ground every quality, the *underlying ground: hypokeimenon, subiectum, substantia.* "Substance," quality, as well as quantity and relation are "categories":

distinctive ways of speaking to beings, addressing a being with regard to what it is *as a being,* whether it be a door or window, table or house, dog or cat, and whether it be brown or white, sweet or sour, big or little.

Metaphysics is defined as the truth of beings as a whole, truth that is enjoined in the words of thinking. These words express the claims of the being as such in its composition—categories. Thus the categories are the basic words of metaphysics and are *therefore* names for the fundamental philosophical concepts. That these categories are silently expressed as claims in our ordinary thoughts and everyday comportment toward beings, or that they are really never experienced, acknowledged, or even conceived of as such tacit claims by most men throughout their "lives," neither these nor other such reasons are sufficient grounds for thinking that these categories are something indifferent, something construed by a philosophy that is supposedly "far removed from life." That the ordinary understanding and general opinion neither knows nor needs to know anything of these categories, merely certifies that something incontrovertibly essential is to be explained here, provided that nearness to essence is the privilege—but also the fate—of only a few. That there exists something like a diesel engine, for example, has its decisive and wholly sufficient ground in the fact that the categories of mechanically and technically useful "nature" were once expressly and thoroughly thought out by philosophers.

There is nothing wrong if the "man in the street" believes that there is a "diesel engine" because Herr Diesel invented it. Not everyone needs to know that the whole business of invention would not have been able to advance one step if philosophy, at the historical moment in which it entered the realm of its nonessence, had not thought the categories of nature and so first opened up this realm for the research and experiments of inventors. Of course, that does not mean that one who knows the true provenance of modern power machinery is thereby in a position to build better motors. But he is perhaps uniquely situated to ask what machine technology *is* within the history of man's relationship to Being.

In contrast, the question of what machine technology means for human progress and culture is of little consequence and ought to be bypassed in any case. For technology signifies exactly what "culture," which is contemporaneous with it, also signifies.

The categories are ways of addressing the being with regard to what the being as such is in its composition. The categories are therefore expressly known as such ways in a meditation on what is already tacitly co-expressed and addressed in the usual modes of addressing and discussing beings. The basic form of our everyday response to beings is assertion—Aristotle's *logos apophantikos,* a saying that is capable of letting the being show itself from itself. Guided by such *logos,* Aristotle was the first to articulate the "categories," which are not expressed in assertions but sustain all assertion. For him it was not a question of a "system" of categories. Coming after Plato, he faced the most ennobling task of first showing *that* such categories belong to the domain of what philosophy (as *prōtē philosophia*) primarily and properly has to ponder. Assertion, *enuntiatio,* is then understood as judgment. The different modes of address—categories—lie hidden in the various modes of judgment. Therefore, Kant in his *Critique of Pure Reason* teaches that the table of categories must be acquired through the guidance of the table of judgments. What *Kant* expresses here—although of course its form had changed in the meantime—is the same as what *Aristotle* had executed more than two thousand years before.

When Nietzsche in section B of note 12 says without further justification that the highest values are "categories of reason," that characterization is once again the same as what Kant taught and Aristotle thought through. The expression "categories of reason" means reason, rational thinking, the judgment of understanding, *logos apophantikos,* "logic"—all things to which the categories stand related in a relationship that is distinctive and that co-determines their essence. The nature of the relationship between the categories and reason—judgmental thinking—is, of course, grasped differently by Aristotle, Kant, and Nietzsche, according to how they define the essence of "reason" and *logos*—that is to say, the essence of man—and how in conjunction with this they experience and explain the being as such, which reveals its articulation in the categories.

But throughout these differences what is essential and telling is preserved—that the determinations of beings as such are secured and

The Uppermost Values as Categories

grounded with respect to *logos,* assertory thinking. As determinations of the being as such, the categories say what the being as a being is. They say the "most universal" thing that can be said of beings: beingness, or Being. The Being of beings is grasped and comprehended on the guidelines of assertion, judgment, or "thinking." This way of defining the truth of beings as a whole, metaphysics, thinks beings by means of categories.

As an earmark of the essence of all metaphysics, therefore, we can inscribe the title *Being and Thinking* or, more specifically, *Beingness and Thinking,* a formulation which stresses that Being is conceived by way of thinking from beings and back to beings as *their* "most universal" element, whereby "thinking" is understood as assertory speech. Such thinking of beings, in the sense of *physei* and *technēi on,* "something present that rises up of itself or is produced," is the guiding thread for the philosophical thinking of Being as beingness.

The title *Being and Thinking* is also valid for irrationalist metaphysics, which is so called because it drives rationalism to its very peak—disburdening itself of it, however, least of all, just as every atheism must busy itself with God more than any theism does.

Because it is a question of the highest determinations of being as a whole in the matter Nietzsche calls "cosmological values," he is also able to speak of categories. That Nietzsche with no further explanation or justification calls these uppermost values "categories" and conceives of them as categories of reason shows how decisively he thinks along the path of metaphysics.

But whether Nietzsche strays from the path of metaphysics by conceiving the categories as *values,* and so describes himself correctly as an "antimetaphysician," or whether he merely brings metaphysics to its ultimate end and thereby himself becomes the last metaphysician, are questions to which we are still under way. The answers to those questions are most closely bound up with the *elucidation* of Nietzsche's concept of nihilism.

The second thing we must point out in our textual analysis of the last sentence in section A is the way in which Nietzsche summarily names the three categories by which beings as a whole have been interpreted. Instead of "meaning" he now says "purpose," instead of "totality" and "systematization" he says "unity," and, most decisively, instead of "truth" and "true world," here he says roundly "Being." Once again, he says all this without offering any explanation. We should not be amazed, however, at the lack of an explanation concerning the concepts and names used here. The sketch that lies before us in this fragment is not a section of a book meant for "publication," nor part of a textbook, but the dialogue of a thinker with himself. Here he is speaking not with his "ego" and his "person" but with the Being of beings as a whole and within the realm of what has already been said in the history of metaphysics.

We, however, his subsequent readers, must first penetrate the domain of metaphysics in order to gauge correctly the weight of the words, of each of their transformations and conceptual formulations, in order to be able to read his simple text *thoughtfully*. For now, we need only keep sight of the fact that Nietzsche grasps "truth" as a category of reason and equates "truth" with "Being." If in turn "Being" is the first and last word about beings as a whole, then Nietzsche's equation of "Being" and "truth" must be announcing something essential for the clarification of his basic metaphysical position, in which the experience of nihilism has its roots.

7. Nihilism and the Man of Western History

What does the final sentence of section A want to say? First, with the categories "purpose," "unity," and "Being" we have invested a *value* in the "world" (that is, in beings as a whole). Second, these categories invested in the world "will be *withdrawn* again by us." And, third, after this retraction of the categories—that is, of values—the world "now" appears *value-less*.

The state identified by the "now" is in no way thought of as final. The "now" does not mean to say that from now on matters shall rest with such value–lessness and such a valueless-aspect of the world. Of course, the title of the piece says simply "Decline of the Cosmological Values," and the first essential definition of nihilism runs "Devaluation of the Uppermost Values." But the concluding sentence, which we are now going to elucidate, not only reveals that the decline of the highest values hitherto does not betoken the end; the language of another perspective speaks within this final sentence. It tells of an investment of values in and a withdrawal of values from the universe of beings, which as it were exists in itself and permits such an investing and withdrawing of values. Values do not fall away of themselves; we withdraw values—first posited by us—from the world. We are actively engaged in valuation and devaluation. Who are "we"?

What is happening here? Nihilism is obviously not a mere unobtrusive collapse of values in themselves somewhere at hand. Nihilism is our deposition of values that are at our disposal with respect to their being posited. By "us" and "we," however, Nietzsche means the man of Western history. He does not mean to imply that the same men who posit values withdraw them again, but that those who posit and those who retract are men from *one* and the *same* Western history. We ourselves, the contemporary representatives of Nietzsche's era, belong to those who are once again withdrawing values that were posited earlier. The deposition of values does not arise from a mere thirst for blind destruction and vain innovation. It arises from the need and necessity to give the world *the* meaning that does not reduce it to a mere passage into the beyond. A world must arise that enables a man to develop his essence from his own fund of values. But for that we need a transition, a way through the predicament in which the world appears value-less but at the same time demands a new value. The passage through the intermediate state must perceive it as such with the greatest possible awareness. To achieve that, it is necessary to recognize the origin of the intermediate state and to bring to light the first cause of nihilism. The decisive will to overcome the intermediate state can only emerge from an awareness of it.

Nietzsche's exposition, which began as an enumeration of the conditions for the emergence of nihilism and as a mere description of its course, now suddenly sounds like a declaration of what we are acting out; indeed, must act out. It is not a question here of historical recognition of past events and their effects on the present. Something imminent is at stake, something barely under way, involving decisions and tasks whose transitional character is interpreted as investing values in and withdrawing values from the world.

But there is more than one kind of "nihilism." Nihilism is not only the process of devaluing the highest values, nor simply the *withdrawal* of these values. The very positing of these values in the world is already nihilism. The devaluation of values does not end with a gradual becoming worthless of values, like a rivulet that trickles into the sand. Nihilism is achieved in the withdrawal of values, in the aggressive removal of values. Nietzsche wants to make clear to us the inner richness of the essence of nihilism. Section B therefore must inspire us to adopt a decisive stance.

If we now review section A with a sharper focus, we are able to detect the various modes of introduction of the three conditions for the emergence of nihilism, which to all appearances are merely being enumerated. In the first paragraph Nietzsche is basically saying that nihilism "will have to enter on the scene" as a psychological state. Here he first names the fundamental condition for the possibility of nihilism—namely, the condition that in general something like a "meaning" is posited as what is sought.

In the second paragraph, he says that nihilism "arises" as a psychological state. Here he identifies the decisive condition that introduces the actual toppling of the highest values, and he arranges matters so that an encompassing, comprehensive totality, a "unity," is posited as meaning, a unity that works through man and establishes and secures human being amidst beings.

In the third paragraph, we find that "Nihilism as a psychological state has yet a *third* and *final* form." Here we preview the advent of something in which nihilism first finds its full essence. This is the positing of a true world beyond, in itself, as the goal and the paradigm of this illusory, earthly world.

The first paragraph names the fundamental condition of the possibility of nihilism, the second its actual beginning, and the third the necessary fulfillment of its essence. This in general is how the history of nihilism *as* history in its essential traits receives its first "portrayal."

Now we can no longer restrain the question touched on earlier as to whether and how the history of the essence of nihilism corresponds to the historical reality one is accustomed to regard historiologically. Nietzsche says nothing about it directly, just as he does not really describe his treatment as the essential history of nihilism. Everything here remains indeterminate. Nonetheless, there are indications that Nietzsche has "actual" history in view, above all where he is discussing the third form of nihilism.

By the positing of a "true world" over against a purely illusory world of becoming, Nietzsche is referring to Platonic metaphysics and in its wake the whole of subsequent metaphysics, which he understands as "Platonism." He takes Platonism to be a "doctrine of two worlds": above this earthly, mutable world, accessible to the senses, there stands a supersensuous, immutable world beyond. The latter is a world continually enduring in "Being," and so is a true world, while the former is illusory. The equation of "truth" and "Being" corresponds to this. As long as Christianity teaches that our world, as a vale of tears, is merely a temporal passage to eternal bliss beyond, Nietzsche can regard Christianity in general as Platonism (the doctrine of two worlds) for the people.

If the third form of the conditions for the emergence and essence of nihilism refers to Plato's philosophy, then we must search for the first and second in *pre*-Platonic philosophy in their corresponding historical forms. In point of fact, we can find the positing of a "unity" for being as a whole in Parmenides' doctrine *hen to on*. Nevertheless, because the first form of the conditions for emergence stands as the grounding condition for the *possibility* of nihilism, governing the whole history of nihilism, we can find no explicit historical testimony for it. But because what we have just said basically holds true for all three conditions, and because these conditions, even when they are correspondingly transformed, exercise some effect on every fundamental metaphysical position, the attempt to demonstrate a historiological correspondence for the three conditions designated does not have all the significance one could ask for, especially when we note that section A is merely the prelude to B.

8. The New Valuation

Section B reads as follows:

> Granted we realize to what extent the world may no longer be *interpreted* in terms of these *three* categories, and that after this insight the world begins to become valueless for us: we then have to ask *whence* our faith in these three categories comes—let us try to see if it is not possible to cancel our faith in *them!* Once we have *devaluated* these three categories, the demonstration that they cannot be applied to the universe is no longer any reason *for devaluating the universe.*
>
> Result: *Faith in the categories of reason* is the cause of nihilism—we have measured the value of the world according to categories *which relate to a purely fictitious world.*
>
> Final result: All the values by means of which we have so far tried to render the world estimable for ourselves and which, after they proved inapplicable, therefore *devaluated* the world—all these values are, psychologically reckoned, results of particular perspectives of utility, for the preservation and enhancement of human constructs of domination; and they have only been falsely *projected* into the essence of things. It is always and everywhere the *hyperbolic naiveté* of man, positing himself as the meaning and standard of value for things.

We have said that a different language is being spoken here, one that has, of course, already been intimated in section A, especially by its last sentence. Now no more is said about how nihilism as a psychological state "will have to enter on the scene"; no longer is there talk of nihilism as a phenomenon found only back in history, as it were. Now we ourselves are involved in the question. Therefore, we now read, "Granted we realize to what extent . . . may no longer be *interpreted*"; we read, "We then have to . . . "; the passage says, "Let us try . . . !"

When we have made the attempt, a wholly new relationship to the "universe" results, the "result" of history is first discerned. That "result" is gathered up in a "final result" by the concluding section.

There are "results" only where there is reckoning and calculation. In fact, Nietzsche's train of thought, as nihilistic, is reckoning. What kind of reckoning it is he specifies in the concluding section: "All these values are, psychologically reckoned, results" of this and that. It is a matter of the "psychological" reckoning and calculation of values, whereby, of course, we ourselves are included in the reckoning. But then to think psychologically means to think everything as a configuration of will to power. To reckon psychologically means to appraise everything on the basis of value and to calculate value on the basis of the fundamental value, will to power—to figure how and to what extent "values" can be evaluated in accord with will to power and so prove valid.

What is demanded in section B, and the purpose for which it is demanded, is the explicit, conscious, and consciously self-justifying attempt to devalue the uppermost values, to depose them as highest values. At the same time, this implies a decision to take seriously the intermediate state that the devaluation of the highest values produces, by simultaneously fixing on our earthly world as the only reality, and a decision *to be* in that decision as a historical one. Nihilism is now no longer a historical process that we as observers merely have before us, outside ourselves, or even behind us; nihilism reveals itself as the history of our era, which imposes its own effective limits on the age, and by which we are claimed. We do not stand in this history as in some uniform space in which any standpoint or position can be assumed at will. That history is itself the manner and mode in which we stand or move, in which we *are*. The devaluation of the highest values hitherto enters the state of deposition and overthrow. But even in an overthrow it is still a question of values that are to determine being as a whole. Through the decline of the highest values hitherto, being in the sense of what is real, what is accessible right here and now, does indeed become valueless. But instead of disappearing, what is accessible validates itself as what has been rendered needful of new values by the overthrow of prior values. Therefore the deposition of previous values

The New Valuation

is already inherently and necessarily on the path toward a new positing of values. By means of the deposition of prior values, the world, formerly the merely earthly world, becomes being as a whole as such. Now, as it were, being as a whole stands outside the difference between the earthly and the beyond. Thus the deposition of the highest values hitherto brings with it a change in being as a whole, such that it becomes questionable where and how one can still speak of beings and of Being. To put it another way, the new positing of values can no longer proceed simply by putting new values in the *same* places—which meanwhile have, of course, become empty—in lieu of the highest values hitherto.

With the downfall of the highest values also comes the elimination of the "above" and the "high" and the "beyond," the former *place* in which values could be posited. Such elimination means that the valuation in itself must become a different one. Even that *for* which the new values are supposed to be values is, after the downfall of the beyond, no longer something this-worldly. But this implies that the *way in which* the values are values, the essence of values, must be transformed. The earth-shaking change behind the devaluation of the highest values hitherto is revealed in the fact that a *new principle of valuation* becomes necessary. But because the devaluation of uppermost values is a conscious deposition of former values, arising from unequivocally known phenomena, the new valuation must have its origin in a new and enhanced consciousness (reckoning).

Hence the principle of a new valuation can become valid only if a new knowledge about the essence of values and the conditions for estimating values is awakened and propagated. The revaluation of all prior values must be accomplished and maintained by the highest awareness of one's own consciousness of essential value and valuation. The decline of prior values first *completes* itself in the new valuation understood in this way.

Nihilism first becomes classical through the revaluation of all values. What distinguishes it is knowledge of the origin and necessity of values, and along with that an insight into the essence of prior values. Here valuation and valuative thought first come to themselves, not simply in the way that an instinctive act also knows and casually observes itself, but rather in such a way that this consciousness becomes an essential moment and a driving force in the whole of behavior. What we describe with the ambiguous name *instinct* now comes to be not merely something of which we were formerly unconscious but now know; consciousness, "psychological reckoning," and calculation now become *instinct proper.*

Whereas in section B nihilism is experienced as a transitional state and made into a standard for thinking and acting, the concluding part of note 12 arrives at the position of classical nihilism. The "final result" is recounted in which being as a whole is newly reckoned and the knowledge of the essence of values and of valuation is expressed without obfuscation. Let us repeat the main sentence of the concluding section:

> All these values are, psychologically reckoned, results of particular perspectives of utility, for the preservation and enhancement of human constructs of domination; and they have only been falsely *projected* into the essence of things. It is always and everywhere the *hyperbolic naiveté* of man, positing himself as the meaning and standard of value for things.

Thus Nietzsche is saying that the essence of values has its ground in "constructs of domination." Values are essentially related to "domination." Dominance is the being in power of power. Values are bound to will to power; they depend on it as the proper essence of power. What is untrue and untenable about the highest values hitherto does not lie in the values themselves, in their content, in the fact that in them meaning is sought, unity posited, and truth secured. Nietzsche sees what is untrue in the fact that these values have been mistakenly dispatched to a realm "existing in itself," within which and from which they are supposed to acquire absolute validity for themselves, whereas they really have their origin and radius of validity solely in a certain kind of will to power.

If we think back from the concluding section of note 12 to its title, "Decline of Cosmological Values," then it becomes clear that the title corresponds to the whole of the note only if we first conceive of nihilism in Nietzsche's sense as history—that is, at the same time conceive of it positively as a preliminary stage of a "new" valuation, so decisively

The New Valuation

that we experience precisely the most extreme nihilism not as a complete downfall but as the transition to new conditions of human existence. Nietzsche preserves this overall insight into the essence of nihilism in a note composed about the time note 12 was written:

> *Overall insight.* All major growth is in fact accompanied by a tremendous *disintegration* and *passing away:* suffering, the symptoms of decline, *belong* to the times of tremendous advance; every fertile and powerful movement of humanity has also *created at the same time* a nihilistic movement. It could turn out to be the sign of crucial and most essential growth, of transition to new conditions of existence, that the *most extreme* form of pessimism, *nihilism* proper, comes into the world. *This I have grasped.* (WM, 112; spring–fall, 1887)

The following note stems from the same period:

> Man is *beast* and *Overbeast:* the higher man is Nonman and Overman: these belong together. With every growth of man in greatness and height, there is also growth in depth and terribleness: one should not will the one without the other—or rather: the more radically we will the one, the more radically we achieve precisely the other. (WM, 1027)

9. Nihilism as History

Following our first elucidation of note 12, the proper task of pondering and thinking through Nietzsche's concept of European nihilism has taken on greater definition. What at the beginning of our reflections was tentatively adumbrated can now be combined for the proper discussion of the essence of nihilism into two lines of questioning—as posed in the following statements. First, nihilism, as Nietzsche thinks it, is the history of the devaluation of the highest values hitherto, as the transition to the revaluation of all prior values, a revaluation that comes to pass in the discovery of a principle for a new valuation, a principle Nietzsche recognizes as the will to power. Second, Nietzsche conceives of the essence of nihilism solely on the basis of valuative thought, and in that form alone does it become an object of his critique and his attempt at an overcoming. But because the valuation has its principle in the will to power, overcoming nihilism by fulfilling it in its classical form develops into an interpretation of being as a whole as will to power. The new valuation is a metaphysics of will to power.

We comprehend the phrase "metaphysics *of* will to power" in a double sense, because the genitive case has the twofold meaning of the objective and subjective genitive. Nietzsche's metaphysics is for one thing metaphysics that has the will to power as the truth of being as a whole for its "object," inasmuch as will to power constitutes the overall character of being as a whole. As the fundamental trait of being as a whole, however, will to power is at the same time the essential definition of man. As such, it lies at the basis of the human coinage of the truth of being as a whole—that is, metaphysics—it is the *subiectum* of metaphysics. For another thing, therefore, Nietzsche's metaphysics is the one in which the will to power is brought to dominance. Such metaphysics itself belongs in the realm of power governed by the will to power and is one of its conditions. The will to power is the object and the subject of a metaphysics thoroughly dominated by valuative thinking. In this univocal sense, the expression "metaphysics *of* will to power" is equivocal.

First, it is necessary to understand nihilism in a unified way as the history of valuations. We are using the term *valuation* here in a broad sense. It includes the positing of the uppermost values, the devaluation of these values as their deposition, and the revaluation of these values as the new positing of values.

Taking up our first line of questioning, we note once again that nihilism is a history. By that we do not mean merely that what we call *nihilism* "has" a "history" inasmuch as it can be traced historically in its temporal course. Nihilism *is* history. In Nietzsche's sense it co-constitutes the essence of Western history because it co-determines the lawfulness of the fundamental metaphysical positions and their relationships. But the fundamental metaphysical positions are the ground and realm of what we know as world history, and especially as Western history. Nihilism determines the historicity of this history. Consequently, for a comprehension of the essence of nihilism there is little to be gained by recounting the history of nihilism in different centuries and depicting it in its various forms. First of all, everything must aim at recognizing nihilism as the lawfulness of history. If one wants to consider this history a "decline," reckoning it in terms of the devaluation of the highest values, then nihilism is not the cause of the decline but its *inner logic,* the lawfulness of events that goes further than mere decline and so also points beyond decline. Hence an insight into the essence of nihilism does not consist in the knowledge of phenomena that can be historically documented as nihilistic—it rests in an understanding of the steps, gradations, and transitions from the initial devaluation up to the inevitable revaluation.

If the highest values are devalued and the feeling arises that the world does not and never did correspond to what we ideally expected of it—if, indeed, the feeling is aroused that everything is going awry, turning into nothing, and that this world is therefore the worst of worlds, a *pessimum*—then there emerges the attitude that in the modern age is usually called "pessimism," the belief that in this worst of worlds life is not worth living or affirming (Schopenhauer). Nietzsche therefore explicitly describes "pessimism" (WM, 9; 1887) as the "prototype of nihilism" (see WM, 37: "Development of *Pessimism into Nihilism*"). But, like nihilism, pessimism too is ambiguous. There is a pessimism of strength and *as* strength; but there is also a pessimism of weakness and *as* weakness. The former does not delude itself, sees the danger, wants no obfuscation: it gazes soberly at the forces and powers that betoken danger. But it also recognizes those conditions that in spite of everything would establish control over things. The pessimism of strength therefore has its position in "analysis." By "analysis," Nietzsche does not mean a disentangling, as a dissecting and unraveling, but the scrutinizing of what "is," a depiction of the grounds for a being's being the way it is. In contrast, pessimism as weakness and decline sees only the dark side of everything, is ready with a reason for each new failure, and fancies itself the attitude that knows in advance how it will all turn out. The pessimism of weakness seeks to "understand" everything and explain it historically, to excuse it, and let it pass. For everything that happens, it has already ferreted out some corresponding precedent. Pessimism as decline takes refuge in "historicism" (see WM, 10).* The pessimism that has its strength in "analysis" and the pessimism that is caught up in "historicism" are opposed to each other in the most extreme way. There is more than one kind of "pessimism." Through pessimism and its ambiguity, therefore, the "extremes" come to appear and preponderate. Thus the "transitional state" that the devaluation of the highest values hitherto produces becomes clearer and more compelling.

From one point of view, it seems that the fulfillment of prior values

---

* Note 10 of *The Will to Power* reads thus:

A. Pessimism as strength—*in what?* in the energy of its logic, as anarchism and nihilism, as analytic.

B. Pessimism as decline—*in what?* as effeteness, as a sort of cosmopolitan fingering, as *tout comprendre* and historicism.

—*The critical tension:* the extremes come to the fore and become predominant.

Actually, WM, 10 is a composite of two notes; the concluding sentence belongs to another page in the notebooks; cf. CM, WII 1 [126] and [128].

is *not* to be attained; the world seems valueless. From the other point of view, the waxing analytical consciousness of the origin of value estimations in will to power guides the inquisitive eye toward the source of new value estimations, although of course without the world gaining in value thereby. With regard to the shaken validity of prior values, however, there could just as well be an attempt to retain their "place," and to fill that old place—the transcendent—with new ideals. According to Nietzsche's treatment, this is what happens in "doctrines of universal happiness," for example, and in "socialism," as well as in "Wagnerian music," the Christian "ideal," and there "where the dogmatic form of Christianity has been abandoned" (WM, 1021). "Incomplete nihilism" arises in this way.

> *Incomplete* nihilism; its forms: we live right in the midst of it.
> Attempts to circumvent nihilism *without* revaluating prior values produce the opposite, make the problem more acute. (WM, 28)

With this it becomes clearer to what extent the "revaluation of all values" belongs to perfected, complete nihilism, and how a peculiar state of uncertainty precedes and accompanies the revaluation. The condition of uncertainty, in which prior values are deposed and new values not yet posited, consists in the fact that there is no truth in itself, although there is still truth. But truth has yet to be newly defined. In the "analytic," the suspicion was already awakened that the "will to truth," as the claim of something binding and authoritative, is a claim of *power,* and as such is sanctioned only by will to power as a configuration of will to power itself. The transitional state being described is "extreme nihilism," which recognizes and expressly states that there is no truth in itself. Again, such nihilism is ambiguous:

> A. Nihilism as a sign of *enhanced power of spirit: active nihilism.*
> B. Nihilism as *decline* and *recession of the power of spirit: passive nihilism.*
> (WM, 22; spring–fall 1887)

Passive nihilism says there is no truth in itself, and lets it go at that. For passive nihilism there is no truth at all. Active nihilism, however, sets out to define truth in its essence on the basis of that which lends all things their determinability and definition. Active nihilism acknowledges truth as a configuration of will to power and as a value of determinate rank.

If will to power is expressly and fully experienced as the ground of the possibility of truth, and if truth is conceived and portrayed as a function of will to power (as justification), then extreme nihilism, as active, is transformed into classical nihilism. But because active nihilism already recognizes and acknowledges will to power as the fundamental trait of beings, nihilism in general is not merely "contemplation" (WM, 24),* is not the mere "no" of judgment. It is the "no" of deed: "one lays his hand to," "one executes." One does not simply regard something as null, he sets it aside, overturns it, and creates an open field. Hence classical nihilism is itself the "ideal of supreme powerfulness" (WM, 14).

Such nihilism emerges from "life" as it used to be, cuts a path "for a new order," and grants whatever wants to die off its "longing for the end." In this way, nihilism makes a clean sweep and at the same time introduces new possibilities. Therefore, referring to the nihilism of a wholly new valuation, a nihilism which makes room by placing all being out into the clear, Nietzsche speaks of "ecstatic nihilism" (WM, 1055). Insofar as the supreme powerfulness of the classic-ecstatic, active-extreme nihilism knows nothing outside itself, recognizes no limits over it, and acknowledges nothing as a measure, classical-ecstatic nihilism could be a *"divine way of thinking"* (WM, 15). In such a form, nihilism is no longer simply a powerless "yearning for nothingness" (WM, 1029), but is the very opposite (see WM, 1010, 1023, 1025).† This reveals the essential fullness of nihilism as articulated in itself: ambiguous early forms of nihilism (pessimism), incomplete nihilism, extreme nihilism, active and passive nihilism, and active-extreme, ecstatic-classical nihilism.

When, how, and to what extent—whether recognized or not—*one*

---

* That is, not merely contemplation of the "In vain!" (cf. WM, 24).

† WM, 1025 invokes that kind of strength that can transmute apparent evil into good, can press everything frightful into its service. WM, 1023 identifies such strength with "pleasure," "felicity," and "progress." WM, 1010 speaks of a new conception of the world's "perfection," one that could even sanction prior misconceptions: "Whatever does *not* correspond to our logic, our 'beautiful,' our 'good,' our 'true,' could be perfect in a *higher* sense than even our ideal."

of these modes of nihilism dominates, or whether they all reign at the same time and produce a thoroughly ambiguous historical condition for an age: these are questions that can be asked only from a position of action and meditation, questions that must be asked here. For us, an indication of the interwoven modes of nihilism suffices to clarify the movement of its essence and its historical character, and at the same time to impress on us anew that by nihilism we do not mean something merely present or, indeed, "contemporary" to Nietzsche's time. The name *nihilism* points to a historical movement that extends far behind us and reaches forward far beyond us.

10. Valuation and Will to Power

Nihilism, however, considered by Nietzsche as the history of valuations, can be understood only if valuation as such is recognized in its essence; that is, in its metaphysical necessity. Therefore, *the primary emphasis of our reflections* shifts to the second line of questioning.

The principal points in this area of inquiry are, first, that Nietzsche thinks nihilism in its origin, development, and overcoming solely in terms of valuative thought; second, that thinking in values belongs to that reality that is defined as the will to power; third, valuative thought is a necessary constituent of the metaphysics of will to power.

But in what does such metaphysics have its historically essential ground? Or, to ask it another way, Where does valuative thinking have its "metaphysical" source? If metaphysics is the truth of beings as a whole and therefore speaks about the Being of beings, from what interpretation of being as a whole does value thinking originate? Our answer is that it originates from a determination of beings as a whole through the basic trait of will to power. It is a correct answe.. But how do we arrive at *this* interpretation of beings, if we insist that it is not an arbitrary and exaggerated opinion occurring only in the head of the eccentric Herr Nietzsche? How do we arrive at a projection of the world as will to power, granted that in such an interpretation of the world Nietzsche must be talking about that toward which the long history of the West, especially the history of the modern age, has been pressing in its most concealed course? What occurs essentially and reigns in Western metaphysics, that it should finally come to be a metaphysics of will to power?

With that question, we move from what is seemingly mere summary and exposition to a "confrontation" with Nietzsche's metaphysics. Presuming that Nietzsche's metaphysics is the fulfillment of Western metaphysics, a confrontation with it will be adequate only if it concerns itself with Western metaphysics in general.

In a thoughtful confrontation with a thinker, it is not a question of opposing one "outlook" to another or of one "standpoint" being "refuted" by another. All that is extraneous and inessential. For us, a confrontation does not mean supercilious "polemic" or vain "critique." Confrontation means meditation on the truth that is up for decision, for a decision not made by us, but one that Being itself, as the history of Being, makes for our own history. Our sole alternatives are either to root about among "outlooks" and adopt "standpoints," among which we must also count the ostensible "freedom from standpoints," or, on the contrary, to break with all adherence to standpoints and outlooks and to take leave of all current opinions and ideas, in order to commend ourselves solely to an original knowing.

Even in our first elucidation of nihilism, we took our impetus from the fact that the name and concept *nihilism* intends thought about Being, although Nietzsche consistently understands nihilism in terms of valuative thought. Although the question about the being as such and as a whole was and is the guiding question of all metaphysics, thinking about values came to predominate *decisively* in metaphysics only recently, and did so only through Nietzsche, in such a way that metaphysics henceforth took a decisive turn toward the fulfillment of its essence.

Partly as a result of Nietzsche's influence, the academic philosophy of the later nineteenth and early twentieth centuries became a "philosophy of value" and a "phenomenology of value." Values themselves appeared to be things in themselves, which one might arrange into "systems." Although tacitly rejecting Nietzsche's philosophy, one rummaged through Nietzsche's writings, especially *Zarathustra,* for such values. Then, "more scientifically" than the "unscientific philosopher-poet" Nietzsche, one organized them into an "ethics of value."

When we discuss valuative thought in this lecture course, we are referring exclusively to Nietzsche's metaphysics. Around the turn of the century, one branch of neo-Kantianism, associated with the names Windelband and Rickert, described itself as "philosophy of value" in a rather narrow and academic sense.* The lasting service of the movement is not its "philosophy of value" but its attitude—remarkable for its time—which preserved and handed down a trace of authentic knowledge about the essence of philosophy and philosophical inquiry against the onslaught of scientific "psychology" and "biology," supposedly the only valid "philosophies." But this stance, which was "traditional" in a good sense, nonetheless prevented the "philosophy of value" from thinking through valuative thought in its metaphysical essence; that is, prevented this movement from really taking nihilism seriously. The movement believed it could elude nihilism by means of a return to Kantian philosophy, but this return was merely a retreat before nihilism and a refusal to look into the abyss it covers.

If Nietzsche's philosophy executes the fulfillment of Western metaphysics, and if for the first time and more originally than in the tardigrade "philosophy of value" valuative thought becomes decisive in Nietzsche's philosophy, then such thinking cannot accidentally and

---

* Wilhelm Windelband (1848–1915), professor of philosophy in Heidelberg from 1903 until his death, and Heinrich Rickert (1863–1936), who taught in Freiburg until assuming Cohen's chair at Heidelberg in 1916, were co-founders of the "Baden" or "Southwest German" School of neo-Kantian philosophy. (Rickert was co-director of Heidegger's doctoral dissertation in 1912–13, and Heidegger dedicated his *Habilitationsschrift* of 1915–16 to him "in most grateful homage.") Although there were differences of emphasis in the work of Windelband and Rickert, both understood philosophy to be the critical-scientific search for values (*Werte*) of universal validity (*Geltung*), primarily in the realm of "culture." In his first logic course at Marburg, in the winter semester of 1925–26, Heidegger discussed the neo-Kantian *value* philosophy of Windelband and Rickert in the context of Rudolf Hermann Lotze's philosophical logic of *validity*. He roundly castigated the former as "the outermost station in the decline of the question concerning truth" and as "the most wrongheaded formulation of the problem." See Martin Heidegger, *Logik: Die Frage nach der Wahrheit*, sections 9–10, especially pp. 82–83 and 91–92. The incipient and gingerly implied criticism of value philosophy in the Foreword to Heidegger's *Habilitationsschrift* had thus after a decade's time become a sardonic total rejection of his former teacher's work. For example, after citing Eduard Spranger's account of Rickert's thought, published in the house journal of neo-Kantian value philosophy (*Logos*, 1923, *12*, 198), Heidegger remarked, "One could almost wax sentimental over such profundity." His discussion here in the Nietzsche lectures is far milder than the earlier caustic treatment, and even includes words of praise for the Baden School. However, it seems clear that Heidegger's confrontation with Nietzsche was delayed throughout the 1920s by Nietzsche's reputation as a "philosopher of value" and by Heidegger's aversion to *Wertphilosophie*.

superficially have forced its way into metaphysics. The question about the origin of valuative thought in metaphysics becomes a question about the essence of values *and* about the essence of metaphysics. Insofar as the latter reaches its fulfillment, our question becomes a decisive question about what defines philosophy in its necessity and grants it its ground.

What is the source of valuative thought, that thinking which gauges everything in terms of values, conceives of itself as an estimation of values, and takes upon itself the task of a new valuation? Nietzsche himself posed the question about the origin of valuative thought and readily answered it, as well. We need only recall the course of his reflections in note 12. There, in section B, Nietzsche explicitly asks where our belief in cosmological values comes from. His answer: From the will of man to secure a value for himself. But how is he supposed to accomplish that if the world in which he belongs does not for its part have value, meaning, purpose, unity, and *truth*—if man cannot subordinate himself to an "ideal"? The concluding part of note 12 expresses the inner connection between valuation and will to power clearly enough. Of course, we have not really grasped the relation by pointing out the reference. However, we may surmise that if a distinctive consciousness is required for the revaluation of values, and thereby a knowledge of what values are all about, Nietzsche must have already brought that inner connection to light in his own way.

Every kind of value positing, including especially the new valuation by which a revaluation of values is to be accomplished, must be related to the will to power. Nietzsche expresses the connection in the first sentence of note 14: "*Values, and their alteration, are related to the growth in power of the one positing the values.*" In accord with the essential definition of will to power provided at the outset, "growth in power" is nothing but power enhancement in the sense of the self-overpowering of power. But therein lies the essence of power. The statement therefore means: Values and their changes, and hence valuation—be it devaluation, revaluation, or the new positing of values—are in every instance determined by the respective nature of the will to power, which for its part defines the one positing—that is, man—in the nature of his human being. Values stem from valuation; valuation corresponds to the will to power. But why and to what extent is the will to power a value positing? What does Nietzsche understand by *value?*

The Will to Power, which is a very confused book with respect to its organization of the posthumous notes, contains under note 715 (dated 1888) a notation of Nietzsche's that answers our question: "The viewpoint of 'value' is the viewpoint of *conditions of preservation* and *enhancement* with regard to complex constructs of relative life-duration within becoming."

According to this note, "value" is a "viewpoint." "Value" is indeed "essentially" the "viewpoint for" (see note 715*). We are not yet asking *for what* value is a point of view; let us first consider *that* "value" is "viewpoint" in general—the sort of thing that, once viewed, becomes a gauge for a seeing that has something in view. Such envisioning is a *reckoning* on something that also must reckon with something else. Thus we immediately place "value" too into conjunction with a "how much" and "so much," with quantity and number. Thus "values" are related to a *"numerical* and *mensural scale"* (WM, 710). There remains only the question of what this scale of increase and diminution is itself related to.

The characterization of value as a "viewpoint" yields one thing that is essential for Nietzsche's concept: as a viewpoint, value is always posited by a seeing. Through the positing, it first comes to be a "point" for the envisioning of something, a point that belongs in the purview of the envisioning of something. Thus values are not from the outset and inherently at hand in themselves, so that they can also occasionally serve as viewpoints. Nietzsche's thinking is lucid and open enough to specify that the viewpoint is "pointed" to the kind of thing it is only through the "punctuation" of the seeing. What is valid does not have validity because it is in itself a value; rather, a value *is* a value because it has validity. It has validity because it has been posited as valid. It is thus posited by an envisioning of something that *through* the envisioning first receives the character of a thing with which one can reckon and that therefore has validity.

Once valuative thought has come on the scene, it must also be

---

* The fourth paragraph of WM, 715 begins, "Value is essentially the viewpoint for the increase or decrease of these centers of domination." Cf. p.66 of the present volume.

Valuation

admitted that values "are" only where there is reckoning, just as there are "objects" only for "subjects." To speak about "values in themselves" is either thoughtlessness, or counterfeiting, or both. "Value," according to its essence, is "viewpoint." There are viewpoints only for a seeing that points and reckons by means of "points."

But what is viewed with value as a gauge? What is that with which we reckon in any given case? What does reckoning essentially envision? Nietzsche says that "the viewpoint of 'value' is the viewpoint of *conditions of preservation* and *enhancement.*" Insofar as we reckon *on* something, there must be something we reckon *with*, something on which preservation and enhancement depend, that promotes or restricts preservation, that provides or denies enhancement. In other words, we must reckon with the sort of thing that conditions. After all we have said thus far, we may suppose that by preservation and enhancement are meant preservation of power and enhancement of power. Power is the "something"; that is, the "thing" that matters, as it were, the thing whose preservation and enhancement is conditioned.

"Values" are the conditions with which power as such must reckon. To reckon on enhancement of power, on the overpowering of the respective stages of power, is the *essence* of will to power. "Values" are in the first place the conditions of enhancement that the will to power has in view. As self-overpowering, will to power is never at a standstill.

In Nietzsche's metaphysics, will to power is a richer name for the overused and vacuous term *becoming.* That is why Nietzsche says that "the viewpoint of 'value' is the viewpoint of *conditions of preservation and enhancement* . . . within becoming." But, in the definition of the essence of value as *condition, what* the values condition still remains undetermined—what sort of thing they make into a thing, if we employ the word *thing* here in the broad sense of "something," which does not compel us to think of tangible things and objects.* But *what*

---

* Heidegger is now taking the verb "to condition" (*bedingen*) quite literally: *be-dingen* would be the making of something into a "thing" (*Ding*). If values are conditions for the preservation and enhancement of power, Heidegger now wants to ask what sorts of things value and power are; that is to say, he wishes to inquire into the ontological status of both the "viewpoint of value" and the "will to power." If the latter is Nietzsche's name for the Being of beings, how can value "be-thing" will to power?

values condition is the will to power. Yes, of course; but will to power, as the fundamental trait of the "real," is not some simple sort of matter, as its name already suggests. Nietzsche is not speaking casually when he says that "value" is the *condition of preservation* and *enhancement* set forth in reckoning. In the real, one is necessarily dealing equally with preservation *and* enhancement; because in order for the will to power as overpowering to be able to surpass a certain stage, that stage must not only be reached, it must also be inwardly, even *powerfully* secured. Otherwise the *over*powering could not be an over*powering*. Only what already has stability and a firm footing can "think" about enhancement. A stage must first be secured in itself before it can be used as a staging area.

Thus what is required for the real in its character as will to power are those values that establish its stability and continuance. But, just as necessarily, it requires the sort of conditions that guarantee an out-beyond-itself, a superelevation of what is real (what is living); it requires values as conditions of enhancement.

In accord with its inmost essence, therefore, the will to power must always and especially posit values of preservation *and* enhancement. Following these two mutually related outlooks, the will to power must look out and beyond, and, so looking, point to view*points,* posit values. The outlook on viewpoints belongs to valuation. What pertains to the will to power as vista and "perspect" Nietzsche calls its "perspectival" character. Will to power is thus *in itself* an envisioning of more power. The "envisioning of" is the path of *perspect* and *purview:* the per-spective belongs to will to power. That is why, in the fragment that is serving as our guide (note 12, concluding section), Nietzsche says, "All these values are, psychologically reckoned, results of particular perspectives." We could also say that all these values are as *values* particular viewpoints of particular purviews of a particular will to power. But insofar as each real thing is real by virtue of the fundamental character of will to power, a single and individual "perspective" belongs to every individual thing. *Beings as such are perspectival.* What we call reality is defined by its perspectival character. Only by keeping this fact constantly in mind can we think the "being" proper within Nietzsche's metaphysics. In the perspectival character of the being, Nietzsche is only expressing what has formed a covert basic trait of metaphysics since Leibniz.

According to Leibniz all being is defined by *perceptio* and *appetitus*, by the representing urge which presses for the *placing-before*, the "representation," of the whole of beings, presses for their *being* first of all and only in such *repraesentatio* and as such *repraesentatio*. In each case, the representing has what Leibniz calls a *point de vue*—a viewpoint. That is what Nietzsche says, too: it is "perspectivism" (the perspectival constitution of the being), "by virtue of which every center of force—and not only man—construes all the rest of the world *from its own viewpoint;* that is, measures, touches, shapes, according to its own force" (WM, 636, from the year 1888; see XIV, 13, from 1884–85: "If one wished to escape from the world of perspectives, he would be going to his doom.") But Leibniz does not yet think these viewpoints as values. Value thinking is not yet so essential and explicit that *values* could be thought as viewpoints of perspectives.

The real that is defined in its reality by the will to power is in every instance an interweaving of perspectives and valuations, a construct of a "complex kind." But it is so because the will to power itself has a complex nature. The complex unity of its essence should once again be brought into view.

If the essence of the power of will is more power, and if power is therefore empowered as overpowering, then something that is overcome as a particular stage of power, and at the same time something that overcomes, both belong to power. What is to be overcome can only be such a thing if it posits a resistance and stands firm and secure, sustaining and preserving itself. In contrast, the overcoming must be able to go up and over to higher stages of power; it requires the possibility of enhancement. The necessary interconnection of preservation and enhancement belongs to the essence of overpowering. The essence of power is itself something intricate. Reality thus defined is permanent and at the same time impermanent. Its permanence is therefore *relative*. Thus Nietzsche says, "The viewpoint of 'value' is the viewpoint of *conditions of preservation* and *enhancement* with regard to complex constructs of relative life-duration within becoming." Gathered together in these constructs are the products of the will to power, whose essence consists in being master and being able to command. That is why Nietzsche also calls these constructs succinctly "constructs of domination" or "centers of domination" (WM, 715): " 'Value' is essentially the viewpoint for the increase or decrease of these centers of domination." It is made explicit in this definition that values as *conditions* of preservation and enhancement are always related to a "becoming" in the sense of waxing and waning power. In no respect are values primarily something "for themselves," having only a subsequent and occasional relation to the will to power. They are what they are—that is, they are conditions—only *as conditioning,* and are therefore posited by the will to power itself as its own conditions of possibility. Thus they provide a standard of measure for the appraisal of degrees of power of a construct of domination and for judging its increase and decrease. When Nietzsche says at the conclusion of note 12 that values are "results of particular perspectives of utility, for the preservation and enhancement of human constructs of domination," use and utility are understood here in their unique relation to power. "Value" is essentially use-value; but "use" must here be equated with the condition of the preservation of power; that is, always at the same time, with the condition of the enhancement of power. According to their essence, values are conditions, and therefore never something absolute.

Values are conditions of "constructs of domination" within becoming; that is, within reality as a whole, whose fundamental character is will to power. The constructs of dominance are configurations of will to power. Nietzsche often calls not only the conditions of these constructs of domination, but even the constructs themselves, *values,* and rightly so. Science, art, the state, religion, and culture all pass as values insofar as they are conditions by virtue of which the classification of becoming—as what alone is real—is carried out. For their part, these values further posit definite conditions for securing their own continuance and development. But becoming itself—that is, reality as a whole—"has no value at all." That is clear now from the definition of the essence of value just given. There is nothing outside of being as a whole that might serve as a condition for it. What is lacking is something whereby it (becoming as a whole) might be measured. *"The overall value of the world cannot be evaluated;* consequently, philosophical pessimism belongs among comical things" (WM, 708, from the years 1887–88).

When Nietzsche says that being as a whole "has no value at all," he does not mean to deliver a disparaging judgment about the world. He merely wants to fend off every evaluation of the whole as a misunderstanding of its essence. The statement "being as a whole has no value at all," thought in the sense of a metaphysics of will to power, is the sharpest rejection of the belief that "values" are something in themselves, hovering over being as a whole and validating it. To say that being as a whole is value-less means that it stands outside every valuing, because through valuing the whole and the absolute would only be made dependent on parts and conditions that are what they are only in terms of the whole. The world of becoming, as will to power, is the un-conditioned. Only *within becoming,* only in relation to individual constructs of power, posited by them and for them, are there conditions; that is, viewpoints of the preservation and enhancement of degrees of power; that is, values. Do values therefore arise from will to power? Certainly. But we would be committing another error in thought if we now wished to understand values as if they were something "alongside" the will to power, as if there were at first the latter, which then posited "values" that would from time to time be pressed into service by it. Values, as *conditions* of preservation and enhancement of power, exist only as something conditioned by the *one* absolute, will to power. *Values are essentially conditioned conditions.*

But values can obviously be conditions of the will to power only if they themselves have the character of power, only if they represent power quanta for reckoning the enhancement of power, in terms of the conscious efforts of the will to power. Hence values, as conditions of the enhancement and preservation of power, are essentially related to man. As viewpoints, they are incorporated into *human* perspectives. Thus Nietzsche says (WM, 713, from 1888),

> *Value* is the highest quantum of power a man is able to incorporate—a man: *not* mankind! Mankind is much more a means than an end. It is a question of the type: mankind is merely the experimental material, a monstrous excess of failures, a field of ruins.

Value is always a quantum of power, posited and measured by the will to power.

Will to power and value positing are *the same*, insofar as the will to power looks toward the viewpoints of preservation and enhancement. Thus valuation cannot be referred back to the will to power as something different from it. The clarification of the essence of value and of valuation only yields a sketch of the will to power. The question of the origin of valuative thought and the essence of value is in no way answered when we demonstrate the inner coherence of valuation and the will to power. It is relegated to the question of the essential origin of will to power. Why is the latter something that inherently posits values? Why does the thought of will to power become dominant *along with* valuative thought in metaphysics? How and why does metaphysics become a metaphysics of the will to power?

11. Subjectivity in Nietzsche's Interpretation of History

In order to survey the scope of this question, we must consider what the dominance of valuative thought in metaphysics signifies. First of all, it leads to the fact that Nietzsche conceives the task of future metaphysics to be the revaluation of all values. At the same time, with no further explanation or rationale, the dominance of valuative thought presupposes as self-evident the fact that all prior metaphysics—that is, all metaphysics that historically preceded the metaphysics of the will to power—has been, even if only tacitly, metaphysics of the will to power. Nietzsche conceives the whole of Western philosophy as a thinking in values and a reckoning with values, as value positing. Being, the beingness of beings, is interpreted as will to power. In a covert yet utterly comprehensible way, the history of metaphysics appears in the light of valuative thought in all of Nietzsche's writings and notes.

We are inclined simply to disregard this fact, or to designate his interpretation of the history of metaphysics as that historiological view that was most available to Nietzsche. Then we would have before us merely one historiological view among others. Thus, in the course of the nineteenth and twentieth centuries, the scholarly discipline of history represented the history of philosophy sometimes within the horizon of Kant's or Hegel's philosophy, sometimes within the philosophy of the Middle Ages. But of course they still *more* frequently represented it within a horizon that, by means of a mixture of radically different philosophical teachings, pretended to a catholicity and universal validity by virtue of which all puzzles vanished from the history of thinking.

But the fact that Nietzsche explains the history of metaphysics from the horizon of will to power arises from his metaphysical thought and is not simply a subsequent historiological insertion of his own "views" into the teachings of earlier thinkers. Rather, the metaphysics of will to power, as a *revaluating* stance toward previous metaphysics, first determines the latter in the sense of valuation and valuative thought. Every confrontation is conducted on the basis of a predetermined interpretation that is banished from all discussion. The metaphysics of will to power does not exhaust itself in the fact that new values are posited over against former ones. It lets everything that has been thought and said in prior metaphysics concerning the totality of being as such appear in the light of valuative thought. For the very essence of history is defined in a new way through the metaphysics of will to power, something that we learned from Nietzsche's doctrine of the eternal recurrence of the same and its innermost relationship with the will to power. Any form of academic history is always only the consequence of a previously posited definition of the essence of history as such.

Hence, Nietzsche speaks of unity, totality, and truth as "highest values"—as if that were the most self-evident thing in the world. That these should be "values" is not simply Nietzsche's belated interpretation. It is the first decisive step of the "revaluation" itself. Properly thought, the revaluation carried out by Nietzsche does not consist in the fact that he posits new values in the place of the highest values hitherto, but that he conceives of "Being," "purpose," and "truth" *as values* and *only* as values. Nietzsche's "revaluation" is at bottom the rethinking of all determinations of the being on the basis of values. In note 12, "purpose," "unity," "totality," "truth," and "Being" are also called "categories of reason." At all events, that is what they *are* for Kant and Fichte, Schelling and Hegel. Even for Aristotle, and for him first of all, the determinations of the being as such are categories, although not "categories of reason"—granted that "reason" here, as with Kant and with German Idealism, is to be understood as the essence of *subjectivity*. Thus, when Nietzsche treats of the determinations of the being, which he conceives as "cosmological values," then what is speaking in this conception is the modern metaphysical interpretation of the definition of the Being of beings as categories of reason. The modern interpretation, however, is transformed by Nietzsche once again, so that now the categories of reason appear as the uppermost values. This interpretation of the definition of the Being of beings, stemming from the most recent times and from recent metaphysics, is traced back to Greek philosophy, because the whole history of Western metaphysics appears as the history of valuations. The earlier fundamental metaphysical positions are not expressed in their own proper truth. They speak the language of a philosophy of will to power understood as valuation.

Moreover, if we consider the demonstration of the essential relatedness between valuation and will to power, then it becomes clear that Nietzsche's interpretation of all metaphysics in terms of valuative thought is rooted in the basic definition of being as a whole as will to power. The latter expression is the key word of *Nietzsche's* metaphysics. Neither Hegel nor Kant, neither Leibniz nor Descartes, neither Medieval nor Hellenistic thought, neither Aristotle nor Plato, neither Parmenides nor Heraclitus knew of will to power as the fundamental character of beings. If, then, Nietzsche sees metaphysics as such and its entire history within the horizon of valuation, that history thereby shifts into a one-sided perspective, and the historiological observation guided by it becomes untrue.

But is there anything at all like an observation of history that is not one-sided but omni-sided? Must not every particular period always examine and interpret the past in terms of *its own* horizon? Won't its historical knowledge be more "alive" the more decisively the given horizon of that particular period is taken as a guide? Did not Nietzsche himself in one of his early writings, the second essay of the *Untimely Meditations,* entitled "On the Use and Disadvantage of History for Life,"* demand and argue with great forcefulness and in detail that history must serve "life," and that it can only do so if it first of all

---

* There are some indications that during the winter semester of 1938–39 Heidegger conducted an informal seminar or "exercise" on the basis of this text. (See the notes on pp. ix–x and 235–36 of the present volume.) In any case, Heidegger was thoroughly familiar with this text even before he wrote *Being and Time,* published in 1927. (See Volume I, p. 247, n. 25.)

frees itself from the illusion of a supposed historiological "objectivity in itself"? If so, then our comment to the effect that on the basis of the questions he poses Nietzsche interprets the history of metaphysics as a history of valuation can scarcely function as an objection or a caution, because it merely confirms the genuineness of his historical thinking. It could even be that by means of Nietzsche's interpretation of metaphysics in terms of valuative thought, prior metaphysics is "comprehended better" than it has been able to comprehend itself, in that his interpretation first lends metaphysics the words to say what it has always wanted to say but could not. If that were how matters stood, then Nietzsche's conception of categories and categories of reason as the highest values and as "values" generally would not be a distortion of historical reality, but would be the release of earlier metaphysical values to their properly creative import, or indeed an enrichment of such import. Finally, if the basis for Nietzsche's conception of all metaphysics, the interpretation of the whole of beings as will to power, moved in the direction of prior metaphysical thinking and brought the fundamental thoughts of metaphysics to completion, then Nietzsche's "image of history" would be justified in every respect and proven to be the only possible and necessary one. In that case, there would be no escaping the opinion that the history of Western thought is running its course as a devaluation of the highest values and, in keeping with the nullification of values and decline of goals, is and must be "nihilism."

One result of such reflections is that the observation that Nietzsche reads his own basic metaphysical position—will to power as the fundamental character of being, valuation, and the origin of valuation within the will to power—back into the prior history of metaphysics may not be used as facile grounds for accusing him of distorting the image of history, or, indeed, for rejecting the legitimacy of valuative thought. Even if we must admit that Nietzsche's interpretation of metaphysics does not coincide with what earlier metaphysics taught, this admission requires substantiation that goes beyond a purely historiological demonstration of the difference between Nietzsche's metaphysics and earlier metaphysics.

It is necessary to show that valuative thought was and had to be alien to earlier metaphysics because such metaphysics could not yet conceive of the being as will to power. If we are to demonstrate this, then we must of course encounter the deeper source of valuative thought, because that is how we remove the illusion that thinking has always already taken place in metaphysics through valuations. If it should be shown to what extent the interpretation of the being as will to power first becomes *possible* on the basis of the fundamental positions of modern metaphysics, then as far as the question of the origin of valuative thought is concerned we would have achieved the important insight that Nietzsche has not and cannot have given an answer to the question of origins.

The reference to note 12 (B) where Nietzsche discusses the origin of our belief in the highest values hitherto, does not advance us any farther. For Nietzsche's account presupposes that valuations stem from the will to power. For Nietzsche, will to power is the ultimate *factum* to which we come. What seems certain to Nietzsche is questionable to us. In a similar way, Nietzsche's derivation of valuative thought is also questionable to us.

In his own way, Nietzsche merely shows that according to their essence values are conditions of the will to power, which the latter posits for itself for its own preservation and enhancement; that is, for the fulfillment of the essence of power. Valuation is included in will to power. But the will to power itself—where does it originate, this projection of beings as a whole that depicts them as will to power? *With this question, we are for the first time thinking about the roots of the origin of valuation within metaphysics.*

If however we now attempt to demonstrate that metaphysics before Nietzsche did *not* interpret the being as will to power and that as a result valuative thought was alien to it, then our plan will be subject to the same objection that was leveled against Nietzsche's interpretation of history. We too must observe and interpret past thought within the horizon of a particular thinking: that is to say, our own. No more than Nietzsche or Hegel can we step out of our history and "times" and, from an absolute standpoint, without any definite and therefore necessarily one-sided point of view, observe what-has-been in itself. The same limitation holds for us as it did for Nietzsche and Hegel, with one additional factor; namely, that perhaps the compass of our thinking does not even have the essentiality—and certainly not the greatness —of the questions posed by these thinkers, so that our interpretation of history even at its best falls short of the heights they attained.

With this thought we are approaching the circle of genuine decisions. The question about the truth of the "image of history" goes farther than the question of historiological correctness and accuracy in employing and interpreting sources. It touches on the question of the truth of our historical situation and the relationship to history prescribed by it. If European nihilism is not simply *one* historical movement among others, if it is *the* fundamental impulse of our history, then the interpretation of nihilism and our stance with respect to it depend on how and whence the historicity of human Dasein is determined for us.

A meditation on that theme can go in several directions. We will choose one suggested by the task of the lecture course. We will follow the path of a historical meditation before we develop a "philosophy of history"; in this way, perhaps, such a philosophy will automatically become superfluous. The path we are constrained to follow, no matter how right or wrong it is on particular points, tends to demonstrate that *prior to* Nietzsche valuative thought was and had to be alien to metaphysics, that nonetheless the emergence of valuative thought was prepared *by metaphysics* in those ages prior to him. But the extent to which we are simply losing ourselves in the distant past by taking this path, or are rather in fact preparing ourselves for the future, are questions we do not need to reckon with either before or after we are on the path, as long as we actually do follow the path. Of course, this inevitably and repeatedly puts in our way an obstacle that arises from the objections we have already cited, objections that have today become clichés: that every observation of history is determined by and related to the present, thus is "relative," thus is never "objective," thus is always "subjective"; that one must resign himself to such subjectivity, and would be better off if he made a virtue out of this lack of "reality," transforming acquiescence in subjectivity into the superiority of one who forces everything past into the service of his own present.

But in order to make the proper contrast between the history of metaphysics as it must first be experienced and Nietzsche's conception of metaphysics, we must on the basis of what has already been said first place his interpretation of the history of metaphysics before us in a comprehensible form. Until now, we have learned only that for Nietzsche valuations have their ground and their necessity in the will to power. Thus in Nietzsche's opinion a definite will to power must also have been definitive for the first positing of the highest values hitherto; that is, for the beginning of metaphysics. The first positing of the highest values has its particularity in the fact that according to Nietzsche the values "purpose," "unity," "truth," have been falsely "projected" into the "essence of things." How did the "projection" come to be? In the sense of Nietzsche's interpretation of history, the question asks, What configuration of the will to power was at work here?

12. Nietzsche's "Moral" Interpretation of Metaphysics

If "truth"—that is, the true and the real—is transposed upward and beyond into a world in itself, then the being proper appears as that to which all human life must be subordinated. The true is what is inherently desired, what ought to be. Human life is therefore worth something, is determined by the correct virtues, only when these virtues exclusively urge and enable us to realize what is commanded and desired—to comply with, and so be subjected to, "ideals."

The man who humbles himself before ideals and strives assiduously to fulfill them is the virtuous, the worthwhile—in a word, the "good man." Understood in Nietzsche's sense, this means the man who wills himself as the "good man" erects transcendent ideals above himself, ideals that offer him something to which he can submit himself, so that in the fulfillment of these ideals he will secure himself an aim for his life.

The will that wills the "good man" is a will to submission beneath ideals that exist in themselves and over which man may no longer have any power. The will that wills the "good man" and his ideals is a will to the power of these ideals and is therefore a will to the impotence of man. The will that wills the good man is of course also will to power, but in the form of the impotence of man's power. The highest values hitherto have this impotence of man's power to thank for their projection into the transcendent and their ascent to a world "in itself" as the only true world. The will that wills the "good man" and in that sense wills "the good" is the "moral" will.

By "morality," Nietzsche usually understands a system of evalua-

"Moral" Interpretation of Metaphysics 77

tions in which a transcendent world is posited as an idealized standard of measure. Nietzsche consistently understands morality "metaphysically"; that is, with a view to the fact that in morality something is decided about the whole of beings. In Platonism, this occurs through the division of beings into two worlds—the transcendent world of ideals, of what ought to be, the true in itself—and the sensible world of unending toil and self-submission to what is valid in itself, which, as absolute, conditions everything. Therefore, Nietzsche can say (WM, 400),

> Thus in the *history of morality* a *will to power* expresses itself, through which the slaves and the oppressed, then the misfits and those who suffer from themselves, and then the mediocre attempt to make those value judgments prevail that are favorable to *them*.

Accordingly, he says (WM, 356), "Modest, industrious, benevolent, temperate: is that how you would have man? the *good man?* But to me that seems simply the ideal slave, the slave of the future." And, further (WM, 358),

> The *ideal slave* (the "good man"). —Whoever cannot posit *himself* as a goal, nor posit any goals for himself at all, bestows honor upon *selflessness*—instinctively. Everything persuades him to this: his wits, his experience, his vanity. And faith too is a form of selflessness.

Instead of selflessness, we could also say a refusal to posit oneself as the one in command and that means impotence to power, "turning one's back on the will to existence" (WM, 11). But impotence to power is merely a "special instance" of the will to power, and that implies that "the highest values hitherto are a special instance of the will to power" (XVI, 428). The positing of these values and their transposition into a transcendent world in itself, to which man is supposed to submit, arises from a "dwarfing of man" (WM, 898). Every metaphysics of the sort that posits a transcendent world as true *above* a sensible world as a world of appearances springs from morality. Hence the statement "It is no more than a moral prejudice that truth is worth more than semblance" (*Beyond Good and Evil*, section 34; VII, 55). In the same book, Nietzsche defines the essence of morality in this fashion: "Morality understood as the doctrine of the relations of dominance under which the phenomenon 'life' comes to be" (section 19; VII, 31). And in *The Will to Power,* note 256: "I understand by 'morality' a system of evaluations that touches on the conditions of a creature's life."

Here Nietzsche understands morality "metaphysically" too, of course, in relation to being as a whole and the possibility of life in general, and not "ethically" with regard to the "conduct of life." But he is no longer thinking about *that* "morality" that conditions Platonism. There is more than one kind of "morality," in Nietzsche's view, and these kinds vary, even in their metaphysical significance. On the one hand, morality in its broadest formal sense means *every* system of evaluations and relationships of dominance; morality here is conceived so broadly that even the new valuations might be called *moral,* simply because they posit conditions of life. On the other hand, and as a rule, Nietzsche means by morality the system of *those* evaluations that are contained in the positing of the absolutely highest values in themselves —in the sense of Platonism and Christianity. Morality is the morality of the "good man," who lives by and within the opposition to "evil," and not "beyond good and evil." To the extent that Nietzsche's metaphysics stands "beyond good and evil," and first fashions that standpoint and occupies it as a fundamental position, he can describe himself as an "immoralist."

This sobriquet in no way means that thinking and pondering are immoral in the sense that they take a stance *against* "good" and *for* "evil." "Without" morality means beyond good and evil. This in turn does not mean outside all law and order, but rather within the necessity of a *new* positing of a different order against chaos.

The morality of the "good man" is the origin of the highest values hitherto. The good man posits these values as unconditioned. In that form, they are the conditions of his "life," which, as impotent in power, demands for itself the possibility of being able to look up to a transcendent world. On this basis we now comprehend also what Nietzsche means in the final section of note 12 by the *"hyperbolic naiveté"* of man.

From a metaphysical point of view, the "good man" of "morality" is the sort of man who suspects nothing of the origin of the values to which he submits himself as to absolute ideals. This *not suspecting* the origin of value therefore prevents a person from any *explicit* reflection on the provenance of values, about the fact that they are conditions of will to power, posited by the will to power itself. "Naiveté" is equivalent to "psychological innocence." According to what was said earlier, this means being untouched by any reckoning of beings and thus of life and its conditions in the will to power. Because the provenance of these values in the power-based evaluation of man remains hidden to the psychologically innocent ("naive") person, the *naive* one takes the values (purpose, unity, totality, truth) as if they had descended to him from elsewhere, from heaven, and stood over against him as something to which he has only to bow. Naiveté as ignorance of the origin of value in human will to power is thus in itself "hyperbolic" (from *hyperballein*). Without knowing it, the "good man" casts values upward beyond himself to something that is "in itself." What is conditioned solely by man himself he takes instead for an absolute that taxes him with demands. Therefore, Nietzsche concludes his assessment of the origin of belief in the highest values and categories of reason, concludes the whole of note 12, with the sentence "It is always and everywhere the *hyperbolic naiveté* of man, positing himself as the meaning and standard of value for things."

In spite of the present discussion of the expression "hyperbolic naiveté," the danger still persists that we might totally misunderstand the important concluding sentence of note 12. It contains the all-too-compressed and therefore easily misinterpreted synopsis of an important thought. By appealing to this statement of Nietzsche's, one could raise the objection that according to its literal meaning Nietzsche is saying the opposite of what *we* have explained as the *essence* of hyperbolic naiveté. If naiveté consists in ignorance of the origin of values in the proper power-based valuation of man, how can it still be "hyperbolic naiveté" to "posit oneself as the meaning and standard of value for things"? The latter is anything but naiveté. It is the supreme consciousness of self-reliant man, explicit will to power, and certainly not in any way impotence to power. If we were forced to understand the statement in this way, then Nietzsche would be saying that "hyperbolic naiveté" consists in being thoroughly *not* naive. We should not attribute such a vacuity to Nietzsche. What, then, does the sentence say? According to Nietzsche's definition of the essence of values, the values posited in ignorance concerning the origin of value must also arise from human positing, which is to say, in the manner in which man posits himself as the meaning and measure of value. Naiveté does not consist in the fact that man posits values and functions as their meaning and as the measure of value. Man remains naive to the extent that he posits values as an "essence of things" that devolves upon him, without knowing that it is *he* who posits them and that the positing is a will to power.

Man remains mired in naiveté as long as he does not really act on the knowledge that he alone is the one who posits values, that only through him can values ever be the conditioned conditions of the preservation, securing, and enhancement of his life. A superficial reading of the statement seduces one to the opinion that Nietzsche—in opposition to the process of naive valuation, which often imposes human values on things and so humanizes all beings—is demanding an experience and definition of beings in which every anthropomorphism would be avoided. But precisely that interpretation of the statement would be erroneous; because the fault in naiveté is not the humanization of things, but the fact that the humanization is not *consciously* carried out. Naiveté is in itself a deficiency in will to power, because it lacks knowledge of the fact that the positing of the world according to the image of man and through man is the only true mode of any interpretation of the world, and therefore something toward which metaphysics must finally, resolutely, and without reservation set its course. The highest values hitherto were able to attain to their rank and validity because man posited himself as the meaning and measure of value for things, but did so unconsciously, believing instead that what had been posited by him was a gift given by the things, a gift that things offered him of their own accord. Of course, the will to power governs in naive valuation, as it does in every valuation. But here the will to power is still impotence to power. Here power does not yet empower as explicitly known, and in control of itself.

That in the positing of the highest values human positings are imposed on things is for Nietzsche something quite correct. The humanization of beings, however, is still innocent and therefore not unconditioned. Because the proper, power-based origin of the highest values hitherto *at first* remains hidden, although with the awakening and expansion of the self-consciousness of man it cannot remain permanently hidden, belief in it must weaken with the growing insight into the origin of values. But insight into the origin of values, of human valuation, and of the humanization of things cannot stop short with the realization that after the unveiling of the origin of value, and after the decline of values, the world seems valueless. In that case, we would be lacking every kind of "value," and therefore the conditions of life, so that life could not *be*. But, in view of the apparent valuelessness of the world, that which has to happen, that in which the revaluation of prior values must consist, is already decided and prescribed by the insight into the origin of values. Nietzsche summarized this new task in a note, stemming from the year 1888, which exhibits the very opposite of hyperbolic naiveté:

> All the beauty and sublimity we have bestowed upon real and imaginary things I will reclaim as the property and product of man: as his fairest apology. Man as poet, as thinker, as God, as love, as power: O, with what regal liberality he has lavished gifts upon things, only to *impoverish* himself and make *himself* feel wretched! His most unselfish act hitherto was to admire and worship and to know how to conceal from himself that it was *he* who created all that he admired. (WM, Introduction to Book II, Part One; XV, 241)

What the note is saying is clear enough. Man should no longer be borrower or lender, nor should he submit himself to what is dispensed by him alone as if it were something foreign to him, as if it were something that man in his misery needed. Instead, man ought to claim everything for himself as his own, something he can do only if first of all he no longer regards himself as a wretch and slave before beings as a whole, but establishes and prepares himself for absolute dominance. But this means that he himself is unconditioned will to power, that he regards himself as the master of such domination, and so consciously decides in favor of every exhibition of power; that is, decides for the continuous enhancement of power. Will to power is the *"principle of a new valuation."* Will to power is not simply the way in which and the means by which valuation takes place; will to power, as the essence of power, is the one basic value according to which anything that is supposed to have value, or that can make no claim to value, is appraised. "All events, all motion, all becoming, as a determination of degrees and relations of force, as a *struggle*" (WM, 552; spring–fall, 1887). What loses the struggle is—because it has lost—untrue and in the wrong. What emerges victorious is—because it has won—true and in the right.

What is being contested, if we want to think of it as a specific substantive goal, is always of less significance. All the aims and slogans of battle are merely the means for waging war. What is being contested is decided in advance: power itself, which requires no aims. It is aim-less, just as the whole of beings is value-less. Such aim-lessness pertains to the metaphysical essence of power. If one can speak of aim here at all, then the "aim" is the aimlessness of man's absolute dominance over the earth. The man of such dominance is the Over-man. It is quite usual to remonstrate with Nietzsche that his image of the Overman is indeterminate, that the character of this man is incomprehensible. One arrives at such judgments only if one has failed to grasp that the essence of the Over-man consists in stepping out "over" the man of the past. The latter needs and seeks ideals and idealizations "above" himself. Overman, on the contrary, no longer needs the "above" and "beyond," because he alone wills man himself, and not just in some particular aspect, but as the master of absolute administration of power with the fully developed power resources of the earth. It is inherent in the essence of this man that any particular substantive aim, any determination of such kind, is always a nonessential and purely incidental means. The absolute determination of Nietzsche's thought about the Overman lies precisely in the fact that he recognizes the essential indeterminateness of absolute power, although he does not express it in this fashion. Absolute power is pure overpowering as such, absolute supersedence, superiority, and command—the singular, the most high.

The sole reason for the inadequate portrayals of the Nietzschean doctrine of the Overman lies in the fact that until now it has not been

"Moral" Interpretation of Metaphysics 83

possible to take the will to power seriously as a metaphysics, to comprehend *metaphysically* the doctrines of nihilism, Overman, and above all the *eternal recurrence of the same* as essentially *necessary* constituents; that is, to think them from within the history and the essence of Western metaphysics.

Nietzsche's note (XV, 241) belongs among the most lucid and in its way most beautiful of his notes. Here he speaks from the noonday brightness of a magnificent attunement by which modern man will be determined as the absolute center and sole measure of beings as a whole. Of course, the note is located in an impossible place in the book of posthumous writings we are using as a text (*The Will to Power*), and, furthermore, is omitted from the consecutive enumeration of aphorisms, and is therefore difficult to find. It stands as the preface to chapter one ("Critique of Religion") of Book II (*Critique of the Highest Values Hitherto*). The insertion of the note in this location is perhaps the clearest evidence for the altogether dubious nature of the book *The Will to Power*. The note we are referring to traverses Nietzsche's basic metaphysical position with simple, confident steps, and therefore ought to have been placed at the front of the entire work, *if* it is appropriate to use it as a foreword at all.

Exactly why we have cited the note will become clear as soon as we give a clearer account of our path of inquiry. In contrast to what *Nietzsche* has revealed as the history of metaphysics, it is necessary to take a *more original look* into the history of metaphysics. The first purpose of such a plan ought to be to make Nietzsche's description and conception of metaphysics clearer. It is a "moral" conception. "Morality" here means a system of evaluations. Every interpretation of the world, be it naive or calculated, is a positing of values and thus a forming and shaping of the world according to the image of man. In particular, that valuation which acts on the basis of insight into the origin of human value and so completes nihilism must explicitly understand and will man as the lawgiver. It must seek the true and the real in the *absolute humanization* of all being.

Metaphysics is anthropomorphism—the formation and apprehension of the world according to man's image. Therefore, in metaphysics as Nietzsche interprets it and above all demands it as future philosophy, *the relationship of man to being as a whole* is decisive. Thus we surmount valuative thought toward a relation that metaphysics as will to power almost forces on us; such metaphysics, to which the doctrine of the Overman belongs, thrusts man as no metaphysics before it into the role of the absolute and unique measure of all things.

13. Metaphysics and Anthropomorphism

Nietzsche's first sustained discussion of his doctrine of will to power in the book *Beyond Good and Evil* (1886) already shows the standard-giving role of the human experience of self and the preeminence of man's self-givenness in every interpretation of the world:

> Granted that nothing else is "given" as real except our world of desires and passions, that we could not descend or ascend to any other "reality" besides the reality of our drives—for thinking is merely a way these drives behave toward one another—: is it not permitted to make the experiment and to ask the question whether this "given" does not *suffice* to understand—on the basis of this kind of thing—the so-called mechanistic (or "material") world? (*Beyond Good and Evil,* section 36)

Nietzsche makes this attempt in his metaphysics of the will to power. When he thinks the material, lifeless world on the basis of man and according to human drives, then he is really giving a "human" interpretation of the living and historical world. We begin to suspect how decisively *valuative thinking,* as the reckoning of all beings according to the basic value of will to power, already has at its essential foundation *this* fact, that in general the being as such is interpreted *after the fashion of* human Being, and not only that the interpretation is fulfilled "through" man.

Thus we shall now temporarily set valuative thinking aside in order to reflect on the relationship of man to beings as such and as a whole, to reflect on the manner and the form *in which* the relationship is defined in the history of metaphysics. Hence we come to an area of questioning that is in fact suggested to us by Nietzsche's own metaphysics and his elucidation of metaphysics but that at the same time leads us into more primordial regions. The latter were known also to prior metaphysics. Thus it sounds almost like a cliché if, for example, we mention that the metaphysics of the modern age is characterized by the special role which the human "subject" and the appeal to the subjectivity of man play in it.

At the beginning of modern philosophy stands Descartes' statement: *Ego cogito, ergo sum,* "I think, therefore I am." All consciousness of things and of beings as a whole is referred back to the self-consciousness of the human subject as the unshakable ground of all certainty. The reality of the real is defined in later times as objectivity, as something that is conceived *by* and *for* the subject as what is thrown and stands over against it. The reality of the real is representedness *through* and *for* the representing subject. Nietzsche's doctrine, which makes everything that is, and as it is, into the "property and product of man," merely carries out the final development of Descartes' doctrine, according to which truth is grounded on the self-certainty of the human subject. If we recall here that in Greek philosophy before Plato another thinker, namely Protagoras, was teaching that man was the measure of all things, it appears as if all metaphysics—not just modern metaphysics—is in fact built on the standard-giving role of man within beings as a whole.

Thus today *one* thought is common to everyone, to wit, an "anthropological" thought, which demands that the world be interpreted in accordance with the image of man and that metaphysics be replaced by "anthropology." In such a demand, a definite decision has already been rendered concerning the relationship of man to beings as such.

What is the position of metaphysics and its history with regard to the relationship? If metaphysics is the truth concerning beings as a whole, certainly man too belongs within them. It will even be admitted that man assumes a special role in metaphysics inasmuch as he seeks, develops, grounds, defends, and passes on metaphysical knowledge—and also distorts it. But that still does not give us the right to consider him the measure of all things as well, to characterize him as the center of all beings, and establish him as master of all beings. It might be thought that the saying of the Greek thinker Protagoras concerning man as the measure of all things, Descartes' doctrine of man as the "subject" of all objectivity, and Nietzsche's thought concerning man as the "producer and possessor" of all beings are perhaps merely exaggerations and extreme examples of particular metaphysical standpoints, and not the temperate and well-balanced thoughts of an authentic knowing. Thus these exceptional cases ought not to be made the rule according to which the essence of metaphysics and its history are defined.

Such an opinion might also aver that the three doctrines that stem from the age of Greek culture, from the beginning of the modern period, and from the present age, are subtle indications that in totally different periods of time and in differing historical situations the doctrine reappears ever more intensely, the doctrine according to which every being is what it is solely on the basis of a humanization by man. Such an opinion might finally pose the question, "Why shouldn't metaphysics affirm once and for all, without reservation, man's unconditional role of dominance, make him into the definitive principle of every interpretation of the world, and put an end to all relapses into naive views of the world?" If matters stand this way, if this expresses the sense of all metaphysics, then Nietzsche's "anthropomorphism" is merely asseverating as undisguised truth what in earlier times was being thought repeatedly, throughout the history of metaphysics, and what was demanded as the principle of all thinking.

With respect to this opinion, and with a view to getting a more unobstructed view of the essence of metaphysics and its history, we would do well first of all to think through the basic features of the doctrines of Protagoras and Descartes. In doing so we must delineate that area of inquiry which in a more original way brings the essence of metaphysics as the truth concerning beings as a whole closer to us and lets us see in what sense the question "What is the being as such and as a whole?" is the guiding question of all metaphysics. The very title of Descartes' major work indicates what it is about: *Meditationes de prima philosophia* (1641), or *Meditations on First Philosophy*. The expression "first philosophy" derives from Aristotle and describes what primarily and properly constitutes the function of what has been given the name *philosophy*. *Prōtē philosophia* is concerned with the highest-ranking and all-pervasive question of what a being is insofar as it is a being: thus, for example, an eagle insofar as it is a bird; that is, a living creature; that is, something that comes to presence of itself. What distinguishes the being as a being?

In the meantime, of course, the question of what the being is appears to have been conclusively answered by Christianity, and the question itself is set aside, from a position essentially superior to arbitrary human opinion and error. Biblical revelation, which according to its own report rests on divine influence ("inspiration"), teaches that the being was created by a personal creator God and is preserved and guided by Him. Through the truth of revelation, promulgated in church doctrine as absolutely binding, the question of what the being is has become superfluous. The Being of a being consists in its being created by God (*Omne ens est ens creatum*). If human knowledge wishes to know the truth concerning beings, the only reliable path left open to it is to adopt and preserve diligently the doctrine of revelation and its transmission by the doctors of the church. Genuine truth is mediated only by the *doctrina* of *doctores*. Truth has the essential character of "doctrinality." The medieval world and its history are constructed on this *doctrina*. The only appropriate form in which knowledge as *doctrina* can express itself is the *Summa,* the collection of doctrinal writings in which the whole content of traditional doctrine is arranged and various scholarly opinions are examined, accepted, or rejected on the basis of their conformity to church doctrine.

Those who treat of beings as a whole in this manner are "theologians." Their "philosophy" is philosophy in name only, because a "Christian philosophy" is even more contradictory than a square circle. Square and circle are at least compatible in that they are both geometrical figures, while Christian faith and philosophy remain fundamentally different.* Even if one wished to say that truth is taught in both, what is meant by truth is utterly divergent. Medieval theologians' having studied Plato and Aristotle in their own way, that is to say, by reinterpreting them, is the same as Karl Marx's using the metaphysics of Hegel for his own political *Weltanschauung.* Viewed correctly, however, the *doctrina Christiana* does not intend to mediate knowledge about beings, about what the being is; rather, its truth is

---

* In a lecture course presented in 1935, Heidegger had employed a different oxymoron, "wooden iron," but his treatment of the issue there is quite similar: cf. Martin Heidegger, *Einführung in die Metaphysik* (Tübingen: M. Niemeyer, 1953), p. 6; see the English translation, *An Introduction to Metaphysics,* tr. Ralph Manheim (Garden City, N.Y.: Doubleday-Anchor, 1961), p. 6.

throughout the truth of salvation. It is a question of securing the salvation of individual immortal souls. All knowledge is tied to the order of salvation and stands in service to securing and promoting salvation. All history becomes the history of salvation: creation, the fall, redemption, last judgment. This itself determines the manner in which (that is, the method by which) what is alone worth knowing is to be defined and mediated. *Schola* ("schooling") corresponds to *doctrina,* and the teachers of the doctrine of faith and salvation are therefore "scholastics."

What is new about the modern period as opposed to the Christian medieval age consists in the fact that man, independently and by his own effort, contrives to become certain and sure of his human being in the midst of beings as a whole. The essential Christian thought of the certitude of salvation is adopted, but such "salvation" is not eternal, other-worldly bliss, and the way to it is not selflessness. The hale and the wholesome are sought exclusively in the free self-development of all the creative powers of man. Thus the question arises as to *how* we can attain and ground a certitude sought by man himself for his earthly life, concerning his own human being and the world. While in the medieval world it was precisely the path to salvation and the mode of transmitting truth (*doctrina*) that was firmly established, now the *quest* for new paths becomes decisive.

The question of "method"—that is, the question about *"finding the way,"* the question about attaining and grounding a certainty secured by man himself—comes to the fore. "Method" here is not to be understood "methodologically," as a manner of investigation or research, but metaphysically, as the way to a definition of the essence of truth, a definition that can be grounded only through man's efforts.

The question of philosophy can therefore no longer simply be "What is the being?" In the context of man's liberation from the bonds of revelation and church doctrine, the question of first philosophy is "In what way does man, on his own terms and for himself, first arrive at a primary, unshakable truth, and what is that primary truth?" Descartes was the first to ask the question in a clear and decisive way. His answer was *Ego cogito, ergo sum,* "I think, therefore I am." And it is no accident that the title of Descartes' chief philosophical works indicate the priority of "method": *Discours de la méthode, Regulae ad directionem ingenii, Meditationes de prima philosophia* (not simply "Prima philosophia"), *Les Principes de la philosophie* (*Principia philosophiae*).

In Descartes' principle *ego cogito, ergo sum,* which we shall discuss with more precision later on, the precedence of the human ego is expressed generally, and with it a new status for man. Man does not simply accept a doctrine on faith, but neither does he procure knowledge of the world merely by following a random course. Something else comes to the fore: man knows himself absolutely and certainly as that being whose Being is most certain. Man comes to be the self-posited ground and measure for all certitude and truth. If initially we think through Descartes' principle no farther than this, then we are immediately reminded of the saying of the Greek sophist Protagoras, Plato's contemporary. According to that saying, man is the measure of all things. Scholars habitually connect Descartes' principle with Protagoras' saying and see in this saying and in Greek sophistic thought in general the anticipation of the modern metaphysics of Descartes; in both instances, the priority of man is almost palpably expressed.

In its general form, the observation is also correct. Nevertheless, Protagoras' fragment says something very different from the import of Descartes' principle. Only the difference of both affords us a glimpse into the *selfsame* that they utter. That selfsame matter is the footing on the basis of which we first get an adequate grasp of Nietzsche's doctrine of man as lawgiver of the world and come to know the origin of the metaphysics of will to power and the value thinking ensconced in it. [For the following, see also *Holzwege*, pp. 94 ff.]*

---

* The remark in brackets was added in 1961. It refers to the eighth appendix to Heidegger's "Die Zeit des Weltbildes," composed prior to the lecture course on nihilism; see *Holzwege* (Frankfurt am Main: V. Klostermann, 1951), p. 344. Section 14 below is a reworking of that appendix, improving it in various details—e.g., the repetition of the four "moments" that determine a metaphysics—and generally sharpening the focus. For an English translation of the earlier text, see Martin Heidegger, *The Question Concerning Technology and Other Essays,* tr. William Lovitt (New York: Harper & Row, 1977), pp. 143–47.

14. The Statement of Protagoras

Protagoras' saying (according to its transmission by Sextus Empiricus) runs thus: *Pantōn chrēmatōn metron estin anthrōpos, tōn men ontōn hōs esti, tōn de mē ontōn hōs ouk estin* (see Plato, *Theaetetus*, 152). An accepted translation reads, "Man is the measure of all things, of things that are, that they are, and of things that are not, that they are not."

One might suppose that it is Descartes who is speaking here. Indeed, the sentence quite clearly betrays the frequently stressed "subjectivism" of the Greek sophists. In order not to confuse matters by bringing modern thoughts into play when interpreting the saying, let us first of all attempt a translation that will be more in keeping with Greek thought. The "translation," of course, already contains the interpretation.

> Of all "things" [of those "things," namely, which man has about him for use, customarily and even continually—*chrēmata, chrēsthai*], the [respective] man is the measure, of things that are present, that they are *thus* present as they come to presence, but of those things to which coming to presence is denied, that they do not come to presence.

The talk here is of beings and their Being. What is meant is the being that comes to presence of itself in the purview of man. But who is "man" here? What does *anthrōpos* mean here? Plato provides an answer to the question in the passage where he is discussing the saying by having Socrates ask the following question (as a rhetorical one):

> *Oukoun houtō pōs legei, hōs hoia men hekasta emoi phainetai toiauta men estin emoi, hoia de soi, toiauta de au soi; anthrōpos de su te kagō?*
> Does he [Protagoras] not somehow understand it *thus:* that each thing which

shows itself respectively to me [also] is for me of such an aspect, but that what shows itself to you is such as it is for you? But are you not a man even as I?

"A man" here is therefore "respective" (I and you and he and she, respectively); everyone can say "I"; the respective man is the respective "I." Thus it is certified in advance—and almost in so many words—that it is a question of man conceived "*ego*istically," that the being as such is determined according to the standard of man so defined, that therefore the truth concerning beings, both with Protagoras and later with Descartes, is of the same essence, gauged and measured by means of the "ego."

Nonetheless, we would be falling prey to a fatal illusion if we wished to presume a similarity of fundamental metaphysical positions here on the basis of a particular similarity in the words and concepts used. The import of these words has been obscured and flattened into the indeterminateness of quite general "philosophical" concepts precisely for purposes of traditional historical comparison with a stock of doctrinal tenets.

But because our path has led us to ask in a fundamental way the question about the relationship of man to the being as such and as a whole, and about the role of man in the relation, we must also establish proper guidelines for distinguishing between Protagoras' saying and Descartes' principle. The guidelines according to which we must differentiate can only be those that determine the essence of a fundamental metaphysical position. We shall single out four of them. A fundamental metaphysical position may be determined:

1. By the way in which man as man is *himself* and thereby knows himself;
2. By the projection of beings on Being;
3. By circumscribing the essence of the truth of beings; and
4. By the way in which each respective man takes and gives "measure" for the truth of beings.

Why and to what extent the selfhood of man, the concept of Being, the essence of truth, and the manner of standard giving determine in advance a fundamental metaphysical position, sustain metaphysics as such, and make it the articulation of beings themselves, are questions that cannot be asked by and through metaphysics. None of the four essential moments of a fundamental metaphysical position just cited can be conceived apart from the others; each of them characterizes the whole of a basic metaphysical position from a single perspective.

Protagoras' statement says unequivocally that "all" being is related to man as *egō* (I) and that man is the measure for the Being of beings. But what is the nature of the relation of beings to the "I," granted that in our retrospective understanding of the saying we are thinking it *in a Greek way* and are not unwittingly inserting representations of man as "subject" into it? Man perceives what is present within the radius of his perception. What is present is from the outset maintained as such in a realm of accessibility, because it is a realm of unconcealment. The perception of what is present is grounded on its lingering within the realm of unconcealment.

We today, and many generations before us, have long forgotten the realm of the unconcealment of beings, although we continually take it for granted. We actually think that a being becomes accessible when an "I" as subject represents an object. As if the open region within whose openness something is made accessible *as* object *for* a subject, and accessibility itself, which can be penetrated and experienced, did not already have to reign here as well! The Greeks, although their knowledge of it was indeterminate enough, nonetheless knew about the unconcealment in which the being comes to presence and which the being brings in tow, as it were. In spite of everything that lies between the Greeks and us by way of metaphysical interpretations of the being, we might still be able to recollect the realm of unconcealment and experience it as that in which our human being has its sojourn. By paying sufficient attention to unconcealment, we can accomplish such recollection even without being or thinking in the Greek way. By lingering in the realm of the unconcealed, man belongs in a fixed radius of things present to him. His belonging in this radius at the same time assumes a barrier against what is not present. Thus, here is where the self of man is defined as the respective "I"; namely, by its *restriction* to the surrounding unconcealed. Such restricted belonging in the radius of the unconcealed co-constitutes the being-oneself of man. By means of the restriction, man becomes an *ego*, but not through delimitation of *such* a kind that the self-representing ego vaunts itself as the midpoint and measure of all that is representable. For the Greeks, "I" is the name for *that* man who joins *himself* to this restriction and thus is *he* himself by himself.

Experienced in a Greek way, the man of the basic relationship with beings is *metron*, "measure," in that he lets his confinement to the restricted radius (restricted for each respective self) of the unconcealed become the basic trait of his essence. That also implies the recognition of a concealment of beings and the admission of an inability to decide about presence and absence, about the outward aspect of beings pure and simple. Therefore Protagoras says (Diels, *Fragmente der Vorsokratiker*, Protagoras, B4), *Peri men theōn ouk echō eidenai, outh' hōs eisin, outh' hōs ouk eisin outh' hopoioi tines idean;* "To know [in a Greek sense this means to 'face' what is unconcealed] something about the gods I am of course unable, neither that they are, nor that they are not, nor how they are in their outward aspect." *Polla gar ta kōluonta eidenai hē t'adēlotēs kai brachys ōn ho bios tou anthrōpou;* "For many are the things which prevent beings as such from being perceived; both the not-openness [that is, the concealment] of beings and also the brevity of the history of man."

Should we be surprised that Socrates says with respect to this prudent remark of Protagoras' (Plato, *Theaetetus*, 152b): *Eikos mentoi sophon andra mē lērein?* "It is to be presumed that he [Protagoras], as a thoughtful man [in his words involving man as *metron pantōn chrēmatōn*], was not simply talking foolishly." The way Protagoras defines the relationship of man to the being is merely an emphatic restriction of the unconcealment of beings to the respective radius of man's experience of the world. The restriction *presupposes* that the unconcealment of beings reigns. Even more, it presupposes that unconcealment was already experienced as such and was long ago taken up into knowledge as the basic character of beings. That occurred in the fundamental metaphysical positions of those thinkers who stand at the beginning of Western philosophy: Anaximander, Heraclitus, and Parmenides. Sophistic thought, whose leading thinker Protagoras is reckoned to be, is only possible on the basis of and as a variation of *sophia*—that is, of the Greek interpretation of Being as presence, and of the Greek definition of the essence of truth as *alētheia* (unconcealment). Man is in each case the measure of presence and unconcealment through his measuredness and restriction to that most intimate open region, without denying the remotest closure and without presuming to make a decision about presence and absence. There is no trace here of the thought that the being as such has to be oriented toward the self-posited ego as subject, that the subject is the judge of all beings and their Being, and that by virtue of this judgeship the subject may with absolute certitude decide about the objectivity of objects. Here, finally, there is no hint of Descartes' procedure, which attempts to prove the very essence and existence of God as absolutely certain. If we think of the four "moments" that determine the essence of metaphysics, we can now say the following about the saying of Protagoras:

1. The "I" is for Protagoras determined by the always limited belonging to beings in the unconcealed. The being-oneself of man is grounded in the reliability of the unconcealed being and its radius.
2. Being has the essential character of presence.
3. Truth is experienced as unconcealment.
4. "Measure" has the sense of the measuredness of unconcealment.

For Descartes and his fundamental metaphysical position, all these moments have a different meaning. His metaphysical position is not independent of Greek metaphysics, but it is essentially removed from it. Because the dependence and distance have as yet never been clearly distinguished, the illusion could easily creep in that Protagoras is, as it were, the Descartes of Greek metaphysics; in the same vein, one was able to assert that Plato is the Kant of Greek philosophy and Aristotle its Thomas Aquinas.

15. The Dominance of the Subject in the Modern Age

By interpreting Protagoras' saying about man as the measure of all things "subjectively"—that is, as if all things were dependent on man as the "subject"—one is misplacing the Greek import of the saying in a fundamental metaphysical position that conceives of man in an essentially different way from the way the Greeks did. But neither is the modern definition of man as "subject" quite so unequivocal as the current application of the concepts "subject," "subjectivity," "subjective," and "subjectivistic" would like to pretend.

We are asking, How do we arrive at an emphatic positing of the "subject"? Whence does that dominance of the subjective come that guides modern humanity and its understanding of the world? The question is justified because up to the beginning of modern metaphysics with Descartes, and even within Descartes' own metaphysics, *every being*, insofar as it is a being, is conceived as a *sub-iectum*. *Sub-iectum* is the Latin translation and interpretation of the Greek *hypo-keimenon* and means what under-lies and lies-at-the-base-of, what already lies-before of itself. Since Descartes and through Descartes, man, the human "I," has in a preeminent way come to be the "subject" in metaphysics. How does man come to play the role of the one and only *subject* proper? Why is the human subject transposed into the "I," so that subjectivity here becomes coterminous with I-ness? Is subjectivity defined through I-ness, or the reverse, I-ness through subjectivity?

According to the concept of its essence, *subiectum* is in a distinctive sense that which already lies-before and so lies at the basis of something else, whose ground it therefore is. We must at first remove the concept "man"—and therefore the concepts "I" and "I-ness" as well—from the concept of the essence of *subiectum*. Stones, plants, and animals are subjects—something lying-before of itself—no less than man is. We ask, For what is the *subiectum* a lying-at-the-base-of, if man becomes *subiectum* in an emphatic way at the beginning of modern metaphysics?

With that, we once again turn to a question we have already touched on: What ground and basis is sought in modern metaphysics? The traditional guiding question of metaphysics—"What is the being?"—is transformed at the beginning of modern metaphysics into a question about method, about the path along which the absolutely certain and secure is sought by man himself for man himself, the path by which the essence of truth is circumscribed. The question "what is the being?" is transformed into a question about the *fundamentum absolutum inconcussum veritatis,* the absolute, unshakable ground of truth. This transformation *is* the beginning of a new thinking, whereby the old order passes into the new and the ensuing age becomes the modern.

We have gathered from these introductory remarks on the distinction between Protagoras' saying and Descartes' principle that man's claim to a ground of truth found and secured by man himself arises from that "liberation" in which he disengages himself from the constraints of biblical Christian revealed truth and church doctrine. Every authentic liberation, however, is not only a breaking of chains and a casting off of bonds, it is also and above all a new determination of the essence of freedom. To be free now means that, in place of the certitude of salvation, which was the standard for all truth, man posits the kind of certitude by virtue of which and in which he becomes certain of himself as the being that thus founds itself on itself. The nature of such a transformation implies that the transformation often pursues its course within the very "language" and representations of what is left behind by the transformation. On the other hand, an unequivocal characterization of the transformation cannot avoid speaking in the language of what is first attained in the transformation. If we say pointedly that the new freedom consists in the fact that man himself legislates, chooses what is binding, and binds himself to it, then we are speaking Kant's language; and yet we hit upon what is essential for the beginning of the modern age. In its unique historical form, this essence is wrought into a fundamental metaphysical position for which freedom becomes essential in a peculiar way (see Descartes, *Meditationes de prima philosophia,* Med. IV). Mere license and arbitrariness are always only the dark side of freedom. The bright side is the claim of something necessary as what binds and sustains. Of course, these two "sides" do not exhaust the essence of freedom, nor do they touch its core. For us, it remains important to see that the sort of freedom whose obverse is the liberation from faith in revelation does not simply lay claim to something generally necessary, but rather makes its claim in such a way that man in each case independently posits what is necessary and binding. But what is necessary here is co-determined by what man, founding himself on himself, requires; that is to say, by the direction and the level of the way man represents himself and his essence. Viewed metaphysically, the new freedom is the opening up of a manifold of what in the future can and will be consciously posited by man himself as something necessary and binding. The essence of the history of the modern age consists in the full development of these manifold modes of modern freedom. Because such freedom implies man's developing mastery over his own definition of the essence of mankind, and because such being master needs power in an essential and explicit sense, the empowering of the essence of power as fundamental reality can therefore become possible only in and *as* the history of the modern age.

Thus it is not the case that earlier epochs also displayed power and that roughly since Machiavelli power has been given one-sided and excessive preeminence; rather, "power" in its correctly understood modern meaning—that is, as will to power—first becomes metaphysically possible as modern history. What reigned previously was something different in its *essence.* But just as one takes "subjectivism" to be something self-evident and then searches history from the Greeks to the present looking for forms of it, so does one trace the history of freedom, power, and truth. That is how historiological comparison blocks the way into history.

That Christianity continues to exist in the development of modern history; has in the form of Protestantism abetted that development; has asserted itself successfully in the metaphysics of German Idealism and romanticism; was in its corresponding transformations, adaptations, and compromises in every instance reconciled with the spirit of the times, and consistently availed itself of modern accomplishments for ecclesiastical ends—all of that proves more forcefully than anything else how decisively Christianity is bereft of the power it had during the Middle Ages *to shape history*. Its historical significance no longer lies in what it is able to fashion for itself, but in the fact that since the beginning of and throughout the modern age it has continued to be that *against which* the new freedom—whether expressly or not—must be distinguished. Liberation *from* the revealed certitude of the salvation of individual immortal souls is in itself liberation *to* a certitude in which man can by himself be sure of his own definition and task.

The securing of supreme and absolute self-development of all the capacities of mankind for absolute dominion over the entire earth is the secret goad that prods modern man again and again to new resurgences, a goad that forces him into commitments that secure for him the surety of his actions and the certainty of his aims. The consciously posited binding appears in many guises and disguises. The binding can be human reason and its law (Enlightenment), or the real, the factual, which is ordered and arranged by such reason (Positivism). The binding can be a humanity harmoniously joined in all its accomplishments and molded into a beautiful figure (the human ideal of Classicism). The binding can be the development of the power of self-reliant nations, or the "proletariat of all lands," or individual peoples and races. The binding can be the development of humanity in the sense of the progress of universal rationality. The binding can also be "the hidden seeds of each individual age," the development of the "individual," the organization of the masses, or both. Finally, it can be the creation of a mankind that finds the shape of its essence neither in "individuality" nor in the "mass," but in the "type." The type unites in itself in a transformed way the uniqueness that was previously claimed for individuality *and* the similarity and universality that the community demands. But the uniqueness of the "type" consists in an unmistakable prevalence of the same coinage, which nonetheless will not suffer any dreary egalitarianism, but rather requires a distinctive hierarchy. In Nietzsche's thought of the Overman, man is not a particular "type"; rather, he is man for the first time prefigured in the essential shape of the "type." Precursors here are the Prussian soldiery and the Jesuit Order, which are characterized by a peculiar meshing of their essential natures, a meshing in which the inner content of the first historical emergence of each can be almost completely ignored.

Within the history of the modern age, and as the history of modern mankind, man universally and always independently attempts to establish himself as midpoint and measure in a position of dominance; that is, to pursue the securing of such dominance. To that end, it is necessary that he assure himself more and more of his own capacity for and means of dominance, and that he continually place these at the disposal of an absolute serviceability. The history of modern mankind, the inner workings of which only in the twentieth century emerged into the full and open space of something incontrovertible and consciously comprehensible, was *mediately* prepared by Christian man, who was oriented toward the *certitude* of salvation. Thus one can interpret certain phenomena of the modern age as a "secularization" of Christianity. In most decisive respects, such talk of "secularization" is a thoughtless deception, because a world toward which and in which one is made worldly already belongs to "secularization" and "becoming-worldly." The *saeculum,* the "world" through which something is "secularized" in the celebrated "secularization," does not exist in itself or in such a way that it can be realized simply by stepping out of the Christian world.

The new world of the modern age has its own historical ground in the place where every history seeks its essential ground, namely, in metaphysics; that is, in a new determination of the truth of beings as a whole and of the essence of such truth. Descartes' metaphysics is the decisive beginning of the foundation of metaphysics in the modern age. It was his task *to ground the metaphysical ground of man's liberation in the new freedom of self-assured self-legislation.* Descartes anticipated this ground in an authentically philosophical sense. That is to say, he thought it out in its essential requirements—not in the sense of a soothsayer who predicts what later occurs, but in the sense that his thought remains the ground for subsequent thought. Prophesying is not the prerogative of philosophy. But neither is philosophy a know-it-all attitude, limping along behind. Common sense has of course eagerly spread the view that philosophy's task is simply to follow up on an age, bringing its past and present to intellectual formulation on the basis of so-called concepts, or even to a "system." People think that with this specification of philosophy's task they are even paying it special homage.

That definition of philosophy does not hold even for Hegel, whose fundamental metaphysical position apparently embraces this conception of philosophy. Hegel's philosophy, which in one respect was a fulfillment, was so only as an anticipation of the areas in which the history of the nineteenth century moved. Thought in terms of metaphysics, the fact that this century took its stand against Hegel on a level beneath Hegelian metaphysics (that is, the level of positivism) is merely proof that it was thoroughly dependent on him and that this dependence was first transformed by Nietzsche into a new liberation.

16. The Cartesian *Cogito* as *Cogito Me Cogitare*

Descartes anticipated the metaphysical ground of the modern age—which is not to say that all subsequent philosophy is simply Cartesianism. But in what way did the metaphysics of Descartes preground the metaphysical ground of the new freedom in the modern age? What kind of ground must it have been? Of such a kind that man could by himself assure himself at all times of that which ensures the advance of every human intention and representation. On the basis of this ground, man must be certain of himself, that is, certain of the surety of the possibilities of his intentions and representations. The ground could not have been anything other than man himself, because the sense of the new freedom forbade him any bond or commitment that did not arise from his own positings.

Everything that is certain of itself must in addition guarantee as certainly given that being *for* which every representation and intention, and *through* which every action, is supposed to be assured. The ground of the new freedom must be what is secure about such security and certitude which, transparent in themselves, satisfy the essential conditions cited earlier. What is the certainty that fashions the ground of the new freedom and so constitutes it? It is the *ego cogito (ergo) sum*. Descartes asserts that the statement is clear and evident indubitable knowledge; that is to say, the first and highest in rank, by which all "truth" is grounded. Some have concluded from this that such knowledge must be clear to everyone in its proper import. But what is forgotten is that this is possible in Descartes' sense only if one simultaneously understands what is meant by "knowledge" here and if one considers that through this principle the essence of knowledge and of truth is newly defined.

What is "new" in the definition of the essence of truth consists in the fact that truth is now "certitude," the full essence of which becomes clear to us only in connection with Descartes' guiding principle. Because one always overlooks the fact that the guiding principle itself first posits the conditions of its understanding and cannot be interpreted according to just any notions, Descartes' principle falls prey to every possible misinterpretation.

Even Nietzsche's opposition to Descartes is entangled in these misinterpretations, something that has its basis in the fact that Nietzsche ineluctably stands under the law of this principle, and that means under Descartes' metaphysics, in a way that no other modern thinker does. We allow "history" to deceive us about this, because "history" can easily establish that between Descartes and Nietzsche lies a span of two-and-a-half centuries. History can point out that Nietzsche openly advocated different "doctrines," that he even criticized Descartes very sharply.

But we do not believe that Nietzsche teaches a doctrine identical to Descartes'. Rather, we are affirming something far more essential, to wit, that he is thinking the *selfsame* in the historical fulfillment of its essence. What begins metaphysically with Descartes initiates the history of its completion through Nietzsche's metaphysics. Naturally, the inception of the modern age and the beginning of its historical completion differ in the extreme, so that of itself, as well as for a historical account, it must appear—and rightly so—that in the face of the expiration of the modern age the most modern times begin with Nietzsche. This is thoroughly true in a quite profound sense, and merely says that the difference between the fundamental metaphysical positions of Nietzsche and Descartes, when described by historical disciplines, extrinsically, is for historical contemplation (that is, a meditation that thinks with a view to essential decisions), the keenest indication of sameness in what is essential.

The position Nietzsche adopts *against* Descartes has its metaphysical ground in the fact that Nietzsche can set about fulfilling its essence absolutely only on the basis of the fundamental Cartesian position, and so must consider Descartes' position to be conditional and imperfect, if not entirely impossible. Nietzsche's misunderstanding of the Cartesian principle is even necessary, for a number of metaphysical reasons. But we do not wish to begin with Nietzsche's misunderstanding of the Cartesian principle. Prior to that, we will attempt a meditation on a law of Being and its truth that governs our own history and will survive us all. In the following portrayal of Cartesian metaphysics, we must bypass a great deal that a thematic discussion of the fundamental metaphysical position of this thinker would not dare overlook. It is simply a question of making a few basic features visible, to permit us insight into the *metaphysical* origin of *valuative thought*.

Ego cogito (ergo) sum—"I think, therefore I am." In a literal sense, the phrase is correctly translated. The correct translation also seems to furnish a correct understanding of the "principle." "I think"—with this assertion, one fact is established; "therefore I am"—with these words, it follows, from the established fact, that I am. On the basis of this logical deduction, I can now be satisfied and rest assured that my existence is thereby "proven." Of course, no thinker of Descartes' stature would need to exert himself to reach that conclusion. And, indeed, Descartes wants to say something else. Our thought can pursue what he wants to say only if we clarify for ourselves what he understands by *cogito, cogitare*.

We translate *cogitare* with "thinking" and thus persuade ourselves that it is now clear what Descartes means by *cogitare*. As if we immediately knew what "thinking" means.* And as if, with our concept of thinking, culled perhaps from some textbook on "logic," we were already certain of confronting *that which* Descartes wishes to assert in the word *cogitare*. In important passages, Descartes substitutes for *cogitare* the word *percipere* (*per-capio*)—to take possession of a thing,

---

* *"Was 'denken' heisst."*—Heidegger's first lecture course at Freiburg after his reinstatement following World War II had as its title *Was heisst Denken?* See the English translation by Fred D. Wieck and J. Glenn Gray, *What Is Called Thinking?* (New York: Harper & Row, 1968). Note that in the ensuing discussion of Cartesian thought "representation" tries to translate *Vor-stellen*. "Pro-pose" would be more literal, as would "pre-sent." But these would confuse *Vor-stellen* with other German expressions, such as *vorschlagen, ansetzen, vergegenwärtigen,* and so on, so that "representation" seems the best rendering.

to seize something, in the sense of presenting-to-oneself by way of presenting-before-oneself, *representing*. If we understand *cogitare* as representing in the literal sense, then we are already coming closer to the Cartesian concept of *cogitatio* and *perceptio*. Words that end with "-tion" often describe two things that belong together: representation in the sense of "representing," and representation in the sense of "something represented." *Perceptio* also has the same ambiguity: *perceptio* has the senses of *percipere* and *perceptum*, the bringing-before-itself and what-is-brought-before-itself and made "visible" in the widest sense. Thus, instead of *perceptio* Descartes often uses the Latin word *idea*, which as a consequence of its use can mean not only what is represented in a representing but also the representing itself, the act and its execution. Descartes distinguishes three kinds of "ideas":

1. *Ideae adventitiae:* something represented which impinges on us; something perceived in things;

2. *Ideae a me ipso factae:* something represented which we purely and arbitrarily imagine by ourselves (imaginings);

3. *Ideae innatae:* something represented in the essential constitution of human representation which accompanies it as already given.

When Descartes grasps *cogitatio* and *cogitare* as *perceptio* and *percipere*, he wants to emphasize that bringing something to oneself pertains to *cogitare*. *Cogitare* is the presenting *to* oneself of what is representable. In such presenting-to lies something definitive, namely, the necessity of a designation for the fact that the represented is not only generally pregiven but is also presented to us as available. The presented-to, the represented—*cogitatum*— is therefore something for man only when it is established and secured as that over which he can always be master unequivocally, without any hesitation or doubt, in the radius of *his own* power to enjoin. *Cogitare* is not only a general and indeterminate representing, but also something that posits itself under the condition that what is presented-*to* no longer permits any doubt about what it is and how it is.

The *cogitare* is always "thinking" in the sense of a "thinking over," and thus a deliberation that thinks in such a way as to let only the indubitable pass as securely fixed and represented in the proper sense. *Cogitare* is essentially a deliberative representing, a representing that examines and checks: *cogitare* is *dubitare*. If we take this "literally," we might easily fall into error. Thinking is not "doubting" in the sense that deliberative thought is everywhere brought to the fore, that every standpoint becomes suspect and all agreement prohibited. Doubting is rather understood as essentially connected with the indubitable, with the undoubted and its securement. What is always doubted in deliberative thinking is whether what is represented is in every instance securely established within the circle of the reckoning power to enjoin. That every *cogitare* is essentially a *dubitare* says nothing other than this: representing is securement. Thinking, which is *essentially* deliberating, accepts nothing as secured and certain—that is, as true— which is not proven before thinking itself to be the sort of thing that has the character of the doubt*less,* whereupon thinking as deliberative doubting is at the same time "finished," and the account is closed.

In the concept of *cogitatio,* there is a general stress on the fact that representing brings the represented *to* the one representing; that therefore the latter, *as* one who represents, in every case "presents" what is represented, calls it to account; that is, grasps it and appropriates it for itself, seizes and secures it. For what? For further representing, which is willed everywhere as securement and which seeks to establish the being as what is secured. But precisely what is to be *secured,* and for what purpose is it to be brought to certitude?

We will discover this when we inquire more essentially into the Cartesian concept of *cogitatio,* because we have *still not* grasped *one* feature of the essence of *cogitatio,* although we have actually touched on it and identified it. We encounter it when we consider that Descartes says that every *ego cogito* is a *cogito* me *cogitare;* every "I represent something" simultaneously represents a "myself," me, the one representing (for myself, in my representing). Every human representing is—in a manner of speaking, and one that is easily misunderstood —a "self-"representing.

The following objection might be raised: If we "represent" the Freiburg cathedral to ourselves—that is, in this case, make it present for ourselves, because at the moment we do not perceive it in the flesh; or if we represent it as standing immediately before us, in the manner of a perception—then we are representing the cathedral and only the cathedral. That is what is represented. We do not, however, represent ourselves, for otherwise we could never represent the cathedral itself, purely for itself, and let ourselves be released to what representing here sets up over against us, the ob-ject [*Gegen-stand*]. Nor in fact does Descartes, by defining the *cogito* as *cogito me cogitare,* mean that with every representing of an object "I" myself, the one representing, am represented as such into the bargain and so become an object. Otherwise every representing would ultimately have to flit constantly back and forth between our objects, between the representing of the properly represented object and the representing of the one who is doing the representing (*ego*). Is the "I" of the one representing therefore merely indistinctly and incidentally represented? No.

Rather, the representing I is far more *essentially* and necessarily *co*-represented in every "I represent," namely as something toward which, back to which, and *before* which every represented thing is placed. For this, I do not need an explicit turning toward and back to me, the one who is representing. In the immediate intuition of something, in every making-present, in every memory, in every expectation, what is represented in such fashion by representation is represented *to me,* placed before *me,* and in such a way that I myself do not thereby really become an object of a representing but am nonetheless presented "to me" in an objective representing, and in fact only in such representing. Since every representing presents the one who is representing and the represented object *to* the representing man, representing man is "co-represented" in a peculiarly unobtrusive way. But this characteristic of representing—that in it representation itself and the representing "I" are "co"-represented and represented "along with" the object—is easily misunderstood as long as we do not more sharply define the essential point on which everything depends. Because in every representing there is a representing person *to* whom what is represented in representation is presented, the representing person is involved with and in every representing—not subsequently, but in advance, in that he, the one who is placing *before,* brings what is represented before *himself.* Because the representing person has already come on the scene, along with what has been represented within representation, there lies in every representing the *essential* possibility that the representing itself take place within the scope of the one representing. Representation and the one who is representing are *co*-represented in human representing. This is not really to say that the I and its representing are, as it were—outside the representing, as additional objects for it—chanced upon and then subsequently introduced into the ambience of what is represented. In truth, the easily misunderstood talk about the *co*-representedness of the one representing and his representing in every act of representation wishes to express precisely the *essential* cohesion of the one representing with the constitution of representation.

That is primarily what the statement *"Cogito* is *cogito me cogitare"* says. Now—after this explanation—we can also describe matters thus: Human consciousness is essentially self-consciousness. The consciousness of my self does not accompany the consciousness of things, as if it traveled alongside the consciousness of things as its observer. The consciousness of things and objects is essentially and in its ground primarily self-consciousness; only as self-consciousness is consciousness of ob-jects possible. For representation as described, the *self* of man is essential as what lies at the very ground. The self is *sub-iectum.*

Even before Descartes, it was noticed that representation and what is represented in it are related to a representing I. What is decisively novel is the fact that this relation *to* the one who is representing and thereby the latter *as such* assumes a definitive role for what should and does come to pass in representation as the placing alongside of beings.*

Still, we have not yet fully surveyed the scope and import of the definition *"Cogito* is *cogito me cogitare."* All willing and asserting, all "affects," "feelings," and "sensations" are related to something willed, felt, or sensed. What relates them is, in the broadest sense, represented

---

* *"Was sich im Vorstellen als Bei-stellen des Seienden begibt und begeben soll."* The sense of the neologism *Bei-stellen* is not clear, but it may well be bound up with the existential structure of *Sein-bei,* the Being-alongside of beings that is characteristic of Dasein as "falling" in the present. See Martin Heidegger, *Being and Time,* sections 12 and 41. This is not to say that the sense of Being-alongside and that of placing-alongside are to be conflated: the first is an existential structure, the second an aspect of Cartesian thought. Their precise relationship poses a knotty problem.

and presented-to. All the modes of comportment mentioned, not just knowing and thinking, are therefore defined in their essence by presentational representation. All these ways of behaving have their Being in such representing; they are such representing; they are representations —*cogitationes*. Man's modes of acting are experienced as his own in and through *being carried out,* experienced as those in which he comports *himself* in such and such a manner. Now for the first time we are in a position to understand the brief answer that Descartes gives to the question *"Quid sit cogitatio?"* He says (*Principia philosophiae,* I, 9):

> *Cogitationis nomine, intelligo illa omnia, quae nobis consciis in nobis fiunt, quatenus earum in nobis conscientia est. Atque ita non modo intelligere, velle, imaginari, sed etiam sentire, idem est sic quod cogitare.*
>
> By the term *cogitatio,* I understand everything we are conscious of along with ourselves, everything which occurs in us for ourselves insofar as we have an accompanying knowledge of it in us. And thus not only are knowing, willing, and imagining, but also sensing, the same as what we call *cogitare.*

If one heedlessly translates *cogitatio* with "thinking" here, then one is tempted to believe that Descartes interpreted all modes of human behavior as thinking and as forms of thinking. This opinion fits in well with the current view concerning Descartes' philosophy, the view that it was "rationalism"—as if what rationalism is did not first have to be determined from a delineation of the essence of *ratio,* as if the essence of *ratio* did not first of all have to be illuminated by the already clarified essence of *cogitatio.* With respect to the latter, it has now been shown that *cogitare* is representing in the fullest sense, that we must conjoin in thought the following essentials: the relation to what is represented, the self-presentation of what is represented, the arrival on the scene and involvement of the one representing with what is represented, indeed in and through the representing.

We should not balk at the formal complexity with which the essence of the *cogitatio* is outlined here. What looks like formal complexity is an attempt to see the simple, unitary essence of representation. This essence reveals that representation places itself in the open region which it traverses as representing, for which reason one can also say—

although this is misleading: representing is a co-representing of oneself. But above all we must realize that for Descartes the essence of representation has shifted its weight to the presenting-to-itself [*das Sich-zustellen*] of what is represented, whereby the human being who is representing decides in advance and everywhere on his own what can and should be accepted as well placed and permanent.

If we heed the essential fullness of the equally essential relations that are there to be seen in Descartes' *cogitatio* and *cogito*, then the foundational role of representation as such *betrays itself* in our elucidation of the essence of *cogitare*. Here is announced *what* the underlying, the *subiectum*, is—namely, the representing—and *for what* the subject is a *subiectum*—namely, for the essence of truth. The essential role of representation—that is, of *cogitatio*—is explicitly expressed in the principle which for Descartes is the principle of all principles, and the founding principle of metaphysics: *ego cogito, ergo sum*. Of this principle he says (*Principia*, I, 7), "Haec cognitio, ego cogito, ergo sum, est omnium prima et certissima, quae cui libet ordine philosophanti occurat"; "This insight, 'I represent, therefore I am' is [in terms of rank] the first and most certain of all, which rises up to meet everyone who duly [in an essentially fitting way] thinks metaphysically."*

The principle *ego cogito, ergo sum* is primary and most certain not in some vague and general way for just any opining and representing. It is primary and most certain *only* for *that* thinking which thinks in the direction of metaphysics and its primary and proper tasks, that is to say, which asks what the being is and in what the truth of beings is unshakably grounded.

---

* The word *metaphysically* is of course also a gloss, presupposing as it does Heidegger's understanding of *philosophanti* as inherently metaphysical inquiry. Cf. the translation by E. S. Haldane and G. R. T. Ross, *The Philosophical Works of Descartes*, 2 vols. (Cambridge, England: Cambridge University Press, [1911] 1967), I, 221: "And hence this conclusion *I think, therefore I am*, is the first and most certain of all that occurs to one who philosophises in an orderly way."

17. Descartes' *Cogito Sum*

Now that we have commented on the essence of *cogitatio*, we will venture an interpretation of the statement that for Descartes constitutes the principle of metaphysics. Recall what was said about *cogitatio*: *cogitare* is *per-cipere*, *cogitare* is *dubitare*; *cogito* is *cogito me cogitare*.

The greatest obstacle to the correct understanding of the principle is Descartes' formulation of it. Because of that formulation—because of the *ergo* ("therefore")—it appears as though the principle were a syllogism composed of a major premise, a minor premise, and a conclusion. Then the principle, separated into its component parts, must have gone as follows: major premise, *Is qui cogitat, existit* [he who thinks, exists]; minor premise, *Ego cogito* [I think]; conclusion, *ergo existo (sum)* [therefore I exist (I am)]. Quite gratuitously, Descartes even calls the principle a *conclusio*. On the other hand, we find a sufficient number of passages that clearly indicate that the principle is not to be thought of in the sense of a syllogism. In addition, many commentators agree that the principle is not "really" a syllogism. Not much is gained by the "negative" observation, however, for it simply gives rise to an equally untenable contrary supposition that the principle is *not* a syllogism but something that provides a sufficient elucidation for everything.

Of course, this supposition could insinuate itself only insofar as the principle has the character of a highest principle. "First principles" do not require a proof, nor are they amenable to being proven. They are said to be utterly transparent in themselves. Why, then, the argument about the principle? Why is this "supreme certitude" so uncertain and dubious in its import? Does it lie in the fact that Descartes thought with too little clarity and did not set to work carefully enough in constructing his "principle"? Or does the difficulty lie in the commentators? They have in the course of time adduced everything that Descartes himself said and everything his opponents said, and again everything that Descartes said in responding to his opponents, and all of it has been discussed endlessly, and yet we still remain in the dark so far as the principle is concerned.

Presumably the reason for this state of affairs is the very same difficulty that always blocks insight into essential philosophical principles: the fact that we do not think simply and essentially enough, that we are too facile and too hasty with our common presuppositions.

Thus we take even the "principle of contradiction" as a "fundamental principle" ("axiom") that is eternally valid in itself; we do not stop to consider that for the metaphysics of Aristotle this principle has an essentially different import and plays a different role from the role it plays for Leibniz, and has yet again a different kind of truth in Hegel's or in Nietzsche's metaphysics. The principle says something essential not only about "contradiction" but also about the being as such and about the kind of truth in which the being as such is experienced and projected. That is also true of Descartes' *ego cogito . . . sum*. But we dare not therefore conclude that everything here is immediately made crystal clear by the magic wand of "self-evidence." We must try to think the *ego cogito . . . sum* through, according to its own lineaments, on the basis of our foregoing commentary on *cogitatio*. In a literal sense, the principle points to the *sum*, "I am," and thus to the knowledge that I am. But if in general this is supposed to show with certainty that I—that is, "I" as *ego*—exist as the one representing in a representation, then there is no need for a syllogism that, from the certain existence of something known, concludes the existence of something previously unknown and uncertain. For in the human representation of an object, and through the object *as* something standing-over-against and represented, that "against-which" the object stands and "before which" it is presented—that is, the one representing—has already presented itself. It has done so in such a way that man, by virtue of such presenting himself to himself as the one representing, can say "I." The "I" in its "I am," or to be more specific, the one representing, is known *in* and for such representing no less than the represented object. The I—as "I am the one representing"—is *so* certainly presented to the representing that no syllogism, no matter how logical, can ever attain the certainty bound up with this presenting to himself of the one representing.

Hence we see at once why the *ergo* cannot be understood as the joining of two elements of a syllogism. The supposed major premise— *Is qui cogitat, est*—can never be the ground for the *cogito sum*, because that premise is first derived from the *cogito sum*, indeed in such a way that the *cogito sum* is thereby reproduced in its essential import, although in an altered form. The "I am" is not first deduced from the "I represent"; rather, the "I represent," according to its *essence*, is what the "I am"—that is, the one representing—has already presented to me. With good reason, we might now omit the confusing *ergo* from the formulation of the Cartesian principle. But if we do include it, then we must interpret it in a different sense. The *ergo* cannot mean "consequently." The principle is a *conclusio,* but not in the sense of a conclusion of a syllogism composed of major and minor premises and a conclusion. It is *conclusio* as the immediate joining together of what essentially belongs together and is securely fixed in such cohesion. *Ego cogito, ergo: sum;* I represent, "and this implies," "therein is already posited and presented by representing itself": I *as being.* The "therefore" does not express a consequence, but points toward that which the *cogito* not only "is" but also knows itself to be in accordance with its essence as *cogito me cogitare.* The *ergo* means nothing more than "and that of itself already says." We can most pointedly express what the *ergo* is supposed to say if we leave it aside, and furthermore if we remove the emphasis on "I" in the word *ego,* because the first-person pronoun is not essential here. Then the principle says: *cogito sum.*

What does the sentence *cogito sum* say? It almost seems to be an "equation." But here we are running a new risk of taking the formulations of one particular domain of knowledge—the equations of mathematics—and transferring them to a principle whose distinguishing feature is to be incommensurate in every way with everything else. The mathematical interpretation of the principle in the sense of an equation suggests itself because the "mathematical" is a standard of measure for Descartes' conception of knowledge and knowing. But it remains for us to ask here, Does Descartes simply take the already present and practiced form of "mathematical" knowledge as the model for all knowledge, or does he on the contrary newly define—in fact, metaphysically define—the essence of mathematics? The second is the case. Therefore we must try again to define more accurately the import of the principle, and above all to answer in this way the question as to what is posited as the *subiectum* "through" the principle.

Is the principle itself the *subiectum* that underlies everything? *Cogito sum* does not merely say that I think, nor merely that I am, nor that my existence follows from the fact of my thinking. The principle speaks of a connection between *cogito* and *sum*. It says that I am as the one representing, that not only is *my* Being essentially determined through such representing, but that my representing, as definitive *repraesentatio*, decides about the being present of everything that is represented; that is to say, about the presence of what is meant in it; that is, about its Being as a being. The principle says that representation, which is essentially represented to itself, posits Being as representedness and truth as certitude. That to which everything is referred back as to an unshakable ground is *the full essence of representation itself*, insofar as the essence of Being and truth is determined by it, as well as the essence of man, as the one representing, and the nature of the definitive standard as such.

The principle *cogito sum*, to the extent that it contains and expresses the essence of *cogitatio*, posits along with the essence of *cogitatio* the proper *subiectum*, which is itself presented only in the domain of *cogitatio* and through it. Because the *me* is implied in *cogitare*, because the relation to the one representing still belongs essentially to representing, because all representedness of what is represented is gathered back *to* it, therefore the one representing, who can thus call himself "I," is subject in an emphatic sense, is, as it were, the subject in the subject, back to which everything that lies at the very basis of representation refers. That is why Descartes can also construe the principle *cogito sum* in the following way: *sum res cogitans*.

This formulation is of course as easily misunderstood as the other. Literally translated, it says, "I am a thinking thing." In that case, man would be confirmed as an object at hand, with the simple result that the attribute "thinking" is assigned to him as a distinguishing property. But with this conception of the principle we would be forgetting that the *sum* is defined as *ego cogito*. We would be forgetting that *res cogitans*, in keeping with the concept of *cogitatio*, would at the same time mean *res cogitata:* what represents *itself.* We would be forgetting that such self-representing co-constitutes the Being of the *res cogitans.* Again, Descartes himself offers a superficial and inadequate interpretation of *res cogitans*, inasmuch as he speaks the language of the doctrines of medieval scholasticism, dividing being as a whole into *substantia infinita* and *substantia finita*. *Substantia* is the conventional and predominant name for *hypokeimenon, subiectum* in a metaphysical sense. *Substantia infinita* is God, *summum ens, creator*. The realm of *substantia f i n i t a* is *ens creatum*. Descartes divides the latter into *res cogitantes* and *res extensae*. Thus all being is seen from the point of view of *creator* and *creatum*, and the new delineation of man through the *cogito sum* is, as it were, simply sketched into the old framework.

Here we have the most palpable example of earlier metaphysics impeding a new beginning for metaphysical thought. A historiological report on the meaning and nature of Descartes' doctrine is forced to establish such results. A historical meditation on the inquiry proper, however, must strive to think Descartes' principles and concepts in the sense he himself wanted them to have, even if in so doing it should prove necessary to translate his assertions into a different "language." Thus *sum res cogitans* does not mean "I am a thing that is outfitted with the quality of thinking," but, rather, "I am a being whose mode *to be* consists in representing in such a way that the representing co-presents the one who is representing into representedness." The Being of that being which I am myself, and which each man as himself is, has its essence in representedness and in the certitude that adheres to it. But this does not mean that I am a "mere representation," a mere thought, and nothing truly actual; it means that the permanence of my self as *res cogitans* consists in the secure establishment of representation, in the certitude according to which the self is brought before itself. But because the *ego cogito*, the "I represent," is not meant as a particular process in an isolated "I," because the "I" is understood as the self, back to which representation as such is essentially referred and in that way is what it is—because of all this, the *cogito sum* in each case says something essentially more. The Being of the one who represents and who secures himself in the representing is the measure for the Being of what is represented as such. Therefore, every being is necessarily measured according to this measure of Being in the sense of certified and self-certifying representedness.

The certitude of the principle *cogito sum* (*ego ens cogitans*) determines the essence of all knowledge and everything knowable; that is, of *mathesis*; hence, of the mathematical. What can therefore be demonstrated and ascertained as a being is only the sort of thing whose placing-alongside guarantees the kind of surety that is accessible through mathematical knowledge and knowledge grounded on mathematics. The mathematically accessible, what can be securely reckoned in a being that man himself is not, in lifeless nature, is *extension* (the spatial), *extensio*, which includes both space *and* time. Descartes, however, equates *extensio* and *spatium*. In that way, the nonhuman realm of finite beings, "nature," is conceived as *res extensa*. Behind this characterization of the objectivity of nature stands the principle expressed in the *cogito sum*: Being is representedness. As one-sided and in many respects unsatisfactory as the interpretation of "nature" as *res extensa* may be, when it is nonetheless thought through in its metaphysical import and measured according to the breadth of its metaphysical project, then it is the first resolute step through which modern machine technology, and along with it the modern world and modern mankind, become metaphysically possible for the first time.

We today are witnesses to a mysterious law of history which states that one day a people no longer measures up to the metaphysics that arose from its own history; that day arrives precisely when such metaphysics has been transformed into the absolute. What Nietzsche already knew metaphysically now becomes clear: that in its absolute form the modern "machine economy," the machine-based reckoning of all activity and planning, demands a new kind of man who surpasses man as he has been hitherto. It is not enough that one possess tanks, airplanes, and communications apparatus; nor is it enough that one has at one's disposal men who can service such things; it is not even sufficient that man only master technology as if it were something neutral, beyond benefit and harm, creation and destruction, to be used by anybody at all for any ends at all.

What is needed is a form of mankind that is from top to bottom equal to the unique fundamental essence of modern technology and its metaphysical truth; that is to say, that lets itself be entirely dominated by the essence of technology precisely in order to steer and deploy individual technological processes and possibilities.

In the sense of Nietzsche's metaphysics, only the Over-man is appropriate to an absolute "machine economy," and vice versa: he needs it for the institution of absolute dominion over the earth.

Descartes, with his principle of the *cogito sum,* forced open the gates of the domain of such a metaphysically comprehended dominion. The principle that lifeless nature is *res extensa* is simply the essential consequence of the first principle. *Sum res cogitans* is the ground, the underlying, the *subiectum* for the determination of the material world as *res extensa.*

Thus the *principle* of the *cogito sum* is the *subiectum*—not the wording of the principle, or the principle considered as a grammatical construct, or taken in its supposedly neutral "meaningful content" that can be thought in itself, but rather the "principle" considered according to what is expressed as essentially unfolding there, and as what sustains it in its proper essence as a principle. What is that? It is *the full essence of representation.* Representation has in itself come to be the establishment and securement of the essence of the truth of Being. Representation presents itself here in its own essential space and posits such space as the standard of measure for the essence of the Being of beings and for the essence of truth. Because truth now means the assuredness of presentation-to, or *certitude,* and because Being means representedness in the sense of such certitude, man, in accordance with his role in foundational representation, therefore becomes the subject in a distinctive sense. In the realm of the dominion of the subject, *ens* is no longer *ens creatum,* it is *ens certum, indubitatum, vere cogitatum, "cogitatio."* *

Now for the first time we can clearly see in what sense the principle *cogito sum* is a "principle" and an "axiom." Following the more or less

---

*That is, "the being that is certain, indubitable, truly represented—the 'representation.'"

correct intuition that in Descartes' thought the "mathematical" *somehow* plays a special role, we recall in this connection that in mathematics certain highest principles or "axioms" occur. These highest principles are then equated with major premises in logical deductions, insofar as mathematical thinking thinks in a "deductive" manner. From here on one presumes without thinking any further about it that the principle *cogito sum,* which Descartes himself singled out as the "first and most certain," must be a highest principle and an "axiom" in the usual sense, the highest major premise, as it were, for all logical deduction. But with this formally correct consideration, which is partly supported by Descartes' own assertions, one overlooks what is essential, to wit, that a new definition of the essence of "ground" and *principium* is first given through the principle *cogito sum.* The *subiectum* is now the "ground" and *principium* in the sense of self-representing representation. Thus a new determination is made concerning the way in which the principle of the *subiectum* is *the* fundamental principle pure and simple. The essence of the fundamental principle now defines itself in and through the essence of "subjectivity." The "axiomatic" now has a different meaning in comparison to the truth of that *axiōma* which Aristotle proclaimed as the "principle of contradiction," applicable to the interpretation of beings as such. The "principial" character of the principle *cogito sum* consists in the fact that the essence of truth and of Being is newly defined, and indeed defined in such a way that the determination itself is addressed as the primary truth, which is also to say, addressed as a being in the proper sense.

Of course, Descartes did not explicitly commit himself concerning the principial character of this principle as the fundamental one. Nonetheless, he possessed a lucid knowledge of its uniqueness. But, through his many efforts to make what was new in his grounding of metaphysics intelligible to his contemporaries by responding to their doubts, Descartes was forced to discourse at the already prevailing level and so to explain his fundamental position superficially, that is, always inappropriately, a contingency that threatens *every essential thinking*— a contingency that is already the consequence of a hidden relationship. Correlative to it is the fact that a thinking also sets *its own* boundaries in *direct proportion* as it presses toward originality.

18. The Fundamental Metaphysical Positions of Descartes and Protagoras

At last we are able to describe Descartes' fundamental metaphysical position according to the four guidelines identified earlier [p.92], and to contrast it with the metaphysical position of Protagoras.

1. In Descartes' metaphysics, in what way *is* man himself, and as what does he know himself? Man is the distinctive ground underlying every representing of beings and their truth, on which every representing and its represented is based and must be based if it is to have status and stability. Man is *subiectum* in the distinctive sense. The name and concept "subject" in its new significance now passes over to become the proper name and essential word for man. This means that every nonhuman being becomes an *object for* this subject. From then on *subiectum* no longer serves as a name and concept for animals, plants, and minerals.

2. What projection of beings on *Being* pertains to such metaphysics? Asked in another way, how is the beingness of beings defined? Beingness now means the representedness of the representing subject. This in no way signifies that the being is a "mere representation" and that the latter is an occurrence in human "consciousness," so that every being evaporates into nebulous shapes of mere thought. Descartes, and after him Kant, never doubted that the being and what is established as a being is in itself and of itself actual. But the question remains what Being means here and how the being is to be attained and made certain through man as one who has come to be a subject. Being is representedness secured in reckoning representation, through which man is universally guaranteed his manner of proceeding in the midst of beings, as well as the scrutiny, conquest, mastery, and disposi-

tion of beings, in such a way that man himself can be the master of his own surety and certitude on his own terms.

3. How is the essence of *truth* circumscribed in such metaphysics? A basic trait of every metaphysical definition of the essence of truth is expressed in the principle that conceives truth as agreement of knowledge with beings: *Veritas est adaequatio intellectus et rei*. But according to what has been said previously we can now easily see that this familiar "definition" of truth varies depending on how the being with which knowledge is supposed to agree is understood, but also depending on how knowledge, which is supposed to stand in agreement with the being, is conceived. Knowing as *percipere* and *cogitare* in Descartes' sense has its distinctive feature in that it recognizes as knowledge only something that representation presents-to a subject as indubitable and that can at all times be reckoned as something so presented. For Descartes too, knowing is oriented toward beings, although only what is secured in the fashion we have described as representing and presenting-to-oneself is recognized *as* a being. That alone is a being which the subject can be certain of in the sense of his representation. The true is merely the secured, the certain. Truth is certitude, a certitude for which it is decisive that in it man as subject is continually certain and sure of himself. Therefore, a procedure, an advance assurance, is necessary for the securing of truth as certitude in an essential sense. "Method" now takes on a metaphysical import that is, as it were, affixed to the essence of subjectivity. "Method" is no longer simply a sequence arranged somehow into various stages of observation, proof, exposition, and summary of knowledge and teachings, in the manner of a scholastic *Summa*, which has its own regular and repetitive structure. "Method" is now the name for the securing, conquering proceeding against beings, in order to capture them as objects for the subject. It is *methodus* in the metaphysical sense that is meant when Descartes in his important posthumously published work *Regulae ad directionem ingenii* postulates as Rule IV: *Necessaria est methodus ad rerum veritatem investigandam*. "Method is necessary [essentially necessary] in order to come upon the trace of the truth [certitude] of beings and to follow this trace." If "method" is understood in this way, then all medieval thinking was essentially methodless.

4. How does man give and take *measure* for the truth of beings in

such metaphysics? This question has already been answered in the preceding. Because man essentially has become the *subiectum*, and beingness has become equivalent to representedness, and truth equivalent to certitude, man now has disposal over the whole of beings as such in an essential way, for he provides the measure for the beingness of every individual being. The essential decision about what can be established as a being now rests with man as *subiectum*. Man himself is the one to whom the power to enjoin belongs as a conscious task. The subject is "subjective" in that the definition of the being and thus man himself are no longer cramped into narrow limits, but are in every respect de-limited. The relationship to beings is a domineering proceeding into the conquest and domination of the world. Man gives beings their measure by determining independently and with reference to himself what ought to be permitted to pass as being. The standard of measure is the presumption of measure, through which man is grounded as *subiectum* in and as the midpoint of beings as a whole. However, we do well to heed the fact that man here is not the isolated egoistic I, but the "subject," which means that man is progressing toward a limitless representing and reckoning disclosure of beings. The new metaphysical position of man as *subiectum* implies that the discovery and conquest of the world, and all the fundamental changes these entail, must be taken up and accomplished by exceptional individuals. The modern conception of man as "genius" has as its metaphysical presupposition the definition of the essence of man as subject. Nevertheless, the cult of genius and its sundry degenerate forms are not what is essential about modern mankind—no more than are "liberalism" and the self-rule of states and nations in the sense of modern "democracies." That the Greeks should have thought of man as "genius" is inconceivable, just as the notion that Sophocles was a "man of genius" is unhistorical. All too infrequently do we reflect that modern "subjectivism" alone has discovered being as a whole, enabled it to be enjoined and controlled, and has made possible the forms and claims of domination that the Middle Ages could not know and that lay beyond the horizon of Greek culture.

We can now clarify what has been said by also distinguishing from each other the fundamental metaphysical positions of Descartes and Protagoras according to the same four guidelines. To avoid repetition, we can put it in the form of a postulation of four brief guiding principles:

1. For Protagoras, man in his selfhood is defined by his belonging in the radius of the unconcealed. For Descartes, man as self is defined by referring the world back to man's representing.

2. For Protagoras, the beingness of beings—in the sense of Greek metaphysics—is a coming to presence in the unconcealed. For Descartes, beingness means representedness through and for the subject.

3. For Protagoras, truth means the unconcealment of what is present. For Descartes, the certitude of self-representing and securing representation.

4. For Protagoras, man is the measure of all things in the sense of a measured restriction to the radius of the unconcealed and to the boundaries of the concealed. For Descartes, man is the measure of all things in the sense of the presumption of the de-limitation of representation for self-securing certitude. The standard of measure places everything that can pass as a being under the reckoning of representation.

If we correctly ponder the difference that has come to light in these fundamental metaphysical positions, then doubt might arise as to whether the same—something equally essential—holds true for both, which would justify our speaking about fundamental positions of *metaphysics* in both cases. But the intent of the contrast is precisely to make clear what is the same—although not identical—in the apparently dissimilar, and thus to make visible the covert unitary *essence* of metaphysics, and in this way to obtain a more *original* concept of metaphysics as opposed to the Nietzschean interpretation of metaphysics, which is merely moral, that is, determined by valuative thought.

But before we attempt the passage to a more original insight into the essence of metaphysics, we must refresh our memory concerning Nietzsche's fundamental metaphysical position, so that the historical connection—not the historiological dependence—between Nietzsche and Descartes may come to light. This we will do by means of a discussion of Nietzsche's position vis-à-vis Descartes.

19. Nietzsche's Position vis-à-vis Descartes

This reference to Nietzsche's position on Descartes' main principle is not intended to call Nietzsche to account for some failing in his interpretation of that principle. Rather, it is a question of our seeing that Nietzsche stands on the ground of metaphysics as laid out by Descartes, and seeing to what extent he must stand on that ground. We cannot deny that Nietzsche rejects the change that Descartes brought to metaphysics, but the question still remains as to why and how Nietzsche arrives at his rejection.

The most important of Nietzsche's notes dealing with Descartes' guiding principle belong among the sketches for his intended major work *The Will to Power*. The editors of the posthumous collection of notes, however, did not include them, which once again sheds some light on the thoughtlessness with which this book was compiled. Nietzsche's relation to Descartes is *essential* for Nietzsche's own fundamental metaphysical position. The *intrinsic* presuppositions of the metaphysics of will to power are determined by that relationship. Because it has gone unnoticed that behind Nietzsche's exceedingly sharp rejection of the Cartesian *cogito* stands an *even more rigorous commitment* to the subjectivity posited by Descartes, the essential historical relationship between these two thinkers—that is, the relationship that determines their fundamental positions—remains in obscurity.

The major part of Nietzsche's observations on Descartes is found in volumes XIII and XIV of the *Grossoktavausgabe*, which contain those notes which, for reasons that are not apparent, were excluded from the posthumous publication. First of all, we will list the passages on which the following discussion is based, by simply enumerating them: XIII, notes 123 (1885); XIV, first half, notes 5, 6, 7 (1885; from the same notebook as the preceding); XIV, second half, notes 160 (1885–86); also, from the posthumous book *The Will to Power*, notes 484, 485, and 533 (all dated spring–fall 1887); see also XII, Part I, note 39 (1881–82). From these notes, it again becomes clear that Nietzsche's confrontations with great thinkers were for the most part undertaken on the basis of philosophical literature *about* these thinkers and therefore, when it comes to particulars, are already questionable, so that it often simply would not pay us to discuss them more thoroughly.

On the other hand, even if we go back to the works of the great thinkers and refer to the full and exact text, that is still no guarantee that the thinking of these thinkers will now be thoughtfully reflected, rethought, and comprehended in a more original manner. The result is that the historian of philosophy, working with great precision, often reports the most incredible things about thinkers he has "researched," while a true thinker can nonetheless use such an inadequate historical report to recognize what is essential, for the simple reason that as a thinker and questioner he is from the start closer to what is to be thought and asked, in an intimacy that can never be achieved by historical inquiry no matter how exact it is. This is true also for Nietzsche's position with respect to Descartes. It is a mixture of mistaken interpretations and essential insights. This, plus the fact that Nietzsche is separated from the great thinkers by the highly complex nineteenth century, so that we lose track of the essential *simple line* running through the historical contexts, makes Nietzsche's relationship to Descartes a very complicated one. Here we restrict ourselves to what is most important.

At the outset, Nietzsche agrees with the familiar interpretation of the principle, which takes *ego cogito,* ergo *sum* as a logical deduction. Underlying the logical deduction is the intention of proving that "I" am, that a "subject" is. Nietzsche believes that Descartes assumes it is self-evident that man may be defined as "I" and that the "I" may be defined as "subject." But of all his arguments against the possibility of the conclusion, many were adduced already in Descartes' time and all have been repeatedly advanced since then: that, in order to be able to arrive at the logical deduction and posit the principle, I must already know what is meant by *cogitare, esse,* and *ergo,* and what "subject"

Nietzsche's Position vis-à-vis Descartes

signifies. According to Nietzsche, and others, because such knowledge is presupposed for and in the principle—granted that it is a conclusion—the principle itself cannot be primal "certitude" and indeed the ground of all certitude. The principle cannot bear the burden that Descartes places on it. Descartes himself answered the objection in his last comprehensive work, *Principia philosophiae* (*Les principes de la philosophie*, I, 10; published in 1644 in Latin, 1647 in the French translation of a friend; see *Oeuvres de Descartes*, Adam and Tannery, Paris, 1897–1910, VIII, 8). The passage has a direct connection with the previously cited characterization of the principle as *prima et certissima cognitio*:

> *Atque ubi dixi hanc propositionem* ego cogito ergo sum, *esse omnium primam et certissimam, quae cuilibet ordine philosophanti occurrat, non ideo negavi quin ante ipsam scire oporteat, quid sit cogitatio, quid existentia, quid certitudo; item quod fieri non possit, ut id quod cogitet, non existat et talia; se quia hae sunt simplicissimae notiones et quae solae nullius rei existentis notitiam praebent, idcirco non censui esse numerandas.*

And where I have said that the principle "I think, therefore I am" is the first and most certain of all, which occurs to anyone who philosophizes in the proper manner, I have not thereby denied that one must "know" [*scire*] in advance of this principle what "thinking," "existence," and "certitude" are, and also that "it cannot be that something that thinks does not exist," and other such things; but because these are the simplest concepts which alone provide knowledge, without what is named in them actually existing as a being, therefore I have taken the position that these concepts are not explicitly to be enumerated [taken into account].*

---

* Heidegger's translation is actually more literal than most renderings. Cf. the translation by Haldane and Ross, I, 222:

"And when I stated that this proposition *I think, therefore I am* is the first and most certain which presents itself to those who philosophise in orderly fashion, I did not for all that deny that we must first of all know *what is knowledge, what is existence, and what is certainty,* and that *in order to think we must be,* and such like; but because these are notions of the simplest possible kind, which of themselves give us no knowledge of anything that exists, I did not think them worthy of being put on record."

One can hardly resist the comment that Heidegger's labors from *Being and Time* (see section 10) through the present Nietzsche lectures represent the effort *to put these things on record.*

Thus Descartes unequivocally concedes that "before" the insight into the *cogito,* knowledge about Being, knowledge itself, and other such things are necessary. But the substantive question remains how this "before" is to be understood, in what the foreknowledge of what is most known is grounded, and on what basis the essence of such knownness of what is most known is to be defined. The passage just quoted is to be understood in this way: The principle, which is posited as an "axiom" and as primal certitude, represents the being as certain (certitude understood as the essence of representation and everything included in it) in such a way that what Being, certitude, and thinking mean is first co-posited through the principle. That these concepts are co-conceived in the principle merely says that they pertain to the import of the principle, but not as something *on which* the principle, along with what it posits, relies for support. Only with the principle— with it first of all—is it stipulated what character the *notissimum* (the most cognizable and recognizable) must possess.

Here we must pay heed to Descartes' preceding fundamental remark, which speaks entirely in Aristotle's idiom (*Physics,* B1) and yet still preserves its own modern tone:

> *Et saepe adverti Philosophos in hoc errare, quod ea, quae simplicissima erant ac per se nota, Logicis definitionibus explicare conarentur; ita enim ipsa obscuriora reddebant.*

> And I have often observed that philosophers err in that they have tried to make what was most simple and knowable through itself clearer by means of conceptual determinations of logic; for in this way they [merely] turned what is clear in itself into something more obscure.

Here Descartes is saying that "logic" and its definitions are not the highest tribunal for clarity and truth. These rest on a different ground —for Descartes, on the ground that is posited through his grounding principle. Above all, priority is given to what is secure and certain, in which the most universal determinations—Being, thinking, truth, and certitude—are of course included.

One could object against Descartes that he does not state clearly enough whether and to what extent the universal concepts that are thought together in the principle get their determination through the principle itself, and that any prior determination of these concepts is impossible if it does not rest on the fundamental certitude of the principle. But this objection—thought through in its implications—would be an objection that concerns *every* fundamental metaphysical position. For it is characteristic of the leading mode of metaphysical thought to take the concept and essence of Being for what is most known and therefore to ask which being is to be experienced, and experienced so that it may be interpreted in a particular way with respect to its Being.

As a preview of what is to come, we can formulate in a basic way what Descartes has to say in answer to the arguments raised: A being must first be established in its truth, after which Being and truth are also conceptually determined. Descartes' principle is such that it immediately expresses the inner ties of Being, certitude, and thinking all at once. In this lies its essence as an "axiom."

If in addition we consider that according to Descartes' own decisive explanations of it the principle ought not to be taken as a logical deduction, then it also becomes clear how the being it secures—representation in its complete essence—in keeping with the principial character of the principle grants certainty about Being, truth, and thinking. Again, what Descartes himself *seems* not to have emphasized sufficiently—that the principle as "axiom" must also be thought "principially," that is, *philosophically*—he actually does indicate by the phrase he has used more than once: *ordine philosophanti*. The principle can be fulfilled and its full content exhausted only if we think along the singular line taken by the search for a *fundamentum absolutum inconcussum veritatis*. This search necessarily ponders *fundamentum, absolutum, inconcussum,* and *veritas,* and in a definite sense thinks all these together with what satisfies the search as the being that is certain and therefore established. The provisional conceptions of Being, knowledge, and representation are also represented in the sense of what is certain and most known. The principle *cogito sum* merely states that they are already represented in such fashion. Nietzsche's objection that Descartes' principle makes use of unproven presuppositions and is therefore not a grounding principle misses the mark in two respects: that to which every principle and every act of knowledge appeal as their essential ground is expressly posited in the principle, first, if the principle is not at all a logical deduction which refers back to higher premises; second, and above all, if according to its essence the principle is itself precisely the *pre-supposing* which Nietzsche fails to notice.

There is another objection that Nietzsche lodges against the principle and that seems more essential, an objection that likewise rests on the presupposition that the principle is a logical deduction. But if we disregard this untenable presupposition, it becomes clear that Nietzsche really has hit on something essential. Nonetheless, his confrontation with Descartes remains opaque on the decisive points, because precisely where his deliberations could carry some weight—if they were adequately thought—they recoil directly on Nietzsche himself. It may be surmised from the start that at the most critical junctures Nietzsche views the Cartesian position from his own, that he interprets it on the basis of will to power. That is to say, in view of what we noted earlier, he "reckons it psychologically." So we should not be surprised if, because of the psychological interpretation of a fundamental position already "subjective" in itself, we fall into a tangle of positions that at first glance cannot be unraveled. We must nonetheless make such an attempt, *because everything depends on conceiving Nietzsche's philosophy as metaphysics; that is, in the essential context of the history of metaphysics.*

Nietzsche believes that through Descartes' principle the "I" and the "subject" are to be posited and secured as conditions of "thinking." But, as a result of the skeptical trend in modern philosophy, it has become easier to believe that contrary to Descartes' intention thinking is the condition of the "subject," which is to say, of the concepts of "subject," "object," and "substance." Nietzsche points to the "skeptical trend" of modern philosophy and in so doing is thinking of "British empiricism," according to which "essential concepts" (the categories) arise from associations and habits of thought.

Of course, Nietzsche knew that the doctrines of Locke and Hume merely represented a coarsening of Descartes' fundamental position, that they tended to obliterate philosophical thinking, and that they arose from a failure to comprehend the beginning of modern philosophy in Descartes. Descartes' observation, which we have cited concerning the universal "concepts" in the *cogito sum,* also contends that the most universal and most known concepts are not only produced as concepts *through* thinking, as all concepts as such are, but rather are attained and determined in their content *along the guideline of* thought and assertion. For Descartes, it is decisive that beingness means representedness, and that truth as certainty signifies establishment in representation.

What Nietzsche believes he must raise against Descartes as a supposedly new perspective, namely, that the "categories" emerge from "thinking," is indeed the decisive principle for Descartes himself. Of course, Descartes was striving for a uniform metaphysical grounding of the essence of thinking as *cogito me cogitare,* while Nietzsche, led on the leash of British empiricism, lapses into a "psychological explanation." By also explaining the categories on the basis of "thinking," Nietzsche agrees with Descartes on the very point on which he believes he must oppose him. Only his *way* of explaining the origin of Being and truth in thinking is different: Nietzsche gives the *cogito sum* a different interpretation.

Without being sufficiently aware of it, Nietzsche agrees with Descartes that Being means "representedness," a being established in thinking, and that truth means "certitude." In this respect, Nietzsche thinks in a thoroughly modern fashion. But he actually believes he is speaking *against* Descartes when he argues that Descartes' principle is *immediate* certitude; that is, is attained and secured through mere cognizance. Nietzsche says that Descartes' quest for unshakable certitude is a "will to truth": " 'will to truth' as an 'I will not be deceived' or as an 'I will not deceive' *or* an 'I will convince myself and be firm,' as forms of will to power" (XIV, second half, note 160).

What is happening here? Nietzsche refers the *ego cogito* back to an *ego volo* and interprets the *velle* as willing in the sense of will to power, which he thinks as the basic character of beings. *But what if the positing of this basic character became possible only on the basis of Descartes' fundamental metaphysical position?* Then Nietzsche's critique of Descartes would be a misunderstanding of the essence of metaphysics. That will come as a surprise only to someone who has not yet realized that such self-mistaking of metaphysics has become a necessity in the stage of its completion. The following sentence makes it clear just how far Nietzsche was thrown off the path of an *original* metaphysical meditation: "The *substance*-concept a consequence of the *subject*-concept: *not* the reverse!" (WM, 485; from the year 1887). Nietzsche understands "subject" here in a modern sense. The subject is the human "I." The concept of substance is never, as Nietzsche believes, a consequence of the concept of the subject. But neither is the concept of the subject a consequence of the concept of substance. The subject-concept arises from the new interpretation of the *truth* of the being, which according to the tradition is thought as *ousia, hypokeimenon,* and *subiectum,* in the following way: on the basis of the *cogito sum* man becomes what is properly foundational, becomes *quod substat,* substance. The concept of the subject is nothing other than a restriction of the transformed concept of substance to man as the one who represents, in whose representing both what is represented and the one representing are firmly founded in their cohesion. Nietzsche mistakes the origin of the "concept of substance" because, in spite of all his criticism of Descartes, and without an adequate knowledge of the *essence of a fundamental metaphysical position,* he takes the fundamental position of modern metaphysics as absolutely certain and stakes everything on the priority of man as subject. Of course, the subject is now conceived as will to power; consequently *cogitatio,* thinking, is also given a different interpretation.

The change is revealed in one of Nietzsche's remarks about the essence of "thinking," a remark that is not jotted down just anywhere, but stands in the context of his explanation of Cartesian certitude as a form of will to power (XIII, note 123): "Thinking is for us a means not of 'knowing' but of describing an event, ordering it, making it available for our use: that is what we think today about thinking: tomorrow perhaps something else."

Thinking is meant purely "economically" here, in the sense of "machine economy." *What* we think is, as something thought, "true" only insofar as it serves the preservation of will to power. But even *how* we think about thinking is measured solely by the same standard. On the basis of this conception of thinking, then, Nietzsche necessarily comes to the conclusion that Descartes was deluding himself when he supposed that an *insight* into the transparency of his principle would secure its certitude. According to Nietzsche, the principle *ego cogito, ergo sum* is only an "hypothesis" assumed by Descartes because it gave "him the greatest feeling of power and security" (WM, 533; from the year 1887).

Now Descartes' principle is suddenly a hypothesis, an assumption, and not primarily a logical deduction as it was when the first objections were raised! Nietzsche's position with respect to Descartes lacks a single, consistent focus. It becomes unequivocal only where Nietzsche no longer engages in a discussion of the substantive content of the principle, but reckons it "psychologically"; that is, understands it as a form of man's self-securing that arises from will to power.

Of course, it would be rash of us to want to conclude from Nietzsche's position that he has in the least abandoned or overcome Descartes' interpretation of Being as representedness, his definition of truth as certitude, and his determination of man as "subject." Descartes' interpretation of Being is adopted by Nietzsche on the basis of his doctrine of the will to power. The adoption goes so far that Nietzsche, without asking for reasons to justify it, equates Being with "representedness" and the latter with "truth." In the equation between "Being" and "truth," which was already apparent in *The Will to Power,* note 12, Nietzsche most unequivocally certifies the rootedness of his fundamental metaphysical position in the *cogito sum.* "Truth" and "Being" mean the same for Nietzsche: specifically, they mean what is established in representing and securing.

But Nietzsche does not acknowledge "Being" and "truth" and their equivalence as the basic truth. That is to say, in *his* interpretation they are not the "highest value"; he tolerates truth only as a necessary value for the preservation of the will to power. It is doubtful—in fact, it is to be denied—that what is represented in representation reveals anything at all about reality; for everything real is a becoming. Every representing, however, as a fixating, occludes becoming and shows it at a standstill, shows it in a way that it "is" *not.* Representation gives only the semblance of reality. What representation takes to be true and existent is therefore essentially in error when measured against the real taken as becoming. Truth is an error, but a necessary error. "*Truth is the kind of error* without which a certain kind of living being [namely man] could not live. The value for *life* ultimately decides" (WM, 493; see also Pascal, *Pensées*, note 18).*

Nietzsche adopts Descartes' fundamental position completely, although reckoning it psychologically; that is, by grounding certitude as "will to truth" on will to power. But does not Nietzsche argue against the concept of "subject" as Descartes thinks it? At any rate, Nietzsche says that the concept of the "I" as subject is an invention of "logic."

And what is "logic"?

Logic is "an imperative, *not* to knowledge of the true, but to the positing and tidying up of a world *which we shall then call true*" (WM, 516; from the year 1887). Here logic is conceived as command and a form of command; that is, as an "instrument" of will to power. Still more decisively, (WM, 512; from the year 1885): "Logic does *not* stem from the will to truth." That is surprising. According to Nietzsche's own conception, truth is indeed what is firm and fixed; but should not logic emerge from this will to fixate and make permanent? According to Nietzsche's own conception, it can only derive from the will to *truth*. If Nietzsche nonetheless says, "Logic does *not* stem from the will to truth," then he must unwittingly mean "truth" in another sense here: not in *his* sense, according to which truth is a kind of error, but in the traditional sense, according to which truth means agreement of knowledge with things and with reality. This concept of truth is the presupposition and principal standard of measure for the interpretation of truth as semblance and error. Then does not Nietzsche's own interpretation of truth as semblance become semblance? It becomes even less than semblance: Nietzsche's interpretation of "truth" as error, by appealing to the essence of truth as agreement with the real, leads to the reversal of his own thinking and thus to its dissolution.

---

* The first paragraph of Pascal's eighteenth "thought" reads as follows: "When we do not know the truth of a thing, it is of advantage that there should exist a common error which determines the mind of man, as, for example, the moon, to which is attributed the change of seasons, the progress of diseases, etc. For the chief malady of man is restless curiosity about things which he cannot understand; and it is not so bad for him to be in error as to be curious to no purpose" (Blaise Pascal, *Pensées* and *The Provincial Letters*, tr. W. F. Trotter, New York: Modern Library, 1941, p. 9).

But we would be taking the confrontation with Nietzsche's fundamental metaphysical position too lightly and leaving everything half-finished if we were to pursue the dissolution of Being and truth solely from this perspective. The tangles from which Nietzsche can no longer extricate himself are at first covered over by the basic notion that everything is sustained, necessitated, and therefore justified by the will to power. This is made explicit in the fact that Nietzsche can simultaneously say that "truth" is semblance and error, but that as semblance it is still a "value." Thinking in values veils the collapse of the essence of Being and truth. Valuative thinking is itself a "function" of the will to power. When Nietzsche says that the concept of the "I" and thus the "subject" is an invention of "logic," then he must have rejected subjectivity as "illusion," at least where it is claimed as the basic reality of metaphysics.

In Nietzsche's thought, however, the argument against subjectivity in the sense of the I-ness of conscious thought nonetheless accords with the absolute acceptance of subjectivity in the metaphysical sense of *subiectum,* an acceptance that is of course unrecognized. For Nietzsche, what underlies is not the "I" but the "body": "Belief in the body is more fundamental than belief in the *soul*" (WM, 491); and "The phenomenon of the *body* is the richer, clearer, more comprehensible phenomenon: to be placed first methodologically, without stipulating anything about its ultimate significance" (WM, 489). But this is Descartes' fundamental position, presupposing that we still have eyes to see; that is, to think metaphysically. The body is to be placed first *"methodologically."* It is a question of method. We know what that means: it is a question of a procedure for defining what everything determinable is referred back to. That the body is to be placed first methodologically means that we must think more clearly and comprehensibly and still more adroitly than Descartes, but do so wholly and solely in his sense. The method is decisive. That Nietzsche posits the body in place of the soul and consciousness alters nothing in the fundamental metaphysical position which is determined by Descartes. Nietzsche merely coarsens it and brings it to the edge—or even into the realm—of absolute meaninglessness. But meaninglessness is no longer an objection, provided only that it remain of some use to the will to power. "Essential: to set out from the *body* and to use it as guideline" (WM, 532). If we ponder this together with the passage already quoted from *Beyond Good and Evil* (note 36), where Nietzsche posits "our world of desires and passions" as the only definitive "reality," we discover clearly enough how decisively Nietzsche's metaphysics is developed as the fulfillment of Descartes' fundamental metaphysical position, except that here everything is transferred from the realm of representation and consciousness (*perceptio*) to the realm of *appetitus* or drives, and thought absolutely in terms of the physiology of will to power.

However, we must also think Descartes' position in a truly *metaphysical* way, and must consider in its complete *inner* scope the *essential* change of Being and truth in the sense of representedness and certainty. Nearly contemporaneous with Descartes, but essentially determined by him, Pascal sought to save man's Christianity, an attempt that not only made Descartes' philosophy seem to be a mere "theory of knowledge" but also caused it to appear as a mode of thought that only served "civilization," but not "culture." But in truth Descartes' thought was concerned with an essential transposition of all of mankind and its history from the realm of the speculative truth of faith for Christian man into the representedness of beings grounded in the subject, a representedness that serves as the essential ground of the possibility of modern man's position of dominance.

In 1637, as a prelude to the *Meditations,* appeared the *Discours de la méthode: Pour bien conduire sa raison et chercher la vérité dans les sciences.* After what has been said above about the modern metaphysical meaning of "method," the title needs no further commentary.

In the sixth part of the *Discourse on Method* Descartes speaks about the parameters of the new interpretation of beings, especially of nature in the sense of *res extensa,* which is represented as "shape and motion" (location and mobility); that is to say, which is supposed to be made predictable and thus controllable. The newly structured concepts, grounded on the *cogito sum,* open up a vista whose development the present age is only now experiencing in its full metaphysical absoluteness. Descartes says (Opp. VI, 61 ff.; see the edition by Etienne Gilson, 1925, p. 61 f.):

Car elles [quelques notions générales touchant la Physique] m'ont fait voir qu'il est possible de parvenir à des connaisances qui soient fort utiles à la vie, et qu'au lieu de cette philosophie spéculative qu'on enseigne dans les écoles, on en peut trouver une pratique, par laquelle connaissant la force et les actions du feu, de l'eau, de l'air, des astres, des cieux et de tous les autres corps qui nous environnent, aussi distinctement que nous connaissons les divers métiers de nos artisans, nous les pourrions employer en même façon a tous les usages auxquels ils sont propres, et ainsi nous rendre comme maîtres et possesseurs de la nature.

For they [the concepts which on the basis of the *cogito sum* determine the modern projection of the essence of nature] have opened for me the prospect that it is possible to attain to insights that are very useful for life, and that, instead of that scholastic philosophy which merely performs a belated conceptual analysis on a given truth, it is possible to find a philosophy that immediately advances to beings and against them, so that we gain knowledge about the power and effects of fire, water, air, the stars, the heavens, and all other bodily things that surround us; indeed, such knowledge [of the elementary, of the elements] will be just as precise as our knowledge of the various activities of our artisans. Thus we will be able to bring such knowledge into use and perfection in the same way for every purpose to which they are suited, so that such knowledge [the modern mode of representing] will in that way make us masters and proprietors of nature.*

---

* Heidegger's translation of this passage contains several glosses that are not placed in brackets. Cf. the translation by Haldane and Ross, I, 119:

For they caused me to see that it is possible to attain knowledge which is very useful in life, and that, instead of that speculative philosophy which is taught in the Schools, we may find a practical philosophy by means of which, knowing the force and the action of fire, water, air, the stars, heavens and all other bodies that environ us, as distinctly as we know the different crafts of our artisans, we can in the same way employ them in all those uses to which they are adapted, and thus render ourselves the masters and possessors of nature.

20. The Inner Connection Between the Fundamental Positions of Descartes and Nietzsche

Nietzsche's position with respect to Descartes' *cogito, ergo sum* is in all respects proof that he *misapprehends* the historically essential inner connection between his own fundamental metaphysical position and that of Descartes. The basis for the necessity of the misapprehension lies in the essence of the metaphysics of will to power, which—without being able to know it yet—obstructs an essentially correct insight into the essence of metaphysics. Of course, we learn that this is so only when a comparative review of the three fundamental metaphysical positions cited lets us see in *one* glance the *selfsame* that governs their essence and at the same time demands their respective uniqueness.

To extract the selfsame in the right way, it might also be advisable to contrast *Nietzsche's* fundamental metaphysical position with Descartes', according to our four guidelines.

1. For Descartes, man is subject in the sense of representing I-ness. For Nietzsche, man is subject in the sense of drives and affects present before us as the "ultimate fact"; that is, in short, the *body*. In such recourse to the body as the metaphysical guideline, all world interpretation is pursued.

2. For Descartes, the beingness of beings is equivalent to representedness through and for the I-subject. For Nietzsche too, "Being" is indeed representedness; but "Being," conceived as permanence, is not sufficient for grasping a proper "being," that is, something that becomes, in its reality as becoming. "Being" as the firm and fixed is merely the semblance of becoming, but a necessary semblance. The

proper character of the Being of the real as becoming is will to power. It requires an explicit and separate demonstration to show how far Nietzsche's interpretation of being as a whole as will to power is rooted in the previously mentioned subjectivity of drives and affects and at the same time is essentially co-determined through the projection of beingness as representedness.

3. For Descartes, truth means the same as secure conveyance of what is represented in self-representing representation; truth is certitude. For Nietzsche, truth is equivalent to taking-for-true. The true is defined by what man makes of the being and what he takes as being. Being [*Sein*] is permanence, fixedness. Taking-for-true is the making-fast of becoming, a fixation through which something permanent is secured for a living creature both in himself and in his surroundings. By virtue of it, he can be secure in his existence and his continuance and thus have control over the *enhancement* of power. For Nietzsche, truth as fixation is the semblance needed by the living creature; that is, by the power center of the "body" as "subject."

4. For Descartes, man is the measure of all beings in the sense of the presumption of the de-limitation of representing to self-securing certitude. For Nietzsche, not only is what is represented as such a product of man, but every shaping and minting of any kind is the product and property of man as absolute lord over every sort of perspective in which the world is fashioned and empowered as absolute will to power.

Therefore, Nietzsche says in his treatise *Toward the Genealogy of Morals,* which was joined to *Beyond Good and Evil* the following year (1887) as a "supplement and clarification" (note 12, section III):

> 'Objectivity'—the latter understood not as 'disinterested apprehending' (which is nonsense and an absurdity), but as the ability *to control* one's pro and con and to apply one or the other of them, so that one knows how to employ a *variety* of perspectives and affective interpretations for knowledge. There is *only* a perspectival seeing, *only* a perspectival 'knowing'; and the *more* affects we allow to express themselves concerning one thing, the *more* eyes, and different eyes, we can use to observe one thing, the more complete will our 'concept' of this thing, our 'objectivity' be.

The more easily one affect or another can be brought into play, the *more* one must look toward *need and utility*—the more one must foresee, reckon, and thus *plan*.

The particular emphasis of the change through which man becomes a "subject" at the beginning of modern metaphysics, and the role that then falls to subjectivity in modern metaphysics, might give rise to the notion that the innermost history of metaphysics and of the change in its basic positions is simply a history of the alteration in man's self-conception. This opinion would correspond completely to contemporary anthropological modes of thought. But it would be an erroneous notion, even though it may seemingly have been suggested and prompted by our earlier discussions; in fact it would be the one error it is necessary to overcome.

Thus at this juncture, having summarized the comparisons between Protagoras and Descartes on the one hand, and between Descartes and Nietzsche on the other, we must provisionally indicate the essential ground of the historicity of the history of metaphysics as a history of the truth of Being. Such an indication at the same time allows us to clarify a distinction that we have already employed several times: the distinction between conditioned and absolute subjectivity. This distinction is also tacitly presupposed by the following remark, presented here as more than a mere assertion: As the fulfillment of modern metaphysics, Nietzsche's metaphysics is at the same time the fulfillment of Western metaphysics in general and is thus—in a correctly understood sense—the end of metaphysics as such.

21. The Essential Determination of Man, and the Essence of Truth

Metaphysics is the truth of beings as such and as a whole. The fundamental positions in metaphysics therefore have their ground in the respective essence of truth and in their respective essential interpretations of the Being of beings. As a metaphysics of subjectivity, modern metaphysics, under whose spell our thinking too stands, or rather inevitably *seems* to stand, takes it as a foregone conclusion that the essence of truth and the interpretation of Being are determined by man as the subject proper. More essentially thought, however, it becomes clear that subjectivity is determined from the essence of truth as "certitude" and from Being as representedness. We saw how representation unfolds its full essence, and how only within it—as the essence of what underlies—man is transformed into the subject in a narrower sense, initially as "I." That man thereby becomes the executor and trustee and even owner and bearer of subjectivity in no way proves that man is the essential ground of subjectivity.

These discussions concerning the origin of subjectivity ought to have moved us closer to a question we must refer to at this point in our reflection. The question asks, Is not any interpretation of man and therefore of the history of human being always only the essential *consequence* of the respective "essences" of truth and of Being itself? If that is so, then the essence of man can never be *adequately* determined in its origin through *the prevailing*—that is, *the metaphysical*—interpretation of man as *animal rationale,* whether one prefers to give priority to *rationalitas* (rationality, consciousness, and spirituality) or to animalitas (animality and corporeality), or whether one merely seeks an acceptable compromise between these two.*

The insight into these relationships was the impetus for the treatise *Being and Time*. The essence of man is determined by Being itself from the essence (understood verbally†) of the truth of Being.

---

* The following passage, containing one of Heidegger's most forceful statements on his major work, *Being and Time*, appears as an inset in the Neske edition (cf. NII, 194–95). The typescript of the lecture course, completed in 1953, indents the passage and places it in brackets. A second set of brackets in red ink was later entered by hand on the typescript page. The implication is that the passage was not read as part of the 1940 Nietzsche lectures. Indeed, the extant holograph of the lecture course does not contain the inset passage. When it was written is therefore impossible to tell: the phrase "the past thirteen years" refers either to 1940 (if the 1953 *Abschrift* be taken as the starting point) or to 1927 (if the year 1940 be taken). The latter solution is probable, since 1927 is the year of publication of *Being and Time*. But when and where Heidegger first formulated the passage is a matter of conjecture. Certain turns of phrase are so reminiscent of Heidegger's "Letter on Humanism" that the late 1940s seems a likely conjecture. But Heidegger's own reference to "the past thirteen years" implies an intention to make the passage contemporaneous to his 1940 lecture course on nihilism.

† *Das Wesen* normally translates the Latin *essentia*, hence is rendered into English as "essence." It also forms the root of *Anwesen*, "coming to presence," which Heidegger takes to be the basic sense of Being (*Sein*) in philosophy. According to Hermann Paul's *Deutsches Wörterbuch* (pp. 591–92 and 796), however, the substantive derives from an Indogermanic root suggesting "to reside," "to dwell," or "to tarry," senses that the verb *wesen* preserves up to Luther and Goethe. As early as *Being and Time* (1927) Heidegger had stressed the verbal character of *Wesen*; for instance, in the phrase "The 'essence' of Dasein lies in its existence" (p. 42 of the German edition). Here "essence" suggests the radically temporalizing projection of Dasein as such, rather than some sort of property or even quiddity of being. During the summer semester of 1927 Heidegger commented at length on the problematic nature of the traditional distinction between *essentia* and *existentia*. See Martin Heidegger, *Grundprobleme der Phänomenologie* (Frankfurt am Main: V. Klostermann, 1975), ch. 2, esp. pp.169–71. In his 1935 lecture course, "Introduction to Metaphysics" (*Einführung in die Metaphysik*, p. 140), Heidegger emphasized the verbal sense of *wesen* as a "governing" or "effecting," while retaining the fundamental reference to "presencing." One of the most detailed statements appears in "The Question Concerning Technology," in Martin Heidegger, *Basic Writings*, ed. D. F. Krell (New York: Harper & Row, 1977), pp. 311–12:

> In the academic language of philosophy "essence" means *what* something is; in Latin, *quid*. *Quidditas*, whatness, provides the answer to the question concerning essence. For example, what pertains to all kinds of trees—oaks, beeches, birches, firs—is the same "treeness." Under this inclusive genus, the "universal," fall all real and possible trees. Is then the essence of technology, enframing, the common genus for everything technological? . . . Enframing, as a destining of revealing, is indeed the essence of

In *Being and Time,* on the basis of the question of the truth of Being, no longer the question of the truth of beings, an attempt is made to determine the essence of man solely in terms of his relationship to Being. That essence was described in a firmly delineated sense as *Da-sein.* In spite of a simultaneous development of a more original concept of truth (since that was required by the matter at hand), the past thirteen years have not in the least succeeded in awakening even a preliminary understanding of the *question that was posed.* On the one hand, the reason for such noncomprehension lies in our habituation, entrenched and ineradicable, to the modern mode of thought: man is thought as subject, and all reflections on him are understood to be anthropology. On the other hand, however, the reason for such noncomprehension lies in the attempt itself, which, perhaps because it really is something historically organic and not anything "contrived," evolves from what has been heretofore; in struggling loose from it, it necessarily and continually refers back to the course of the past and even calls on it for assistance, in the effort to say something entirely different. Above all, however, the path taken terminates abruptly at a decisive point. The reason for the disruption is that the attempt and the path it chose confront the danger of unwillingly becoming merely another entrenchment of subjectivity; that the attempt itself hinders the decisive steps; that is, hinders an adequate exposition of them in their essential execution. Every appeal to "objectivism" and "realism"

---

technology, but never in the sense of genus and *essentia.* If we pay heed to this, something astounding strikes us: it is technology itself that makes the demand on us to think in another way what is usually understood by "essence." But in what way? If we speak of the *Hauswesen* and *Staatswesen* we do not mean a generic type; rather we mean the ways in which house and state hold sway, administer themselves, develop, and decay—the way in which they essentially unfold [*wesen*]. . . . It is from the verb *wesen* that the noun is derived. *Wesen* understood as a verb is the same as *währen* [to last or endure], not only in terms of meaning, but also in terms of the phonetic formation of the word.

But such enduring is not permanent. *Währen* is the same as *gewähren,* the "granting" of Time and Being within the history and destiny of Being. The verbal *wesen* of the "truth of Being" is in fact history as such. See D. F. Krell, "Work Sessions with Martin Heidegger," in *Philosophy Today,* 1982, *26* (2–4), 126–38. In what follows, *wesen,* when used as a verb, will be rendered as "essentially unfold" or "occur essentially."

remains "subjectivism": the question concerning Being as such stands outside the subject-object relation.

In the prevailing Western interpretation of man as *animal rationale*, man is first experienced within the compass of *animalia, zōa,* living creature. Then *ratio, logos,* is attributed to the being that has thus come forward as the chief property and distinguishing feature of *its* animality, as opposed to that of mere animals. Of course, in *logos* lies the relation to beings, which we gather from the connection between *logos* and *katēgoria*. But this relation does not attain prominence as such. Rather, *logos* is conceived as a capability that makes higher and broader knowledge possible for the living creature "man," while animals remain "irrational" creatures, *a-loga*. Metaphysics knows and *can* know nothing about whether and how the essence of truth and of Being, and a relationship to that essence, define the essence of man in such a way that neither animality nor rationality, neither the body nor the soul, neither the spirit nor all these together suffice for a primordial conception of the essence of man.

If the appropriate "essence" of truth—rather than a conception of man—is decisive for the essential definition of subjectivity, then subjectivity in each case must allow itself to be defined in terms of the respective essence of truth by which it is measured. However, the appropriate essence of truth comes to be recognized by how untruth is determined in it and from it, and in what respect untruth is comprehended.

It is no accident, and has nothing to do with "theory of knowledge," that in Descartes' proper major work, the *Meditations on Metaphysics,** we find a meditation—the fourth—entitled *"De vero et falso"* ["On the True and the False"]. Untruth is conceived as *falsitas* (falsehood), and falsehood as *error, erring*. Error occurs when in representation something is presented-to the one representing that does not satisfy the conditions of presentability, that is to say, of indubitability and certitude. The fact that man errs and so is *not* in immediate, continuous, and full possession of the true certainly

---

* What is meant, of course, is the *Meditationes de prima philosophia*. Heidegger chooses the word *metaphysics* in order to emphasize that Descartes' major work on "first philosophy" is not a contribution to "epistemology" but an event in the history of Being.

signifies a limitation of his essence; consequently the subject, as which man functions within his representing, is also limited, finite, conditioned by something else. Man is not in possession of absolute knowledge; thought from a Christian point of view, he is not God. But insofar as he does know, he is also not simply a nullity. Man is a *medium quid inter Deum et nihil*—a definition of man that Pascal, in a different way and from another perspective, later appropriated and made into the kernel of his definition of the essence of man.

However, although being-able-to-err is a lack for Descartes, it is also a certification that man is free, is a being founded on himself. *Error* directly attests to the priority of subjectivity, so that from the viewpoint of subjectivity a *posse non errare,* an ability not to err, is more essential than a *non posse errare,* the inability to err at all. Where no possibility of error exists, there is either—as in the case of a stone—no relationship to truth at all, or—as in the case of an essence that is absolutely knowing, that is, creative—a binding into pure truth that excludes all subjectivity, that is, all reversion of a self back to itself. In contrast, the *posse non errare,* the possibility and the capacity of *not* erring, means *at one and the same time* the relationship to truth but also the factuality of error and thus entanglement in untruth.

In the further course of the development of modern metaphysics, untruth becomes (with Hegel) a stage and a mode of truth itself, which means that subjectivity, in its reversion of self back to itself, is the sort of essence that cancels and conducts [*aufhebt*] untruth into the unconditioned realm of absolute knowledge, a process through which untruth first comes to appear as something conditioning and finite. Here all error and everything false is but the one-sidedness of what in and for itself is true. The negative *belongs* to the positivity of absolute representation. Subjectivity is absolute representing, which in itself mediates, cancels, and conducts everything that conditions. It is absolute spirit.

For Nietzsche, subjectivity is likewise absolute, albeit in a different sense, one that is in keeping with his different determination of the essence of truth. Here truth itself is in its essence error, so that the distinction between truth and untruth falls away. The distinction is consigned to the command decision of will to power, which absolutely enjoins the respective roles of various perspectives according to the need for power. Because the power of disposing over the true and the untrue, the verdict concerning the respective roles of error, semblance, and the production of semblance for the preservation and enhancement of power remain solely with the will to power itself, the power-based essence of truth is, according to Nietzsche, "justification."* Of course, in order to grasp the Nietzschean sense of the word *justification* we must immediately put aside any ideas about "justice" that stem from Christian, humanistic, enlightenment, bourgeois, and socialist morality. "Justification as a constructive, exclusive, and annihilative way of thought, advancing beyond evaluations: *the supreme representative of life itself*" (XIII, note 98). And "*Justification,* as function of a perspicacious power which looks beyond the narrow perspectives of good and evil, thus has a wider horizon of *advantage*—the intention of preserving something that is *more* than any given person" (XIV, first half, note 158).

That "something" to whose preservation justification is exclusively tied, is the will to power. Such novel "justification" no longer has anything to do with deciding about right and wrong according to a true relationship of measure and rank that would subsist of itself. Rather, the new justification is active, and above all "aggressive"; it posits what is to be considered right and wrong solely from the viewpoint of its own power.

For example, when the British recently blew to smithereens the French fleet docked at Oran it was from *their* point of view "justified"; for "justified" merely means what serves the enhancement of power.†

---

* The word *Gerechtigkeit* is usually rendered as "justice" or "righteousness," especially as an attribute of the Judeo-Christian God. Nietzsche writes about it often, early and late, and always with ambivalence: *Gerechtigkeit* is the virtue closest to intellectual probity, which may be identified with "the grand righteousness" of philosophers (see *Beyond Good and Evil,* note 213); yet "justice" and "righteousness" have their origins in moralizing-reactionary will to power, they do the work of rancor. To emphasize the active, critical, genealogical aspect of Nietzsche's usage, *Gerechtigkeit* has been translated here as "justification." Heidegger regards it as one of the five fundamental terms of "Nietzsche's metaphysics" (see NII, 314–33, in Volume III of the present series).

† Heidegger is referring to the British ultimatum and attack of July 3, 1940, an event that had just occurred and which therefore should not be confused with the battle (November 7–8, 1942) that ensued upon the Allied landing in North Africa. Heidegger

At the same time, what this suggests is that *we* dare not and cannot ever justify that action; in a metaphysical sense, every power has *its own* right and can only come to be in the wrong through impotence. But it belongs to the metaphysical tactics of every power that it cannot regard any act of an opposing power from the *latter's* power perspective, but rather subjects the opposing activity to the standard of a universal human morality—which has value only as propaganda, however.

In accordance with the essence of truth as justification, the subjectivity of that will to power which justification "represents" is absolute. But absoluteness now has a different meaning than it does in Hegel's metaphysics, for example. The latter posits untruth as a stage of one-sidedness taken up into truth. Nietzsche's metaphysics directly posits untruth in the sense of error as *the* essence of truth. Truth—so qualified and conceived—fashions for the subject an absolute power to enjoin what is true and what is false. Subjectivity is not merely *de*limited from every limit, it is itself what now enjoins every kind of restriction and delimitation. It is not the subjectivity of the subject that first transforms the essence and the position of man in the midst of beings. Rather, being as a whole has already experienced a different interpretation through that in which subjectivity finds its origin; that is, through the *truth* of beings. By virtue of the transformation of the human being into the subject, the history of modern mankind does not merely receive new "contents" and areas of activity; rather, the course of history itself takes a different direction. To all appearances, everything is merely discovery of the world, research into the world, portrayal of the

---

found the event compelling for probably two reasons: first, the French forces were—and the British knew them to be—largely incapable of defending themselves in the event of an attack; second, the "moral status" of the French, a defeated ally caught in the shadowy realm of collaboration, was a delicate issue throughout Europe during the weeks following the fall of France. Nevertheless, whatever Heidegger's reasons, I am not inclined to temper my sardonic treatment of this ostensible example of Nietzschean *Gerechtigkeit* (in D. F. Krell, "Nietzsche and the Task of Thinking: Martin Heidegger's Reading of Nietzsche," unpublished doctoral dissertation, Duquesne University, 1971, pp. 62–63, 77–79), an example that remains alien to the letter and spirit of Nietzschean will to power. Otto Pöggeler also comments on Heidegger's reference, more equably than I, in his *Philosophie und Politik bei Heidegger* (Freiburg and Munich: K. Alber, 1972), pp. 33–34.

world, arrangement of the world, and dominion over the world in which man extends himself, and in such extension stretches his essence thin, flattens it, and loses it. In truth, however, these are matutinal appearances of those basic features with which the unconditioned subjectivity of mankind is stamped.

22. The End of Metaphysics

In order to grasp Nietzsche's philosophy as metaphysics and to circumscribe its place in the history of metaphysics, it is not enough to explain historiologically a few of his fundamental concepts as being "metaphysical." *We must grasp Nietzsche's philosophy as the metaphysics of subjectivity.* What was said concerning the expression "metaphysics of will to power" is also valid for the phrase "metaphysics of subjectivity." The genitive is ambiguous, having the sense of a subjective and objective genitive, in which the words *objective* and *subjective* maintain emphatic and rigorous significance.

Nietzsche's metaphysics, and with it the essential ground of "classical nihilism," may now be more clearly delineated as a *metaphysics of the absolute subjectivity of will to power*. We do not say merely "metaphysics of absolute subjectivity," because this determination also applies to Hegel's metaphysics, insofar as it is the metaphysics of the absolute subjectivity of self-knowing will; that is, spirit. Correspondingly, Hegel determines the nature of absoluteness from the essence of reason existing in and for itself, which he always thinks as the unity of knowing and willing, although never in the sense of a "rationalism" of pure understanding. For Nietzsche, subjectivity is absolute as subjectivity of the body; that is, of drives and affects; that is to say, of will to power.

The essence of man always enters into these two forms of absolute subjectivity in a way that is different in each case. The essence of man is universally and consistently established throughout the history of metaphysics as *animal rationale*. In Hegel's metaphysics, a speculatively-dialectically understood *rationalitas* becomes determinative for subjectivity; in Nietzsche's metaphysics, *animalitas* is taken as the guide.

Seen in their essential historical unity, both bring *rationalitas* and *animalitas* to absolute validity.

The absolute essence of subjectivity necessarily develops as the *brutalitas* of *bestialitas*. At the end of metaphysics stands the statement *Homo est brutum bestiale*. Nietzsche's phrase about the "blond beast" is not a casual exaggeration, but the password and countersign for a context in which he consciously stood, without being able to peer through its essential historical connections.

But to what extent metaphysics, when considered from the themes we have discussed, is brought to essential completion, and to what extent its essential history is at an end, require a separate discussion.

Here once again, we must emphasize the following: our talk of the end of metaphysics does not mean to suggest that in the future men will no longer "live" who think metaphysically and undertake "systems of metaphysics." Even less do we intend to say that in the future mankind will no longer "live" on the basis of metaphysics. The end of metaphysics that is to be thought here is but the beginning of metaphysics' "resurrection" in altered forms; these forms leave to the proper, exhausted history of fundamental metaphysical positions the purely economic role of providing raw materials with which—once they are correspondingly transformed—the world of "knowledge" is built "anew."

But then what does it mean, "the end of metaphysics"? It means the historical moment in which *the essential possibilities* of metaphysics are exhausted. The last of these possibilities must be that form of metaphysics in which its essence is reversed. Such a reversal is performed not only in actuality, but also *consciously*—although in different ways —in Hegel's and in Nietzsche's metaphysics. In the view of subjectivity, the *conscious* act of reversal is the only one that is *real;* that is, appropriate to subjectivity. Hegel himself says that to think in the manner of his system means to attempt to stand—and walk—on one's head. And Nietzsche very early describes his philosophy as the reversal of "Platonism."

The fulfillment of the essence of metaphysics can be very imperfect in its realization, and does not need to preclude the continued existence of previous fundamental metaphysical positions. Reckoning in terms of various fundamental metaphysical positions and their individual doctrines and concepts remains a likelihood. But such reckoning does not take place indiscriminately. It is guided by the *anthropological* mode of thinking which, *no longer comprehending the essence of subjectivity,* prolongs modern metaphysics while vitiating it. "Anthropology" as metaphysics is the transition of metaphysics into its final configuration: "world view" [*Weltanschauung*].

Of course, the question of whether and how all the essential possibilities of metaphysics can be surveyed at once has yet to be decided. Might not the future still be open to metaphysical possibilities of which we suspect nothing? Surely, we do not stand "above" history, least of all "above" the history of metaphysics, if it is really the essential ground of all history.

Were history a thing, then it might be plausible for one to insist that he must stand "above it" in order that he might know it. But if history is not a thing, and if we ourselves, existing historically, are implied along with history *itself,* then perhaps the attempt to stand "above" history is an effort that can never reach a standpoint for historical decision. The statement concerning the end of metaphysics is of course a historical decision. Presumably, our meditation on the more original essence of metaphysics brings us into proximity to the standpoint for the decision mentioned. Such meditation is equivalent to insight into the way European nihilism essentially unfolds in the history of Being.

23. Relations with beings and the Relationship to Being. The Ontological Difference

The comparison of the three fundamental metaphysical positions of Protagoras, Descartes, and Nietzsche has at least in part prepared us to answer the question we have been holding in check. What, in the fundamental metaphysical positions we have characterized, is the selfsame—what is it that everywhere sustains and is indicative? It is obviously something that in each comparison of the three fundamental positions was seen to be that one-and-the-same regarding which we were interrogating the positions, in order to distinguish what was proper to each of them. We have already highlighted this one-and-thesame in naming the four guidelines that steered the entire comparison. They comprise:

1. The way in which man is himself.
2. The projection of the Being of beings.
3. The essence of the truth of beings.
4. The manner in which man takes and gives measure for the truth of beings.

Now the question arises: Have we just arbitrarily bound these four guidelines together, or do they themselves have an inner connection such that in each one the other three are already posited? If the second alternative applies, and if therefore the four guidelines do indicate a unified articulation, this gives rise to a further question: How does the articulation circumscribed by these four guidelines stand with respect to what we called the relations of man with beings?

The first guideline considers man as he himself is, as a being who knows himself and knowingly is *this* being who consciously distinguishes himself from every being he himself is *not*. Included in such being-himself is the fact that man stands within some kind of truth about beings, indeed about the being he himself is *and* the beings he himself is *not*. Thus the first guideline includes the third: the truth of beings. The second is already thought along with the third, for the truth of beings must uncover and represent these beings in what they are as beings; that is, in their Being. The truth of beings contains a projection of the Being of beings. But, insofar as man, himself a being, maintains himself in the projection of Being and stands in the truth of beings, he must either *take* the truth of beings as a measure for his being-himself, or must *give* a measure for the truth of beings out of his own being-himself. The first guideline contains the third, in which the second is included, but also at the same time embraces the fourth in itself. Correspondingly, one can show in terms of the second, and also in terms of the third, the cohesion of the remaining guidelines.

The four guidelines characterize the unity of an as yet nameless articulation. But how does the latter relate to what we have vaguely called the relation of man to beings? If we consider the relation more precisely, it becomes clear that it cannot subsist or be absorbed in the relation of man as subject to the being as object. For once the subject-object relation is restricted to the modern history of metaphysics, it no longer holds in any way for metaphysics as such, especially not for its beginning with the Greeks (specifically, with Plato). The relation in which we seek the more primordial essence of metaphysics does not at all concern the relation of man as a self and as a somehow self-existent being to the other remaining beings (earth, stars, plants, animals, fellow men, works, facilities, gods).

Metaphysics speaks of beings as such and as a whole, thus of the *Being* of beings; consequently, a relationship of man to the *Being* of beings reigns in it. Nonetheless, still unasked is the question of whether and how man comports himself to the *Being* of beings, not merely to *beings*, not simply to this or that thing. One imagines that the relation to "Being" has already been sufficiently defined by the explanation of man's relations with beings. One takes both the relations with beings and the relationship to Being as the "selfsame," and indeed with some justification. The fundamental trait of metaphysical thought is intimated in such an equivalence. Because the relationship to Being is scarcely thought beyond relations with beings, and even when it is, is always taken as their shadow, the essence of these very relations also remains obscure. According to the third guideline, metaphysics is the truth "of" beings as a whole. It likewise remains unasked in what relation man stands to truth and to its essence. Finally, in the fourth guideline, according to which man posits the measure for the determination of a being as such, there is concealed a question of how the being *as such* can be brought into view by man at all, can be experienced and preserved in its determinateness, no matter whether man here takes the role of subject or of some other essence.

Although unexpressed and at first perhaps even inexpressible, the one-and-the-same is already experienced and claimed in advance in the four guidelines: the relationship of man to Being. The unitary articulation indicated by the four guidelines is nothing other than man's relations with beings, the essential structure of these relations. Perhaps the primary and uniquely experienced relation of man to beings is what it is only because man as such stands in *relationship to Being*. How could man comport himself to beings—that is, experience beings as being—if the relationship to Being were not granted him?

Let us immediately try to clarify this with a specific illustration. Suppose that every trace of the essence of history were hidden and that every elucidation of what history as such *is* were missing: then the being that we call historical being would also remain concealed. Then not only would historiological inquiry, communication, and tradition never be able to come into play, there would never be any historical experience anywhere and, prior to it, no historical decision or action. Nonetheless, we experience historical events and acknowledge historiological reports as if they were self-evident.

The most essential aspect of all this, the fact that we operate within a perhaps quite indefinite and confused knowledge of the historicity of history, does not trouble us—nor does it need to trouble everyone. But *our* not being troubled does not deprive the *Being* of beings in the form of what is historical of anything essential. It becomes all the more strange when we recognize that *such* essentiality does not even require the general awareness of the public in order to radiate its essential fullness. Such strangeness increases the questionableness of what we are here pointing to, the *questionableness* of Being and thereby the questionableness of the relationship of man to Being.

Therefore, what we were pointing to with the vague expression "relations of man with beings" is in its essence the relationship of man to Being.

But what is this relationship itself? What "is" Being, granted that we can and must distinguish it from beings? How does it stand with the *differentiation* of Being from beings; how does man stand vis-à-vis the differentiation? Is man first of all man, and does he in addition "have" a relationship to Being? Or does the latter constitute the essence of man? If it does, then of what essence "is" man if his essence is defined in terms of that relationship? Has the essence of man ever yet been defined in terms of the relationship to Being? If not, why not? If so, why is the relationship as inconceivable to us, as incomprehensible and indiscernible, as Being itself? We can at any time encounter, pinpoint, and investigate beings—historical matters, for example. But "Being"? Is it an accident that we scarcely grasp it, and that with all the manifold relations with beings we forget the relationship to Being? Or is metaphysics and its dominance the reason for the obscurity that enshrouds Being and man's relationship to it? How would it be if it were the essence of metaphysics to establish the truth of beings, and thus necessarily to be sustained by the relationship of man to Being, but *not* to ponder the relationship itself, not even to be able to ponder it?

The relationship of man to Being is obscure. Nonetheless, we everywhere and continually stand within it wherever and whenever we comport ourselves toward beings. When and where would we—ourselves beings—*not* comport ourselves toward beings? We keep hold of beings and at the same time hold ourselves in the relationship to Being. Only in that way is being as a whole our foothold and halting place. This is to say that *we stand in the differentiation of beings and Being*. Such differentiation sustains the relationship to Being and supports relations with beings. It prevails, without our being aware of it. Thus it appears to be a differentiation whose differences are not differentiated by anyone, a differentiation for which no differentiator "is there" and no region of differentiation is constituted, let alone experienced. One might almost surmise and maintain correctly that with what we call the "differentiation" between Being and beings we have invented and contrived something that "is" not and that above all does not need "to be."

But a glance at metaphysics and into its history soon teaches us otherwise. The differentiation of beings and Being shows itself as that selfsame from which all metaphysics arises and also, in arising, inevitably escapes, that selfsame which it leaves behind as such, and outside its domain, which it never again expressly considers and no longer needs to consider. The differentiation of beings and Being makes possible every naming, experiencing, and conceiving of a being as such. In Greek, the being is called *to on;* addressing a being as being and, furthermore, grasping a being take place in *logos.* One can therefore circumscribe the essence of metaphysics, which explicitly brings beings as such to word and concept, in the name "onto-logy." The name, even though it is formed from Greek words, does not stem from the period of Greek thought, but was coined in the modern age; it was employed by the German scholar Clauberg, for example, who was a disciple of Descartes' and a professor in Herborn.*

Following the basic position of metaphysics and its scholastic formations, various opinions concerning the knowledge of beings and Being attach to the term *ontology.* Today *ontology* has once again become a fashionable term; but its time seems to be over already. We therefore ought to recall its simplest application, based on the Greek meaning of the words: *ontology*—addressing and grasping the Being of beings. With this name, we are not identifying a particular branch of metaphysics, nor a "direction" of philosophical thought. We take the title

---

* The term *ontology* apparently was coined by Goclenius in 1613, then taken up by the Cartesian philosopher Johannes Clauberg (1622–1665) into his *Metaphysica de ente sive Ontosophia* of 1656, and finally established in the German language around 1730 by the Leibnizian rationalist Christian Wolff (1679–1754). Attacked and eclipsed by Kant's transcendental philosophy, "ontology" emerged once again at the forefront of philosophical inquiry only with Martin Heidegger and his onetime Marburg colleague Nicolai Hartmann (1882–1950), author of *Zur Grundlegung der Ontologie* (1935) and *Neue Wege der Ontologie* (1942).

so broadly that it simply indicates an event, the event in which the being is addressed as such; that is, addressed in its Being.

"Ontology" is grounded on the differentiation of Being and beings. The "differentiation" is more appropriately identified by the word *difference*, in which it is intimated that beings and Being are somehow set apart from each other, separated, and nonetheless connected to each other, indeed of themselves, and not simply on the basis of an "act" of "differentiation." Differentiation as "difference" means that a *settlement* [Austrag] between Being and beings exists. We shall not say from where and in what way the settlement comes about; we mention the difference at this point merely as an occasion for and an impetus toward an inquiry concerning the settlement. The differentiation of Being and beings is intended as the ground of the possibility of ontology. But the "ontological difference" is introduced not in order to resolve the question of ontology but to identify what, as the heretofore unasked, first makes all "ontology," that is, metaphysics, fundamentally questionable. The reference to the ontological difference identifies the ground and the "foundation" of all onto-logy and thus of all metaphysics. The naming of the ontological difference is to imply that a historical moment has arrived in which it is necessary and needful to ask about the ground and foundation of "onto-logy." Thus in *Being and Time* there is talk of "fundamental ontology." Whether another "foundation" is to be laid under metaphysics as if under a building already standing, or whether other decisions about "metaphysics" are to result from meditation on the "ontological difference," need not be discussed here. The reference to the "ontological difference" wishes only to point out the inner connection of our present meditation on a more original concept of metaphysics to what we communicated earlier.

The differentiation of Being and beings—although taken for granted everywhere—is the unknown and ungrounded ground of all metaphysics. All enthusiasm for metaphysics and all efforts to produce "ontologies" as doctrinal systems, but also every critique of ontology within metaphysics—all these merely attest to an accelerating *flight* in the face of the unknown ground. For one who knows of it, however, the ground is so *worthy* of question that it even remains an open question whether the very thing we call *differentiation,* the settlement between Being and beings, can be experienced in an essentially appropriate way on the basis of such a designation.

Every designation is already a step toward interpretation. Perhaps we have to retrace this step once again. That would mean that the settlement cannot be grasped if we think it formally as "differentiation" and wish to search out an "act" of the differentating "subject" for such differentiation. Once again, however, our designation is perhaps at first the *only* possible *basis* for bringing the generalized selfsameness of all metaphysics into view, not as some neutral quality, but as the decisive ground that historically guides and shapes every metaphysical inquiry. The fact that metaphysics generally thinks Being in the same way, although the Being of beings is variously interpreted in the playspace of presencing, must have its ground in the essence of metaphysics.

But *does* metaphysics think Being in the same way? There are several pieces of testimony that say it does, pieces which at the same time are related to each other and thus display their provenance from what we first identified as the differentiation of Being and beings.

Even the name for Being that was already familiar at the beginning of metaphysics, in Plato—namely, *ousia*—betrays how Being is thought; that is to say, in what way it is differentiated from beings. We need only translate the Greek word in its literal *philosophical* meaning: *ousia* means being*ness* and thus signifies the universal in beings. If we simply assert of a being—for instance, of a house, horse, man, stone, or god—that it is in being, then we have said what is most universal. Being*ness,* therefore, designates the most universal of universals, the most universal of all, *to koinotaton,* the highest genus, the "most general." In contrast to what is most universal of all, in contrast to Being, a being is "particular," "individual," and "specified" in a certain way.

The differentiation of Being from beings appears here to depend on and consist in looking away from ("abstracting") all the particularities of beings, in order to retain the most universal as the "most abstract" (the most removed). With such differentiation of Being from beings nothing is said about the inner content of the essence of Being. It merely reveals the way in which Being is differentiated from beings, specifically, by way of "abstraction," which is also quite normal for our representing and thinking of ordinary things and connections among things, and is in no way reserved for the consideration of "Being."

It cannot surprise us, therefore, when we frequently encounter the assurance in metaphysics that of Being itself nothing further can be predicated. One can even prove this assertion with "rigorous logic." For if something were to be predicated of Being, then that predicate would have to be *still more* universal than Being. But, because Being is the most universal of all, such an attempt contradicts its essence. As if by calling it "the most universal" anything would be said about the essence of Being! At best, what this tells us is the way in which one thinks "Being"—namely, through a generalization concerning beings —but not what "Being" means. But by defining Being as what is most universal, all metaphysics nonetheless certifies the fact that it posits itself on the basis of a peculiar kind of differentiation of Being and beings. Furthermore, if metaphysics always affirms that Being is the most universal and therefore emptiest concept, and so a concept not to be determined any further, it remains true that every fundamental metaphysical position does think Being according to an interpretation all its own. Of course, this easily gives rise to the mistaken notion that, because Being is the most universal, the interpretation of Being also proceeds on its own and requires no further grounding. In the interpretation of Being as the most universal, nothing is said about Being itself, but only about the way in which metaphysics thinks about the *concept* of Being. That metaphysics thinks about it so remarkably thoughtlessly —that is, from the viewpoint and in the manner of everyday opinion and generalization—proves quite clearly how decisively every meditation on the differentiation of Being and beings is utterly remote to metaphysics, although metaphysics everywhere makes use of the differentiation. All the same, the differentiation also comes to appear everywhere within metaphysics, indeed, in an essential form which governs the articulation of metaphysics in all its fundamental positions.

Being, the beingness of beings, is thought as the *a priori,* the *prius,* the prior, the precursory. The *a priori,* the prior in its ordinary temporal significance, means an older being, one that emerged previously and came to be, and was, and now no longer comes to presence. If it were a question here of the temporal sequence of beings, then the word and its concept would need no special elucidation. But what is in question is the differentiation of Being and beings. The *a priori* and the prior are predicated of Being as words that distinguish Being. The Latin word *prius* is a translation and interpretation of the Greek *proteron*. Plato, and later Aristotle, first discussed the *proteron* with particular reference to the beingness of beings (*ousia*). Here we must forego an explicit presentation of Platonic and Aristotelian thoughts concerning *proteron* from the dialogues and treatises of these thinkers. A rather more general and freer commentary must suffice. Of course, even that cannot be done without at some point entering briefly into a few of the main features of Plato's doctrine of the Being of beings. Discussing the *a priori* with the intention of characterizing the differentiation of Being and beings ought at the same time to insure that nothing irrelevant is introduced in thinking about the *a priori,* but rather that something all-too-near is for the first time conceived and yet grasped only within definite limits, which are the limits of philosophy; that is, the limits of metaphysics. In terms of the matter, therefore, our foregoing discussions have already dealt with what will be brought to language in the following special treatment of the *a priori.*

24. Being as *A Priori*

If we compare two colored things with respect to their coloration and say that they are alike, then we are establishing the equality of the coloration. Such establishment mediates for us a knowledge of things that are. In the sphere of everyday cognition and treatment of things such establishment suffices. But if we meditate on the cognition of similar coloration with respect to what might be further revealed in such knowledge, then something remarkable takes place, something Plato first approached with measured steps.* We say that the coloration—or simply these colored things—are alike. With regard to the two similar things, we first of all—and for the most part continue—to overlook the likeness. We pay no heed to the fact that we can make out both colored things *as* alike, can examine them with respect to their being alike or different at all, only if we already "know" what likeness means. If we supposed with all seriousness that "likeness," equality, is not at all "represented" (that is, not "known") to us, then we might *perhaps* continue to perceive green, yellow, or red, but we could never come to know *like* or different colors. Likeness, equality, must previously have been made known to us, so that in the light of likeness we can perceive something like "similar beings."

Because it is made known *beforehand,* equality and likeness must be "prior" to what is alike. But we will now object that we really first— that is, previously—perceive like colors, and only afterward—if at all— recognize that we are thereby thinking likeness and equality. We cautiously add the "if at all" because many people establish many things as alike and never in all their "lives" consider, and do not need to consider, that with this perception and for its sake they are already "repre-

---
* See, for example, *Phaedo,* 74–76.

senting" likeness. Actually, then, likeness and equality are subsequent and not prior. In a certain sense, this is accurate, and nonetheless does not touch on the theme we are dealing with here, the *a priori*. We must therefore ask more precisely in what sense colored things are "prior" and "equality" is later, or in what sense likeness is prior and similarly colored things are "subsequent."

It is said that like things are *given* prior to likeness and equality, and that it takes a special reflection to bring the subsequent "givenness" to us. Only afterward can we "abstract" likeness from previously perceived like things. But this popular explanation remains superficial. The matter at hand cannot be sufficiently clarified as long as we do not bring it into an established radius of inquiry. We might with the same —indeed, with greater—justice say the reverse: Likeness and equality in general are "given" to us beforehand, and only in the light of such givenness can we first ask whether two things are alike in this or that respect. How could an investigation and a determination be initiated with respect to equality if equality were not somehow in view, thus given beforehand? The question remains: What do "given" and "givenness" mean here and in what we said earlier? If we think in Greek fashion, we obtain from the Greek thinkers a primal and lucid illumination of the matter under consideration. They tell us that similarly colored existing things are *proteron pros hēmas,* "they are prior, or previous, particularly with reference to us" who perceive them. What is meant, however, is not that the things must have already "existed" before us, but that when they are viewed in relationship to us, with reference to our everyday perception and observation, they are revealed prior; that is, in their explicit coming to presence as such. Prior to what? Prior to likeness and equality. In the sequence of steps in our perception, we first perceive similar existing things and then *afterward* perhaps, although not necessarily, explicitly perceive likeness and equality. But the unequivocal result is that likeness and equality and all Being are subsequent to beings, and so are not *a priori*. Certainly they are subsequent—that is, subsequent *pros hēmas*—with regard to us, in the manner and sequence in which we find our way to something that is expressly known, pondered, and investigated by us. In the temporal order of explicit comprehension and observation carried out

Being as A Priori 161

by us, the beings—for example, similar existing things—are *proteron,* prior to likeness and equality. In the order indicated, beings are—now we can also say "with respect to us"—"prior" to Being. The order according to which the previous and the subsequent are determined here is the sequence of *our knowing.*

But the *a priori* is supposed to contain a distinctive determination of *Being.* In its ownmost essence, Being must be defined on its own terms, independently, and not according to what *we* comprehend it and perceive it to be. *Pros hēmas,* with reference to *our* approach to beings, beings are prior as what is known beforehand and often solely, in contrast to Being as the subsequent. If, however, we contemplate whether and to what extent beings and Being *essentially unfold* of themselves, according to their own proper essence, then we are not asking how it stands with Being *pros hēmas,* with regard to the way *we* explicitly grasp Being and beings. Instead, we are asking how it stands with Being insofar as Being "is." The Greeks primally and primordially conceived Being as *physis*—as rising forth from itself and thus essentially self-presenting in upsurgence, self-revealing in the open region. If we inquire into Being with regard to itself as *physis,* therefore *tēi physei,* then the result is: *tēi physei,* Being is *proteron,* before beings, and beings are *hysteron,* subsequent.

The *proteron* has a twofold sense: first, *pros hēmas*—in the order of temporal sequence in which *we* expressly grasp beings and Being; and second, *tēi physei*—in the order in which Being essentially unfolds and beings "are."

How are we to understand this? Basically, we have already provided an answer. In order to achieve clarity here, we need only continue our effort to think every Greek utterance about beings and Being in truly Greek fashion, so far as we can do so in retrospect. For the Greeks (Plato and Aristotle), Being means *ousia,* the presence of what endures in the unconcealed. *Ousia* is an altered interpretation of what initially was named *physis. Tēi physei,* from the point of view of Being itself— that is, viewed from the presence of what endures in the unconcealed, likeness, for example, or equality—is *proteron,* pre-vious [*vor-herig*] compared to things that are alike. Equality already unfolds essentially in the unconcealed; likeness "is" before we, with our perceiving, ex-

plicitly view, observe, and indeed consider like things as like. In our comportment toward similar things, equality has already come into view in advance. Equality, Being-alike, as Being—that is, as presence in the unconcealed—is what stands essentially in view, and in such a way that it first brings "view" and "the open" with it, holds them open, and grants visibility of similar beings. Plato therefore says that Being as presence in the unconcealed is *idea,* visibleness. *Because Being is presence of what endures in the unconcealed, Plato can therefore interpret Being,* ousia *(beingness), as* idea.* "Idea" is not the name for "representations" that we as "I-subjects" have in our consciousness. That is a modern thought, whereby moreover what is modern is diluted and distorted. *Idea* is the name for Being itself. The "ideas" are *proteron tēi physei,* the pre-vious as presencing.

In order to grasp the Platonic or Greek essence of *idea,* we must eliminate *every* reference to the modern determination of *idea* as *perceptio* and thus the relation of idea to the "subject." The most pertinent aid in doing so is the recollection that in a certain sense *idea* says the same thing as *eidos,* a name that Plato also uses frequently in place of *idea. Eidos* means the "outward appearance." But *we* understand the "outward appearance" of a thing in a modern sense as the perspective that we form for ourselves concerning a thing. Considered in a Greek sense, the "outward appearance" of a being, for example, a house, thus the houselike, is that wherein this being comes to appear; that is, to presence; that is, to Being. The "outward appearance" is not—as the "modern" sense would have it—an "aspect" for a "subject," but that in which the thing in question (the house) has its subsistence and from which it proceeds, because it continuously stands there; that is, *is* there. Viewed in terms of individually existing houses, then, the houselike, the *idea,* is the "universal" vis-à-vis the particular,

---

* See Martin Heidegger, "Plato's Doctrine of Truth," in *Wegmarken* (Frankfurt am Main: V. Klostermann, 1967), esp. pp. 130–31 and 135–36. The remarks on Plato in these Nietzsche lectures, along with those on Nietzsche in the Plato essay (e.g., pp. 133, 139, and 142), remind us that Heidegger concentrates on precisely these two thinkers during the decade—the 1930s—dedicated to the question of the essence of truth. See Heidegger's "Foreword to All Volumes" in Volume I of this series, p. xvi, and my "Analysis" to that volume, pp. 251–53.

Being as A Priori

and so *idea* immediately receives the characterization of *koinon,* something common to many individuals.

Because every individual and particular has its presence and subsistence, hence its Being, in its *idea,* the *idea,* as that which confers "Being," is for its part the proper being, *ontōs on.* In contrast, the individual house, and thus every particular being, merely lets the *idea* appear in a particular way, and thus appear in a limited and impaired way. Plato therefore calls individually existing things the *mē on:* that is, not simply nothing, but an *on,* a being, although in a way that it properly ought not to be, precisely the sort of thing to which the full designation *on* must, strictly speaking, be refused—the *mē on. Idea* and only *idea* always distinguishes the being as a being. Consequently, *idea* first and foremost makes its appearance in everything that comes to presence. According to its own essence, Being is the *proteron,* the *a priori,* the prior, although not in the order in which it is grasped by us, but with regard to what first *shows itself to us,* what first of all and on its own comes to presence toward us into the open.

In terms of our theme, the most appropriate German translation for *a priori* is obtained when we call the *a priori* the *Vor-herige* [previous]. *Vor-herige* in the strict sense says two things at once: the *vor* means "beforehand," and *her* means "from out of itself toward us"— the *Vor-herige.* If we think the authentic meaning of *proteron tēi physei,* the *a priori* as the *Vor-herige,* the word loses the misleading "temporal" significance of "prior" by which we understand "temporal" and "time" as ordinary time reckoning and temporal sequence, the succession of beings. But the *a priori,* when rightly conceived as the previous, first reveals its *time-*ly essence in a more profound sense of "time," which our contemporaries do not presently *wish* to see, because they do not see the concealed essential connection between Being and Time.

What is stopping them? Their own structures of thought and their covert entanglement in disordered habits of thought. They do not wish to see because otherwise they would have to admit that the foundations on which they continue to build one form of metaphysics after another *are no foundations at all.*

Through his interpretation of Being as *idea*, Plato was the first to identify Being with the character of the *a priori*. Being is the *proteron tēi physei;* consequently, the *physei onta;* that is, beings, are subsequent. Viewed from the standpoint of beings, Being as the previous not only accrues to the being but also reigns over it, and shows itself as something that lies above beings, *ta physei onta.* The being, as what is defined by Being in the sense of *physis,* can be comprehended only by a knowing and cognizing that thinks the character of such *physis.* The knowledge of beings, of *physei onta,* is *epistēmē physikē.* What becomes the theme of such knowledge of beings is therefore called *ta physika.* *Ta physika* thus becomes the name for beings. Being, however, in accord with its apriority, lies above beings. In Greek, "above" and "beyond" are called *meta.* Cognition and knowledge of Being is (*proteron tēi physei*) what is essentially *a priori*—the *Vor-herige*—and must therefore, when seen from beings or *physika,* surpass them; that is to say, the knowledge of Being must be *meta ta physika;* it must be metaphysics.

According to the meaning of the matter under consideration, the name *metaphysics* means nothing other than knowledge of the Being of beings, which is distinguished by apriority and which is conceived by Plato as *idea.* Therefore, *meta-physics begins* with Plato's interpretation of Being as *idea.* For all subsequent times, it shapes the essence of Western philosophy, *whose history, from Plato to Nietzsche, is the history of metaphysics.* And because metaphysics begins with the interpretation of Being as "idea," and because that interpretation sets the standard, all philosophy since Plato is "idealism" in the strict sense of the word: Being is sought in the idea, in the idea-like and the ideal. With respect to the founder of metaphysics we can therefore say that all Western philosophy is Platonism. *Metaphysics, idealism,* and *Platonism* mean essentially the same thing. They remain determinative even where countermovements and reversals come into vogue. In the history of the West, Plato has become the prototypal philosopher. Nietzsche did not merely *designate* his own philosophy as the reversal of Platonism. Nietzsche's thinking *was* and *is* everywhere a single and often very discordant dialogue with Plato.

The incontestable predominance of Platonism in Western philosophy ultimately reveals itself in the fact that philosophy *before* Plato, which as our earlier discussions have shown was not yet a metaphysics —that is to say, not a developed metaphysics—is interpreted with reference to Plato and is called pre-Platonic philosophy. Even Nietzsche adopts this point of view when he interprets the teachings of the early thinkers of the West. His remarks about the pre-Platonic philosophers as "personalities," together with his first book, *The Birth of Tragedy*, have strengthened the prejudice still current today that Nietzsche's thought is essentially determined by the Greeks. Nietzsche himself had a much clearer view, and in his final book, *Twilight of the Idols*, expressed himself concerning it in a segment called "What I Owe to the Ancients." Here he says, in section 2 (VIII, 167): "To the Greeks I do not by any means owe similarly strong impressions; and—to come right out with it—they *can* not be for us what the Romans are. One does not *learn* from the Greeks." Nietzsche by that time had clear knowledge of the fact that the metaphysics of will to power conforms only to Roman culture and Machiavelli's *The Prince*.* For the thinker of will to power, the only essential figure among the Greeks was the historical thinker Thucydides, who reflects on the history of the Peloponnesian War; thus, in the passage cited earlier, which contains Nietzsche's sharpest words *against* Plato, Nietzsche says, "My *cure* for all Platonism was always Thucydides." But Thucydides, the thinker of *history*, was not able to overcome the Platonism reigning at the basis of Nietzsche's thought. Because Nietzsche's philosophy is metaphysics, and all metaphysics is Platonism, at the end of metaphysics, Being must be thought as value; that is, it must be reckoned as a merely conditioned conditioning of beings. The metaphysical interpretation of Being as value is prefigured in the beginning of metaphysics. For Plato conceives Being as *idea*. The highest of ideas, however—and that means *at the same time* the essence of all ideas—is the *agathon*. Thought in a Greek sense, *agathon* is what *makes suitable*, what befits a being and makes it possible for it to be a being. Being has the

---

* Cf. Heidegger's formulation in 1936 (Volume I, p. 7), which is more cautious. There he asserts that the "world of the Greeks" remains "decisive for the whole of Nietzsche's life, although in the last years of his wakeful thinking it had to yield some ground to the world of Rome."

character of making possible, is the condition of possibility. To speak with Nietzsche, Being is a *value*. Was Plato therefore the first to think in values? That would be a rash conclusion. The Platonic conception of *agathon* is as essentially different from Nietzsche's concept of value as the Greek conception of man is from the modern notion of the essence of man as subject. But the history of metaphysics proceeds on its path from Plato's interpretation of Being as *idea* and *agathon* to an interpretation of Being as will to power, which posits values and thinks everything as value. Because of it, we today think exclusively in "ideas" and "values." Because of it, the new order of metaphysics is not only intended as a revaluation of all values but is carried out and established as such.

But all these remarks are only descriptions of the fundamental fact that the differentiation of beingness and beings forms the proper framework of metaphysics. The characterization of Being as the *a priori* grants the differentiation a unique coinage. Thus in the various formulations of apriority that are reached in particular fundamental metaphysical positions by virtue of an interpretation of Being, which is at the same time an interpretation of ideas, there is also a guideline for a more accurate delineation of the role that the differentiation of Being and beings always plays, without really being thought as such. Of course, in order to grasp the formulations of the apriority of Being, especially in modern metaphysics, and to think them in the context of the origin of valuative thought, Plato's doctrine of *idea* as the essential character of Being must be more decisively thought through in yet another respect.

25. Being as *Idea*, as *Agathon*, and as Condition

The interpretation of Being as *idea* made immediately compelling the analogy between grasping beings and seeing. The Greeks, particularly since the time of Plato, also conceived knowledge as a kind of seeing and viewing, a state of affairs suggested by the expression "theoretical," an expression that is still common today. In it, the words *thea*, "view," and *horan*, "seeing" (compare with *theater* and *spectacle*) speak. One believes he has given the fact a profound explanation when he assures us that the Greeks were to a special degree visually oriented and were a "visual people." It is easily shown that this popular explanation cannot be an explanation at all. It is supposed to explain why the Greeks explicated the relationship to beings through seeing. But that can have its sufficient reason only in an interpretation of Being which was decisive for the Greeks. Because Being means presence and permanence, "seeing" is especially apt to serve as an explanation for the grasping of what is present and what is permanent. In seeing, we have the perceived "over against" us in a strict sense, provided that an interpretation of beings does not already underlie our seeing. The Greeks did not explain relations with beings through seeing because they were "visual people"; they were "visual people," so to speak, because they experienced the Being of beings as presence and permanence.

This would be the place to discuss the question of why no sense organ, taken separately, can have precedence over the others in the experience of beings. What would remain to be considered is that no sensation is ever able to perceive a being *as* a being. At the end of Book VI of his great dialogue *The Republic*, Plato attempts to elucidate the relationship of knowing to the being that is known by bringing that relationship into correspondence with seeing and being seen. Supposing that the eye is endowed with the capacity to see, and supposing that colors are present in things, the faculty of sight will nonetheless not see, and colors will not become visible, if a third thing is not introduced that according to its essence is destined to make both seeing and visibility possible. That third thing, however, is *to phōs*, light, and the source of light, the sun. It confers a brightness in which things become visible and eyes see.

A corresponding situation prevails in our knowing as grasping a being in its Being; that is, its *idea*. Knowing would not be able to know and the being could not be known—that is, perceived as unconcealed —if there were not some third element that granted to the one knowing his capacity to know, and granted unconcealment to what is known. That third element, however, is *hē tou agathou idea*, "the idea of the Good." The "Good" takes the sun as its image. But the latter not only expends light, which as brightness makes seeing and visibility and thus unconcealment possible. The sun also confers warmth, through which the capacity for seeing and the visible things first *become* "beings," or, in the Greek view, first become the kind of things that can each in its own way come to presence into the unconcealed. Correspondingly, the "idea of the Good" is not only something that confers "unconcealment," on the basis of which knowing and knowledge become possible, but is also what makes knowing, the knower, and beings as beings possible.

Thus it is said of *agathon, esti epekeina tēs ousias presbeiai kai dynamei.* "The Good is above and beyond even Being in worth and power; that is to say, in *basileia*, dominion"—not merely above and beyond unconcealment.

What does Plato mean here by *agathon*, the "Good"? There is much disagreement among commentators about this doctrine of Plato's. In the Christian era, Plato's *agathon* was taken to mean the *summum bonum;* that is, *Deus creator*. Plato, however, speaks of the *idea tou agathou*. He thinks the *agathon* as *idea*, as the idea of ideas, in fact. It is a Greek thought—and here all theological and pseudotheological tricks of interpretation shatter. But now, to be sure, the substantive

Being as Idea, Agathon, *Condition*

difficulties of Platonic thought begin to appear: *idea* means Being; beingness, *ousia,* is *idea.* At the same time, however, we hear that *hē idea tou agathou* is *epekeina tēs ousias,* "beyond even beingness." That can only mean that if the *agathon* remains rooted in the basic character of *idea,* then it constitutes the proper essence of beingness.

In what does the essence of beingness consist; that is to say, in what does the essence of the visuality of the idea consist? The "idea" itself gives the answer when Plato calls it *agathon.* We say "the Good" and think of "good" in Christian-moral fashion as meaning well-behaved, decent, in keeping with law and order. For the Greeks, and for Plato too, *agathon* means the suitable, what is good for something and itself makes something else worthwhile. It is the essence of *idea* to make suitable; that is, to make the being as such possible, that it may come to presence into the unconcealed. Through Plato's interpretation of *idea* as *agathon* Being comes to be what makes a being fit *to be* a being. Being is shown in the character of making-possible and conditioning. Here the decisive step for all metaphysics is taken, through which the *a priori* character of Being at the same time receives the distinction of being a condition.

However, we now know that Nietzsche conceives *values* as conditions of the possibility of the will to power; that is, as conditions for the basic character of beings. Nietzsche thinks the beingness of beings essentially as condition, making possible, making suitable, *agathon.* He thinks Being in a thoroughly Platonic and metaphysical way—even as the subverter of Platonism, even as the antimetaphysician.

Then are all those correct who conceive of Plato's *agathon* and the "ideas" in general as values? By no means. Plato thinks Being as *ousia,* as presence and permanence, and as visuality—not as the will to power. It might be tempting to equate *agathon* and *bonum* with value (see *Duns Scotus' Doctrine of Categories and Meaning,* 1916).* The

---

* Heidegger's *Habilitationsschrift* appears now in Martin Heidegger, *Frühe Schriften* (Frankfurt am Main: V. Klostermann, 1972), pp. 131–353. Heidegger's reference to the work here is mysterious. For the problem of the Good (*bonum*), mentioned only on pp. 158 and 174, is expressly left out of account. The decisive reference—not listed in the volume's index of topics—is the following parenthetical remark on p. 207, n. 1: "In *this* investigation, which has to do solely with *theoretical* objectivity, the *bonum* remains outside of consideration." Heidegger's admission betrays the principal shortcoming of his

equation bypasses in thought what lies between Plato and Nietzsche; bypasses, that is, the entire history of metaphysics. To the extent that Nietzsche conceives of values as conditions—indeed, as conditions of "beings" as such (or, better, as conditions of the actual, of becoming)—he is thinking Being Platonically as beingness. Of course, that still does not explain why Nietzsche thinks these conditions of the being as "values" and thus gives the *a priori* character of Being a different significance as well. With Plato's interpretation of Being as *idea*, philosophy as metaphysics begins. Through Plato's determination of the *essence* of *idea* in the sense of *agathon*, Being and its apriority become explicable as what makes possible, as the condition of possibility. The prototype of valuative thought is completed at the beginning of metaphysics. Value thinking becomes the carrying through of the completion of metaphysics. But valuative thought was every bit as foreign to Plato as the interpretation of man as "subject."

The *a priori* is not a quality of Being, but is itself the pre-vious [*Vor-herige*] in its essence, insofar as the latter must be understood in reference to the *alētheia* that belongs to it, however much it is to be thought in its own terms. But already at the beginning, with Parmenides and Heraclitus, *alētheia* is thought in terms of *noein*. Thus the *a priori* shifts into the differentiation between the previous and the subsequent in knowledge; that is, in perception. At the same time, Being is in a certain sense necessarily experienced as the utmost being [*das Seiendste*]; Being is *ontōs on*, while "beings" become *mē on*.

With regard to such true being (Being taken as a being), the *a priori* immediately becomes a property; that is to say, the truth of the essence

---

second dissertation, a shortcoming intimated in the Introduction and Conclusion of the work itself: although that work falls under the influence of Rickert and Cohen's *Wertphilosophie* (see pp. 200–07 and 352), it does not explore the realms of medieval mysticism, moral theology, and asceticism—that is, the realms of the "Good"—which alone would enable the work to advance from the gray-on-gray of epistemology to the full palette of "the living spirit" in *cultural history* and in *metaphysics* (pp. 147–48 and 347–53). Such an advance would in fact lead back to Aristotle, and thence to Plato and the *agathon*, thus closing the circle of *theoretical* inquiry into *the Good*. The problem of theory, apriority, and the Good later receives prolonged and intense treatment in Martin Heidegger, *Metaphysische Anfangsgründe der Logik im Ausgang von Leibniz*, a lecture course taught during the summer semester of 1928 at Marburg (Frankfurt am Main: V. Klostermann, 1978), pp. 183–87, 235–38, and 284.

Being as Idea, Agathon, *Condition* 171

of Being as *physis, alētheia*, withdraws into concealment. The "ideas" are installed in "God's" thought and ultimately in *perceptio*. The *idea*, then, is itself something placed in a sequence relative to which it is distinguished as *proteron*. The sequence is determined as the *differentiation* of Being and beings. With regard to the differentiation, and from the viewpoint of Being, Being is prior to beings, because as *idea* it is *what conditions*. Within the differentiation, through which Being has become "visible," beings at the same time become conceptually "prior" with respect to knowledge and cognition.

More essentially thought, however, Being as *physis* does not at all require a "sequence" by which one can decide about its before and after, its previous and subsequent; because it is in itself a pro-ceeding [*Her-vor-gehen*] into its lighting; as going forth it is the fore-going [*Vor-herige*]; it is what essentially unfolds of itself into the lighting and what through the lighting first comes toward man.

This* would be an opportunity to define the fundamental metaphysical position of Aristotle, for which the traditional contrast with Plato is quite insufficient. For Aristotle once again attempted—although by passing through Platonic metaphysics—to think Being in the primordial Greek way and, as it were, to retrace the step Plato had taken with the *idea tou agathou*, whereby beingness receives the character of what conditions and makes possible, *dynamis*. As opposed to that, Aristotle thinks Being in a more Greek way—if such an expression is permissible—by thinking it as *entelecheia* (see "On the Essence and the Concept of *Physis*: Aristotle, *Physics* B 1"). † What this signifies cannot be said in a few words. We can only note that Aristotle is neither a Platonist gone wrong nor a precursor

---

* The present passage appears as an inset in the Neske edition (NII, 228). In the 1953 typescript, which shows some variations of the text as reproduced in Neske, the passage is indented, although without brackets. In the holograph of the 1940 lecture course, the passage appears on a loose sheet inserted into the lecture text, and appears there in brackets. The implication is that the passage was not read as part of the lecture course but is a contemporaneous reference to Heidegger's then recently completed work on Aristotle's concept of *physis*.

† Heidegger adds in brackets the bibliographical reference to "Biblioteca 'Il Pensiero,' 1960." The essay, composed in 1939, appears now in *Wegmarken*, pp. 309–71. See the English translation by Thomas J. Sheehan, "On the Being and Conception of *Physis* in Aristotle's *Physics* B, 1," *Man and World*, 1976, 9(3), 219–70.

of Thomas Aquinas. Nor is his philosophical accomplishment summed up in the nonsense often ascribed to him, that he fetched Plato's ideas from their being-in-themselves and lodged them in the things themselves. Despite its distance from the beginning of Greek philosophy, Aristotle's metaphysics is in essential respects a kind of swing back toward the beginning within Greek thought. That Nietzsche never—apart from his thoughts about the essence of tragedy—established an intimate relationship with Aristotle's metaphysics that would be equivalent to his perdurant relationship with Plato, is something that would merit our thinking it through in its essential grounds.

26. The Interpretation of Being as *Idea*, and Valuative Thought

According to Plato's doctrine, Being is *idea*, visuality, presence as outward appearance. What stands in such outward appearance becomes and is a being insofar as it comes to presence there. However, because the highest of ideas is at the same time conceived as *agathon*, the essence of all such ideas undergoes a decisive interpretation. The idea as such, that is, the Being of beings, receives the character of *agathoeides,* of what makes something suitable for . . . ; namely, what makes the being suitable to be a being. Being receives the essential trait of what makes possible. From that point on—that is, from the beginning of metaphysics—a peculiar ambiguity enters into the interpretation of Being. In a certain sense, Being is pure presence, and yet it is at the same time the making possible of beings. Thus as soon as the being itself presses forward and draws all human comportment to itself and claims it, Being must retreat in favor of beings. Of course, Being still remains what makes possible, and in that sense is the previous, the *a priori*. But the *a priori,* although it cannot be denied, by no means has the weight of *what* it continually makes possible, the beings themselves. The *a priori,* in its beginning and essence the pre-vious, thus becomes an addendum, which in view of the hegemony of beings is barely tolerated as the condition for the possibility of beings.

The ambiguity of Being as Idea (pure presence and making-possible) also announces itself in the fact that through the interpretation of Being (*physis*) as *idea* the reference to "seeing" evokes human knowing. As the visual, Being is presence, but at the same time is what man brings before his eyes.

How is it, then, if there comes a moment when man frees himself to himself, as to the one being who represents by bringing everything before himself, as the tribunal of continuance? Then the *idea* becomes the *perceptum* of a *perceptio;* becomes what the representing of man brings before itself, precisely as what makes the to-be-represented possible in its representedness. Now the essence of *idea* changes from visuality and presence to representedness for and through the one who is representing. Representedness as beingness makes what is represented possible as the being. Representedness (Being) becomes the condition of the possibility of what is represented and presented-to and thus comes to stand; that is, the condition of the possibility of the object. Being—Idea—becomes a condition over which the one representing, the subject, has disposal and must have disposal if objects are going to be able to stand over against him. Being is conceived as a system of necessary conditions with which the subject, precisely with regard to the being as the objective, must reckon in advance on the basis of his relations with beings. *Conditions* with which one must necessarily *reckon*—how could one not eventually call them "values," "the" values, and account for them *as* values?

The essential origin of valuative thought in the original essence of metaphysics, and of the interpretation of Being as *idea,* and *idea* as *agathon,* has now been clarified.

We see that in the history of the provenance of valuative thought the transformation of *idea* into *perceptio* becomes decisive. Only through the metaphysics of subjectivity is the at first largely veiled and reserved essential trait of *idea*—the trait of being something that makes possible and conditions—transposed into the free region and then put into uninhibited play. What is innermost in the history of modern metaphysics consists in the process through which Being preserves the uncontested essential trait of being the condition of the possibility of beings; that is, in a modern sense, the possibility of what is represented; that is, of what stands over against us; that is, objects. Kant's metaphysics takes the decisive step in that process. His metaphysics is *the midpoint* within modern metaphysics, not only in terms of temporal reckoning but also in its essential history, in the way it takes up the beginning in Descartes, as altered in the dialogue with Leibniz. Kant's fundamental metaphysical position is expressed in the principle that Kant himself defined in the *Critique of Pure Reason* as the highest principle in his grounding of metaphysics (A 158, B 197). The principle states, "The conditions of the *possibility of experience* in general are at the same time conditions of the *possibility of the objects of experience.*"

Explicitly and definitively named here as the "conditions of possibility" are what Aristotle and Kant call *categories*. According to our earlier explanation of the term, what is meant by the categories are the definitions of the essence of beings as such; that is to say, beingness or Being—what Plato comprehends as "ideas." According to Kant, Being is the condition of the possibility of beings, is their beingness. Corresponding to the basic modern notion of representedness, beingness and Being mean objectiveness (objectivity). The highest basic principle of Kant's metaphysics says that the conditions of the possibility of representing what is represented are also—that is to say, are nothing else but—conditions of the possibility of what is represented. They constitute representedness. But this is the essence of objectivity, and the latter is the essence of Being. The basic principle says: Being is representedness. But representedness is presentedness-to, in such a way that the one representing can be sure of what is thus brought into place and brought to stand. Security is sought in *certitude*. Certitude defines the essence of *truth*. The ground of truth is representing; that is, "thinking" in the sense of *ego cogito;* that is, of *cogito me cogitare*. Truth as representedness of the object, objectivity, has its ground in subjectivity, in self-representing representation; but this is due to the fact that representing itself is the essence of Being.

Man *is,* however, in that he represents in this particular way; that is, as a creature of reason. Logic, as the unfolding of the essence of "Logos" in the sense of unifying representing, is the essence of beingness and the ground of truth as objectivity.

Kant does not simply repeat what Descartes had already thought before him. Kant is the first to think transcendentally, and he explicitly and consciously conceptualizes what Descartes posited as the beginning of inquiry against the horizon of the *ego cogito*. In Kant's interpretation of Being, the beingness of beings is for the first time expressly thought as a "condition of possibility," thus clearing the way for the development of value thinking in Nietzsche's metaphysics. Nevertheless, Kant does not yet think Being as value. But neither does he any longer think Being in Plato's sense, as *idea*.

Nietzsche defines the essence of value as the condition of the preservation and enhancement of will to power, and in such a way that such conditions are posited by will to power itself. Will to power is the fundamental character of beings as a whole, the "Being" of beings, and precisely in the broad sense which recognizes becoming too as Being, if indeed becoming "is not nothing."

Metaphysical thinking in values—that is to say, the interpretation of Being as a condition of possibility—is prepared in its essential features through various stages: through the beginning of metaphysics with Plato (*ousia* as *idea*, *idea* as *agathon*), through Descartes' transition (*idea* as *perceptio*), and through Kant (Being as the condition of the possibility of the objectivity of objects). Nonetheless, these remarks are not sufficient to make the metaphysical origin of value thinking wholly visible even in basic outline.

Of course, it has become clear to what extent Being was able to accede to the role of "making possible" and of "condition of possibility." But why and how do the "conditions of possibility" become values; how does beingness come to be a value? Why does everything that conditions and everything that makes possible (meaning, aim, purpose, unity, order, truth) slip into the character of value? This question seems to render itself superfluous as soon as we remember that Nietzsche interprets the essence of value as a *condition*. "Value" is then but another name for "condition of possibility," for *agathon*. But even as another name it still requires a justification for its emergence and for the preeminence it has everywhere in Nietzsche's thought. A name always hides within itself an interpretation. Nietzsche's concept of value certainly thinks the conditional, but not only the conditional, and no longer in the sense of the Platonic *agathon* and the Kantian "condition of possibility."

In "value," what is valued and evaluated is thought as such. Holding-something-for-true and taking and positing something as a "value" is estimating. But estimating also means assessing and comparing. We often think that "estimating" (for example, in estimating distances), as opposed to an exact account, is merely an approximate discernment and determination of a connection between things, relationships, or people. In truth, however, estimating underlies every "accounting" (in the narrow sense of a numerical e-"valuation").

The essential estimating is reckoning, whereby we grant the word the particular meaning that reveals a fundamental kind of behavior: reckoning as to reckon *on* something, to "count" on a man, to be certain of his allegiance and readiness; reckoning as to reckon *with* something, to take the force of its impact and its scope into consideration. Reckoning means positing that in accordance with which everything we reckon on and with is to play a role. Reckoning thus understood is a self-imposed positing of conditions in such a way that the conditions condition the Being of beings. The positing of conditions *is* as reckoning and certifies itself *as* reckoning in the midst of beings as a whole, and thus certifies itself and its relation *to* beings *from out of* beings. In that way, reckoning, when it is understood essentially, comes to be the representing and presenting-to of the condition of the possibility of beings; that is, of Being. Such essential "reckoning" first makes planning and reckoning in a purely "calculative" sense both possible and necessary. Essential reckoning is the basic character of estimating, through which everything evaluated and valued as conditioning has the character of "value."

But when does the representing of the Being of beings come to be an essential reckoning and estimating? When do "conditions" come to be what is evaluated and valued; that is, come to be values? Only when the representing of beings as such comes to be that representing which absolutely posits itself on itself and has to constitute of itself and for itself all the conditions of Being; only when the basic character of beings has become the sort of essence that itself demands reckoning and estimating as an essential requirement for the Being of beings. That happens when the basic character of beings is revealed as will to power. Will to power is the essence of willing. Nietzsche writes in 1884: "In every willing there is *estimating*" (XIII, note 395). Earlier we showed in terms of the fullness of the essence of will to power to what extent will to power is of itself a value estimating. Now, from the essence of estimating as absolute reckoning, its essential affinity to will to power has emerged.

27. The Projection of Being as Will to Power

How does the projection of Being as will to power come about? Granted that every projection of Being is cast in such a way that Being joins what essentially unfolds to its truth, then the response to the question we have raised is tantamount to the experience of the most concealed history of Being. We are ill-prepared for such an experience. The answer we are looking for can only be replaced by comments that are barely distinguishable from a historiological report of various interpretations of the Being of beings, while the nature and intent of these remarks is to carry out a historical meditation on the history of the truth of beings.

In the Platonic interpretation of the beingness of beings as *idea*, there is no hint of an experience of Being as "will to power." But even Descartes' grounding of metaphysics on representing as the *sub-iectum* merely seems to imply a revision of the Greek *idea* into the Latin *idea* as *perceptio*, and seems to think Being as representedness in which certitude becomes essential, although here too the character of will to power fails to appear. Kant's doctrine of the objectivity of objects unequivocally shows how the projection of beingness as representedness seeks to develop the essence of the latter and still knows nothing of a will to power. Transcendental subjectivity is the inner presupposition for the absolute subjectivity of Hegel's metaphysics, in which the "absolute idea" (the self-appearing of absolute representing) constitutes the essence of actuality.*

---

* In order to transpose the tone of the word *Wirklichkeit*, heretofore rendered as "reality," out of all empiricist and positivist registers, we will from now on render it as "actuality." The "action" of that word also rescues a bit of the related German words *Wirkung*, "effect" or "impact," and *Werk*, "work."

Does not Nietzschean "will to power" therefore descend on metaphysics without historical precedent as an arbitrary explanation of beings as a whole? But let us recall that Nietzsche himself explained Descartes' principle on the basis of the will to truth, and the will to truth as a kind of will to power. Consequently, Descartes' metaphysics is indeed a metaphysics of will to power, albeit an unwitting one. The question, however, does not aim to ask whether the will to certitude can be interpreted as will to power and thus be historically counted as a preliminary stage of the will to power. The question remains whether Being as representedness, according to its essential import, is a preliminary stage of the will to power, which, experienced as the basic character of beings, first permits certitude to be explained as a will to fixation, the latter to be explained as a form of will to power. "Idea," representedness, objectivity contain nothing of the will to power in themselves.

But is not representedness what it is in and through representing? Hasn't representing become visible as the fundamental essence of the *subjectivity* of the *subiectum?* Certainly, but in an essentially complete way only when we know to what extent subjectivity is not only the determining ground for beings as objectivity and objectiveness, but also at the same time the ground of the essence of beings in their actuality. Only when we consider beingness as actuality does the connection with effect and impact reveal itself; that is, the connection with the empowering of power as the essence of will to power. Consequently, an inner relationship obtains between beingness as subjectivity and beingness as will to power. We need only ponder the fact that the metaphysics of subjectivity has its decisive beginning in the metaphysics of Leibniz. Every being is *subiectum,* a monad. Every being is also an *obiectum,* an object determined by a *subiectum.* The beingness of beings becomes ambiguous through subjectivity. Being means objectivity and at the same time actuality; one stands for the other, and both belong together. The essence of actuality is effectiveness (*vis*); the essence of objectivity as representedness is visuality (*idea*). Leibniz brings the interpretation of *subiectum* (*substantia* as *monas*) in the sense of the *vis primitiva activa* (effectiveness) into contrapuntal relation with the medieval differentiation of *potentia* and *actus,* in such a way of course that *vis* is neither *potentia* nor *actus,* but is in an original way both at once—as the unity of *perceptio* and *appetitus*. The differentiation of *potentia* and *actus* points back to Aristotle's distinction between *dynamis* and *energeia*. Furthermore, Leibniz himself often explicitly indicates the connection between the *vis primitiva activa* and the "entelechy" of Aristotle.*

Thus it seems we have found the historical (or merely historiological?) thread along which we can pursue the historical provenance of the projection of beings as will to power. We have up to now comprehended metaphysics too exclusively as Platonism and have as a result undervalued the no less essential historical influence of Aristotle's metaphysics. Aristotle's basic metaphysical concept, *energeia*, "energy," points "energetically" enough toward the will to power. "Energy" pertains to power. But the question remains whether "energy" so understood touches even in the vaguest way on the essence of Aristotle's *energeia*. The question remains whether Leibniz' own reference to the connection between *vis* and *energeia* did not transform the essence of *energeia* in the direction of modern subjectivity, after Aristotelian *energeia* had already received its first reinterpretation through the medieval notion of *actus*. But what remains more essential than insight into these transformations and the "impact"—sustained by them—of Aristotelian thought on Western metaphysics is the fact that originally embraced in the essence of *energeia* is what later, as objectivity and actuality, separates and then comes together in an interplay, and is consolidated as the essential determinations of beingness in modern metaphysics. The essential historical connection between *energeia* and will to power is both more hidden and richer than it might appear from

---

* Twelve years before his lectures on nihilism, during the second "logic" course at Marburg (summer semester 1928), Heidegger had treated the question of Leibnizian *vis* in some detail. (As an exercise in interpretation of texts, this last Marburg lecture course is perhaps Heidegger's supreme effort of the 1920s.) The text of that course has been ably edited—as far as one can determine without access to the original notes—by Klaus Held as vol. 26 of the *Gesamtausgabe* (bibliographical information on p. 170 n.). On the monad as *vis primitiva*, see section 5a, esp. pp. 96–105; for Leibniz' explicit references to Aristotelian *entelecheia*, see pp. 104–05; and for *vis* as representational, *vor-stellend*—that is to say, for the relationship between *appetitus* and *perceptio*, which is so essential for Heidegger's interpretation—see section 5c, pp. 111–22.

The Projection of Being as Will to Power

the superficial correspondence of "energy" (force) and "power." We can now give only a rough indication of what is involved.

Through Leibniz all being becomes "subjectival"—that is, in itself eager to represent, and thus effective. Immediately and mediately (through Herder), Leibniz' metaphysics shaped German "humanism" (Goethe) and Idealism (Schelling and Hegel). Because Idealism above all grounded itself on transcendental subjectivity (Kant) and because at the same time it thought in a Leibnizian manner, the beingness of beings, through a peculiar melding and intensification in the direction of the absolute, was thought in Idealism as both objectivity and effectiveness. Effectiveness (actuality) is conceived as knowing will (or willful knowing); that is to say, as "reason" and "spirit." Schopenhauer's main work, *The World as Will and Representation,* with its altogether superficial and scanty analysis of Platonic and Kantian philosophy, gathers up in one all the basic directions of the Western interpretation of beings as a whole, although everything there is uprooted and cast down to a level of understanding befitting the positivism then on the rise. Schopenhauer's main work became for Nietzsche the proper "source" for the shape and direction of his thought. Nonetheless, Nietzsche did not take the projection of beings as "will" from Schopenhauer's "books." Schopenhauer could "captivate" the young Nietzsche only because the fundamental experiences of the awakening thinker found their first inevitable supports in such metaphysics.

Again, the basic experiences of the thinker never stem from his disposition or from his educational background. They take place in terms of Being's essentially occurring truth. To be transposed into the domain of truth constitutes what we usually know exclusively in a historical-biographical and anthropological-psychological way as the "existence" of a philosopher.

That the Being of beings becomes operative as will to power is not the result of the emergence of Nietzsche's metaphysics. Rather, Nietzsche's thought has to plunge into metaphysics because Being radiates its own essence as will to power; that is, as the sort of thing that in the history of the truth of beings must be grasped through the projection as will to power. The fundamental occurrence of that history is ultimately the transformation of beingness into subjectivity.

We are inclined to ask here whether absolute subjectivity, in the sense of limitless reckoning, is the ground for the interpretation of beingness as will to power. Or, on the contrary, is the projection of beingness as will to power the ground for the possibility of the dominance of the absolute subjectivity of the "body," through which the proper effects of actuality are first liberated? In truth, this either-or remains inadequate. Both are valid, yet neither is accurate, and even both together do not attain to the history of Being, which grants to the whole history of metaphysics what essentially unfolds as its proper historicity.

We would like to develop a sense for just this one thing: that Being itself essentially unfolds as will to power and therefore demands of thinking that it perfect itself in the direction of that unfolding as estimating; that is, that it absolutely reckon with, on, and in terms of conditions; that is, that it think in values.

But we must also keep something else in mind; namely, that Being as will to power arises from the determination of the essence of *idea* and therefore itself entails the differentiation of Being and beings, but in such a way that the differentiation, unexamined as such, forms the basic structure of metaphysics. Insofar as we do not trivialize metaphysics as a doctrine, we experience it as the articulation of the differentiation of Being and beings as "enjoined" by Being. But even where "Being" is interpreted in such a way that it rarifies into an empty but necessary abstraction, so that it then appears in Nietzsche (VIII, 78) as the "last wisp of evaporating reality" (that is to say, of the Platonic *ontōs on*), the differentiation of Being and beings reigns—not in the thought processes of the thinker, but in the essence of the history in which he himself is thinking and in which he is and has to be.*

---

* Cf. Heidegger's remarks during the summer semester of 1935 (in *Einführung in die Metaphysik*, p. 27; English translation, p. 29). In retrospect, Nietzsche's caustic reduction of Being to a "vapor and a fallacy" appears to have provoked, almost singlehandedly, Heidegger's ensuing lecture courses (1936–1940) on Nietzsche.

28. The Differentiation Between Being and beings, and the Nature of Man

We cannot withdraw from the differentiation of Being and beings, not even when we ostensibly refuse to think metaphysically. Everywhere we go we are continually moving on the path of the differentiation, a path that carries us from beings to Being and from Being to beings, in every comportment toward beings of whatever kind and rank, whatever certitude and accessibility they may have. Therein lies an essential insight into what Kant says about "metaphysics": "Thus in all men, as soon as their reason has become ripe for speculation, there has always existed and will always continue to exist some kind of metaphysics" (Introduction to the second edition of the *Critique of Pure Reason*, B 21). Kant is speaking about reason, about its ripening into "speculation"; that is, he is speaking about theoretical reason, representation, insofar as it undertakes to enjoin the beingness of all beings.

What Kant says here about metaphysics as a developed and self-developing "speculation" of reason, to wit, that it is a "natural disposition" (B 22), is wholly valid for that on which all metaphysics is grounded. That ground is the differentiation of Being and beings. Perhaps such differentiation is the proper core of the disposition of human nature toward metaphysics. But then the differentiation would actually be something "human"! Why shouldn't the differentiation be something "human"? That would provide the best and the ultimate explanation for the possibility and necessity of the demand voiced by Nietzsche—that philosophers finally act on the humanization of all things.

If the natural metaphysical disposition of man, the very core of that disposition, is the differentiation of Being and beings, in such a way that metaphysics arises from it, then by referring back to the differentiation we have reached the origin of metaphysics and at the same time attained a more original concept of metaphysics.

What we have just been examining in an indeterminate way, the relations of man with beings, is at bottom nothing other than the differentiation of Being and beings, which belongs to man's natural disposition. Only because man differentiates in such a way can he comport himself toward beings in the light of differentiated Being; that is, sustain relations with beings; which is to say, be metaphysically determined and defined by metaphysics.

However, *is* the differentiation of Being and beings the natural disposition—indeed the core of the natural disposition—of man? But what is man? In what does human "nature" consist? What does "nature" mean here, and what does "man" mean? Whence and in what way should human nature be defined? Doubtless, we must accomplish a delineation of the essence of man's nature if we wish to prove the disposition toward metaphysics in it, if we are going to identify the differentiation of Being and beings as the very core of that disposition.

But could we ever determine the essence of man (his nature) without heeding the differentiation of Being and beings? Does the differentiation occur only as a consequence of man's nature, or is man's nature and essence first and foremost determined on the basis of and out of the differentiation? In the second case, the differentiation would not be an "act" that man, already existing, also performs among others; rather, man could be man only insofar as he maintained himself in the differentiation, because he is sustained by it. Then the essence of man must have been built on a "differentiation." Is this not a fantastic thought? Is it utterly fantastic for the reason that the differentiation itself, essentially nebulous, is, as it were, a castle in the air?

All we know is that here we are approaching a domain, or perhaps only the frontier, of a decisive question which philosophy hitherto has shunned—that is to say, which it really could not even shun, because that would mean that it had already encountered the question of differentiation. We suspect, perhaps, that behind the confusion and noise broadcast by the "problem" of anthropomorphism looms the decisive question, which, like every question of its kind, conceals in itself a peculiar abundance of questions linked to it.

We ask the question once again within the limits of what is most germane to our task:

Is all metaphysics grounded in the differentiation of Being and beings?

What is that differentiation?

Is the differentiation grounded in the nature of man, or is the nature of man grounded in the differentiation?

Is even this either-or inadequate?

What does grounding mean here in each case?

Why are we thinking here in terms of grounds and asking about the "ground"?

Is not the groundable also an essential feature of Being? Thus, in all these formulations of the question, are we asking about man's relation to Being, over which no question can vault, but which nonetheless has not yet been questioned in any question? For we always find ourselves immediately forced to take man as a given, as a nature at hand on which we then impose the relation to Being. Corresponding to that is the inevitability of anthropomorphism, which even gets its metaphysical justification from the metaphysics of subjectivity. Doesn't the essence of metaphysics thereby become inviolable as the domain into which no philosophical inquiry may trespass? At best, metaphysics can relate itself to itself and thus for its part finally satisfy the essence of subjectivity.

Such meditation of metaphysics upon metaphysics would then be "metaphysics of metaphysics." In fact, such a thing is mentioned by the thinker who in the history of modern metaphysics occupies a position between Descartes and Nietzsche, a position that cannot be circumscribed in a few words.

Kant traces metaphysics as a "natural disposition" back to the "nature of man." As if the "nature of man" were unequivocally determined! As if the truth of that determination and the grounding of the truth were utterly unquestionable! We might of course now point out that Kant himself (see *Kant and the Problem of Metaphysics,* 4th ed., pp. 199 ff.) wishes to refer the basic questions of metaphysics and philosophy back to the question "What is man?" Through a properly conducted interpretation of Kantian philosophy, we might even show that Kant analyzed the "inner nature" of man and thereby made use of the differentiation of Being and beings, that he claimed something as the essence of human reason which points in the direction of the differentiation. For Kant proves how human understanding in advance, *a priori,* thinks in categories, and that through these an objectivity of objects and an "objective knowledge" are made possible.

And yet Kant does not ask what the reason is for our thinking in categories. He takes such thinking as a fact of human reason; that is to say, of human nature, which even for Kant is defined in the old traditional sense by the designation *Homo est animal rationale*—"Man is a rational animal."

But, since Descartes, reason has been conceived as *cogitatio*. Reason is the faculty of "principles," a faculty that represents in advance what defines everything representable in its representedness, to wit, the Being of beings. Reason would then be the faculty of the differentiation of Being and beings. And, because reason characterizes the essence of man, while according to modern thought man is the subject, the differentiation of Being and beings as well as the faculty for the differentiation is revealed as a property and perhaps the basic constituent of subjectivity. For the essence of that particular *subiectum* which is distinguished at the beginning of modern metaphysics is representation itself in its full essence: "reason" (*ratio*) is merely another name for *cogitatio*.

Even with these reflections we still have not made any progress. We have entered the realm of a question that is still undecided, indeed is yet to be asked, a question that, briefly put, asks: Is the differentiation of Being and beings grounded on the nature of man, so that his nature can be specified from the differentiation, or is the nature of man grounded on the differentiation? In the second instance, the differentiation itself would no longer be anything "human" and could not be subsumed under a "faculty of man" either in "potency" or in "act." That kind of arrangement became ever more current in modern thought, so that it finally proclaimed anthropomorphism or "biologism," or whatever other name this sort of thinking goes under, as absolute truth evident even to the most thoughtless.

How and in what respect we achieve a more original concept of metaphysics depends on our mastering the decisive question just referred to. Only now is it clear what such a concept of metaphysics is searching for: not for an improved or more "radical" concept, as if "radicalism" were always inherently more significant. Rather, we are seeking to advance into the ground of metaphysics because we wish to experience in it the differentiation of Being and beings, or more precisely, what the differentiation as such sustains in itself, namely, the relation of man to Being.

We therefore can ask the decisive question correctly only if we have first experienced in a more meaningful way what we have termed the "differentiation of Being and beings."

29. Being as the Void and as Abundance

We said that the differentiation was the path that at all times and places in every comportment and every attitude leads from beings to Being and from Being to beings. We formulate this in an image that prompts us to imagine that beings and Being are found to stand on opposite banks of a stream we cannot and perhaps never could identify. For where are we going to find a basis for this? Or, to stay with the image, could something that neither is a being nor belongs to Being somehow flow between beings and Being? But let us not permit the unreliability of "images" to keep us from the experience of what we call the *differentiation*. Above all, let us now consider more decisively what has engaged us in the foregoing deliberations ever since we began discussing "nihilism."

We speak about "Being," refer to "Being," hear the word, and repeat it again and again. It is almost like a passing remark. *Almost*, but not entirely. There always remains an aura of knowledge—even when we merely append to the echoing word a reminder that we are "thinking" something with it. Of course, what we understand by it is something altogether tenuous and vague, but in the next breath it leaps out at us as most familiar. "Being" [*das Sein*], viewed as a part of speech, is a substantive formed by making the verb *sein* into a noun, by placing *das* before it. The verb *sein* is the "infinitive" of "is," which is all too familiar to us. We do not need a lecture on nihilism and its frequent use of the noun *das Sein* in order to perceive at once that with every remark we utter we *still* more frequently and continuously, in every usage of the word "is," say *Sein*. "Is" drifts about as the most threadbare word in language, although it sustains all saying, and not only in the sense of spoken language. The "is" speaks even in every tacit comportment toward beings. Everywhere, even where we do not speak, we still comport ourselves toward beings as such and to the sort of thing that "is," that is in a particular way, that is not yet or is no longer, or that simply is not.

The uniformity of this used-up though often unused "is" conceals a rarely considered abundance behind the sameness of the sound and shape of the word.* We say, "This man is from Schwabenland"; "This book is yours"; "The enemy is in retreat"; "Red is portside"; "God is"; "There is a flood in China"; "The cup is silver"; "The earth is"; "The farmer is (as we say in dialect) afield"; "The potato bug is in the patch"; "The lecture is in Room 5"; "The dog is in the garden"; "This is a devil of a man"; "Above all peaks / is repose."

In each case, the "is" has a different meaning and range in what it says. "The man is from Schwabenland" means that he *comes from* there. "The book is yours" signifies: *belongs* to you. "The enemy is in retreat" says that he *has set out* in retreat. "Red is portside" means that portside is what the color *signifies*. "God is"; we experience Him as *really present*. "There is a flood in China"; it *prevails*. "The cup is of silver"; it *consists* of. "The farmer is afield"; he *has taken up his sojourn there*. "The potato bug is in the patch"; *has spread* there in its harmfulness. "The lecture is in Room 5"; *will take place*. "The dog is in the garden"; *is rooting about*. "This is a devil of a man"; he *behaves* like someone possessed by a demon. "Above all peaks / is repose"; repose *"is found"? "will take place"? "comes to rest"? "prevails"?* or *"lies"?* or *"holds sway"?* No paraphrase will work here. Nonetheless, the same "is" speaks here—simple, and at the same time irreplaceable, uttered in those few lines that Goethe wrote in pencil on the windowframe of a wooden hut on the Kickelhahn at Ilmenau (see the letter to Zelter, September 4, 1831).†

Yet it is remarkable that in explaining the familiar "is" we should waver and hesitate before this phrase of Goethe's, and finally give it up

---

* Many of the following examples—and the issue they are all meant to illustrate—derive from Heidegger's 1935 lecture course, "Introduction to Metaphysics." See *Einführung in die Metaphysik*, p. 68; English translation, pp. 74–75.

† Goethe's poem, written on the evening of September 6, 1780, and later designated as a second "Wanderer's Nocturne," reads as follows:

entirely and simply repeat the words once again. "Above all peaks / is repose." We attempt no explanation of the "is," not because it would be too complicated, difficult, or indeed hopeless to understand, but because the "is" is so simply spoken here, *still more* simply than every other kind of familiar "is" that is interspersed carelessly and constantly in our everyday speech. But what is simple in the "is" of Goethe's poem is far removed from a void indeterminacy that cannot be grasped. The simplicity of rare abundance speaks in the poem. The series of different statements in which we were able to interpret immediately each "is" from a particular point of view also testifies to this same abundance, although in a different way and only as a rough indication. The uniformity of "is" and "to be" thus proves to be a gross illusion that simply fastens on the identical sound and spelling of the word. Nor is it enough anymore to offer here the assurance that "is" belongs among the "multivalent" words; for it is not merely a question

---

        Über allen Gipfeln
        Ist Ruh,
        In allen Wipfeln
        Spürest du
        Kaum einen Hauch;
        Die Vögelein schweigen im Walde.
        Warte nur, balde
        Ruhest du auch.

In translation:

        Above all peaks
        Is repose,
        In the treetops
        You trace
        Scarcely a breath;
        The songbirds are silent in the wood.
        Only wait, for soon
        You too will repose.

See the commentary by Erich Trunz and Elizabeth M. Wilkinson in Goethe, *Gedichte* (Munich: C. H. Beck, 1974) pp. 533–34; the poem itself appears on p. 142.

Goethe's letter to Zelter of September 4, 1831, tells of his return that summer to the hut, where he found the inscription he had made a half-century earlier. "After so many years one beheld: the enduring, and the obliterated. What had gone well returned to cheer me, what had gone awry was forgotten, overcome." See *Goethes Briefe* (Hamburg: Chr. Wegner, 1967), IV, 442.

Being as the Void and as Abundance

of varied meanings. An abundance in the sayability of Being is indicated that first makes possible what we, looking at it logically and grammatically, tend to account for in terms of "multivalence." What is under discussion here are not the words *is* and *to be,* but what they say, what comes to words in them: Being. Once more we stop at the same point in our meditation: "Being," indefinite and trivialized—and yet understandable and understood. We could put it to the test by taking a poll to establish what you listeners thought of each time the "is" was spoken; but these results would only confirm that in the "is" "Being" passes like a fleeting echo, while at the same time touching us in some respect, and saying something essential—perhaps what is most essential.

However, should we infer from the many meanings and many possible interpretations of the "is" an abundance of essence in Being? Does not the manifoldness of the "is" stem from the fact that in the statements just quoted various kinds of beings are contextually meant: the man, the book, the enemy, God, China, the cup, the earth, the farmer, the dog? Must we not rather conclude the opposite of all this: Because the "is" and "Being" are in themselves indeterminate and empty, they can lie ready for various kinds of filling? The putative manifoldness of definite meanings in the "is" therefore proves to be the opposite of what was supposed to be shown. Being must keep its meaning. If we restrict ourselves exclusively to the literal meaning of the words *is* and *to be,* then even this literal meaning must with all its utter vacuity and indeterminacy nonetheless have the kind of univocity that ing. If we restrict ourselves exclusively to the literal meaning of the words *is* and *to be,* then even this literal meaning must with all its utter vacuity and indeterminacy nonetheless have the kind of univocity that of itself permits a transformation into manifoldness. But the celebrated "universal" significance of "Being" is not the reified emptiness of a huge receptacle into which everything capable of transformation can be thrown. What misleads us in the direction of this notion is our long-accustomed way of thinking that thinks "Being" as the most universal determination of all, and that therefore can admit the manifold only as the sort of thing that fills the vast empty shell of the most universal concept.

Instead, we wish to concentrate on something else. We think "Being" and the "is" in a peculiar indeterminacy and *at the same time* experience them in a fullness. This Janus-head [*Doppelgesicht*] of "Being" might perhaps put us on the trail of Being's essence, and in any case prevent our employing abstraction, the simplest of all instruments of thought, to explain what is most essential in everything to be thought and experienced. But now we must also elucidate the duplicity of "Being" beyond a mere reference to it, without succumbing to the danger of substituting for abstraction an equally popular instrument of thought as a final answer, to wit, dialectic. Dialectic is always introduced the moment opposition is mentioned.

Being is what is emptiest and at the same time it is abundance, out of which all beings, known and experienced, or unknown and yet to be experienced, are endowed each with the essential form of its own *individual* Being.

Being is most universal, encountered in every being, and is therefore most common; it has lost every distinction, or never possessed any. At the same time, Being is the most singular, whose uniqueness cannot be attained by any being whatever. Over against every being that might stand out, there is always another just like it; that is, another being, no matter how varied their forms may be. But Being has no counterpart. What stands over against Being is the nothing, and perhaps even that is still in essence subject to Being and to Being alone.

Being is most intelligible, so that we pay no heed to the effortless way we maintain ourselves in the comprehension of it. The most intelligible is at the same time what is least comprehended and is apparently incomprehensible. On what basis would we comprehend it? What "is there" outside of it from which we could attribute a determination to it? The nothing is least of all suitable for a determining, because it "is" indeterminate, "is" indeterminateness itself. The most intelligible defies all intelligibility.

Being is most in use; it is what we call on in every action and from every standpoint. For we everywhere hold ourselves in being and comport ourselves toward beings. Being is used up and yet at the same time is unthought in its advent at every moment.

Being is what is most reliable; it never unsettles us with doubt. We

Being as the Void and as Abundance

occasionally wonder whether this or that being is or is not; we often consider whether a particular being is one way or another. Being, without which we can never wonder about beings in any respect whatsoever, offers us a reliance whose reliability cannot be surpassed anywhere. And yet Being offers us no ground and no basis—as beings do—to which we can turn, on which we can build, and to which we can cling. Being is the rejection [*Ab-sage*] of the role of such grounding; it renounces all grounding, is abyssal [*ab-gründig*].

Being is the most forgotten, so boundlessly forgotten that the very forgottenness is sucked into its own vortex. We all habitually hasten toward beings; scarcely anyone ponders Being. If he does, then the emptiness of what is most universal and intelligible absolves him from the commitment he had momentarily considered making. But what is most forgotten is at the same time most in remembering, which alone allows us to enter and inhabit the past, present, and future.

Being is the most said, not only because the "is" and all the forms of the verb "to be" are perhaps most often expressed, but because in *every* verb, even when its conjugated forms do not use the word "Being," Being is nonetheless said. Every verb, and not just every verb but also every substantive and adjective, all words and articulations of words, say Being. What is most said is at the same time the most reticent in the special sense that it keeps its essence silent, perhaps is reticence itself. No matter how loudly and how often we say "is" and name "Being," such saying and that name are perhaps only seemingly proper names for what is to be named and said. For every word as such is a word "of" Being, in fact a word *"of"* Being not only insofar as it talks "about" Being or "of" Being but a word "of" Being in the sense that Being expresses itself in each word and precisely in that way keeps its essence silent.

Being reveals itself to us in a variety of oppositions that cannot be coincidental, since even a mere listing of them points to their inner connection: Being is both utterly void and most abundant, most universal and most unique, most intelligible and most resistant to every concept, most in use and yet to come, most reliable and most abyssal, most forgotten and most remembering, most said and most reticent.

But are these, rightly considered, opposites in the essence of Being itself? Are they not opposites merely in the way *we* comport ourselves toward Being, in representing and understanding, in using and relying on, in retaining (forgetting) and saying? But even *if* they were opposites *only* in our relation to Being, we would still have attained what we were seeking: the determination of our relation to Being (not merely to beings).

That relation is revealed as discordant. The question still remains whether the discordancy of our relation to Being lies in us or in Being itself; the answer to that question may once again decide something important about the essence of the relation.

Still more pressing than the question of whether the opposites identified lie in the essence of Being itself, or whether they merely arise out of *our* discordant relation to Being, *or whether this relation of ours to Being in fact springs from Being itself,* since it abides by Being—more pressing than these indubitably decisive questions is the following: Viewed with respect to matters as they stand, *is* our relation to Being a discordant one? Do we comport ourselves toward Being so discordantly that the discord completely dominates *us;* that is to say, our comportment toward beings? We must answer in the negative. In our comportment, we merely stand on one side of the opposites: Being is for us the emptiest, most universal, most intelligible, most used, most reliable, most forgotten, most said. We scarcely even heed it, and therefore do not know it *as* an opposition to something else.

Being remains something neutral for us, and for that reason we scarcely pay attention to the differentiation of Being and beings, although we establish all our comportment toward beings on the basis of it. But it is not only we today who stand outside that still unexperienced discord of the relation to Being. Such "standing outside" and "not knowing" is characteristic of all metaphysics, since for metaphysics Being necessarily remains the most universal, the most intelligible. In the scope of Being metaphysics ponders only the multifaceted and multilayered universals of various realms of beings.

Throughout the whole history of metaphysics, from the time Plato interpreted the beingness of beings as *idea* up to the time Nietzsche defined Being as value, Being has been self-evidently well preserved as the *a priori* to which man as a rational creature comports himself.

Being as the Void and as Abundance

Because the relation to Being has, as it were, dissolved in indifference, the *differentiation* of Being and beings also cannot become questionable for metaphysics.

By this state of affairs, we first come to know the metaphysical character of today's historical epoch. "Today," reckoned neither by the calendar nor in terms of world-historical occurrences, is determined by the period in the history of metaphysics that is most our own: it is the metaphysical determination of historical mankind in the age of Nietzsche's metaphysics.

Our epoch reveals a particularly casual matter-of-factness with respect to the truth of beings as a whole. Being is either explained in the conventional Christian theological explanation of the world, or else being as a whole—the world—is defined by an appeal to "ideas" and "values." "Ideas" reminds us of the beginning of Western metaphysics in Plato. "Values" intimates a reference to the end of metaphysics in Nietzsche. But "ideas" and "values" are not thought any further in their essence and in their essential provenance. The appeal to "ideas" and "values" and their positing constitute the most familiar and most intelligible framework for interpreting the world and for guiding one's life. Such indifference to Being in the midst of the greatest passion for beings testifies to the thoroughly *metaphysical* character of the age. The essential consequence of this situation is revealed in the fact that historical decisions are now consciously, willfully, and totally transferred from the separate areas of earlier cultural activities—politics, science, art, society—into the realm of *Weltanschauung*. *Weltanschauung* is that configuration of modern metaphysics which becomes inevitable when its fulfillment in the conditionless begins. The consequence is a peculiar uniformity of our heretofore multifarious Western European history, a uniformity that announces itself metaphysically in the coupling of "idea" and "value" as the standard paraphernalia for the interpretation of the world in terms of *Weltanschauung*.

Through the coupling of idea with value, the character of Being and its differentiation from beings vanishes from the essence of the Idea. That here and there in learned circles and within the scholarly tradition there is talk of Being, of "ontology" and metaphysics, is merely an echo in which there no longer resides any history-making force. The power of *Weltanschauung* has taken possession of the essence of metaphysics. That is to say, what is proper to all metaphysics, the fact that the differentiation of Being and beings which sustains metaphysics itself essentially and necessarily remains an unquestioned matter, a matter of indifference for it, this fact now comes to be what *distinguishes* metaphysics as *Weltanschauung*. This is the basis of the fact that complete, absolute, undisturbed, and undistracted dominion over beings can develop only with the beginning of the fulfillment of metaphysics.

The age of the fulfillment of metaphysics—which we descry when we think through the basic features of Nietzsche's metaphysics—prompts us to consider to what extent we first find ourselves in the history of Being. It also prompts us to consider—prior to our finding ourselves—the extent to which we must experience history as the release of Being into machination, a release that Being itself sends, so as to allow its truth to become essential for man out of man's belonging to it.*

---

* *Die Loslassung des Seins in die Machenschaft.* The "machination" meant here is not a conspiracy of Being, although the word does suggest the duplicity of the Janus-head. The "making," contriving, or planning referred to is that of reckoning and calculative thought in the age of "machine" technology. Heidegger concludes his lecture course on nihilism by invoking the possibility (fully discussed in "The Question Concerning Technology," 1953) that meditation on our technical doings—as a way of revealing beings—may compel a reflection on *alētheia* and on the history of Being.

Part Two

NIHILISM AS DETERMINED BY THE HISTORY OF BEING

Nietzsche's acknowledgment of the being as the most elemental factor (as will to power) does not conduct him to the thought of Being as such. Nor does he attain that thought by way of an interpretation of Being as a "necessary value." Nor does the thought of the "eternal return of the same" become the impetus to ponder eternity as a moment arising from the precipitance of luminous presencing, recurrence as the manner of such presencing, and both in accord with their essential provenance arising out of in-cipient "Time."

When Nietzsche clings to his acknowledgment of will to power in the sense of the "ultimate fact" as his fundamental philosophical insight, he acquiesces in the description of Being as one of those beings that are distinguished according to the genus "fact." Factuality as such is not pondered. Nietzsche's adherence to his fundamental insight is precisely what blocks him from the path that leads to thinking Being as such. The fundamental insight does not see the way.

In Nietzsche's thought, however, the question of Being itself cannot even be raised, because Nietzsche has already given an answer to the question of Being (in its sole known sense, as the Being of beings). "Being" is a value. "Being" means the being as such; that is, the permanent.

However extensively and from whatever point of view we prefer to interrogate Nietzsche, we do not find that his thought thinks Being from its truth as the essential occurrence of Being itself, in which Being is transformed and whereby it loses its name.

The meditation we have now engaged in gives rise to the general suspicion that we assume Nietzsche's thinking ought to think Being as such in its ground, that it neglects to do so and is therefore inadequate. We have nothing like that in mind. Rather, it is simply a matter of bringing ourselves from our thinking toward the question of the truth of Being into proximity to Nietzsche's metaphysics, in order to experience his thought on the basis of the supreme fidelity of his thinking. It is far from the intention of our effort to disseminate a perhaps more correct version of Nietzsche's philosophy. We are thinking his metaphysics solely in order to be able to inquire into what is worthy of question: *In Nietzsche's metaphysics, which for the first time experiences and thinks nihilism as such, is nihilism overcome or is it not?*

By asking whether or not it accomplishes the overcoming of nihilism, we are passing judgment on Nietzsche's metaphysics. However, we will let even this judgment go. We are simply asking, and addressing the question to ourselves, whether and how the proper essence of nihilism is revealed in Nietzsche's metaphysical experiencing and overcoming of nihilism. What we are asking is whether in the *metaphysical* concept of nihilism its essence can be experienced, whether its essence can be grasped at all, or whether that might not require a different rigor of saying.

In such questioning, we are of course supposing that the nothing exercises its essence in what we call *nihilism,* specifically in the sense that basically there "is" nothing to beings as such. We are in no way subjecting Nietzsche's thinking to an inappropriate or excessive claim. Insofar as Nietzsche experiences nihilism as the history of the devaluation of the highest values, and thinks of the overcoming of nihilism as a countermovement in the form of the revaluation of all previous values, and does so in terms of the expressly acknowledged principle of valuation, he is directly thinking *Being;* that is, beings as such; and in this way he understands nihilism mediately as a history in which something happens with beings as such.

Strictly speaking, it is not *we* who impute something to someone else; rather, we place *ourselves* under the claim of language. Language demands that in the word *nihilism* we think the *nihil,* the nothing, simultaneously with the thought that in beings as such something transpires. Language demands not only that we correctly comprehend mere words as lexical artifacts, but that we heed the matter expressed in and with the word. We submit ourselves to the claim of the name *nihilism* to think a history in which the being as such stands. In its own way, the name *nihilism* names the *Being* of beings.

Nietzsche's metaphysics is based on the explicitly implemented, fundamental insight that the being as such *is,* and that only the being that is acknowledged in this way grants thought a guarantee of its possibility as *being* thinking, no matter what it may be thinking about. Nietzsche's fundamental experience says that the being *is* a being as will to power in the mode of the eternal recurrence of the same. As a being in this form, it is *not* nothing. Consequently, nihilism, to the degree there is supposed to be nothing to beings as such, is excluded from the foundations of such metaphysics. Thus—it would seem—metaphysics has overcome nihilism.

Nietzsche acknowledges the being as such. Yet, in such an acknowledgement, does he also recognize the Being of beings, and indeed It itself, *Being,* specifically *as Being?* He does not. Being is determined as value and is consequently explained in terms of beings as a condition posited by the will to power, by the "being" as such. Being is not acknowledged as Being. Such "acknowledging" means allowing Being to reign in all its questionableness from the point of view of its essential provenance; it means persevering in the question of Being. But that means to reflect on the origin of presencing and permanence and thus to keep thinking open to the possibility that *"Being," on its way to the "as Being," might abandon its own essence in favor of a more primordial determination.* Any discussion of "Being itself" always remains interrogative.

For representing, which in value thinking aims at validity, Being is already outside the horizon of the *questionability* of the "as Being." There "is" nothing to Being as such: Being—a *nihil.* However, if we grant that beings are thanks to Being, and that Being never is thanks to beings; and if we also grant that Being cannot be nothing in the face of beings, then does not nihilism also, or perhaps first of all, put itself properly into play where not only is there nothing to beings but also nothing to Being? Indeed. Where there is simply nothing to beings, one might find nihilism, but one will not encounter its *essence,* which first appears where the *nihil* concerns Being itself.

The essence of nihilism is the history in which there is nothing to Being itself.

Our thinking, or better expressed, our reckoning and accounting according to the principle of noncontradition, can hardly wait to offer the observation that a history which is, but in which there is nothing to Being itself, presents us with an absolute absurdity. But perhaps Being itself does not trouble itself about the contradictions of our thought. If

Being itself had to be what it is by grace of a lack of contradiction in human thought, then it would be denied in its own proper essence.

Absurdity is impotent against Being itself, and therefore also against what happens to it in its destiny—that within metaphysics there is nothing to Being as such.

More essential than reckoning with absurdities is finding out to what extent there is nothing to Being itself in Nietzsche's metaphysics.

Therefore, we say that Nietzsche's metaphysics is nihilism proper. But does Nietzsche need us with our hindsight to calculate such a thing against his thinking? In describing the way Nietzsche himself sees the various forms and stages of nihilism,* we touched on the concluding sentence of note 14 (dated 1887) from *The Will to Power*, which runs: " 'Nihilism' as ideal of *the supreme powerfulness* of spirit, of superabundant life—partly destructive, partly ironic." However, the "recapitulation," which has been cited already, begins (WM, 617): "To *stamp* Becoming with the character of Being—that is the supreme *will to power.*"

Such thinking—that is, thinking *Becoming* as the *Being* of the totality of beings, thinking "will to power" in terms of the "eternal recurrence of the same"—is what the spirit of Nietzsche's metaphysics achieves as the ideal of its supreme powerfulness. It therefore corresponds to the supreme form of "nihilism." In that Nietzsche's metaphysics thinks a complete revaluation of all previous values, it completes the devaluation of the highest values hitherto. In this way, it belongs "destructively" within the course of the prior history of nihilism. But insofar as the revaluation is carried out expressly *in terms of the principle* of valuation, such nihilism pretends to be what it no longer is in *its own* sense: as "destructive," it is "ironic." Nietzsche understands his metaphysics as the most extreme nihilism; indeed, in such a way that it is no longer even a nihilism.

---

* The reference here is not to the lecture course on "European Nihilism" but is presumably to the essay "Nietzsche's Metaphysics," which also refers to WM, 14 and 617. (Cf. NII, 281–82, 288, and 327, included in Volume III of the present series.) The references below to "justification" and, indeed, to all five "major rubrics" of Nietzsche's metaphysics seem to refer to that essay.

We have said, however, that Nietzsche's metaphysics is nihilism proper. This implies not only that Nietzsche's nihilism does not overcome nihilism but also that it can never overcome it. For it is precisely in the positing of new values from the will to power, by which and through which Nietzsche believes he will overcome nihilism, that nihilism proper first proclaims that there is nothing to Being itself, which has now become a value. As a result, Nietzsche experiences the historical movement of nihilism as a history of the devaluation of the highest values hitherto. On the same basis, he represents overcoming as revaluation and carries it through, not only in a new valuation but also in such a way that he experiences will to power as the principle of the new—and ultimately of all—valuation. Value thinking is now elevated into a principle. Being itself, as a matter of principle, is not admitted as Being. According to its own principle, in this metaphysics there is *nothing* to Being. How can what is worthy of thought be given here with Being itself, namely, Being as—Being? How could an overcoming of nihilism occur here, or even make itself felt?

Consequently, Nietzsche's metaphysics is not an overcoming of nihilism. It is the ultimate entanglement in nihilism. Through value thinking in terms of will to power, it of course continues to acknowledge beings as such. But, by tying itself to an interpretation of Being as value, it simultaneously binds itself to the impossibility of even casting an inquiring glance at Being as Being. By means of the entanglement of nihilism in itself, nihilism first becomes thoroughly complete in what it is. Such utterly completed, perfect nihilism is the fulfillment of nihilism proper.

But if the essence of nihilism is the history in which there is nothing to Being itself, then neither can the essence of nihilism be experienced and thought as long as in thinking and for thinking there is indeed nothing to Being itself. Fulfilled nihilism definitively shuts itself off from the possibility of ever being able to think and to know the essence of nihilism. Is this not to say that the essence of nihilism remains closed to Nietzsche's thought? How dare we assert such a thing?

Nietzsche clearly asks, "What does nihilism mean?" and he answers succinctly, *"That the uppermost values devaluate themselves"* (WM, 2).

No less clearly and succinctly, however, the note shows that Nietzsche asks about what he experiences as nihilism in terms of an "interpretation," and that he interprets what is thus examined from the viewpoint of his value thinking. Consequently, Nietzsche's question about the meaning of nihilism is a question that for its part still thinks nihilistically. Even in his very manner of questioning, therefore, Nietzsche does not attain to the realm of what the question of the essence of nihilism seeks; that is, *whether* and *in what way* nihilism is a history that applies to Being itself.

However, insofar as for Nietzsche nihilism professes to be an occurrence of devaluation and decline, of enervation and death, Nietzsche's experience appears at least to confirm the negativity in nihilism. Instead of a "no" to beings as such, Nietzsche demands a "yes." He contemplates an overcoming of nihilism. But how is that possible as long as the essence of nihilism is not experienced?

Hence, *before* any overcoming, it is necessary to have the kind of confrontation with nihilism that will for the first time bring to light the essence of nihilism. If we grant that there is some way in which human thought is to participate in that confrontation with the essence of nihilism, which concerns Being itself, then such thinking must for its part first be stunned by the essence of nihilism. Therefore, with regard to the kind of metaphysics which first of all experiences and thinks nihilism as a general historical movement, but which at the same time for us begins to be the fulfillment of nihilism proper, we must ask in what the phenomenon of nihilism proper, and specifically its fulfillment, which is of immediate historical concern to us, has its ground.

Nietzsche's metaphysics is nihilistic insofar as it is value thinking, and insofar as the latter is grounded in will to power as the principle of all valuation. Nietzsche's metaphysics consequently becomes the fulfillment of nihilism proper, because it is the metaphysics of will to power. But, if that is so, then metaphysics as the metaphysics of will to power is indeed the ground of the *fulfillment* of nihilism proper, although it can in no way be the ground of proper nihilism *as such*. That ground, though still incomplete, must already reign in the *essence* of prior metaphysics, which is of course not the metaphysics of will to power, although it does experience beings as such and as a whole as *will.* Even if the essence of willing which is thought here is obscure in many respects, perhaps even necessarily obscure, we can see that, from the metaphysics of Schelling and Hegel, back beyond Kant and Leibniz to Descartes, the being as such is at bottom experienced as *will.*

Of course, that does not mean that the subjective experience of human will is transposed onto beings as a whole. Rather, it indicates the very reverse, that man first of all comes to know himself as a willing subject in an essential sense on the basis of a still unelucidated experience of beings as such in the sense of a willing that has yet to be thought. Insight into these connections is indispensable for an experience of the history of nihilism proper, an experience of its essential history. Those connections cannot be explained here, however. For the moment, that task is not a pressing one. What was said about nihilism proper in describing Nietzsche's metaphysics as a fulfillment of nihilism must have already awakened thoughtful readers to another supposition: that the ground of nihilism proper is neither the metaphysics of will to power nor the metaphysics of will, but simply metaphysics itself.

Metaphysics as metaphysics is nihilism proper. The essence of nihilism *is* historically as metaphysics, and the metaphysics of Plato is no less nihilistic than that of Nietzsche. In the former, the essence of nihilism is merely concealed; in the latter, it comes completely to appearance. Nonetheless, it never shows its true face, either on the basis of or within metaphysics.

These are disturbing statements. For metaphysics determines the history of the Western era. Western humankind, in all its relations with beings, and even to itself, is in every respect sustained and guided by metaphysics. In the equation of metaphysics and nihilism one does not know which is greater—the arbitrariness, or the degree of condemnation of our entire history heretofore.

But in the meantime we should also have noticed that our thinking has still scarcely responded to the essence of nihilism proper, let alone thought it adequately enough for us to reflect meditatively on the statements made about metaphysics and nihilism, so that afterward we might pass judgment on them. If metaphysics as such is nihilism proper, while the latter, in accord with its essence, is incapable of thinking its own essence, how could metaphysics itself ever encounter its own essence? Metaphysical representations of metaphysics necessarily lag behind that essence. The metaphysics of metaphysics never attains to its essence.

But what does *essence* mean here? We are not adopting the idea of "essentialities" from the word. In the name *essence* [*Wesen*] we perceive what occurs essentially [*das Wesende*]. What is "the essence" of metaphysics? How does it essentially unfold? How does the relationship to Being reign in it? That is the question. Our attempt to answer it in the radius of our meditation on Nietzsche's metaphysics is necessarily inadequate. Furthermore, insofar as our thinking proceeds from metaphysics, our attempt always remains tied to what is questionable. All the same, we must hazard a few steps. Let us concentrate on the question which Aristotle expressed as the enduring question for thought: What is the being?

Every question specifies as a question the breadth and nature of the answer it is looking for. At the same time, it circumscribes the range of possibilities for answering. In order to ponder the question of metaphysics adequately, we first of all need to consider it as a question, without considering the answers that have devolved on it in the course of the history of metaphysics.

In the question "What is the being?" we ask about the being as such. The being as a being *is* such thanks to Being. In the question "What is the being as such?" we are thinking of Being, and specifically of the Being of beings, that is to say, of what beings are. What they are—namely, the beings—is answered by their what-being, *to ti estin*. Plato defines the whatness of a being as *idea* (see *Plato's Doctrine of Truth*). The whatness of being, the *essentia* of *ens*, we also call "the essence." But that is no incidental and harmless identification. Rather, in it is hidden the fact that the Being of beings—that is to say, the way in which beings essentially occur—is thought in terms of whatness. "Essence" in the sense of *essentia* (whatness) is already a metaphysical interpretation of "essence," which asks about the "what" of beings as such. And, of course, "essence" here is always thought as the essence of beings. The Being of beings is examined *in terms of* beings as what is thought *toward* beings. Thought as what? As the *genos* and the *koinon,* as that from which every being in its being thus-and-so receives the common What.

Because the being is interrogated as such, it is also experienced with respect to the simple fact that *it is*. Therefore, a further question at once arises from the question of what the being as such is: Among all beings as beings, which one most nearly corresponds to what is defined as the What of the being? The being that corresponds to whatness, the *essentia* of beings as such, is what truly exists. In the question "What is the being?" the truly existing is thought at the same time with respect to *essentia* and *existentia*. In that way, the being is determined *as such;* that is, determined as to *what* it is and as to the fact *that* it is. *Essentia* and *existentia* of the *ens qua ens* answer the question "What is the being as such?" They define the being in its Being.

Accordingly, how does metaphysics comport itself to Being itself? Does metaphysics think Being itself? No, it never does. It thinks *the being* with a view to Being. Being is first and last what answers the question in which the being is always what is interrogated. What is interrogated is not Being as such. Hence, Being itself remains unthought in metaphysics, not just incidentally, but in accord with metaphysics' own inquiry. By thinking the being as such, the question *and* the answer necessarily think on the basis of Being; but they do not think about Being itself, precisely because in the most proper sense of the metaphysical question Being is thought as the being in its Being. Inasmuch as metaphysics thinks the being on the basis of Being, it does not think Being *as Being.*

To think on the basis of Being does not yet mean going back to Being, thoughtfully recalling it in its truth. Being remains unthought in the kind of thinking that, as metaphysical, passes for thinking pure and simple. That Being itself remains unthought in metaphysics as such is a remaining-unthought of a peculiar, distinctive, and unique kind.

The metaphysical question does not extend to Being itself. How could we expect it to ponder Being itself? However, dare we say that the question of metaphysics does not go far enough in its questioning, that it does not go far enough beyond beings? We leave that question open, simply because we have not yet decided whether or not metaphysics might in fact determine Being as such. We should not forget the characterization of Being which from the beginning of metaphysics and throughout its history is thought under the subsequent term *a priori*. The term says that Being is prior to beings. But in that way Being is thought precisely and solely on the basis of the being and for the being, whether metaphysics prefers to explain the *a priori* as materially prior, or as something precursory in the order of knowledge and of the conditions of the object.

As long as the Being of beings is thought as the *a priori*, that determination itself prevents any reflection on Being as Being from perhaps discovering how far Being as Being enters into the *a priori* relation to beings, whether that relation merely chances on and accompanies Being, or whether Being itself is the relation, and what Being and relation mean. That every metaphysics, even the reversal of Platonism, thinks the Being of beings as the *a priori*, merely certifies that metaphysics as such leaves Being unthought.

Of course, metaphysics acknowledges that beings are not without Being. But scarcely has it said so when it again transforms Being into a being, whether it be the supreme being in the sense of the first cause, whether it be the distinctive being in the sense of the subject of subjectivity, as the condition of the possibility of all objectivity, or whether, as a consequence of the coherence of both these fundamental conditions of Being in beings, it be the determination of the supreme being as the Absolute in the sense of unconditioned subjectivity.

The grounding of Being—which is barely remembered—in the utmost being among beings proceeds from the metaphysical question about the being as such. It discovers that beings are. The fact that Being essentially occurs brushes by it. But the latter experience indiscernibly attains the path of the metaphysical question which in Leibniz' subsequent formulation inquires, "Why are there beings at all, and why not rather nothing?"*

---

* Leibniz' formulation appears in section 7 of *The Principles of Nature and of Grace, Founded on Reason* (1714), in the translation of Robert Latta (revised by Philip P. Wiener) as follows:

7. Thus far we have spoken as simple *physicists:* now we must advance to *metaphysics*, making use of the *great principle*, little employed in general, which teaches

This question inquires into the first cause and highest existent ground of beings. It is the question of the *theion,* a question that had already arisen at the beginning of metaphysics in Plato and Aristotle; that is to say, arisen from the essence of metaphysics. Because metaphysics, thinking the being as such, is approached by Being but thinks it on the basis of and with reference to beings, metaphysics must therefore say *(legein)* the *theion* in the sense of the highest existent ground. Metaphysics is inherently theology. It is theology to the extent that it says the being as being, the *on hēi on.* Ontology is simultaneously and necessarily theology. In order to recognize the fundamentally ontotheological character of metaphysics,† we do not need to orient ourselves toward the purely scholastic concept of metaphysics. On the contrary, the scholastic concept is merely a doctrinal formulation of the essence of metaphysics thought metaphysically.

The names *ontology* and *theology* as they are used here do not possess the identical senses they have in the scholastic concept of meta-

---

that *nothing happens without a sufficient reason;* that is to say, that nothing happens without its being possible for him who should sufficiently understand things, to give a reason sufficient to determine why it is so and not otherwise. This principle laid down, the first question which should rightly be asked, will be, *Why is there something rather than nothing?* For nothing is simpler and easier than something. Further, suppose that things must exist, we must be able to give a reason *why they must exist so* and not otherwise.

Heidegger employs the first "Why?" question at crucial junctures in a number of his essays and lectures, for example, as the culmination of "What Is Metaphysics?" (1929; cf. also the 1949 "Introduction" to the inaugural lecture, *Wegmarken,* p. 210) and as the opening question of *Introduction to Metaphysics* (1935). I have altered the traditional English translation to capture the peculiar stress on the *potius quam,* or *plutôt que,* which Heidegger during his lectures on Leibniz at Marburg in 1928 found to be of the greatest importance. See *Metaphysische Anfangsgründe der Logik im Ausgang von Leibniz,* p. 141 and "Vom Wesen des Grundes," *Wegmarken,* pp. 65 and 68.

† Cf. Heidegger's 1957 lecture, "The Onto-Theo-Logical Constitution of Metaphysics," in Martin Heidegger, *Identität und Differenz* (Pfullingen: G. Neske, 1957), pp. 31–67; English translation by Joan Stambaugh in *Identity and Difference* (New York: Harper & Row, 1969), pp. 42–74. The Harper & Row edition also reprints the German text, pp. 107–43. In this lecture, Heidegger considers Hegel—especially the Hegel of *The Science of Logic*—as the apotheosis of ontotheology. In the antecedent Nietzsche lectures, the phrase is associated principally with Leibniz. Recall the delightful precursor of Heidegger's phrase in Voltaire's *Candide,* where it is averred of Pangloss that "he taught *la métaphysico-théologo-cosmolonigologie."*

physics. Rather, "ontology" defines the being as such with respect to its *essentia*, and is found in psychology, cosmology, and theology. Yet "theology" too, rightly thought, reigns in both cosmology and psychology (or anthropology) as well as in *metaphysica generalis*.

As an *ontology*, even Nietzsche's metaphysics is *at the same time* theology, although it seems far removed from scholastic metaphysics. The ontology of beings as such thinks *essentia* as will to power. Such ontology thinks the *existentia* of beings as such and as a whole theologically as the eternal recurrence of the same. Such metaphysical theology is of course a negative theology of a peculiar kind. Its negativity is revealed in the expression "God is dead." That is an expression not of atheism but of ontotheology, in that metaphysics in which nihilism proper is fulfilled.

But if metaphysics as such does not think Being itself because it thinks Being in the sense of the being as such, ontology and theology, on the basis of their mutual dependence on each other, both must leave Being itself unthought. Theology derives the *essentia* of the being from ontology. Ontology, whether knowingly or not, transposes the being with respect to its *existentia*, that is, as what exists, into the first cause [*Grund*], which theology goes on to represent. The onto-theological essence of metaphysics thinks the being from the viewpoint of *essentia* and *existentia*. These determinations of the Being of beings are as it were thoughtfully intimated, but not thought in terms of Being itself, neither separately nor both together in their difference. That difference and everything it encompasses, as unthought, suddenly becomes determinative for metaphysical thinking—as though it had fallen out of the sky. Maybe it did. But then we would need to consider what that means with regard to Being itself.

The manifold yet scarcely explicated *coherence* of ontology and theology in the *essence* of metaphysics is enunciated with particular clarity where metaphysics, following the thrust of its own name, identifies the fundamental trait by which it knows the being as such. That is *transcendence*.

On the one hand, the word *transcendence* designates the transition of the being into what it is as a being in its whatness (its qualification). The surpassment to *essentia* is transcendence as the transcendental.

Kant, by critically limiting the being to an object of experience, equated the transcendental with the objectivity of the object. On the other hand, however, transcendence at the same time means the transcendent, which in the sense of the first existent cause of the being as existent surpasses the being, and in surmounting it looms over it in the perfect plenitude of what is essential. Ontology represents transcendence as the transcendental. Theology represents transcendence as the transcendent.

The unitary ambiguity named by transcendence and grounded in the—in terms of its provenance—obscure differentiation of *essentia* and *existentia* reflects the onto-theological essence of metaphysics. By virtue of its essence, metaphysics thinks the being by surpassing it transcendentally-transcendently, but only in order to represent the being itself; that is, to return to it again. Being is, as it were, skimmed over representationally in the transcendental-transcendent act of surpassing. The thinking that surpasses always passes over Being itself in thought, not as an oversight, but in such a way that it does not enter into Being as such, into what is questionable about its truth. Metaphysical thought does not enter into Being itself because it has *already thought* Being, namely as the being, insofar as the being is.

Being itself necessarily remains unthought in metaphysics. Metaphysics is a history in which there is essentially nothing to Being itself: *metaphysics as such is nihilism proper.*

The experience of the nihilistic essence of metaphysics that we have now indicated is still not sufficient for thinking the proper essence of metaphysics in an essentially correct way. This first of all requires that we experience the essence of metaphysics on the basis of Being itself. But, supposing that our thought is on the way toward this experience, approaching it from afar, then it must first of all have learned what it means to say that Being itself remains unthought in metaphysics. Perhaps that is all our thought has to learn in advance.

Being remains unthought in metaphysics because metaphysics thinks the being as such. What does it mean to say that the being as such is thought? It implies that the being itself comes to the fore. It stands in the light. The being is illumined, is itself unconcealed. The being stands in unconcealment. The latter is the essence of truth, which appears at the outset and then immediately disappears again.

In what truth does the being stand, if it is thought as the being in metaphysics? Obviously, metaphysics itself is the truth of the being as such. What is the essential mode of such unconcealment? Does metaphysics ever say anything about the essence of truth, in which and out of which it thinks the being, anything about the truth as which metaphysics itself essentially occurs? Never. Or are we talking this way, to all appearances presumptuously, merely because up to now we have searched in vain for what metaphysics says about the essence of the truth in which it stands? Have we been searching in vain merely because we have been asking inadequate questions?

If that is the case, then we must set things aright. The reference to Nietzsche's metaphysical concept of justification provisionally showed that Nietzsche was incapable of recognizing the justification thought by him either in the truth of its essence in general or as the essential character of the truth of his metaphysics. Is the reason for that incapacity the fact that his metaphysics is the metaphysics of will to power, or merely that it is metaphysics?

The reason is that metaphysics leaves Being itself unthought. By thinking the being as such it skims over Being in thought so as to pass it by in favor of *the being,* to which it returns and with which it remains. Thus metaphysics thinks the being as such; but it never ponders the *"as such" itself.* The "as such" implies that the being is unconcealed. The *hēi* in *on hēi on,* the *qua* in *ens qua ens,* the "as" in "the being as a being," *name unconcealment, which is unthought in its essence.* Language harbors such significant matters so inconspicuously in such simple words, if words they are. In its naming, the "as such" skims over the unconcealment of the being in its Being. But because Being itself remains unthought, the unconcealment of beings too remains unthought.

What if in both cases what is unthought were the selfsame? Then the unthought unconcealment of the being would be unthought Being itself. Then Being itself would unfold essentially as such unconcealment—as revealing.

Once again, and in an even more essential manner, what remains unthought in metaphysics, which is itself the truth of beings as such, has shown itself. It is finally time to ask how the "unthought" itself is to be thought. Along with this remaining-unthought, we are at the same time invoking the history in which there is nothing to Being itself. By contemplating the "unthought" in its essence, we come closer to the essence of nihilism proper.

If Being itself is unthought, that seems to be the fault of thinking, inasmuch as thinking is unconcerned with Being itself. Thinking omits something. Meanwhile, metaphysics thinks the Being of beings. It knows Being in terms of its own fundamental concepts *essentia* and *existentia*. But it knows Being only in order to recognize beings as such on the basis of it. In metaphysics, Being is neither bypassed nor overlooked. Nonetheless, the *metaphysical* view of Being does not allow for it as something explicitly thought; for that, Being as Being itself would have to be admitted by metaphysics as what metaphysics is to think. Being remains in the glare of concepts, indeed in the radiance of the absolute concept of speculative dialectics—and nonetheless remains *unthought*. Thus one might conclude that metaphysics repudiates Being as what is to be thought expressly.

Such a repudiation would, of course, presuppose that metaphysics had already somehow admitted Being itself into its domain as what is to be thought. Where is such admittance to be found within the history of metaphysics? Nowhere. Also absent, therefore, are any traces of a repudiation of Being as what is expressly to be thought.

Even where it does not *express* itself as ontotheology, metaphysics asserts and knows itself as a thinking that always and everywhere thinks "Being," although only in the sense of the being as such. Of course, metaphysics does not recognize this "although only." And it does not recognize it, not because it repudiates Being itself as to-be-thought, *but because Being itself stays away.* But if that is so, then the "unthought" does not stem from a thinking that neglects something.

How are we to understand the fact that Being itself stays away? Perhaps in the sense that Being halts somewhere, like a being, and, for whatever reasons, perhaps because it has lost its way, does not reach us? Except that in and for metaphysics Being stands in view, as the Being of beings.

In the meantime, it has become clearer that Being itself occurs essentially as the unconcealment in which the being comes to presence. Unconcealment itself, however, remains concealed as such. With reference to itself, unconcealment as such keeps away, keeps to itself. *The matter stands with the concealment of the essence of unconcealment. It stands with the concealment of Being as such. Being itself stays away.*

Thus matters stand with the concealment of Being in such a way that the concealment conceals itself in itself. The staying away of Being is Being itself *as this very default.** Being is not segregated somewhere off by itself, nor does it also keep away; rather, the default of Being as such is Being itself. In its default Being veils itself with itself. This veil that vanishes for itself, which is the way Being itself essentially occurs in default, is the nothing as Being itself.

Do we sense what occurs essentially in the nothing which is now to be thought? Do we dare think the possibility that the nothing is infinitely different from vacuous nullity? In the present case, the characterization of the essence of nihilism proper, in which there is nothing to Being itself, would have to contain something more than a merely negative conclusion.

Being remains unthought in metaphysics as such. This now suggests that Being itself stays away; as such default, Being itself essentially unfolds.

Insofar as the "un-" of unconcealment, with reference to itself, keeps away from unconcealment, staying with the concealment of Being, default evinces the character of *concealing*. In what sense must such concealing be thought? Is concealing simply a veiling or is it at the same time a storing away and preserving? The default "of" Being itself is such always in relation to beings. In its default is Being withheld from beings? Is the withholding in fact a refusal? We are only asking questions here, asking what we can surmise with respect to the default of Being itself. If we grant that Being itself *"is"* the *default,* then we will have to rely on Being, and on how Being strikes our thinking, to ascertain from it what features essentially occur in the default. For

---

* *Das Ausbleiben des Seins ist das Sein selbst* als dieses Ausbleiben. The jurisprudential term *default* will now help to translate *das Ausbleiben,* the "staying away" of Being, its *failure to appear* as such in the history of metaphysics.

the present, we will concentrate solely on what pertains to the default of Being itself. Nor are we hesitant to admit that the discussion of Being as just that—Being—still speaks an inadequate language, insofar as, in our perpetual references to Being itself, it is addressed with a name that continues to talk past Being as such.

In making this remark, we are voicing the assumption that Being—thought as such—can no longer be called "Being." Being as such is other than itself, so decisively other that it even "is" not. When put into words, all this sounds dialectical. In terms of the matter, it is otherwise.

Whether or not the concealing is a self-refusing preserving of Being itself, something like a self-withdrawal essentially occurs in it, and in such a way that it somehow remains in view, namely, as the Being of beings. The withdrawal, in which form Being itself occurs essentially, does not rob the being of Being. Nonetheless the being, precisely and only when it is a being, stands in the withdrawal of Being itself. We might say that the being is abandoned by Being itself. The abandonment by Being applies to beings as a whole, not only that being which takes the shape of man, who represents beings as such, a representing in which Being itself withdraws from him in its truth.

Being itself withdraws. The withdrawal happens. The abandonment by Being of the being as such takes place. When does it happen? Now? Only yesterday? Or a long time ago? How long has it been? Since when? Since the being came into the unconcealed as the being itself. Metaphysics has prevailed ever since this unconcealment occurred; for metaphysics is the history of the unconcealment of the being as such. Since that history came to be, there has historically been a withdrawal of Being itself; there has been an abandonment by Being of beings as such; there has been a history in which there is nothing to Being itself. Consequently, and from that time on, Being itself has remained unthought.

Since that time, however, nihilism proper has also been essentially unfolding, covertly, as accords with its essence. Let us now consider the name *nihilism* insofar as it names the *nihil*. We think the nothing as it applies to Being itself. We think the "applying" itself as what is historical. We think the historical as what happens in the history of

Being itself, whereby what occurs essentially in such historicity is likewise determined by Being itself.

The essence of nihilism proper is Being itself in default of its unconcealment, which is as its own "It," and which determines its "is" in staying away.*

Perhaps now it may be clear to us, at least in a few respects, that the remaining-unthought of Being as such, which we mentioned earlier, derives from the default of Being itself, a default that Being itself "is." Nevertheless, we would be overstating the case if we went on to put forth the proposition that remaining-unthought lies in Being itself and not in thinking. Does thinking therefore belong *with* the default of Being? Depending on the way it is thought, an affirmation of this question can hit upon something essential. However, it can also miss it. In the same way the proposition which asserts that remaining-unthought lies in Being itself can say too much and yet express what is alone essential.

Thinking does not belong with the default of Being as such in the sense that it observes the default, as though Being itself were one thing off by itself somewhere and thinking another that, founded on itself, either troubles itself or not about Being in its unconcealment as such. Thinking is not an independent activity over against Being, certainly not in such a way that, as the representational activity of the subject, it would already sustain Being as what is most universally represented by it and in it.

Apart from the fact that this description mistakes the simple appearance and proper intent of thinking as such, locating Being in the representing subject's domain of disposition would not allow us to see or

---

* Heidegger's use of the *Es*, "It," here and below foreshadows the theme of *Ereignis*, the propriative event, by which there is / it gives (*Es gibt*) Time and Being. Crucially important is the matrix of the thought of *Ereignis* in the history of nihilism: throughout the history of metaphysics, for which Being amounts to nothing, the unconcealment of Being remains *itself* withdrawn in concealment. For precisely that reason, the "itself" and "It" resist all depiction. Heidegger's capitalization of the latter is not meant to refer to a supreme being, or to a being of any kind. Prophylactic against all reification of the It are Heidegger's remarks on the finitude of *Ereignis* during his Todtnauberg Seminar on "Time and Being." See *Zur Sache des Denkens* (Tübingen: M. Niemeyer, 1969), pp. 53 and 58. Cf. Volume I of this series (*The Will to Power as Art*), p. 156 n.

understand whether and how Being as such in its unconcealment withdraws from thinking *along with* unconcealment as long as, and to the extent that, thinking already represents the being as such, that is, its Being. On the contrary, thinking belongs to Being itself, insofar as thinking, true to its essence, maintains access to something that never comes to Being as such from just anywhere, but approaches *from* Being itself, indeed as It itself, and "is" Being itself *withal*. What is that?

What we are asking about here, and what we must experience in its simplicity, we already identified without noticing it when we proceeded to describe the default "of" Being as a feature of Being itself. We said that Being itself is not something that keeps itself isolated somewhere. From what could Being separate itself in any case? Not from the being, which dwells in Being, although Being persists in a difference with respect to beings. Not from Being, which Being itself "is" as Being itself. Rather, in staying away, there comes to be a relation to something like a place, away from which the staying away remains what it is: the default of unconcealment as such. That place is the shelter in which the default of unconcealment essentially persists. But if it is precisely concealment that remains in the staying away of unconcealment as such, then the staying of concealment also retains its essential relation to the same place.

The staying away of unconcealment as such and the staying of concealment essentially occur in a shelter which is the very abode for the proper essence of both. But the staying away of unconcealment and the staying of concealment do not subsequently search about for an abode; rather, the abode occurs essentially with them as the advent that Being itself is. The advent is in itself the advent of their abode. The locale of the place of Being as such is Being itself.

That locale, however, is the essence of man. It is not man for himself as subject, insofar as he merely busies himself with his human affairs, considering himself as one being among others, and always, when he is explicitly concerned with Being, immediately explaining it solely from the viewpoint of beings as such. But to the extent that man already comports himself to Being even when he knows it exclusively in terms of beings, he is comporting himself to Being. Man stands in the relationship of Being itself to him, to man, to the extent that as man he comports himself to beings as such. *Being bestows itself by betaking itself into its unconcealment—and only in this way is It Being—along with the locale of its advent as the abode of its default.* This "where," as the "there" of the shelter, belongs to Being itself, "is" Being itself and is therefore called *being-there* [*Da-sein*].

"The *Dasein* in man" is the essence that belongs to Being itself. Man belongs to that essence in such a way that he has to be such Being. *Da-sein* applies to man. As his essence, it is in each case his, what he belongs to, but not what he himself makes and controls as his artifact. Man becomes essential by expressly entering into his essence. He stands in the unconcealment of beings as the concealed locale within which Being essentially occurs in its truth. He stands in this locale, which means that he is ecstative in it, because he is as he is always and everywhere on the basis of the relationship of Being itself to his essence; that is, to the locale of Being itself.

As the relation to Being, whether it is to the being as such or to Being itself, ecstative inherence in the openness of the locale of Being is the essence of thinking. The essence of thinking experienced in this way, that is, experienced on the basis of Being, is not defined by being set off against willing and feeling. Therefore, it should not be proclaimed purely theoretical as opposed to practical activity and thus restricted in its essential importance for the essence of man.

If in our meditation on the essence of nihilism we have been talking about the unthought, it is always the unthought of a thinking that is determined by the essence of Being. Thinking is taken as the activity of the intellect. The issue for the intellect is understanding. The essence of thinking is the understanding of Being in the possibilities of its development, which are conferred by the essence of Being.

From the abode of its advent—It being this abode—Being itself applies to man along with his essence. As the one approached by Being, man is the one who thinks. The "whether it be this, whether it be that," in which the essential possibility of being one way or the other is revealed for thinking, stands in a *certain* way in *man's* thinking; but it rests on Being itself, which can itself withdraw as such and *does withdraw* by *showing* itself in beings as such. But because it concerns the essence of man, even that possibility of thinking is in some sense

Nihilism and the History of Being

founded on his essence, which as the locale of Being in turn rests on Being itself.

In that way man, as the one who thinks, can relate himself to beings as such. Thinking therefore brings Being in the form of a being as such to language. Such thinking is metaphysical. It does not repudiate Being itself, but neither does it keep to the default of Being as such. Of itself, thinking does not correspond to the withdrawal of Being.

However, the twofold omission of repudiation and correspondence is not nothing. Rather, it happens not only that Being as such stays away, but that its default is thoughtlessly misplaced and suppressed by thinking. The more exclusively metaphysics gains control of the being as such and secures itself in and by the being as the truth "of Being," the more decisively has it already dispensed with Being as such. Being is the condition of beings, posited by the being as such, and as this condition is one value among others.

The default of Being itself is expressly, if unknowingly, misplaced in its default by the nature of metaphysical thinking, as thinking in values, whereby the very misplacing does not know itself as such. The nothing of Being itself is sealed in the interpretation of Being as value. It belongs to this sealing that it understand itself as the new "yes" to beings as such in the sense of the will to power, that it understand itself as the overcoming of nihilism.

Thought in terms of the *essence* of nihilism, Nietzsche's overcoming is merely the *fulfillment* of nihilism. In it the full essence of nihilism is enunciated for us more clearly than in any other fundamental position of metaphysics. What is authentically its own is the default of Being itself. But insofar as the default occurs in metaphysics, such authenticity is not admitted *as* the authenticity of nihilism.* Rather, the default as such is precisely what is omitted in metaphysical thought, and in such a way that metaphysics omits even the omission as its own act. The default is covertly left to itself by means of the

---

*"Authenticity" here translates *das Eigentliche*. Heidegger's prior references to *der eigentliche Nihilismus* have been rendered as "nihilism proper." It is still the issue of what is *proper* to nihilism as such that Heidegger explores here, even if the requirements of English compel a return to the problematic renderings "authenticity" and (for *das Uneigentliche*) "inauthenticity."

omission. Precisely in the way it takes place, the authenticity of nihilism *is not* something authentic. To what extent? Nihilism takes place as metaphysics in its own inauthenticity. However, such inauthenticity is not a lack of authenticity but its fulfillment, because it is the default of Being itself and because it devolves upon Being to see that the default remains entirely itself. The authenticity of nihilism historically takes the form of inauthenticity, which accomplishes the omission of the default by omitting this very omission. What with its unqualified affirmation of beings as such, it does not and cannot get involved with whatever might concern Being itself. The full essence of nihilism is the original unity of its authenticity and inauthenticity.

If therefore nihilism is experienced and brought to concepts within metaphysics, metaphysical thought can treat only the inauthenticity of nihilism, and that only in such a way that the inauthenticity *is not experienced as such* but is explained according to the procedures of metaphysics. The omission of the default of Being as such appears in the shape of an explanation of Being as value. Reduced to a value, Being is derived from the being as a condition for it as such.

Nihilism—that there is nothing to Being itself—always means precisely this for metaphysical thought: there is nothing to the being as such. *The very path into the experience of the essence of nihilism is therefore barred to metaphysics.* Insofar as metaphysics in every case decides for either the affirmation or the negation of the being as such, and sees both its beginning and its end in the corresponding elucidation of the being from its existing ground, it has unwittingly failed to notice that Being itself stays away *in the very priority of the question about the being as such.* In staying away, Being abandons the thinking of metaphysics to its own nature, which is precisely to omit the default as such and not to involve itself in the omission. Insofar as such thought, which has become historical as metaphysics, belongs in its essence to Being itself, insofar as it thinks on the basis of the unconcealment of the being as such, the inauthenticity of nihilism is also determined by Being itself.

Inauthentic nihilism is inauthenticity in the essence of nihilism, precisely insofar as nihilism fulfills authenticity. A difference unfolds in the essential unity of nihilism. The inauthenticity of nihilism is not eliminated from its essence. That indicates that nonessence belongs to essence. One might think that the relationship between the authenticity and inauthenticity of nihilism is a particular instance of a universally valid connection between essence and nonessence, so that the former can serve as an example of the latter. But the statement "Nonessence belongs to essence" is by no means a formal, universal assertion of ontology concerning an essence which is represented metaphysically as "essentiality" and appears definitively as *"idea."* In the word (*verbum*) "essence," taken as a verb, the statement thinks Being itself in the way in which it is, a default as such that dwells in an omission and thus is preserved. However, the omission itself occurs essentially in accord with the concealment of the unconcealment of Being in what is withdrawn. Thus thinking, which as metaphysical represents the being as such by way of the omission, is as unlikely to pay attention to the omission as it is incapable of experiencing the abandonment of beings as such by Being itself.

If we think the essence of nihilism in the way we have attempted, then we think it from Being itself as the history of Being, which Being itself "is" as Being. However, the essence of nihilism in the history of Being still does not reveal those features that usually describe what one means by the familiar term *nihilism:* something that disparages and destroys, a decline and downfall. The essence of nihilism contains nothing negative in the form of a destructive element that has its seat in human sentiments and circulates abroad in human activities. The essence of nihilism is not at all the affair of man, but a matter of Being itself, and thereby of course also a matter of the *essence* of man, and only in *that* sequence at the same time a human concern. And presumably not merely one among others.

Though what has been identified as negative within the proximate phenomenon of nihilism in its usual sense does not belong to the essence of nihilism, that in no way implies that the actuality of destructive phenomena should be overlooked, denied, or explained away as irrelevant. Rather, it becomes necessary to ask about the source of these destructive phenomena in their essence, not merely about causal relations concerning their effects.

But how will we even pose the decisive question if we have not first pondered the essence of nihilism and at the same time brought ourselves to ask whether the staying away of the question concerning the essence of nihilism does not partly occasion the dominance of those phenomena? Is it the case that the dominance of destructive nihilism and of our not asking, not being able to ask, about the essence of nihilism ultimately derive from a common root?

If that were so, then there would be little to be gained by maintaining that if the essence of nihilism does not consist in what is negative, then it is automatically something positive. For the positive shares a domain with its opposite. Ascent versus decline, waxing versus waning, exaltation versus degradation, construction versus destruction, all play their roles as counterphenomena in the realm of beings. The essence of nihilism, however, applies to Being itself, or, more appropriately expressed, Being applies to the essence of nihilism, since Being itself has brought it to pass in history that there is nothing to Being itself.

We could now, especially if we have adequately thought through the foregoing discussion of nihilism, profess that the negative phenomena referred to do not immediately pertain to the essence of nihilism, since they do not reach that far. Nevertheless, we continue to insist that something "negative" must reign in the essence of nihilism. Otherwise how could this name, which we would like to take seriously in its naming, still have anything to say? The preceding determination of the essence of nihilism has laid all the stress on the difference between authenticity and inauthenticity in nihilism. The "in-" of inauthenticity brings the negative to the fore.

Certainly it does. But what does "the negative" mean? Are we not appealing to a notion that is indeed familiar, but also a mere commonplace? Does one believe that inauthenticity in nihilism is bad, even malignant, in contrast to authenticity as good and just? Or does one take authentic nihilism to be bad, malignant, and inauthentic nihilism, if not as good, then at least as nonmalignant?

Even discounting their rashness, these opinions would be equally erroneous. Both judge authenticity and inauthenticity in the essence of nihilism superficially. Furthermore, they use standards of judgment whose appropriateness must first be decided. This much ought to have become clear by now: with the essential question we have posed we are moving in the realm of Being itself, which we can no longer explain and judge from any other standpoint, granted that the way of thinking we have attempted is at all adequate. If the "in-" in the essence of nihilism does come forward, then it also lets itself be thought only from the *unity* of that essence. The unity reveals a difference which the "in-" accentuates. But whether the "in-" and the "not" have their essence in the difference, or whether the negative in the "in-" is simply ascribed to the difference, and only as a consequence of a negation, still remains concealed.

But what is it in the essential unity of nihilism that provides an occasion and a footing for such negation? The question cannot be answered immediately. We therefore content ourselves with the insight that something differentiated reigns in the essence of nihilism, something differentiated that applies to Being itself. The "in-" does not merely or primarily rest on a negation and its negativity. But if the basic feature of what is negative in the sense of something destructive is entirely absent from the essence of nihilism, then the intention to overcome nihilism immediately as something that is supposedly purely destructive appears in a strange light. Still more curious, of course, would be the notion that a thinking that refuses the immediate overcoming of a nihilism which is thought essentially must therefore affirm nihilism in the ordinary sense.

What does "overcoming" mean? To overcome signifies: to bring something under oneself, and at the same time to put what is thus placed under oneself behind one as something that will henceforth have no determining power. Even if overcoming does not aim at sheer removal, it remains an attack against something.

To *want* to overcome nihilism—which is now thought in its essence —and to *overcome* it would mean that man of himself advance against Being itself in its default. But who or what would be powerful enough to attack Being itself, no matter from what perspective or with what intent, and to bring it under the sway of man? An overcoming of Being itself not only can never be accomplished—the very attempt would revert to a desire to unhinge the essence of man. The hinge of that essence consists in the fact that Being itself, in whatever way, even as staying away, lays claim to the essence of man. That essence is the abode which Being itself provides for itself, so that it might proceed to such an abode as the advent of unconcealment.

To want to overcome Being itself would mean unhinging the essence of man. One could understand the impossibility of such a plan as if it were an absurd gesture of thought, which as such thinks *on the basis* of Being while wanting to launch an attack *against* Being; as if such a plan were any more absurd (provided there are degrees here) than that effort of thought which, in thinking—which is surely in being—tries to deny beings as such. But what is at stake here is not merely whether thinking, taken for itself, contradicts itself in its own activity and so lacks any basic rules for itself, thereby falling into absurdity. Quite often human thought is entangled in contradiction and nonetheless remains on a path where it meets with success.

It is not merely or primarily that in advancing against Being itself thinking falls into what is logically impossible, but that with such an attack on Being it rises to renounce Being itself, and pursues the surrender of man's essential possibility. That pursuit, despite its absurdity and logical impossibility, could be fatefully realized.

Nor is the essential matter the fact that in the attempt to advance against the default of Being as such, and thus against Being itself, we are not abiding by the rules of thought; it is rather that Being itself is not admitted as Being; that, on the contrary, it is omitted. In such omission, however, we recognize the essential feature of nihilism. To want to assail the default of Being itself directly would mean not heeding Being itself as Being. The overcoming of nihilism willed in such a way would simply be a more dismal relapse into the inauthenticity of its essence, which distorts all authenticity. But how would it be if the overcoming did not directly assail the default of Being itself and stopped trying to measure up to Being itself, while advancing upon the omission of the default? The omission, in the form of metaphysics, is the work of human thought. Would it not be possible for thought to advance upon its own failure, namely, the failure to think Being itself in its unconcealment?

The necessity of such an effort can scarcely be contested, but such a necessity must first be experienced. That of course implies that man experience the omission as such; that is, the inauthenticity in the essence of nihilism. But how can he do so without first being struck by what is authentic—by the default of Being in its unconcealment?

Meanwhile, Being does not merely keep to itself in its unconcealment, as though to reserve this for itself; rather, in accord with the essential relationship of Being itself to the essence of man, Being at the same time also determines the fact that its omission takes place in and through human thought. Even an overcoming of the omission could occur only mediately from man's point of view; that is, in such a way that Being itself first of all would immediately prompt the essence of man to experience the *default* of Being's unconcealment as such for the first time *as an advent* of Being itself, and to ponder what is thus experienced.

If we heed the essence of nihilism as an essence of the history of Being itself, then the plan to overcome nihilism becomes superfluous, if by overcoming we mean that man independently subject that history to himself and yoke it to his pure willing. Such overcoming of nihilism is also fallacious in believing that human thought should advance upon the default.

Instead of such overcoming, only one thing is necessary, namely, that thinking, encouraged by Being itself, simply think to encounter Being in its default as such. Such thinking to encounter rests primarily on the recognition *that Being itself withdraws, but that as this withdrawal Being is precisely the relationship that claims the essence of man, as the abode of its (Being's) advent.* The unconcealment of the being as such is bestowed along with that abode.

Thinking to encounter does not omit the default of Being. But neither does it attempt to gain control of the default and to brush it aside. Thinking to encounter follows Being in its withdrawal, follows it in the sense that it lets Being itself go, while for its own part it stays behind. Then where does thinking linger? No longer where it lingered as the prior, omitting thought of metaphysics. Thinking stays behind by first taking the decisive *step back,* back from the omission—but back to where? Where else than to the realm that for a long time has been granted to thinking by Being itself—granted, to be sure, in the veiled figure of the *essence* of man.

Instead of rushing precipitously into a hastily planned overcoming of nihilism, thinking, troubled by the essence of nihilism, lingers a while in the advent of the default, awaiting its advent in order to learn how to ponder the default of Being in what it would be in itself. In the default as such, the unconcealment of Being conceals itself as the essential occurrence of Being itself. But insofar as Being is the unconcealment of beings as such, Being has nonetheless already addressed itself to the essence of man. Being has already spoken out for and insinuated itself in the essence of man insofar as it has withheld and saved itself in the unconcealment of its essence.

Addressing in this way, while withholding itself in default, *Being is the promise of itself.* To think to encounter Being itself in its default means to become aware of the promise, as which promise Being itself "is." It is, however, in staying away; that is to say, insofar as there is nothing to it. This history—that is, the essence of nihilism—is the destiny of Being itself. Thought in its essence and authenticity, nihilism is the promise of Being in its unconcealment in such a way that it conceals itself precisely as the promise, and in staying away simultaneously provides the occasion for its own omission.

In what does the essence of nihilism consist if such authenticity is at the same time thought with regard to inauthenticity? The inauthenticity in the essence of nihilism is the history of omission; that is, of the concealing of the promise. Granted, however, that Being itself saves itself in its default, then the history of the omission of the default is precisely the preservation of that self-saving of Being itself.

What is essential to the inauthenticity of nihilism is not something base or deficient. The essential occurrence of the nonessence in essence is nothing negative. The history of the omission of the default of Being itself is the history of the preservation of the promise—in the sense that such self-preservation is concealed in what it is. It remains concealed because it is occasioned by the self-concealing withdrawal of Being itself and in that way is imbued by Being with its preserving essence.

That which according to its essence preservingly conceals, and thus remains concealed in its essence and entirely hidden, though nonetheless it somehow appears, is in itself what we call *the mystery.* In the inauthenticity of the essence of nihilism, the mystery of the promise occurs, in which form Being is Itself, in that it saves itself as such. The history of the secret, the mystery itself in its history, is the essence of the history of the omission of the default of Being. The omission of Being itself in the thought of beings as such is the history of the unconcealment of beings as such. That history is metaphysics.

The essence of metaphysics consists in the fact that it is the history of the secret of the promise of Being itself. The essence of metaphysics, which is thought on the basis of Being itself in its history, is the essential factor in the nonessence of nihilism that pertains to the unity of the essence of nihilism. As in the case of the essence of nihilism, therefore, the essence of metaphysics may not be assessed either positively or negatively. But if the plan for an immediate overcoming of nihilism hurries on by its essence, then the intention to overcome metaphysics is also null and void, unless the talk of overcoming metaphysics embraces a meaning that intends neither to disparage nor to eliminate metaphysics.

Metaphysics first attains its essence when it is thought in the way we have attempted to think it, in terms of the history of Being. Its essence is withdrawn from metaphysics itself, and is withdrawn in accord with metaphysics' own essence. Every metaphysical concept of metaphysics assists in barring metaphysics from its own essential provenance. Thought in terms of the history of Being, "the overcoming of metaphysics" always means simply surrendering the metaphysical interpretation of metaphysics. Thinking abandons the pure "metaphysics of metaphysics" by taking the step back, back from the omission of Being in its default. In the step *back,* thinking has already set out on the path of thinking to *encounter* Being itself in its self-withdrawal. That self-withdrawal, as the self-withdrawal of Being, still remains a mode of Being—an advent. By thinking to encounter Being itself, thinking no longer omits Being, but admits it: admits it *into* the originary, revealing unconcealment of Being, which is Being itself.

A little while ago we stated that Being itself remains unthought in metaphysics. In the meantime, we have more clearly illustrated what happens in such remaining-unthought and what takes place as remaining-unthought itself: it is the history of Being itself in its default. Metaphysics belongs within that history. In its essence, metaphysics first approaches thinking from its provenance in the history of Being. Metaphysics is the inauthenticity in the essence of nihilism, and takes place in an essential unity with the authenticity of nihilism.

Until now, the dissonance of something negative—in the sense of destructive—has sounded in the name *nihilism*. Until now, metaphysics has been taken as the supreme region in which the most profound matters are thought. Presumably, the dissonance in the name *nihilism* and the prestige of metaphysics are both genuine, and in that way necessary, semblances. The illusion is inevitable. Metaphysical thought cannot overcome it.

Is it also indomitable for the thinking that thinks the history of Being? The apparent dissonance in the name *nihilism* could indicate a more profound accord that would be determined not from metaphysical heights but from a different domain. The essence of metaphysics reaches deeper than metaphysics itself, indeed reaches into a depth that belongs to a different realm, so that the depth no longer corresponds to a height.

According to its essence, nihilism is the history of the promise, in which Being itself saves itself in a mystery which is itself historical and which preserves the unconcealment of Being from that history in the form of metaphysics. The whole of the essence of nihilism, to the extent that—as the history of Being—it bestows itself as an abode for the essence of man, grants thinking everything that is to be thought. Consequently, what is given to thinking as to be thought we call *the enigma*.

Being, the promise of its unconcealment as the history of the secret, is itself the enigma. Being is that which of its essence gives only that essence to be thought. It, Being, *gives food for thought,* and indeed not just sometimes or in a particular respect, but always and from every point of view, because essentially the fact that It, Being, hands thinking over to its essence—this is a mark of Being itself. Being itself is the enigma. This does not mean (provided such a comparison is fitting here) that Being is the irrational, from which everything rational rebounds, so as to tumble into incapacity for thought. Rather, Being, as what gives food for thought—that is, gives what is to be thought—is also the unique matter which of itself and for itself raises the claim of being what is to be thought; it "is" as this very claim. In the face of Being itself, the unworthy game of hide and seek which is supposed to be played between the irrational and the rational is exposed in all its mindlessness.*

Nevertheless, is not the essence of nihilism in the history of Being the mere product of an enthusiastic thinking into which a romantic philosophy flees, escaping from true reality? What does the essence of nihilism thus thought signify as opposed to the reality—which alone is effective—of actual nihilism, which sows confusion and strife everywhere, which instigates crime and drives us to despair? What is the nothing of Being which we have considered in the face of the actual an-nihil-ation [*Ver-nichts-ung*] of all beings, whose violence, encroaching from all sides, makes almost every act of resistance futile?

We hardly need to illustrate in detail the spreading violence of actual nihilism, which we all personally experience to a sufficient degree, even without an ivory-tower definition of its essence. Furthermore, Nietzsche's experience, in spite of the one-sidedness of his interpretation, deals with "actual" nihilism so forcefully that by comparison our attempt at determining the essence of nihilism appears insubstantial, not to say utterly useless. When every divine, human, material, and natural thing is threatened in its existence, who would want to trouble himself about something like the omission of the default of Being itself, even granting that such a thing takes place and is not merely the subterfuge of a desperate abstraction?

If only a connection between actual nihilism, or even the nihilism experienced by Nietzsche, and the essence of nihilism as thought here were at least perceptible. Then we would remove from the essence of nihilism the undeniable impression of complete unreality, which seems to be even greater than the admittedly enigmatic nature of this essence.

The question remains, in fact emerges for the first time, whether the

---

* The above paragraph sets the tone for Heidegger's 1951–52 lecture course "What Calls for Thinking?" In the *Spiegel* interview of September 23, 1966, Heidegger complained that in Germany the resulting publication was the least read of all his books; in a conversation with J. Glenn Gray he noted that it was a book he himself had to re-read, since "it contained almost all of my ideas."

"essence" of Being comes from beings, whether the being, as actual, in all its concatenations, is capable of determining actuality, Being, or whether the effectuality that stems from Being itself calls forth everything actual.

Does what Nietzsche experiences and thinks, namely, the history of the devaluation of the highest values, stand for itself? Does not the essence of nihilism in the history of Being essentially unfold within that history? That Nietzsche's metaphysics interprets Being as a value is the effectual, actual omission of the default of Being itself in its unconcealment. What comes to language in the interpretation of Being as value is the eventuating inauthenticity in the essence of nihilism, an inauthenticity that does not know itself and nonetheless only *is* in essential unity with the authenticity of nihilism. If Nietzsche really experienced a history of the devaluation of the highest values, then what is experienced in that way, together with the experience itself, is the *actual* omission of the default of Being in its unconcealment.

The omission *is* as actual history and takes place as that history within the essential unity of the inauthenticity and authenticity of nihilism. That history is nothing alongside "essence." It is the essence itself, and this alone.

Nietzsche appends to his interpretation of nihilism (*"that the uppermost values devaluate themselves"*) an explanation: "The aim is lacking; the 'why?' receives no answer" (WM, 2).

Let us consider the question the "why?" raises here more precisely with regard to what it interrogates and what it asks for. It interrogates beings as such and as a whole, asking them why they are in being. As a metaphysical question, it asks about the being that might be a ground for what is and for the way in which it is. Why does the question about the highest values contain the question about what is supreme? Is it only the *answer* to the question that is lacking? Or is the question itself defective as the question which it is? It is defective as a question because in asking about the existent ground of beings it fails to ask about Being itself and its truth. The question has already failed *as a question* —not simply because it lacks an answer. The inadequate question is no mere mistake, as though some flaw or other had slipped past it. The question misplaces itself. It places itself in a region without prospect, against whose horizon all merely possible answers are bound to fall short.

But as Nietzsche confirms, the fact that the answer to the question "why?" really is lacking, and that where it is still given it remains ineffective from the point of view of being as a whole, the fact that all this is so, and the way in which it is so, implies something else. The question governs all questioning even when it remains without an answer. The exclusive, actual dominance of the question, however, is nothing other than the actual omission of the default of Being itself. Considered from such a viewpoint, is the essence of nihilism something abstract? Or is the essential unfolding of the history of Being itself *the* occurrence on the basis of which all history now takes place? That historiography, even one with the prestige and scope of Jacob Burckhardt's, knows nothing and can know nothing at all of this—is this proof enough that the essence of nihilism "is" *not?*

If Nietzsche's metaphysics interprets Being as a pure value in terms of beings and in accord with the sense of will to power; if Nietzsche in fact thinks the will to power as the principle of a new valuation and understands and wills the latter as the overcoming of nihilism; then metaphysics' utmost entanglement in the inauthenticity of nihilism comes to language in the desire to overcome. It does so in such a way that the entanglement closes itself off from its own essence and thus, under the guise of an overcoming of nihilism, transposes nihilism into the effectuality of its deracinated nonessence.

The putative overcoming of nihilism first establishes the dominion of an absolute omission of the default of Being itself in favor of the being in the form of valuative will to power. Through its withdrawal, which nonetheless remains a relationship to beings, in which form "Being" appears, Being itself releases itself into will to power. As will to power, the being seems to reign above and over all Being. In such reigning and radiating of Being, which is concealed with respect to its truth, the default of Being occurs essentially in such a way that it permits the most extreme omission of itself. It thus aids and abets the advance of the purely actual—of those popularly acclaimed realities— which prides itself on being what is, while at the same time presuming itself to be the measure for deciding that only what is effectual—what is palpable and makes an impression, what is experienced and its expression, what is useful and its success—should pass as being.

In the most extreme form of the inauthenticity of nihilism, which apparently comes to appear of itself, the essential unity of nihilism in the history of Being essentially unfolds. *Granted that the unconditioned appearance of the will to power in the whole of beings is not nothing, is the essence of nihilism in the history of Being, an essence that reigns concealed in this appearance, merely a product of thought or even something utterly fantastic?*

Does not the fantasy—if we are going to talk about it at all—consist more in our indulging the habit of accepting any isolated set of negatively interpreted appearances as results of a nihilism which we do not experience in its essence, taking these appearances as what alone is actual, and throwing to the winds what occurs essentially in the actual, as though it were nothing at all? What if this truly fantastic notion, full of good faith and desirous of order, were one of a kind with nihilism, which it imagines it has not been touched by, or has been absolved from?

The essence of nihilism in the history of Being is not something produced in thought, nor does it hover rootlessly above actual nihilism. Rather, what one takes to be "the real" is something that comes to be only on the basis of the essential history of Being itself.

Of course, the difference between inauthenticity and authenticity which reigns in the essential unity of nihilism could diverge into the most extreme disjunction of inauthentic from authentic. Then, in keeping with its own essence, the essential unity of nihilism would have to conceal itself in what is most extreme. It would have to disappear, as though it were nothing at all, in the unconcealment of the being as such, which everywhere passes for Being itself. It would then have to appear as if in truth there were nothing to Being itself, provided that such a thought could still occur at all.

If he were to consider what has been said up to now, who would not suppose Being itself capable of such a possibility? Who, if he thinks, could escape being affected by the most extreme withdrawal of Being, sensing that in the withdrawal there is an exaction by Being—*Being itself as such exaction*—which applies to man in his essence? That essence is nothing human. It is the abode of the advent of Being, which as advent grants itself an abode and proceeds to it, so that precisely as a result *"There is / It gives Being."* * The essence of nihilism in the history of Being takes place as the history of the secret. The essence of metaphysics proceeds as the mystery.

The essence of nihilism is an enigma for thinking. This has been admitted. However, the admission does not belatedly and of itself yield something that it was previously able to enjoin for itself. The admission merely places itself in insistence; that is, into the tarrying inherence in the midst of the self-veiled truth of Being. Only through such insistence is man capable of maintaining his essence as the one who, in his essence, thinks.

When thinking dispatches itself into thought, it stands already in the admission of the enigma of the history of Being. At the moment thinking thinks, Being has already been intended for it. *The mode of this primordial summoning is the default of the unconcealment of Being in the unconcealed being as such.*

For a long time, thinking did not heed this. That prevented it from discerning that the phenomena of nihilism in the ordinary sense are unchained by the release of Being. Such release surrenders the default of the unconcealment of Being to an omission through metaphysics, which at the same time and in a concealed fashion prevents the advent of self-concealing Being. Insofar as nihilistic phenomena emerge from the release of Being, they are evoked by the predominance of the being itself, and they in turn effect the disjunction of the being from Being itself.

In the occurrence of the default of Being itself, man is thrown into the release of the being by the self-withdrawing truth of Being. Representing Being in the sense of the being as such, he lapses into beings, with the result that by submitting to beings he sets himself up as the

---

* *So dass* "Es"—*demzufolge und nur so*—"das Sein gibt." The translation tries to capture both the idiomatic and the literal senses of the German *Es gibt*—"there is," "it gives." Note that Heidegger's formulation of the *Es gibt* throughout these pages differs from his later interpretation of *Ereignis*. The present formulation tends to equate the "It" with Being, whereas Heidegger's final efforts leave the "It" of the granting unnamed. Yet these pages too voice the suspicion that the word *Being* names the enigma inadequately, and that the word may therefore have to be surrendered.

being who in the midst of beings representationally and productively seizes upon them as the objective. In the midst of beings, man freely posits his own essence as certainty for and against the being. He seeks to accomplish this surety in the being through a complete ordering of all beings, in the sense of a systematic securing of stockpiles, by means of which his establishment in the stability of certainty is to be completed.

The objectification of all being as such, on the basis of man's insurrection on behalf of the exclusive self-willing of his will, is the essence of that process in the history of Being by which man sets forth his essence in subjectivity. In accord with subjectivity, man installs both himself and what he represents as world into the subject-object relation, which is sustained by subjectivity. *All transcendence, whether it be ontological or theological, is represented relative to the subject-object relation.* Through the insurrection into subjectivity even theological transcendence and thus the supreme being of beings—one calls it, indicatively enough, "Being"—shifts into a kind of objectivity, specifically, the objectivity of the subjectivity of moral-practical faith. It makes no difference in the essence of this fundamental metaphysical position concerning the human essence whether man takes that transcendence seriously as "providence" for his religious subjectivity or takes it merely as a pretext for the willing of his self-seeking subjectivity.

There is no reason for astonishment over the fact that both these opinions about providence, opinions which when viewed individually are opposites, should prevail at the same time alongside each other, for both stem from the same root of the metaphysics of subjectivity. As metaphysics, they leave Being itself unthought in its truth from the outset. As the metaphysics of subjectivity, however, they make Being in the sense of the being as such into the objectivity of representing and pro-posing. The pro-posing of Being as a value posited by the will to power is merely the final step of modern metaphysics, in which Being comes to appearance as will to power.

But the history of metaphysics, as the history of the unconcealment of the being as such, is the history of Being itself. The modern metaphysics of subjectivity is the granted closure of Being itself, which in the default of its truth causes the omission of that default.* The essence of man, however, which in a covert way is the abode of Being itself in its advent, an abode that belongs to Being itself, becomes more and more omitted the more essentially the advent is preserved in the form of the withdrawal of Being. Man becomes uncertain when confronting his own essence, which lingers with Being itself in the withdrawal, without being able to discover the source and essence of his uncertainty. Instead, he seeks primal truth and permanence in self-certainty. He therefore strives for self-assurance, which he himself provides in the midst of beings, which are always surveyed with regard to what they can offer by way of new and continuous possibilities of surety. What becomes evident thereby is that, of all beings, man is transposed into uncertainty in a special way. This allows us to assume that man, particularly in his relation to his own essence, is at stake. With that, the possibility glimmers that all being as such could occur essentially as a game in which everything is at stake, and that being itself is such "world-play."

In the years he was working toward his planned *magnum opus*, Nietzsche summarized the fundamental thoughts of his metaphysics in the following poem. It belongs in the sequence of "Songs of the Outlaw Prince," which was published in the second edition (1887) of the book *The Gay Science* as an "Appendix" (V, 349)†:

---

* In the expression "the granted closure of Being itself," *die Zulassung des Seins selbst*, we find the paradox of the oblivion of Being stated most pointedly. *Zu-lassen* means "to leave closed"; *Zulassen* means "to grant entry," "admit." Being remains closed to the metaphysics of subjectivity, and yet is somehow granted—as closure, default, omission.

† The poem appears in CM, vol. V, Division 2, p. 323, as follows:

An Goethe

Das Unvergängliche
Ist nur dein Gleichnis!
Gott der Verfängliche
Ist Dichter-Erschleichnis . . .

Welt-Rad, das rollende,
Streift Ziel auf Ziel:
Not—nennt's der Grollende,
Der Narr nennt's—Spiel . . .

To Goethe

The Ever-enduring
Is but your conceit!
And God, the alluring,
A poet's retreat.

World-wheel, spinning by,
Skims goals on its way:
Calamity! is rancor's cry;
The jester calls it Play!

World-play, the ruling,
Mixes "Seems" with "To Be":
Eternally, such fooling
Mixes *us* in—the melee!

Let the following remarks suffice in place of the detailed interpretation of the poem that belongs here but that would repeat much of what was said earlier. The last stanza enables us to see that "world-play" as "the ruling" thinks on the basis of will to power. The latter posits "Being" as the condition of its securing of permanence. The will to power posits "Being" at the same time in unity with "semblance" (art) as the condition of its own enhancement. Both Being and semblance are mixed with each other. The blending, however, the way in which will to power *is,* the poem calls "eternal fooling," and the "world-

---

Welt-Spiel, das herrische,
Mischt Sein und Schein:—
Das Ewig-Närrische
Mischt *uns*—hinein! . . .

Nietzsche's poem, especially its concluding stanza, holds a special place in Heidegger's esteem. The sole extant typescript of the essay "Nietzsche's Metaphysics" (1940; see Volume III of this series) shows a second title page with the words, "Nietzsche's Metaphysics, Interpreted on the Basis of the Lines. . . ." (Heidegger then reprints the concluding stanza of "To Goethe.") A handwritten note at the top of this sheet refers to "the winter semester of 1938–39," indicating perhaps—although this is uncertain—a three-hour "exercise" with the title "Toward an Interpretation of Nietzsche's Second *Untimely Meditation,* 'On the Use and Disadvantage of History for Life.' " Strangely, the typescript of "Nietzsche's Metaphysics" makes no mention of the stanza in question. It may well be that the materials on which Heidegger based his seminar on "world-play" are lost—unless these few lines of the "nihilism" essay rescue their substance.

wheel, spinning by." It is the eternal recurrence of the same, which posits no indestructible aims, but merely "skims goals on its way."

Insofar as man is, he is a configuration of will to power. He is mixed by the blending power of the world-wheel "into" the whole of becoming-being.

In the metaphysical domain of the thought of will to power, as the eternal recurrence of the same, all that is left to express the determination of the relationship of man to "Being" is the following possibility:

> Eternally such fooling
> Mixes *us* in—the melee!

Nietzsche's metaphysics thinks the playful character of world-play in the only way it can think it: out of the unity of will to power and eternal recurrence of the same. Without a perspective on this unity, all talk about world-play remains vacuous. But for Nietzsche these are thoughtful words; as such, they belong to the language of his metaphysics.

The unity of will to power and eternal recurrence of the same rests on the coherence of *essentia* and *existentia,* whose differentiation remains obscure with respect to its essential provenance.

The unity of will to power and eternal recurrence signify that the will to power is in truth the will-to-will, a determination in which the metaphysics of subjecticity* attains the peak of its development, its fulfillment. The metaphysical concept of "world-play" identifies the affinity in the history of Being between what Goethe experienced as "nature" and Heraclitus as *kosmos* (see Fragment 30). †

---

* *Subiectität.* At this point, Heidegger inserts a reference to his essay "Metaphysics as History of Being" (1941). See Martin Heidegger, *The End of Philosophy,* tr. Joan Stambaugh (New York: Harper & Row, 1973), pp. 46–49, and NII, 450 ff.

† Fragment 30 reads, "This cosmos, the same for all, was created neither by god nor man, but always was, is, and shall be ever-living fire, kindling in measures, dwindling in measures." Heidegger refers to it in his essay "Aletheia," *Early Greek Thinking,* pp. 115 and 117, and it is one of the mainstays of Eugen Fink's "cosmological" interpretation of Heraclitus. See Martin Heidegger and Eugen Fink, *Heraclitus Seminar 1966/67,* tr. Charles Seibert (University, Ala.: University of Alabama Press, 1979), sections 2, 5, and 6. Cf. John Sallis and Kenneth Maly, eds., *Heraclitean Fragments: A Companion Volume to the Heidegger/Fink Seminar on Heraclitus,* published by the University of Alabama Press in 1980, p. 8 and throughout. Curiously, Heidegger does not here refer

In the sometimes visible, sometimes undescried reigning of world-play, thought metaphysically, the being at times reveals itself as the will-to-will as such, and at times conceals itself again. Everywhere, the being as such has brought itself into an unconcealment that lets it appear as what posits itself on itself and brings itself before itself. That is the fundamental trait of subjecticity. The being as subjecticity omits the truth of Being itself in a decisive way, insofar as subjecticity, out of its own desire for surety, posits the truth of beings as certitude. Subjecticity is not a human product: rather, man secures himself as the being who is in accord with beings as such, insofar as he wills himself as the I-and-we subject, represents himself to himself, and so presents himself to himself.

That the being as such is in the mode of subjecticity and that man searches high and low in the midst of beings, seeking means of securing his certainty, in all cases merely testifies that in the history of its default Being keeps to itself with its unconcealment. *Being itself occurs essentially as such keeping to itself.* The essence of Being itself does not take place behind or beyond beings, but—provided the notion of such a relationship is permissible here—*before* the being as such. Therefore, even the presumed actuality of nihilism in the ordinary sense falls behind its essence. That our thinking, which for centuries has been accustomed to metaphysics, still does not perceive this is no proof for the opposite conclusion. In fact, we ought to ask here in a general way whether proofs of thought, of whatever kind they may be, are what is essential—or whether what is essential are hints of Being.

But how can we be certain of these hints? Even this question, which sounds so serious and poised, arises from a claim that still belongs to the realm of the metaphysics of subjecticity. This does not mean that it may be disregarded. Rather, it is necessary to ask whether the call for criteria of certitude has considered and pondered everything that belongs within the radius of what must be heard.

The essential unfolding of nihilism is the default of Being as such. In staying away, it promises itself in its unconcealment. The default

---

to Fragment 52, "Aion is a child at play, playing at draughts; dominion is the child's." See Martin Heidegger, *Nietzsche, vol. II: The Eternal Recurrence of the Same*, section 11 (NI, 333–34); *Holzwege*, p. 258; and *Der Satz vom Grund* (Pfullingen: G. Neske, 1957), pp. 187–88.

abandons itself to the omission of Being itself in the secret of history. As history, metaphysics keeps the truth of Being concealed in the unconcealment of the being as such. As the promise of its truth, Being keeps to itself with its own essence. The admission of the omission of the default takes place on the basis of its keeping to itself. From the respective distance of the withdrawal, which conceals itself in any given phase of metaphysics, such keeping to itself determines each epoch of the history of Being as the *epochē* of Being itself.

But when Being itself withdraws into its remotest withholding, the being as such arises, released as the exclusive standard for "Being," into the totality of its dominion. Beings as such appear as will to power, whereby Being as will fulfills its subjecticity. The metaphysics of subjectivity omits Being itself so decisively that it remains concealed in value thinking and can barely allow value thinking to be known as or to pass for metaphysics at all. While metaphysics plunges into the vortex of its omission, the latter, unrecognizable as such, is established for the truth of beings in the form of the securing of permanence; it completes the closing off of the truth of beings as such from the truth of Being. But, in accord with the prevailing blindness of metaphysics to itself, the closing off appears as a liberation from all metaphysics (see *Twilight of the Idols,* "How the 'True World' Finally Became a Fable"; VIII, 82 f.).*

In this way, the inauthenticity in nihilism reaches absolute predominance, behind which the authenticity—and along with authenticity and its relation to inauthenticity the *essence* of nihilism—remains submerged in the inaccessible and unthinkable. In our epoch of the history of Being, only the consequences of the predominance of the inauthenticity in nihilism take effect, although never *as* consequences, but simply as nihilism itself. Nihilism therefore reveals only destructive features. These are experienced, furthered, or resisted in the light of metaphysics.

Antimetaphysics and the reversal of metaphysics, but also the defense of previous metaphysics: these constitute the sole occupation of the long-eventuating omission of the default of Being itself.

The struggle over nihilism, for it and against it, is engaged on a field

---

* See the first volume of this series, *The Will to Power as Art,* section 24.

staked out by the predominance of the nonessence of nihilism. Nothing will be decided by this struggle. It will merely seal the predominance of the inauthentic in nihilism. Even where it believes itself to be standing on the opposite side, the struggle is everywhere and at bottom nihilistic—in the usual destructive sense of the word.

The will to overcome nihilism mistakes itself because it bars itself from the revelation of the *essence* of nihilism as the history of the default of Being, bars itself without being able to recognize its own deed. The mistaking of the essential impossibility of overcoming metaphysics within metaphysics, or even through the reversal of metaphysics, could go so far that one might take the denial of that possibility as an affirmation of nihilism, or even as a complacent observation of the course of nihilistic decadence that will not lend a hand to stop it.

Because the default of Being is the history of Being and thus is authentically existing history, the being as such, especially in the epoch of the dominance of the nonessence of nihilism, lapses into the unhistorical. The sign of this lapse is the emergence of the historical sciences, which advance a claim to be the definitive representation of history. They take history to be of the past, and explain it in its emergence as a causally demonstrable continuum of effects. The past, objectified by recounting and explaining, appears against the horizon of that present which in each case performs the objectification; at its culmination, the present explains itself as the product of the past occurrence itself. One believes one knows what facts and factuality are, and what sorts of beings take the form of the past, because through historical research objectification is always bringing forward some kind of factual material, and it knows how to put it in a frame of reference that is topical and, above all, "relevant" to the present.

Our historical situation is being analyzed everywhere. It is the point of departure and the goal for the mastery of beings, in the sense of securing man's standpoint and status within them. Historical research consciously or unconsciously stands in service to the will of human cultures to establish themselves among beings according to a comprehensible order. The will to nihilism as normally understood, and to its campaign, as well as the will to an overcoming of nihilism, become operative in the historiological reckoning of historiologically analyzed spirit and of world-historical situations.

Sometimes historical research also asks what history is, but always merely as an "also," and therefore belatedly and by the way, always as if historiological representations of history could furnish a determination of the essence of history by making sufficiently broad generalizations. When philosophy takes up the inquiry, however, and attempts to set forth an ontology of the happening of history, it persists in the metaphysical interpretation of beings as such.

History as Being—indeed, as coming from the essence of Being itself—remains unthought. Every historiological meditation of man on his condition is therefore metaphysical, and thus pertains to the essential omission of the default of Being. It is necessary to contemplate the metaphysical character of history as a discipline if we are going to measure the impact of historiological thought, which at times considers itself authorized to enlighten, if not to rescue man, who is at stake in the age of the self-fulfilling nonessence of nihilism.

Meanwhile, following the claims and demands of the age, the effective completion of academic history has advanced from being a scientific discipline to journalism. If it is understood correctly, and not in a disparaging way, "journalism" identifies the metaphysical securing and establishment of the everydayness of our dawning age, everydayness in the form of solid historical research; that is to say, research that works as hastily and reliably as possible, through which everyone is provided with the ever-useful objectivities of the day. At the same time, it reflects the self-completing objectification of beings as a whole.

The epoch of the unconditioned and complete objectification of everything that is begins with the self-fulfilling metaphysics of subjectivity, which corresponds to the most extreme withdrawal of the truth of Being, because it obscures the withdrawal until it is unrecognizable. In that objectification, man himself and every aspect of human culture is transformed into a stockpile which, psychologically reckoned, is incorporated into the working process of the will-to-will, even if some people view that process as free, while others interpret it as purely mechanical. Both mistake the covert essence in the history of Being, that is, the nihilistic essence, which when expressed in the language of metaphysics is always something "spiritual." Even the fact that in the process of the absolute objectification of beings as such mankind has become a "human resource," ranked behind natural resources and raw materials, does not betray a supposedly materialistic preference for matter and energy over the human spirit. It is grounded in the unconditioned character of objectification itself, which must bring every stockpile, no matter what its nature, into its own possession and must secure this possession.

The absolute objectification of the being as such results from the self-fulfilling dominion of subjectivity. This occurs essentially as the most extreme release of the being as such into the omission of Being itself; in that way Being refuses its default to the extreme and as such refusal dispatches Being in the form of beings as such—dispatches it as the destiny of the complete concealment of Being in the midst of the thoroughgoing securing of beings.

History, concealed in its historicity, is still interpreted historiologically—that is always to say, metaphysically—albeit from different if not indeed necessarily opposing standpoints. The positing of aims in all ordering, the assessment of the value of the human, establishes for itself a public according to the positings of value thinking, and procures for that public its legitimacy.

Just as the unconcealment of the being, the truth of the being, has come to be a value, so has the kind of unconcealment known as publicity become—in the essential sequence of this interpretation of the essence of truth—a necessary value for securing the permanence of the will to power. In each case publicity yields metaphysical or, what is the same thing here, antimetaphysical explanations of what is to be considered being and what nonbeing. But the being, thus objectified, is nonetheless not what *is*.

What is, is what takes place. What takes place has already taken place. That does not mean that it is past. What has already taken place is only what has gathered itself into the essence of Being, into the having-occurred-essentially [*das Ge-Wesen*], from which and as which the advent of Being itself is—even if in the form of the self-withdrawal that stays away. The advent holds the being as such in its unconcealment and leaves unconcealment to the being as the unthought Being

Nihilism and the History of Being

of beings. What happens is the history of Being, Being as the history of default. The latter pertains to the essence of man, specifically insofar as man in our time has neither recognized nor acted on the admission that his essence has been withheld from him. The default of Being comes toward the essence of man in such a way that in his relationship to Being man unwittingly turns away from it, understanding Being solely in terms of beings, wanting to have every question regarding "Being" understood in that way.

Had the admission of man into his essence in the history of Being already taken place, he surely would have been able to experience the essence of nihilism. Such an experience would have induced him to consider that what is commonly known as nihilism is what it is on the basis of the completed dominion of the nonessence of its essence. That nihilism does not allow itself to be overcome is implicit in the essential provenance of nihilism in the metaphysical sense. It does not allow itself to be overcome, not because it is insuperable, but because all wanting-to-overcome is inappropriate to its essence.

The historical relation of man to the essence of nihilism can only consist in his thoughtfully undertaking to think to encounter the default of Being itself. Such thinking of the history of Being brings man face to face with the essence of nihilism; in contrast, all wanting-to-overcome puts nihilism behind us, but only in such a way that in the still-dominant horizon of metaphysically determined experience nihilism rises up around us unperceived, ever more terrible in its power, beguiling our thoughts.

Thinking in terms of the history of Being lets Being arrive in the essential space of man. Because the essential domain is an abode with which Being as such provides itself, thinking in terms of the history of Being lets Being occur essentially as Being itself. Thinking takes a step back from metaphysical representing. Being lightens as the advent of the keeping-to-itself of the refusal of its unconcealment. What is identified with "lighting," "arriving," "keeping to itself," "refusal," "revealing," and "concealing" is one and the same essential occurrence, namely, Being.

Nevertheless, the name *Being* at the same time loses its naming power in the step back, because it always unwittingly says "presence and permanence," determinations to which the *essentially occurring* character of Being can never be attached as a mere addendum. On the other hand, the attempt to think Being as Being with regard to the tradition must go to utmost extremes in order to experience whether and why Being no longer allows itself to be defined as—"Being." That limitation does not extinguish thinking, but transforms it into that essence which is already predetermined by the withholding of the truth of Being.

When metaphysical thinking takes the step back, it dispatches itself to liberate man's essential space. But such liberation is occasioned by Being in order that we think to encounter the advent of its default. The step back does not cast metaphysics aside. Rather, now for the first time thinking has the essence of metaphysics before it and around it in the radius of its experiences of the being as such. The provenance of metaphysics in the history of Being remains what is to be thought. In this way the essence of metaphysics is preserved as the secret of the history of Being.

The default of Being is its withdrawal, its keeping to itself with its unconcealment, which it promises in its refusing, self-concealing. Thus Being essentially occurs as promise in the withdrawal. But that is a relating: in it Being itself lets its abode come to it, that is, draws it forth. As such relating, Being never, even in the default of its unconcealment, relents from unconcealment, which in keeping to itself is released solely as the unconcealment of the being as such. As the advent that never abandons its abode, Being is the unrelenting. In this way, it is compelling. Being occurs essentially in this way to the extent that as the advent of unconcealment it requires unconcealment, not as something alien, but as Being. Being needs an abode. Requiring an abode, Being lays claim to it.

Being is compelling in a twofold, harmonious sense: it is unrelenting and needful in relating to an abode that essentially occurs as the essence to which man belongs, man being the one who is needed. What is doubly compelling is, and is called, the need. In the advent of the default of its unconcealment, Being itself is need.*

---

* Being "needs" (*braucht*) an abode, and thus "uses" (also: *braucht*) man. But when Being advenes in default of unconcealment, it can only be "needy," its history a

Nihilism and the History of Being

But need veils itself by staying away. At the same time the default is hidden by the omission of the truth of Being in the history of metaphysics. Within the unconcealment of the being as such, which the history of metaphysics determines as the fundamental occurrence, the need of Being does not come to the fore. The being *is*, and gives rise to the illusion that Being is without need.

But the needlessness that establishes itself as the dominion of metaphysics brings Being itself to the utmost limit of its need. Need is not merely what compels in the sense of the unyielding claim that occupies an abode by using it as the unconcealment of the advent; that is, by letting it unfold essentially as the truth of Being. The relentlessness of its usage extends so far in the default of its unconcealment that the abode of Being—that is, the essence of man—is omitted; man is threatened with the annihilation of his essence, and Being itself is endangered in its usage of its abode. By extending so far into default, Being consigns itself to the danger that the need, in which form it compellingly unfolds, never becomes for historical man the need that it is. At its outermost limit, the need of Being comes to be the need of needlessness. The predominance of the still-veiled needlessness of Being, which in its truth is the doubly compelling need of an unrelenting usage of the abode, is nothing other than the absolute preeminence of the fully developed nonessence in the essence of nihilism.

As the veiled and extreme need of Being, however, needlessness reigns precisely in the age of the darkening of beings, our age of confusion, of violence and despair in human culture, of disruption and impotence of willing. Both openly and tacitly, boundless suffering and measureless sorrow proclaim the condition of our world a needful one. All the same, at the basis of its history it is needless. Yet in the history of Being this is its supreme and at the same time most concealed need. It is the need of Being itself.

But how can the need as such expressly involve man—and involve him specifically in his essential distance from himself? What can man

---

"calamity" (*die Not*). "Need" is thus twofold, referring to the "destitute time" in which we live but also to the "usage" of Being as such in every epoch. Heidegger discusses this difficult matter further in "The Anaximander Fragment," *Early Greek Thinking*, pp. 52–59.

do, if in truth the need is a need of Being itself? The need of Being itself, which the essence of nihilism embodies historically and which—perhaps—will bring its authenticity to advent, is patently not a need in the sense that man might meet it by controlling and restraining it. How should he meet it if he does not even know it? And would not restraint be a relation that is altogether contrary to the essence of such need?

To correspond to the need of needlessness can only mean above all else to assist in experiencing needlessness for the first time as the essential occurrence of need itself. That would require that we point toward the need-less quality of need, which in turn requires that we experience the omission of the default of Being itself. In what is thus experienced, it is appropriate to think the essence of nihilism as the history of Being itself. But that means to think to encounter the advent of the self-withdrawal of Being in relation to its abode; that is to say, the advent of the essence of historical man.

But what vista opens up here? To think to encounter the extreme need of Being suggests that we broach the extreme threat to man; that is, the danger that threatens to annihilate his *essence*. It means thinking what is dangerous. Then the path of contemplation would be fortunate in having arrived at that "dangerous thinking" which the human world, already sufficiently confused, still condemns as irresponsible and groundless. The glorification of danger and the misuse of force—do they not reciprocally enhance each other?

Nietzsche's oft-repeated phrase about "living dangerously" belongs to the realm of the metaphysics of will to power; it calls for an active nihilism, which is now to be thought as the absolute dominion of the nonessence of nihilism. But danger as the risk of the uncontrolled implementation of force, and danger as the threat of the annihilation of man's essence, although they both derive from the default of Being itself, are not identical. Yet neglecting to think about the omission of the need of Being itself, an omission that takes place as metaphysics, is blindness in the face of needlessness as the essential need of man. Such blindness comes from unconfessed anxiety in the face of the anxiety that experiences with trepidation the default of Being itself.

When it is viewed with respect to the duration of the history of

Being, it may well be that blindness in the face of the extreme need of Being, in the form of the needlessness that prevails in the midst of crowds of beings, is still more hazardous than the crass adventures of a merely brutal will to violence. The greater danger consists in optimism, which recognizes only pessimism as its opponent. But both are value assessments in relation to beings and among beings. Both move in the realm of metaphysical thinking and institute the omission of the default of Being. They increase needlessness, and, without being able to meditate on it, merely see to it that needlessness is not and cannot be experienced *as need.*

The need of Being consists in the fact that it is doubly compelling, but that in its default it is accompanied by the danger of the annihilation of man's essence, insofar as Being occasions the omission of its own default. Need-lessness signifies that the need, which Being itself essentially unfolds as, remains veiled—a destiny that endangers need by elevating it to the utmost extremity and perfecting it as the need of needlessness.

However, if historical man were capable of thinking needlessness as the need of Being itself, then he could presumably discover what *is* in the history of Being.* In the era of the fulfilled nonessence of nihilism, man might then for the first time learn that what "is," *is*—in the sense of an "is" determined by the truth of Being. For he would already have thought on the basis of Being itself. Man would discover what emerges from needlessness as need in terms of the history of Being, what in that way has already arrived in its provenance but comes to presence in a concealed advent; that is, from the viewpoint of metaphysical experience, comes to absence. Metaphysically considered, absence means the exact opposite of presencing as Being: nonbeing in the sense of vacuous nothingness. What is it that emerges from the need of needlessness into the unthought of Being itself—that is to say, amid beings as such—in such a way that it passes for nothingness?

---

* The use of the verb *is* in this and the following sentence points forward to Heidegger's lecture series to the Bremen Club in 1949 entitled *Einsicht in das, was Ist,* "Insight into What Is." The four lectures were "The Thing," "The Enframing" (later entitled "The Question Concerning Technology"), "The Danger," and "The Turning."

The default of the unconcealment of Being as such releases the evanescence of all that is hale in beings. The evanescence of the hale takes the openness of the holy with it and closes it off. The closure of the holy eclipses every illumination of the divine. The deepening dark entrenches and conceals the lack of God. The obscure lack lets all beings stand in the unfamiliar, even though the being, as what is objectified in limitless objectification, seems to be a secure possession and is everywhere well-known. The unfamiliarity of beings as such brings to light the homelessness of historical man within beings as a whole. The "where" of a dwelling in the midst of beings as such seems obliterated, because Being itself, as the essential occurring of every abode, fails to appear.

The partly conceded, partly denied homelessness of man with regard to his *essence* is replaced by the organized global conquest of the earth, and the thrust into outer space. Homeless man—thanks to the success of his management and ordering of ever greater numbers of his kind—lets himself be driven into flight in the face of his own essence, only to represent this flight to himself as a homecoming to the true humanity of *homo humanus,* and to make humanity part of his own enterprise. The pressure of the actual and effectual increases. Needlessness in relation to Being is entrenched in and through the increased demand for beings. The more the being requires beings, the less it craves the being as such; even less is it inclined to heed Being itself. The destitution of beings with respect to the unconcealment of Being is complete.

The epoch of the concealment of Being in the unconcealment of the being in the form of will to power is the age of the accomplished destitution of the being as such. However, this age first begins to establish the dominion of the nonessence of nihilism in its completeness. The historical course of our era entertains the illusion that man, having become free for his humanity, has freely taken the universe into his power and disposition. The right way seems to have been found. All that is needed is to proceed rightly and thus to establish the dominion of justification as the supreme representative of the will-to-will.

The essence of the destitution of this era in the history of Being consists in the need of needlessness. Because it is more essential, and older, the destiny of Being is less familiar than the lack of God. As such a destiny, the truth of Being refuses itself in the midst of the throng of beings and nothing but beings. What is unfamiliar in our absent-present need closes itself off thanks to the fact that everything actual, the being itself which concerns the man of our era and carries him along with it, is thoroughly familiar to him; but precisely on that account, not only is man unacquainted with the truth of Being, but wherever "Being" crops up he proclaims it the specter of sheer abstraction, thus mistakes it and repudiates it as vacuous nothingness. By surrendering all remembrance, instead of ceaselessly recollecting the essential historical fullness of the *words* "Being" and "to be," he hears mere *terms,* whose empty reverberations he rightly finds irritating.

The unfamiliarity of the need of needlessness does close itself off; it does extend its misconstrued reign in the omission of Being itself. But the unfamiliarity of the need derives from what is simple. Such simplicity bodies forth in the stillness of Being's default, which *remains* still. However, man in the age of fulfilled metaphysics hardly encounters in thought what is simple. To the extent that he is able to think Being as such, he immediately encumbers it with the freight of a metaphysical concept, whether he takes the latter seriously as the labor of a limited comprehension, or frivolously as the mere sport of a futile grappling. In any case, metaphysical knowledge, whether as a positive investment or a negative withdrawal, is enriched only by the labors of scientific knowledge.

But thinking, which encounters in inquiry the default of Being, neither is grounded on science nor can it ever find its way by setting itself off against science. Whenever it *is,* thinking rests in the occasioning of, and is as an occasion from, Being itself, insofar as it involves itself in the unconcealment of Being.

To the extent that a thinking of Being, according to its own essence in the history of Being, can experience what remains for it to experience only in the need of needlessness; that is, can experience need itself as the destiny of the default of Being in its truth; to that extent it necessarily dispatches itself—still under the dominance of metaphysics, and within its unlimited sphere of control—with those first steps that lead it toward the drawing pull of Being on the essence of man, a drawing in the form of withdrawal.

Thinking of Being is so decisively caught up in the metaphysical thought of the being as such that it can only grope its way with the help of a staff borrowed from metaphysics. Metaphysics helps and hinders at the same time. It makes the passage more difficult, not because it is metaphysics, but because it maintains its own essence in what is unthinkable. The essence of metaphysics, however, the fact that in concealing it shelters the unconcealment of Being and thus is the *secret* of the history of Being, first of all permits the experience of thinking the history of Being passage into the free region. The truth of Being itself essentially occurs as the free region.

If needlessness is the most extreme need and *is* precisely as if it were not, then in order for the need to be compelling in the realm of man's essence, man's capacities must first be directed toward the needlessness. To experience needlessness as such is a necessity. Granted, however, that it is the need of Being as such, and granted that Being as such is entrusted preeminently and only to thinking, then the matter of Being—that in its unconcealment it is the Being of beings—passes over to thinking. For thinking, Being itself in its unconcealment and thus unconcealment itself must become questionable; but this is to happen in the age of metaphysics, through which Being is devalued into a value. Yet the worth of Being, as Being, does not consist in being a value, even the supreme value. Being essentially occurs in that it—the freedom of the free region itself—liberates all beings to themselves. It remains what is to be thought by thinking. But the fact that the being *is* as if Being "were" *not* unrelenting in its usage of the abode, as if it "were" *not* the compelling need of truth itself—this fact constitutes the dominion of needlessness entrenched in metaphysics as fulfilled.

ANALYSIS AND GLOSSARY

Analysis

By DAVID FARRELL KRELL

At the outset, three extracts to broach the themes of will to power, nihilism, and the nothing.

First, Ulysses to the Greek princes on the plains of Troy:

> Take but degree away, untune that string,
> And, hark, what discord follows! each thing meets
> In mere oppugnancy: the bounded waters
> Should lift their bosoms higher than the shores,
> And make a sop of all this solid globe:
> Strength should be lord of imbecility,
> And the rude son should strike his father dead:
> Force should be right; or, rather, right and wrong,—
> Between whose endless jar justice resides,—
> Should lose their names, and so should justice too.
> Then everything includes itself in power,
> Power into will, will into appetite;
> And appetite, an universal wolf,
> So doubly seconded with will and power,
> Must make perforce an universal prey,
> And last eat up himself.
>
> SHAKESPEARE, *Troilus and Cressida*, I, iii

Second, Hyperion to Bellarmine:

O you hapless creatures, who feel it, but who do not like to speak of what defines man; you who are transfixed by the nothing that governs us; you who thoroughly comprehend that we are born for nothing, that we love a nothing, believe in the nothing, toil away for nothing, in order gradually to pass over into the nothing;—what can I do to prevent your collapsing when you contemplate it in earnest? ... O, I can fall on my knees, wring my hands, and plead (with whom I know not) that there be other thoughts. But I cannot suppress the crying truth. Have I not convinced myself twice over? When I gaze into life, what is the end of it all? Nothing. When my spirit ascends, what is the highest height of all? Nothing.

HÖLDERLIN, Hyperion, I, 1

Third, the merciless Melville, raising the curtain on a shivering author and delivering himself of "some philosophical remarks":

Some hours pass. Let us peep over the shoulder of Pierre, and see what it is he is writing there, in that most melancholy closet. ... "A deep-down, unutterable mournfulness is in me. Now I drop all humorous or indifferent disguises, and all philosophical pretensions. ... Away, ye chattering apes of a sophomorean Spinoza and Plato, who once didst all but delude me that the night was day, and pain only a tickle. Explain this darkness, exorcise this devil, ye cannot. Tell me not, thou inconceivable coxcomb of a Goethe, that the universe cannot spare thee and thy immortality, so long as—like a hired waiter—thou makest thyself 'generally useful.' ...

"Cast thy eye in there on Vivia; tell me why those four limbs should be clapped in a dismal jail ... and himself the voluntary jailor! Is this the end of philosophy? ...

"I hate the world, and could trample all lungs of mankind as grapes, and heel them out of their breath, to think of the woe and the cant,—to think of the Truth and the Lie! ..."

From these random slips, it would seem, that Pierre is quite conscious of much that is so anomalously hard and bitter in his lot, of much that is so black and terrific in his soul. Yet that knowing his fatal condition does not one whit enable him to change or better his condition. Conclusive proof that he has no power over his condition. For in tremendous extremities human souls are like drowning men; well enough they know they are in peril; well enough they know the causes of that peril; nevertheless, the sea is the sea, and these drowning men do drown.

HERMAN MELVILLE, Pierre, Or, The Ambiguities, XXII, iii

I. THE STRUCTURE AND MOVEMENT OF THE LECTURE COURSE AND ESSAY

Heidegger's 1940 lecture course, "Nietzsche: *The Will to Power (European Nihilism),*" comprises twenty-nine unnumbered sections.[1] Although no other divisions appear, this course too (see Volume I in this series) may be seen as unfolding in three stages. The first stage (sections 1–9) offers an account of nihilism, will to power, and valuation in Nietzsche's thought; the second (sections 10–20) interprets valuation and the metaphysics of will to power in terms of the modern metaphysics of subjectivity; the third (sections 21–29) postulates the end of such metaphysics—although not the cessation of nihilism—and calls for an inquiry into the history of Being. Here too, as in Volume I, the first and last sections of the central part serve as hinges for the triptych, so that my Analysis will have to pay special heed to them: section 10, "Valuation and Will to Power," and section 20, "The Inner Connection Between the Basic Positions of Descartes and Nietzsche." Yet even these cursory delineations of the structure of Heidegger's lecture course on nihilism betray the movement of that course. Beginning with a criticism of Nietzsche's valuative thought as the culmination of Western metaphysics since Plato, and advancing through a detailed account of the "modernity" of such thought—that is to say, its Cartesian heritage—Heidegger's lectures conclude with an effort to redefine in a nonvaluative mode of thought the relationship of Being and Man in the epoch of metaphysics' fulfillment, the epoch of nihilism.

Heidegger begins (in section 1) by distinguishing Nietzsche's understanding of nihilism in terms of the collapse of all transcendent values from other, more "symptomatic" uses of the word and by defining Nietzsche's understanding of the being in terms of will to power. The latter is acknowledged as the source of all valuation. But because power is essentially enhancement, any revaluation of values must itself revert to perpetual becoming, hence to eternal recurrence. Finally, the affirmation of eternal recurrence, Nietzsche's principal thought, demands

---

[1] Throughout the English translation numbers have been added to facilitate reference.

a new type of humanity, namely, Overman. These five expressions (nihilism, revaluation of all values, will to power, eternal recurrence of the same, and Overman) yield five complementary perspectives on Nietzsche's metaphysics.

At the very outset Heidegger proposes his thesis that Nietzsche's "classical" nihilism itself precludes the possibility of a thoughtful encounter with the *nihil*, described as "the veil that conceals the truth of the Being of beings." Heidegger now (section 2) raises the question of valuative thought and the "validity" of values in terms of the question of their Being; he asserts that nihilism has to do, not primarily with the collapse of "values," but with the fact that all being is experienced as *being nothing* (section 3). Heidegger ventures the assertion that the essence of nihilism consists in *not* taking the question of the *nihil* seriously, and that in this respect the history of nihilism is coterminous with the history of metaphysics. The latter, up to and including Nietzsche, unfolds as the nonessence of Being.

In a lengthy note (WM, 12), Nietzsche defines nihilism as the collapse of "cosmological" values such as purpose, unity, truth, and Being. Nietzsche reckons the impact of that collapse "psychologically" in terms of the inapplicability of the "categories of reason" to the world (sections 4–6). Although the three forms of nihilism defined by Nietzsche cannot be aligned with particular historical epochs, Nietzsche's own position in the history of nihilism may be defined (section 7) as an *active,* transitional position. Its activity (section 8) consists in actively knowing—that is, reckoning—the source of all valuation as will to power. Section 9 summarizes the foregoing in two statements:

> First, nihilism, as Nietzsche thinks it, is the history of the devaluation of the highest values hitherto, as the transition to the revaluation of all prior values, a revaluation that comes to pass in the discovery of a principle for a new valuation, a principle Nietzsche recognizes as the will to power. Second, Nietzsche conceives of the essence of nihilism solely on the basis of valuative thought, and in that form alone does it become an object of his critique and his attempt at an overcoming. But because the valuation has its principle in the will to power, overcoming nihilism by fulfilling it in its classical form develops into an interpretation of being as a whole as will to power. The new valuation is a metaphysics of will to power.

Now the long middle section of the course commences, seeking in the history of metaphysics the origin of the convergence of will to power and valuative thought. In section 10, Heidegger asks, "What occurs essentially and reigns in Western metaphysics, that it should finally come to be a metaphysics of will to power?" The principal clue to an answer is the role of valuative thought in modern metaphysics, value thinking being the essence and fulfillment of the metaphysics of subjectivity. As conditions of will to power, values must assure not only the stability and continuance, but also the enhancement, of will to power. Values, whose validity can be ascertained only by a calculative thinking, revert to "viewpoints" and "perspectives," terms that have been current in the history of metaphysics since Leibniz. Values are "conditioned conditions"; valuation and will to power are the same. Only in that sense can values "condition" will to power, since the latter constitutes the basic trait of beings. At the end of section 10, Heidegger restates the questions that will dominate the central portion of his course: "Why does the thought of will to power become dominant *along with* valuative thought in metaphysics? How and why does metaphysics become a metaphysics of the will to power?"

That Nietzsche calls the highest values "categories of reason" testifies to his remaining within the orbit of modern metaphysics (section 11), although he thinks "category" differently from the way Hegel, Kant, and certainly Aristotle do. But Heidegger now makes the important concession that he himself cannot overcome the limitation of his own point of view in the history of Being in order to ascertain precisely where Nietzsche stands. For Nietzsche's interpretation of metaphysics on the basis of a genealogy of *morals* (section 12) is something altogether unique in the history of philosophy. Although it does arise from the tradition that asserts the anthropomorphic origins of metaphysics, a tradition that extends from Protagoras through Descartes (section 13), Nietzsche's "humanization" of metaphysics and morals is sufficiently radical to constitute the end of the tradition. For Protagoras and the Greeks in general, man is a restricted radius of measured unconcealment of beings (section 14); for Descartes, man is the *subiectum* proper; that is, the ground of the representation of beings in terms of truth as certitude (sections 15–18). Released from the Greeks' limited radius, modern man is leashed to the task of his own liberation and self-determination. On the quest of security in certitude, he pursues the goal of power, power to unconditioned dominion over the earth. As the philosopher of power, Nietzsche fails to recognize the dependence of his interpretation of beings as will to power on Descartes' own fundamental position (section 19): Nietzsche too interprets Being as representedness. This failure derives from a "self-mistaking" that is essential to the completion of metaphysics: "Thinking in values conceals the collapse of the essence of Being and truth." Placing the body in the position of consciousness as methodologically primary alters nothing in that "self-mistaking."

Section 20, "The Inner Connection between the Fundamental Positions of Descartes and Nietzsche," summarizes the middle section of the course and introduces the third cluster of themes—Being, truth, and the ontological difference in the history of metaphysics. The paradoxical thesis of the central portion of Heidegger's course is that although Nietzsche misapprehends the essential inner connection between his metaphysics of will to power and Descartes' metaphysics of subjectivity, Nietzsche's metaphysics "fashions for itself an essentially correct insight into the essence of metaphysics." Referring to the four criteria that ascertain the character of a fundamental metaphysical position (see section 14), namely, the understanding of *man,* the projection of *beings* upon *Being,* the understanding of *truth,* and the *measure* for the truth of beings, Heidegger now compares Nietzsche's and Descartes' positions. First, Descartes posits *man* as the representing subject, while for Nietzsche the body's "drives" and "affects" are decisive. Second, with regard to beings in their *Being* (or beingness), Descartes insists on their representedness (*Vorgestelltheit*), while Nietzsche stresses the inadequacy of all representation of becoming. Even so, however, Nietzsche's emphasis on perspectival will to power reverts to the understanding of Being as representedness. Third, *truth* for Descartes is certitude of representation, whereas for Nietzsche it is taking-for-true; that is, a futile permanentization. Nonetheless, an understanding of truth as representation seems to underlie Nietzsche's critique of Descartes. Fourth, Descartes removes the limits from the Greek understanding of man as *measure,* making the representing sub-

Analysis

ject the absolute ground of certitude; Nietzsche rejects man as epistemological measure, but only to affirm the Overman as will to power which is absolutely empowered to assume lordship over the earth. Heidegger emphasizes that the differences between Descartes' and Nietzsche's positions—for they are not identical—cannot be reduced to a straightforward alteration in man's conception of himself; the innermost history of metaphysics is rather "a history of the truth of Being." The following thesis brings section 20 to a close and introduces the final third of the lecture course: "As the fulfillment of modern metaphysics, Nietzsche's metaphysics is at the same time the fulfillment of Western metaphysics in general and is thus—in a correctly understood sense—the end of metaphysics as such."

Heidegger insists (section 21) that the role of the human being as subject is not a subjective decision on man's part; it results from the understanding of Being as representedness and of truth as certitude. That understanding has man in its grip and has become man's stranglehold on the world. Whereas Hegel's thought may be described as a metaphysics of absolute subjectivity which in one sense constitutes the end of metaphysics, Nietzsche's is a metaphysics of the absolute dominion of will to power, constituting the "full ending" (*Vollendung*) of metaphysics (section 22). The metaphysics of Hegel celebrates rationality; that of Nietzsche bestiality. Both together exhaust the traditional sense of humanity. But the phrase "end of metaphysics" means that the essential possibilities of metaphysics too are exhausted. "At the end of metaphysics stands the statement *Homo est brutum bestiale*." But that end is just beginning.

Heidegger can claim no "bird's-eye view" of our present age, but he nonetheless calls for a "decision." The standpoint for such a decision is recognition of the way European nihilism essentially unfolds in and as the history of Being. The four guidelines mentioned earlier (sections 14 and 20) express in their unity that essential unfolding. They exhibit as their unifying ground the ontological difference, here (section 23) defined as the distinction between man's relationship to Being and his sundry relations with beings. Heidegger calls the differentiation between Being and beings the "settlement." The principal proviso of that settlement in the history of metaphysics is the *a priori* character of

Being (section 24), seen from the point of view and for the sake of beings. The *a priori* is defined early on as the Idea of the Good, the earliest prototype of Nietzsche's value thinking, although not its replica (section 25). "Idea" is interpreted as the "condition" of beings with a view to their visuality, to human seeing and knowing, hence, in the modern age, to *perceptio*. "Idea" must be reckoned with as a condition of the representedness (Being) of objects. But ideas as conditions can only become *values:* thus the movement from Plato, through Descartes, Leibniz, Kant, and Hegel, to Nietzsche (section 26). Being as *idea* can be projected, can essentially unfold, only as will to power (section 27). Yet the very possibility of "idea," "condition," and "value" lies in the differentiation between Being and beings (section 28), for that differentiation constitutes the metaphysical in man. The nature of man is grounded in the differentiation—as our language suggests when it (section 29) employs the "is" of Being so abundantly that even in the age of *Weltanschauung* nothing appears beyond its scope. But the scope of "Being," Janus-headed, duplicitous, vacuous yet rich in possibility, becomes the crucial mystery for the epoch of nihilism.

Heidegger's essay or brief treatise, "Nihilism as Determined by the History of Being," maps more thoroughly than any other text in the *Nietzsche* volumes Heidegger's path of thought toward the "Letter on Humanism" (see Heidegger's "Foreword to All Volumes" in Volume I of this series). The central theme of that "Letter"—namely, the relationship of Being and human being—along with a host of related themes such as nihilism, valuative thought, ontotheology, the history of Being as abandonment and withdrawal, Da-sein as the abode of Being's advent, and the essence of Da-sein as meditative thinking, receive detailed treatment here. Roughly speaking, the movement of Heidegger's essay is *from* Nietzsche's valuative thought *to* the thought that encounters Being in withdrawal *via* the "step back" out of metaphysics into the history of Being.

Heidegger begins with the complaint that neither the metaphysics of will to power nor the thought of eternal recurrence develop adequately the question of Being and Time. But he immediately concedes the irrelevance of such a complaint, and, responding to the fidelity of

Nietzche's own thinking, asks whether in Nietzsche's metaphysics nihilism as such is overcome. Prior to that, of course, he must ask how nihilism is experienced there. Because Nietzsche's metaphysics insists that the being *is* (as) will to power in the mode of eternal recurrence, nihilism *appears* to be overcome there: in Nietzsche's metaphysics there is ultimately no room for the nothing. But acknowledgment of beings does not think Being; it misses the *essence* of nihilism. "The essence of nihilism is the history in which there is nothing to Being itself." Nietzsche's metaphysics is nihilism proper, for it insists that Being is a "value," hence, ironically, that there is "nothing to it." It is thus the fulfillment of the metaphysics that began with Plato.

The "essence" or "essential unfolding" of nihilism as metaphysics takes center stage in Heidegger's inquiry. Metaphysics establishes essences in terms of "whatness," and thus interprets beings in terms of other beings and their beingness, never raising the question of Being *as* Being. Metaphysics is onto-theology. Nietzsche's thought too is onto-theological, although as fulfilled nihilism it is "negative" onto-theology, neither transcendental nor transcendent in character. Like all prior metaphysics, Nietzsche's metaphysics neglects to think *unconcealment* as the truth of Being. Being remains in default. The history of Being comes to nothing. The emphasis falls equally on all these terms: Being *remains* in default; history *comes* to nothing. Heidegger recognizes that the word *Sein* itself misses what is to be thought here. He therefore attempts to think the default of Being as such with the help of a metaphorics of sojourn: "advent," "locale," "abode," "shelter." All these are names for *Da-sein*, ecstatic inherence in openness, the essence of which is to think Being. The relation of Being to Man is thus the crucial problem.

In Heidegger's discussion of that problem, the terms "authenticity" and "inauthenticity," nihilism "proper" and nihilism *manqué*, "essence" and "nonessence" are thoroughly relativized, because the omission of the default of Being (in metaphysical thought) is the *Gift* of duplicitous Being itself. Thus "the full essence of nihilism is the original unity of its authenticity and inauthenticity." The full essence of nihilism in the history of Being therefore may not be identified with "destructive nihilism," but is itself something essentially differentiated.

That difference cannot be expunged. But human thought can advance toward the omission of the default of Being, provided it has experienced the necessity of such an advance, as "promise," "mystery," and "enigma," by thinking to encounter it. Thinking encounters the withdrawal of Being but does not pursue it; it remains behind, takes the "step back," descends to a depth "which no longer corresponds to a height." It eschews all forms of objectification, especially those endemic to the historical disciplines, and all willfulness, including the will to overcome nihilism. The withdrawal of Being assumes a particularly striking form with the insight that in the step back "Being" loses its power to name, "because it always unwittingly says 'presence and permanence,' determinations to which the *essentially occurring* character of Being can never be attached as a mere addendum." Thus, in the end as at the beginning, the thinker of Becoming penetrates to the thinker of Being. The Heidegger-Nietzsche confrontation culminates in a shared recognition of *need* and *danger* in the present historical age.

II. CONTEXTS

It is with trepidation that I write anything at all about the contexts of nihilism, for they are invariably intricate and highly explosive. Whatever the context in question, nihilism remains bewildering and hazardous. It has therefore been a painful embarrassment for me to read a number of contemporary monographs and essays on nihilism by professional philosophers for whom the matter is ultimately quite simple. Such essays boil down to the remonstrance, "If you people would only put away such dangerous and destructive writers as Nietzsche and Heidegger, and go back to the truly inspirational philosophers of our tradition, embracing the timeless wisdom of their texts (as elucidated in my own modest commentaries), all of this nihilism business would vanish like a bad dream." What is painful is not the condemnation of "dangerous" thinkers but the adulation of "safe" ones. To proclaim any Socrates "safe" is to outdo Alcibiades in violence; it is to proffer the deadliest of draughts. What is embarrassing is the assumption that by doing what they have been taught to do in graduate schools philosophers are redeeming the world. Against such pomposity and covert violence the following lines from Yeats's "Nineteen Hundred and Nineteen" are effective—and they introduce the most troubling of contexts.

> Now days are dragon-ridden, the nightmare
> Rides upon sleep: a drunken soldiery
> Can leave the mother, murdered at her door,
> To crawl in her own blood, and go scot-free;
> The night can sweat with terror as before
> We pieced our thoughts into philosophy,
> And planned to bring the world under a rule,
> Who are but weasels fighting in a hole.

In the *Spiegel* interview of September 23, 1966, Heidegger himself invokes the most distressing context. There he twice identifies his Nietzsche lectures of the late 1930s and early 1940s as one of the principal sites of his confrontation (*Auseinandersetzung*) with National Socialism.[2] The context is grievously distressing for at least two reasons: first, the unspeakable consequences of Nazism, what has come to be called "the holocaust"; second, the way the retrospective illusion causes us to jumble the multiple facets of German fascism—the racism and anti-Semitism, the relentless propaganda, the mass enthusiasm masking mass despondency, industrial and military mobilization, chauvinism and xenophobia, police terror and the death camps—into a nightmarish composite portrait we call *nihilism*. Our initial question, formulated with little thought and a great deal of passion, is

---

[2] *Der Spiegel*, 1976, *30* (23), 204. An English translation of the interview by Maria P. Alter and John D. Caputo appears in *Philosophy Today*, 1976, *20* (4-4), 267-84. The *Spiegel* interview is an important document because it is one of the rare places where Heidegger speaks of his political engagement in the 1930s. Yet Heidegger is less than candid about many matters; for example, his and Frau Heidegger's relations with the Jaspers and Husserl households. Heidegger's defensive attitude throughout the interview precludes genuine self-criticism, so that the piece often seems self-serving when what is called for is profound forthrightness. Unfortunately, the documents that would shed most light on Heidegger's political blunder—namely, his extensive correspondence with figures such as Jaspers, Karl Löwith, and Hannah Arendt—will not be made available to scholars for some time.

"How could Heidegger have been mixed up in all of this—or in any of it?"

Such a question cannot be answered to the satisfaction of passion, and perhaps even less to the satisfaction of thought. For one thing, we lack an adequate notion of National Socialism, one that can differentiate among the various years, places, and circumstances of the movement. Otto Pöggeler writes,

> It is altogether inappropriate to treat National Socialism as an indissoluble, homogeneous unit, and then to take it as a mere instance of European fascism and a countermovement to Communism. National Socialism, with its insistent grasp after world rule and its attempt to annihilate European Jewry, is utterly unique. But neither can the later totalitarian system simply be equated with the early "resurgence" of those desperate persons who responded to the movement, or with the elements that crystallized about such resurgence.[3]

Yet it is important to reiterate the particular attraction National Socialism exercised on Heidegger, an attraction, it is true, that began to wither soon after he had taken up his duties as rector of the University of Freiburg.[4] That attraction may be glimpsed in what Ernst Bertram and Karl Jaspers—who went opposite ways in the 1930s—say concerning the fate of Germany in the twentieth century. In his influential work, *Nietzsche: Attempt at a Mythology*, Bertram includes a chapter entitled "German Becoming."[5] There he elaborates on the tradition that begins with Luther and continues through Lessing, Herder, Goethe, Schiller, Novalis, Hölderlin, Jean Paul, Hebbel, Stifter, and Nietzsche, a tradition in which poets and educators in the

---

[3] Otto Pöggeler, "Heideggers Begegnung mit Hölderlin," in *Man and World*, 1977, 10 (1), 25. Pierre Trotignon, *Heidegger: Sa vie, son oeuvre* (Paris: Presses Universitaires de France, 1965), p. 3, quotes Helvétius as saying, "L'aurore de la tyrannie n'annonce jamais les meurtres."

[4] I presuppose that the reader is familiar with the chronology of Heidegger's political engagement, although the extent and character of his involvement is disputed everywhere and on all points. For a brief account, see my "General Introduction" to Martin Heidegger, *Basic Writings* (New York: Harper & Row, 1977), pp. 27–28. In addition to the sources cited there, see the fine critical account by Karsten Harries, "Heidegger as a Political Thinker," in M. Murray, ed., *Heidegger and Modern Philosophy*, (New Haven, Conn.: Yale University Press, 1978), pp. 304–28.

[5] Ernst Bertram, *Nietzsche: Versuch einer Mythologie* (Berlin: Georg Bondi, 1918).

German lands prod the nation *to become* what it must be, to develop through *Erziehung* and *Bildung* a German "essence." For, politically and historically speaking, the German "essence" is precisely a lack of Being. Hence the almost desperate clinging to Becoming, the hope in transition and transformation, the longing after something ill-defined and ever unattained.[6] In the eighth chapter of his *Philosophical Autobiography,* Karl Jaspers recounts the crisis of German "Becoming" in the current century. In the course of his reflections he comments on the frenzied search for a German "essence":

> Other nations accuse us of unending reflection on what it means to be German, of wanting so badly to *be* German; they insist that we turn what is natural into something artificial and forced. . . . But for Germans the question is . . . unfortunately unavoidable.[7]

---

[6] Cf. Heidegger's remarks in *The Will to Power as Art,* the first volume of this translation, pp. 103–4, which pertain to the task of German "Becoming." Heidegger is discussing Hölderlin's conceptual pair "holy pathos" and *"Junonian sobriety* of representational skill," related to Nietzsche's later distinction between the "Dionysian" and "Apollonian," respectively:

> The opposition is not to be understood as an indifferent historical finding. Rather, it becomes manifest to direct meditation on the destiny and determination of the German people. . . . It is enough if we gather from the reference that the variously named conflict of the Dionysian and the Apollonian, of holy passion and sober representation, is a hidden stylistic law of the historical determination of the German people, and that one day we must find ourselves ready and able to give it shape. . . . By recognizing this antagonism Hölderlin and Nietzsche early on placed a question mark after the task of the German people to find their essence historically. Will we understand this cipher? One thing is certain: history will wreak vengeance on us if we do not.

Cf. *Der Spiegel,* p. 214; English translation, p. 281. While it is tempting to regard the German fascination with Becoming as *sui generis,* as something specifically German, and while that fascination (visible in Heidegger's words here) does display traits found nowhere else, we would do well to reflect on parallel situations in nineteenth- and twentieth-century Eurasia and America; for example, in the ideologies of Pan-Slavism, of the "glory" of the French nation, or of the divinely sanctioned "manifest destiny" of the United States to extend its frontiers endlessly. We can no longer be confident that American faith in the New Frontier or the politicized nostalgia for the Old Frontier will have less devastating consequences for world history than the earlier German faith in Becoming. And there seems to be no one to inscribe a question mark between such nostalgia and the gathering vengeance.

[7] Karl Jaspers, *Philosophische Autobiographie,* new, expanded edition (Munich: R. Piper, 1977), pp. 76 ff.

Hardly an explanation—more a confession of impotence in the face of a long and tyrannical tradition. Indeed, Jaspers displays a helpless fascination for "grand politics" in his 1936 *Nietzsche*,[8] and even in his autobiography he celebrates "the grand politics of the philosophers" extending from "Plato and Kant, and on to Hegel and Kierkegaard and Nietzsche." "A philosophy shows what it is," he concludes, "in its political manifestation."[9] But now to the crisis.

With the outbreak of World War I, the Germans, perhaps more acutely than other European peoples, sensed that they had been caught up in, or "thrown into," a turbulent stream of "relentless, uncomprehended" events. The initial problem for reconstruction after the war was therefore how to achieve some modicum of comprehension concerning what had happened. Because of Versailles, of course, that comprehension tended to be defensive or, through overcompensation, offensive, self-inflating, and self-assertive. Jaspers credits Max Weber's "national thinking" with whatever political insight he (Jaspers) attained. Weber had insisted that Germany was to fulfill a special mission in Europe: Germany would rescue the liberal tradition in Western political thought from the Soviet "lash" and from Anglo-Saxon "conventionalism." Russian Bolshevism was feared as the more formidable enemy—its victory in Germany would spell the virtual end of European liberalism. Germany would therefore have to confront "its momentous world-historical task" (Jaspers), the task of salvaging the threatened "between."[10] It would have to assume leadership in *der grossen Politik,* understood not in terms of Ludendorff's militarism but as a diplomacy based on a volatile mixture of shrewdness and liberal principles—precisely the kind of diplomacy practiced by "Paul Arnheim" (i.e., Walther Rathenau) in *The Man Without Qualities,* Robert Musil's brilliant portrayal of prewar Austria-Hungary. Yet one remark by Jaspers is revealing, even devastating in the present context:

---

[8] Karl Jaspers, *Nietzsche: Einführung in das Verständnis seines Philosophierens* (Berlin: W. de Gruyter, 1936), Book II, ch. 4.

[9] K. Jaspers, *Philosophische Autobiographie,* p. 85.

[10] Cf. Martin Heidegger, *Einführung in die Metaphysik,* pp. 28–29; English translation by Ralph Manheim, *An Introduction to Metaphysics,* pp. 31–32. Cf. a more cryptic reference to the "between" in MHG 39, 289.

he confesses that he felt unequal to Weber's political mission and that he never discussed politics during the Weimar years, feeling that he had no right to do so—because he had not been a soldier![11] So much for a *grosse Politik* not disfigured by militarism.

The contrast between Weber's *nationales Denken* and the realities of Weimar Germany was no less devastating. In the everyday life of the Republic, amid the newspapers scattered on the breakfast table, such thinking could only express its contempt for the tepid liberalism, contentious socialism, and reactionary conservatism of the day.[12] Heidegger took part in the impatient search for something *authentic* in public life. He yearned for a "fundamental change," *Aufbruch* or *risorgimento,* that would totally recast the social, political, and academic order in Germany. Pöggeler, alluding to an analysis by Ernst Bloch, expresses the attraction of National Socialism for young intellectuals such as Heidegger in the following way:

> In the early years National Socialism had its positive aspect—which attracted many—in the fact that during a period that witnessed the destruction of every tradition that had once granted meaning—destruction by the new forces of the world economy and technology, destruction by the hectic promotions of the new mass media—and during a period that witnessed the uprooting of the old peasant and bourgeois classes of society, it promised to rescue and even to renew a sense of "homeland."[13]

In addition to Heidegger's participation in the general disaffection with Weimar political life, a disaffection the Nazis knew well how to cultivate and manipulate, one must also stress his hopes for university reform. At the outset of his discussion with *Spiegel* editors Rudolf Augstein and Georg Wolff, Heidegger mentions his conversations with a Freiburg colleague in 1932-33 concerning the "hopeless" situation of university students at that time; this is perhaps another way of saying what Heidegger had insisted in his inaugural lecture at Freiburg in 1929, "What Is Metaphysics?" There he bemoaned the fragmentation of the various faculties which represented disciplines that had lost all

---
[11] Jaspers, *Philosophische Autobiographie,* p. 71.
[12] See Otto Pöggeler, *Philosophie und Politik bei Heidegger* (Freiburg and Munich: K. Alber, 1972), p. 109.
[13] Pöggeler, "Begegnung," p. 25.

connection to their "essential ground," to wit, philosophy. The amorphous and utterly contingent configurations of *Wissenschaft* had to disturb a man who at least to some extent still thought of himself as a proponent of scientifically rigorous phenomenology; the fragmentation of the faculties and the absence of common goals, methods, and intentions in the university had to trouble an admirer of Wilhelm von Humboldt's university reforms. (Precisely what sorts of faculty reforms Heidegger had in mind, precisely what proposals he laid before Rust, the *Reichsminister* of Culture, in November 1933, we are not told.) At all events, in order to prevent the accession of a mere functionary of the Culture Ministry to the rectorship—that is to say, in order to preserve whatever autonomy and even "self-assertion" the university could aspire to—Heidegger gave way to the importunities of his younger colleagues and accepted the nomination to the rectorship.[14]

Heidegger's involvement in National Socialism in 1933-34 thus stemmed from two related sets of motives: first, a genuine hope that the promised "resurgence" would grant the nation a new sense of direction and the university a possibility for academic reform; second, the fear that if he did not accept the rectorship the university would lose whatever autonomy it still possessed. Heidegger's private ambitions surely colored both sets of motives, but the strength and quality of those ambitions is hard to judge. In any case, when Heidegger assumed the post it became clear to him that he would not be able to succeed in any of his plans "without compromises."[15] While resisting the most abusive actions of the students' branch of the *Sturmabteilung,* Heidegger spoke out vigorously in support of the *Führer* and his aggressive policies. Those dreary documents collected so assiduously by Guido Schneeberger record a different "voice"; in fact, in them the voice of

---

[14] Heidegger several times mentions his "younger colleagues" during the *Spiegel* interview, and this seems to be important. Himself a product of the provinces, with none of the advantages of family connections and social status to aid his rise in the academic world, Heidegger could hardly have been immune to the allure of academic prestige and power; as rector, Heidegger placed as many of those younger, more sympathetic colleagues in positions of power, such as deanships, as he could, and even opened various faculty meetings to student representatives, all to the chagrin of the older, more established professors.

[15] *Der Spiegel,* p. 198.

Martin Heidegger recedes, drowned in a crescendo of "the They." Ironically, the notion of *das Man* is often criticized for its imputed "elitist" and "protofascist" asocial tendencies; the rehabilitation of the notion may be furthered when we realize that Heidegger himself was fully capable of subsumption under it. For a time.

As rector, then as professor of philosophy, Heidegger soon sensed that National Socialism had perverted the drive to resurgence by making so atavistic, cynical, and demagogic a notion as race the center of its ideology. In his 1934–35 lecture course on Hölderlin he inveighed against such crass "biologism," attacking one of Rosenberg's ideological prototypes in supremely sardonic style:

> Herr Kolbenheyer, who is a writer, says that poetry "is a biologically necessary function of the *Volk.*" We do not need a great deal of intelligence to discern that the same is true of digestion. Digestion too is an essential biological function of a people—especially of a healthy people.[16]

But to what extent do the Nietzsche lectures themselves represent a confrontation with National Socialism? Heidegger's resistance to "biologism" is of course visible throughout, as is his rejection of the "official" Nietzsche, the monumentalized Nietzsche promulgated by Frau Förster and embraced by the Nazi leadership.[17]

One of the most influential perpetrators of the "official" Nietzsche was Alfred Baeumler, professor of philosophy in Berlin from 1933 to 1945 (note the place and dates, which tell it all), author of *Nietzsche,*

---

[16] Quoted by Pöggeler in "Begegnung," p. 24; cf. pp. 44–45. The "writer" Heidegger here derides is Erwin Guido Kolbenheyer, author of several novels and of *The Philosophy of the Lodge (Bauhütte),* the latter published in 1925. Kolbenheyer developed a brand of "metabiology" that lent itself easily to the *völkisch*-racist ideology of National Socialism. Heidegger labels him a *Schriftsteller* in order to scorn his pretensions to "metaphysics." The quoted passage now appears in Martin Heidegger, *Hölderlins Hymnen 'Germanien' und 'Der Rhein'* (Frankfurt am Main: V. Klostermann, 1980), MHG 39, 27.

[17] Walter Kaufmann has told the grim tale of the "Nietzsche legend" so well in the Prologue and the tenth chapter of his *Nietzsche: Philosopher, Psychologist, Antichrist* (Princeton, N.J.: Princeton University Press, 1950), pp. 3 ff. and 252 ff., that there is no need to recapitulate it here. I will restrict my discussion to matters directly pertinent to Heidegger's *Nietzsche.*

Philosopher and Politician.[18] At the outset of his first lecture course on Nietzsche,[19] Heidegger vigorously criticized Baeumler's adoption and political adaptation of "will to power" and his scornful rejection of "eternal recurrence." Heidegger insisted that these two teachings did not contradict one another, as Baeumler had claimed. He then added,

> But even if we concede that here we have a contradiction which cannot be transcended and which compels us to decide in favor of either will to power or eternal recurrence, why does Baeumler then decide *against* Nietzsche's most difficult thought, the peak of his meditation, and *for* will to power? The answer is simple: Baeumler's reflections on the relationship between the two doctrines do not press toward the realm of actual inquiry from either side. Rather, the doctrine of eternal recurrence, where he fears "Egypticism," militates against his conception of will to power, which, in spite of the talk about metaphysics, Baeumler does not grasp metaphysically but interprets politically.[20]

Baeumler's conception of politics is perhaps best betrayed by his affirmation of Nietzsche's ostensible world view—namely, "heroic realism"—and of the pseudo-Heraclitean world of Becoming, "of struggle and victory."[21] Baeumler devotes his energies in the second half of his book to an explanation of why Nietzsche merely *seems* to be anti-German—Nietzsche, who says in a hundred different ways, "The man is blond and stupid: he must be German." Baeumler's reassuring discovery is that Nietzsche is anti-German only because Roman-Christian-Mediterranean elements have infiltrated *Deutschtum,* and that Nietzsche wishes to revert to "Germanic undercurrents" and strictly "Nordic elements" in founding a new German state.[22] The great transformation in Nietzsche, from philosopher to politician, occurs when in the autumn of 1888 he alters the title of his projected major work from *The Will to Power* to *The Revaluation of All*

---

[18] Alfred Baeumler, *Nietzsche der Philosoph und Politiker* (Leipzig: P. Reclam, 1931).
[19] See Volume I of this translation, pp. 22–23.
[20] Ibid., p. 22.
[21] Baeumler, *Nietzsche,* p. 15.
[22] Ibid., pp. 88 ff.

Values.[23] Presumably from 1888 on Nietzsche dedicates himself to his political mission. Germany is to become Europe's "leader," and not in any "idealistic" sense. "He does not wish to make Germany into a nation of thinkers and poets again; he does not speak of a kingdom of the German Spirit or of the Christmas tree of the German Soul. . . . He wants to guide the Germans *zur grossen Politik.*"[24]

By now, of course, the grand style of art and "grand politics" have parted company irrevocably: not *Dichten* and *Denken,* which he reduces to Christmas-tree tinsel, but another vision dances in Baeumler's head. He capitulates to that vision three years later in an article entitled "Nietzsche and National Socialism."[25] There he identifies Nietzsche and Hitler as opponents of democratic-parliamentarian bourgeois society and government: "If we transpose Hitler's position with respect to the Weimar Republic to a lonely thinker of the nineteenth century, then we have Nietzsche." —It is pointless and unpleasant to go on, but let me at least reprint Baeumler's grandiloquent peroration:

> When we see German youth today marching under the symbol of the swastika, we recall Nietzsche's *Thoughts Out of Season,* in which our youth is summoned for the first time. It is our greatest hope that the state stands open to our youth. And when we greet them with the call *"Heil Hitler!"* we greet at the same time Friedrich Nietzsche.

One reader of Baeumler's *Nietzsche, Philosopher and Politician,* who had borrowed the copy deposited in Freiburg's university library some time before I did, could not resist jotting down on the title page the lament of Ophelia, "O, what a noble mind is here o'erthrown!" He or she was not referring to Baeumler's mind.

---

[23] Ibid., p. 153. See also Baeumler's ordering of the *Nachlass,* entitled *Die Unschuld des Werdens,* 2 vols., 2nd ed. (Stuttgart: A. Kröner, 1978), II, 313. In his Introduction to the volumes (I, xvii–xviii) Baeumler calls the Nietzsche of "revaluation" a "destroyer in the grandest style," "brandishing his sword" and dying a heroic death. Heidegger's rejection of Baeumler's political interpretation may also be mirrored in Heidegger's critique of the project of revaluation and of value thinking as such: surely Baeumler shows how low the project of revaluation can go.

[24] Baeumler, *Nietzsche,* p. 166.

[25] In the *Nationalsozialistische Monatshefte,* edited by Alfred Rosenberg, 1934, 5(49), 289–98. The following two quotations appear on pp. 290 and 298.

I reprint so much of Baeumler's disturbing *bavardage*, not to distract the reader from Heidegger's own involvement in National Socialism, or to minimize it, but to make clear the context in which Heidegger had to address the students attending his Nietzsche lectures. What they heard from Heidegger was something different—it was in fact totally *out of context*.

Related to the most troubling context, yet coming closer to the matter of Heidegger's own career of thought, is Hannah Arendt's thesis that the *Nietzsche* volumes reflect a "reversal" in Heidegger's thought that took place between 1936 and 1940.[26] Professor Arendt surrenders to the temptation "to date the 'reversal' as a concrete autobiographical event precisely between Volume I and Volume II."[27] But she is unable or unwilling to specify such an event: the "catastrophic defeat" of Nazi Germany in 1945, mirrored according to Arendt in "The Anaximander Fragment," may not be confused with this earlier unspecified event. Presumably, that earlier event would have to do with Heidegger's growing disaffection from National Socialism, even though Heidegger himself insists that the disaffection had burgeoned by 1934, two years before the first Nietzsche lecture.

Whatever the ostensible "event" that would insert itself as a wedge between the *Nietzsche* volumes, and however futile speculations about it must be, the reason behind Arendt's "temptation" merits critical discussion. Her own reason, "put bluntly," is that "the first volume explicates Nietzsche by going along with him, while the second is written in a subdued but unmistakably polemical tone."[28] To be sure, one senses a difference between the lectures and the treatises in

---

[26] Hannah Arendt, *The Life of the Mind*, 2 vols. (New York: Harcourt Brace Jovanovich, 1977–1978), II, 172 ff. It would be churlish of me not to admit that in what follows I have singled out what appears to be one of the weaker and ultimately less interesting theses in Arendt's section on Heidegger and the "will-not-to-will." There are astonishing lapses there, such as the initial claim that "Nietzsche's name is nowhere mentioned in *Being and Time*." (For a list of the references, see my Analysis to Volume I of this series, p. 247.) Yet there are gems as well, such as Arendt's reading of "The Anaximander Fragment." The lapses are signs of haste, testimony perhaps of the death that was too impatient; the gems are testimony to her intelligence and incredible vitality.
[27] Ibid., pp. 172–73.
[28] Ibid., p. 173.

Heidegger's *Nietzsche,* although the division into lectures and treatises does not in any case coincide with the division between Volume I and Volume II; and it is true that the lectures engage themselves with Nietzsche's texts intimately and at great length, whereas the treatises tend to formulate, foreshorten, differentiate, and delimit positions. But whether the *polemos* ever becomes a *polemic* is doubtful. Surely in the lecture on "European Nihilism," contained in the *second* volume of the German edition, Heidegger "goes along" with Nietzsche as far as he ever goes in previous lecture courses; and surely the very first lecture course, "Will to Power as Art," contains some of Heidegger's keenest criticisms of Nietzsche.

Nevertheless, what Hannah Arendt is trying to indicate is what both she and J. L. Mehta, along with many others, call a "change of mood" in Heidegger's writings during the 1930s. Mehta describes the mood of *Being and Time* and other "early" writings in terms of a "Promethean, aggressive attitude, in which man thinks of himself as destined to take truth and reality by storm, as it were."[29] Among the key words for the Promethean attitude would be *Wissenschaft,* "science," as the destiny of Dasein in the Western world, and particularly in the "between" of Germany; *Selbstbehauptung,* "self-assertion," both of the university and of the man who wills to know; *Wesenswille,* the will to assert the essence of one's self and one's nation; and *Entscheidung,* a resolute decision-making in service to that essence. Among these key words, *Selbstbehauptung* and *Wille* do play a role in the first volume of Heidegger's *Nietzsche* that they no longer play in the second. In the first volume of the English translation (sections 7-10), Heidegger discusses the will at great length. There, as Arendt notes, will is

---

[29] J. L. Mehta, *The Philosophy of Martin Heidegger* (New York: Harper & Row Torchbooks, 1971), pp. 110-11. I refer to this edition throughout, but readers should be aware of the larger volume, *Martin Heidegger: The Way and the Vision* (Honolulu: University of Hawaii Press, 1976), one of the very best books on Heidegger available. Mehta quickly qualifies the remark I have cited here by noting the essential role of *Seinlassen,* "letting-be," in Heidegger's "early" work as well. He observes correctly that the essay "On the Essence of Truth" is devoted entirely to the notion of "letting." Mehta therefore resists the reductive tendency of his own thesis, which would divide Heidegger's thought into two sequences, one marked by *Angst,* the other graced by *Gelassenheit.*

identified with the authentic self of Dasein, with steadfast resoluteness, and even with "care," the essence of finite transcendence as such.[30] As for the term *Selbstbehauptung,* Heidegger writes in that same volume,

> Life not only exhibits the drive to maintain itself, as Darwin thinks, but also is self-assertion. The will to maintain merely clings to what is already at hand, stubbornly insists upon it, loses itself in it, and so becomes blind to its proper essence. Self-assertion, which wants to be ahead of things, to stay on top of things, is always a going back into its essence, into the origin. *Self-assertion is original assertion of essence.*[31]

Professor Arendt is right about the fact that the detailed descriptions of the act of willing and of self-assertion in *Nietzsche I* are absent from the later treatises in *Nietzsche II.*[32] Indeed, there are other subtle differences she does not mention. For example, Heidegger's 1936–37 discussion of "the event of nihilism" invokes *die grosse Politik.*[33] Here Heidegger refers to those forces that grant the "historical existence of peoples" their coherence and power, forces that "sustain and propel preparation of the new realm, the advance into it, and the cultivation of what unfolds within it, forces which induce it to undertake bold deeds." By 1940 the German nation had amply demonstrated the quality of its bold deeds. While the second volume of *Nietzsche* is not devoid of political references, the public realm invoked there is dark indeed, and there is no talk of grand politics.[34]

---

[30] Arendt, p. 176.

[31] Volume I of this series, pp. 60–61. These words are highly reminiscent of Heidegger's *Rektoratsrede,* "The Self-Assertion of the German University," which is dominated by the terms *Selbstbehauptung* and *Wille* (usually in the verbal form *wollen*). See Martin Heidegger, *Die Selbstbehauptung der deutschen Universität* (Breslau: W. G. Korn, 1933), throughout.

[32] Note that in the lecture course contained in the present volume (p. 33), Heidegger does *not* identify with the human being's "self-assertion" in the midst of beings. *Selbstbehauptung* is here equated with the valuative thought against which Heidegger inveighs.

[33] See Volume I of this series, pp. 157–58, for this and the following quotation.

[34] This difference is also reflected in the fact that although "deeds which found the state" are elevated to the rank of works of art in the 1935 lectures "On the Origin of the Work of Art," the postwar lecture "The Question Concerning Technology," which contraposes art to technology, leaves "the state" utterly out of account. See Martin Heidegger, *Der Ursprung des Kunstwerkes* (Stuttgart: P. Reclam, 1960), pp. 68–69;

Yet to style the Heidegger of *Nietzsche I* as "Promethean" and the Heidegger of *Nietzsche II* as the meek prophet of "releasement" and "tranquil detachment" is far too crude a reduction. The very designation "Promethean" is misleading in the extreme. Both Mehta and Arendt use the word to portray a heaven-storming, aggressively self-assertive Heidegger; yet the passage in the *Rektoratsrede* to which they appeal displays a Prometheus who has "failed" to master his fate. *Technē d'anankēs asthenestera makroi*, "But knowledge is far less powerful than necessity."[35] Both Prometheus and Nietzsche are cited in the rectoral address as witnesses of man's helplessness in the midst of beings, his utter subjection to what is uncertain, concealed, and questionable. As such, they are figures that tend to restrain the generally will-full exhortations of the *Rektoratsrede*. However, it remains true that the later treatises on Nietzsche often turn their back on the richness of Nietzsche's central thought, the eternal recurrence of the same, and treat will to power as a metaphysical construct or "a will to rule and dominate rather than as an expression of the life instinct."[36] Will to power there becomes indistinguishable from the "essentially destructive" will-to-will and the accomplished subjectivism and nihilism of planetary technology. Heidegger's developing insight into the metaphysico-technological matrix of the will-to-will and his struggle to escape that matrix and to advance the thought of letting-be surely can be witnessed in the years 1936 to 1946; surely, the political debacle and national disaster can only have spoken for such a move. The desperately somber tone of the second part of the present volume, the essay composed in 1944–46—so much darker than the tone of the first part written in 1940—testifies to the impact of political catastrophe

---

English translation by Albert Hofstadter in *Poetry, Language, Thought* (New York: Harper & Row, 1971), p. 62. Cf. the whole of "Die Frage nach der Technik" in Martin Heidegger, *Vorträge und Aufsätze* (Pfullingen: G. Neske, 1954); English translation by William Lovitt, *The Question Concerning Technology* (New York: Harper & Row, 1977), also contained in *Basic Writings*, pp. 283–317.

[35] Mehta's reference (p. 112) is more cautious: following Walter Schulz, he refers to the figure of Prometheus as an incarnation of "heroic nihilism," representing "the self-assertion of Dasein in its impotence and finitude." See Heidegger, *Selbstbehauptung*, pp. 8–9; on Nietzsche, cf. p. 12.

[36] Arendt, p. 177, for this and the following.

on thinking. Yet it is crucial to recognize that the origins of Heidegger's insight, struggle, and advance go far back; they resist easy "dating" and all biographical reductionism. Professor Mehta is therefore wise to ascribe any "reversal" or shift in mood—which in any case he dates circa 1935—not to a shattering personal experience but to Heidegger's "study of Nietzsche."[37]

Not that the study of Nietzsche stands in isolation. Interwoven with it are a number of involvements that effect the altered *Stimmung* of Heidegger's thought: the critique of *Wissenschaft* and of the subjectivist philosophy of modernity, a critique that does not leave Heidegger's own project of fundamental ontology unscathed; the turn to Schelling, whom ten years earlier in a fit of phenomenological pique Heidegger had derided as a "mere *littérateur*";[38] the overpowering attraction to Hölderlin, for whom poetizing was anything but willful self-assertion; and the expanding influence of arts and letters in general on a man who once had styled himself an "ahistorical mathematician."[39] These preoccupations, along with Heidegger's prolonged confrontation with Nietzsche, are the quieter but more decisive events of the 1930s, these the more fertile contexts.

III. QUESTIONS

If in Heidegger's view Nietzsche's metaphysics of will to power and valuative thought prevent him from encountering the *nihil* as such, what kind of thinking does Heidegger propose for such an encounter? What role does the nothing play in Heidegger's own texts before and after the Nietzsche lectures? If those lectures derive from "the one experience out of which *Being and Time* is thought,"[40] and yet if they spurn "fundamental ontology" in order to promote inquiry into the history of Being, how are we to conceive of *the* "fundamental

---
[37] Mehta, p. 112.
[38] See Jaspers, *Philosophische Autobiographie*, p. 96.
[39] See Martin Heidegger, *Frühe Schriften* (Frankfurt am Main: V. Klostermann, 1972), p. 3.
[40] Martin Heidegger, "Nietzsches Wort 'Gott ist tot,'" in *Holzwege* (Frankfurt am Main: V. Klostermann, 1950), p. 195; English translation by William Lovitt, *Question*, p. 56.

experience" of Heidegger's thought? What does that experience have to do with the nothing?

It would be misleading to single out this or that "place" in *Being and Time* as the locus of the problem of the *nihil*. It would be no exaggeration to say that the nothing plays a principal role in virtually every phase of the analysis of Dasein, whether under the aspect of worldhood or selfhood, and at virtually every critical juncture of Heidegger's methodical inquiry into the meaning of Being. Readers will recall, for instance, the negativity implied in the reduction of *Zuhandenheit* to *Vorhandenheit*, being "on hand" to sheer being "at hand": Heidegger uses such words as *loss, disturbance,* and *breach* to describe that transition. But two sections of *Being and Time* (section 40, "The Fundamental Mood of Anxiety as an Exceptional Disclosure of Dasein," and section 58, "Understanding the Call, and Guilt") do thematize the problem. In section 40, Heidegger describes the everyday drift of Dasein as a flight "in the face of itself," a flight that allows Dasein to get "behind" itself, as it were, and so attain awareness of its existence. That in the face of which Dasein wishes to flee, that before which it experiences anxiety, is its being in the world as such. Anxiety is not fear of this or that being which may be on or at hand; intramundane entities are not "relevant" to the experience of anxiety. What threatens in anxiety cannot be located: it is nowhere, and it is nothing. "It was really nothing," we say, and on occasion we mean it. The no-thing that is no-where indicates that region in which beings—ourselves and others—can be disclosed. Such disclosure is the primal event of world, and of our being in the world. That *in the face of which* we are anxious is the world as such; that *about which* we are anxious is the possibility of our being there at all.[41] Why should the possibility of my

---

[41] The most important structural device in section 40 is Heidegger's alternation of *Angst-vor* and *Angst-um*, the first expressing the moment of world as a relational totality, the second the moment of Dasein as the capacity to be, possibility-being, or being *in* a world. The convergence of these two moments is one of the most dramatic and methodologically decisive junctures in *Being and Time*. For the very core of being-in is *disclosure*, and the phenomenon of anxiety, as disclosive, proves to be decisive for the analysis of Dasein as both disclosed and disclosing. Heidegger italicizes the following words: *"The existential selfsameness of the disclosing with what is disclosed, in such a way that in the latter world is disclosed as world, and being-in as individualized, pure, and*

being in the world make me anxious? Because I am not the *ground* of my own capacity to be there; because it is eminently possible that I *not* be there. In the second division of *Being and Time* (section 62; SZ, 308) Heidegger writes,

> The indefiniteness of death is disclosed originally in anxiety.... Anxiety clears away every obfuscation of the fact that Dasein has been abandoned to itself. The nothing with which anxiety brings us face to face unveils the nullity that defines Dasein in its very *ground,* unveils that ground itself as thrownness into death.

The uncanny circle of anxiety, the nothing, death, disclosure, and nullity-as-ground constitutes the core of the second division of *Being and Time,* "Dasein and Temporality." Although much of the language employed there is fatal to Heidegger's efforts—"the call," "conscience," "guilt," and "resoluteness" all allowing existential analysis to slip back into the categories of Christian theology and moral philosophy—Heidegger continued to probe the nexus of *ground* and *nullity* during all the later phases of his career.[42]

Section 58 of *Being and Time* takes up the problem of ground *as* nullity. While trying to subordinate to existential analysis the juridical and moral interpretations of guilt as an apparent "lack" or "deficiency" in the Being of Dasein, Heidegger defines the character of such negativity in the following way: to be Dasein is "to be the ground of a Being which is determined by a not," "to be the ground of a nullity." The "not" nestles in all the existential structures of Dasein and in all the dimensions of care: as thrown, Dasein has *not* brought it on itself to exist; as projecting itself into this or that possibility, Dasein chooses this but *not* that; as falling or drifting through its quotidian routine, Dasein for the most part is *not* attuned to its own capacity to be, a capacity that in any case has *not* been granted it as its own. Nullity permeates care, which may be defined as "the (nugatory) being a ground of a nullity" (SZ, 285). That paradoxical formula results from

---

thrown capacity-to-be, makes it clear that with the phenomenon of anxiety an exceptional mood has become thematic for our interpretation." See Martin Heidegger, *Sein und Zeit,* 12th ed. (Tübingen: M. Niemeyer, 1972), p. 188. Cited in the text as SZ, 188.

[42] For a basic bibliography of that nexus in the "later phases," see p. 284, footnotes 56–57.

the paradox of existence: "The self, which as such is to establish the ground of itself, can *never* master that ground; and yet by existing it is to take upon itself its being a ground" (SZ, 284). In spite of Heidegger's later disavowals, we know where Jean-Paul Sartre unearthed his striking formulations of *mauvaise-foi,* the being that "must be what it is not and not be what it is," or of *la réalité humaine,* which "rises in being as perpetually haunted by a totality which it is without being able to be it."[43] Heidegger himself does not flit from one dramatic description to the next, however, but immediately invokes the problem of the "ontological sense of nullity," which, he admits, "remains obscure":

> True, ontology and logic have exacted a great deal from the not and have thereby made its possibilities visible in piecemeal fashion, without unveiling the not itself ontologically. Ontology came across the not and made use of it. But is it so obvious that every not signifies a *negativum* in the sense of a lack? Is its positivity exhausted in the fact that it constitutes "passing over" something? Why does all dialectic take refuge in negation, without grounding something like negation *itself* dialectically, indeed, without being able to pinpoint negation *as a problem?* Has the *ontological origin* of nullity ever been declared a problem at all? Or, *prior to that,* has anyone ever sought *the condition* on the basis of which the problem of the not and its nullity, the very possibility of that nullity, might be posed? And where else are such conditions to be found *if not in the thematic clarification of the meaning of Being in general?*[44]

---

[43] Jean-Paul Sartre, *Being and Nothingness,* tr. Hazel Barnes (New York: Philosophical Library, 1956), pp. 67, 90.

[44] SZ, 285–86. In his doctoral dissertation, "The Doctrine of Judgment in Psychologism" (University of Freiburg, 1914; now in *Frühe Schriften*), Heidegger had already recognized the troublesome nature of the negative in logic: if judgment is a relation—namely, a relation of validity (*Gelten*)—negative judgments appear to truncate the relation, cancel validity, and destroy judgment as such. The young Heidegger tries to solve the dilemma by removing the negative from the copula to the predicate (instead of "The book is not yellow," one might say "Not-being-yellow is true of the book"). Unsatisfied with such logistical legerdemain, which only postpones the problem, Heidegger asks, "Can we penetrate still further into the essence of negation?" Negation must be allowed to affect the copula, to separate subject and predicate, even if such separation—which seems to presuppose a relationship of some kind—remains mysterious. Heidegger's acceptance here of the Lotzean theory of four distinct modes of actuality, of which *Geltung* is one, prevents him from pushing on to the existential-ontological problem of negation. Decisive advances will occur during the Marburg years both prior to *Being and*

After the publication of *Being and Time* in the spring of 1927, Heidegger devoted his attention to the related problems of the not (*das Nicht*), negation (*die Verneinung*), nullity (*die Nichtigkeit*), and the nothing (*das Nichts*). All these converged in the crucial problem of ground (*der Grund*). At the same time, Heidegger's thinking underwent what he himself called "a meta-ontological turn."[45] His project of "fundamental ontology" would now have to seek its own fundament or ground in the history of metaphysics, which inquired not only into human Being or Dasein but also into, and beyond, beings as a whole (*das Seiende im Ganzen*). In his lecture courses at Marburg during the summer semesters of 1927 and 1928—which I cannot discuss here at length[46]—Heidegger focused not only on the experience of anxiety as an opening onto the groundlessness of Dasein but also on the nothing itself as the source of "the ontological difference." The nothing was, after all, the "not" of "things"; that is, of beings as a whole. Heidegger even spoke of the world as a *nihil originarium*. The nothing would be the common *ground* of the radical finitude of man, of Being, and even of Time itself. But what could "ground" mean for a philosophy that experienced keenly its own radical finitude? That question reverberates through all three principal texts from this period (*Kant and the Problem of Metaphysics*, "On the Essence of Ground," and "What Is Metaphysics?"). Although each of these merits discussion here, I will for reasons of economy consider only the last mentioned: Heidegger's inaugural lecture at the University of Freiburg in 1929, *Was ist Metaphysik?*[47]

Time (see Martin Heidegger, *Logik: Die Frage nach der Wahrheit* [Frankfurt am Main: V. Klostermann, 1976], section 12, esp. p. 141) and immediately following it (see Martin Heidegger, *Die Grundprobleme der Phänomenologie* [Frankfurt am Main: V. Klostermann, 1975], section 16d, esp. p. 283.

[45] See Martin Heidegger, *Metaphysische Anfangsgründe der Logik im Ausgang von Leibniz* (Frankfurt am Main: V. Klostermann, 1978), esp. pp. 196–202.

[46] For a detailed treatment of this period of Heidegger's career, see D. F. Krell, *Intimations of Mortality*, chapter two, "Fundamental Ontology, Meta-Ontology, Frontal Ontology," pp. 31–43.

[47] The inaugural lecture (cf. footnote 50) has provoked a flurry of irate responses. Apart from the two best-known replies—Günther Grass's parody at the close of *The Dog Years* and Rudolf Carnap's scornful reduction of it in "Overcoming Metaphysics Through Logical Analysis of Language," tr. Arthur Pap, in A. J. Ayer, ed. *Logical*

In his inaugural lecture Heidegger carefully balances the existential-ontological and meta-ontological aspects of the question of the nothing. Anxiety, along with other moods, reveals the nothing; but the nothing points toward beings as a whole. It does so not merely as the complete "negation" of beings in ensemble but as "nihilation" (*das Nichten, die Nichtung*). The latter is not annihilation of beings, however, but an indication of their slipping away from Dasein. Paradoxically, such slippage attunes Dasein to beings as a whole in the region of openness. Openness is the work of nihilation: only when the quotidian flight toward beings is suspended, only when beings as a whole withdraw in such a way that they draw attention to their departure, can the Being of beings, the bare "is-ness" of things, assert itself. Although the phenomenon of anxiety still retains its privileged position with respect to nihilation, the withdrawal of beings as a whole may also be sensed in other exceptional moods such as profound boredom or intense joy. (Rilke, we recall from Volume I of this series, pp. 116–17, identifies joy in beauty as terror before what we but barely endure.) In section 26 of "Song of Myself," Walt Whitman invokes an experience of nihilation that combines an astonishing variety of moods:

> The orchestra whirls me wider than Uranus flies,
> It wrenches such ardors from me I did not know I possess'd them,
> It sails me, I dab with bare feet, they are lick'd by the indolent waves,
> I am cut by bitter and angry hail, I lose my breath,

Positivism (New York: Free Press, 1959, pp. 60–81) —and apart from the vast expository literature on Heidegger, one might also note the protracted (but singularly unhelpful) "Discussion" in the *Zeitschrift für philosophische Forschung*, 1949–1951, 4–6. The best indication of the helplessness of most commentators is Gertrud Kahl-Furthmann, *Das Problem des Nicht*, 2nd ed. (Meisenheim am Glan: A Hain, [1934] 1968). This is a broadbased account of "the not" in Western logic and metaphysics from Parmenides to Heidegger. Yet it is a pedestrian work, on whose path Heidegger constitutes the major stumbling block. (See the Foreword to the second edition, p. vi.) The book ignores the essential coherence of *Sein* and *Nichts* in "What Is Metaphysics?" (see p. 309) and proclaims as its great discovery the "error" Heidegger commits when he capitalizes the "n" of *nichts*, thus "confusing" an indefinite pronoun for a substantive (pp. 311–12). The book does achieve a fleeting moment of truth, however, when Frau Kahl-Furthmann concedes, "A plethora of unanswered questions remains, making it impossible for us to derive from Heidegger's analysis of the nothing results which would advance our own investigation."

Steep'd amid honey'd morphine, my windpipe throttled in fakes of death,
At length let up again to feel the puzzle of puzzles,
And that we call Being.

William James, exalting the "hoary loafer" who composed "Crossing Brooklyn Ferry," refers to a similar sort of experience. "There is life," he writes, "and there, a step away is death. There is the only kind of beauty there ever was." James continues,

> To be rapt with satisfied attention, like Whitman, to the mere spectacle of the world's presence, is one way, and the most fundamental way, of confessing one's sense of its unfathomable significance and importance. But how can one attain to the feeling of the vital significance of an experience, if one have it not to begin with? There is no receipt which one can follow. Being a secret and a mystery, it often comes in mysteriously unexpected ways. It blossoms sometimes from out of the very grave wherein we imagined that our happiness was buried.[48]

Whether and to what extent other moods duplicate the characteristics of anxiety—its bewildering calm, speechlessness, and uncanniness in the face of the slipping away of beings as a whole—remains an intriguing existential-ontological problem.[49] The meta-ontological significance of attunement remains nonetheless clear: "Being held out into the nothing," Dasein is in some way "out beyond" beings. By grace of nihilation, Dasein is trans-ontical, is (finite) transcendence. By grace of nihilation, Dasein is *meta-physical*. "Metaphysics is the

---

[48] William James, "On a Certain Blindness in Human Beings," in Joseph L. Blau, ed. *Pragmatism and Other Essays*, (New York: Washington Square, 1963), pp. 263–64. I introduce these lyric and pragmatic American sources to suggest that "nihilation" need not merely be the result of Heidegger's failure to locate "fixed" semantic and syntactic "units" for "protocol sentences" and "empirical propositions" about "possible experience." See Rudolf Carnap, "Overcoming Metaphysics," pp. 60–81. Although Carnap's conjecture (p. 80) "that metaphysics is a substitute, albeit an inadequate one, for art" remains thought-provoking, especially because he cites Nietzsche as the one who "almost entirely" avoids confusing science with artistic expression, it does seem as though nihilation—celebrated in art and interrogated in thought—remains a "possible experience." Indeed, for Heidegger, nihilation is the possibility of experience as such.

[49] See Heidegger's analysis of "profound boredom" and "melancholy," in MHG 29/30, Part One and pp. 270–71.

basic occurrence of Dasein. It is Dasein itself."[50] But such transcendence, selfhood, and freedom as are at the disposal of Dasein are not metaphysical in the traditional ontotheological sense; they manifest themselves in the interstices of beings as *negation,* and in sundry contexts of beleaguered human behavior as *nihilation.* Nihilation is both broader and deeper than negation:

> Unyielding antagonism and stinging rebuke have a more abysmal source than the measured negation of thought. Galling failure and merciless prohibition require some deeper answer. Bitter privation is more burdensome.[51]

It is therefore comprehensible that metaphysics, spawned in the opening of the nothing, should leave its own origins in obscurity and busy itself with beings. While the classical metaphysical proposition *ex nihilo nihil fit*—from nothing, nothing comes to be—is essential for the fundamental conception of Being in antiquity, the sense of the *nihil* itself "never really becomes a problem."[52] The Platonistic, Aristotelian, and Plotinian conceptions of becoming (*genesis*) and matter (*hyle*) as properly nothing (*to mē on*), become as it were the cracked looking-glass for Western conceptions of Being. In the Augustinian transformation of the ancient principle, which now reads *ex nihilo fit—ens creatum,* from nothing comes created being, a second crack intersects the first and forms what Schelling will call "the cross of the Intellect."[53] Hegel's *Logic* only appears to draw the consequences of the resulting distorted reflection: it equates pure Being and pure Nothing as "concepts" that are equally immediate and

---

[50] Martin Heidegger, "Was ist Metaphysik?" in *Wegmarken* (Frankfurt am Main: V. Klostermann, 1967), p. 18; in *Basic Writings,* p. 112.

[51] Heidegger, *Wegmarken,* p. 14; *Basic Writings,* p. 107.

[52] Heidegger, *Wegmarken,* p. 16; *Basic Writings,* p. 109.

[53] See F. W. J. Schelling, *Sämmtliche Werke* (1860), VII, 373, n. 2. For Schelling's God, that crack becomes a wound from which the Absolute will never recover. Schelling calls that wound "the will of ground," *der Wille des Grundes* (p. 375). From this gaping "ground," in spite of all that Schelling can do to anneal it, flows "a source of sadness," a "profound, indestructible melancholy in all life" (p. 399). Heidegger, who was teaching courses on Schelling immediately before and after the Nietzsche lectures, recognized the wound—the fatal split between *Grund* and *Existenz*—as the demise of Schelling's God *and* his system. See Martin Heidegger, *Schellings Abhandlung über das Wesen der menschlichen Freiheit (1809),* ed. Hildegard Feick (Tübingen: M. Niemeyer, 1971), esp. p. 194.

indeterminate, then proceeds to derive Becoming from their interpenetration, in strict conformity with the metaphysical tradition. For Heidegger too, Being and the nothing belong together, although not merely as concepts, "because Being itself is essentially finite and reveals itself only in the transcendence of Dasein which is held out into the nothing."[54] Being itself, *das Sein,* is finite, pervaded by the nothing. At this juncture, *Sein* and *Dasein* become wholly indistinguishable; indeed, Heidegger now speaks of "the nothing of *Dasein*" in which alone beings as a whole can come to themselves in their own way; that is to say, a finite way. *Sein, Dasein,* and *das Seiende im Ganzen* converge in nihilation. But if that is so, then the introduction of beings as a whole as a "new" horizon for fundamental ontology, the meta-ontological turn, seems to turn us back toward the same cluster of problems. As Heidegger himself puts it: in the question of Being, horizons form only to dissolve.[55] Not into new *grounds,* but into old *questions,* for example, that posed by Leibniz in his *Principles of Nature and of Grace, Founded on Reason* (1714): "Why are there beings at all, and why not rather nothing?"

Heidegger lets that same question resound in his 1944–46 treatise, "Nihilism as Determined by the History of Being" (p. 208, above). In fact it can be heard throughout the Nietzsche lectures in Heidegger's emphasis on Nietzsche's experience of nihilism—the futility of the "why?" question, and the "coming to nothing" of beings as a whole and Being itself. The Leibnizian question is furthermore a leitmotif in a number of lectures and essays immediately prior to, and directly subsequent to, the Nietzsche lectures.[56] All the same, I want to pursue the enigma of the nothing not in these but in several later texts where the Leibnizian question concerning beings fades before the question of Being.[57] Study of these later texts discloses the lasting quality of the

---

[54] Heidegger, *Wegmarken,* p. 17; *Basic Writings,* p. 110.
[55] See Heidegger, *Anfangsgründe,* p. 198.
[56] In addition to the sources just cited, see Heidegger's *Einführung in die Metaphysik* (lectures given in 1935), esp. pp. 18–24; English translation, pp. 19–25. See also the 1943 "Afterword" and 1949 "Introduction" to "What Is Metaphysics?" in *Wegmarken,* pp. 99–108, 195–211. Finally, see the 1946–47 "Letter on Humanism," *Wegmarken,* esp. pp. 176–78, 189–91; in *Basic Writings,* pp. 225–27, 237–38.
[57] Martin Heidegger, "Zur Seinsfrage," first published in 1955, now in *Wegmarken,*

issue of ground and nullity. Such study makes it impossible to assent to that interpretation of Heidegger's career which asserts that the problem of the nothing pertains to an "existentialist" phase that is soon tranquilized into "releasement" by "thankfulness to Being." If one interpretation deserves another—to counter it—then mine would be as follows: Heidegger's thought, early and late, inquiring into the finitude of human being (as being-toward-death and as mortal), the finitude of philosophy (including both fundamental ontology and "the other thinking"), the finitude of Being (as revealing-concealing) and of Time (as presencing-absencing), and the finitude of *Ereignis* itself, brings Nietzsche's accomplishment—ecstatic nihilism—to an apotheosis.

Heidegger grapples with the relation of ground to nullity once again in his 1955–56 lecture course on the "principle of sufficient reason," *Der Satz vom Grund*. That course offers us a matchless opportunity to trace the development of Heidegger's thoughts on ground from the period of *Being and Time* through his later thought.[58] Without being able to attempt such a tracing here, I at least want to indicate one of Heidegger's strategies in the later lecture course. He stresses the principle of sufficient reason, *Nihil est sine ratio*, "Nothing is without grounds," as it is normally asserted: "*Nothing* is *without* grounds." Curiously, when we stress the word "nothing" we tend to pass *through* it, to think it *away*, to proceed to beings *without* it—the nothing. Oddly, when we stress the nothing the principle sounds wholly positive, conclusive, self-evident. It lays a claim on all beings which is utterly transparent: *Nihil . . . sine* executes a perfectly choreographed dialectic, a negation of negation that guarantees universal rationality. But Heidegger now alters the emphasis, ironically downplaying the nothing and invoking the ostensibly fully positive identity of being and reason: "Nothing *is* without *grounds*." Finally, he inserts a hiatus into the principle, which now proclaims something disconcerting:

---

pp. 213–53; "Bauen Wohnen Denken" (1951), "Das Ding" (1950), and "Dichterisch Wohnet der Mensch" (1951), now in *Vorträge und Aufsätze*, pp. 145–204; English translations in *Poetry, Language, Thought*, pp. 145–86 and 213–29; and Martin Heidegger, *Der Satz vom Grund* (Pfullingen: G. Neske, 1957), complete.

[58] From the period of *Being and Time*, see "Vom Wesen des Grundes," in *Wegmarken*, pp. 21–71, and the lecture course on which that essay was based, reprinted as *Anfangsgründe*.

"Nothing *is*—without *grounds,*" *Nichts* ist—*ohne* Grund. The identity between Being and the rationalist project of ground, the identity of *einai* and *noein,* precisely when it is stressed, is undercut by the scarcely heard "Nothing . . . without."

True, when all is said and done, Heidegger is here only playing with words, or worse, is letting words play with him. He knows that. For Heidegger such play is in earnest, and goes for the highest stakes—it is the child's play that rules the world:

> The question evoked by our leap into the altered emphasis of the principle of sufficient reason asks: Can the essence of play be defined appropriately in terms of Being as ground, or must we think Being and ground, Being as abyss [*Ab-Grund*], in terms of the essence of play, indeed, of that play to which we mortals are introduced, being mortal only because we dwell in proximity to death, which, as the uttermost possibility of Dasein, is capable of the supreme lighting of Being and of Being's truth? Death is the still unthought standard of the immeasurable, that is, of that supreme play to which man is introduced on earth, and in which he is at stake.[59]

So much for a Heidegger II who would rescue us from Heidegger I: the circle of themes in *Being and Time* (anxiety, the nothing, death, disclosure, and nullity-as-ground) is never broken. It never traces a line one might cross.

To the *Festschrift* for Heidegger's sixtieth birthday Ernst Jünger contributed an essay entitled *Über die Linie,* "Over the Line." The "line" in question was the boundary demarcating the historical region of nihilism from the still uncharted domain where a new relationship to Being might become possible. Five years later, Heidegger contributed to the *Festschrift* for Jünger's sixtieth birthday an open letter entitled *Über 'Die Linie,'* "About 'The Line.'"

Heidegger's title liberates the *Über* from the quotation marks and thus focuses on the question of "the line" as such. It transmutes Jünger's title and his intention: the *Über* is no longer a command to cross over the boundary but a question about the boundary itself. For Heidegger, nihilism is not a matter that can be left behind by a crossing; there is no promised land *trans linea,* no meta-level hovering over the

---

[59] Heidegger, *Satz vom Grund,* pp. 186–87.

Analysis

terrain of the nothing. Heidegger's title is not *trans linea* but *de linea*: his essay does not cross the line but moves about (*peri*) the periphery of the zone or dimension where the *nihil* comes to the fore. Much about the two *Festschrift* essays is similar. For example, Nietzsche is the principal witness for both, invoking nihilism as the "uncanniest of guests" and defining it as the collapse of the uppermost values. But the major difference between the two essays emerges in Heidegger's droll comment on that "guest":

> He is called the *unheimlichste* ["uncanniest"] because, as the unconditioned will-to-will, he wills *Heimatlosigkeit* ["homelessness"] as such. It doesn't help to show him the door because for a long time, and quite unseen, he has been making himself at home.[60]

Whereas Jünger's essay on nihilism—like most of the others I have seen—adopts a "medical attitude," venturing a diagnosis, risking a prognosis, and prescribing a predictable therapy, Heidegger's letter promises considerably less: "With regard to the *essence* of nihilism there is no prospect of, and no meaningful claim to, a cure."[61] The *essence* of actual, destructive nihilism (which in the context of the present volume we would have to call the *nonessence* of the nothing) is a complex matter that cannot be reduced to definitions. Its zone is world-historical, its scope planetary. But Heidegger tries to shift attention from the multiple appearances of nihilism to its essential provenance. He abjures all reactive and restorative efforts, all attempts to vulcanize the blasted balloon tires of "value," in order to inquire into "the questionableness of man's metaphysical position."[62] Both his abjuration and his incipient inquiry derive from an insight into the peculiar quandary that language gets into when it speaks of the nothing. Jünger speaks the same language whether he is contemplating this or that "side" of the "line." Heidegger remarks,

> There is a kind of thinking that endeavors to cross over the line. What language does the basic plan of such thinking speak? Shall a rescue operation lead the language of the metaphysics of will to power, *Gestalt*, and

---
[60] Heidegger, "Zur Seinsfrage," *Wegmarken*, p. 215.
[61] Ibid.
[62] Ibid., p. 220.

values across the critical line? Why should we want to do that, if it is the language of metaphysics itself (whether of the living or the dead God) which *as* metaphysics has erected those barriers that obstruct passage across the line and so prevent the overcoming of nihilism? If that is how matters indeed stand, then would not a crossing of the line necessarily have to involve a transformation of saying; would it not demand a transformed relation to the essence of language?[63]

But the metamorphosis of saying and the transformed relation to the essence of language here assume a disconcerting form. Heidegger begins to write the word "Being," which according to a long tradition is the word that says the very opposite of "nothing" and so would be the key word for overcoming nihilism, as ~~Being~~. Whereas Jünger envisions a new "turn to Being" as the prerequisite for a successful crossing of the line, Heidegger "crosses out" Being. It appears that the thinker whose sole passion it was to raise anew the question of Being now surrenders his own question to nihilation. For what would it mean to ask about ~~Being~~?

The motivation for Heidegger's crossing of Being is not capitulation to nihilism. It springs from an active resistance to the customary way of posing the question of the "relationship" of Being and Man. That is the question in which both parts of the present volume culminate. Heidegger notes,

> We always say *too little* about "Being itself" when, uttering "Being," we leave out of account presencing *to* the human *presence* [*das An-wesen* zum *Menschen*wesen], thereby ignoring the fact that the latter presence itself participates in constituting "Being." We always say *too little* about man as well when, uttering "Being" (N.B.: not human being), we posit man for himself and only then bring what we have posited into relation to "Being." ... The talk about "Being" drives representational thought from one quandary into another, without the source of such helplessness ever showing itself.[64]

The "individualizing" and "separating" words *Sein* and *Mensch* are hence to be dispatched. Between ~~Being~~ and ~~Man~~ there can be no

---

[63] Ibid., p. 233.
[64] Ibid., pp. 235-36.

relation, not even full identity. In ~~Being~~ and ~~Man~~ we confront a duplicitous convergence that is neither identity nor difference in the usual sense. But with the nihilation of Being and Man there seems to be *nothing* left. Or can we scratch the nothing as well, and so, as though there were ~~nothing~~ to it, slip unobtrusively over the line? What would grant us the power to scratch the nothing?

It is so little a question of dispatching the nothing that we must rather say the very opposite: a transformed relation to the essence of language, as the sole way "to the question of Being," must allow the nothing to advene and to take up residence among and within mortals.[65] But by mentioning the "mortals" we invade the dimension of *the fourfold* as discussed in the essays "Building Dwelling Thinking," "The Thing," and "Poetically Man Dwells." In fact, Heidegger explicitly directs the reader of *Zur Seinsfrage* to these essays, with the hint that the fourfold will tell him something essential about "the line."

If we try to sketch the fourfold as envisioned in these essays, to make of it a kind of pictogram and rebus, we establish a periphery about the dimension of Being:

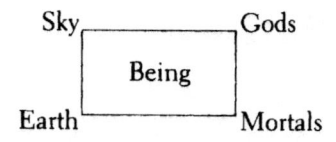

```
Sky ─────────── Gods
   │   Being   │
Earth ────────── Mortals
```

Accordingly, the crossing of Being would be, not mere *Durchstreichung*, but a *Durchkreuzen*—not a crossing *out*, but a crossing *through*:

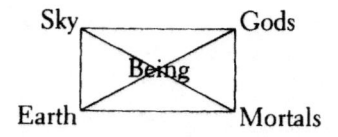

```
Sky ─────────── Gods
   │╲ ~~Being~~ ╱│
   │ ╳ │
Earth ────────── Mortals
```

---

[65] Ibid., p. 238.

By virtue of the crossing, each member of the fourfold could proceed not only about the periphery of the dimension but toward its very center. The cohesion of the fourfold thus would depend on the nihilation of Being. ~~Being~~ would express the finite transcendence of Dasein; mortal Dasein would be the same as ~~Sein~~. But because it is the thinking by mortals that thinks the other three along with itself, mortal Dasein could be said to inhabit the heart of the fourfold dimension of ~~Being~~ in a special way. Does that mean that mortals can, perhaps like the original androgynes, roll up that inclined plane to the Sky, then across to the Gods, reducing divinity, nature, and history to elements of its self-contained autonoesis? If not, how is the unity of the fourfold sustained? What is this "crossing"?

While it is true that a sacrificial vessel ("The Thing") is not a broken hammer (*Being and Time*), such things remain the accoutrements of mortal man, on this earth. They, and the mortals, have their specific gravity. Mortality is joined by the nothing—so that the crossing cannot be a matter of clambering up divided-lines and ladders of love—joined by the nothing in both its *living* and its *naming*. With respect to naming, or rather, his reticence about naming the dimension,[66] Heidegger testifies to the lack of an irrefragable standard of measure for speech. A late poem of Hölderlin contains the lines:

> Is there a measure on earth? There is
> None.

With respect to the living, Heidegger writes,

> Mortals are men. Men are called mortals because they can die. To die means to make death possible as death. . . . Death is the shrine of the nothing, of that which is never in any respect a mere being, but which all the same comes to presence as the very mystery of Being itself. As the shrine of the nothing, death shelters the presencing of Being in itself. . . . The mortals are who they are, as mortal, presencing in the shelter of Being. They are the presencing relation to Being as Being.[67]

Perhaps Heidegger should have written, "the presencing relation to

---

[66] Heidegger, "Dichterisch Wohnet der Mensch," *Vorträge und Aufsätze*, p. 195.
[67] Heidegger, "Das Ding," *Vorträge und Aufsätze*, p. 177.

Being as B̶e̶i̶n̶g̶." As for human beings, the preceding passage has already crossed them through, not by outfitting them with a cross of the Intellect, but by addressing them as mortals, the ones for whom death is, in the words of *Being and Time,* "ownmost, nonrelational, and insurmountable," at once "certain and indefinite."[68] There is no crossing over the line. There is no line. Only the zone or dimension whose very openness and anonymity require the shelter, the protective screen, of nihilation. To advance *de linea,* about the periphery, then to cross through, is to confront and accompany the nothing. Without dreaming of escape.

But when I read over the above lines, which try to compress the contents of several of Heidegger's essays into a few lines, complete with pictures, and to follow the trajectory of Heidegger's thought back to the one experience that spawned *Being and Time,* back to *the* fundamental experience of Heidegger's thought *as such,* I am struck by their resemblance to the ridiculous bathos of Pierre's scribblings. As though both naming and living were consumed in writing! As though writing itself were the crossing! Of B̶e̶i̶n̶g̶ Jacques Derrida writes,

> This erasure is the last inscription of an epoch. Under its traced lines the presence of a transcendental signified is effaced—while remaining legible. Effaces itself while remaining readable; destroys itself while making manifest the very idea of a sign. Inasmuch as it de-limits ontotheology, metaphysics of presence, and logocentrism, this last inscription is also the first.[69]

The first, that is to say, of a new epoch of writing.

Indeed, the question of the *nihil* has struck not only contemporary philosophy but also contemporary literature and literary criticism. I am thinking for example of a recent statement by three inquisitive critics who, peering into Dedalus' "cracked looking-glass of a servant" (a second looking-glass, or the same one?), descry the "shattered image" of contemporary criticism as a whole:

> What one sees . . . is *dispersal:* a broken, discontinuous, jagged series of fragments stripped of all illusory, mystifying *images* of unity, revealed in all its particularity and unevenness—not the One, the Word, Identity, but the

---
[68] Heidegger, *Sein und Zeit,* pp. 263–65.
[69] Jacques Derrida, *De la grammatologie* (Paris: Éditions de Minuit, 1967), p. 38.

many, words, difference. The one who stares into the mirror is unmasked: there he finds the same figures of disruption, of failed recuperation, of the nostalgic desire to *create* or *project* a unified image of critical activity—where none is to be found. We can connect nothing with nothing, one might say.[70]

I am thinking too of a recent thought-provoking essay by J. Hillis Miller, "The Critic as Host."[71] In the second section of his paper Miller raises the question of nihilism with respect to deconstructive criticism, tracing the very path we have traveled here, from Nietzsche to Ernst Jünger to Heidegger. Miller too experiences the nothing, not as a disease he hopes to eradicate, but as a permanent though hardly comfortable symbiosis of "parasite and host" in the critical encounter. Whether it be in a self-subverting text of metaphysics, a poem, or a piece of criticism, "nihilism is the latent ghost encrypted within any expression of a logocentric system."[72] Yet, to repeat, it is not an apotropaic ritual that Miller is looking for, neither exorcism nor pacification. "Deconstruction does not provide an escape from nihilism, nor from metaphysics, nor from their uncanny inherence in one another. There is no escape."[73]

---

[70] William V. Spanos, Daniel T. O'Hara, and Paul A. Bové, Introduction to "The Problems of Reading in Contemporary American Criticism: A Symposium," *boundary 2*, 1979, 8(1), 8.

[71] In Harold Bloom et al., eds., *Deconstruction and Criticism* (New York: Seabury Press, 1979), pp. 217–53.

[72] Miller, p. 228.

[73] However, deconstruction does, according to Miller, (p. 231),

move back and forth within this inherence. It makes the inherence oscillate in such a way that one enters a strange borderland, a frontier region which seems to give the widest glimpse into the other land ("beyond metaphysics"), though this land may not by any means be entered and does not in fact exist for Western man. By this form of interpretation, however, the border zone itself may be made sensible, as quattrocento painting makes the Tuscan air visible in its invisibility. The zone may be appropriated in the torsion of the mind's expropriation, its experience of an inability to comprehend logically. This procedure is an attempt to reach clarity in a region where clarity is not possible. In the failure of that attempt, however, something moves, a limit is encountered. This encounter may be compared to the uncanny experience of reaching a frontier where there is no visible barrier, as when Wordsworth found he had crossed the Alps without knowing he was doing so. It is as if the "prisonhouse of language" were like that universe finite but unbounded which some modern cosmologies posit.

Analysis

Toward the close of his letter to Ernst Jünger, Heidegger again invokes Nietzsche—"in whose light and shadow all of us today, with our 'pro-Nietzsche' or 'contra-Nietzsche,' are thinking and writing."[74] Nietzsche responded to the call to reflect on the fate and fatality of humanity's inheritance of the earth.

> He followed that call along the path of metaphysical thinking which was his lot, and he collapsed while under way. So it seems, at least, to the historian's eye. Perhaps he did not collapse, however, but went as far as his thinking could go.[75]

"As far as his thinking could go. . . ." The phrase still seems to betray a residual judgment or *evaluation* of Nietzsche, as though Heidegger had crossed the line to the meta-level of the historian's unrestricted vision, the level that would permit a final settling of accounts with Nietzsche. Yet that is not the case. A thinking that goes as far as it can—Heidegger never claimed such success for his own thought.

> The fact that Nietzsche's thought left to posterity such weighty and difficult matters should remind us in a different and more rigorous way than ever before of the long provenance of the question of nihilism which stirred in him. The question has not become any easier for us.[76]

My Analysis in the first volume of Heidegger's *Nietzsche* opened with an innocent though perhaps preposterous anecdote: because the

---

One may move everywhere freely within this enclosure without ever encountering a wall, and yet it is limited. It is a prison, a milieu without origin or edge. Such a place is therefore all frontier zone without either peaceful homeland, in one direction, land of hosts and domesticity, nor, in the other direction, any alien land of hostile strangers, "beyond the line."

Cf. Maurice Blanchot, "The Limits of Experience: Nihilism," in David B. Allison's excellent collection, *The New Nietzsche: Contemporary Styles of Interpretation* (New York: Delta Books, 1977), pp. 121–27. Blanchot calls nihilism "an extreme that cannot be gotten beyond," but also "the only true path of going beyond": "Nihilism is the impossibility of coming to an end and finding an outcome in this end. . . . Nihilism would be identical with the will to overcome Nihilism *absolutely.*" Finally, for a discussion of nihilism in the context of Heidegger's remarks on p. 48 of the present volume, see D. F. Krell, "Results," in *The Monist*, 1981, *64* (4), 467–80.

[74] Heidegger, "Zur Seinsfrage," *Wegmarken* p. 252.
[75] Ibid., pp. 252–53.
[76] Ibid., p. 253.

designer of the German volumes printed merely the two names *heidegger* and *nietzsche* on the spine of the books, and because Nietzsche was, as he himself had said, "born posthumously," no one could tell which was the author and which the title. By the time we have worked through the lecture and essay on nihilism we cannot but have noticed that these volumes are shaped as much by their subject as by their author. In one of his notes on nihilism Nietzsche pledges to relate "the history of the next two centuries." Heidegger is well within the scope of that "history," as are those now translating or reading the volumes. It will not surprise us therefore, since Heidegger has prepared us well for it, that our own questions to Heidegger's text revert to Nietzsche's texts—as though the matter for further thought were nietzsche's heidegger.

> Perhaps what we must do is, not remove Nietzsche from the Heideggerian reading, but on the contrary deliver him over to it totally, subscribe to that interpretation without reservation. In a *certain manner,* and precisely at the point where the content of the Nietzschean discourse is all but lost in the question of Being, the form of that discourse recovers its absolute strangeness. At that point Nietzsche's text finally calls for another kind of reading, one more faithful to his type of writing: since *what* Nietzsche wrote, he wrote.[77]

---

[77] Derrida, pp. 32–33.

Glossary

abandonment	*die Verlassenheit*
abode	*die Unterkunft*
absence	*die Abwesenheit*
absolute	*unbedingt, absolut*
abyss, abyssal	*der Abgrund, abgründig*
to accomplish	*vollbringen*
actual	*wirklich*
to address	*ansprechen*
advent	*die Ankunft*
affect	*der Affekt*
appearance	*der Schein, die Erscheinung*
articulation	*das Gefüge*
aspect, outward	*das Aussehen,* eidos
at hand	*vorhanden*
authentic	*eigentlich*
basic experience	*die Grunderfahrung*
basic occurrence	*das Grundgeschehen*
basically, at bottom	*im Grunde*
becoming	*das Werden*
Being	*das Sein*
being(s), the being	*das Seiende*
being(s) as a whole	*das Seiende im Ganzen*
beingness	*die Seiendheit*
belonging	*die Zugehörigkeit*
claim	*die Ansprechung, der Anspruch*

coherence, cohesion	die Zusammengehörigkeit
coinage	die Prägung
completion	die Vollendung
concealing	die Verbergung
concealment	die Verborgenheit
conception	der Begriff, die Auffassung
configuration	die Gestalt
confrontation	die Auseinandersetzung
continuance	die Beständigkeit
countermovement	die Gegenbewegung
default	das Ausbleiben
to define	bestimmen
definitive	massgebend
deliberative thought	das Bedenken, dubitare
de-limitation	die Ent-schränkung
destiny	das Geschick
to determine	bestimmen
difference	die Differenz, der Unterschied
differentiation	die Unterscheidung
discordance	der Zwiespalt
disjunction	die Abkehr
disposition	die Verfügung
distinction	der Unterschied
dominance, dominion	die Herrschaft
to doubt	bezweifeln, dubitare
drawing pull	der Bezug
drive	der Trieb
ecstative	ekstatisch
effectiveness	die Wirksamkeit
encounter in thought	entgegendenken
enframing	das Ge-stell
enhancement	die Steigerung
enigma	das Rätsel
to enjoin	über etwas verfügen

essence	*das Wesen*
essential determination	*die Wesensbestimmung*
essential unfolding	*wesen* (verbal)
to estimate	*schätzen (ab-, ein-)*
eternal recurrence of the same	*die ewige Wiederkehr des Gleichen*
eternal return	*die ewige Wiederkunft*
event	*das Ereignis*
exaction	*die Zumutung*
explicit(ly)	*ausdrücklich, eigens*
expression	*der Ausdruck*
expressly	*eigens*
feeling	*das Gefühl*
fixation	*die Festmachung*
force	*die Kraft*
fore, to come to the	*zum Vorschein kommen*
forgottenness	*die Vergessenheit*
form	*die Form, die Gestalt*
free region	*das Freie*
fulfillment	*die Vollendung*
fullness, plentitude	*die Fülle*
fundamental experience	*die Grunderfahrung*
fundamental metaphysical position	*die metaphysische Grundstellung*
genuine	*echt, eigentlich*
to grasp	*begreifen, fassen*
ground(s)	*der Grund*
grounding question	*die Grundfrage*
guiding question	*die Leitfrage*
hale	*das Heilsame*
to harbor, shelter	*bergen*
to heed	*achten, beachten*
hierarchy	*die Rangordnung*

historicity	die Geschichtlichkeit
history of Being	die Seinsgeschichte
to hold sway	walten
idea	die Idee, idea
illusion	der Anschein
impact	das Erwirken, die Tragweite
in-cipient	an-fänglich
inherence	das Innestehen
insistence	die Inständigkeit
jointure	der Fug
justification	die Gerechtigkeit
to keep to itself	ansichhalten
lawfulness	die Gesetzlichkeit
to lighten	lichten
lighting	die Lichtung
to linger, tarry	verweilen
locale	die Ortschaft
main, major work, magnum opus	das Hauptwerk
matter (of thought)	die Sache (des Denkens)
measure	das Mass
measuredness	die Mässigung
to mediate	vermitteln
to meditate	besinnen
mood	die Stimmung
mystery, secret	das Geheimnis
need	das Brauchen, die Not
the nothing	das Nichts
vacuous nothingness	das leere Nichts
nullity	die Nichtigkeit

Glossary

oblivion	die Vergessenheit
occur essentially	wesen (verbal)
on hand	zuhanden
the open (region)	das Offene
openness	die Offenheit
origin	der Ursprung, die Herkunft
original	ursprünglich
outset, at the	anfänglich
outward appearance (or aspect)	das Aussehen, eidos, idea
perfection	die Vollendung
permanence	die Beständigkeit
the permanent	das Beständige
phenomena	die Erscheinungen
to place alongside	bei-stellen
playspace	der Spielraum
to ponder	bedenken
presence	die Anwesenheit
presencing, becoming present	das Anwesen
what is present	das Anwesende
to present to	zu-stellen
presumption	die Anmassung
to prevail	walten, herrschen
pre-vious	das Vor-herige, a priori
primordial	anfänglich, ursprünglich
proper	eigentlich
to be proper to	gehören
pro-posing	das Vor-setzen
proposition	der Satz
provenance	die Herkunft
proximity	die Nähe
radiance	das Scheinen
to radiate	scheinen
real, actual	wirklich

reality	die Realität, die Wirklichkeit
realm	der Bereich
to recall thoughtfully	an-denken
refusal	die Verweigerung
to reign	walten
rejection	die Ab-sage
relation	die Beziehung
relation(s) with beings	das Verhältnis zum Seienden
relationship to Being	der Bezug zum Sein
representable	vorstellbar
representation	die Vorstellung, das Vorstellen
representing	das Vorstellen
repudiation	die Abwehr
restriction	die Beschränkung
revealing	die Entbergung
to rule	walten
secret, mystery	das Geheimnis
to secure	sichern
securement	die Sicherstellung
securing of permanence	die Bestandsicherung
to seem	scheinen
the selfsame	das Selbe
self-assertion	die Selbstbehauptung
semblance	der Schein
settlement	der Austrag
shelter	die Bleibe
stability	der Bestand
standard	massgebend
statement	der Satz
to stay away	ausbleiben
stockpile	der Bestand
strength	die Kraft
subjecticity	die Subiectität
subjectivity	die Subjektivität
subsistence	der Bestand

suitable	*tauglich*, agathon
supersensuous	*übersinnlich*
surety	*die Sicherung*
surpassment	*der Überstieg*
the transcendent, supersensible	*das Übersinnliche*
transformation	*der Wandel*
transition	*der Übergang, der Überstieg*
the true	*das Wahre*
truth	*die Wahrheit*, alētheia
ultimately	*im Grunde*
the unconcealed	*das Unverborgene*
unconcealment	*die Unverborgenheit*
unconditioned	*unbedingt*
the underlying	*das Zugrundeliegende, das Zum Grunde Liegende*
upsurgence	*das Aufgehen*, physis
usage	*das Brauchen, der Brauch*
valuation	*die Wertsetzung*
valuative thought	*der Wertgedanke*
value estimation	*die Wertschätzung*
value thinking	*das Wertdenken*
viewpoint	*der Gesichtspunkt, der Blickpunkt*
visuality	*die Sichtsamkeit*, idea
to will, want	*wollen*
will to power	*der Wille zur Macht*
will-to-will	*der Wille zum Willen*
withdrawal	*der Entzug*
withholding	*der Vorenthalt*